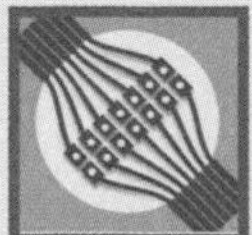

Improving Your Skills Feature Boxes

Practice IT Feature Boxes

- **Managing Now** *in-text examples* offer insights into today's management world and the technology that is influencing it.
- **Experiential Exercises** *at the end of every chapter* ask students to go beyond management theory to actually apply what they've learned in the chapter.
- **Chapter-Closing Case Study** is a detailed case study that asks students to apply what they have learned in the chapter to a real-world scenario.
- ***Online Study Center*** Look for this *icon* in the margin of your text. It alerts you that the content being covered in that chapter will be covered in the **Managing Now! LIVE simulation**.

To Samantha

Vice President, Executive Publisher: George Hoffman
Executive Sponsoring Editor: Lisé Johnson
Senior Marketing Manager: Nicole Hamm
Development Editor: Julia Perez
Cover Design Manager: Anne S. Katzeff
Senior Photo Editor: Jennifer Meyer Dare
Senior Project Editor: Nancy Blodget
Editorial Assistant: Jill Clark
Art and Design Manager: Jill Haber
Senior Composition Buyer: Chuck Dutton

Cover photo credits
Main image: © Bryan F. Peterson/CORBIS
Lower left image: © Stockbyte/Getty Images
Lower right image: © David Oliver/Getty Images

Additional photo credits are listed on page 516.

Printed in the U.S.A.

Library of Congress Control Number: 2007924351

Instructor's exam copy:
ISBN-13: 978-0-618-83347-4
ISBN-10: 0-618-83347-1

For orders, use student text ISBNs:
ISBN-13: 978-0-618-74163-2
ISBN-10: 0-618-74163-1

2 3 4 5 6 7 8 9—CRK—11 10 09 08 07

managing NOW!

Gary Dessler
Florida International University

Jean Phillips
Rutgers University

Houghton Mifflin Company Boston New York

BRIEF CONTENTS

CONTENTS

PREFACE

Information technology is a familiar aspect of our lives. We use computers, e-mail, software, cell phones, iPods, fax machines, flash drives, scanners, and BlackBerry®-type devices every day. We search for travel information on Expedia, download airline tickets from AA.com, and register for and take college courses online. Computerized diagnostic tools analyze our autos' problems, point-of-sale computers at Target process our credit-card purchases, and computerized traffic systems manage our trips to work.

Perhaps not so obvious is the extent to which managers rely on information and information technology to run their companies. For example, how does Seattle-based Starbucks Coffee Company, with over 12,000 stores globally, control what's happening in each of those stores? Its "XPR" global information system monitors point-of-sale measures at each store and triggers reports back to Seattle when a store's measures move out of control. Caterpillar Corporation needed a better way for its employees to share their knowledge. The company installed a new Web-based system that its employees now use to collaborate and share knowledge via chatroom-type discussions and e-mail bulletin boards. Michael Dell and thousands of other managers use "digital dashboards" with computerized desktop graphs and charts to get real-time information on how their companies' plans are progressing. Procter & Gamble no longer relies on its own engineers to create new products. Its *InnovationNet* Web portal enables 18,000 outside experts to share their ideas with P&G's engineers, and thus bolster the firm's innovation efforts. The bottom line is that in any aspect of managing now, it's impossible to be world-class without using information technology.

Managing Now

Managing Now! is a basic management textbook for the Principles of Management course. The book competes with the many popular principles books now on the market and basically follows the familiar management process theme. However, *Managing Now!* recognizes that the nuts and bolts of what managers do is qualitatively altered by the Internet and IT. In practice, we think this means that basic management textbooks need to be more explicit at showing how the Internet and IT change how managers carry out tasks such as planning, organizing, and managing interunit relations.

Throughout history, some things in management have not and will not quickly change. Managers still plan, organize, lead, and control. And they still get things done through people—by communicating, leading, appraising, and coaching.

This is a book on management. We therefore focus our attention on what managers should know about planning, organizing, leading, controlling, and dealing with people. However, managers now manage in a fast-changing and highly competitive global environment. To succeed here, they use information technology devices including software systems, cell phones, and PDAs to do their jobs. We therefore include in this book discussions about how managers use these devices. Every chapter shows, with "Managing Now" examples, how the manager plans, organizes, leads, and controls, in light of the Internet, IT, and ever-changing technology.

Syllabus Flexibility

Managing Now! also includes several new topics, including certain selected topics in Chapters 5 (the role of information systems/IT, knowledge management, and the Internet in managing companies), 9 (managing supply chains and operations), 16 (building community, culture, and teamwork), and 17 (encouraging sharing and collaboration).

However, we recognize that few professors have the luxury of assigning 17 full chapters. We've therefore included summary descriptions of core technology topics such as supply chain, enterprise, and knowledge management systems in Chapter 1, as well as in Chapters 5 (Information and Knowledge Management) and 9 (Managing Operations and Supply Chains). We touch on collaboration in several chapters, including Chapters 3 (Managing in a Global Environment), 9 (Managing Operations and Supply Chains), and 17 (Managing Trust and Collaboration). The professor can therefore assign this book without covering one or more of Chapters 5 , 9, and 17, with no loss of continuity.

The Human Element Remains Crucial

Interestingly, the Internet and information technology haven't diminished the manager's leadership role—quite the opposite. When Brady Corp. installed a new Web-based ordering system, its managers wisely anticipated that the system would fail unless they had employees in self-managing teams with the skills and commitment to do the new high-tech jobs. Listening, communicating, motivating, and encouraging trust and collaboration have never been more important. *Managing Now!* fully addresses, comprehensively and with the most recent research findings, the human side of managing, including a new and unique chapter (17), Managing Trust and Collaboration.

The Book's Learning Features

We've included many exciting learning features in each chapter. Each chapter starts with an opening vignette, which challenges students to solve an actual management problem. The chapter's *Practice IT* feature then shows how the manager used information technology to solve the problem.

Each chapter also starts with *Behavioral Objectives* that are broken out into the Learn It, Practice It, and Apply It models. Students are not just given a list of theoretical objectives. They are also urged to put these concepts into practice. The Learn It objectives refer to the major concepts in the text. The Practice It objectives refer students to the end-of-chapter exercises and case study. And, finally, the Apply It objectives refer students to the online simulation, Managing Now! LIVE.

Online Study Center
ACE the Test
Managing Now! LIVE

The Managing Now! LIVE simulation highlights and reviews key topics from each chapter and provides self-paced interactive tools for reinforcing and practicing what students will learn in the book. The simulation mirrors the pedagogically sound Learn It, Practice It, and Apply It models.

Boxed *Window on Managing Now* features illustrate how actual managers have used IT to improve their operations. Various *Managing Now* chapter outline headings highlight managers' use of technology in real situations. Boxed *Improving Your Skills* features provide readers with practical managerial skills.

Finally, each chapter concludes with a numbered summary, discussion questions, experiential exercises, and a case study with questions. All of these features are meant to reinforce concepts from within the chapter and make students practice what they've learned in the chapter.

Acknowledgments

We are very grateful to the many people who supported us in making *Managing Now!* a reality. At Houghton Mifflin, we are grateful to George Hoffman and Lisé Johnson for their advice, dedication, intelligence, insight, creativity, and courage in bringing this book to the market. Thanks to Julia Perez and Nancy Blodget for making the book's editorial and production process a smooth and pleasant one. We thank Nicole Hamm and the Houghton Mifflin marketing and sales staff for their hard work and dedication to making adopters aware of *Managing Now!*.

We are grateful to *Managing Now!*'s academic reviewers for their support, diligence, and many helpful suggestions.

John Anstey, *University of Nebraska, Omaha*
Karen Barr, *Penn State, Beaver Campus*
Bret Becton, *Winthrop University*
James D. Bell, *Texas State University*
Keith Benson, *Winthrop University*
Mauritz Blonder, *Hofstra University*
Bruce Bloom, *DeVry University, Chicago*
Lon Doty, *San Jose State University*
Bret R. Fund, *Penn State University*
Melissa Gruys, *Wright State University*
Rebecca Guidice, *University of Nevada, Las Vegas*
J.W. Haddad, *Seneca College of Applied Arts and Technology*
James Hess, *Ivy Tech State University*
Nancy B. Higgins, *Montgomery College*
Phillip Jeck, *University of Central Oklahoma*
Carol Jensen, *Northeast Iowa Community College*
Stephen Jones, *Southwest Missouri State University*
Cynthia Lengnick-Hall, *University of Texas, San Antonio*
Susan Looney, *Delaware Technical & Community College*
Grace McLaughlin, *University of California, Irvine*
Mark Miller, *Carthage College*
LaVelle Mills, *West Texas A&M University*
Benham Nakhai, *Millersville University of Pennsylvania*
Muhammed Obeidat, *Southern Poly State University*
Leah Ritchie, *Salem State College*
Stephen Schuster, *California State University, Northridge*
Marianne Sebok, *Community College of Southern Nevada*
Mansour Sharifzadeh, *California State Poly University, Pomona*
Leslie Shore, *Concordia University*
Gary Springer, *Texas State University, San Marcos*
Charles Stubbart, *Southern Illinois University*
Robert Tanner, *California State University, East Bay*

On a personal note, we want to thank our families. Gary's mother, Laura Dessler, was always a source of support, and would have been very proud to see and hold this book. His wife Claudia's managerial expertise helped make it possible for Gary to concentrate on his writing. As usual, the advice and support of his son, Derek, the best people manager he knows, were invaluable. Jean's husband, Stan, and sons, Tyler and Ryan, provided the love and support that enabled Jean to complete her work on this book.

Gary Dessler
Jean Phillips

About the Authors

Gary Dessler is a Founding Professor in the College of Business at Florida International University, where he teaches courses in human resource management, management, and strategic management, and where he also served for twelve years as associate dean and department chair. He has degrees from New York University (B.S.), Rensselaer Polytechnic Institute (M.S.), and the Baruch School of Business of the City University of New York (Ph.D.). Dessler's other books include *Management: Modern Principles and Practices for Tomorrow's Leaders,* Revised Third Edition (Houghton Mifflin 2007), *Framework for Human Resource Management* (Prentice Hall), and *Winning Commitment: How to Build and Keep a Competitive Workforce* (McGraw-Hill). Students around the world use his best-selling *Human Resource Management,* Tenth Edition (Pearson/Prentice Hall 2005) in various languages, including Chinese. He has published articles on employee commitment, leadership, and quality improvement in journals, including *Academy of Management Executive* and *SAM Advanced Management Journal.* He is a visiting professor at Renmin University of China and served for three years on the Institute of International Education's national selection committee for the Fulbright student awards. Dessler consults in strategic planning, management, and human resource management.

Jean Phillips is a professor in the School of Management and Labor Relations at Rutgers University. For over fifteen years, she has taught classroom and hybrid classroom/online courses in strategic human resource management, organizational behavior, management, staffing, and teams and leadership in the United States and in Singapore. Jean earned both her B.A. and Ph.D. in Business Administration from Michigan State University. Her research interests focus on recruitment and staffing, leadership and team effectiveness, and issues related to learning organizations. Her work has appeared in *Academy of Management Journal, Journal of Applied Psychology, Organizational Behavior and Human Decision Processes, Personnel Psychology, Small Group Research, Business and Psychology,* and *International Journal of Human Resource Management.* Jean was among the top 5% of published authors in *Journal of Applied Psychology* and *Personnel Psychology* during the 1990s and received the 2004 Cummings Scholar Award from the Organizational Behavior Division of the Academy of Management. She has served on the Editorial Boards of *Journal of Applied Psychology, Journal of Management,* and *Personnel Psychology.* She is a member of the Academy of Management and the Society for Industrial and Organizational Psychology. Her consulting work includes the creation and evaluation of strategic staffing programs, coaching on enhancing leadership and team performance, and strategic human resource management.

MANAGING AND THE EVOLUTION OF MANAGEMENT

1

CHAPTER OUTLINE

J. Crew

At first, J. Crew was a real success story. Starting as a direct-mail retail business, its distinctive, collegiate lifestyle catalogs were a hit. As catalog sales grew, J. Crew began opening stores with jeans, shirts, and chinos priced a bit above stores like The Gap. Sales grew fast. But soon, J. Crew was struggling. Competitors were siphoning off its customers. J. Crew struggled with an identity crisis, made worse by a revolving door of top managers. Perhaps more unnerving, a new generation of retail managers at Zara, Benneton, and H&M was using high-tech computerized systems to track daily store sales and to produce and deliver almost overnight the fashions that were selling best—tasks that often took J. Crew weeks or months to complete. With its sales, profits, and prospects diminishing, Texas Pacific Group, a private investment company, bought control of J. Crew. They tried for several years to revive the J. Crew brand. Then, a few years ago, they hired Millard Drexler, The Gap Inc.'s former CEO and a famously successful retail manager. The question was, What steps should he take to turn J. Crew around? ■

J. Crew's new CEO had to turn the company around.

BEHAVIORAL OBJECTIVES

After studying this chapter, you should be able to:

Show that you've learned the chapter's essential information by

- Defining *manager* and *organization*.
- Listing and describing five things a manager can learn from the evolution of management thought.
- Defining *information technology* and *information system*.

Show that you can practice what you've learned here by

- Reading the opening vignette and giving three examples of what the new manager may do.
- Reading the exercises and answering the question, "Do I have what it takes to be a manager?"
- Reading the chapter case study and listing the manager's specific management tasks.
- Reading the chapter case study and explaining what environmental forces are influencing the situation.

Online Study Center
ACE the Test
Managing Now! LIVE

Show that you can apply what you've learned here by

- Watching the simulation video and identifying the various functions the manager performs.

What Managers Do

Online Study Center
ACE the Test
Managing Now! LIVE

Managers can have the most remarkable effects on organizations. A few years ago, Avon Products was struggling.[1] Its whole back-end operation—buying from suppliers, taking orders, and distributing products to sales reps—lacked automation. Sales reps took orders by hand. One-third of the orders went out wrong.

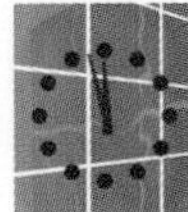

WINDOW ON MANAGING NOW
Andrea Jung Turns Avon Around

Within two years of becoming CEO, Andrea Jung had turned Avon around. She did it by overhauling "everything about the way Avon does business: how it advertises, manufactures, packages, and even sells its products."[2] She started with a turnaround plan. It included launching a new line of businesses, developing new products, building the sales force, and selling Avon products at retail stores. Next, she told R&D, "You've got two years. I need a breakthrough . . . ."[3] By the end of the year, Avon's new Retroactive, an anti-aging cream, sold $100 million. Jung also reorganized Avon. She created an "office of the chairman." Now, many of the divisions that had their own managers report instead directly to her office. The effect was to flatten Avon's chain of command (by cutting out a layer of managers). This, Jung said, ". . . will significantly increase speed and flexibility in decision making . . . ."[4]

Next, Jung appointed a new chief operating officer to get Avon's global operations under control. The company sells worldwide, and each Avon facility around the world had its own unique computer system. In Poland, Germany, and the United Kingdom, for instance, the shipping was manual. In other countries, it was computerized. The computer systems in one country couldn't communicate with another's. At Avon's headquarters, managers didn't know what each country's factories had in stock or were shipping. No one could plan the next day's production levels. Things were slipping out of control. Avon sends out about 50,000 orders each day, and one-third of them went out wrong.

To solve this, Avon installed a single "supply chain management system" in all its countries' facilities. This system combines special software with new hardware and telecommunications devices such as handheld PDAs. Now, every night, this new system ". . . collects supply chain information from Avon's 29 markets; information such as inventory, future sales demands, transport schedules, and sales history."[5] This information, along with the system's built-in planning software, automatically creates daily production and distribution plans for all of Avon's facilities. It also enables Avon sales reps to work collaboratively across borders. For example, if a customer in Germany needs a product that is out of stock there, the rep might see that it's available in Paris and have it shipped from France. The new high-tech system helped cut $400 million in costs.[6] Andrea Jung's effective management turned Avon around.

Customers no longer just wanted products like Avon's that made them look good; they also wanted healthier skin. Yet Avon spent a fraction of what competitors L'Oréal and Estée Lauder spent on research and development. The company had to take action. It appointed Andrea Jung as CEO. Within two years, she added new products, raised Avon's sales by tens of millions of dollars, and boosted profitability by automating operations and cutting costs. The Window on Managing Now feature shows how she did this.

The effect of good management is amazing. Take an underperforming—even chaotic—situation and install a skilled manager, and he or she can soon get the enterprise humming. In the New Orleans turmoil after Hurricane Katrina hit several years ago, no one in government seemed to know what to do. People were starving on rooftops, begging passing planes for help. The U.S. Army sent in Lieutenant General Russell Honore. He swiftly established a chain of command, decided what had to be done, prioritized those tasks, assigned officers to do them, and created a communications structure through which he maintained control.

● **FEMA vs. Wal-Mart** That storm brought out the best and the worst in several management teams.[7] Most people still remember that even days after Katrina hit New Orleans, the U.S. government's Federal Emergency Management Agency (FEMA) was still trying to organize its rescue efforts. Compare that to Wal-Mart's response. Many people are understandably upset today with Wal-Mart management's labor relations actions in the past few years, for instance, with respect to low wages. However, in the case of Katrina, Wal-Mart's other management actions were quite effective. Six days *before* Katrina hit, Wal-Mart's emergency operations center managers made plans to shut and guard potentially endangered stores, and they worked out how they would reopen and restock them. Emergency merchandise began moving to distribution sites close to New Orleans but outside Katrina's likely path. Twelve hours before the National Weather Service issued its hurricane warning, Wal-Mart's own meteorologists told Wal-Mart's emergency operations managers that Katrina would hit. Its stores hunkered down. Then, once Katrina passed, hundreds of Wal-Mart trucks rolled out to restock stores, with desperately needed food, water, and supplies. Wal-Mart's labor relations policies are a serious issue. But after Katrina, one police officer surveying the devastation said that the city's only lifeline was the Wal-Mart.

Manager effects like these don't occur just in big companies. Right now, managers at thousands of small businesses—diners, dry cleaners, motels—are running their businesses well, with courteous, prompt, first-class service; high-morale employees; and a minimum of problems like cold dinners, or pants not pressed on time.

● **The Ineffective Manager** Yet the opposite can be true. Take an enterprise that's been managed well for years—say, a neighborhood stationery store—and watch as a new, less-competent owner takes over. Shelves are suddenly in disarray, products are out of stock, bills are unpaid. One study of forty manufacturing firms concluded that effective management was more important than factors like market share, firm size, industry average rate of return, or degree of automation.[8] Another study concluded that organizations with better managers had lower turnover rates and higher profits and sales per employees.[9] About 90 percent of the new businesses started this year will fail within five years; Dun & Bradstreet says that the reason is usually poor management. The aim in this book is for you to be a better manager. Let's start with some definitions.

Organization Defined

organization: a group of people with formally assigned roles who work together to achieve the group's stated goals

All these enterprises—Avon, the diner, the dry cleaner, even the New Orleans rescue effort—are *organizations.* An **organization** consists of people with formally assigned roles who work together to achieve stated goals. Organizations need not be just business firms. The word applies equally well to colleges, local governments, and nonprofits like the Red Cross. The U.S. government is an organization—certainly a not-for-profit one—and its head manager, or chief executive officer, is the president. All organizations have several things in common.

First, organizations are (or should be) *goal-directed.* Thirty strangers on a bus from New York to Maine are not an organization, because they're not working together to accomplish some singular aim.

Organizations are also (one hopes) *organized* because everyone has a job to do, and people know who does what. Even a local dry-cleaning business has an *organizational structure.* Employees know who does what (pressers press, for instance, and cleaners clean) and how the work (the incoming clothes) should flow through the store and get cleaned and pressed.

But as we just saw, whether organizations achieve their goals or not depends on how the organizations are managed. This is because organizations, by their nature, cannot simply run themselves. Who would ensure that each employee knew what to do? Who would ensure that all employees work together, more or less harmoniously? Who would decide the goals? The answer is, the manager.

Management Defined

manager: a person who plans, organizes, leads, and controls the work of others so that the organization achieves its goals

management: the group of people—the managers—who are responsible for accomplishing an organization's goals through planning, organizing, leading, and controlling the efforts of the organization's people; also the totality of managerial actions, people, systems, procedures, and processes in place in an organization

Management expert Peter Drucker said that management "... is the responsibility for contribution."[10] In other words, managers are responsible for making sure that the company achieves its goals. Specifically, a **manager** is someone who is responsible for accomplishing an organization's goals, and who does so by planning, organizing, leading, and controlling the efforts of the organization's people. **Management** most often refers to the group of people—the managers—who are responsible for accomplishing an organization's goals through planning, organizing, leading, and controlling the efforts of the organization's people. However, management also refers to the totality of managerial actions, people, systems, procedures, and processes in place in an organization (such as when someone says, "the management of that crisis was totally inept").

Three Aspects of Managerial Work Our definitions of management highlight three key aspects of managerial work. First, a manager is always *responsible for contribution*—on his or her shoulders lies the responsibility for accomplishing the organization's goals. Therefore, while managers may apply management theories, managing is never just theoretical. The manager is responsible for getting things done. That is why former Honeywell CEO and successful manager Lawrence Bossidy named his book *Execution: The Discipline of Getting Things Done.*

Second, managers always get things done *through other people.* The owner/entrepreneur running a small florist shop without the aid of employees is not managing. Only when she starts hiring people and trying to get things done through them can she call herself a manager. She'll have to train and motivate her new employees and put controls in place so that the person who closes the store won't borrow part of the day's receipts.

The third aspect of managerial work refers to what managers actually do (and why some people turn out to be better at managing than others). That third aspect is that *managers must be skilled at planning, organizing, leading, and controlling* if they are to accomplish the organization's goals through other people. Management writers traditionally refer to the manager's four basic functions—planning, organizing, leading, and controlling—as the **management process**. They include:

management process: the manager's four basic functions of planning, organizing, leading, and controlling

- *Planning.* Planning is setting goals and deciding on courses of action, developing rules and procedures, developing plans (for both the organization and those who work in it), and forecasting (predicting or projecting what the future holds for the firm).
- *Organizing.* Organizing is identifying jobs to be done, hiring people to do them, establishing departments, delegating or pushing authority down to subordinates, establishing a chain of command (in other words, channels of authority and communication), and coordinating the work of subordinates.
- *Leading.* Leading is influencing other people to get the job done, maintaining morale, molding company culture, and managing conflicts and communication.
- *Controlling.* Controlling is setting standards (such as sales quotas or quality standards), comparing actual performance with these standards, and then taking corrective action as required.

Some people think that managing is easy and that anyone with half a brain can do it. But if it is so easy, why do 90 percent of new businesses fail within five years due to poor management? Why did FEMA drop the ball when Katrina hit? The words about management and managing in this book are easy to read. However, don't let that lull you into thinking that managing is easy.

Application Example: You Too Are a Manager Managing is something we're often called upon to do every day. In business, for instance, even a nonmanagerial employee may have to manage once in a while. The marketing manager might ask a marketing analyst to head a team analyzing a product's potential. Everyone who works should know the basics of managing.

Furthermore, life sometimes requires management skills. For example, suppose that you and some friends want to spend the summer in France. They've asked you to manage the trip. Where would you start? (Resist the urge to delegate the job to a travel agent, please.) Start with *planning.* You will need to plan the dates the group is leaving and returning, the cities and towns in France to visit, the airline to take you there and back, how the group will get around in France, and where to stay while you are there.

You might divide the work and create an *organization.* For example, put Rosa in charge of checking airline schedules and prices, Ned in charge of checking hotels, and Ruth in charge of checking the sites to see in various cities as well as the transportation between them. However, the job won't get done without supervision. For example, Ned can't schedule hotels unless he knows from Ruth what sites to see and when. You will either have to schedule weekly manager's meetings or coordinate the work of these people yourself.

Leadership can also be a challenge. Rosa is a genius with numbers, but she tends to get discouraged. You'll have to make sure she stays focused.

Finally, you will have to ensure that the whole project stays in *control.* At a minimum, make sure that all those airline tickets, hotel reservations, and itineraries are checked so there are no mistakes. Now let us consider another real-life *managing* example.

● **Application Example: Meg Whitman Builds eBay** It took Meg Whitman barely five years from the time eBay's founders hired her to take eBay from almost nothing to billions in sales. She did it by effectively applying the management process. In terms of *planning*, in 2000, she said that eBay would achieve $3 billion a year in revenue by 2005, and it did.

She *organized* the company. She split eBay into twenty-three main business categories (such as sports, and jewelry and watches). Then Whitman assigned executives to manage each category (and many of their 35,000 subcategories). She also organized a customer-support group that employs close to half of eBay's employees.

As a *leader*, she's reportedly soft-spoken, participative, humble but firm. Behind that quiet exterior is someone who keeps tight *control*. eBay reportedly measures almost everything, from how much time each user remains on the site to eBay's take rate (the ratio of revenues to the values of goods buyers and sellers traded on eBay). Whitman even monitors eBay's discussion boards to see what users are saying.

By 2006, faced with intense competition, eBay's growth rate was slowing. Many of eBay's most successful online sellers were exploring other ways to market their products. One that sold 1,000 pairs of shoes a day on eBay was promoting its own website and partnering with new websites that provide comparison prices. Newer companies like Google were introducing competing services, such as Froogle. As one analyst put it, "they've reached a point in their growth where things are beginning to shift against [eBay]."[11] Even a top CEO like Meg Whitman can't afford to relax for a moment. She knows that only the most agile and best-run companies survive.[12]

Table 1.1 summarizes some differences between traditional CEOs and the sorts of talents it takes to run today's e-businesses such as eBay. With technology and competition changing so fast, it takes someone who thrives on ambiguity and change and who can make good decisions very fast.

TABLE 1.1

CEOs of e-Businesses Need Some Special Skills

Traditional Company's CEO	eBay, Google-Type Company E-CEO
Encouraging employees	Evangelizing to employees
Alert to change	Obsessed with change
Cordial	Brutally frank
Infotech literate	Infotech superliterate
Fast decisions	Superfast decisions
Can handle ambiguity	Thrives on ambiguity
A paragon of good judgment	Also a paragon of good judgment
Average age: fifty-seven	Average age: thirty-five
Rich	Really rich

Source: Adapted from *Fortune*, 24 May 1999, p. 107.

What Else Do Managers Do?

Planning, organizing, leading, and controlling are the heart of what managers do, but there is more to the manager's job. For example, when Apple CEO Steve Jobs presented the new video iPod a while ago, he was acting as Apple's *spokesperson.*

Mintzberg's Managerial Roles Professor Henry Mintzberg studied what managers actually do. Mintzberg found that in a typical day, managers didn't just plan, organize, lead, and control. Instead, they also filled these various roles:

- *The figurehead role.* Every manager spends some time performing ceremonial duties.
- *The leader role.* Every manager must function as a leader, motivating and encouraging employees.[13]
- *The liaison role.* Managers spend a lot of time in contact with people outside their own departments, essentially acting as the liaison between their departments and other people within and outside the organization.
- *The spokesperson role.* The manager is often the spokesperson for his or her organization.
- *The negotiator role.* Managers spend a lot of time negotiating; the head of an airline, for instance, might try to negotiate a new contract with the pilots' union.

The Manager as Innovator In today's fast-changing world, managers also have to make sure their companies can innovate new products and react quickly to change. Therefore, management experts Sumantra Ghoshal and Christopher Bartlett say that successful managers must also improve their companies' abilities to be more innovative.[14] Effective managers do this in three ways:

- They *encourage entrepreneurship.*[15] In their study of successful companies, Ghoshal and Bartlett found that successful managers got employees to think of themselves as entrepreneurs. For example, the managers made sure employees had the support and rewards they needed to create and run their own projects. (We discuss entrepreneurship in Chapter 4.)
- They *build competence.* Bartlett and Ghoshal also found that successful managers make sure employees had the skills and competencies to be innovative and to run their own operations.[16] They encourage them to take on more responsibility, provide the education and training they need, allow them to make mistakes without fear of punishment, and coach them.[17]
- They *promote a sense of renewal.* Successful managers also foster what Bartlett and Ghoshal call renewal.[18] Effective managers take steps to guard against complacency. They encourage employees to question if they might do things differently.

Effective managers want all their employees to be innovative. For example, one South Carolina manufacturer uses a machine that now runs five times faster than anticipated when the firm ordered it. The employees made over 200 small improvements to boost its efficiency.[19]

Types of Managers

There are different types of managers. We may classify managers based on their *organization level* (top, middle, first line), their *position* (manager, director, or vice president, for instance), and their *functional title* (such as sales manager or vice president for finance). (*Function* refers in this instance to business function, such as sales, accounting, production, and human resources.)

executives: the managers at the top of an organization

In Figure 1.1, the managers at the top level, of course, are the firm's top management. These are the company's **executives**. Typical positions here are president, senior vice president, and executive vice president. Functional titles here include senior vice president for sales and chief financial officer (CFO).

Beneath the top management level (and reporting to it) may be one or more levels of middle managers. The positions here usually include the words *manager* or *director* in the titles. (In larger companies like IBM, managers report to

FIGURE 1.1

Types of Managers

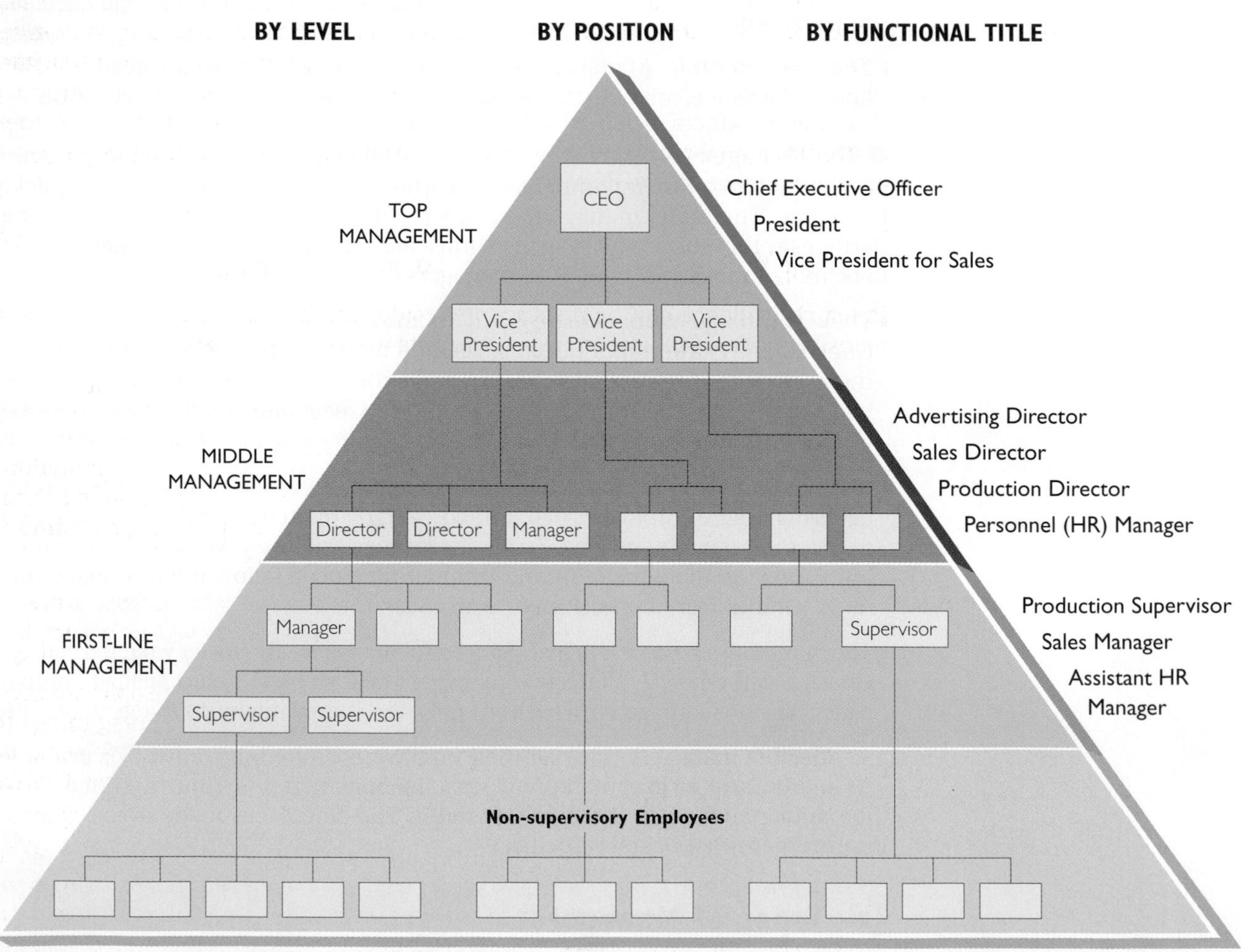

directors, who in turn report to top managers like vice presidents.) Examples of functional titles here include production manager, sales director, human resources (HR) manager, and finance manager. Finally, **first-line managers** are at the lowest rung of the management ladder. Positions here include supervisor or assistant manager. Functional titles include production supervisor and assistant marketing manager.

first-line managers: managers at the lowest rung of the management ladder

Similarities and Differences in What Managers Do

All managers have much in common. They all plan, organize, lead, and control. And all managers at all levels and with every functional title also spend most of their time with people—talking, listening, influencing, motivating, and attending meetings.[20] In fact, even chief executives (whom you might expect to be somewhat insulated from other people, up there in their executive suites) spend about three-fourths of their time dealing directly with other people.[21]

However, there are two main differences among the management levels. First, top and middle managers both have managers for subordinates. In other words, they are in charge of other managers. First-line supervisors have workers—nonmanagers—as subordinates. Second, top, middle, and first-line managers use their time differently. Top managers tend to spend more time planning and setting goals (like "double sales in the next two years"). Middle managers then translate these goals into specific projects (like "hire two new salespeople and introduce three new products") for their subordinates to execute. First-line supervisors then concentrate on directing and controlling the employees who actually do the work on these projects day to day.

Do You Have the Traits to Be a Manager?

Research evidence can help someone decide whether management might be a plausible occupation to pursue.[22] It suggests that managers have certain traits.

Personality and Interests Career counseling expert John Holland says that personality (including values, motives, and needs) is an important determinant of career choice. Specifically, he says that six basic personal orientations determine the sorts of careers to which people are drawn. Research with his Vocational Preference Test (VPT) suggests that almost all successful managers fit into at least one of two (or both) personality types or orientations:

- *Social orientation.* Social people are attracted to careers that involve working with others in a helpful or facilitative way. (So managers as well as others, like clinical psychologists and social workers, would exhibit this orientation.) Socially oriented people usually find it easy to talk with all kinds of people; are good at helping people who are upset or troubled; are skilled at explaining things to others; and enjoy doing social things like helping others with their personal problems, teaching, and meeting new people.[23] It's hard to be a manager if you're not comfortable dealing with people.
- *Enterprising orientation.* Enterprising people tend to like working with people in a supervisory or persuasive way. They like influencing others. Enterprising people often characterize themselves as being good public speakers, as having reputations for being able to deal with difficult people, as successfully organizing the

work of others, and as being ambitious and assertive. They enjoy influencing others, selling things, serving as officers of groups, and supervising the work of others. Managers need to be comfortable influencing others.

Comptencies Edgar Schein says that career planning is a process of discovery. He says that each person slowly develops an occupational self-concept, in terms of what his or her talents, abilities, motives, and values are.

managerial competence: the motivation and skills required to gain a management position, including intellectual, emotional, and interpersonal skills

career anchor: a dominant concern or value that directs an individual's career choices and that the person will not give up if a choice must be made

People in different occupations have different competencies. Based on his study of MIT graduates, Schein says that managers have a strong **managerial competence career anchor.**[24] These people show a strong motivation to become managers, "and their career experience enables them to believe that they have the skills and values necessary to rise to such general management positions." A management position with high responsibility is their ultimate goal. Every career decision they make pivots around the fact that they know they have this managerial competence career anchor. A career anchor, says Schein, is a dominant concern or value that directs an individual's career choices and that the person will not give up if a choice must be made.

These managerially oriented people see themselves as competent in three specific areas. One is *analytical competence.* They have the ability to identify, analyze, and solve problems under conditions of incomplete information and uncertainty. A second is *interpersonal competence:* the ability to influence, supervise, lead, manipulate, and control people at all levels. Third is *emotional competence.* They were stimulated, not exhausted, by emotional and interpersonal crises.

Achievements Psychologists at AT&T conducted two long-term studies of managers. The aim was to determine how their premanagement achievements related to their subsequent success (or lack thereof) as managers at AT&T.[25] Those managers who went to college rose (on average) much faster and higher in management than did those who did not attend college. People with higher college grades showed greater potential for promotion early in their careers, and they rose higher in management than did those with lower grades. Those who had attended better-quality colleges at first ranked higher as potential managers. However, within several years, college quality had little effect on who was promoted.

Managers who majored in humanities and social sciences moved faster up the corporate ladder.[26] Business majors ranked second. Math, science, and engineering majors ranked third. Why? At least in this study, the humanities majors scored the highest in decision making, intellectual ability, written communication skills, creativity in solving business problems, and motivation for advancement. Both the humanities/social science majors and the business majors ranked higher in leadership ability, oral communication skills, interpersonal skills, and flexibility than did the math, science, and engineering majors.[27]

AT&T's managers are dealing with rapid technological change in their industry.

Findings like these may just be unique to this specific group of managers—or to AT&T. However, the findings do suggest that, whatever the major, it's important for managers and future managers to work on improving decision making, creativity, and written communication skills.

The Managerial Skills

Online Study Center
ACE the Test
Managing Now! LIVE

Successful managers like Andrea Jung and Lieutenant General Russell Honore don't just have the right personality traits and competencies. They also have the right skills. For example, Jung's planning skills helped her set Avon on the right path. Honore's organizational skills helped him turn New Orleans's disastrous situation around. Managers need three sets of skills: technical, interpersonal, and conceptual.[28]

Technical Skills

First, managers have to be technically competent with respect to planning, organizing, leading, and controlling. For example, they should know how to develop a plan, write a job description, and design an incentive plan. Chapters 2 to 17 focus on these management skills. In today's high-tech environment, managers also must know when and how to use the manager's new technological tools. Chapters 5, 6, and 8 focus on these skills, for example, on how managers use decision-making software. Finally, managers should be competent in their areas of expertise. For example, accounting managers need accounting skills. Your other business courses will help develop these latter skills.

Interpersonal Skills

Researchers at The Center for Creative Leadership in Greensboro, North Carolina, studied why managers fail, and they came to some useful conclusions. Some managers simply didn't do their jobs. These managers thought more about being promoted than about excelling on their current jobs.[29] However, most of the failures were interpersonal. These managers had abusive or insensitive styles, disagreed with upper management about how to run the business, left a trail of bruised feelings, or didn't resolve conflicts among subordinates.

Second, managers must therefore have good interpersonal skills. Interpersonal skills "include knowledge about human behavior and group processes, ability to understand the feelings, attitudes, and motives of others, and ability to communicate clearly and persuasively."[30] These skills include tact and diplomacy, empathy, persuasiveness, and oral communications ability. Because managing in today's Internet environment requires getting employees and alliance partners to work together, encouraging collaboration and trust is also crucial. Chapters 13 to 17 will help you learn these skills.

Conceptual Skills

Third, studies also show that effective leaders tend to have more cognitive ability. In other words, their intelligence (and subordinates' perception of that intelligence) tend to be highly rated.[31] Conceptual (or cognitive) skills "include analytical ability, logical thinking, concept formation, and inductive reasoning."[32] Conceptual skills manifest themselves in good judgment, creativity, and in the ability to see the big picture in a situation.

Intelligence is one thing; good judgment is another. Many high-IQ people have wobbly judgment. And many people of lower IQ have great judgment. As Lawrence Bossidy puts it, "If you have to choose between someone with a staggering IQ and elite education who is gliding along, and someone with a lower IQ but who is absolutely determined to succeed, you'll always do better with the second person."[33] Chapter 5 will help you hone conceptual skills.

The Evolution of Modern Management

Online Study Center
ACE the Test
Managing Now! LIVE

To understand how to manage today, it is useful to know something about how management evolved over time, since much of what managers do today is surprisingly similar to what even ancient managers did. One ancient Egyptian father told his child this about managerial planning: "The leader ought to have in mind the days that are yet to come."[34] In terms of control, the pharaoh's vizier (manager) got this advice: "Furthermore, he shall go in to take counsel on the affairs of the king, and there will be reported to him the affairs of the two lands in his house every day."[35] We can learn from what worked and did not work for the managers who came before us. For example, the word *bureaucracy* originally referred to an efficient way to get things done!

The Classical and Scientific Management School

Modern management concepts and techniques had their roots in the Industrial Revolution hundreds of years ago. Before that, businesses tended to be small. When machines replaced human labor, business boomed. However, success created a problem—how to manage these new, large enterprises. At this time, there were no management principles, no management gurus, and no management textbooks (or business schools).

Businesspeople therefore turned for management techniques to military and religious organizations, the only big organizations they knew. These organizations had (and still tend to have) centralized, top-down decision making, rigid chains of command, specialized divisions of work, and autocratic leadership. Entrepreneurs thus organized their new businesses along the same lines.[36]

As their companies grew, business owners sought principles they could apply to solve their management problems by asking questions like, "How should we organize our departments?" and "How many employees should a manager supervise?" Out of this environment emerged what we call today the classical school of management.

Frederick Winslow Taylor and Scientific Management Frederick Winslow Taylor was among the first of the classical management writers. Writing mostly in the early 1900s, he developed a set of principles and practices that he called scientific management. Taylor's basic theme was that managers should scientifically study how work was done to identify the one best way to get a job done. He based his theory of scientific management on four principles:

1. *The one best way.* Management, through scientific observation, must find the one best way to perform each job.
2. *Scientific selection of personnel.* Management must uncover each worker's limitation, find his or her "possibility for development," and give each worker the required training.
3. *Financial incentives.* Taylor knew that putting the right worker on the right job would not ensure high productivity. He proposed financial incentives, with each worker paid in direct proportion to how much he or she produced.

The Gilbreths were scientific management pioneers.

4. *Functional foremanship.* Taylor called for a division of work between manager and worker such that managers did all planning, preparing, and inspecting, and the workers did the actual work. Specialized experts, or functional foremen, would be responsible for specific aspects of a job, such as choosing the best machine speed and inspecting the work.[37]

● **Frank and Lillian Gilbreth and Motion Study** The work of this husband-and-wife team also illustrates the classical/scientific management approach. Born in 1868, Frank Gilbreth began as an apprentice bricklayer, and he soon became intrigued by the idea of improving efficiency.[38] In 1904, he married Lillian, who had a background in psychology. Together, they invented motion-study principles to scientifically analyze tasks. Two principles were "The two hands should begin and complete their motions at the same time," and "The two hands should not be idle at the same time except during rest periods."[39]

● **Henri Fayol and the Principles of Management** The work of Henri Fayol also illustrates the classical approach. Fayol had been an executive with a French iron and steel firm for thirty years before writing *General and Industrial Management.* In his book, Fayol said that managers performed five basic functions: planning, organizing, commanding, coordinating, and controlling (sound familiar?). He also outlined a list of management principles he had found useful. Fayol's fourteen principles include his famous principle of unity of command: "For any action whatsoever, an employee should receive orders from one superior only."[40]

● **Max Weber and the Bureaucracy** Max Weber's work was first published in Germany in 1921. At the time, managers still had few principles they could apply in managing organizations. Weber therefore created the concept of an ideal or pure form of organization, which he called **bureaucracy**. Bureaucracy, for Weber, was the most efficient form of organization. Managers, he said, would do well to organize their companies along these lines:

bureaucracy: to Max Weber, the ideal way to organize and manage an organization; generally viewed today as a term reflecting an unnecessarily rigid and mechanical way of getting things done

1. A well-defined hierarchy of authority
2. A clear division of work
3. A system of rules covering the rights and duties of all employees
4. A system of procedures for dealing with the work situation
5. Impersonality of interpersonal relationships
6. Selection for employment and promotion based on technical competence.[41]

The Behavioral School

The classical management experts' principles gave managers at the time rules they could use to better run their companies. However, the principles themselves, while valuable, tended to ignore the human element at work. "Design the most highly specialized and efficient job you can," assumed the classicist, and "plug in the worker, who will then do your bidding if the pay is right." The basic (if implicit) assumption was that pay and working conditions alone determined workers' productivity.

By the 1920s, things were changing. People moved from farms to cities and became more dependent on each other for goods and services. Businesses mechanized their factories, and jobs became more specialized, monotonous, and interdependent.[42] The Great Depression began. These events made people wonder: Are hard work, individualism, and maximizing profits—the building blocks of classical management—really as beneficial as they were thought to be? Soon, government became more involved in economic matters. Social reformers worked both at establishing a minimum wage and at encouraging trade unions.

● The Hawthorne Studies In 1927, what we call today the Hawthorne studies began at the Chicago Hawthorne plant of the Western Electric Company. Researchers from Harvard University conducted several studies, one of which is known as the relay assembly test room studies. The researchers isolated a group of workers in a separate room. Then the researchers began changing the working conditions (for instance, modifying the length of the workday and the morning and afternoon rest breaks). Surprisingly, these changes did not greatly affect the workers' performance. The researchers concluded that employee performance depended on factors other than working conditions or pay—a stunning discovery at the time.

In short, the researchers found that it was the workers' social situations, not just their working conditions, that influenced how they behaved at work. Most notably, the researchers discovered that their study had inadvertently made the workers feel they were special. The research observer had changed the workers' situation by "his personal interest in the girls and their problems."[43] Scientists call this phenomenon the Hawthorne effect. It's what happens when the scientist, in the course of an experiment, inadvertently influences the participants.

The Hawthorne studies were a turning point in the study of management. They proved that employee morale and showing an interest in employees had a big effect on employee performance. The human relations movement, inspired by this realization, was born. It emphasized that workers had social needs that the organization had to accommodate.

● Changing Environment Hawthorne wasn't the only reason for this new point of view: the environment was also changing. Having grown large and then made their companies more efficient, many managers were turning to research and development (R&D) to develop new products. For example, after World War II, companies such as U.S. Rubber and B.F. Goodrich (which had concentrated on tire manufacturing) began developing and marketing new products such as latex, plastics, and flooring.

The new R&D and product diversification influenced management theory in several ways. For one thing, efficiency was no longer a manager's only concern. With more diversified product lines to keep track of, managers had to *decentralize*—that is, set up separate divisions to manage each new product. That meant relying on these new divisions' managers and employees to make more decisions. And with the need to encourage employees to innovate, managers had to let even lower-level employees make more decisions. Thus, because of the Hawthorne findings and the other changes taking place after World War II, managers started taking a much more people-oriented approach to managing employees.

● Douglas McGregor: Theory X and Theory Y The work of Douglas McGregor is a good example of this new approach. According to McGregor, the classical organization was not just a relic of ancient times. Instead, it also reflected certain basic assumptions about human nature.[44] McGregor arbitrarily classified these assumptions as Theory X. Theory X assumptions held that most people dislike work and responsibility and prefer to be directed; that they are motivated not by the desire to do a good job but simply by financial incentives; and that therefore most people must be closely supervised, controlled, and coerced into achieving organizational objectives.

McGregor questioned this view. He felt that management needed new practices and ways of organizing to deal with diversification, decentralization, and participative decision making. These new management practices had to reflect a new set of assumptions about human nature, assumptions McGregor called Theory Y. Theory Y held that people wanted to work hard, could enjoy work, and could exercise substantial self-control. You could trust your employees if you treated them right.

Chris Argyris established many of the principles that led managers to take a more people-oriented view of how to manage organizations.

● **Rensis Likert and the Employee-Centered Organization** What new management practices do these Theory Y assumptions call for? Writing at this time, the researcher Rensis Likert concluded that effective organizations differ from ineffective ones in several ways. The classical writers' "job-centered organizations" focus on specialized jobs, efficiency, and close supervision of workers. Post-Hawthorne "employee-centered organizations" should "focus their primary attention on endeavoring to build effective work groups with high performance goals."[45] Therefore, said Likert, "widespread use of participation is one of the more important approaches employed by the high-producing managers."[46] He said that managers should let workers participate in making important work-related decisions.

● **Chris Argyris and the Mature Individual** Chris Argyris reached similar conclusions, but he approached the situation differently.[47] Argyris argued that healthy people go through a maturation process. Gaining employees' compliance by assigning them to highly specialized jobs with no decision-making power and then closely supervising them encourages workers to be dependent, passive, and subordinate. He said that it's better and more natural to give workers more responsibility and broader jobs.

The Administrative School

The administrative school experts include Chester Barnard and Herbert Simon. Chester Barnard was president of what was then New Jersey Bell Telephone Company and, at various times, president of the Rockefeller Foundation and chair of the National Science Foundation. In terms of devising a management theory, he focused on what managers could do to make employees willing to contribute their individual efforts to the organization.

How do you get the employees to "contribute their individual efforts"?[48] Barnard proposed what he called a person's zone of indifference. He said that each person has a range of orders (a "zone of indifference") he or she will willingly accept without consciously questioning their legitimacy.[49] Barnard said the manager had to provide sufficient inducements (and not just financial ones) to make each employee's zone of indifference wider.

Herbert Simon also viewed getting employees to do what the organization needed them to do as a major issue facing managers. How can managers influence employee behavior? According to Simon, managers can ensure that employees carry out tasks in one of two ways. They can impose control by closely monitoring subordinates and insisting that they do their jobs as ordered (using the classicists' approach, in other words). Or managers can foster employee self-control by providing better training, encouraging participative leadership, and developing commitment and loyalty (thus, take a more behavioral approach).[50]

The Management Science School

More recently, management theorists began to apply quantitative techniques to solving management problems. Writers usually refer to this movement as management science (or operations research). It is "the application of scientific methods, techniques, and tools to problems involving the operations of systems so as to provide those in control of the system with optimum solutions to the problems."[51]

The Management Science Approach Historian Daniel Wren says that operations research/management science has "... roots in scientific management."[52] Like Taylor and the Gilbreths, today's management scientists use research and analysis to find optimal solutions to management problems. Modern-day management scientists, of course, use much more sophisticated mathematical tools and computers. And management science's goal is not to try to find a "science of management" but "to use scientific analysis and tools to solve management problems."

The Systems Approach Management science evolved along with the systems approach. A system is an entity—a hospital, city, company, or person, for instance—that has interdependent parts (or subsystems) and a purpose. Systems-approach practitioners advocate viewing organizations as systems with interrelated subsystems. Focusing on the interrelatedness of the subsystems (and between the subsystems and the firm's environment) provides useful insights. For example, it suggests that a manager can't change one subsystem without affecting the rest. Hiring a new production manager might have repercussions in the sales and accounting departments.

Similarly, according to systems experts, managers can't properly organize and manage their companies without understanding the firms' environments. For example, when the tire companies diversified into new products, they abruptly faced more diverse markets and competitors. That prompted these companies to split themselves into separate divisions so each division could focus on its own market. That got management experts thinking that the organization and how you manage it must be contingent (rely) on the environment.

The Situational/Contingency School

Studies in England and the United States soon began to emphasize the need for a situational or contingency approach to management. The essence of this approach was that both the organization and how its managers should manage it depended (were contingent) on the company's environment and technology.

For example, two British researchers, Tom Burns and G. M. Stalker, studied several industrial firms in England. They concluded that whether what they called a mechanistic or an organic management approach was best depended on the company's environment. In a textile mill they studied, it was important to have long, stable production runs. That way, management didn't have to shut down the huge textile machines. Management had to keep sales and demand stable. In such a stable environment, Burns and Stalker found that within the company, a mechanistic (or classical) management approach worked best. Managers emphasized efficiency, specialized jobs, and making everyone stick to the rules.

In contrast, Burns and Stalker found that the main focus in high-tech firms was innovating new products. These companies therefore faced relatively innovative, fast-changing environments (with more new products and more quickly changing competitors, for instance). In these firms, the important thing was learning as fast as possible what competitors were doing and being able to respond quickly by letting even lower-level employees make fast decisions. These firms used the more flexible, people-oriented, organic management approach. They emphasized innovation, did not confine employees to specialized jobs, and did not stress sticking to the rules.

With business becoming increasingly high-tech, it would soon turn out that this organic management approach would become more prevalent. With that in mind, let us turn to managing today.

Modern Management Schools of Thought

Things change fast in business today. Just months after going public, Google faced new competition. Yahoo! poured millions into building its search capabilities. Microsoft was perfecting its own search engine. Amazon (fearing Google's new Froogle shopping site) introduced a new search engine. And, not to be outdone, Google introduced Gmail to lure surfers from Yahoo! and Microsoft.[53] After about one year in business, Friendster.com, the social networking site, had about 1 million unique visitors per month. Introduced a year later, myspace.com went from nothing to 14 million visitors per month.

Rapid change like this is not limited to high-tech companies. For example, between 1997 and 2006, Coca-Cola Co. had three CEOs—extraordinary turnover for this firm. Why? Coke faces bigger global competitors, and huge customers like Wal-Mart are now dictating stronger terms. (For example, Wal-Mart made Coca-Cola introduce a new Splenda-based Diet Coke.) Carbonated drinks still account for most of Coke's business, but consumers are increasingly purchasing noncarbonated drinks.[54]

Managing under such fast-changing conditions is a challenge. Ford Motor Company announced its new Way Forward plan in March 2006 to return to profitability; in June, they had to revise that plan because of shrinking sales. Then, in September 2006, William Ford, Ford's CEO, stepped down in favor of bringing in a new CEO, a president from Boeing named Al Mulally. Mr. Mulally had experience managing under conditions of rapid change.

Several factors explain why the manager's environment is changing so fast. These factors include globalization, technological change, and the changing nature of work.

globalization: the extension of a firm's sales, ownership, or manufacturing to new markets abroad

Competition Is Global **Globalization** refers to extending a company's sales, ownership, and/or manufacturing to new markets abroad.[55] Toyota produces the Camry in Kentucky, while Dell produces and sells personal computers in China. In 2006, Google extended its reach into China by instituting its new Google China instant messenger service. Free trade areas—agreements that reduce tariffs and barriers among trading partners—further encourage international trade.

More globalization means more competition, and more competition means more pressure to improve—to lower costs; to make employees more productive; and to do things better, faster, and less expensively. When Carrefour opens stores in Chile, the local retailers either improve or leave. Similarly, Ikea changed the ground rules for local U.S. furniture stores when it opened in New Jersey. As one expert says, "The bottom line is that the growing integration of the world economy into a single, huge marketplace is increasing the intensity of competition in a wide range of manufacturing and service industries."[56]

Managers react in various ways. Some, like Levi Strauss, outsource or transfer operations abroad to seek cheaper labor and to tap what *Fortune* magazine calls "a vast new supply of skilled labor around the world."[57] Others, as we'll see, adapt by applying world-class management practices. Many of these practices, such as flexible manufacturing and computerized links between a company and its suppliers, rely on technology.

● Technological Advances Force Managers to Change New high-tech products and services are changing the face of business. Thousands of new Web-enabled businesses exist, including (to choose just three) file-sharing sites, blog sites, and social networking sites like myspace.com.[58] Managers rely on information technology, for instance, in the form of personal digital assistants (PDAs) to do their jobs.

Technology is triggering turmoil. In 2006, America's second-largest newspaper chain, Knight-Ridder, was sold. Part of its problem was new high-tech competition. Websites such as Monster and Hot Jobs had drawn off many employment ad users, while sites like Craigslist siphoned classified ad users. Early in 2006, SBC Communications bought AT&T, which then bought BellSouth. The purchases reflect technological change. For example, demand for Voice over Internet Protocol (VoIP) phone calls is booming, which displaces demand for land-line and even cell-phone calls. This accelerates a revolution among land-line and cell-phone firms, many of which have gone out of business trying to compete on this fast-changing playing field.[59]

● The Nature of Work In turn, using new technology to the fullest usually requires changing how people work. For example, one bank installed special software that made it easier for customer-service representatives to handle customers' inquiries. Seeking to capitalize on the new software, the bank upgraded the customer-service representatives' responsibilities. The bank gave them new training, taught them how to sell more of the bank's services, gave them more authority to make decisions, and raised their wages. Here, the new computer system improved profitability.

A second bank installed a similar system but did not change the workers' jobs. Here, the system did help each service representative handle a few more calls. But this second bank saw few of the performance gains that the first bank did by turning its reps into motivated, highly trained salespeople.[60]

As Microsoft Corporation chair Bill Gates put it, "In the new organization, the worker is no longer a cog in a machine but is an intelligent part of the overall process. Welders at some steel jobs now have to know algebra and geometry to figure weld angles from computer-generated designs."[61] This means managers must be skilled at managing *knowledge work* and *human capital*.[62] Knowledge work is work that depends on employees' training, knowledge, and expertise. Human

Managers need a new approach when managing knowledge workers like the person pictured here.

capital refers to the sum total of all the knowledge, education, training, skills, and expertise of a firm's workers.[63] Today, "the center of gravity in employment is moving fast from manual and clerical workers to knowledge workers, who resist the command and control model that business took from the military 100 years ago."[64] In other words, managers need new principles and tools for managing knowledge workers.

● **Modern Management Thought** Trends like these prompted modern management writers to propose new theories of how to manage. The basic theme of these experts is *managing change and innovation.* Two McKinsey & Co. consultants, Thomas Peters and Robert Waterman Jr., were among the first. They studied what they called eight excellent companies. They concluded that these firms were excellent because managers here followed several simple principles: a bias toward action, simple form and lean staff, continued contact with customers, productivity improvement via people, operational autonomy to encourage entrepreneurship, one key business value, doing what they know best, and simultaneous loose and tight controls (in other words, making sure that employees buy into the company's values so that they are able to control themselves).[65]

Rosabeth Moss Kantor studied companies like IBM. She concluded that more successful companies generally had fewer management levels and a greater responsiveness to change, and they entered into more partnerships with other companies.[66] As mentioned earlier in this chapter, Sumantra Ghoshal and Christopher Bartlett argue that successful managers foster innovation by encouraging entrepreneurship.

Several modern management writers say that, with innovation so important, the best companies are *intelligent enterprises,* or *learning organizations.* James Brian Quinn studied what he calls intelligent enterprises. These companies (like Google) depend on converting their employees' intellectual resources (such as engineering knowledge) into services and products. Companies like these, says Quinn, must leverage—take maximum advantage of—their intellectual capital. They do this by ensuring that ideas can flow quickly among employees, such as by encouraging informal communications.[67]

Similarly, Peter Senge argues for creating learning organizations, "organizations where people continually expand their capacity to create the results they truly desire . . . and where people are continually learning how to learn together."[68] Learning organizations' managers do this by encouraging systems thinking, personal mastery (empowering employees to make decisions), building a shared vision, and team learning.[69]

The bottom line is that modern management theorists argue for a more agile, responsive, lean, fast-acting approach to management. Figure 1.2 helps summarize their thinking. A fast-changing global environment means more competition, change, and unpredictability. Managers have responded by making their companies more streamlined and agile, leaner, and faster-acting. The following discussion lists a few specific features of managing in today's fast-changing environment, according to their thinking.

● **Smaller, More Entrepreneurial Organizational Units** It is easier to stay in touch with employees when the organization is not too big. Toyota therefore keeps its plants down to several hundred employees. T. J. Rogers, president of Cypress Semiconductor, believes that large companies stifle innovation. When developing a new product, he creates a separate start-up company under the Cypress umbrella.[70]

FIGURE 1.2

Why Companies Need to Be More Flexible and World Class

Factors including globalized competition, technology revolution, new competitors, and changing tastes produce more uncertainty, more choices, and more complexity. The result is that organizations must be responsive, smaller, flatter, and oriented toward motivating knowledge workers.

● **Team-Based Organizations** Managers extend this small-is-beautiful philosophy to how they organize the work itself. Most companies today organize at least some of their operations around small, self-managing teams. GM's Saturn Corporation subsidiary is an example. Work is organized around work teams of ten to twelve employees. Each team is responsible for a complete task, such as installing door units or maintaining automated machines. The teams don't have traditional supervisors. Instead, highly trained workers do their own hiring, control their own budgets, monitor the quality of their own work, and generally manage themselves.

Worker empowerment: Rooms Control Clerk at the front desk, the New York Marriott, Brooklyn.

● **Empowered Decision Making** For self-managing teams to manage themselves, they need the authority and training to do so. Empowering employees (giving them the training and authority) is therefore central to what managers do today.

● **Flatter Organizational Structures, Knowledge-Based Management** It can take a long time for a request from a front-line employee to get to the top of the typical tall, multilayered organization like GM. By empowering their employees (and letting them make their own decisions), companies can eliminate layers of management. Instead of seven or eight tall management layers, there may be only three or four flat layers.[71]

New Bases of Management Power In today's team-based and empowered organizations, managers can no longer rely on their formal authority to get employees to follow them.[72] Peter Drucker put it this way: "You have to learn to manage in situations where you don't have command authority, where you are neither controlled nor controlling."[73] Yesterday's manager thought of him- or herself as a manager or boss. The new manager is a sponsor, a team leader, or an internal consultant.[74]

An Emphasis on Vision In companies with fewer bosses, formulating a clear vision of where the firm is heading becomes more important. Peter Drucker says today's companies require "clear, simple, common objectives [a vision] that translate into particular actions."[75] The vision is like a signpost. Even without a lot of supervisors to guide them, employees can steer themselves by the company's vision.[76] Technology is another feature of managing now.

Managing Now

Online Study Center
ACE the Test
Managing Now! LIVE

Information technology is now a familiar aspect of our lives. We use computers, e-mail, software, cell phones, iPods, fax machines, flash drives, scanners, and BlackBerries© to assist with our daily chores. We search for travel information on Expedia, download airline tickets, and register for and take college courses online. Computerized diagnostic tools analyze our autos' problems, point-of-sale computers at Zara process our credit-card purchases, and computerized traffic-flow systems control our trips to work.

The Company of the Future Is Here Now

information technology (IT): any processes, practices, or systems that facilitate the processing and transporting of information

Perhaps not so obvious is the vast number of ways in which managers rely on information technology to succeed in today's fast-changing world. Modern management theorists' prescriptions for streamlined, agile, lean, faster-acting companies would be hard to achieve without information technology.[77] **Information technology (IT)** refers to any processes, practices, or systems that facilitate processing and transporting information. It includes both the hardware (such as computers, iPods, cell phones, and servers) and the software systems used to make these devices work. Like the managers and professionals on this book's cover, managers today simply could not do their jobs—or do them as well—without the aid of information technology. Here are some examples of the managerial applications of information technology we'll discuss in this book, showing how managers use information technology.

- The Spanish retailer Zara doesn't need the expensive inventories that burden competitors like The Gap. Zara operates its own Internet-based worldwide distribution network linked to the checkout registers at its stores around the world. This lets it continuously monitor store sales. When it sees a particular garment flying off the shelves of one of its stores, its flexible manufacturing system swings into action. It dyes the required fabric, manufactures the item, and speeds it to that store.[78]
- Accountants PriceWaterhouseCooper maintains electronic bulletin boards on more than 1,000 different company projects. About 18,000 of its employees in

twenty-two countries use these bulletin boards to get updates on matters such as how to handle specialized projects on which they are working.

- The team that developed the Boeing 787 made extensive use of videoconferencing for meeting with engine suppliers and airlines around the world to discuss the new aircraft's design.
- Managers make extensive use of mySpace.com-like virtual online communities. For example, to win a $300 million navy ship deal, Lockheed-Martin established a virtual design environment with two major shipbuilders via a private intranet. Eventually, about 200 global suppliers also connected to the network via special, secure Internet links. This allowed secure transfer of design, project management, and even financial data back and forth via simple browser access.
- Procter & Gamble's R&D executive, Larry Huston, knew his firm had to reach out to get more and better new-product ideas. Procter & Gamble (P&G) now uses various information technology tools to connect itself to various sources of new-product ideas. For example, InnovationNet is an intranet Web portal for 18,000 Procter & Gamble innovators in research and development, engineering, market research, purchasing, and patents. One P&G senior vice president calls it a sort of global lunchroom. It lets 18,000 P&G employees worldwide exchange ideas.
- With about 10,000 stores and 34 million transactions a week, Seattle-based Starbucks Coffee Company's managers must make sure they stay in control of what's happening at each of their stores. That's why Starbucks uses a global information technology system to monitor transactions in each of its stores. Its system (called XPR) remotely monitors an assortment of metrics at each store. XPR then triggers reports when any of the metrics for a store seem to be moving in unusual ways. For example, the system monitors point-of-sale activities and then triggers reports if a particular register seems to be recording too many free refills. That helps Starbucks's executives stay in control, even from thousands of miles away.
- Aiming to improve its service, Safeway Supermarkets installed special point-of-sale computerized registers. Their suppliers now get real-time information regarding sales of their products, which they need in order to replenish Safeway's shelves using just-in-time inventory management. Some Safeway customers receive handheld devices in order to communicate to Safeway, prior to leaving home, the items they need to purchase.
- Wal-Mart recently had its top 100 suppliers start attaching radio frequency identification (RFID) tags to shipments. These help Wal-Mart and its supply chain partners keep track of inventory as it moves from manufacturer to warehouse to stores.[79]
- Information technology is critical to UPS's success. Its drivers use handheld computers to capture customers' signatures along with pickup, delivery, and time-card information and automatically transmit this information back to headquarters via a wireless telephone network. UPS and its customers can then monitor and control the progress of packages throughout the delivery process.
- Caterpillar Corporation needed a better way for its employees to share their knowledge. The company recently introduced its Knowledge Network, a Web-based system that Caterpillar employees use to collaborate and share knowledge.

Using the Knowledge Network, Caterpillar employees can more easily communicate and participate in chatroom-type discussions, and post best ideas on community bulletin boards.

- A "digital dashboard" presents the manager with computerized desktop graphs and charts so he or she can get a picture of where the company has been and where it's going. For example, a top manager's dashboard for Southwest Airlines might display daily trends for activities such as airplane turnaround time, attracting and keeping customers, and on-time flights. This keeps the manager in control. For example, if ground crews are turning planes around slower today, financial results tomorrow may decline unless the manager takes action.

Some Important Management Information Systems

information system: the interrelated components working together to collect, process, store, and disseminate information to support decision making, coordination, analysis, and visualization in an organization

Information Systems All the examples listed above depend on information systems. **Information system** refers to the interrelated components working together to collect, process, store, and disseminate information to support decision making, coordination, analysis, and visualization in an organization. Managerial information systems support managerial decision making and control. Caterpillar uses a "knowledge management information system" to capture and compile the information that it needs. Safeway uses a "supply chain management information system" to automate its purchases from suppliers. The following discussion lists some important information systems that managers use (we discuss these in more detail in Chapter 5).

decision support system (DSS): a set of computerized tools that helps managers make decisions

Decision Support Systems A **decision support system (DSS)** is a set of computerized tools that helps managers make decisions. The DSS helps the manager make decisions in two ways. It helps that person access the data he or she needs (for instance, on which products sold best last year). And it provides user-friendly software to analyze that data.

enterprise resource planning (ERP) system: a companywide integrated computer system comprised of compatible software modules for each of the company's separate departments

Enterprise Resource Planning Systems An **enterprise resource planning (ERP) system** is a companywide integrated computer system. It is comprised of compatible software modules for each of the company's separate departments (such as sales, accounting, finance, production, and human resources). Often Internet-based, the ERP modules are designed to communicate with each other and with the central system's database. That way, information from all the departments is readily shared by the ERP system and is available to employees in all the other departments. ERP strips away the barriers that typically exist among a company's stand-alone departmental computer systems. The name notwithstanding, enterprise resource planning systems are not primarily planning systems. We'll generally refer to them as enterprise systems in this book.

With an enterprise system, activities that formerly required human intervention (such as production telling accounting that it should bill a customer because an order just shipped) occur automatically. By integrating the separate departmental modules, enterprise systems can do things for managers that the separate departmental systems (sales, production, finance, and human resources) could not do on their own. For example, when a customer buys a Dell computer online, Dell's ERP automatically records the sale, orders the necessary parts, schedules production, orders UPS to deliver the finished product, and has Dell's accounting department send the customer a bill. The accompanying

Practice IT
J. Crew

After hitting turbulence in the 1990s, J. Crew sold out to Texas Pacific Group, which brought in The Gap Inc.'s former CEO Millard Drexler to turn the company around. One of Drexler's first steps was to articulate a new plan for J. Crew, which had struggled with an identity crisis for several years. Drexler took J. Crew back to its preppy roots and also began offering more upscale merchandise, including $550 tuxedo jackets for men.

However, Drexler knew that in the increasingly competitive retail industry, having the right image was not enough. J. Crew was now competing with huge multinational companies like Zara, H&M, and, in some markets, even with Target and Wal-Mart. Companies like these had hugely efficient information technology-based systems. At Target, for instance, every time an item moved through a point-of-sale register, digital signals went out to its suppliers and transportation companies, automatically signaling them to replenish the items. Zara's technology systems were, in a way, even more impressive. Zara does almost all its own designing and manufacturing in its plant in Spain. When it receives the overnight digital signals about what customers are buying each day, management springs into action. Zara then quickly designs, produces, and delivers to each store similar, complementary items. Drexler knew J. Crew's success depended in part on installing such management information systems.

J. Crew's new chief intelligence officer (CIO) Paul Fusco decided to install an enterprise system from one of the largest suppliers of such systems, SAP. J. Crew began by installing separate SAP enterprise modules for each of its departments. They started with financial systems and then moved on to human resources and inventory management and replenishment.

The new enterprise system made J. Crew a more agile and efficient company. For example, by automating its purchase order system, J. Crew reduced the time required to fill an order and get it to the store by about three weeks. More important, the new system gives J. Crew's headquarters merchandise managers and buyers a real-time view of what's selling and what's not. This changed the firm's whole planning system. Previously, it took two to three days for J. Crew's buyers and merchandisers to find out what was selling in each store. That made it impossible to accurately gauge exactly what to design and produce. Now, sales and inventory data move digitally from every store to headquarters every night. As Fusco says, "[I]t's so important when the buyers and merchandisers arrive each morning for them to have a complete view of what's sold the previous day . . . having a better view of yesterday helps our merchants to make more informed decisions."[80]

Millard Drexler's J. Crew turnaround has been a huge success. For 2005, J. Crew had profits of $3.8 million, compared with a loss of just over $100 million in the previous year. And in July 2006, J. Crew's new owners sold off some of their stock in one of the largest initial public offerings in the previous five years, raising about $350 million. In three years, Drexler had turned the company around, using effective management skills supported by information technology.

supply chain management systems: systems to help a company manage its relationship with its suppliers and retailers by providing information to help suppliers, purchasing firms, distributors, and logistics/transportation companies coordinate, schedule, and control a company's procurement, production, inventory management, and delivery services

Practice IT feature shows how Millard Drexler used an enterprise system to help turn J. Crew around.

● **Supply Chain Management Systems** **Supply chain management systems** help the company manage its relationship with its suppliers and retailers. They provide information to help suppliers, purchasing firms, distributors, and logistics/transportation companies coordinate, schedule, and control a company's procurement, production, inventory management, and delivery services. For many firms today, much of their fame rests on their supply chain management systems. Target keeps its costs famously low largely because its point-of-sale computers automatically notify vendors like Levi's and P&G when it's time to replace merchandise.

Window on Managing Now
Virtual Integration at Dell Computer

Michael Dell built Dell Computer by using supply chain and customer relationship technology to "blur the traditional boundaries ... among suppliers, manufacturers, and the end users."[81]

For most computer companies, the manufacturing process is like a relay race: components come in from suppliers, these components are assembled into computers, and the computers are then handed off for distribution through wholesalers and retailers (such as CompUSA) to the ultimate customers. Dell's system changes all that. For example, Dell interacts with and sells to customers directly, so it eliminates the activities of the wholesalers and retailers in the traditional distribution chain.

Virtual integration—linking Dell with its suppliers and customers via the Internet—speeds things up even more. Computerized information from Dell continually updates suppliers regarding the number of components they should deliver every morning. The outside suppliers thus actually start to look and act more like an inside part of Dell. Similarly, instead of stocking its own monitors, "[w]e tell Airborne Express or UPS to come to Austin and pick up 10,000 computers a day and go over to the Sony factory in Mexico and pick up the corresponding number of monitors. And while we're all sleeping, they match up the computers and the monitors, and deliver them to the customers ... [O]f course, this requires sophisticated data exchange."[82]

The result of this virtual integration is a lean, efficient, and fast-moving operation. It can turn on a dime when the products demanded by customers change.

customer relationship management systems: systems to help companies manage all the processes involved with interacting with customers, such as taking orders, answering technical questions, and sending bills

● Customer Relationship Management Systems **Customer relationship management systems** help companies manage all the processes involved with interacting with customers, such as taking orders, answering technical questions, and sending bills.[83] For example, when a customer calls with a problem, Dell's customer relationship management system shows the technician what system the customer owns. It then leads the technician through a sequence of diagnostic questions to solve the problem.

knowledge management: any efforts aimed at enabling a company's managers and employees to better access and utilize information available anywhere in their companies

● Knowledge Management **Knowledge management** refers to any efforts aimed at enabling a company's managers and employees to better access and utilize information available anywhere in their companies.[84] When an organization has information and either doesn't know it has that information or can't access it, it suffers a breakdown in knowledge management.

Knowledge management is enormously important today. Think of how wasteful it is for an engineer to spend three days writing a quote for a customer, only to then discover that her predecessor filed a similar quote. One advisory firm estimates that *Fortune* 500 companies lose at least $31.5 billion per year by not sharing knowledge.[85] In today's competitive business environment, it's usually the company with the best information that is the most successful. As a result, many managers today embrace knowledge management systems.

knowledge management systems: systems to organize and make available important knowledge, wherever and whenever a manager or employee needs it

Knowledge management systems organize and make available important knowledge, wherever and whenever the manager or employee needs it. We'll see in Chapter 5 that some knowledge management systems focus on accessing, compiling, and organizing and reviewing knowledge that's already written down and stored away in some form in the company. For example, Merck has vast amounts of knowledge stored away in its computers, like what combinations of drugs they've tested in the past and what the results were. Others focus on helping the company capture new knowledge. For instance, they make it easier for a repairperson to electronically record how he or she solved a customer's computer problem.

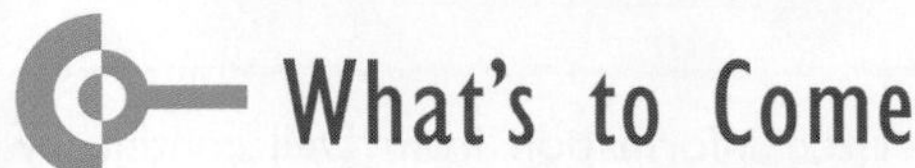

What's to Come

Throughout history, some things in management have not and will not quickly change. Managers still plan, organize, lead, and control. And they still deal with people—communicating, leading, appraising, and coaching them.

This is a book on management; therefore, we focus on what managers should know about planning, organizing, leading, and controlling, and dealing with people. However, we have seen that managers now manage in a fast-changing and highly competitive global environment. To succeed here, managers simply have no choice but to effectively use information technology (IT) devices and systems, including software systems, cell phones, RFIDs, and PDAs. We therefore include in this book many examples of the Internet and IT tools that managers use today to plan, organize, lead, and control. We place some of these examples, like the accompanying one on Dell Computer (on page 25), in the Practice IT and Window on Managing Now features.

CHAPTER SUMMARY

1. An organization consists of people who have formally assigned roles and who must work together to achieve the organization's goals. Organizations needn't be just business firms.
2. Organizations are run by managers. A manager is someone who plans, organizes, leads, and controls the people and the work of the organization so that the organization achieves its goals.
3. Management writers traditionally refer to the manager's four basic functions of planning, organizing, leading, and controlling as the management process.
4. We can classify managers based on organizational level (top, middle, first-line), position (executives, managers or directors, supervisors), and functional title (vice president of production, sales manager). All managers get their work done through people and by planning, organizing, leading, and controlling. Top managers spend more time planning and setting goals. Lower-level managers concentrate on implementing goals and getting employees to achieve them.
5. Managers play other roles too—for instance, figurehead, leader, liaison, spokesperson, negotiator. They also engage in entrepreneurial, competence-building, and renewal processes.
6. Almost everything a manager does involves interacting with and influencing people. The bottom line is that the leading, or people, side of what managers do is not just another step in the management process; it is an integral part of the manager's job.
7. Managers and their organizations now confront rapid change and intense competition. Trends contributing to this include globalization, technological advances, and an emphasis on knowledge work.
8. Modern management theorists' prescriptions for streamlined, agile, lean, faster-acting companies would be hard to achieve without information technology. Information technology (IT) refers to any processes, practices, or systems that facilitate processing and transporting information.
9. Information system refers to the interrelated components working together to collect, process, store, and disseminate information to support decision making, coordination, analysis, and visualization in an organization. Managerial information systems support managerial decision making and control.

DISCUSSION QUESTIONS

1. Is your professor responsible for managing this class? Why or why not?
2. Is your management class an organization? Why or why not?
3. Give examples of each of the four functions of management.
4. Give examples of top, middle, and first-level managers at your college or university.
5. What are four things a manager today can learn and apply from studying management history?
6. Briefly describe four differences between classical and behavioral approaches to managing.
7. What accounts for the fact that companies must be agile today?
8. List ten examples of information technology you would typically expect to deal with on the job.
9. What information technology tools do you use? List at least three ways in which managers use these for planning, organizing, leading, or controlling.

EXPERIENTIAL EXERCISES

1. Most people tend to think of organizations as pyramid-shaped hierarchies, with authority and decision making flowing from the top down. The boss gives the orders, and the employee does the work. As this chapter points out, today's changing environment demands new forms of organization. In a team of four to five students, graphically depict some of the newer organizational designs mentioned in this chapter. First, draw the shapes you think represent the organization charts of the new team-focused organizations. Then write a brief (one- to two-page) summary describing what you have drawn and what you think the implications of these designs are for planning, organizing, leading, and controlling organizations today.
2. While most organizations do tend to be hierarchies with bosses telling employees what to do, colleges and universities have long been somewhat different. For example, many universities traditionally have faculty senates that make decisions about what new programs to approve, and on what bases the university will evaluate and appraise professors. Similarly, many universities have students evaluate the faculty—still an unusual arrangement even in progressive companies. As a team, answer the following questions: (a) In a university in which students evaluate the faculty and the faculty is "the boss" when it comes to deciding on new programs, how can you determine who the "managers" and "employees" are? (b) What five specific recent environmental trends do you think have had the most pronounced effect on the methods used to manage your college or university today? (c) List several ways in which you believe these trends have influenced the way in which the college or university's managers plan, organize, lead, and control.
3. Write a short essay on this topic: the tasks I've performed that I most enjoyed, was proudest of, and was most successful at. (Perhaps, if you're lucky, one task fills the bill!) Now do the same for the task or tasks you least enjoyed, were least proud of, and were least successful at. Now answer this question: based on what you know about what managers do and what it takes to be a manager, do you think you have what it takes to be a manager?

CASE STUDY

No Rules, Just Right

Chris Sullivan and the founders of Outback Steakhouse, Inc., developed a unique vision for a restaurant concept and the management system that would make it work. Having worked for other chain restaurants in the past, Sullivan and his team wanted to do things very differently. They wanted a restaurant that was a fun place for employees to work.

Sullivan and his cofounders had originally planned to build just a few restaurants and then play a lot of golf. Things didn't work out that way. The company they created captured the imagination and appetites of the public. Within its first six years, Outback Steakhouse had become the fastest-growing restaurant chain in the casual-dining segment of the restaurant industry. Outback's management team took the company public. It has won numerous awards for business growth, including Entrepreneur of the Year awards from both *Inc.* magazine and the Kauffman (Entrepreneurship) Foundation.

Part of Outback's success has come from its unorthodox management system. First, Sullivan and his colleagues wanted restaurateurs to be able to make a career as store managers. In many restaurant chains, the best-paying positions are in the corporate office, not directly serving customers. Top store managers in those systems leave the restaurant to move to corporate to make a good salary.

To attract managers, Outback offered very strong financial packages (in many cases offering the manager equity in the local restaurant), assignment to a location for a minimum of five years, and a work environment serving dinner only. Outback's unique employment benefits aren't just for management. Recently, the company rolled out a benefits program for part-time employees. In contrast to many other companies, the less you make at Outback, the less you are required to pay for health insurance.

Sullivan insists that one key for a successful restaurant is for the local team to have fun. Local Outback managers have noted that one of the first questions CEO Sullivan asks them when visiting their location is, "Are you still having fun?" Management's casual style and its fiercely entrepreneurial culture echo the corporate motto: "No rules, just right."

DISCUSSION QUESTIONS

1. Based on this case, what management roles does Sullivan fulfill?
2. List at least ten specific management tasks Sullivan will have to attend to in a typical week.
3. Is Sullivan using a classical or a behavioral management approach, and why do you think he is doing so, given his environment and situation?
4. What environmental forces are acting to influence Outback's business and management style, for good or for ill?

ETHICAL AND SOCIAL ISSUES 2

Sarbanes-Oxley Act of 2002

Managers today run big legal risks if they don't manage their companies ethically.[1] For example, the federal Sarbanes-Oxley Act now requires that publicly traded companies' CEOs and CFOs personally certify the accuracy of their companies' financial statements and that their firms' internal controls are adequate.[2] This means the managers must be able to show they've done their best to ensure that all their employees are acting ethically.

To do this, managers must provide employee ethics training (among other things) and prove that employees actually got trained. However, offering and following up on such training programs can be expensive, particularly when hundreds of employees are involved. So when DTE Energy needed ethics training for its 14,000 employees, its managers wanted a cost-effective program. What should they do? You should have a good answer after reading this chapter. ■

Franklin Raines, the CEO of the Business Roundtable business association, leads a group of managers in an ethics training program.

BEHAVIORAL OBJECTIVES

After studying this chapter, you should be able to:

Show that you've learned the chapter's essential information by

- Explaining what is meant by ethical behavior.
- Describing the organizational factors that influence ethical behavior at work.
- Listing five ways in which a supervisor can personally improve the ethical behavior of his or her subordinates.
- Answering the question, "To whom is the company responsible?"
- Listing the bases for diversity.

Show that you can practice what you've learned here by

- Reading the opening vignette about the Sarbanes-Oxley Act and DTE Energy and recommending an ethics training system for the company.
- Reading the end-of-chapter exercises and explain how you would handle the ethical challenge.
- Reading the chapter case study and explain what you would do if you were the manager, and why.

Show that you can apply what you've learned here by

- Watching the simulation video, identifying the ethical situations, and determining appropriate actions.
- Studying the video scenario and explaining how the manager could use information technology (IT) to encourage ethical behavior in the company.

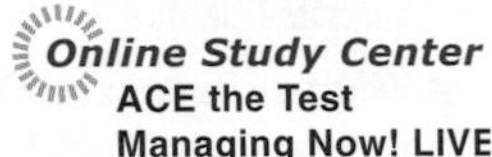

Ethics in an Age of Information Technology

Online Study Center
ACE the Test
Managing Now! LIVE

The U.S. Justice Department recently tried to force Google to hand over a week's worth of Internet searches. Google refused. Yet the day the story broke, Google's stock fell almost 10 percent. This drop seemed to reflect the fact that if Google ever did have to agree to such a request, users felt it would invade their privacy.[3]

In fact, this case had little to do with privacy. The government said it didn't seek personally identifiable information. And Google said its main concern was that supplying the information might give competitors some insight into Google's trade secrets. Still, just the idea that the government's request might somehow strip away Google users' privacy was enough to trigger widespread concern. Users were concerned about their privacy. And perhaps they were concerned about the ethics of Google letting them think that all those searches they inputted were private, when in fact they were all filed away, potentially available for all to see.

The idea that websites and even employers are tracking what people do has focused new interest on *ethics*. Ethics are the principles of conduct that govern an individual or a group.[4] Someone can tell when a situation involves ethics from two observations. First, ethical decisions always involve *normative decisions*. These are decisions where the manager must decide if something is good or bad, right or wrong. Second, ethics always involve *moral decisions*. These are decisions (like those involving lying or stealing) that society views as having serious moral consequences.

● Ethical or Not? Sometimes it's clear what the ethical thing to do is, but often it is not. Sometimes it's fairly clear. One guideline is that if the decision makes the person feel ashamed or remorseful, or involves a matter of serious consequence such as murder, then chances are it is unethical. For example, you are the purchasing manager, and your biggest supplier offers you a $10,000 all-expenses-paid trip to play golf in Scotland, but asks you not to tell your boss. Most people would (rightly) assume that taking the trip is unethical.

On the other hand, many ethical decisions are judgment calls, and here it's not so clear what is ethical and what is not. Conflicts of interest often fall in this category. Conflicts of interest arise when someone who represents Party A in dealings with Party B has a hidden relationship with Party B. For example, a big supplier (who you know your firm is thinking of dropping in favor of another) offers you (the purchasing manager) some help in getting admitted to a graduate program by calling his friend, the dean. What would you do? Similarly, some doctors accept expensive free dinners and trips from drug companies, although they contend (perhaps correctly) that accepting those gifts cannot affect whether and how much they prescribe those companies' drugs.

There are countless other ethical judgment calls. For example, at election time, many newspapers size up the accuracy and honesty of political ads. How far can a candidate (or company) go in embellishing the truth or stating facts out of context in ads? It's an ethical judgment call. As another example, most people would say that lying is bad. But if a person who plans to cause harm asks you where his victim is, would lying still be bad? Perhaps not.[5] The fact that ethics may be situational complicates things even more. For example, bribery in some countries is so widespread that people in those countries don't view it as wrong.

Ethics and the Law

Why not just follow the law? It may seem odd, but the law is not a perfect guide about what is ethical. Something may be legal but not ethical, and something may be ethical but not legal. Charging a naïve customer an exorbitant price may be legal but unethical. Insulting the government may be ethical by society's broader norms but still illegal in some countries. Patrick Gnazzo, vice president for business practices at United Technologies Corp. (and a former trial lawyer), put it this way: "Don't lie, don't cheat, don't steal. We were all raised with essentially the same values. Ethics means making decisions that represent what you stand for, not just what the laws are."[6]

If it's not just legal constraints, why do people do the right thing? One ethicist explains this by suggesting people fall along a continuum, from selfish egoists to people of integrity. Some must be forced to be ethical, while some do so voluntarily. At one end, the selfish egoist basically says, "I'll do whatever I think I can get away with."[7] To stop or slow them down, governments pass laws, and many managers do follow these legal standards. Other managers and professionals voluntarily comply with the professional standards of their professions or professional associations. For example, the professional association of executive recruiters has rules regarding how long a recruiter should wait before approaching a manager he or she placed in a position about a second new position. Finally, some people do not need laws or standards to get them to do the right thing. They are people of integrity who do what they honestly believe is right.[8]

Compare your ethics answers to those of Americans in one survey by answering the quiz in Figure 2.1. You'll find the answers on page 58.

● Managing Now: Ethics and Information Technology An Internet spam gang recently sent misleading e-mails to businesses and consumers in the United States. Most people saw this as unethical. Microsoft helped catch the spammers. It used thousands of trap accounts with addresses on its e-mail service.[9]

For all its benefits, modern information technology does prompt new ethical concerns. A short list of concerns includes intellectual property piracy, computer crimes (including hacking, viruses, and cyberterrorism), security and reliability of intellectual property and of records and forms, spamming, online marketing to children, and privacy.[10]

security: a company's attempts to prevent inappropriate access to the company's resources

privacy: an individual's expectation that what he or she does will remain secret

Of these, one survey found that business managers ranked IT-related **security** and **privacy** as the two main technology-related issues they face. "Security refers to a company's attempts to prevent inappropriate access to the company's resources. Privacy refers to an individual's expectation that what he or she does will remain secret."[11] IT issues raise serious ethical concerns

FIGURE 2.1

The *Wall Street Journal* Workplace Ethics Quiz

The spread of technology into the workplace has raised a variety of new ethical questions, and many old ones still linger.

OFFICE TECHNOLOGY	GIFTS AND ENTERTAINMENT	TRUTH AND LIES
1. Is it wrong to use company e-mail for personal reasons? ☐ Yes ☐ No	7. What's the value at which a gift from a supplier or client becomes troubling? ☐ $25 ☐ $50 ☐ $100	15. Due to on-the-job pressure, have you ever abused or lied about sick days? ☐ Yes ☐ No
2. Is it wrong to use office equipment to help your children or spouse do schoolwork? ☐ Yes ☐ No	8. Is a $50 gift to a boss unacceptable? ☐ Yes ☐ No	16. Due to on-the-job pressure, have you ever taken credit for someone else's work or idea? ☐ Yes ☐ No
3. Is it wrong to play computer games on office equipment during the workday? ☐ Yes ☐ No	9. Is a $50 gift FROM the boss unacceptable? ☐ Yes ☐ No	
4. Is it wrong to use office equipment to do Internet shopping? ☐ Yes ☐ No	10. Of gifts from suppliers: Is it OK to take a $200 pair of football tickets? ☐ Yes ☐ No	
5. Is it unethical to blame an error you made on a technological glitch? ☐ Yes ☐ No	11. Is it OK to take a $120 pair of theater tickets? ☐ Yes ☐ No	
6. Is it unethical to visit pornographic Web sites using office equipment? ☐ Yes ☐ No	12. Is it OK to take a $100 holiday food basket? ☐ Yes ☐ No	
	13. Is it OK to take a $25 gift certificate? ☐ Yes ☐ No	
	14. Can you accept a $75 prize won at a raffle at a supplier's conference? ☐ Yes ☐ No	

SOURCE: Adapted from *Wall Street Journal*, 21 October 1999, pp. 81–84. Ethics Officer Association, Belmont, Mass.: Ethics Leadership Group, Wilmette, Ill. Surveys sampled a cross-section of workers at large companies and nationwide.

cookies: small files deposited on a visitor's hard drive to track the person's visits

● **Privacy and IT** As the Managing Now section notes, privacy is now more of a concern than in the past because information technology facilitates collecting, processing, and disseminating vast quantities of employee and consumer information.[12] For example, websites use **cookies** to track users' online behavior. They do this to see which targeted ads are most effective and to maintain passwords and other personalization features at many websites.[13]

Most consumers don't like cookies. For example, in a survey, 64 percent of 150 Internet users said cookies represented an invasion of their privacy. Fifty-two percent disable cookies before using the Web. About 39 percent delete cookies on a weekly basis, and 25 percent do so monthly.[14] DoubleClick Inc. uses cookies to track users' online habits. Several years ago, it created controversy by matching identifiable personal information with previously anonymous user profiles.[15]

Cookie-related ethical issues can be tricky. For example, if a consumer willingly sends a website personal information, then collecting that information is ethical. On the other hand, a monitoring program that secretly gathers this information to use for identity theft is unethical. But suppose the person willingly gives information to one site. That site then sells it to another site, which in turn uses it to promote its own Web services to the individual. In this situation, it isn't clear that what the websites did was ethical or not.[16]

Two events brought the privacy/ethics issue into focus for many people. Passage of the post-9/11 Patriot Act basically entails a tradeoff of some privacy for added security. However, some in Congress argued that the government's monitoring of some domestic phone calls without judicial consent was both illegal and unethical. Others questioned whether librarians should have to transfer user lists to law enforcement officials.

Similarly, passage of the Health Insurance Portability and Accountability Act (HIPAA) affected many people. This act established national standards for maintaining and electronically transferring patients' health-care information. It stemmed in part from concerns that the health-care industry was not doing enough to protect patients' privacy.[17]

● **Employee Monitoring and IT** Electronically monitoring employees raises similar privacy and ethics concerns. For example, electronic performance monitoring (EPM) means having supervisors electronically monitor the amount of computerized data an employee is processing per day. It's estimated that as many as 26 million U.S. workers have their performance monitored electronically. This fact has already triggered congressional legislation aimed at requiring that employees receive precise notification of when they will be monitored.

Electronic performance monitoring is also becoming more sophisticated. Thanks to cell phones and wireless communication, employers like United Parcel Service (UPS) use GPS units to monitor the whereabouts of their deliverypeople. A federal law now requires all new cell phones to have GPS capabilities; this should expand the number and range of employees that employers keep tabs on.[18] Many more employers, like Bronx Lebanon Hospital in New York, use biometric scanners, for instance, to ensure that the employee who clocks in in the morning is really who he or she claims to be.[19]

Air-Trak employee using global positioning software to track an employee's movements.

Monitoring is spreading. For example, one survey by the Society of Human Resource Management found that about two-thirds of companies monitor e-mail activity, three-fourths monitor employee Internet use, and about two-fifths monitor phone calls.[20] Another survey of 192 companies concluded that 92 percent check their employees' e-mail and Internet use at work. Twenty-two percent monitor employees' online activities all the time.[21]

There are two main legal restrictions on workplace monitoring: the Electronic Communications Privacy Act (ECPA) and common-law protections against invasion of privacy. Congress intended the ECPA to restrict interception and monitoring of oral and wire communications. Common-law protections against invasion of privacy are not written down in laws, but reflect many years' worth of judges' decisions.[22]

Employers do have legitimate reasons for electronically monitoring employees. As one example, employees who use their company computers to swap and download music files can ensnare their employers in illegal activities.[23] Monitoring can also improve productivity, as when UPS tracks the whereabouts of their drivers.

Security and IT Information technology also raises serious computer security concerns. The Australian Stock Exchange recently had to review its online practices when a security breach allowed people using its website to view the details of other users' stock-market activity.[24] Several credit-card-processing companies recently had data on millions of clients stolen. Employees understandably worry that nonauthorized persons may gain access to their private personnel files. Similarly, most people know that what an attorney and his or her client discuss is supposed to be confidential. Yet when an e-mail message bounces from computer to computer through the Internet, it's more like a postcard than a sealed letter.[25]

Piracy Information technology has created whole new industries devoted to pirating copyrighted music, books, and movies. A walk through video stores in some foreign countries would reveal thousands of pirated music and movie performances. And many people routinely download and trade copyrighted files with friends or use pirated software at work. Does morality forbid downloading? Some say no, that the Internet should make transfers free. Others argue that it's immoral (and thus unethical) to violate copyrights by downloading and sharing music or movies.[26]

Reducing IT's Ethical Concerns Technical and legal safeguards can reduce piracy, privacy, and security concerns up to a point. For example, techniques for improving security include encrypting e-mail messages, installing firewalls and antivirus software, instituting access control techniques for preventing unauthorized access, making the computer itself physically secure by using passwords, attaching a privileged notice to each e-mail, and using digital signatures on e-mails.

However, most ethical issues come back to the ethics of people. What about the entrepreneur who's thinking of saving some money by illegally duplicating a program for his or her employees to use? Or, say, the employee whose company is monitoring his or her e-mail messages, or the consumer who's submitting personal information to a website? In most cases, the ethics of those involved—the entrepreneur, the people doing the monitoring, and those managing the website—are the only real safeguards.

What Influences Ethical Behavior at Work?

Several years ago, MCI-WorldCom's CFO pleaded guilty to helping hide the company's true financial condition. The government accused him of having subordinates make fraudulent accounting entries and of filing false statements with the Securities and Exchange Commission (SEC). Why would a star CFO do this? Because, he said, he thought he was helping MCI: "I took these actions, knowing they were wrong, in a misguided attempt to preserve the company to allow it to withstand what I believed were temporary financial difficulties."[27]

Managers can learn some lessons from MCI-WorldCom. Even gifted managers fail if they make the wrong ethical choices. And even honest managers find it easy to convince themselves that what they're doing is not really wrong.

As the example from WorldCom shows, there is no simple answer to the question, What influences ethical behavior at work? It is not just an issue of personal honesty. Basically, to quote just one source, "[E]thical decisions are the result of the interaction of the person and the situation."[28] Let us look more closely at what this means.

Individual Factors

Certainly, people do bring to their jobs their own ideas of what is morally right and wrong, and this influences what they do. Managers use a variety of devices, from polygraph (lie detector) machines (now banned in most cases) to written honesty tests to uncover such tendencies.

Personal ethical tendencies are important. For example, researchers surveyed CEOs of manufacturing firms. The aim was to explain the CEOs' intentions to engage (or to not engage) in two questionable business practices: soliciting a competitor's technological secrets and making payments to foreign government officials to secure business. The researchers concluded that the CEOs' personal tendencies more strongly affected their decisions than did environmental or organizational pressures.[29]

Several personal traits seem to predispose people to possibly making ethical mistakes. Age is one factor. One study surveyed 421 employees to measure the degree to which age, gender, marital status, education, dependent children, region of the country, and years in business influenced responses to ethical decisions. (Decisions included "doing personal business on company time" and "calling in sick to take a day off for personal use.") Older workers in general had stricter interpretations of ethical standards and made more ethically sound decisions than did younger employees. Other studies have found this ethical generation gap.[30]

Researchers in another study asked graduate and undergraduate students to complete a questionnaire containing eleven statements. Each statement described a common but probably unethical behavior concerning intellectual property. The good news was that the students did label as highly unethical those behaviors that had to do with personal privacy or property theft. The bad news was that those behaviors that had to do with theft of the company's property or privacy did not elicit the same negative reactions. Instead, the students tended to be neutral about whether these behaviors were ethical or not.[31]

Another study focused on how different people react to protecting intellectual property and privacy rights. Machiavellian personalities—those who took some pleasure in manipulating others—were more likely to view ignoring the intellectual property and privacy rights of others as acceptable.[32]

● **Self-Deception** Personal tendencies are also important because self-deception has a bigger influence in ethical choice than most people realize. To sum this up, "Corrupt individuals tend not to view themselves as corrupt."[33] They rationalize their unethical acts as being somehow okay. As the president of the Association of Certified Fraud Examiners puts it, people who have engaged in corrupt acts ". . . excuse their actions to themselves, by viewing their crimes as non-criminal, justified, or part of a situation which they do not control."[34]

Table 2.1[35] summarizes six ways managers rationalize away the corruptness of their corrupt acts. For example, consider the "appeal to higher loyalties" rationalization. Here the manager might say, "I'm doing this to protect the company." In one real example, three former executives pleaded guilty to federal charges in what authorities then called the largest and longest accounting fraud in history; the fraud had lasted for twelve years. The managers said they had done what they did to keep their company's stock price high.[36]

TABLE 2.1
How Managers Rationalize Their Corrupt Behavior

Strategy	Description	Examples
Denial of responsibility	The actors engaged in corrupt behaviors perceive that they have no other choice than to participate in such activities.	"What can I do? My arm is being twisted." "It is none of my business what the corporation does in overseas bribery."
Denial of injury	The actors are convinced that no one is harmed by their actions; hence, the actions are not really corrupt.	"No one was really harmed." "It could have been worse."
Denial of victim	The actors counter any blame for their actions by arguing that the violated party deserved whatever happened.	"They deserved it." "They chose to participate."
Social weighting	The actors use two basic approaches to reduce the perceived importance of corrupt behaviors: (1) condemn the condemner and (2) selective social comparison.	"You have no right to criticize us." "Others are worse than we are."
Appeal to higher loyalties	The actors argue that their violation of norms is due to their attempt to realize a higher-order value.	"We answered to a more important cause." "I would not report it because of my loyalty to my boss."
Metaphor of the larger	The actors rationalize that they are entitled to indulge in deviant behaviors because of their accrued credits (time and effort) in their jobs.	"We've earned the right." "It's all right for me to use the Internet for personal reasons at work. After all, I work overtime."

Source: Vikas Anand et al., "Business as Usual: The Acceptance and Perpetuation of Corruption in Organizations," *Academy of Management Executive,* 2004, vol. 18, no. 2, p. 41.

Organizational Factors

In a famous study first conducted at Yale University some years ago, researcher Stanley Milgram showed that, given the right situation, even ethical people do unethical things.[37] In this case, numerous undergraduate students were willing to inflict what they erroneously thought was pain on fellow students in a misguided effort to help the researcher conduct his study. One conclusion we can draw is that misplaced loyalties distort peoples' ethical choices. Most of the apparently sadistic students felt they were, in effect, "just following orders." A second is that the organization and its leaders have a big influence on whether people behave ethically. Pressure, the boss, and the firm's culture are three such factors.

Pressure to Perform Putting employees under undue pressure fosters ethical compromises. A study by the American Society of Chartered Life Underwriters found that 56 percent of all workers felt some pressure to act unethically or illegally, and that the problem seems to be getting worse.[38]

Table 2.2 shows the principal causes of ethical compromises as reported by six levels of employees and managers. Dealing with scheduling pressures was the

TABLE 2.2
Principal Causes of Ethical Compromises

	Senior Management	Middle Management	Front-Line Supervisor	Professional Nonmanagement	Administrative, Salaried	Hourly Employees
Meeting schedule pressure	1	1	1	1	1	1
Meeting overly aggressive financial or business objectives	3	2	2	2	2	2
Helping the company survive	2	2	4	4	3	4
Advancing the career interests of my boss	5	4	3	3	4	5
Feeling peer pressure	7	7	5	6	5	3
Resisting competitive threats	4	5	6	5	6	7
Saving jobs	9	6	7	7	7	6
Advancing my own career or financial interests	8	9	9	8	9	8
Other	6	8	8	9	8	9

Note: 1 is high; 9 is low.

Source: O. C. Ferrell and John Fraedrich, *Business Ethics,* 3rd ed. (Boston: Houghton Mifflin, 1997), p. 28. Adapted from Rebecca Goodell, *Ethics in American Business: Policies, Programs, and Perceptions* (Ethics Resource Center, 1994), p. 54. Reprinted with permission of the Ethics Resource Center.

number 1 reported cause of ethical lapses. Meeting overly aggressive financial or business objectives and helping the company survive were two other top causes. Advancing my own career or financial interests ranked toward the bottom of the list.

● The Boss's Influence The leader's actions may be "the single most important factor in fostering corporate behavior of a high ethical standard."[39] In other words, employees tend to take their ethical signals from their bosses. Yet only about 27 percent of employees in one poll strongly agreed that their organizations' leadership is ethical.[40] One writer gives these examples of how supervisors knowingly (or unknowingly) lead subordinates astray ethically:

- Tell staffers to do whatever is necessary to achieve results.
- Overload top performers to ensure that work gets done.
- Look the other way when wrongdoing occurs.
- Take credit for others' work or shift blame.[41]

When managers do set the wrong tone, it often starts at the top. The National Commission on Fraudulent Financial Reporting concluded that "more than any other key individual, the chief executive sets the tone at the top that affects integrity and ethics and other factors of a positive, controlled environment."[42]

Some top managers react to ethical crises in admirable ways. When he found out that a rogue group of Procter & Gamble (P&G) investigators were going through competitor Unilever's garbage for information, former P&G CEO John Pepper was reportedly shocked. He ordered the campaign to stop, and he fired the managers responsible for hiring the spies. Then, he blew the whistle on his own company. He had P&G inform Unilever of what his firm had done. Unilever demanded, among other things, that Procter & Gamble retain a third-party auditor to make sure it does not take advantage of the documents its spies stole from Unilever's trash.[43]

● The Organizational Culture Employees also get signals about what is acceptable behavior from the *culture* of the organization in which they work. We may define **organizational culture** as the characteristic traditions, norms, and values employees share. Values are basic beliefs about what you should or shouldn't do and about what is and is not important. Google's founders famously wrote "Do no evil" in the firm's prospectus when they took their company public on the stock market. They wanted "Do no evil" to be a basic value or rule employees applied when making decisions on behalf of Google.

organizational culture: the characteristic traditions, norms, and values that employees share

Google's organizational culture.

Managers shape organizational cultures in many ways. They do so consciously, for example, by using symbols (such as incentives to reward ethical behavior), offering stories about ethical employees, and holding ceremonies to reward employees who did the right thing. Writing the values up as rules or codes (as Google did) also illustrates using symbols.

Managers sometimes shape culture unconsciously. Thus, the manager who unthinkingly accepts expensive dinners from a supplier in violation of company rules may send the signal to subordinates that unethical behavior really isn't that bad.

Encouraging Ethical Behavior at Work

Online Study Center
ACE the Test
Managing Now! LIVE

Just as there is no single cause of unethical behavior at work, there's no one silver bullet to prevent it. Instead, managers must take several steps to ensure ethical behavior by their employees.[44]

Publish an Ethics Code

ethics code: the principles, values, and guidelines a company wants its employees to adhere to

The first step is usually to adopt an ethics code. An **ethics code** lays out the principles, values, and guidelines the company wants its employees to adhere to.[45] One study found that 56 percent of large firms and about 25 percent of small firms had corporate ethics codes.[46] As an example, IBM's ethics code has this to say about tips, gifts, and entertainment:

> No IBM employee, or any member of his or her immediate family, can accept gratuities or gifts of money from a supplier, customer, or anyone in a business relationship. Nor can they accept a gift or consideration that could be perceived as having been offered because of the business relationship. "Perceived" simply means this: if you read about it in the local newspaper, would you wonder whether the gift just might have had something to do with a business relationship? No IBM employee can give money or a gift of significant value to a customer, supplier, or anyone if it could reasonably be viewed as being done to gain a business advantage.[47]

The ethics code is often part of (and, in most cases, the same as) a code of conduct. The latter addresses not just ethics but also closely related matters such as respecting the environment.

Basically, all publicly traded companies doing business in the United States must have ethics codes.[48] The Sarbanes-Oxley Act (passed after a series of top corporate management ethical lapses a few years ago) requires companies to declare if they have a code of conduct. Federal sentencing guidelines reduce penalties for companies convicted of ethics violations if they have codes of conduct. Both the New York Stock Exchange and NASDAQ require listed companies to follow their exchanges' corporate governance rules.

Codes of conduct are also a global phenomenon (see Figure 2.2). Nations and groups of nations (including Japan, South Africa, the European Union, and the

FIGURE 2.2

Codes of Conduct

- Asian Pacific Economic Cooperation Forum Business Code of Conduct (www.cauxroundtable.org)
- Caux Round Table Principles for Business (www.cauxroundtable.org)
- European Corporate Code of Conduct (European Union Parliament, www.europa.eu.int)
- Fair Labor Association Workshop Code of Conduct (www.fairlabor.org)
- Global Sullivan Principles (http://globalsullivanprinciples.org)
- ILO Tripartite Declaration of Principles Concerning Multinational Enterprises and Social Policy (www.ilo.org)
- OECD Guidelines for Multinational Enterprises—2000 (www.corporate-accountability.org)
- OECD, Principles of Corporate Governance—2004 (www.oecd.org)
- Rules of Conduct on Extortion and Bribery in International Business Transactions (International Chamber of Commerce, www.iccwbo.org)
- United Nations Universal Declaration of Human Rights (www.un.org)

SOURCE: Adapted from Standards of Corporate Social Responsibility by Social Venture Network, 1999, www.svn.org/.

Asian Pacific Economic Cooperation Forum) have corporate codes they expect companies to follow. These codes generally do not carry the weight of law. However, they do set out what these countries view as acceptable corporate behavior. As such, ". . . They are slowly defining the terms and conditions of a company's license to operate—around the world."[49]

Businesspeople also hope that an antibribery treaty signed by thirty-four trading nations will reduce the incidence of corruption. Some executives also advocate a global corporate ethics standard under the auspices of the International Standards Organization (ISO). The ISO now provides international quality (ISO 9000) and environmental (ISO 14,000) standards. "We want a simple, effective way to operate [ethically] internationally—one that meets all the criteria of doing business overseas, whether it's proving assurance of quality or ethical business practices," says one executive.[50] ISO ethical standards would provide a detailed list of criteria companies must meet to prove that they do business ethically.

Codes of conduct tend to include several common principles. After reviewing various international codes of conduct, researchers concluded that most codes address the eight principles listed in Figure 2.3.

FIGURE 2.3

Eight Common Code of Conduct Principles

I.	Fiduciary principle: act as a fiduciary for the company and its investors. Carry out the company's business in a diligent and loyal manner, with the degree of candor expected of a trustee.[51]
II.	Property principle: respect property and the rights of those who own it. Refrain from theft and misappropriation, avoid waste, and safeguard the property entrusted to you.
III.	Reliability principle: honor commitments. Be faithful to your word and follow through on promises, agreements, and other voluntary undertakings, whether or not embodied in a legally enforceable contract.
IV.	Transparency principle: conduct business in a truthful and open manner. Refrain from deceptive acts and practices, keep accurate records, and make timely disclosures of material information while respecting the obligations of confidentiality and privacy.
V.	Dignity principle: respect the dignity of all people. Protect the health, safety, privacy, and human rights of others. Adopt practices that enhance human development of the workplace, the marketplace, and the community.
VI.	Fairness principle: engage in free and fair competition, deal with all parties fairly and equitably, and practice nondiscrimination in employment and contracting.
VII.	Citizenship principle: act as responsible citizens of the community. Respect the law, protect public goods, cooperate with public authorities, avoid improper involvement in politics and government, and contribute to community betterment.
VIII.	Responsiveness principle: engage with parties who may have legitimate claims and concerns relating to the company's activities, and be responsive to public needs while recognizing the government's role and jurisdiction in protecting the public's interest.

TABLE 2.3
Six Steps to Effectively Implementing an Ethics Code

1. Distribute the code of ethics to all employees, subsidiaries, and associated companies.
2. Assist employees in interpreting and understanding the application and intent of the code.
3. Specify management's role in the implementation of the code.
4. Inform employees of their responsibility to understand the code, and provide them with the overall objectives of the code.
5. Establish grievance procedures.
6. Provide a conclusion or closing statement, such as this one from Cadbury Schweppes: The character of the company is collectively in our hands. Pride in what we do is important, and let us earn that pride by the way we put the beliefs set out here into action.

Source: O. C. Ferrell and John Fraedrich, *Business Ethics*, 3rd ed. (Boston: Houghton Mifflin, 1997), p. 176. Adapted from Walter W. Manley II, *The Handbook of Good Business Practice* (London: Routledge, 1992), p. 16.

It is customary for the firm to set forth its ethics code in the form of written documents.[52] Table 2.3 summarizes six steps for effectively implementing an ethics code.

● **Are Ethics Codes Effective?** Enron was a large gas and power trading company that basically imploded in the face of allegations of top management misconduct. Eventually, several of its managers plead guilty. Yet Enron's ethics code was readily available on the company's website. It said, among other things, "As a partner in the communities in which we operate, Enron believes it has a responsibility to conduct itself according to certain basic principles." Those values include "respect, integrity, communication and excellence."[53]

However, in most cases, ethics codes do have a positive impact on employees' ethical behavior. One study consisted of interviews with 766 subjects over a two-year period.[54] The researchers drew two main conclusions. First,

> Respondents who worked for companies having a code of ethics judge subordinates, co-workers, themselves and especially supervisors and top managers to be more ethical than respondents employed in organizations not having a formal code of ethics. . . .[55]

Second, it seemed to be the mere presence of the code (rather than its content) that was important.

> In fact, we found that although most respondents could not recall specific features of their company's ethics code, employees of companies having a code had very different perceptions of ethical climate and behavior than employees of companies lacking a code. . . .[56]

What Managers Do to Encourage Ethical Behavior

Having an ethics code doesn't guarantee employees will act ethically, as Enron discovered. Instead, managers need to implement and enforce the code's ethical

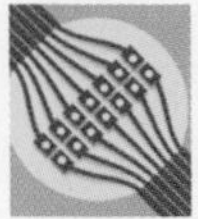
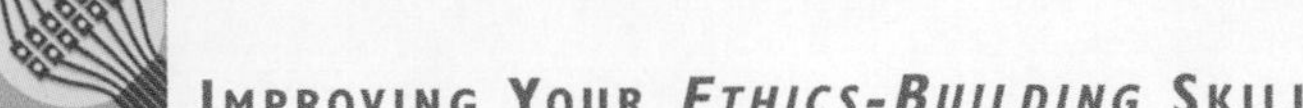

IMPROVING YOUR *ETHICS-BUILDING* SKILLS

There is much that you, as a manager, can do to make it more likely that your employees behave ethically.

Walk the Talk

First, we've seen in this chapter that the leader's actions are the biggest element in determining whether employees' ethical standards stay high. Supervisors therefore need to walk the talk when it comes to behaving ethically and enforcing ethics rules.

Unfortunately, supervisors sometimes send the wrong cues. For example, telling subordinates they should do "whatever it takes" to get the job done, overloading subordinates, and ignoring incidents of wrongdoing help set the stage for ethical misdeeds.

Even for experienced supervisors, knowing where to draw the ethical line sometimes isn't easy. Questions to ask include, Is what you're about to do legal? Is it right? How do you think you'll feel afterward? How would you react if you saw your actions described in the newspaper?

Clarify Your Expectations

Make it clear what your expectations are with respect to the ethical values you want subordinates to follow. If your company has a corporate ethics code, emphasize, from your subordinate's first day, that you expect him or her to follow that code.

Some managers use stories and examples to make their ethical expectations come alive. The examples may be local, as when they describe the lengths to which someone in the company went to do the right thing. The news is always a good source, as when that MCI-WorldCom executive said that he knew he was doing wrong, but he was trying to save the company.

However, clarifying expectations doesn't mean just talking about them. Strong statements may reduce the risk of legal and ethical violations. But those statements are meaningless if subordinates see that you or your company does not back them up with enforcement.

Screen Out the Problem Employees

To some extent, the easiest way to avoid ethical lapses is to screen out potential problem employees before you hire them. Some companies use honesty tests to screen out ethically undesirable applicants, but testing is not your only option.

To the degree possible, make sure you've checked out the person you're thinking of hiring with careful background and reference checks. There's generally nothing wrong with asking all candidates some very direct questions. For example, Have you ever observed someone stretching the rules at work? What did you do about it? Have you ever had to go against company guidelines or procedures to get something done? Have you ever stolen anything at work?

Support Ethics Training

We've seen that, for all practical purposes, ethics training is mandatory today. Federal sentencing guidelines from

principles. Here, three main things—top management commitment, training, and enforcement—are important.

Top Management Commitment We saw that employees tend to take their ethical signals from their bosses. As two researchers put it, "To achieve results, the chief executive officer and those around the CEO need to be openly and strongly committed to ethical conduct, and give constant leadership in tending and renewing the values of the organization."[57] Lockheed Martin Corporation appointed a chief ethics officer, Nancy Higgins, as executive vice president of ethics and business conduct to emphasize top management's commitment to ethics.[58]

Train Employees Training plays an important role in publicizing a company's ethics principles and in encouraging employees to adhere to them. For

1991 reduced penalties for employers accused of misconduct who had implemented codes of conduct and ethics training. An amendment to those guidelines, which became effective in 2004, outlines stricter ethics training requirements.

In most firms, the manager's responsibility here is to make sure his or her employees are participating in the ethics training program and doing so seriously. Packaged ethics training programs are also widely available online. For example, skillsoft.com and netG.com offer such programs.

Ensure Fair and Unbiased Performance Appraisals

How the supervisor handles the employees' periodic performance appraisals is important. Unfairness and bias in the appraisal sends a strong signal that ethics is secondary in the company or to the supervisor. To send the signal that fairness and ethics are paramount, the employees' standards should be clear, employees should understand the basis upon which you're appraising them, and you should perform the appraisals objectively and fairly.

Use Rewards and Discipline

Because behavior tends to be a function of its consequences, it is the manager's (and the company's) responsibility to ensure that the firm rewards ethical behavior and penalizes unethical behavior. In fact, when the company does not deal swiftly with unethical behavior, it's often the ethical employees (not the unethical ones) who feel punished.

Strive to Build an Atmosphere of Fairness, Justice, and Respect

Ethics always involve questions of right and wrong and of society's moral standards. Therefore, employees tend to associate unfair, unjust, disreputable behavior with unethical companies and supervisors. They tend to associate fair, just, respectful behavior with ethical companies and supervisors.

Some workplace unfairness is blatant. For example, some supervisors are workplace bullies, yelling at or ridiculing subordinates, humiliating them, and even making threats. Behavior like this is not just unfair, but unethical too. Many firms therefore have antiharassment policies. For example, "It is the policy of this company that all employees, customers, and visitors are entitled to a respectful and productive work environment, free from behavior and language constituting workplace harassment."

Yet in practice, it's not gross behavior like workplace bullying that's the problem. Instead, it's the many small day-to-day opportunities where the manager should have been fair but was not. To the extent that the manager carries out his or her hiring, training, appraisal, reward, discipline, and termination responsibilities with honesty, fairness, and respect, he or she can foster a feeling among employees that they're working in a place that values ethical behavior and where ethical behavior must be the norm.

example, based on one survey, 89 percent of surveyed ethics officials said that their companies use the new-hire orientation to convey ethics codes, and 45 percent use annual refresher training sessions. Figure 2.4 on page 44 shows other findings from this survey.

● **Measure and Enforce** One study of effective ethics programs found that all these firms used surveys or audits to monitor actual compliance with ethical standards.[59] Board members and employees should then discuss the results.[60] Managers should address any ethical lapses by enforcing the firm's ethics code. As one study of ethics concludes, "Strong statements by managers may reduce the risk of legal and ethical violations by their work forces, but enforcement of standards has the greatest impact."[61] The accompanying feature, Improving Your *Ethics-Building* Skills, focuses on what the individual manager/supervisor can do to encourage ethical behavior.

FIGURE 2.4

The Role of Training in Ethics

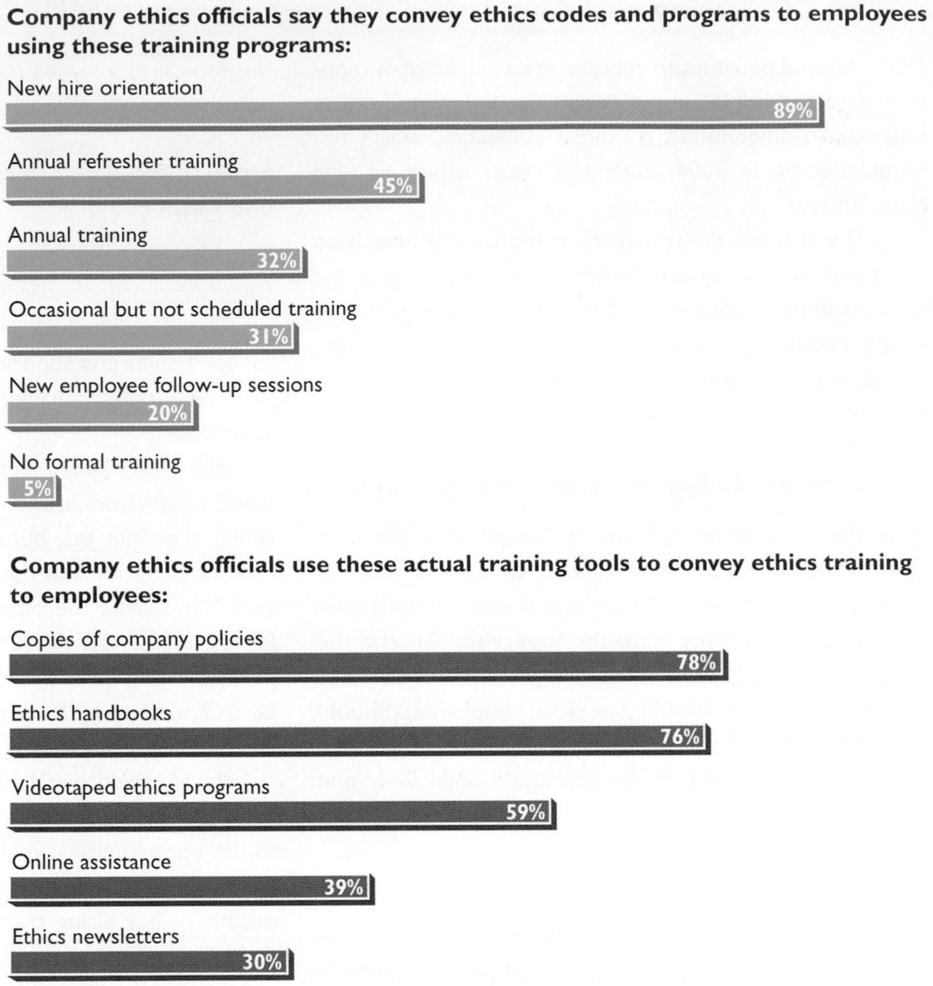

Company ethics officials say they convey ethics codes and programs to employees using these training programs:

Training program	Percent
New hire orientation	89%
Annual refresher training	45%
Annual training	32%
Occasional but not scheduled training	31%
New employee follow-up sessions	20%
No formal training	5%

Company ethics officials use these actual training tools to convey ethics training to employees:

Training tool	Percent
Copies of company policies	78%
Ethics handbooks	76%
Videotaped ethics programs	59%
Online assistance	39%
Ethics newsletters	30%

SOURCE: Susan Well, "Turn Employees into Saints," adapted from *HRMagazine*, December 1999, p. 52.

Managing Now: Using Information Technology to Encourage Ethical Behavior

Turner Broadcasting System Inc. noticed that employees at its CNN London business bureau were piling up overtime claims. CNN installed new software to monitor every webpage every worker used. Overtime expenses soon plunged. As the firm's network security specialist puts it, "If we see people were surfing the Web all day, then they don't have to be paid for that overtime."[62]

As at CNN, information technology is a double-edged sword for employee ethics. It enables employees to spend time at work on personal pursuits—shopping online or sending messages to friends, for instance. (UPS caught one employee using the company computer to run a personal business.) However, as we saw earlier in this chapter, information technology also enables employers to monitor their employees' behavior as never before.

● The Wireless Revolution Internet monitoring is just one example of how managers use technology to keep closer tabs on their employees. When cable

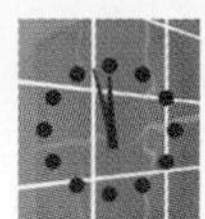

WINDOW ON MANAGING NOW
Complying with Sarbanes-Oxley and Other Regulations

Particularly for larger firms, complying with Sarbanes-Oxley (SOX) would be prohibitively expensive without IT support. For example, SOX requires that top managers certify, through a series of sign-off procedures, that the company has complied with its financial statement accuracy and whistle-blower requirements. Enterprise-based financial-software packages enable managers to quickly analyze each department's compliance procedures, and to organize the financial data for documentation and sign-off.[63]

Sarbanes-Oxley is just one of the many national and international laws and regulations with which companies must comply. For example, Adaptec Corp. provides data storage to many companies and government agencies, many abroad. Particularly for high-technology companies such as Adaptec, complying with global trade regulations is quite complex. The software company SAP's "Global Trade Services" software package helps Adaptec to comply. For example, this system automatically compares Adaptec's business partners around the world with the "restricted party" lists various governments publish. The package's Export Control System checks for embargos and then automatically performs the necessary export license activities. Says one Adaptec manager, "Many of our orders, destinations, and business partners have to be screened the day of the shipments . . . We now have that data in a single, integrated system for a more easily accessible electronic record."[64]

Similarly, IT helps international employers comply with local employment, payroll, safety, and recording regulations in each country in which they operate.[65] For example, software packages combined with special data-input devices help companies comply with federal money-laundering regulations by automatically identifying and classifying suspicious cash-flow activities. Others help financial companies comply with banking regulations such as the Home Mortgage Disclosure Act.[66] The European Union requires most publicly traded companies to issue consolidated financial statements consistent with International Financial Reporting Standards. Compliance here would be impossible without using financial-software packages for planning, budgeting, financial reporting, and cost and profitability management.

repairperson Johnny Cupid starts his service truck, his employer BellSouth knows exactly where he is. Thanks to BellSouth's new global positioning satellite (GPS) units, BellSouth supervisors know every time Cupid stops at a stoplight and where he is as he makes his daily rounds. "I feel like they got their eye on me all the time," he says. "I can't slow down anywhere anymore."[67] A BellSouth spokesperson says, "GPS was not installed as an employee monitoring system. It's an efficiency tool, just like the wireless laptops and cellphones our technicians have." However, union workers filed about fifty grievances about the system in one recent year. Cupid says, "I love my job (but) I don't need any more stress."

As at BellSouth, managers generally don't use IT just to check up on employees but to improve efficiency. The Window on Managing Now feature shows how managers use information technology to comply with government regulations.

Lockheed Martin relies on IT for managing its ethics compliance programs. For example, Lockheed uses its intranet to help its 160,000 employees take ethics and legal compliance training online. Each short course addresses topics ranging from insider trading to sexual harassment. The system also keeps track of who is (and is not) taking the required courses.

Lockheed's special electronic ethics software also keeps track of how well the company and its employees are doing in terms of maintaining high ethical standards.[68] For example, the program helped top management see that in one year, 4.8 percent of the company's ethics allegations involved conflicts of interest. It

PRACTICE IT

DTE Energy's Web-Based Ethics Training System

Complying with Sarbanes-Oxley means that publicly traded companies need a cost-effective way of training employees and of certifying that they really were trained. So when DTE Energy, with 14,000 employees, needed ethics training, it turned to a Web-based program from Integrity Interactive Corp. of Waltham, Massachusetts. Now, all the company's employees have easy access through their computers to a standardized ethics training program. DTE can also easily track who has taken the training and who has not. The employees can take the training when they want to, and the company can monitor their progress. As one officer at Integrity Interactive said, it would have been easy in the 1990s for companies to resist ethics training by saying

> [W]e have 30,000 employees and 40% turnover. There's no way to train all these people in our code of conduct and ethical compliance . . . The Internet has taken that excuse away. It is now physically possible to reach anyone, anywhere on the globe—and what's more, to prove that you're doing it.[69]

shows that it takes just over thirty days to complete an ethics violation internal investigation.[70] It also shows that several years ago, 302 Lockheed employees were sanctioned for ethical violations. The accompanying Practice IT feature shows how DTE Energy uses information technology for ethics training.

Social Responsibility Now

Online Study Center
ACE the Test
Managing Now! LIVE

For years, environmental activists linked General Electric (GE) with wasting energy and dumping toxic wastes in New York's Hudson River. Today, GE is actively pursuing socially responsible energy and environmental policies. The company is appraising its managers based on their environment-friendly performance. Every GE business unit must cut its greenhouse gas, or carbon dioxide, emissions. Under GE's Ecomagination strategy, it aims to double its revenues from renewable energy such as hydrogen fuel cells within several years.[71]

General Electric isn't doing this just because social responsibility makes for good public relations. GE found that most of its customers believe that rising fuel costs and environmental regulations will soon make alternative fuels and a cleaner environment a necessity. As one of the world's premier corporations, GE's new stance says much about how managers view social responsibility now. As several writers put it:

> [M]ore and more companies are accepting corporate citizenship as a new strategic and managerial purpose requiring their attention. Once seen as a purely philanthropic activity—a source of general goodwill, with no bottom-line consequence—citizenship is moving from the margins of concern to the center at leading companies.[72]

Figure 2.5[73] summarizes the new attitude and approach.

Social Responsibility Defined

Corporate social responsibility refers to the extent to which companies should and do direct resources toward improving segments of society other than the firm's owners. In essence, "Theories of corporate social responsibility suggest that there needs to be a balance between what business takes from society and what it gives back in return."[74] Socially responsible behavior might include creating jobs for

FIGURE 2.5

Old and New Company Attitudes

OLD ETHIC	NEW ETHIC
▪ Do the minimum required by law ▪ Keep a low profile ▪ Downplay public concerns ▪ Reply to shareholders' inquiries when necessary ▪ Communicate on a need-to-know basis ▪ Make decisions on the bottom line and laws alone	▪ Do the right thing ▪ Show you are doing the right thing ▪ Seek to identify and address public concerns ▪ Be responsible to shareholders ▪ Communicate openly ▪ Integrate all of the above into decision making

SOURCE: Adapted from Dunphy, D., Griffiths, A., & Benn, S., *Organizational Change for Corporate Sustainability* (New York: Routledge, 2003), p. 11.

minorities, controlling pollution, improving working conditions for one's employees abroad, or supporting educational facilities or cultural events, for example.[75]

To Whom Is the Company Responsible?

The topic of social responsibility continues to provoke lively debate. On one point all or most agree: "The socially responsible corporation is a good corporation."[76] In other words, acting in a socially responsible manner means being ethical, doing the right thing with respect to issues such as pollution or charitable contributions.

The question is, Is a company that tries to do its best for only its owners any less ethical than one that tries to help customers, vendors, and employees, too? The answer depends on what you believe is the purpose of a business. Many perfectly ethical people believe that a company's only social responsibility is to its stockholders. Others disagree.

● **Managerial Capitalism** The classic view is that a corporation's main purpose is to maximize profits for stockholders. Today, this view is most notably associated with economist and Nobel laureate Milton Friedman. He said:

> The view has been gaining widespread acceptance that corporate officials and labor leaders have a "social responsibility" that goes beyond the interest of their stockholders or their members. This view shows a fundamental misconception of the character and nature of the free economy. In such an economy, there is one and only one social responsibility of business—to use its resources and engage in activities designed to increase its profits so long as it stays within the rules of the game, which is to say, engages in open and free competition, without deception and fraud. . . .[77]

Friedman said that the firm's profits belong to the stockholders, the company's owners, and to them alone.[78] He also said that the stockholders deserve their profits because these profits derive from a voluntary contract among the various corporate stakeholders. For example, the community receives taxes, suppliers are paid, employees earn wages, and so on. Everyone gets his or her due, and additional social responsibility is unnecessary.

● **Stakeholder Theory** An opposing view is that business has a social responsibility to serve *all* the corporate stakeholders affected by its business decisions. A **corporate stakeholder** is "any group which is vital to the survival and success of the corporation."[79]

corporate stakeholder: any group that is vital to the survival and success of the corporation

As shown in Figure 2.6, experts in this area traditionally identify six stakeholder groups: stockholders (owners), employees, customers, suppliers, managers,

FIGURE 2.6

A Corporation's Major Stakeholders

One view of social responsibility is that a firm must consider and serve all the stakeholders that may be affected by its business decisions.

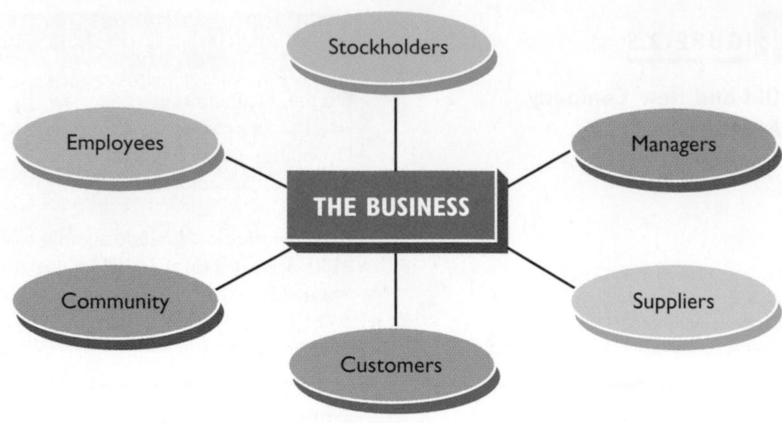

and the local community.[80] Stakeholder theory holds that the rights of these groups must be ensured, and, further, the groups must participate, in some sense, in decisions that substantially affect their welfare.[81]

moral minimum: the position that states that the purpose of the corporation is to maximize profits without committing any harm

● **The Moral Minimum** Between the extremes of Friedman's capitalism and stakeholder theory lies an intermediate position. **Moral minimum** advocates agree that the purpose of the corporation is to maximize profits but say that in doing so, it must conform with the moral minimum. This means that the firm should be free to strive for profits so long as it commits no harm.[82] A business would certainly have a social responsibility not to produce exploding cigarette lighters or operate chemical plants that poison the environment. However, it's unlikely that the firm's social responsibilities would extend to donating to charity or educating the poor, for instance. The bottom line is that when it comes to being socially responsible, there are many points of view.

Why Are Companies Socially Responsible?

Employees of the DeCoro sofa plant in Shenzhen, China, recently got into a fist-fight with the plant's Italian managers, who had fired them the week before. The workers were protesting their firing. Hundreds of plant workers soon took to the streets to protest what they said was unfair treatment by the managers.

Russian workers protest at a Coca-Cola plant in St. Petersburg.

The incident prompted management to retain experts to administer the plants' first social audit. Prompted by accusations of sweatshop working conditions at other plants in the 1990s, *social audits* aim to verify that plants are meeting both local labor laws and buyers' codes regarding things like safety conditions. Yet many buyers, including giants like Nike, reportedly know that some plant managers falsify the information they give the social auditers.[83]

In practice, the lengths to which a manager goes to be socially responsible depends on four things. It depends, first, on *how ethical the person* is. Ethical people can surely adhere to Friedman's stockholder-oriented managerial capitalism theory, but even Friedman said that the manager must play by the rules. No ethical managerial capitalist would knowingly commit unethical acts, say, by selling medicines that tests have shown to be deadly.

Second, how socially responsible the company is depends on *top management's philosophy*—whether they believe in managerial capitalism, stakeholder theory, or the moral minimum, for instance. The original Ben and Jerry (of Ben & Jerry's Ice Cream) were famous for buying milk from local Vermont farmers, although their prices were higher than those of other regions.

Third, as at the sofa plant, outside monitors and *pressure groups* help to nudge the process along. As another example, when shoppers in several Home Depot stores heard, "Attention shoppers, on aisle 7 you'll find mahogany ripped from the heart of the Amazon," store managers scampered to find pranksters with megaphones.[84] There were none. Rainforest Action Network activists had cracked Home Depot's intercom system's security code.

Finally, as explained above, *economic realities* like rising fuel costs and environmental regulations require that managers like those at GE pursue socially responsible aims to support their companies' strategic needs.

Companies usually don't go from being socially irresponsible to socially responsible overnight. Instead, they evolve. Figure 2.7[85] illustrates the typical evolution. Firms move from defensive to grudging compliance, and then on to affirmatively making the changes a valued part of management's strategic plans.

FIGURE 2.7

The Five Stages in Social Responsibility for an Organization

When it comes to developing a sense of corporate responsibility, organizations typically go through five stages.

Stage	What Organizations Do	Why They Do It
DEFENSIVE	Deny practices, outcomes, or responsibilities	To defend against attacks to their reputation that in the short term could affect sales, recruitment, productivity, and the brand
COMPLIANCE	Adopt a policy-based compliance approach as a cost of doing business	To mitigate the erosion of economic value in the medium term because of ongoing reputation and litigation risks
MANAGERIAL	Embed the societal issue in their core management processes	To mitigate the erosion of economic value in the medium term and to achieve longer-term gains by integrating responsible business practices into their daily operations
STRATEGIC	Integrate the societal issue into their core business strategies	To enhance economic value in the long term and to gain first-mover advantage by aligning strategy and process innovations with the societal issue
CIVIL	Promote broad industry participation in corporate responsibility	To enhance long-term economic value by overcoming any first-mover disadvantages and to realize gains through collective action

How to Improve the Company's Social Responsiveness

Managers improve their companies' social responsiveness by instituting policies and practices that encourage socially responsible behavior. These include social audits, whistle-blowing, joining responsibility advocacy groups, and staying in touch with stakeholders.

The Social Audit One important step is to ascertain just how socially responsible the firm really is. Some firms measure this by using a rating system called a **corporate social audit**.[86] This is a review and analysis of the firm's social responsibility, usually based on a checklist that addresses issues such as "How many accidents have you had this year?" "What percent of your profits go to community services?" and "What portion of your managers are minority or women?" The DeCoro plant's social audit is typical of those used at facilities throughout China's Pearl River Delta, which contains many of China's industrial cities. Auditors come in for a few hours or days. They review payroll records, interview employees, check fire escapes, and take similar actions.[87]

corporate social audit: a review and analysis of a firm's social responsibility

The Sullivan Principles for Corporate Labor and Community Relations in South Africa is the classic audit example.[88] The Reverend Leon Sullivan was an African American minister and General Motors (GM) board of directors member. For several years during the 1970s, he had tried to pressure the firm to withdraw from South Africa, whose multiracial population was divided by government-sanctioned racist policies known as apartheid.

As part of that effort, Sullivan codified a set of principles "to guide U.S. business in its social and moral agenda in South Africa."[89] The code provided measurable standards by which one could audit U.S. companies operating in South Africa. For example, there were standards for nonsegregation of the races in all eating, comfort, and work facilities.[90]

Whistle-Blowing Sarbanes-Oxley strengthens the rights of whistle-blowers, people who report their employers' questionable activities to authorities.[91] For example, SOX gives whistle-blowers the right to sue in federal court if employers retaliate against them.

Many firms have a reputation for actively discouraging whistle-blowing. Yet doing that may be short-sighted. As one writer put it, whistle-blowers "represent one of the least expensive and most efficient sources of feedback about mistakes the firm may be making."[92] Other firms find that trying to silence whistle-blowers backfires.[93] Once the damage has been done—whether it is asbestos hurting workers or a chemical plant making the community ill—the cost of making things right can be enormous.[94] When John Pepper, CEO of P&G, discovered that some rogue P&G employees were spying on a competitor, he followed a laudable course: he blew the whistle on his own company and told Unilever about P&G's transgression.

CEO John Pepper took the correct step of divulging his company's ethical lapse as soon as he became aware of it.

Social Responsibility Networks Other firms, such as Rhino Records, join organizations like the Social Venture Network (www.svn.org) and Businesses for Social Responsibility (www.bsr.org). These organizations promote socially responsible business practices and help managers to establish socially responsible programs.[95]

Managing Now Managers use the Internet to support their social responsibility efforts. For example, Shell Oil Company maintains an Internet-based stakeholder Web forum. The website makes it easy for anyone with an interest in Shell's operations—consumers, people living near Shell refineries, and owners of Shell-branded gas stations, for instance—to make their opinions known. This helps Shell be more socially responsive, by making it easier for management to engage with parties who have legitimate concerns.[96]

Managing Diversity

Online Study Center
ACE the Test
Managing Now! LIVE

Of all the firm's nonowner stakeholders, perhaps none has so obvious a claim on receiving socially responsible treatment as do its employees. To a great extent, the company is its employees, since they largely determine if the firm will succeed. So the care, courtesy, integrity, and humanity the firm applies in managing its employee diversity is a measure of how socially responsible it is.

managing diversity: planning and implementing organizational systems and practices to manage people so that the potential advantages of diversity are maximized while the potential disadvantages are minimized

Managing diversity means "planning and implementing organizational systems and practices to manage people so that the potential advantages of diversity are maximized while its potential disadvantages are minimized."[97] Managing diversity refers to questions like, How much effort should a manager make to employ minorities? How ethnically diverse should the company be? and, How much effort should employers make to manage the resulting diversity?

Diversity management is increasingly important for several reasons. Treating employees equitably is, first, an *ethical and moral* matter. There are also *equal-employment laws* for those employers that require some added motivation. From a practical point of view, the *workforces* of many industrialized countries, including the United States, are increasingly diverse, and employers have little choice but to recruit and then productively assimilate women and minorities. Furthermore, in an increasingly diverse and globalized business environment, smart employers *capitalize* on their diversity. For example, Longo Toyota in El Monte, California, built a sixty-person salesforce that speaks more than twenty languages. This is a powerful competitive advantage in demographically diverse Southern California. Having a smoothly functioning diverse workforce is also advantageous for companies that routinely do business abroad. As the *Wall Street Journal* recently put it, "As companies do more and more business around the world, diversity isn't simply a matter of doing what is fair or good public relations. It's a business imperative."[98]

Today, therefore, the aim of diversity management is not just to get diverse employees to work together but to create "a workplace where differences can be learned from and leveraged."[99] Leveraging—capitalizing on—diversity can pay big dividends. For example, starting with low percentages, people of color recently held 17 percent of PepsiCo's mid- and top-level jobs, and women held 29 percent. PepsiCo learned from and leveraged its newly diverse management pool. For example, in one recent year, new diversity-driven products such as guacamole-flavored Doritos (Hispanic) and wasabi-flavored snacks (Asian) accounted for about one percentage point of PepsiCo's 8 percent revenue growth.

Bases for Diversity

What is "diversity"? In one study, most respondents listed race, gender, culture, national origin, disability, age, and religion as the demographic building blocks that represent diversity. They are what people often think of when they are asked what diversity means.[100]

diverse: composed of two or more groups (when referring to a workforce), each of whose members are identifiable and distinguishable based on demographic or other characteristics

A workforce is **diverse** when it is composed of two or more groups, each of whose members are identifiable and distinguishable based on the following demographic or other characteristics:[101]

- *Racial and ethnic groups.* African Americans, Pacific Islanders, Asian Americans, Native Americans, and other people of color comprise about 25 percent of the U.S. population.
- *Women.* Women represent about 48 percent of the U.S. workforce.
- *Older workers.* By 2005, the average age of the U.S. worker was forty, up from an average of thirty-six, and reflecting the gradual aging of the workforce.
- *People with disabilities.* The Americans with Disabilities Act makes it illegal to discriminate against people with disabilities who are qualified to do the job. This act has highlighted the large number of people with disabilities in the U.S. workforce.
- *Sexual/affectional orientation.* Experts estimate that 5 to 20 percent of the population is gay. This may make gays a larger percentage of the workforce than some racial and ethnic minorities.[102]
- *Religion.* Domestic and world events are underscoring differences, similarities, and tensions relating to the diversity of religions among most employees in a given firm.

Winning with diversity: the night crew at Home Depot.

Barriers in Dealing with Diversity

Demographic differences can create behavioral barriers that inhibit collegiality and cooperation. Managers who want to manage diversity must address these barriers if they want their employees to work together productively. The barriers include stereotyping and prejudice, ethnocentrism, discrimination, tokenism, and gender-role stereotypes. Managing diversity starts with understanding these barriers.

stereotyping: a process in which someone ascribes specific behavioral traits to individuals based on their apparent membership in a group

prejudice: a bias that results from prejudging someone based on some trait

Stereotyping and Prejudice Stereotyping and prejudice are two sides of the same coin. **Stereotyping** is a process in which someone ascribes specific behavioral traits to individuals based on their apparent membership in a group.[103] **Prejudice** is a bias that results from prejudging someone based on some trait.

Most people develop lists of behavioral traits that they associate with certain groups. For example, stereotypical male traits might include strong, aggressive, and loud; female traits might include cooperative, softhearted, and gentle.[104] When someone allows traits like these to determine how he or she reacts to members of one of these groups, then we say the person is prejudiced.

Ethnocentrism Ethnocentrism is prejudice on a grand scale. It is a tendency to view members of one's own group as the center of the universe and other social groups less favorably. For example, in one study, managers attributed the good performance of some minorities less to their ability and more to help they received from others. Conversely, they attributed the performance of nonminorities to their abilities.[105]

discrimination: taking specific actions toward or against a person based on the person's group

Discrimination Discrimination is prejudice in action. Whereas prejudice means a bias toward prejudging someone based on that person's traits, **discrimination** means taking specific actions toward or against the person based on the person's group.[106]

In many countries, including the United States, it is illegal to discriminate at work based on a person's age, race, gender, disability, or country of national origin (with some very specific exceptions, such as when hiring men to play male roles in a movie). But in practice, discrimination is still a barrier to managing diversity. For one thing, discrimination is often subtle. For example, many argue that an invisible "glass ceiling," enforced by an old-boy network and friendships built in places like exclusive clubs, effectively prevents women from reaching the top ranks of management.

tokenism: appointing one or a small group of women or minority-group members to high-profile positions, rather than more aggressively seeking full representation for that group

Tokenism **Tokenism** occurs when a company appoints one or a small group of women or minority-group members to high-profile positions, rather than more aggressively seeking full representation for that group. Tokenism is a diversity barrier when it slows the process of hiring or promoting more members of the minority group.

Token employees often fare poorly. Research suggests, for instance, that token employees face obstacles to full participation, success, and acceptance in the company. The extra attention their distinctiveness creates magnifies their good or bad performance.[107]

gender-role stereotypes: the tendency to associate women with certain (frequently nonmanagerial) jobs

Gender-Role Stereotypes Discrimination against women goes beyond glass ceilings. Working women also confront **gender-role stereotypes**, the tendency to associate women with certain (frequently nonmanagerial) jobs. In one study, attractiveness was advantageous for female interviewees when the job was nonmanagerial. When the job was managerial, there was a tendency for a woman's attractiveness to reduce her chances of being hired.[108]

How to Manage Diversity

Diversity can be a blessing or—if mismanaged—a problem. Bringing together people with different values and views can ensure they attack problems in a richer, more multifaceted way. On the other hand, if barriers such as stereotypes and tokenism flourish, diversity can make it harder to create smoothly functioning teams.[109] To repeat, managing diversity means taking steps to maximize diversity's potential advantages while minimizing the potential barriers—such as prejudice and bias—that can undermine the functioning of a diverse workforce. The manager can take several steps.

Legal Actions Managing diversity usually involves both legally mandated and voluntary actions. There are, of course, many legally mandated actions. For example, employers should avoid discriminatory employment advertising (such as "young man wanted for sales position") and prohibit sexual harassment.

However, legally required steps are rarely enough to blend diverse employees into a productive team. Other voluntary steps and programs are required. As summarized in Figure 2.8, these include providing strong leadership, assessing the situation, providing diversity training and education, changing the culture and management systems, and evaluating the diversity program.

Provide Strong Leadership Top executives of firms with exemplary diversity management reputations champion diversity. For example, they take strong

FIGURE 2.8

Activities Required to Better Manage Diversity

ACTIVITIES AT THE HEART OF A DIVERSITY MANAGEMENT PROGRAM				
Leadership	**Assess Your Situation**	**Education**	**Changes in Culture and Management Systems**	**Evaluate**
▪ Top management commitment and support ▪ Steering and advisory groups ▪ Communications strategy	▪ Comprehensive organizational assessment ▪ Baseline data ▪ Benchmarking	▪ Awareness training ▪ Development of in-house expertise ▪ Orientation programs ▪ Advanced training	▪ Recruitment ▪ Orientation ▪ Performance appraisal ▪ Compensation and benefits ▪ Promotion ▪ Training and development	▪ Evaluation ▪ Accountability ▪ Continuous improvement

personal stands on the need for change, become role models for the behaviors required for the change, issue a statement that defines what they mean by diversity, and provide financial and other support to implement the changes.[110]

After settling a class-action suit by black employees, Coca-Cola took steps to improve its diversity management record. For example, it established a formal mentoring program. It also is spending $500 million to support minority suppliers.[111]

● **Assess Your Situation** For example, use surveys to measure current employee attitudes and perceptions toward different cultural groups in the company. Conduct audits of your minority and female hiring and staffing practices.

● **Provide Diversity Training and Education** "The most commonly utilized starting point for . . . managing diversity is some type of employee education program."[112] A one- to two-day seminar involving a diverse group of employees is typical. Topics include, What does diversity mean to you? What does it mean to our organization?[113]

● **Change the Culture and Management Systems** Managers have to walk the talk if they want employees to take diversity management seriously. For example, change the performance appraisal procedure to appraise supervisors based partly on their success in minimizing intergroup conflicts. Institute mentoring programs. **Mentoring** is "a relationship between a younger adult and an older, more experienced adult in which the mentor provides support, guidance, and counseling to enhance the protégé's success at work and in other arenas of life."[114] Mentoring can contribute to the success of diversity management. Why attract a diverse workforce and then leave the new people to sink or swim?[115]

mentoring: a relationship between a younger adult and an older, more experienced adult in which the older adult provides support, guidance, and counseling to enhance the protégé's success at work and in other arenas of life

Sending signals about how management feels about diversity can cut both ways. For example, six women filed a sexual discrimination class-action suit in federal court against Wal-Mart.[116] Among other things, they asserted that they did not get the raises or promotions their male colleagues received. They also said they were exposed to hostile comments and actions by male employees (including, allegedly, offers to "get one of them pregnant").

Wal-Mart denies any systematic discrimination and has policies forbidding sexual harassment of any kind. However, some lawyers argue that it's not what Wal-Mart says, it's what it does. They argue that Wal-Mart has long had a policy of vigorously defending itself in such lawsuits. They say such actions could prompt some employees to believe that Wal-Mart may not actually take sexual harassment seriously.

● **Evaluate the Diversity Program** For example, do your surveys suggest an improvement in employee attitudes toward diversity? How many employees have entered into mentoring relationships? Do these relationships appear to be successful?

● **Managing Now** The manager assessing the effectiveness of his or her company's equal-employment and diversity efforts has numerous measures to use. These include, for example, the number of diversity-related (sexual harassment, age discrimination, and so forth) legal claims per year, the percentage of minority/women promotions, and measures for analyzing the survival and loss rate among diverse employee groups.

Even for a company with just several hundred employees, keeping track of metrics like these is expensive. Managers therefore tend to rely on technology. For example, the typical diversity management software package provides management with several diversity-related software options. These provide information relatively efficiently. The typical package calculates for the manager things like the cost per diversity hire, a workforce profile index, the amount of voluntary turnover among diverse employee groups, and the effectiveness of the firm's employment agencies' diversity initiatives.

Recruiting a More Diverse Workforce

It is useless to talk about diversity management if the company does not effectively recruit and retain a diverse team of employees. Without a diverse workforce, there is no diversity to manage.

Managers do not just recruit diverse employees out of altruism or because it is the socially responsible thing to do. The U.S. population is becoming more diverse, and thus more applicants are minorities or women. Federal, state, and local laws also generally require equality in employment. This means hiring people based on their abilities to do the job, not based on their ethnicity, age, gender, or other trait such as disability. Furthermore, as we noted earlier, having a diverse workforce is becoming a practical necessity as companies do more and more business around the world.

● **Fine-Tuning Recruitment Efforts** Recruiting a diverse workforce usually requires fine-tuning recruitment and retention efforts to the diverse employees' needs. For example, older workers sometimes particularly value having more free time and flexible work hours. Firms such as Wrigley Company let workers over age sixty-five shorten their workweeks and use minishifts to let these workers work less than full-time. Recruiting single parents similarly requires understanding that they often need to have flexible work arrangements. They also need supervisors who are supportive of their dual roles as employees and single parents. To the extent that some minorities or recent immigrants may need special training, many firms institute special remedial training. For example, Aetna Life and Casualty provides remedial training in basic arithmetic and writing.

Women workers, married or not, often carry the heavier burden of caring for the children and obviously have childbearing responsibilities that men do not.

Many progressive firms, such as the accounting firm KPMG, therefore make it easier for females to, say, restart their careers after returning from even lengthy maternity leaves, or to remain employed (if they so choose) in positions that don't involve the time commitments of being full-time partners in the firm. In any case, recruiting (and retaining) a diverse workforce calls for having a comprehensive plan in place for providing the employment support these employees need.

CHAPTER SUMMARY

1. Managers face ethical choices every day. Ethics refer to the principles of conduct governing an individual or a group. Ethical decisions always include judgments of good and bad and of serious moral issues.
2. Being legal and being ethical are not necessarily the same thing. A decision can be legal but still unethical, or ethical but still illegal.
3. Organizational factors influencing ethical behavior include pressure, the boss, and the organization's culture.
4. To improve your ethics-building skills, walk the talk; clarify your expectations; screen out the problem employees; support ethics training; ensure fair and unbiased performance appraisals; use rewards and discipline; and strive to build an atmosphere of fairness, justice, and respect.
5. Information technology has prompted new ethical concerns, particularly related to security (controlling access to company resources) and privacy. In terms of privacy, electronic performance monitoring and wireless-based monitoring of employee location and performance allow employers to keep close tabs on what their employees are doing. Similarly, the majority of companies monitor e-mail activity and employee Internet use.
6. Information technology also raises serious security concerns. For example, nonauthorized employees or outsiders could gain access to employees' personal data.
7. Technical and legal safeguards can reduce privacy and security concerns, up to a point. However, the ethics of those managing the company may be the only real safeguards.
8. Ethics policies and codes send a strong signal that top management is serious about ethics and are signs that it wants to foster a culture that takes ethics seriously.
9. Organizational culture is the characteristic traditions, norms, and values employees share. Values are basic beliefs about what you should or should not do and what is and is not important. Managers need to "walk the talk" to set the right culture.
10. Employers' use of information technology to maintain high ethical standards goes well beyond employee monitoring and employee training. For example, it would be prohibitively expensive without IT support for most companies to comply with the standards in the Sarbanes-Oxley Act regarding financial statement accuracy and whistle-blower requirements. Similarly, IT enables companies engaged in foreign trade to automatically perform the necessary export license activities and to comply with local employment, payroll, safety, and recording regulations in each country in which they operate.
11. People differ in answering the question, To whom should the corporation be responsible? Some say solely to stockholders, and some say to all stakeholders. Some take an intermediate position: they agree that the purpose of the corporation is to maximize profits, but that it is subject to the requirement that it must do so in conformity with the moral minimum.
12. As business becomes more global and the workforce becomes more diverse, it becomes more important to manage diversity so that its benefits can be leveraged while minimizing potential barriers. Potential barriers to managing diversity include stereotyping, prejudice, and tokenism. Managing diversity involves taking steps such as providing strong leadership, assessing the situation, providing training and education, changing the culture and systems, and evaluating the diversity program.

DISCUSSION QUESTIONS

1. What is ethical behavior?
2. Explain why information technology is a double-edged sword with respect to ethical behavior in organizations.
3. What are two technology-related ethical issues business managers face? Give examples of each.
4. What individual factors contribute to one's ethical or unethical behavior?
5. What are the organizational factors that influence ethical behavior at work?
6. What are eight common code of conduct principles?
7. What are important managerial methods for encouraging ethical behavior?
8. What are three ways in which managers use information technology to improve ethical behavior in organizations?
9. To whom is the company responsible? Include the three main points of view addressed in the chapter.
10. Why are companies socially responsible?
11. How is the subject of managing diversity changing today?

EXPERIENTIAL EXERCISES

1. Obtain the ethics code for your college. Then determine to what extent it covers the eight common code of conduct principles discussed in this chapter. Do you think the college's code is effective? Why or why not?

2. Most students (and faculty members, for that matter) would not want unauthorized individuals gaining access to the personal information the college has on file for them. In teams of three or four students, compile a list of the information technology tools the college uses to ensure that its students' records are secure. Particularly for professors teaching online courses, employee performance monitoring (or, more accurately in this case, student performance monitoring) is very important. After all, the professor wants to make sure that students log on to do the online activities. And professors want to make sure that exams are also properly monitored. In your teams of three or four students, compile a list of ways in which the online teaching system your college uses monitors student performance online.

3. You work for a medical genetics research firm as a marketing person. You love the job. The location is great, the hours are good, and the work is challenging and flexible. You receive a much higher salary than you ever anticipated. However, you've just heard via the rumor mill that the company's elite medical team has cloned the first human, the firm's CEO. It was such a total success that you have heard that they may want to clone every employee so that they can use the clones to harvest body parts as the original people age or become ill. You are not sure you endorse the cloning of humans. You joined the firm for its moral and ethical reputation. You feel that the image presented to you was one of research and development of life-saving drugs and innovative medical procedures. The thought of cloning was never on your mind, but now it must be. In teams of four or five students, answer the following questions: What, if any, is the ethical decision to be made? What would you do? Why?

4. You are taking a month's holiday in Europe. During your first week there, you became very ill with a recurring ailment for which you have been previously treated with limited success in the United States. It is a chronic condition that is inhibiting your ability to advance your career. The doctors who treated you in Europe have given you some medication that is legal there but has not been approved for use in the United States by the U.S. Food and Drug Administration. You feel better than you have in years. Because the European drug laws allow this drug to be purchased across the counter without a prescription, you are able to buy a year's supply. However, you know that it is listed as an illegal drug in the United States and you must pass through customs. If your decision is to smuggle the drug in and you are successful, what will you do in a year?

CASE STUDY

Allstate's Disappearing Agents

Like many companies, Allstate faces pressure to be cost-competitive and to provide new services to its customers. It also faces pressure for continuous improvement in its financial performance from its shareholders. Assume that for Allstate to survive and prosper, it needs to respond to both customers and shareholders. What responsibilities does it have toward another important group of stakeholders, its employees? Several years ago, the Allstate Corporation announced a series of strategic initiatives to expand its selling and service capabilities, buy back company shares to raise its stock price, and cut expenses by reducing the workforce. As part of its restructuring, Allstate would transfer its existing agents to an exclusive independent contractor program, whereby Allstate agents would become basically self-employed independent contractors. This would markedly reduce the need for Allstate to provide agency support staff. In its press release on this initiative, Allstate management also announced it would eliminate 4,000 current non-agent positions by the end of 2000, or approximately 10 percent of the company's nonagent workforce.

Said Allstate's CEO, "Now, many of our customers and potential customers are telling us they want our products to be easier to buy, easier to service and more competitively priced. We will combine the power of our agency distribution system with the growth potential of direct selling and electronic commerce. . . . This unique combination is without parallel in the industry and will make Allstate the most customer-focused company in the marketplace."

Proponents of this type of restructuring might argue that Allstate is simply taking the steps needed to be competitive. They might even say that if Allstate did not cut jobs to create the cash flow needed to fund new competitive initiatives, it might ultimately fail as a business, putting all 54,000 of its employees at risk.

Yet Allstate's program raises concerns. One analyst noted that by encouraging customers to purchase insurance products directly via the Internet, Allstate could threaten the commissions of its more than 15,000 agents. The announcement of cost cutting came one day after Allstate announced it would meet its regular quarterly dividend of $0.15 per share. The company has raised its dividend annually since 1993.

DISCUSSION QUESTIONS

1. Is reducing the number of employees in a company in and of itself unethical? Why or why not? Is it socially responsible (or irresponsible)?
2. If you decided it was generally ethical, what would the company have to do to make the employee dismissals unethical?
3. What responsibilities does a company like Allstate have toward its employees?
4. Is there a moral dimension to the question of marketing Allstate insurance via the Internet? If so, what is it?

Answers to *Wall Street Journal* Ethics Quiz

The quiz is on page 32.

1. 34% said personal e-mail on company computers is wrong.
2. 37% said using office equipment for schoolwork is wrong.
3. 49% said playing computer games at work is wrong.
4. 54% said Internet shopping at work is wrong.
5. 61% said it's unethical to blame your error on technology.
6. 87% said it's unethical to visit pornographic sites at work.
7. 33% said $25 is the amount at which a gift from a supplier or client becomes troubling, while 33% said $50, and 33% said $100.
8. 35% said a $50 gift to the boss is unacceptable.
9. 12% said a $50 gift *from* the boss is unacceptable.
10. 70% said it's unacceptable to take the $200 football tickets.
11. 70% said it's unacceptable to take the $120 theater tickets.
12. 35% said it's unacceptable to take the $100 food basket.
13. 45% said it's unacceptable to take the $25 gift certificate.
14. 40% said it's unacceptable to take the $75 raffle prize.
15. 11% reported they lie about sick days.
16. 4% reported they take credit for the work or ideas of others.

MANAGING IN A GLOBAL ENVIRONMENT

3

Tramco, Inc.

Tramco, Inc. is a small company with big ideas. With only about 100 employees, Wichita, Kansas–based Tramco designs and manufactures the big conveyors that food-processing firms like General Mills use to move ingredients around their factories.[1] But like almost all small-business managers today, Tramco's managers knew that to continue to grow, they had to take their company abroad. After all, many of their huge U.S. customers already had factories abroad, and Tramco wanted to serve them there. And there were also thousands of local food companies abroad that Tramco's managers knew would buy Tramco's products, if Tramco could provide local service. The problem was that Tramco's conveyors are so big and heavy that it costs as much to pack and ship one as it does to manufacture it. So Tramco had a dilemma. It could not just hire salespeople abroad, get orders, and then ship the huge conveyors. But with only about 100 employees, Tramco wasn't big enough to build its own factories abroad. What should they do? ■

Leon Trammell (center), Chairman of Tramco, had to decide how he and his firm's managers should take Tramco's business abroad.

BEHAVIORAL OBJECTIVES

After studying this chapter, you should be able to:

Show that you've learned the chapter's essential information by

- Explaining the economic, legal/political, sociocultural, and technological issues managers should consider when expanding abroad.
- Listing the special challenges a manager faces in leading and motivating employees abroad.

CHAPTER OUTLINE

➤ Listing the reasons why you would (or would not) be a good global manager.
➤ Giving examples of how to use information technology (IT) to improve global communications.

Show that you can practice what you've learned here by
➤ Reading the opening vignette about Tramco, Inc. and suggesting what IT tools they should use, and why.
➤ Reading the end-of-chapter exercises and explaining what global strategy the company should pursue, and why.

Show that you can apply what you've learned here by
➤ Watching the simulation video and identifying the key implementation issues facing the global business.
➤ Watching the simulation video and identifying what cultural adaptations need to be made when expanding globally.

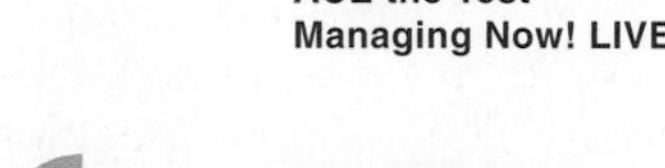

Globalization

Outside Anchorage, Alaska, just off Northern Lights Boulevard, is FedEx's new Anchorage hub. This enormous facility handles FedEx air shipments between North America and China. With package delivery growing relatively slowly in North America, China presents FedEx with enormous growth possibilities. In one recent year, the revenue FedEx generated from its package-delivery business to and from China increased by about 50 percent.[2] Like many companies today, most of FedEx's growth comes from international operations. Most businesses today are therefore involved in international business. The main purpose of this chapter is to enable you to better understand what it's like managing in a global environment.

Globalization Defined

Globalization (as noted in Chapter 1) is the tendency of firms to extend their sales, ownership, and/or manufacturing to new markets abroad. As with Tramco and FedEx, managers expand their services abroad to take advantage of new opportunities. Sony, Apple, and Nike are some firms that market and manufacture all over the world. For these firms and most others, managing is increasingly global.

Globalization is a two-way street. General Motors (GM) manufactures and sells cars in China, and China's Shanghai Auto is planning to manufacture and sell cars in the United States. In South Africa, numerous small wood furniture producers use the Internet to work with trading partners around the world. In South Korea, a special government program subsidizes small companies that want to use information technology to boost their share of global commerce. Raju Mirchandani, born in Dubai, recently expanded abroad by opening a branch of his New York–based "Bar and Books" in the Czech Republic.[3]

The Pros and Cons of Globalization

Globalization is thus not just for manufacturing firms.[4] For example, soon after it bought MySpace.com, News Corp. began laying plans to take the site abroad, to Britain and Europe, and soon to Asia. Going abroad will obviously hold some challenges for MySpace. For example, political and legal constraints against

Many U.S. companies are outsourcing call center services to centers like this one in India.

unrestricted blogging may be an issue in China, and each country must have its site in its own language.[5]

It's hard to overemphasize how important globalization is today to just about every business and manager in America (and around the world), and to every employee and consumer. In his recent book *The World Is Flat,* columnist Thomas Friedman explains how communications technology now makes it easy for companies everywhere (like Tramco) to compete just about anywhere. This has had a startling effect on businesses. As we noted in Chapter 1, more globalization means more competition, and more competition means more pressures to improve—to lower costs, to make employees more productive, and to do things better and less expensively. Globalization is great for firms like Tramco and FedEx, whose managers had the foresight and skills to capitalize on global opportunities. It's also great for consumers, who can now buy almost everything—from conveyors to cars to computers—less expensively thanks to globalization-driven competition.

But there's also another side to globalization.[6] All that improved productivity is coming from somewhere, and in many cases, it's coming from reductions in the numbers of managers and employees that companies need to compete. In 2006, Ford Motor Company instituted a plan, called Way Forward, that lays out how Ford would return to profitability, in part by reducing its workforce by over 25,000 employees, selling assets, and boosting productivity. GM has a similar plan. Meanwhile, Toyota's North American sales continue to expand, putting it on track to soon become the largest seller of cars in America. Globalization also triggered outsourcing. **Outsourcing** refers to the business practice of having workers abroad do jobs (such as handling customer-service questions) that employees in a company's home office previously did. American companies had outsourced about 830,000 service-sector jobs as of 2005.[7] No company or manager or employee today—even one safely situated in America's heartland, like Tramco—is not affected in a big way by globalization. Globalization shows up in the prices of the products we buy, the companies we choose to buy from, whether our employers stagnate or grow, and indeed how hard we work and whether we keep our jobs. Everyone should understand the global environment in which we live.

outsourcing: the business practice of having workers abroad do jobs (such as handling customer-service questions) that employees in a company's home office previously did

How and Why Do Companies Conduct Business Abroad?

Online Study Center
ACE the Test
Managing Now! LIVE

Companies like Tramco expand abroad for several reasons: to expand sales, obtain new foreign products, cut labor costs, and perhaps seek foreign partnerships for broader strategic reasons. Tramco expanded to follow its customers abroad. In 2006, Google expanded its China presence by initiating its Google China instant-messaging service. In 2005, IBM sold its personal computer (PC) division to the Chinese firm Lenova, in part to cement firmer ties with the booming China market.

Once they decide to expand abroad, managers like those at Tramco must decide *how* to expand. (Remember that Tramco, faced with the difficulty of shipping its products overseas, had to decide what its options were.) Options include exporting, licensing, franchising, foreign direct investment, joint ventures/strategic alliances, and wholly-owned subsidiaries.

Exporting

exporting: selling abroad, either directly to target customers or indirectly by retaining foreign sales agents and distributors

Exporting is often a manager's first choice when expanding abroad, because it is a relatively simple and easy approach. **Exporting** means selling abroad, either directly to customers or indirectly through agents and distributors. Agents, distributors, or other intermediaries handle more than half of all exports. They are generally local people familiar with the market's customs and customers.

The manager can check business reputations of potential local representatives via local agencies of the U.S. State Department. A U.S. Commerce Department trade specialist will provide advice regarding generating overseas business. For example, advertising in *Commercial News USA,* a government publication, will inform about 100,000 foreign agents, distributors, buyers, and government officials about U.S. products. The Small Business Exporters Association (www.sbea.org) is another good source.[8]

Exporting has pros and cons. It avoids the need to build factories abroad, and it is a relatively quick and inexpensive way of going international.[9] It's also a good way to test the waters in the host country and to learn more about its customers' needs. Transportation and tariff costs and poorly selected representatives are potential problems.

More and more companies rely on e-commerce to directly sell their products abroad, but even this can produce surprises. One European country wanted the Internet "closed" on Sundays to avoid competing unfairly with local merchants who closed that day.[10] Another country asked Lands' End to revise its guarantee, which it said was too good for local shops to compete with. And while getting an online order from, say, Japan may be exciting, the Better Business Bureau says that nondelivery is a chronic complaint, usually because the e-exporter is not familiar with foreign shipping requirements.

Licensing

licensing: an arrangement whereby a firm (the licensor) grants a foreign firm the right to use intangible property

If someone with a great idea wants to let someone else use the same idea, he or she might want to grant that person a license. Music companies grant licenses all the time. For instance, if Universal wants to let MGM use one of its songs in a movie, it will grant a license for that use. **Licensing** is an arrangement whereby the licensor (let's say, Universal) grants another firm (let's say, MGM) the right to exploit intangible (intellectual) property, such as patents, copyrights, manufacturing processes, or trade names, for a specific period. The licensor usually gets royalties—a percentage of the earnings—in return.[11]

Licensing is particularly useful when doing business abroad because it enables a firm to generate income abroad from its intellectual property without actually producing or marketing the product or service there. If a company in Kansas has a patent on a new device, one way for it to make money on that patent abroad is to license the patent's foreign rights to a company abroad.

Franchising

franchising: the granting of a right by a company to another firm to do business in a prescribed manner

If you've eaten in McDonald's by the Spanish Steps in Rome, you've experienced franchising as another way to do business abroad. **Franchising** is the granting of a right by a company to another firm to do business in a prescribed manner.[12]

Franchising and licensing both involve granting rights to intellectual property. Both are also quick and lower-cost ways to expand abroad. However, franchising tends to be much more restrictive. The franchisee must generally follow strict guidelines in running the business. McDonald's, for instance, is very fussy about franchisees following all its rules. The franchisee must also make substantial investments in a physical plant (such as a fast-food restaurant). Licensing tends to be limited to publishers and manufacturers—to letting others use a copyrighted or patented idea. Franchising is more common among service firms, such as restaurants, hotels, and rental services, that want to let investors (called franchisees) open businesses under the franchiser's name.

Foreign Direct Investment and the Multinational Enterprise

foreign direct investment: operations in one country owned and controlled by entities in a different country

At some point, managers find that capitalizing on international opportunities requires direct investment. **Foreign direct investment** refers to having operations in one country owned and controlled by entities in a different country. Companies make foreign direct investments in several ways. A foreign firm might build facilities in another country, as Toyota did when it built its Camry plant in Georgetown, Kentucky. Or a firm might buy property or operations, as when Wal-Mart bought control of the Wertkauf stores in Germany (it sold them and left Germany several years later, when the investment did not pan out). *Foreign portfolio investments* are investments by a company (or government) in a foreign firm's financial instruments (such as bonds or common stock). Strictly speaking, foreign direct investment means owning more than 50 percent of the operation. But in practice, a firm can gain effective control by owning less than half.

Foreign purchases of businesses trigger large and small changes. For example, when the Italian bank UniCredito Italiano Group purchased Boston's Pioneer Group, one of its first changes was installing an Italian espresso machine in Pioneer's offices. The Milan bank also installed videoconferencing equipment so managers on both sides of the Atlantic can interact live. Pioneer group managers have begun learning Italian. And the companies integrated their Italian and U.S. investment teams, which then went on to launch several global funds.[13]

Joint Ventures and Strategic Alliances

strategic alliance: a formal agreement between potential or actual competitors to achieve common strategic objectives

Managers often form strategic alliances or joint ventures when making forays into foreign markets (usually as a way to expand abroad without making a huge investment). **Strategic alliances** are formal cooperative agreements between potential or actual competitors, agreements that are of strategic importance to the alliance members.[14] Airline alliances, such as American Airlines' One World alliance with Japan Airlines and others, are examples. The airlines don't share investments, but they do share seating on some flights, and they let passengers use alliance members' airport lounges.[15] Each airline gets the advantage of being able to offer its own passengers an expanded overseas network without having to develop its own fleet of planes and flights abroad.[16] Perhaps a strategic alliance with a manufacturer abroad is an option for Tramco, Inc.

Window on Managing Now
Shanghai GM

Global joint ventures would be impractical without information technology such as computers, cell phones, fax, and software. As we mentioned, Shanghai Auto has a joint venture with General Motors, called Shanghai GM. The company's manufacturing process involves assembling vehicles from parts and partially assembled components it imports from around the world. Before Shanghai GM installed its new supply chain management software system, Shanghai GM's parts suppliers could not get real-time knowledge of what cars Shanghai GM had scheduled to assemble. And Shanghai GM did not know what parts its vendors already had in stock. This meant Shanghai GM had to order parts far in advance and then stock these parts, sometimes for several weeks.

Shanghai GM's managers found a better way. They used information technology (including new software systems and the Internet) to link together all the partners of the joint venture's worldwide supply chain (this includes its parts suppliers, shippers, and warehouses, for instance). Shanghai GM and its vendors and carriers now use an Internet portal to get continuous real-time production schedules showing what vehicles are to be produced, as well as updates on the availability of various parts. This dramatically reduced the amount of time managers had to leave for ordering vehicle components and reduced how much inventory Shanghai GM had to keep in stock.[17] This helped ensure that Shanghai GM is an efficient, world-class joint venture.

joint venture: the joining of two or more companies to form a separate company so that each party contributes assets, owns the entity to some degree, and shares risk

With a **joint venture**, two or more companies jointly form a separate company in which each party contributes assets, and each shares both ownership and risk.[18] Companies execute joint ventures every day. For example, the big Indian media company, Zee Telefilms, formed several partnerships with Time Warner. The firms call their joint venture Zee Turner. It will distribute both partners' television programs in India and neighboring countries.[19]

Partners usually form joint ventures to quickly gain advantages that would otherwise take time to acquire. Shanghai Auto and GM formed Shanghai General Motors. GM wanted to quickly produce Buicks for sale in China. Shanghai Auto wanted to learn how to build world-class cars.[20] The Window on Managing Now feature shows how technology helped make their venture a success.

A joint venture lets a firm gain useful experience in a foreign country by using the expertise and resources of a locally knowledgeable firm. As already mentioned, GM and Shanghai Auto formed a joint venture near Shanghai to build GM cars for China. Joint ventures also help both companies share the cost of starting a new operation. One downside is that the joint-venture partners each risk giving away their proprietary secrets. And sharing control and decision making can lead to conflicts, and thus requires careful planning regarding who does what.

Joint ventures can be a necessity. In China, foreign companies that want to enter regulated industries (like telecommunications) must use joint ventures with Chinese partners. The partnership of Britain's Alcatel and Shanghai Bell to make telephone-switching equipment is an example.[21]

Successful Joint Ventures Experts from consultants McKinsey & Co. estimate that companies have launched over 5,000 joint ventures worldwide in the past few years, but that these ventures' success rate is barely 50 percent.[22] Their study shows that in organizing a joint venture, managers need to follow several guidelines:

- *Achieve strategic alignment.* Organize the joint venture so that each corporate partner derives from the venture the strategic benefits it desires. For example, when Starbucks formed a coffee venture with PepsiCo, Starbucks sought to

Shanghai Auto and GM formed Shanghai General Motors to quickly gain manufacturing and sales advantages that would otherwise take time to acquire.

expand its brand into carbonated coffee, and PepsiCo wanted to expand from sodas to coffee. In assessing results, the partners therefore had to pay careful attention to improvements in Starbucks' share of the carbonated beverage market and in PepsiCo's share of the coffee market.

- *Create a governance system.* Give the joint venture's managers enough autonomy so they can make decisions quickly enough to be competitive, but not so much autonomy that they can trap either corporate partner in large, unwelcome commitments.
- *Manage economic interdependencies.* Outline clearly each partner's contributions in terms of capital, people, and material and other resources.
- *Build the organization.* Decide cooperatively which managers will actually staff the joint venture and what roles they may continue to play in their previous joint-venture parent firms.

Wholly-Owned Subsidiaries

wholly-owned subsidiary: a firm that is owned 100 percent by a foreign firm

Sometimes, the best way to go abroad is to open or own one's own facility. A **wholly-owned subsidiary** is one owned 100 percent by the foreign firm. In the United States, Toyota Motor Manufacturing, Inc., and its Georgetown, Kentucky, Camry facility is a wholly-owned subsidiary of Japan's Toyota Motor Corporation. Wholly-owned subsidiaries let the company do things exactly as it wants (subject to local laws and regulations, of course).

The Language of International Business

international business: any firm that engages in international trade or investment; also business activities that involve the movement of resources, goods, services, and skills across national boundaries

international trade: the export or import of goods or services to consumers in another country

international management: the performance of the management process across national boundaries

multinational corporation (MNC): a company that operates manufacturing and marketing facilities in two or more countries, and whose managers, located mostly in the firm's home country, coordinate the MNC's operation

To do business abroad, the manager should also know the vocabulary of international business. An **international business** is any firm that engages in international trade or investment. *International business* also refers to those activities, such as exporting goods or transferring employees, that require moving resources, goods, services, and skills across national boundaries.[23] **International trade** is the export or import of goods or services to consumers in another country. **International management** is the performance of the management functions of planning, organizing, leading, and controlling across national borders. As myspace.com's managers expand abroad, for instance, they necessarily engage in international management.

A multinational corporation is a special type of international business. A **multinational corporation (MNC)** is one that operates manufacturing and marketing facilities in two or more countries. Managers of the parent firm, whose owners are mostly in the firm's home country, coordinate the MNC's operations.

Firms like GE and GM have long been multinational corporations. However, thousands of small firms are MNCs, too. An MNC operates in two or more countries and often adapts its products and practices to each one. Often, however, the MNC's behavior may still reflect its national roots. When Germany's DeutscheBank bought a British bank, the British managers' high-incentive pay prompted tension between them and their new German bosses.

The Manager's International Environment

Online Study Center
ACE the Test
Managing Now! LIVE

Tensions like those between the British managers and their new German bosses illustrate a fact of life when doing business abroad. Countries differ in terms of economic, legal, and political systems and also in their cultures. Differences like these translate into different ways of doing business. Managers at firms like Tramco and myspace.com ignore such differences at their peril because the differences shape the manager's plans, organization, leadership style, and controls. We'll address countries' economic, legal/political, sociocultural, and technological environments.

The Economic Environment

First, managers should understand the economic environments of the countries they are considering entering. This includes each country's economic system, economic development, exchange rates, trade barriers, and economic integration and free trade.

The Economic System Countries differ in the extent to which they adhere to capitalistic economic ideals and policies like America's. For example, America's is a market economy. In a pure market economy, supply and demand determine what is produced, in what quantities, and at what prices. Managers here have freedom of choice to compete and set prices without government intervention.

At the other extreme, North Korea is a pure command economy. Countries like these base their yearly production and price targets on five-year plans set by the government. Then the government establishes specific production goals and prices for each sector of the economy (for each product or group of products), as well as for each manufacturing plant. Managers from abroad usually need government approval before entering these markets and forming partnerships with local firms.

mixed economy: an economy in which some sectors are left to private ownership and free-market mechanisms, while others are largely owned and managed by the government

In a **mixed economy**, some sectors have private ownership, while the government owns and manages others.[24] For example, France is a capitalist country. However, it has a mixed economy. The government owns shares of industries like telecommunications (France Telecom) and air travel (Air France).

Economic systems in transition can trigger social instability. Free-market economies depend on commercial laws, banking regulations, protection of private property, and an effective independent judiciary and law enforcement. When Russia moved to capitalism a number of years ago, it lacked much of this political and legal infrastructure. Early business owners there had to cope not just with competitors but also with criminals and lax law enforcement.

Economic Development Countries also differ in degree of economic development. For example, some countries, such as the United States, Japan, Germany, France, Italy, and Canada, have large, mature economies and extensive industrial infrastructures. The latter includes telecommunications, transportation, and regulatory and judicial systems. These countries' gross domestic products range from about $700 billion for Canada to $8.5 trillion for the United States. Other countries, such as Mexico, are less developed. Economists often measure an economy's size by *gross domestic product.* **Gross domestic product (GDP)**, a

gross domestic product (GDP): the market value of all goods and services that have been bought for final use during a period of time, and, therefore, the basic measure of a nation's economic activity measure of economic activity, is the market value of all goods and services bought for final domestic use during a period.

Some countries (like China) are growing much faster than others (like the United States). The growth rate of mature economies averages around 3 to 4 percent per year. On the other hand, China is growing at about 9.5 percent per year (10.5 percent in 2005–2006). Many managers at firms like General Electric (GE) are therefore boosting their investments in high-growth, high-potential countries.[25] Being relatively less-developed may suggest the potential for rapid development and growth. However, it can also mean inadequate roadways, communications, and regulatory and judicial infrastructures.

exchange rate: the rate at which one country's currency can be exchanged for another country's currency

● Exchange Rates Like anyone traveling or doing business abroad, managers engaged in international business must also juggle exchange rates. The **exchange rate** for one country's currency is the rate at which someone can exchange it for another country's currency. As the value of the dollar dropped against Europe's euro in 2003–2006, Europeans found it easier to purchase American products and properties. European manufacturers found it harder to compete against the cheaper American goods. British travelers flocked to the United States to buy clothes and even vacation homes (because the strong British pound could buy so many weak American dollars). On the other hand, some Americans were shocked to find it could cost $40 to buy a pasta meal in London's Piccadilly Circus (because it took so many American dollars to buy one British pound's worth of food).

trade barrier: a governmental influence that is usually aimed at reducing the competitiveness of imported products or services

tariff: a government tax on imports

quota: a legal restriction on the import of particular goods

● Trade Barriers The Gap store in Paris's Passy area (across the Seine from the Eiffel Tower) sells jeans that someone could buy for two-thirds the price in mid-town Manhattan. Why? In part because trade barriers distort the prices companies must charge for their products. **Trade barriers** (such as tariffs and quotas) are governmental influences aimed at reducing the competitiveness of imported products or services. Countries often use such barriers to make their domestic products look more attractive. **Tariffs**, the most common trade barrier, are governmental taxes levied on goods shipped internationally.[26] The exporting country collects export tariffs. Importing countries collect import tariffs. For instance, a China textile manufacturer might have to pay an import tax, or duty, to the United States in order to bring its textiles into the United States. Even people flying internationally—say, to the United States—must pay a duty to bring in many items, such as watches. Countries through which the goods pass collect transit tariffs. Other countries impose **quotas**—legal restrictions on the import of specific goods.[27] Managers thinking of doing business abroad ignore taxes like these at their peril.

subsidies: direct payments a country makes to support a domestic producer

Nontariff trade barriers exist, too. For example, cars imported to Japan must meet a complex set of regulations and equipment modifications. Side mirrors must snap off easily if they contact a pedestrian. Some countries make payments called **subsidies** to domestic producers. These are government payments that can make inefficient domestic producers more competitive.

free trade: the situation in which all trade barriers among participating countries are removed so that there is an unrestricted exchange of goods among these countries

● Economic Integration and Free Trade Economic integration and free trade are two big determinants of the economic situation international managers face. **Free trade** means all trade barriers among participating countries are removed.[28] Free trade occurs when two or more countries agree to allow the free flow of goods and services. Trade is unimpeded by trade barriers such as tariffs.

economic integration: the result of two or more nations minimizing trade restrictions in order to obtain the advantages of free trade

free trade area: a type of economic integration in which all barriers to trade among members are removed

customs union: a situation in which trade barriers among members are removed and a common trade policy exists with respect to nonmembers

common market: a system in which no barriers to trade exist among member countries, a common external trade policy that governs trade with nonmembers is in force, and factors of production, such as labor, capital, and technology, move freely among members

Economic integration means that two or more nations obtained the advantages of free trade by minimizing trade restrictions.

There are several levels or degrees of economic integration: free trade areas, custom unions, and common markets. In a **free trade area**, member countries remove all barriers to trade among them so that they can freely trade goods and services among member countries. A **customs union** is the next higher level of economic integration. Here, members dismantle trade barriers among themselves while establishing a common trade policy with respect to nonmembers. In a **common market**, no barriers to trade exist among members, and a common external trade policy is in force. In addition, factors of production, such as labor, capital, and technology, move freely between member countries, as shown in Figure 3.1. We'll look at some examples next.

More regions are pursuing economic integration. Back in 1957, founding members France, West Germany, Italy, Belgium, the Netherlands, and Luxembourg established the European Economic Community (EEC), now called the European Union (EU). Their Treaty of Rome called for the formation of a free trade area, the gradual elimination of tariffs and other barriers to trade, and the formation of a customs union and (eventually) a common market. Soon, the EEC further reduced its trade barriers.[29] By 1995, Austria, Finland, and Sweden became the thirteenth, fourteenth, and fifteenth members, respectively, of the EU. In 2002, the EU admitted ten more members, including some formerly Soviet Union countries, such as Poland. On January 1, 2002, the EU's new currency, the euro, went into circulation. It entirely replaced twelve EU countries' local currencies.

Brunei, Indonesia, Malaysia, the Philippines, Singapore, Thailand, and Vietnam comprise the Association of Southeast Asian Nations (ASEAN).[30] There is

FIGURE 3.1

Levels of Economic Integration

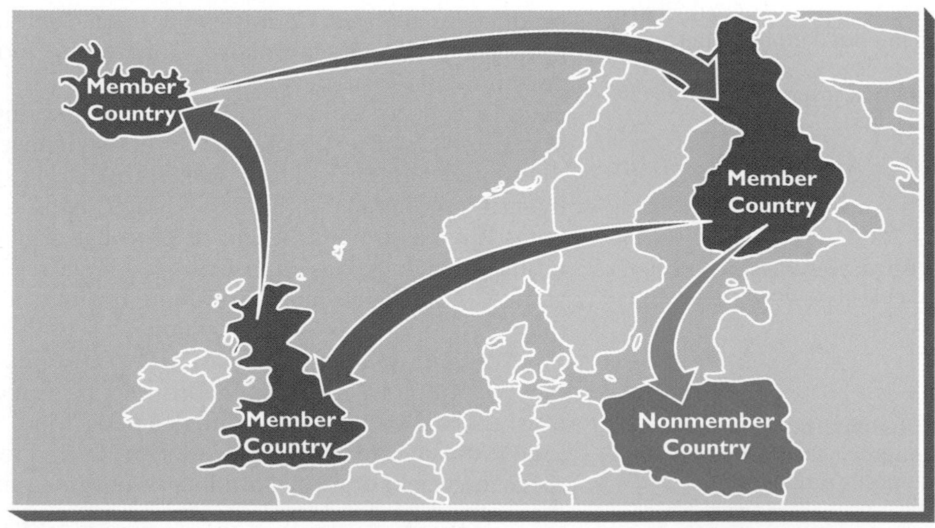

also the Asia Pacific Economic Cooperation (APEC) forum. Members include Australia, Chile, China, Japan, Malaysia, Mexico, Singapore, and the United States.[31] Africa also has several regional trading groups, including the Southern African Development Community, the Common Market for Eastern and Southern Africa, and the Economic Community of West African States.

Canada, the United States, and Mexico established the North American Free Trade Agreement (NAFTA). NAFTA creates the world's largest free trade market, with a total output of about $11 trillion.

● **The World Trade Organization (WTO)** Governments work together to encourage free trade in other ways (not just by fostering free trade areas, in other words).[32] The General Agreement on Tariffs and Trade (GATT) was one example. Formed in 1947 by twenty-three countries, by the mid-1990s, 117 countries were participating. The World Trade Organization (WTO) replaced GATT in 1995, and it now has over 130 members. One of the WTO's important functions is granting most favored nation (or normal trade relations) status for countries. This means that the WTO countries' "most favorable trade concessions must apply to all trading partners."[33]

When China received most favored nation status, it got the benefits of normal trade relations with WTO partners, but it also had to reduce its own trade barriers. Several U.S. companies, including New York Life Insurance Company and Metropolitan Life Insurance Co., quickly got the green light to set up 50-50 joint ventures with Chinese partners once China joined the WTO.[34] More recently, the New York Stock Exchange got China's permission to open a business office there.

Even for WTO members, some trade barriers fall faster than others. With WTO membership, China will see its import duties on cars fall drastically (to about 25 percent).[35] However, *within* China, Shanghai still has big license fees on cars from neighboring provinces so that Shanghai can protect its locally built Volkswagen.

● **The Impact of Economic Integration** Economic integration (such as NAFTA and the EU) has a big effect on managers. By removing trade barriers such as tariffs, it promotes regional trade because it becomes easier for companies from one country to do business in another. It thus boosts competition. So, in Europe, airlines (like British Airways) and telecommunications firms (like France Telecom) now face competition from Air France and DeutscheTelecom. Establishing free trade zones also puts firms from nonmember countries at a disadvantage. Many U.S. managers formed joint ventures with European partners to make it easier for them to sell in the EU.

In general, economists believe that free trade improves the standard of living of a country's citizens by encouraging competition and therefore providing better products at lower prices. The other side of the coin is that business managers now must be much more skillful at managing their companies to compete.

The Legal and Political Environment

Global political and legal differences can blindside even the most sophisticated managers and companies. After spending billions of dollars expanding into Germany, for instance, Wal-Mart managers were surprised to learn that Germany's commercial laws discourage advertising or promotions that involve competitive price comparisons. They soon had to leave Germany. In 2006, the European Union was locked in a dispute with Microsoft, which the EU accused of not making it easy enough for other firms to design compatible software products.

● **Legal Systems** Countries differ fundamentally in their approaches to the law. For example, companies like MGM and Warner Music find it difficult to protect their intellectual property in some Asian countries where copyright laws (if they exist) are not enforced with the same zeal as they are in Europe and the United States. Similarly, a U.S. manager, if arrested in France, may be surprised to find that French law holds him guilty until proven innocent—the opposite of the United States.

Global managers should familiarize themselves with such differences. In France, labor laws can make it difficult to fire and lay off employees, and employers in France, Germany, and the Netherlands usually must consult with powerful work councils before reorganizing or relocating employees.[36] Similarly, legal terms such as *trade secrets* and *confidential information* aren't necessarily enforceable in some countries around the world, even if the manager puts the words into his or her international contracts.[37]

Legal considerations influence how managers expand abroad.[38] In India, for instance, a foreign investor may own only up to 40 percent of an Indian industrial company, whereas in Japan, up to 100 percent of foreign ownership is allowed.[39] Some managers go global by appointing sales agents or representatives in other countries. But in Algeria, agents can't represent foreign sellers. Other countries view agents as employees subject to those countries' employment laws.[40]

International law consists mostly of agreements embodied in treaties and other types of agreements. International law governs things like intellectual property rights. Intellectual property piracy (fake brands) can be a big problem where the legal system is inadequate or inadequately enforced. For example, Procter & Gamble (P&G) estimates that about 20 percent of all its products sold in some countries are fake.[41]

● **Political Systems** Going abroad also means sizing up the political systems and risks with which the manager must cope. Thus, democratic countries usually provide a more open environment in which to run businesses than do dictatorships. Sometimes, the company's fate can change unexpectedly as the political winds shift. For example, some time ago, the Coca-Cola Company was very successful in Uzbekistan. One reason, perhaps, was that it opened the plant in partnership with the Uzbekistan president's son-in-law. When the president's daughter separated from her husband, the bottling company's Uzbek fortunes diminished.[42]

The manager also must take many practical risks into account. Examples include the problems a firm's employees might run into being robbed or arrested while traveling abroad. A new website (www.assessyourinternationalrisk.org) helps managers size up their international risks.[43]

The Sociocultural Environment

Global managers also quickly discover that people around the world react to events in varied but characteristic ways. For example, one study found that Japanese, German, and U.S. managers tended to take different approaches when resolving workplace conflict.[44] The Japanese prefer the power approach, which meant tending to defer to the party with the most power. Germans used a more legalistic, stick-to-the-rules approach. U.S. managers tend to try to take into account all parties' interests and to work out a solution that maximizes everyone's benefits.

Cultural differences like these should influence how managers conduct business abroad. When it opened its new production plant in Valenciennes, France, Toyota had to explain to the French Labor Ministry why management banned the traditional red wine at lunchtime in the company cafeteria. The reasons given were health and working conditions.[45]

On the other hand, Starbucks broke some traditions when it opened its first Tokyo store. Starbucks (pronounced STAH-buks-zu in Japanese) redefined the way the Japanese drink coffee. Its nonsmoking, bright, sofa-filled stores are in marked contrast to the dimly lit, smoke-filled stores where many Japanese traditionally drink their coffee from tiny cups.[46]

The Technological Environment

technology transfer: the transfer, often to another country, of the knowledge required to manufacture a product, apply a process, or render a service; does not extend to the mere sales or lease of goods

Doing business abroad often requires **technology transfer**, which basically means transferring knowledge, such as how to design or manufacture some product, or how to apply some process or render some service.[47] Let's say that Dell builds a computer factory in China staffed with local Chinese managers and workers. The plant's success depends on more than the bricks and mortar and machines. For example, Dell must also carefully train all the workers to use Dell's technology—such as its methods for ordering computer parts and for reporting problems. Similarly, Tramco (from this chapter's opening vignette) must have some way to transfer its knowledge of how to produce its conveyors if it decides to have a company abroad manufacture them.

"STAH-buks-zu" broke some traditions when it opened its first Tokyo store.

Successful Technology Transfer Successful technology transfer depends on several factors. First, one needs a *desirable and suitable technology*. For instance, one Miami company transferred to another country the machines from a plant that was a bit out-of-date in America but still usable in the lower-cost labor country abroad. *Social and economic conditions* must then favor the transfer. Pollution-reducing technology might be economically useless in a country where pollution reduction is low priority. Finally, technology transfer depends on the willingness and *ability* of the receiving party to use and adapt the technology.[48] In China, for instance, many multinational hotel chains are spending millions of dollars to train their local employees to apply the hotel chains' philosophy, for instance, for giving excellent service.

Sometimes technology transfers more quickly than the manager originally planned. For example, thanks to joint ventures with Volkswagen (VW) and GM, Shanghai Auto now produces over 650,000 cars per year in ultramodern factories in and around Shanghai. The company is already one of *Fortune*'s 500 largest companies in the world, with total revenues well over $12 billion. However, for top management at Shanghai Auto, that is only the beginning. The company's CEO says that Shanghai Auto will be producing 2 million vehicles by 2010.

Technology transferred from GM and VW helped Shanghai Auto achieve this. For example, when Shanghai Auto's joint venture with GM (Shanghai General Motors) started business, the joint venture received licenses to use GM's technical know-how. GM's technical computer systems, blueprints, and other supporting information helped Shanghai Auto create the manufacturing machines and systems for its new high-tech factory.[49] That helped Shanghai Auto to eventually grow out of its dependence on joint ventures and to someday compete with its joint-venture partners on their own turf.

Distance and Global Management

As you can see, it's not just vast distances that global managers must deal with. They also face economic, legal/political, sociocultural, and technological barriers. In fact, such factors are often as or more important than geographic distance in determining a foreign venture's success. One researcher says that managers should take into account four factors before expanding abroad: (1) cultural distance (such as languages and religions), (2) administrative distance (such as absence of shared monetary or political associations), (3) geographic distance (such as physical remoteness), and (4) economic distance (such as differences in consumer incomes). All of these—not just physical distance—influence the difficulty the company can expect to encounter (see Figure 3.2). The more distant the new country is on each of the four measures, the more difficult it may be to expand into it. MySpace will probably find it more challenging to expand into China than into England.

FIGURE 3.2

Determinants of Global Distance

ATTRIBUTES CREATING DISTANCE			
Cultural Distance	**Administrative Distance**	**Geographic Distance**	**Economic Distance**
▪ Different languages ▪ Different ethnicities; lack of connective ethnic or social networks ▪ Different religions ▪ Different social norms	▪ Absence of shared monetary or political association ▪ Political hostility ▪ Government policies ▪ Institutional weakness	▪ Physical remoteness ▪ Lack of a common border ▪ Lack of sea or river access ▪ Size of country ▪ Weak transportation or communication links ▪ Differences in climates	▪ Differences in consumer incomes ▪ Differences in costs and quality of: • natural resources • financial resources • human resources • infrastructure • intermediate inputs • information or knowledge

SOURCE: Adapted from Pankaj Ghemawat, "Distance Still Matters," *Harvard Business Review*, September 2001, p. 140.

Managing Now: Global Communications

Distance—be it physical distance, cultural distance, or another type of distance—has always been a major stumbling block to doing business abroad. This is because distance complicates everything the manager does, from controlling local operations to coaching employees.

Telecommunications tools like the telephone and e-mail reduce these problems. Instant messaging enables geographically dispersed employees to communicate inexpensively in real time. With Voice over Internet Protocol (VoIP) technology, calls that would usually go over phone lines are redirected through the Internet, which makes it easier and less expensive for companies to add or delete phones, and to combine voice and e-mail systems. Telecommunications—the electronic transmission of data, text, graphics, voice (audio), or image (video) over any distance—also facilitates transferring technical information. Ford designers at the company's Dearborn, Michigan, headquarters use computers to design new cars. Digitized designs then go electronically to Ford's Turin, Italy, design facility. There, the system automatically reproduces the designs and creates mockups of them. As another example, PricewaterhouseCoopers maintains electronic bulletin boards on more than 1,000 different company projects. About 18,000 of its employees in twenty-two countries use these electronic bulletin boards to get updates on matters such as how to handle specialized projects.[50]

Face-to-Face Global Communications However, dealing with sensitive topics or trying to be persuasive usually requires more personal, "rich" media, and this is where modern IT-based systems are invaluable to global managers.[51] Being able to see the other person usually makes it easier to communicate in any situation. And in some societies—including many in Asia—people are much more comfortable with rich media. This means communicating with people whose expressions and gestures they can actually see. Examples of useful IT tools here include videoconferencing, group decision support systems, and virtual communities. These all support global communications and make it possible for virtual teams—geographically dispersed teams who communicate primarily online and via telecommunications—to do their jobs. We'll look at each.

Videoconferencing Companies use videoconferencing to facilitate communications of geographically dispersed members of work teams. For example, the team that developed the Boeing 787 made extensive use of videoconferencing for meetings with engine suppliers and airlines around the world to discuss the new aircraft's design.[52] The links may be by phone or they may be satellite-based; or they may use one of the popular PC-based video technologies.[53] Videoconferencing has become very sophisticated. For example, Hewlett-Packard's new life-size Halo Collaboration Studio makes videoconferencing so clear that it makes people look as if they're on the other side of the table, although they may be half a world away.

decision support system (DSS): an interactive, computer-based communications system that facilitates the solution of problems by a virtual decision-making team

Workgroup Support Systems Workgroup support systems are technology-based systems that make it easier for workgroup members to work together. Team members might meet at a single site, or they may be dispersed around the world. A group **decision support system (DSS)** is an interactive, computer-based communications system that facilitates the solution of problems by a virtual decision-making team.[54] The group DSS lets team members interact via their PCs and use several software tools to assist in decision making and project completion. These software tools include electronic questionnaires, electronic brainstorming tools, idea organizers (to help team members compile ideas generated during brainstorming), and tools for voting or setting priorities (so that recommended solutions can be weighted and prioritized). A **group scheduling system** provides a shared scheduling database for geographically disbursed group members. Each group member puts his or her daily schedule into the shared database, which then helps to identify and set the most suitable times for meetings. A **workflow automation system** uses an e-mail type of system to automate the flow of paperwork.[55] For example, if a proposal requires four signatures, the workflow automation system can send it electronically from mailbox to mailbox for the required signatures.

group scheduling system: a system that provides a shared scheduling database for geographically disbursed group members

workflow automation system: an e-mail type of system to automate the flow of paperwork

Collaborative Writing Systems Collaborative writing systems let group members create long written documents (such as proposals) while working at a network of interconnected computers. As team members work on different sections of the proposal, each member has automatic access to the rest of the sections and can modify his or her section to be compatible with the rest. For example, each member of a global team with access to Oracle Project Collaboration software can easily keep track of such things as assigned tasks, issues, and deliverables. It enables global team members (both within and outside the company) to work together more efficiently and to make better and more effective project-related decisions.[56]

Virtual Communities One Friday night, about eighty young people met in a Tokyo club to exchange business cards and to learn more about some of the other people in their Japan-based myspace.com-like virtual online community.[57] Back online, they spend hours discussing matters of mutual interest.[58]

Global companies also use virtual communities. For example, as the prime contractor in an effort to win a $300 million navy ship deal, Lockheed-Martin "established a virtual design environment with two major shipbuilders, via a private internet existing entirely outside the firewalls of the three individual companies."[59] Eventually, about 200 global suppliers also connected to the network via special, secure Internet links. This Internet-based network "allows secure transfer of design, project management, and even financial data back and forth among the extended design team via simple browser access, with one homepage as its focal point." Lockheed got the contract.

Internet-Based Communications Schlumberger, which manufactures oil-drilling equipment and electronics, has headquarters in New York and Paris. The company operates in eighty-five countries, and in most of them, employees are in remote locations.[60] How does the company keep communications costs low for such a global operation? Here's how experts describe the company's system:

> Using the Internet, Schlumberger engineers in Dubai (on the Persian Gulf) can check e-mail and effectively stay in close contact with management at a very low cost. In addition, the field staff is able to follow research projects as easily as can personnel within the United States. Schlumberger has found that since it converted to the Internet from its own network, its overall communications costs are down. . . . The main reason for the savings is the dramatic drop in voice traffic and in overnight delivery service charges. . . .[61]

Planning, Organizing, and Controlling in a Global Environment

Online Study Center
ACE the Test
Managing Now! LIVE

International management means carrying out the four management functions we discuss in this book—planning, organizing, leading, and controlling—to achieve the company's international aims. As we've seen, managing in a global environment can present managers with some special challenges. We'll look at some of these challenges in the following discussion, starting with the global manager's traits, and then focusing on planning, organizing, and controlling in a global environment. This should also provide you with a better feel for what planning, organizing, leading, and controlling involve on a day-to-day basis.

The Global Manager

Not everyone is competent to manage in a global arena. Saying you appreciate cultural differences is one thing; being able to act on it is another. Global managers therefore tend to be, first, cosmopolitan in how they view people and the world. Some define *cosmopolitan* as "belonging to the world; not limited to just one part of the political, social, commercial or intellectual spheres; free from local, provincial, or national ideas, prejudices or attachments."[62] Global managers must be comfortable living and working anywhere in the world, and being cosmopolitan helps them to do so.

Sir Howard Stringer is a global executive endeavoring to manage Sony Corporation while dividing his time between the United States, Europe, and Japan.

Sir Howard Stringer, chief executive officer of Sony Corp., is probably as "global" as a manager can be. Born in Wales, Sir Howard manages Tokyo-based Sony Corp. by telecommuting from his offices in New York while still often visiting his family in Oxfordshire, England.[63]

Sir Howard got the Sony CEO job partly based on his success turning around Sony USA. Under his watch, Sony USA eliminated 9,000 jobs and $700 million in costs. He also made other numerous changes, including merging Sony's music business with Bertelsmann's BMG label.

Now that he is CEO of Sony Corp., Sir Howard's strategies will probably include centralizing some Sony activities such as research and development to cut costs, and focusing more on high-value products such as video games. He also wants Sony's employees and professionals from divisions such as engineering and media to work more closely together. But as a true global manager, Sir Howard knows that in a Japanese culture that favors harmony, he can't push the idea of maximizing shareholder value too hard. As a true global manager, he will adapt his leadership style to the culture of the Japanese.

Like Sir Howard, cosmopolitan people are sensitive to what is expected of them in any context, and they have the flexibility to deal intelligently and in an unbiased way with people and situations from other cultures. One needn't have traveled extensively or be multilingual like Sir Howard to be cosmopolitan, although such experiences help. The important thing is to be sensitive to other people's perspectives and to consider them in your own behavior.[64]

In addition to being cosmopolitan, global managers also have what some experts call a global brain. They are flexible enough to accept that, at times, their own ways of doing business are not the best. For example, Volkswagen formed a partnership with Skoda, a Czech carmaker. VW trained Skoda's managers in Western management techniques. However, it followed Skoda's suggestions about how to conduct business in the Czech Republic.[65] Being willing to apply the best solutions from different systems is what experts mean by having a global brain.

This global point of view (or its absence) tends to reflect itself in a manager's global philosophy. For example, an **ethnocentric** (home-base-oriented) management philosophy may manifest itself in an ethnocentric or "stay at home" home-market-oriented firm. A **polycentric** philosophy may translate into a company that is limited to several individual foreign markets. A **regiocentric** (or geocentric) philosophy may lead managers to create more of a global production and marketing presence.

ethnocentric: a management philosophy that leads to the creation of home-market-oriented firms

polycentric: a management philosophy oriented toward pursuing a limited number of individual foreign markets

regiocentric: a management philosophy oriented toward larger areas, including the global marketplace; also called geocentric

Would Your Company Choose You as an International Executive? What do companies look for in their international executives? One study focused on 838 lower-, middle-, and senior-level managers from six international firms in twenty-one countries. The researchers studied the extent to which employers could use personal characteristics such as sensitivity to cultural differences to distinguish between managers who had high potential as international executives and those whose potential was not so high. Fourteen personal characteristics successfully distinguished those identified as having high potential from those identified as lower performing.

Table 3.1 lists the fourteen characteristics with sample items. For each, indicate (by placing a number in the space provided) whether you strongly agree (7), strongly disagree (1), or fall somewhere in between. The higher you score, the more likely you would have scored high as a potential global executive in this study.[66]

planning: the process of setting goals and courses of action, developing rules and procedures, and forecasting future outcomes

Planning in a Global Environment

Planning means setting goals and identifying the courses of action for achieving those goals. The company's strategic plan lays out how the company will move from the business it is in now to the type of business it wants to be. GM wanted to expand into China. Its strategy was to do so by forming a joint venture with Shanghai Auto.

Mattel discovered that children everywhere wanted the same blond Rapunzel Barbie.

Going global helps to illustrate the sorts of strategic decisions managers need to make. For example, one big global strategy question is whether to offer standardized or localized products abroad. In deciding this, common sense does not always suffice. Instead, the manager needs to study the matter carefully. For years, Mattel Inc. adapted its Japan Barbie doll to what it assumed were local tastes, with black hair, Asian features, and Japanese-type clothes.[67] Several years ago, Mattel's consumer research group discovered a surprising fact. Most kids around the world actually wanted the original Barbie, with her blond hair and blue eyes. So recently, when Mattel introduced its Rapunzel Barbie with long blond hair, it also introduced the same doll on the same day in fifty-nine countries. The Window on Managing Now feature (page 78) shows how managers use software and other IT components to improve their localization decisions.

As another planning example, expanding abroad also takes careful feasibility planning. French retailer Carrefour conducts feasibility studies before entering new markets. For example, it avoids entering developing markets—such

TABLE 3.1
Characteristics of More Successful International Managers

Scale	Your Score	Sample Item
Sensitive to cultural differences.		When working with people from other cultures, works hard to understand their perspectives.
Business knowledge.		Has a solid understanding of our products and services.
Courage to take a stand.		Is willing to take a stand on issues.
Brings out the best in people.		Has a special talent for dealing with people.
Acts with integrity.		Can be depended on to tell the truth, regardless of circumstances.
Is insightful.		Is good at identifying the most important part of a complex problem or issue.
Is committed to success.		Clearly demonstrates commitment to seeing the organization succeed.
Takes risks.		Takes personal as well as business risks.
Uses feedback.		Has changed as a result of feedback.
Is culturally adventurous.		Enjoys the challenge of working in countries other than his or her own.
Seeks opportunities to learn.		Takes advantage of opportunities to do new things.
Is more open to (less sensitive about) criticism.		Appears brittle—as if criticism might cause him or her to break. (Reverse scored, so 1 is "strongly agree" for this item.)
Seeks feedback.		Pursues feedback even when others are reluctant to give it.
Is flexible.		Doesn't get so invested in things that he or she cannot change when something doesn't work.
TOTAL SCORE		

as Russia—that don't have reliable legal systems.[68] Even in more traditional markets, Carrefour won't proceed without at least a year's worth of on-site research. In China, "Carrefour takes care to chop vegetables vertically—not laterally—so as not to bring bad luck to superstitious shoppers."[69]

Organizing in a Global Environment

Organizing means identifying the jobs to be done, establishing departments, delegating or pushing authority down to subordinates, and creating a chain of command and mechanisms for coordinating employees' efforts. In general, the firm's stage of internationalization determines how it organizes its international

Window on Managing Now
Global Clustering

Managers today increasingly use "clustering" to make better decisions about whether to offer standardized or localized products. Clustering means identifying commonalities among customers based on their local tastes, and then combining (or clustering) common customers together. The clustered customers still get their locally preferred products or services. The company gets improved economies by clustering together several customers with similar tastes and preferences.

For example, Best Buy clusters stores in terms of several typical types of customers. For example, "Jill" is a busy mother who is the chief buyer for her household and wants quick, personalized help navigating the world of technology. Stores aimed at appealing to "Jill" have uncluttered, wider aisles, warmer lighting, and more technology-related toys for children.

Clustering relies on information technology.[70] Clustering requires being able to quickly access and analyze huge amounts of sales information across the company's global operations. The company needs to analyze who buys what and how buyers are similar to or different from each other. Information technology makes this possible. For example, with information on details like style and size constantly streaming back to the retailer Zara's global headquarters from point-of-sale computers, personal digital assistants (PDAs), and special software in stores, companies like Zara have developed methods for analyzing data on local buying patterns. This enables them to group these buying patterns into clusters—groups of stores that get similar merchandise and store layouts.

efforts. Thus, a company at the earliest stages of internationalization (or with few globally qualified managers) will more likely opt for managing its international operations out of a headquarters import-export or international department.

There is a typical evolution as the company becomes more international. In a *domestic organization,* each company division handles its own foreign sales. In response to increasing orders from abroad, the firm may move to an *export-oriented structure.* Here, one department (often called an import-export department) coordinates all international activities such as licensing, contracting, and managing foreign sales.

In an *international organization,* management splits the company into domestic and international divisions. The international division focuses on production and sales overseas, while the domestic division focuses on domestic markets. Reynolds Metals, for instance, set up six worldwide businesses, each with a U.S.-focused group and a separate international group. In a *multinational organization,* each country where the firm does business has its own subsidiary. Royal Dutch Shell has separate subsidiaries for Shell Switzerland and Shell U.S.A. (as well as many other countries).[71]

Other things affect how the manager organizes his or her international operations. Top management's philosophy is another consideration. For example, some CEOs are more globally oriented, while some are more local (ethnocentric) in their philosophical outlooks. The manager who believes that his or her country's ways are best is less likely to delegate much authority to remote local managers. Geographic distance is also important. Practical experience shows that it's harder to keep track of things that are happening far away. The following Managing Now section shows how Porsche uses information technology to help headquarters managers make better local decisions.

PRACTICE IT
Tramco, Inc.

Wichita, Kansas–based Tramco wants to supply its conveyors abroad, but the conveyors are so big and heavy that it costs as much to pack and ship one as it does to manufacture it. So they can't economically ship them. And with only about 100 employees, Tramco can't start building its own factories in countries around the world.

Tramco was able to use technology to solve its problem. First, it entered into strategic partnership agreements with manufacturers in several countries, who agreed to build the conveyors according to Tramco's specifications. The engineering design work on these huge conveyors is highly specialized and proprietary, so Tramco wanted to do that design work in its own Wichita offices. By installing special three-dimensional computerized design equipment at its own offices and at each partner abroad, Tramco's engineers in Kansas can design the conveyor and electronically transmit the design to the partner, which then manufactures it. It's easy for Tramco's engineers and the local manufacturer-partners' production teams to discuss and fine-tune designs electronically. Thanks to its new technology, Tramco is now truly a global company, with customers and manufacturing partners around the world. It's hard to see how Tramco could have accomplished this without information technology.

Managing Now: Porsche Centralizes Information technology also makes it easier to centralize decision making in one headquarters location (as opposed to letting managers at remote sites make these decisions). For example, Porsche's local warehouses used to supply parts to local dealers. If a warehouse was out of stock, there could be a delay. Now, Porsche uses information technology to link all its worldwide parts distribution and warehouse facilities. Therefore, its new central global logistics-planning center always knows who has what parts where. Now, when an order for a part comes in from a dealer, that order goes to the global logistics-planning center. This center handles the scheduling based on its information regarding global availability of those parts.[72] The Practice IT feature shows how Tramco expanded abroad.

Controlling in a Global Environment

Coca-Cola once had a rude surprise when several European countries made it take its beverages off store shelves. Coke has high standards for product quality and integrity, but controlling what's happening at every plant worldwide is a challenge. Chemicals had possibly seeped into the beverages at one of Coke's European plants.

Controlling means monitoring actual performance to ensure it is consistent with the standards the manager set. This is difficult enough when the employees are next door. Geographic distance complicates the problem, and the other distances (cultural and legal, for instance) complicate it even more. Among other things, the global manager should carefully address two factors: what to control and how to control it. The following presents some examples.

Deciding What to Control Particularly given the geographic distances involved, the global manager has to choose the activities he or she will control with great care. The manager could, of course, try to micromanage everything abroad—from hiring and firing to product design, sales campaigns, and cash management. However, micromanaging at long distances is not practical—even with the Internet, keeping track of people far away is not easy.

In practice, the amount of autonomy the local manager gets is usually *least* for financial and capital decisions and *most* for personnel decisions.[73] Production and marketing decisions tend to fall in the middle. In one study of 109 U.S., Canadian, and European multinational corporations, "these firms exercised stricter financial control, and allowed greater local freedom for labor, political, and business decisions. The home offices also usually made the decisions to introduce new products and to establish R&D facilities."[74]

Deciding How to Maintain Control The global manager also must decide how to control his or her global operations. Most managers today use computerized information systems. For many years, Kelly Services, Inc., let its offices in each country operate with their own individual billing and accounts receivable systems. However, according to Kelly's chief technology officer, "we are consolidating our operations in all countries and subsidiaries under a standard [information system]. . . . All our customers expect us to deliver consistent practices, metrics, and measurement. Establishing global standards is an important part of meeting and exceeding that expectation."[75]

Global managers also endeavor to foster their employees' self-control and employee commitment. Global managers do use computerized systems, financial and operating reports, and personal visits to help control their international operations.[76] However, methods like these are limited when thousands of miles separate boss and subordinate. Particularly in global companies, there's wisdom in making sure employees want to do what is right—and that they know what's expected of them in terms of the company's values and goals.

In other words, global companies have to make sure their managers and employees buy into and are really committed to "the way we do things around here."[77] Many firms, like Shell Oil and GE, therefore spend millions of dollars each year bringing managers together for special training sessions where the firm's core values (such as "ethics is all-important") are stressed. The Window on Managing Now feature illustrates how Dräger Safety uses information technology to support its control efforts.

Leading and Motivating in a Multicultural Environment

Online Study Center
ACE the Test
Managing Now! LIVE

Many people are probably less skilled at dealing with cultural differences than they think they are. Most people might say, "of course, there are cultural differences among people from different cultures." Yet many, once abroad, would blunder into simply treating the people there the same as the people at home.[78] The problem stems from what international management writers call the universality assumption of motivation: "These [motivation] theories erroneously assume that human needs are universal."[79] For example, an American manager in Chile might assume that employees there are as enthusiastic about participative leadership—having the boss ask what the workers think is best—as are those in the United States, although they might not be.

Such assumptions are not uniquely American. Everyone everywhere tends to assume that everyone thinks and feels more or less like they do. But, in fact, people and cultures are different in many ways. We'll briefly look at how cultural differences influence how managers in international arenas motivate and lead employees.

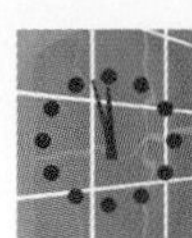

WINDOW ON MANAGING NOW
Dräger Safety

Dräger Safety, based in Lubec, Germany, is the world's largest supplier of personal-protection, gas-testing, and diving equipment, with operations in thirty-three countries.[80] Several years ago, Dräger faced a problem controlling its worldwide sales and inventory operations. Each of its facilities around the world basically had its own software system. For instance, if managers at headquarters wanted to know what the company's total inventory was, headquarters employees had to collect the separate, incompatible reports from each of the company's facilities and summarize them for management.

This lack of comparable information was hurting Dräger's competitiveness. As Dräger's chief financial officer put it, "it got to the point where sales reps dreaded going to customer sites . . . the customer would spend a whole hour berating them about late deliveries and missed appointments." For instance, warehouses found it difficult to monitor the status of a product after it shipped, and the trucking company found it difficult to forecast when Dräger would have a particular order ready to ship.

Dräger installed a new software system that enables its managers to better control its global production. For example, it installed a special enterprise software system that integrated and made compatible the systems each of its facilities had been using. Now, all Dräger's suppliers, facilities, and customers are linked together to Dräger's global database.

Figure 3.3 summarizes the new system. Dräger's suppliers, locations, and customers can all connect to the common global database and thereby monitor product and shipping status. Dräger salespeople can now give customers accurate shipping estimates. Customers now get accurate shipping information. Furthermore, Dräger headquarters management can now access the global database for producing sales forecasts, production plans, and purchasing plans and for compiling budgets and financial reports. At Dräger, IT—a combination of computers, special software, cell phones, PDAs, and fax, for instance—made successful globalization possible.

FIGURE 3.3

An Oracle-Based Supply Chain

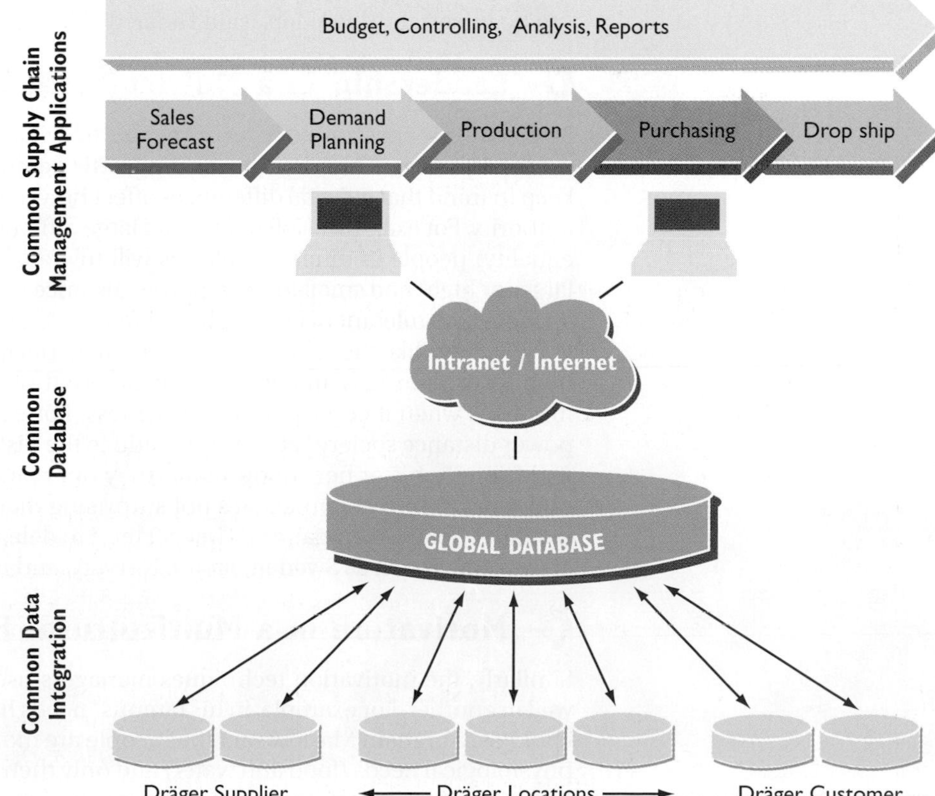

SOURCE: Adapted from Business Benefits Series, "Dräger Safety Re-Engineers Global Supply Chain, Builds Centralized Logistics and IT Infrastructure Yielding Three-Year ROI of 193%," www.oracle.com, accessed March 2006. Reprinted by permission of Oracle Corporation.

Values

values: basic beliefs about what is important and unimportant, and what one should and should not do

One way people around the world differ is in terms of their values. **Values** are basic beliefs we hold about what is good or bad, important or unimportant. Values (such as West Point's famous "Duty, honor, country") are important to managers because our values shape how we behave. When Professor Geert Hofstede studied managers around the world, he found that societies' values differ in several ways:

- *Power distance.*[81] Power distance is the extent to which the country's less powerful members accept and expect that power will be distributed unequally.[82] At the time, Hofstede concluded that acceptance of such inequality was higher in some countries (such as Mexico) than it was in others (such as Sweden).
- *Individualism versus collectivism.* In individualistic countries like Australia and the United States, "all members are expected to look after themselves and their immediate families."[83] In collectivist countries like Indonesia and Pakistan, society expects people to care for each other more.
- *Masculinity versus femininity.* According to Hofstede, societies differ also in the extent to which they value assertiveness (which he called "masculinity") or caring ("femininity"). For example, Austria ranked high in masculinity; Denmark ranked lower.
- *Uncertainty avoidance.* Uncertainty avoidance refers to whether people in the society are uncomfortable with unstructured situations in which unknown, surprising, novel incidents occur. People in some countries (such as Sweden, Israel, and Great Britain) are relatively comfortable dealing with uncertainty and surprises. People living in other countries (including Greece and Portugal) tend to be uncertainty avoiders, said Hofstede.[84]

Leadership in a Multicultural Environment

Leadership means influencing someone to willingly work toward achieving the firm's objectives. The manager dealing with people from other cultures needs to keep in mind that cultural differences affect how managers exercise their leadership authority. For example, Hofstede found large differences in the "power distance" (inequality) people in different cultures will tolerate.[85] Figure 3.4 lists countries with large (or high) and small (or low) power-distance rankings. For example, Argentines appear more tolerant of large power differences, Swedes less so.

Findings like these have practical managerial implications. For one thing, they help to explain why managers from different countries seem to have different mindsets when it comes to doing business. For example, if a manager in a "large power distance society" attempts to reduce the distance by acting more accessible and friendly, his or her subordinates may not react well to such friendliness from their boss.[86] In that context, it's not surprising that leaders in some countries (for instance, Spain, Portugal, and Greece) tend to delegate less authority than do leaders in others such as Sweden, Japan, Norway, and the United States.[87]

Motivation in a Multicultural Environment

Similarly, the motivation techniques managers use in one country may not work well in another. For example, in his famous "needs hierarchy theory," American psychologist Abraham Maslow said that people are motivated first to satisfy their basic physiological needs (food and water) and only then will they be motivated to satisfy (in ascending order) their security, social, self-esteem, and self-actualization

FIGURE 3.4

Countries Ranked Based on How Much Power Distance People Tolerate

HIGH POWER DISTANCE (Inequality more acceptable)	Argentina Brazil Belgium Chile Colombia France Greece Hong Kong India Iran Italy Japan Mexico Pakistan Peru Philippines Portugal Singapore Spain Taiwan Thailand Turkey Venezuela Yugoslavia
POWER DISTANCE	
LOW POWER DISTANCE (Inequality less acceptable)	Australia Austria Canada Denmark Finland Germany Great Britain Ireland Israel Netherlands New Zealand Norway Sweden Switzerland U.S.A.

SOURCE: Adapted from G. Hofstede, *Culture's Consequences* (Beverly Hills, Calif.: Sage Publications, 1984).

(becoming the person you believe you are capable of becoming) needs. However, he based his theory on Americans. In other societies, people's needs don't necessarily revolve around the self as much as around social relationships. Thus, in China, social needs might come first, then physiological, security, and finally self-actualization needs. Not surprisingly, in Asia, paying an incentive to a work team for how well it performs is very popular. In America, individual incentives are more popular.[88]

Interpersonal Communications in a Multicultural Environment

Communication refers to exchanging information so that the manager creates a common basis of understanding. Cultural differences influence communication in obvious and subtle ways. Language barriers are one obvious problem. An American manager negotiating a deal in England can generally make him- or herself understood using English, but he or she might need an interpreter in France. Even when the other party speaks some English, problems can arise. For example, using an idiom (such as "you bet it is") may be incomprehensible to the Swiss person with whom you're speaking. Furthermore, as General Motors once discovered, words that sound or look the same (such as *Nova,* which means "won't go" in Spanish) may have different meanings in different countries.

The problem is not just the words. As much as 90 percent of what people "say" is nonverbal, conveyed via facial expressions and signs and motions of one sort or another. Here is where the novice international manager can really get into trouble. Table 3.2 shows what some typical nonverbal behaviors mean in various countries. Subtle differences like these can make international management an adventure! The Improving Your *Cultural Intelligence* Skills feature presents other examples of global cultural differences.

TABLE 3.2

Implications of Various Nonverbal Behaviors in Different Cultures

Nonverbal Behavior	Country	Meaning
Thumbs up	United States	An approval gesture/okay/"Good job!"
	Middle East	A gesture of insult
	Japan	A sign indicating "male"
	Germany	A sign for the count of 1
A finger circulating next to the ear	Argentina	A telephone
	United States	"Crazy!"
A raised arm and waggling hand	United States	Goodbye
	India, South America	Beckoning
	Much of Europe	A signal for no
Showing the back of the hand in a V-sign	England	A rude sign
	Greece, Middle East	A sign for the count of 2
Showing a circle formed with index finger and thumb	United States	"Very good!"
	Turkey	Insult gesture/accusation of homosexuality
Eye contact, gazing	United States	A sign of attentiveness
	Japan	A rude behavior/an invasion of privacy
	Most Asian countries	Sign of disrespect to senior people
Widening eye	United States	An indication of surprise
	Chinese	An indication of anger
	Hispanic	Request for help
	French	Issuance of challenge
Nodding the head up and down	Western countries	A sign for agreement/yes
	Greece, Bulgaria	A sign for disagreement/no

Source: Adapted from Kamal Fatehi, *International Management* (Upper Saddle River, N.J.: Prentice Hall, 1996), Table 6.1, p. 194.

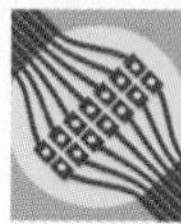

Improving Your *Cultural Intelligence* Skills

In practice, there is more to being multicultural than just using the right mannerisms and idioms. Two researchers say that being truly multicultural (having "cultural intelligence") requires that the person also have what they call the right cognitive, physical, and emotional/motivational cultural skills. Figure 3.5 presents a short cultural intelligence test.

Figure 3.5

Diagnosing Cultural Intelligence

These statements reflect different facets of cultural intelligence. For each set, add up your scores and divide by four to produce an average. Work with large groups of managers shows that for purposes of your own development, it is most useful to think about your three scores in comparison to one another. Generally, an average of less than 3 would indicate an area calling for improvement, while an average of greater than 4.5 reflects a true "Cultural Quotient" (CQ) strength.

Rate the extent to which you agree with each statement, using the scale:
1 = strongly disagree, 2 = disagree, 3 = neutral, 4 = agree, 5 = strongly agree.

_____ Before I interact with people from a new culture, I ask myself what I hope to achieve.

_____ If I encounter something unexpected while working in a new culture, I use this experience to figure out new ways to approach other cultures in the future.

_____ I plan how I'm going to relate to people from a different culture before I meet them.

\+ _____ When I come into a new cultural situation, I can immediately sense whether something is going well or something is wrong.

Total _____ ÷ 4 = ☐ COGNITIVE CQ

_____ It's easy for me to change my body language (for example, eye contact or posture) to suit people from a different culture.

_____ I can alter my expression when a cultural encounter requires it.

_____ I modify my speech style (for example, accent or tone) to suit people from a different culture.

\+ _____ I easily change the way I act when a cross-cultural encounter seems to require it.

Total _____ ÷ 4 = ☐ PHYSICAL CQ

_____ I have confidence that I can deal well with people from a different culture.

_____ I am certain that I can befriend people whose cultural backgrounds are different from mine.

_____ I can adapt to the lifestyle of a different culture with relative ease.

\+ _____ I am confident that I can deal with a cultural situation that's unfamiliar.

Total _____ ÷ 4 = ☐ EMOTIONAL/MOTIVATIONAL CQ

Source: Christopher Earley and Elaine Mosakowski, "Cultural Intelligence," *Harvard Business Review,* October 2004, p. 143.

For example, the Cognitive Skills component of someone's cultural intelligence in the figure is reflected in statements like the following: "When I come into a new cultural situation, I can immediately sense whether something is going well or something is wrong." One point these experts emphasize is that succeeding with people of other cultures really takes being sensitive to who they are and to how they do things. As they say,

. . . Your actions and demeanor must prove that you have already to some extent entered their world. Whether it's the way you shake hands or order a coffee, evidence of an ability to mirror the customs and gestures of the people around you will prove that you esteem them enough to want to be like them. By adopting people's habits and mannerisms, you eventually come to understand in the most elemental way what it is like to be them.[89]

CHAPTER SUMMARY

1. Companies can pursue several approaches when it comes to extending operations to foreign markets: exporting, licensing, and franchising are popular alternatives. At some point, a firm may decide to invest funds in another country. Joint ventures and wholly-owned subsidiaries are two examples of foreign direct investment.
2. An international business is any firm that engages in international trade or investment. Firms are globalizing for many reasons, the three most common being to expand sales, acquire resources, and diversify sources of sales and supplies. Other reasons for pursuing international business include reducing costs or improving quality by seeking products and services produced in foreign countries and smoothing out sales and profit swings.
3. Free trade means removing all barriers to trade among countries participating in the trade agreement. Its potential benefits have prompted many nations to enter into various levels of economic integration, ranging from a free trade area to a common market.
4. Globalizing production means placing parts of a firm's production process in various locations around the globe. The aim is to take advantage of national differences in the cost and quality of production and then integrate these operations in a unified system of manufacturing facilities around the world. Companies are also tapping new supplies of skilled labor in various countries. The globalization of markets, production, and labor coincides with the rise of a new type of global manager, someone who can function effectively anywhere in the world.
5. International managers must be skilled at weighing an array of environmental factors. Before doing business abroad, managers should be familiar with the economic systems, exchange rates, and level of economic development of the countries in which they plan to do business. They must be aware of import restrictions, political risks, and legal differences and restraints. Important sociocultural differences also affect the way people in various countries act and expect to be treated. Values, languages, and customs are examples of elements that distinguish people of one culture from those of another. Finally, the relative ease with which the manager can transfer technology from one country to another is an important consideration in conducting international business.
6. With respect to planning the products it sells, the company can offer standardized products worldwide, or products more specifically designed for local preferences. Many companies group customers into clusters to gain some of the advantages of both standardization and localization. Feasibility planning is also important to global managers.
7. Particularly given the geographic distances involved, the global manager has to choose the activities he or she will control with great care. Micromanaging at long distances is not practical—even with the Internet, keeping track of people far away is not easy. In practice, the amount of autonomy the local manager gets is usually *least* for financial and capital decisions and *most* for personnel decisions.
8. The company's international organization reflects the firm's degree of globalization. In a domestic organization, each division handles its own foreign sales. In response to increasing orders from abroad, the firm may move to an export-oriented structure.

In an international organization, management splits the company into domestic and international divisions. In a multinational organization, each country where the firm does business has its own subsidiary.

9. Leading, motivating, and communicating abroad are susceptible to what international management writers call the universality assumption—the tendency to assume that everyone everywhere thinks and feels more or less like we do. People around the world actually hold different values in areas such as power distance, individualism versus collectivism, masculinity versus femininity, and uncertainty avoidance, and they often have different needs and ways of communicating.

DISCUSSION QUESTIONS

1. If you owned a small U.S. business and wanted to expand sales to Europe, explain briefly how you would go about doing so.
2. Why does globalization affect businesses and employees in the United States?
3. What do we mean by economic integration?
4. What is the European Union?
5. How do managers generally organize for international business? What do their organizining decisions depend on?

EXPERIENTIAL EXERCISES

1. You have just taken an assignment to assess the feasibility of opening a branch of your company's business in Russia. Your company manufactures and sells farming equipment. Working in teams of four or five, prepare a detailed outline showing the main topic headings you will have in your report, including a note on the management tools you will use to get the information you need for each topic.
2. While Google's strategy of exporting its e-mail and other tools from the United States to various countries seems to be working well, management is now concerned that local competitors may start eating into its business. Working in teams of four or five, use the discussions in this chapter to specify the global strategy (localize or not?) you believe Google should pursue now. What global organization structure would that imply?
3. Spend several minutes using the tools and what you learned so far in this book to list ten reasons why you would (or would not) be a good global manager.
4. Many rightfully believe that it is the business school's responsibility to familiarize business students with what it takes to be an effective global manager. In teams of four or five, compile a list, based on this course and any others you've taken, of what your business school is doing to cultivate a better appreciation of the challenges of doing business internationally.

CASE STUDY

U.S. Bookseller Finds a Strong Partner in German Media Giant

When Barnes & Noble was exploring ways to become more competitive in its battle with Amazon.com, there were hundreds of U.S. companies to which it could turn. Research demonstrated that the cultural differences that characterize cross-border ventures made them far more complicated than domestic ones. So Barnes & Noble surprised competitors when it chose to form an Internet joint venture with the German media giant Bertelsmann.

Bertelsmann was best known among college students for its record label and music club, BMG (now both owned by Sony). At the time, BMG Entertainment was second in the market with $1.9 billion in sales. Bertelsmann's holdings include Random House, the world's largest English-language book publisher, and Offset Paperback, a firm that manufactures nearly 40 percent of all the paperback books sold in the United States. Bertelsmann had also actively pursued e-commerce on its own.

To fund the original barnesandnoble.com, the two created a separate company and conducted an initial public offering (IPO) to raise capital. The offering raised $421 million for the new venture after commissions and expenses, making it the largest e-commerce offering in history. Since launching its online business in May 1997, barnesandnoble.com has quickly become one of the world's largest e-commerce retailers. The company has successfully capitalized on the recognized brand value of the Barnes & Noble name to become the second largest online retailer of books.

DISCUSSION QUESTIONS

1. What may have motivated Barnes & Noble to partner with the German firm Bertelsmann? In general terms, what advantages would Barnes & Noble gain by having an international partner in such an endeavor? Suggest the pros and cons of this partnership.
2. Specify the basic global strategy you believe barnesandnoble.com should pursue, and explain why. How, in very general terms, would you organize this venture?
3. With all its experience in e-commerce, why wouldn't BMG just set up its own competitor to Amazon .com?
4. List three specific planning, organizing, leading, and controlling issues Barnes & Noble's managers probably faced in establishing this new joint venture.
5. Write a one-page essay on the following topic: cultural factors our Barnes & Noble managers should keep in mind when dealing with our colleagues at Bertelsmann.

MANAGING ENTREPRENEURSHIP AND INNOVATION

4

CHAPTER OUTLINE

Procter & Gamble

Just about everyone uses products from Procter & Gamble (P&G) every day. Some of its hundreds of famous brands include, just for a start, Bounty, Crest, Clairol, Duracell, Gillette, Head & Shoulders, Ivory, Old Spice, Pampers, and Swiffer. Like almost every company, the only way P&G can stay ahead of the competition is to keep coming up with new and improved products. Whether it's a new multiblade razor, a superwhitening toothpaste, or a Swiffer mop (which did not even exist a few years ago), innovation is the name of the game at P&G. The problem is that companies like P&G can't rely on just their own research labs to come up with the necessary new products. "The R&D model that most companies are following is broken," says Larry Huston, the firm's head of research and development.[1] Instead, P&G also wants to tap the ideas of its millions of consumers, distributors, and retailers, as well as any scientists who might want to contribute. The question for Larry Huston is, How should P&G do this? ■

Just about everyone uses a P&G product every day.

BEHAVIORAL OBJECTIVES

After studying this chapter, you should be able to:

Show that you've learned the chapter's essential information by

- Explaining why you do (or do not) have the traits to be an entrepreneur.
- Listing the pros and cons of four forms of business ownership.
- Listing what a person should keep in mind with respect to buying a business or franchise.

- Explaining managing innovation, new product development, and life-cycle management, using examples.

Show that you can practice what you've learned here by

- Reading the opening vignette and explaining how to answer Larry Huston's question.
- Reading the chapter case study and listing what an entrepreneur is doing right and doing wrong with respect to starting a business.
- Reading Experiential Exercise 2 and explaining why you would or would not buy that franchise.

Show that you can apply what you've learned here by

- Watching the simulation video and identifying how the manager recognizes, manages, and creates innovation for a sustained competitive advantage.

Online Study Center
ACE the Test
Managing Now! LIVE

Introduction: Entrepreneurship and Innovation

P&G is a great company, but chances are most people reading this book won't work for P&G, or for other giant companies like GM either. Most people work for small, entrepreneurial firms, firms with no more than perhaps 100 or so employees. And many business school graduates also go out and start their own businesses, or buy small businesses, or start franchises. Therefore, business students definitely should be familiar with small-business management.

Small entrepreneurial companies are important for another reason. Small firms are engines of inventiveness and innovation, the sort of inventiveness and innovation that produces the floods of new products that any society needs to grow and to thrive. After all, all those Google, MySpace, and Youtube dotcoms didn't come out of some giant company's lab. (Twenty-somethings Chad Hurley and Steven Chen created Youtube in about one year.) And even most of the great and most innovative products around today (like the Apple computer, or even Gillette razors) originally came out of the work of a small band of people working together, often in the proverbial garage. The bottom line is that business students and management majors should know something about managing small entrepreneurial companies and about innovation.

In fact, innovation is a much more important topic for business success than most people realize. Xerox Corporation revolutionized the document-duplicating market with its first Xerox machine. It then watched feebly as Canon captured market share with innovative new-product improvements. Kodak owned the photographic film market for almost 100 years. It then watched helplessly for years as first Polaroid and then digital photography revolutionized the photography market. Americans once shopped for bargains in stores owned by companies named W. T. Grant and Woolworth's. Then Sam Walton entered the scene with a new approach that basically put these giants and many small mom-and-pop retail businesses out of business.

Creative Destruction The economist Joseph Schumpeter used the term *creative destruction* to describe the process through which entrepreneurs and companies introduce radical innovations like these that transform industries.[2] Basically, to paraphrase Schumpeter, no industry and no products are immune to being put out of business by some revolutionary new product; or new equipment; or new methods of organization, management, or communication. For example, think about the thousands of bookstores that Amazon put out of business with its first Internet website. Note how Monster is killing the market for newspaper help-wanted ads. And consider how even Microsoft, long the king of the hill of personal computers, is fighting to stay dominant now that people increasingly find and use the software they need online. For example, in June 2006, Google announced a new service that lets users access (online and for free) a spreadsheet package that rivals Microsoft's Excel program.

Schumpeter's creative destruction theory neatly sums up a fact of management life, and one we'll discuss at more length later in this chapter. The development and life of every product, no matter how innovative it is when first introduced, follows what businesspeople call a *product life cycle.* An inventor or entrepreneur gets a new-product idea, develops it, introduces it to the market (to those buying the product), and then hopefully watches sales take off. Next, he or she turns (again, hopefully) to innovating improvements to the product as the market matures, for instance, as competitors like Canon and Wal-Mart clamber in. Finally, as changing tastes and even more innovative new products cause the market for the original product to decline, our inventor/entrepreneur needs to decide what to do. What does P&G do as things get more and more competitive in the toothpaste market? Keep adding new innovations (whiteners, and so on)? Get out of producing toothpaste altogether?

In this chapter, we'll focus on two inseparable topics, entrepreneurship and innovation. No company that fails to innovate can survive, no matter how skilled its managers are in their other endeavors. And it is most often through the efforts of entrepreneurs that truly innovative new products and services arise to challenge the status of the former kings of the hill. We'll begin with entrepreneurship.

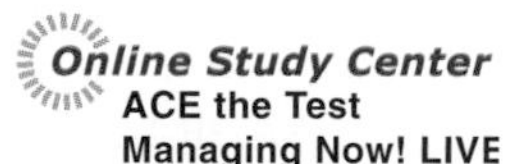

Entrepreneurship Today

entrepreneurship: the creation of a business for the purpose of gain or growth under conditions of risk and uncertainty

entrepreneur: someone who creates new businesses for the purpose of gain or growth under conditions of risk and uncertainty

Early in their careers, Steve Jobs, Michael Dell, and Donna Karan were all entrepreneurs. **Entrepreneurship** is the creation of a business for the purpose of gain or growth under conditions of risk and uncertainty.[3] An **entrepreneur** is thus someone who creates new businesses under risky conditions.[4] Entrepreneurship "requires a vision and the passion and commitment to lead others in the pursuit of that vision [and] a willingness to take calculated risks."[5] Figure 4.1 neatly sums up what entrepreneurship is all about. In the pantheon of management, entrepreneurs are unique. Entrepreneurs "build something of value from practically nothing."[6] Innovation, the creating of value, growth, and uniqueness, characterizes the entrepreneur's efforts. Many business students plan to and will start new businesses (and have to manage them) once they leave school.

Entrepreneurs and Small-Business Management

Because entrepreneurs create something out of nothing, it stands to reason that the firms they create usually start small. Most people therefore tend to associate entrepreneurs with small businesses, although that link is, in reality, a bit tenuous. David Neeleman, JetBlue's founder and CEO, is certainly an entrepreneur. However, the business he's running is not and never really was very small. On the other hand, someone who buys and runs a successful dry-cleaning business probably is not an entrepreneur in the strictest sense. That person is a small-business owner/manager. It's creating a business from nothing that distinguishes the entrepreneur.

small-business management: planning, organizing, leading, and controlling a small business

Small-business management refers to planning, organizing, leading, and controlling a small business. The U.S. Small Business Administration (SBA) sets

FIGURE 4.1

Common Themes in Definitions of Entrepreneurship

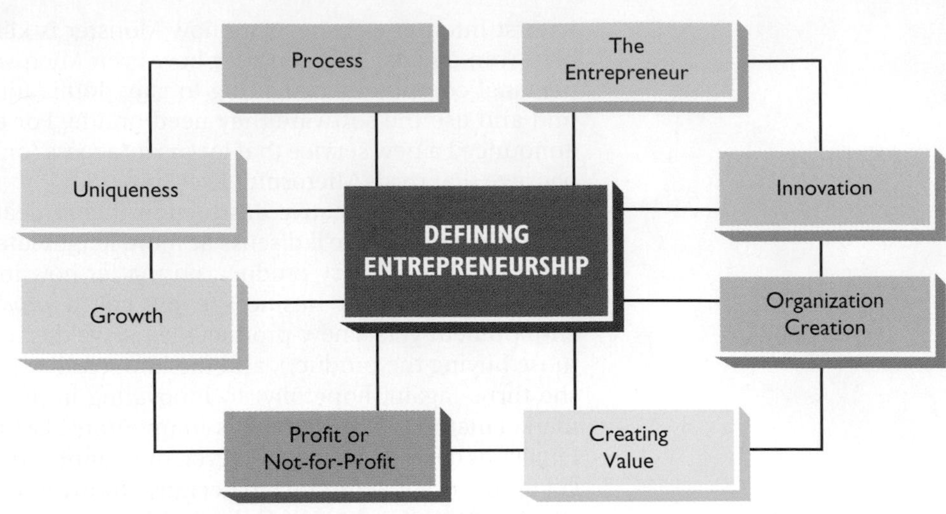

SOURCES: Adapted from Mary Coulter, *Entrepreneurship in Action* (Upper Saddle River, N.J.: Prentice Hall, 2001), p. 4; based on W. B. Gartner, "What Are We Talking About When We Talk About Entrepreneurship?" *Journal of Business Venturing, 5,* 1990, pp. 15–28.

size limits by industry when it defines which businesses are small enough to be eligible for SBA-guaranteed loans. Generally, manufacturing or wholesaling firms with fewer than 100 employees are small businesses. Retailing or service firms with annual sales under $5 million are small businesses.

Successful entrepreneurs like Neeleman tend to be good small-business managers because the firms they start either grow successfully or die. However, successful small-business managers needn't necessarily exhibit the flair for innovation—for creating new businesses under risky conditions—which is the hallmark of the entrepreneur. Small-business owners who inherit or buy small businesses and run them successfully need to be good managers. Entrepreneurs, on the other hand, don't just have to run their businesses; they must also have the flair for starting a business from scratch.

The Environment of Entrepreneurship

Entrepreneurs like taking risks, but that doesn't mean they are foolish. Good entrepreneurs continuously size up their opportunities and constraints—their environments.

Some countries are more conducive to entrepreneurship than others. The country's level of *economic freedom* is one important factor.[7] Some countries make it easier to be entrepreneurial than do others. Table 4.1 shows a portion of the Heritage Foundation's index of economic freedom. For instance, in Hong Kong, Singapore, Ireland, and the United States, entrepreneurs encounter relatively few barriers in starting and growing their businesses. At the other extreme, pity the entrepreneur who wants to start a business in Cuba or North Korea. Here, the combination of governmental and bureaucratic impediments and high taxes are enough to stifle almost any new business idea.

Periods of increased *economic activity* (boom times) tend to be associated with increased business creation ("timing is everything" is how one entrepreneur put this). As the U.S. economy boomed in the late 1990s, the number of businesses created jumped (see Figure 4.2). Business creation also outpaced the number of firms that closed down. However, the number of businesses that closed down rose, too (perhaps because boom times also mean that struggling entrepreneurs have other employment opportunities to pursue).

TABLE 4.1
The Index of Economic Freedom: Selected Locales

Overall Rank	Country	Overall Score*
1	Hong Kong	1.35
2	Singapore	1.55
4	Ireland	1.80
4	United States	1.80
9	United Kingdom	1.85
45	France	2.70
60	Mexico	2.90
72	Saudi Arabia	3.00
153	Cuba	4.75
155	North Korea	5.00

*Low overall score means higher economic freedom.

Source: Adapted from "The Index of Economic Freedom: Selected Locales," © 2001, The Heritage Foundation, 214 Massachusetts Ave NE, Washington, D.C., 20002–4999, at www.heritage.org.

Technological advances (whether steam engine, railroad, telephone, computer, or the Web) also trigger bursts of business creation. For example, the growth in percentage of patents issued by the U.S. Patent and Trademark Office rose from the single digits in the early 1990s to over 32 percent in 2000 as Web businesses took off.[8] Many of these patents translated into new-business ideas.

In practice, dozens of other environmental (outside) opportunities and constraints influence the budding entrepreneur's willingness and ability to create a new business. A short list of other environmental factors includes venture capital

FIGURE 4.2

Business Turnover, 1990–2003

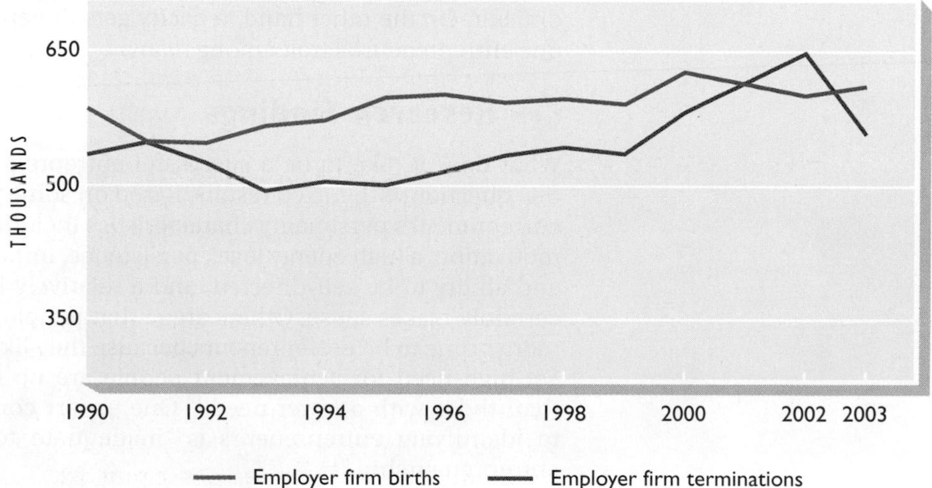

SOURCES: U. S. Small Business Administration, Office of Advocacy, from data provided by the U.S. Bureau of the Census and the U.S. Department of Labor, ETA.

availability, a technically skilled labor force, accessibility of suppliers, accessibility of customers, the availability of lenders, accessibility of transportation, the attitude of the area's population, and the availability of supporting services (such as roads, electric power, and accounting firms).[9]

Why Entrepreneurship Is Important

When it comes to its impact on the U.S. economy, the phrase *small business* is a little misleading.[10] For example, small businesses as a group account for most of the 600,000 or so new businesses created every year, as well as for most of the growth of companies (small firms grow much faster than big ones). Small firms also account for about three-quarters of the employment growth in the U.S. economy—in other words, small businesses create most of the new jobs in the United States.

More than half of the people working in the United States—68 million out of 118 million—work for small firms. That's why one recent U.S. president's report noted, "a great strength of small businesses is [their] role in renewing the American economy."[11] Small businesses are "an integral part of the renewal process" through which businesses arise to replace those that fail. In doing so, they provide employment opportunities for tens of millions of people. Indeed, as we said, the vast majority of students graduating today will start or work for smaller firms.

Small businesses also account for much of the product and technological innovation in America today. For example, "new small organizations generate 24 times more innovations per research and development dollar spent than do *Fortune* 500 organizations, and they account for over 95 percent of new and 'radical product development.'"[12]

What It Takes to Be an Entrepreneur

Several years ago, someone asked H. Ross Perot, who had made hundreds of millions of dollars starting Electronic Data Systems Inc. and then Perot Systems Inc., what his advice would be for people who hoped to be entrepreneurs. Perot said, "Never give up, never give up, never give up." His advice highlights an entrepreneurial dilemma. On the one hand, there's no doubt that tenacity is a crucial trait for entrepreneurs, because creating something out of nothing is so difficult. On the other hand, tenacity gets the entrepreneur only so far. It is only one entrepreneurial trait among many.

Research Findings

What does it take to be a successful entrepreneur? Psychologists have studied this question with mixed results. Based on some studies, researchers say that the entrepreneur's personality characteristics include self-confidence, a high level of motivation, a high energy level, persistence, initiative, resourcefulness, the desire and ability to be self-directed, and a relatively high need for autonomy.[13] This certainly makes sense. Others argue that people high in the need to achieve are more prone to be entrepreneurs because they like to set goals and achieve them. Yet high-need-for-achievement people are no more likely to start businesses than those with a lower need.[14] One expert concludes that the trait approach to identifying entrepreneurs is "inadequate to explain the phenomenon of entrepreneurship."[15]

Recent studies are more positive. Some studies focus on the proactive personality. Proactive behavior reflects the extent to which people ". . . take action to influence their environments."[16] One study of 107 small-business owners found some support for the notion that proactive personality contributes to innovation in some circumstances.[17]

Still others study what they call the dark side of the entrepreneur. They say less positive traits drive entrepreneurs, traits like the need for control, a sense of distrust, the need for applause, and a tendency to defend one's operations.[18] This approach doesn't paint a pretty picture of how some entrepreneurs behave. With respect to the need for control, for instance, "a major theme in the life and personality of many entrepreneurs is the need for control. Their preoccupation with control inevitably affects the way entrepreneurs deal with power relationships and the consequences for interpersonal action. . . . An entrepreneur has a great inner struggle with issues of authority and control."[19]

Anecdotal Evidence

A few behaviors do seem to arise consistently in anecdotal and case studies of successful entrepreneurs. As we mentioned earlier, tenacity is one. Entrepreneurs face so many barriers when creating a business that if they're not tenacious, they're bound to fail.

Intensity—the drive to pursue a goal with passion and focus—is another trait that often pops up. For example, Sky Dayton started EarthLink in the mid-1990s, and the firm is now one of the largest Internet service providers.[20] One friend, who watched him surfing, says Dayton "took the sport up with a vengeance. He's as intense and fearless in surfing as he is in business."

Should You Be an Entrepreneur?

Is entrepreneurship for you? To gauge your potential, try taking the short proactive personality survey in Figure 4.3. You might also answer the following questions, compliments of the U.S. Small Business Administration:

- *Are you a self-starter?* No one will be there prompting the entrepreneur to develop and follow through on projects.

- *How well do you get along with different personalities?* Business owners need to develop good working relationships with a variety of people, including customers, vendors, employees, bankers, and accountants. Will you be able to deal with a demanding client, an unreliable vendor, or a cranky employee?

- *How good are you at making decisions?* Small-business owners make decisions constantly and often quickly, under pressure, and independently.

- *Do you have the physical and emotional stamina to run a business?* Can you handle twelve-hour workdays, six or seven days a week?

- *How well do you plan and organize?* Research shows that good plans could have prevented many business failures. Furthermore, good organization—not just of employees but also of finances, inventory, schedules, production, and all the other details of running a business—can help prevent problems.

- *Is your drive strong enough to maintain your motivation?* Running a business can wear you down. You'll need strong motivation to help you survive slowdowns, reversals, and burnout.

FIGURE 4.3

Is Entrepreneurship for Me?

Instrument

Respond to each of the 17 statements using the following rating scale:

1 = Strongly disagree
2 = Moderately disagree
3 = Slightly disagree
4 = Neither agree nor disagree
5 = Slightly agree
6 = Moderately agree
7 = Strongly agree

1. I am constantly on the lookout for new ways to improve my life.	1 2 3 4 5 6 7
2. I feel driven to make a difference in my community—and maybe the world.	1 2 3 4 5 6 7
3. I tend to let others take the initiative to start new projects.	1 2 3 4 5 6 7
4. Wherever I have been, I have been a powerful force for constructive change.	1 2 3 4 5 6 7
5. I enjoy facing and overcoming obstacles to my ideas.	1 2 3 4 5 6 7
6. Nothing is more exciting than seeing my ideas turn into reality.	1 2 3 4 5 6 7
7. If I see something I don't like, I fix it.	1 2 3 4 5 6 7
8. No matter what the odds, if I believe in something, I will make it happen.	1 2 3 4 5 6 7
9. I love being a champion for my ideas, even against others' opposition.	1 2 3 4 5 6 7
10. I excel at identifying opportunities.	1 2 3 4 5 6 7
11. I am always looking for better ways to do things.	1 2 3 4 5 6 7
12. If I believe in an idea, no obstacle will prevent me from making it happen.	1 2 3 4 5 6 7
13. I love to challenge the status quo.	1 2 3 4 5 6 7
14. When I have a problem, I tackle it head-on.	1 2 3 4 5 6 7
15. I am great at turning problems into opportunities.	1 2 3 4 5 6 7
16. I can spot a good opportunity long before others can.	1 2 3 4 5 6 7
17. If I see someone in trouble, I help out in any way I can.	1 2 3 4 5 6 7

Scoring Key

To calculate your proactive personality score, add up your responses to all statements, except item 3. For item 3, reverse your score.

Analysis and Interpretation

This instrument assesses proactive personality. That is, it identifies differences among people in the extent to which they take action to influence their environments. Proactive personalities identify opportunities and act on them; they show initiative, take action, and persevere until they bring about change. Research finds that the proactive personality is positively associated with entrepreneurial intentions. Your total score will be between 17 and 119. The higher your score, the stronger your proactive personality. For instance, scores above 85 indicated fairly high proactivity.

SOURCES: Adapted from T. S. Bateman and J. M. Crant, "The Proactive Component of Organizational Behavior: A Measure and Correlates," *Journal of Organizational Behavior*, March 1993, pp. 103–118; J. M. Crant, "The Proactive Personality Scale as a Predictor of Entrepreneurial Intentions," *Journal of Small Business Management*, July 1996, pp. 42–49.

- *How will the business affect your family?* The first few years of a business start-up can be hard on family life. The strain of an unsupportive spouse may be hard to balance against the demands of starting a business. There also may be financial difficulties until the business becomes profitable, which could take years.[21]

Getting Started in Business

Online Study Center
ACE the Test
Managing Now! LIVE

Overcoming all the challenges that stand in the way of going from nothing to something requires tackling at least four main tasks along the way: (1) coming up with the idea for the business, (2) deciding how to get into that business, (3) deciding on a form of business ownership, and (4) getting funded.

Coming Up with the Idea for the Business

Lance Fried is a successful entrepreneur whose insight created an all-new product, and whose management skills then built a successful company around that product.

Most entrepreneurs don't come up with the ideas for their businesses by doing an elaborate analysis of what customers want.[22] Between 43 percent and 71 percent of those responding to one survey said that they got the ideas for their businesses through their previous employment. Ralph Lauren supposedly got his idea for the Polo line of clothes while working at Brooks Brothers.[23] After work experience, serendipity was the source that 15 to 20 percent of respondents mentioned. They just stumbled across the business idea. A handful of respondents got their ideas from hobbies or from a "systematic search for business opportunities."[24]

Speaking of serendipity, consider Lance Fried. He got the idea for his business pretty much by accident. His friend dropped an iPod into a cooler of water and ice, ruining it. Fried, who's in the habit of watching the surfers near his home in Del Mar, California, got his brainstorm. The prototype for a waterproof MP3 player was soon ready. His target customers were people who would use them while surfing, swimming, or snowboarding. He invested his savings to get his business started. Fried's business plan called for starting small and for selling through small specialty shops, thus building his product's reputation. He introduced his product at a big trade show, and hundreds of people came by to try it. He cleverly left the players at the bottom of a fish tank with the earphones hung over the top, so anyone stopping by could listen. Dozens of shops ordered his product. *Surfer* magazine put it at the top of its holiday wish list. Lance Fried's business took off.

Methods for Getting into Business

Entrepreneurs get into business in several ways: through a family-owned business, by starting a business from scratch, by buying a business, or by buying a franchise.

Taking Over the Family-Owned Business Perhaps the easiest way to get into business is to take over the family business. A family-owned business "is one that includes two or more members of a family with financial control of the company."[25] About 90 percent of all businesses in the United States are family-owned and -managed. They employ more than 50 million people and account for over half of the country's economic output.[26]

Balancing family and business pressures is not easy. As Dan Bishop, president of the National Family Business Association, has said, "A family is based on emotion, nurturing, and security, but a business revolves around productivity, accomplishment, and profit."[27] The owner may be torn between doing what's best for the business and a desire to help a child who may not have what it takes to succeed.

Many owners do little planning to help ease the burden for heirs. One survey showed that only 45 percent of the owners of family firms had selected successors.[28]

At a minimum, the owner of the family business should make his or her succession plans clear. "The children should know if they will take over management or if the business will be sold to an outsider. If they spend years working in the business only to find it sold to an outsider, they may have trouble finding positions in other companies."[29]

Starting a New Business When most people think of entrepreneurs, it's their role as the starter of a new business that comes to mind. (That was the route Lance Fried chose.) It is in starting a new business that the entrepreneur supplies the spark that makes something out of nothing. This spark brings a new business to life, complete with customers, suppliers, permits, accountants, and lawyers.

Because the endeavor will require so much of the entrepreneur's money and time, starting a small business is not something to take lightly. To prepare, the entrepreneur should:

1. *List the reasons for wanting to go into business.* Some of the most common reasons are that you want financial independence and creative freedom, and you want to use your skills and knowledge more fully.
2. *Determine what business is right for you.* Ask yourself, What do I like to do with my time? What technical skills have I learned? What do others say I am good at? Will I make enough to support my family?
3. *Identify the niche your business will fill.* Research and answer questions such as: What business am I interested in starting? What services or products will I sell? Is my idea practical, and will it really work? What is my competition? What is my business's advantage over existing firms?
4. *Conduct a prebusiness review.* Now answer questions like these: What insurance coverage will I need? What equipment or supplies will I need? What are my resources? What financing will I need? Where will my business be located?

Answers to these questions will help you create a business plan. The business plan should serve as a blueprint for the business. According to the Small Business Administration, "[The plan] should detail how the business will be operated, managed and capitalized."[30] We'll discuss business planning in a moment.

franchise: a license to use a company's business ideas and procedures and to sell its goods or services

franchiser: a firm that licenses other firms to use its business idea and procedures and to sell its goods or services in return for royalty and other types of payments

franchisee: a firm that obtains a license to use a franchiser's business ideas and procedures and that may get an exclusive right to sell the franchiser's goods or services in a specific territory

Buying an Existing Business Buying an existing business is a double-edged sword. At least in theory, buying an existing business means the buyer will know what the existing market is, as well as what the company's revenues, expenses, and profits (or losses) are. Buying a business can also mean getting into business faster and with less effort than starting a business from scratch.

On the other hand, as one cynical management consultant once put it, "There's always a reason why the business owner wants to sell, and the reason is never good." One risk is that the figures the owner reports may be inflated. Another is that the owner may know or sense that things are about to go wrong.

Buying a Franchise To some extent, buying a **franchise** gives the entrepreneur the best of both worlds. A **franchiser** is a firm that licenses other firms to use its business idea and procedures and to sell its goods or services in return for royalty and other types of payments. A **franchisee** is a firm that obtains a license to use a franchiser's business ideas and procedures and that may get an exclusive right to sell the franchiser's goods or services in a specific territory. Each franchisee

franchising agreement: a document that lays out the relationship between the franchiser and franchisee

owns his or her franchise unit. The **franchising agreement** is a document that lays out the relationship between the franchiser and franchisee. The agreement creates a franchise, a franchiser, and a franchisee.[31]

Franchising can be a good way to get into business. The franchisee usually gets the right to start his or her business from scratch without the excess baggage of the problems associated with an existing business. Yet the franchisee gets much of the preparatory work done by the franchiser and (hopefully) gets a business that is based on a proven business model. Other benefits include name recognition, management training and assistance, economies in buying, financial assistance, and promotional assistance. On the other hand, some franchisers don't put the thought and care into developing the franchise idea that familiar ones like McDonald's do. In such cases, the unsuspecting buyer can end up investing his or her life savings in a dud. One expert suggests looking for the following details when evaluating a franchise opportunity:

1. Select a franchising company with a reputation for distributing quality products and services to ultimate customers. Franchisers like Dunkin' Donuts and McDonald's are famous for their emphasis on providing high-quality products and services—they're not there just to sell franchises.
2. Pick a franchiser that is dedicated to franchising. Avoid franchisers with large numbers of company-owned stores—or that distribute the product or services through other channels, such as supermarkets.
3. Pick a franchiser that provides products or services for which there is an established market demand.
4. Pick a franchiser that has a well-accepted trademark.
5. Evaluate your franchiser's business plan and marketing methods.
6. Make sure your franchiser has good relationships with its franchisees.
7. Deal with franchising companies that provide sales and earnings projections that demonstrate an attractive return on your investment.
8. Meet with your accountant and lawyer, and carefully review the franchiser's Uniform Franchise Offering Circular, a document required by the U.S. Federal Trade Commission (FTC). The FTC oversees the interstate activities of the franchise industry. Its Uniform Franchise Offering Circular rules require franchisers to disclose all essential information about the business.[32]

The checklist in Figure 4.4 provides additional guidance for evaluating the franchise and the franchiser.

Forms of Business Ownership

In creating the business entity, the entrepreneur needs to decide what the entity's form of ownership will be. The four main forms of business ownership are the sole proprietorship, the partnership, the corporation, and the limited liability company.

sole proprietorship: a business owned by one person

● The Sole Proprietorship

The **sole proprietorship** is a business owned by one person. About 70 percent of businesses in the United States are sole proprietorships.

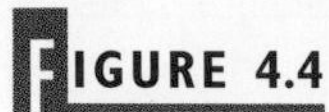

Checklist for Evaluating a Franchise Opportunity

The Franchise

☐ 1. Did your lawyer approve the franchise contract you are considering after he studied it paragraph by paragraph?
☐ 2. Does the franchise call on you to take any steps that are, according to your lawyer, unwise or illegal in your state, county, or city?
☐ 3. Does the franchise give you an exclusive territory for the length of the franchise agreement or can the franchisor sell a second or third franchise in your territory?
☐ 4. Is the franchisor connected in any way with any other franchise company handling similar merchandise or service?
☐ 5. If the answer to the last question is yes, what is your protection against this second franchisor organization?
☐ 6. Under what circumstances can you terminate the franchise contract and at what cost to you, if you decide for any reason at all that you wish to cancel it?
☐ 7. If you sell your franchise, will you be compensated for your goodwill, or will the goodwill you have built into the business be lost by you?

The Franchisor

☐ 8. How many years has the firm offering you a franchise been in operation?
☐ 9. Has it a reputation for honesty and fair dealing among the local firms holding its franchise?
☐ 10. Has the franchisor shown you any certified figures indicating exact net profits of one or more going firms that you personally checked yourself with the franchisee?
☐ 11. Will the firm assist you with
a. A management training program?
b. An employee training program?
c. A public relations program?
d. Capital?
e. Credit?
f. Merchandising ideas?
☐ 12. Will the firm help you find a good location for your new business?
☐ 13. Is the franchising firm adequately financed so that it can carry out its stated plan of financial assistance and expansion?
☐ 14. Is the franchisor a one-person company or a corporation with an experienced management trained in depth (so that there would always be an experienced person at its head)?
☐ 15. Exactly what can the franchisor do for you that you cannot do for yourself?
☐ 16. Has the franchisor investigated you carefully enough to assure itself that you can successfully operate one of its franchises at a profit both to it and to you?
☐ 17. Does your state have a law regulating the sale of franchises, and has the franchisor complied with that law?

You—the Franchisee

☐ 18. How much equity capital will you have to have to purchase the franchise and operate it until your income equals your expenses? Where are you going to get it?
☐ 19. Are you prepared to give up some independence of action to secure the advantages offered by the franchise?
☐ 20. Do you really believe you have the innate ability, training, and experience to work smoothly and profitably with the franchisor, your employees, and your customers?
☐ 21. Are you ready to spend much or all of the remainder of your business life with this franchisor, offering its product or service to your public?

Your Market

☐ 22. Have you made any study to determine whether the product or service that you propose to sell under the franchise has a market in your territory at the prices you will have to charge?
☐ 23. Will the population in the territory given to you increase, remain static, or decrease over the next five years?
☐ 24. Will the product or service you are considering be in greater demand, about the same, or less demand five years from now than today?
☐ 25. What competition exists in your territory already for the product or service you contemplate selling?
a. Nonfranchise firms?
b. Franchise firms?

SOURCE: *Franchise Opportunities Handbook* (Washington, D.C.: U.S. Government Printing Office, 1988).

The sole proprietorship is simple to start. The owner usually just has to register the firm's name at the county courthouse and perhaps get the necessary municipal business license.[33] As sole owner, there are no other owners with whom to share the rewards or setbacks. Sole proprietors are their own bosses. Because the sole proprietor *is* the firm, he or she pays only personal income taxes on its profits. There is no income tax on the firm as a separate entity.

On the other hand, the sole proprietor has unlimited financial liability. *Unlimited liability* means that the business owner is responsible for any claims against the firm that go beyond what the owner has invested in the business. Sole proprietors, therefore, risk losing everything they own if their businesses go bust. Furthermore, there is no other owner with whom to share the management burden.

partnership: an association of two or more persons to carry on as co-owners of a business for profit

partnership agreement: an oral or written contract between the owners of a partnership. It identifies the business, and it lays out the partners' respective rights and duties.

general partnership: a partnership in which all partners share in the ownership, management, and liabilities of the firm

limited partnership: a partnership in which one or more, but not all, partners (the limited partners) are liable for the firm's debts *only to the extent of their financial investment in the firm*

● The Partnership Some entrepreneurs therefore opt to form a partnership. Under the Uniform Partnership Act, a **partnership** is "an association of two or more persons to carry on as co-owners of a business for profit." People form a partnership by entering into a partnership agreement. A **partnership agreement** is an oral or written contract between the owners of a partnership. It states the name, location, and business of the firm. It also specifies the mutual understanding of each owner's duties and rights in running the business, the method for sharing the profits or losses, and the policies for withdrawing from the business and dissolving the partnership.

In a **general partnership**, all partners share in the ownership, management, and liabilities of the firm. A **limited partnership** is a business in which one or more, but not all, partners (the limited partners) are liable for the firm's debts *only to the extent of their financial investment in the firm.* This helps the firm's general partners (who actually run the business) attract investment dollars from people who do not want unlimited liability—or who do not want to get involved in managing the firm.

The partnership has four main advantages. There are few restrictions on starting one. There are several partners, so a partnership permits the pooling of funds and talents. The partnership also provides more chance to specialize. For example, the outside person can specialize in sales, while the inside person can specialize in running the business. Finally, like a sole proprietorship, the owners, not the firm, are taxed only individually.

Unlimited liability is a main disadvantage. In general partnerships, all partners have unlimited liability for the partnership's debts. In a limited liability partnership, the limited partners are personally liable only up to the amount they invest in the business.

corporation: a legally chartered organization that is a separate legal entity, apart from its owners. A corporation comes into being when the incorporators (founders) apply for and receive a charter from the state in which the firm is to reside.

● The Corporation A **corporation** is a legally chartered organization that is a separate legal entity, apart from its owners. A corporation comes into being when the incorporators (founders) apply for and receive a charter (license) from the state in which the firm is to reside. The shareholders (or stockholders) own the corporation. Each owns a part interest in the entire corporation.

Limited financial liability is the corporation's main advantage over sole proprietorships and partnerships. Usually, the most an owner/shareholder can lose is what he or she paid for the shares. This makes it much easier for the company to raise money. Furthermore, because the corporation is a separate legal entity, it has permanence. The death or imprisonment of a shareholder does not mean the end of the corporation.

Taxation is a big disadvantage. In sole proprietorships and partnerships, the owners pay the company's income taxes individually—the government does not also separately tax the companies themselves. Corporations are entities separate from their owners. Therefore, the corporation generally pays federal and state taxes on its profits. If the corporation then pays cash dividends to shareholders from its after-tax profits, the shareholders pay personal income taxes on the dividends. Corporations can avoid double taxation by forming an **S corporation**. An S corporation has the option of being taxed like a partnership. It pays no income taxes as a firm.

S corporation: a corporation that has the option of being taxed like a partnership and that pays no income taxes as a firm

The Limited Liability Company The **limited liability company (LLC)** is a cross between a partnership and a corporation. Like a corporation, the LLC limits the liability of its owners (called members) from personal liability for the company's debts and liabilities. At the same time, the limited liability company's earnings are not subject to separate corporate taxes. The government taxes it as if it is an individual proprietorship or partnership.[34]

limited liability company (LLC): a cross between a partnership and a corporation

angels: wealthy individuals interested in the high-risk/high-reward potentials to be derived from the creation of a new venture

Getting Funded

Generating ideas for the business and deciding on a legal form are all theoretical if the entrepreneur can't find the money to actually start the business. How will I fund my business? is, therefore, a question the entrepreneur should be thinking about. Even experienced businesspeople make mistakes. The developers of the Royal Palm Crowne Plaza Resort in South Florida completed their new hotel—but two years late and with cost overruns of $16 million. To reduce that debt, they had to sell about 150 of the 422 hotel rooms as condominiums.[35]

One of the swimming pools at the Royal Palm Crowne Plaza Resort in Miami Beach.

The two basic sources of business finance are debt and equity. Equity finance represents an ownership in the venture. Debt, of course, is borrowed capital.

Equity For the typical new small business, much of the initial capital traditionally comes from the founder. Family and friends are usually the second biggest source. No one knows the entrepreneur like his or her family and friends. One hopes that this familiarity translates into the faith required to help that person start a business.

Outside equity—either from wealthy private investors (so-called angels) or from venture capital firms—are two other possibilities. **Angels** are wealthy individuals interested in the high-risk/high-reward potentials to be derived from the creation of a new venture. **Venture capitalists** professionally manage pools of investor money. They specialize in evaluating new venture opportunities and taking equity stakes in worthy businesses. A public offering—selling stock to the public—is usually an option open to relatively few new ventures. When the company first sells stock to outside owners, the firm has gone public. The process is called the **initial public offering (IPO)**. Investment bankers are professionals that walk the entrepreneur through the various registration requirements, thus enabling the company to publicly offer stock.[36]

venture capitalists: professionals who manage pools of investor money, and who specialize in evaluating new venture opportunities and taking equity stakes in worthy businesses

initial public offering (IPO): the process that occurs the first time a company sells stock to outside owners

Debt Debt, or borrowed capital, is the second main source of business finance. An entrepreneur with good personal credit and a sound business plan may be able to obtain a business loan from a commercial bank. However, banks are not in the venture capital business. The entrepreneur usually guarantees loans like these with his or her personal assets and promise to repay.

Many entrepreneurs dip deeply into their personal debt-paying capacity to support the business. By one estimate, the debts of smaller businesses are divided roughly equally among (1) business credit lines (loans from banks, or from vendors who are willing to wait a while to get paid) and loans, (2) business credit-card debt, and (3) personal credit-card debt.[37] Asset-based debt is a popular type of business loan. It is debt collateralized (guaranteed) by one or more specific assets of the business. If the business doesn't pay, the lender takes the asset.

● **The Small Business Administration (SBA)** Many entrepreneurs turn to the Small Business Administration (SBA) for assistance in obtaining bank financing. Most of these SBA loans are in the form of so-called 7-A loans. The SBA basically guarantees up to 90 percent of the outstanding loan; the loan itself comes from a commercial bank. However, the businessperson typically must personally guarantee the entire loan, too.

Writing the Business Plan

Whether raising capital from friends or the SBA, the entrepreneur will have to provide a business plan. *Planning* means "setting goals and choosing courses of action for achieving those goals." The entrepreneur should have a good idea of what financial and other business goals he or she wants to achieve and how he or she plans to reach those goals. Those investing in the business will certainly want to see what the entrepreneur's plans are for the business.

Business planning usually starts with the manager asking, What business are we in? The company needs a clear idea of what specific products it's going to sell and how the business will differ from the competition. The owners can't intelligently choose suppliers, employees, advertising campaigns, or business partners if they don't know what business they are in. They also cannot make financial projections for sales, costs, and profits if they don't see quite clearly what business they are in. Compass Records illustrates why such clarity of vision is important.

Alison Brown, co-owner of Compass Records.

● **Compass Records** Alison Brown and Garry West, both musicians, got their idea for starting Compass Records while talking before a show they were attending in Stockholm.[38] Today, Compass Records is booming. Over the last ten or so years, the company has released more than 100 albums, ranging from "collections of centuries old ballads by the British folksinger Kate Rusby to an album of soukous by the Congolese singer guitarist Samba Ngo."[39]

What business is Compass Records in? Compass has built up an audience of listeners by focusing like a laser on roots music/folk music—from whatever country. As Alison Brown says, "Whether we're doing Celtic or Bluegrass or singer-songwriter, it all has that common thread running through it."[40]

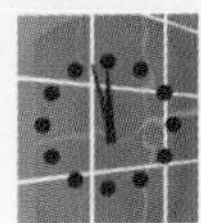

Window on Managing Now
Choosing a Web-Based Business

The Internet makes it easier to get into business. For example, an entrepreneur can create a virtual bookstore or other business for a fraction of the time and cost that it would take to create a bricks-and-mortar version. In fact, eBay grew so fast in part by becoming the online marketplace where entrepreneurs could sell their wares.

In terms of deciding what one's business should be, the secret of small-business Web success seems to be choosing a niche. One expert calls this "the fragmentation of the Web."[41] For example, Harris Cyclery is a successful New England business. Sheldon Brown, the veteran mechanic who runs Harris Cyclery, avoids head-on competition with bigger online bicycle retailers by focusing on hard-to-find replacement parts. He also cultivates a competitive advantage by offering free advice over the Web.[42] Ron Davis, who owns and manages a chain of apparel stores called The Shoe Horn, also created a website, but he kept it highly focused. He sells dyed wedding shoes online.[43] He knows what his business is and sticks to it.

Highly focused online entrepreneurs can use giant websites to help them get their businesses started. Thanks to sites like eBay and Froogle, even tiny businesses can offer their products to huge audiences online.

Sticking to that vision has taken Compass Records into some interesting musical niches. Its first release was an album of music played on a didgeridoo, a wood instrument indigenous to Australia. Other titles "have included sets by the progressive jazz bassist Victor Wooten, the Czech Bluegrass band Druha Trava and the neopop duo Swan Dive."[44] The partners know exactly what business they are in. Their business is not "music" but "roots music/folk music." Because they do know what business they're in, it is easy for them to make plans—regarding what musicians to choose; how and where to record, market, and publicize their records; and roughly speaking, what they can expect in terms of revenues, expenses, and sales when they sign an artist. See the Window on Managing Now feature for another example of the need for business planning.[45]

business plan: a plan that lays out what the business is, where it is heading, and how it plans to get there

The **business plan** lays out in detail what the business is, where it is heading, and how it plans to get there. Figure 4.5 summarizes the contents of a typical business plan.

● **Creating the Business Plan** Developing the business plan helps the entrepreneur understand his or her options and anticipate problems. The entrepreneur does not want to find out six months after opening that labor costs are twice as high as anticipated and that the store's economics, therefore, make it unlikely that the business can survive. Furthermore, no banker, angel, or financier will make cash infusions without a business plan.

Experts in writing business plans emphasize the importance of doing this job right. You need to pay particular attention to four tasks: (1) clearly define the business, (2) provide evidence of management capabilities, (3) provide evidence of marketing capabilities, and (4) offer an attractive financial arrangement.[46] As one expert says, "Most entrepreneurs and small-business owners can prepare a B or B+ business plan without too much trouble. That would be fine if investors would fund B or B+ plans. Investors, however, fund only A or A+ plans. . . ."[47] The Window on Managing Now feature on page 106 shows one way to accomplish this.

FIGURE 4.5

Contents of a Good Business Plan

Introduction
A basic description of the firm—name, address, business activity, current stage of development of the firm, and plans for the future.

Executive Summary
An overview of the entire business plan, summarizing the content of each section and inviting the reader to continue.

Industry Analysis
A description of the industry the firm is competing in, focusing on industry trends and profit potential.

Management Section
A description of the management team and whether it is complete—and, if not, when and how it will be completed.

Manufacturing Section
A description of the complexity and logistics of the manufacturing process and of the firm's production capacity and current percentage of capacity use.

Product Section
A description of the good or service, including where it is in its life cycle (for example, a new product or a mature product); of future product research and development efforts; and of the status of patent or copyright applications.

Marketing Section
A marketing plan, including a customer profile, an analysis of market needs, and a geographic analysis of markets; a description of pricing, distribution, and promotion; and an analysis of how the firm's marketing efforts are different from competitors' efforts.

Financial Section
Financial statements for the current year and the three previous years, if applicable; financial projections for the next three to five years; and assumptions for sales, cost of sales, cash flow, pro forma balance sheets, and key statistics, such as the current ratio, the debt/equity ratio, and inventory turnovers.

Legal Section
Form of ownership (proprietorship, partnership, or corporation) and a listing of any pending lawsuits filed by or against the firm.

SOURCE: Adapted from *Business Plan Pro* (Palo Alto, Calif.: Palo Alto Software).

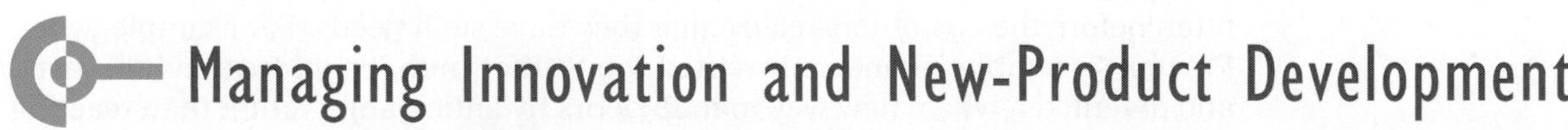

Managing Innovation and New-Product Development

Online Study Center
ACE the Test
Managing Now! LIVE

Entrepreneurs and small entrepreneurial companies don't have monopolies on new ideas and innovation. Innovation plays a crucial role in helping all firms, not just small ones, to survive and expand. We'll look at how managers manage the innovation process in this and the following sections. We begin by defining what innovation is and what it is not. Innovation does not just mean inventing

WINDOW ON MANAGING NOW
Using Computerized Business-Planning Software

There are several business-planning software packages to assist the entrepreneur in writing A+ plans. For example, Business Plan Pro, from Palo Alto Software, contains all the information and planning aids you need to create a business plan. It contains, for example, thirty sample plans, step-by-step instructions (with examples) for creating each part of a plan (executive summary, market analysis, and so on), financial planning spreadsheets, easy-to-use tables (for instance, for making sales forecasts), and automatic programs for creating color three-dimensional charts for showing things like monthly sales and yearly profits.

Business Plan Pro's Planning Wizard takes the entrepreneur "by the hand" and helps him or her develop a business plan step by step. The result is an integrated plan, complete with charts, tables, and professional formatting. For example, click "start a plan," and the Planning Wizard presents a series of questions, including, "Does your company sell products, services or both?" "Would you like a detailed or basic business plan?" "Does your company sell on credit?" Then as you go to each subsequent part of the plan—such as the executive summary—the Planning Wizard shows instructions with examples, making it easy to create your own executive summary (or other plan section). The Planning Wizard even helps the entrepreneur translate his or her financial and other projections (such as for numbers of items sold) into easy-to-understand tables and charts.[48]

something new. Many new inventions end up withering on some research and development department's shelf. Innovation means something more. Innovation means uncovering a valuable need, inventing a new or improved product or service to fill that need, and then developing and introducing the new product or service so that it succeeds in the marketplace.[49]

Innovation in Practice For example, IBM's employees produced more U.S. patents than any other company between 1993 and 2005, at a cost of about $6 billion per year in research and development expenditures alone. Even a company as large as IBM could not afford this unless it led to saleable products. Innovation at IBM therefore "requires applying those technologies to critical customer problems and then bringing them to market in a form that customers can easily use."[50] Innovation is therefore not just a job for engineers, inventors, and entrepreneurs. It also requires effective management, for instance, in identifying the need, developing and testing the new idea, and making sure that the structure and people are in place to get the product to market.

The process of innovation is more complicated than it might appear at first. For example, ideally, companies can't just wait to react to what customers say they want. Suppose customers don't yet realize what they need? And waiting till the need is obvious may give competitors the time to innovate the same (or better) new-product ideas. The preferred approach is to anticipate the customers' needs, often before the customers realize that they have such needs. For example, when Procter & Gamble engineers invented the Swiffer mop, they identified the need and invented a whole new way to mop floors by anticipating rather than reacting to its customers' needs.[51]

As small entrepreneurial companies evolve into large multinational ones, they must guard against losing their entrepreneurial flair. Growth can bring bureaucracy, for instance, in terms of stratified, compartmentalized, slow-moving decisions. Many once-successful entrepreneurial companies, including Polaroid, Kodak, and Xerox, basically became, for a time, victims of their own success. Growth led to misplaced self-confidence and a dramatic reduction in these firms'

FIGURE 4.6

The Eight Stages in New-Product Development

Idea Generation	Idea Screening	Concept Development and Testing	Marketing Strategy Development	Business Analysis	Product Development	Test Marketing	Commerciali-zation

creative output. Google's small entrepreneurial teams seem, at least for now, to be coming up with more innovative new products and services than does Microsoft's more plodding, hierarchical approach.

The Eight-Stage New-Product Development Process

To help ensure they have a steady stream of new and innovative products, managers often establish a formal new-product development process for their companies, often under the guidance of a new-product development (R&D) officer and department. This new-product development process typically consists of eight main stages.[52] Figure 4.6 summarizes these eight stages.

1. In the first stage, *idea generation,* the company uses consumer research and creativity to produce the ideas that become the raw material of the new-product development process.

2. It may take thousands of new-product ideas to produce just one saleable new product. Most companies do not have the resources to put thousands of new-product development ideas into development. The purpose of the second stage, *idea screening,* is to reduce the many possible new-product ideas down to a more manageable few. Managers here might ask questions such as, Does this product really makes sense for our customers?

3. In the third stage, *concept development and testing,* the new-product development department translates each surviving new-product idea into a more tangible concept and then tests it. For example, Gillette researchers may have an idea for a new razor that combines the simplicity of a manual razor with some of the advantages of an electric one. In this concept development and testing stage, Gillette's development experts translate this raw idea into a more workable product concept—say, a cross between a five-blade manual razor and a simple battery-driven device, one that vibrates the razor's head. Gillette then tests this product concept. For instance, it asks consumers questions such as, How do you like this battery-driven razor compared with the manual razor you're using now?

4. Having an idea—even one that seems to appeal to the markets—is only the beginning of the process of innovating a successful new product. The best idea will fail if the company isn't successful in introducing it to the market. Therefore, *marketing strategy development* is the fourth step in the process. Marketing strategy development means laying out a marketing plan for the potential new product. This plan includes the target customers (for instance,

in terms of age, income, and education) and the probable target price, sales, and market share and profit goals.

5. In the fifth stage, *business analysis,* the manager examines the target market and the potential new product's pricing, sales, market share, and pricing goals to determine how likely it is that this new product will succeed.
6. Assuming the answer is yes, the new-product process moves into its sixth stage, *product development.* In creating the very successful RAZR cell phone, Motorola scientists and engineers worked with production engineers and marketing specialists to create the actual prototypes for the product. The product development stage should answer the question, Can we turn this product idea into a workable, saleable new product?
7. For most companies, the vast expense involved in gearing up to produce and sell the new product means it is prudent to test-market it first. *Test marketing* is the seventh new-product development stage. For example, Kraft Foods might test-market a new cheese in one or two small U.S. cities before rolling out full production and marketing nationwide. This gives Kraft managers an opportunity to test and improve physical characteristics of the product. It also lets the manager test aspects of the marketing plan for the product, such as whether the price is too high, too low, or just right.
8. Now the manager is just about set to introduce the new product. In this eighth stage, *commercialization,* the manager actually implements the marketing plan by introducing the new product into the market. If the manager has done his or her homework, the commercialization will be successful. The company will have successfully innovated, from idea, to development, to commercialization.

Fostering Innovation

Managers traditionally use three methods—intrapreneurship, business incubators, and new-product development teams—to foster increased innovation. We look at these next.

Corporate Intrapreneurship Entrepreneurship is not just for entrepreneurs. Large companies also work hard at being entrepreneurial. Managers of giant companies understand that entrepreneurial activities drive innovation and that big-company bureaucracy can stifle such activities. Thus, they work hard to institute policies and practices that encourage what they call intrapreneurship within their big firms. For example, intrapreneurial activities within Cisco Systems led to the creation of several spinoff companies (including Cordis Corp. and Equinox) that together produced almost $700 million for Cisco.[53] Similarly, QUALCOMM Corporation's intrapreneurial activities led to the wireless Web company Handspring. Sun Microsystems' intrapreneurial activities helped it create and spin off several successful companies, including Caldera Systems.

intrapreneurship: the development, within a large corporation, of internal markets and relatively small autonomous or semiautonomous business units that produce products, services, or technologies that employ the firm's resources in a unique way

Intrapreneurship means producing innovative ideas and products in big corporations by organizing innovation around small, usually autonomous business units, and by taking steps to empower employees to be more entrepreneurial and innovative.[54] Intel provides an example of what is involved.

Intel's and Sunlight's New-Business Initiatives The idea for Intel's new, in-house new-business initiative "... came from our employees, who kept telling us they wanted to do entrepreneurial things. . . .[55] Intel is in the microprocessor business. However, its new-business intrapreneurship initiative is earmarked

QUALCOMM Corporation's intrapreneurial activities led to the wireless Web company Handspring.

specifically for encouraging nonmicroprocessor businesses. Part of Intel's intrapreneurship effort involves providing budding Intel employee-inventors with the spare time and some financial support to pursue their ideas. For example, Intel engineer Paul Scagnetti came up with the idea for a handheld computer that helps people record and plan their fitness regimens. Intel gave him the funding to launch his product, the Vivonic fitness planner.

Intrapreneurship applies equally well to introducing new services as it does to introducing new products. For example, the group benefits department of Canada's Sunlight Financial Insurance Company has over 3,100 employees in eleven locations in Canada. To help innovate new services, it also has a small, intrapreneurial sixty-person group that works independently. Its job is to come up with and create new insurance services, for instance, for university professors.[56] As the vice president of group benefits says, this small unit ". . . and the others we have like it operate with great independence and often act as a sort of laboratory creating, refining and launching new products."[57]

● **Business Incubators** Some entrepreneurs and managers turn to business incubators to help develop their new-product ideas. As its name implies, employees in a business incubator center provide the advice, support, and resources that the manager needs to nurture the new idea. Some companies establish their own business incubators; other incubators are university-based. IBM established dozens of business innovation centers around the world. In these centers, specially trained IBM engineering, financial, and other employees work with IBM customers. They help the latter capitalize on IBM products and services in commercializing their own companies' new-product ideas.[58]

● **New-Product Development Teams** The usual new-product development process resembles a relay race. Each department, such as research and development (R&D), does its part of the job. It then hands off the project to the next department, for instance, from R&D to marketing, to finance, and then to production. The problem with this sequential process is that it tends to be slow at identifying potential problems and at making the required changes. For example, if production wants to make a change, that change needs to be backed up to and approved by each preceding department.

More companies are therefore reorganizing their new-product development processes around small, multifunction teams.[59] Teams comprised of employees from R&D, finance, sales, production, and engineering work together on developing and commercializing a new-product idea. Then, new-product development is no longer a relay race. Instead, the team members work interactively and collaboratively to fine-tune and finalize their new-product idea.[60]

Innovation Now

Online Study Center
ACE the Test
Managing Now! LIVE

Innovation today is becoming more collaborative and technology-based. We discuss how in this final section.

Innovation and Collaboration

Traditional new-product development tends to be inward-looking. Employees in R&D or new-product development think up and evaluate ideas for new products. They may not check with customers and suppliers until it's time to test-market the product.

Managers are now moving away from that inward-looking model. Instead of just asking their customers, suppliers, and dealers for help in test-marketing new-product ideas, they are tapping them as sources for new-product ideas. Kraft Foods Inc. recently launched a program to encourage unsolicited new-product-idea submissions from customers and others.[61]

Kraft's CEO calls this "open innovation." Other experts call it "collaborative new-product and process development" (NPPD) and "open market innovation." IBM speaks of creating "innovation ecosystems" comprised of solution providers, independent software developers, consultants, venture capitalists, academics, and industry thought leaders.[62] In any case, the main aim of collaboration is to tap the ideas of a wider community and thus to solicit more and better new-product ideas.

Why Collaboration? At Kraft and other firms, diminishing innovation prompted CEOs to look outside their companies for new ideas. For example, Kraft has its own research and development units for developing new products. However, the only big new product they've had in years was DiGiorno pizza. A study by consultants Booz Allen Hamilton Inc. concluded that there was no relationship between a company's growth rate and the amount it spent on research and development. Firms like Merck felt that their own R&D was becoming too insular, too Merck-oriented. The solution: Dr. Peter Kim, Merck's new R&D head, hired many

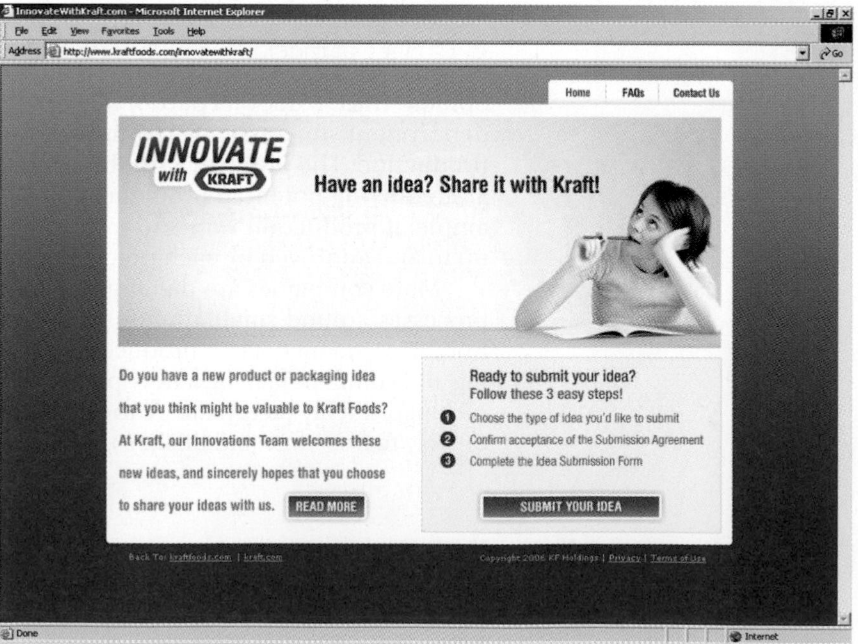

SOURCE: © 2006 Kraft Foods Inc. All rights reserved.

new outside scientists. He also instituted procedures that enable hundreds of independent, outside scientists to help Merck identify and develop new potential drugs.[63]

We'll see that companies like Kraft and Merck use a variety of tools, often Internet-based, to make it easier to tap the ideas of outsiders, be they freelance scientists and inventors, customers, suppliers, universities, or others.[64] As one example, links on Kraft's corporate website now make it easier for outsiders to submit ideas online or via a toll-free telephone number.

Innovation and Learning

Tapping the ideas of people both inside and outside the firm requires that firms such as Kraft be good at learning—for instance, at learning what customers want, what competitors are doing, and which ideas one's suppliers and employees believe might work and which to discard.[65] As one expert said,

> [A]n organization's innovative potential is strongly influenced by its access to customer and competitor intelligence, by its awareness of its internal organizational and technological capabilities, and by its understanding of external demands posed by governmental policies, environmental regulations, laws, and socioeconomic trends. . . . Progressive firms have recognized this and are implementing new organizational structures, communication technologies, and incentives systems in order to grow their collaborative potential in important areas.[66]

We will see in Chapter 10 that managers can take many steps to improve their companies' abilities to learn. Many reduce the number of management layers in the chain of command. This way, the managers at the top are closer to the customers rather than isolated in their executive suites by layers of subordinates. Most also help their employees do a better job of gathering, analyzing, and communicating information about new-product ideas. For example, the firm might give repairpeople laptop computers and encourage them to share ideas for learning about and solving particular customer problems.

Managing Now: Using Information Technology for Innovation

When a company embraces collaborative new-product development, it needs a way to link together and tap the input of many people. It wants input from independent experts like scientists who might be able to contribute. And it wants input from its own supply chain members such as its dealers, customers, and suppliers.

Companies use information technology–based systems to enable this kind of collaboration. The basic idea is to allow ideas to flow freely among all the parties. Companies are using a variety of information technology–based systems for enabling this kind of collaboration. A short list would include virtual PC-based video brainstorming sessions (among people in different locations), e-mail, request for assistance notices on bulletin boards, videoconferencing, and computer-aided design tools. The latter enable geographically dispersed employees to work in a virtual environment to collaboratively create and fine-tune new-product designs. Many companies use even more powerful tools. The Practice IT feature shows how Procter & Gamble uses information technology to facilitate collaborative innovation.

Practice IT
Collaborative Innovation at P&G

Procter & Gamble's R&D head, Larry Huston, knew his firm had to reach out to get more and better new-product ideas. P&G now uses several information technology tools to connect itself to various sources of new-product ideas.[67]

InnovationNet

This is an intranet Web portal for 18,000 Procter & Gamble innovators in research and development, engineering, market research, purchasing, and patents. One P&G senior vice president calls it a sort of global lunchroom. It lets those 18,000 P&G employees worldwide exchange ideas.

InnoCentive

This virtual laboratory posts scientific problems from its thirty idea-seeking corporate members (including P&G) to a proprietary network of about 30,000 registered solvers around the world. Each posting at www.Intelincentive.com includes a promised cash incentive for coming up with the solution.

NineSigma Inc.

This company helps its fifty or so clients (including P&G) prepare technical briefs describing projects or problems they want solved. NineSigma then sends these briefs (without identifying the corporate customer) to researchers around the world for possible solutions.

YourEncore Inc.

This is a network of about 400 retired scientists and engineers. P&G and other YourEncore corporate sponsors pay them for specific, short-term job assignments aimed at helping the YourEncore Inc. sponsors develop new products.[68]

● **Self-Organizing** Intranet portals like P&G's InnovationNet (which links its 18,000 innovators) can make it easy for subsets of these experts to self-organize. The portal enables them to identify like-minded colleagues and to share information about projects of mutual interest without centralized, detailed managerial guidance.[69]

Product Life-Cycle Management

No new product sells forever. Instead, all products move through a product life cycle from development to expansion, maturity, and decline.[70] In stage 1, the company develops and test-markets the new product and then introduces it to the market. Stage 2 is a period of rapid expansion as the new product, with little competition, quickly expands its sales. Competition picks up in stage 3 (maturity), and the growth rate of both sales and profitability flatten. Finally, the product enters its fourth stage, the decline stage, as both sales and profitability start to trend down.

Managers face different challenges at each stage of a product's life cycle. For example, in stage 1 (development), the main challenges are creating, developing, and testing the new-product idea, and introducing the product to the market. In the second stage, the expansion stage, the manager, facing little competition, can focus on marketing the new product to as many new customers as possible. In the third stage, the maturity stage, competition becomes intense, and the manager turns to making incremental, innovative improvements to keep the product selling. In the fourth stage, the decline stage, the total market for the product begins to shrink, and the manager must decide whether to stay in the business or to introduce a dramatically new stage 1 product to meet the market's new needs.

Managing Now: Product Life-Cycle Management Software

For companies like Sony or Dell that produce hundreds or thousands of different products and models, each in different life-cycle stages, keeping track of all the different components that comprise each product and model is a daunting task.[71] For example, Sony has over 3,000 main product groups and over 54,000 identifiable products. That can translate into millions of separate components.

The huge number of components complicates the new-product development process for a firm like Sony or Dell.[72] Ideally, companies like these don't want to start from scratch every time they design a new product. Instead, they want to keep costs down by reusing, if possible, proven components from their existing products. However, doing so presents three challenges.

- One challenge is keeping track of all those current products' components.
- Another is enabling the companies' designers to see how, for instance, they might recycle a component from an existing Sony laptop to serve some purpose in Sony's new video game.
- A third is to show suppliers how the components they previously supplied for product A are now going to be used (in a slightly modified fashion) in the company's new product B.

Challenges like these don't concern only companies that are trying to innovate brand-new products. They also concern managers who are trying to update existing products. To address every product's inevitable life-cycle maturity and decline, every company continually fine-tunes its existing products, for instance, by upgrading memory capacity. So Dell's designers, for example, face the three component-recycling challenges, not just for the new products they're developing but also for innovating and improving their existing products. How can managers at Dell or Sony make sure they're doing the best job of recycling existing products' components?

Product Life-Cycle Software Keeping track of all these components is a mammoth task if done manually. The preferred alternative is to use product life-cycle management software. *Product life-cycle management software* is a suite of software applications that helps managers design, manufacture, and manage the evolution of their products.[73]

Product life-cycle management (PLM) software applications support innovation in many ways. For example, if Dell's engineers want to design a new computer, the company's product life-cycle management software helps them keep track of and reuse the parts of previous designs. This in turn helps Dell minimize new-product and component development costs. It also helps Dell keep operational surprises and problems to a minimum. By enabling designers to reuse existing components, PLM software also reduces the amount of time it takes to get the new product to the market and improves the efficiency of the whole new-product innovation process. It does this in part by enabling the company's suppliers to track product changes via the firm's new-product development intranet, and thereby inform them automatically when a component is to be improved and/or reused in a new product.

CHAPTER SUMMARY

1. Entrepreneurship is the creation of a business for the purpose of gain or growth under conditions of risk and uncertainty, and an entrepreneur is someone who creates new businesses under risky conditions.
2. Some environments are more conducive to entrepreneurship than others. The level of economic freedom is one consideration. Others include the ability to streamline, downsize, and fire employees at will; technological advances; the level of economic activity; globalization, and other environmental factors, such as venture capital availability; a technically skilled labor force; the accessibility of suppliers; the accessibility of customers; the availability of lenders; the accessibility of transportation; the attitude of the area's population; and the availability of supporting services (such as roads, electric power, and accounting firms).
3. Small businesses as a group account for most of the new businesses created every year as well as for most of the growth of companies (small firms grow much faster than do big ones). Small firms also account for about three-quarters of the employment growth in the U.S. economy—in other words, small businesses create most of the new jobs in the United States.
4. A few behaviors seem to arise consistently in anecdotal/case descriptions of successful entrepreneurs, including tenacity and intensity—the drive to pursue a goal with passion and focus.
5. Most entrepreneurs seem to stumble upon their ideas for a business. Most of those responding to one survey said that they got their ideas for their businesses through their previous employment. Serendipity was the next source that most respondents mentioned. A relative handful got their ideas from hobbies or from a systematic search for business opportunities.
6. In creating the business entity, the entrepreneur needs to decide what the ownership structure will be. The four main forms of business ownership are the sole proprietorship, the partnership, the corporation, and the LLC. Taxation and limiting the owner's liability are always big considerations in choosing an ownership form.
7. Innovation means uncovering a valuable need, inventing a new or improved product or service to fill that need, and then developing and introducing the new product or service so that it succeeds in the marketplace. Today, most big companies rely more on collaborative innovation, which involves reaching out with IT tools to those inside and outside the company for good ideas.
8. Product life-cycle management software is a suite of software applications that helps managers design, manufacture, and manage the evolution of their products.

DISCUSSION QUESTIONS

1. Why is entrepreneurship important?
2. Do you know of anyone involved in a family business, and if so, do they experience any of the family business issues we discussed in this chapter? Which ones?
3. If you were interested in buying a franchise, how would you get started?
4. According to your state and county officials, what is involved in incorporating where you live?
5. Why do you think you would (or would not) make a good entrepreneur?
6. List ten innovative products introduced by P&G over the past five years.

EXPERIENTIAL EXERCISES

1. Using the information in this chapter, write a one-page paper on the topic "Why I would (or would not) make a good entrepreneur."
2. At the library or on the Internet, review sales information on two popular franchises of your choice. Then, in teams of three or four people, evaluate

the pros and cons of these franchise businesses, and answer the question, Should I invest in this franchise?

3. The dean of your business school is eager to expand her college's programs to new markets. She has decided to try to establish a new online MBA program. She has asked you to conduct an informal, quick feasibility study. In teams of four or five, outline what you would cover in such a study, and then explain why you believe her new program is or is not a good idea.

4. In teams of four or five people, choose a consumer products company such as P&G and list the innovative products they've introduced in the past three years. What was it about these products that you consider innovative?

CASE STUDY

Getting By with a Little Help from His Mother's Friends

Andrew Morris had almost everything he needed to start his Caribbean grocery store in a New York City suburb. He had an MBA from Columbia University, a business plan, and a $50,000 loan from the European American Bank. However, after he negotiated the rent on a 1,600-square-foot retail space in Hempstead, New York, he found he did not have enough cash left for inventory, payroll, marketing, and licenses. Thanks to his mother and her friends, he was able to secure an additional $15,000 in resources, which enabled him to stock the shelves with dozens of kinds of hot sauce, curry, and reggae music that the growing Caribbean community craves.

Morris got the money from his mother's *susu,* a kind of club or fund developed by West Indian housewives to provide rotating credit for big-ticket household purchases. A *susu,* which means "partner," typically has about twenty members, most of them either relatives or close friends. Each week, every member contributes a fixed sum, or *hand,* into the fund for a twenty-week period. Any time during those twenty weeks, each member is entitled to borrow an amount, or *draw,* to use interest-free during that time. For example, if a twenty-member *susu* has a set weekly contribution of $100, each member pays $100 into the fund every week—or pays a total of $2,000 over twenty weeks. Each member is then also able to draw $2,000 at any point during that period. Essentially, the *susu* is a kind of planned savings program that pools money to help members of the group who need help with cash flow. The Caribbean *susu* is not really a unique concept in the United States. Asian Americans and other ethnic groups have also developed informal lending networks for their members.

Andrew Morris has dipped into his mother's *susu* a number of times to help his business grow. He used the money to pay a sales tax obligation; purchase a commercial oven to cook Jamaican meat patties; produce a special Easter promotion with traditional cheese and sweetbread sandwiches; and expand his inventory to include unusual but popular items, such as Jamaican Chinese soy sauce. "It's a cash-flow boon," Morris says. After seven years of ongoing *susu* support, Morris's store now has annual revenues of over $1 million. Morris is now counting on *susu* support to help it expand into distributing coffee and developing a website. "[The *susu* is] no longer just a Christmas club," he says. "It's a way of life."[74]

DISCUSSION QUESTIONS

1. Andrew Morris has approached you for help. List what you believe he is doing right and doing wrong with respect to starting his business. What do you think accounts for the fact that he ran out of money before he opened, even though he had a business plan? What remedy or remedies would you suggest at this point?
2. Develop a one-page outline showing Andrew Morris how you would suggest he conduct an informal business feasibility study.
3. List the activity areas for which Andrew Morris should establish controls.
4. What other alternative means for obtaining financing would you recommend for Andrew Morris, and what are their pros and cons when compared to continuing to use his mother's *susu*?

5 INFORMATION AND KNOWLEDGE MANAGEMENT

CHAPTER OUTLINE

Caterpillar Inc.

"Knowledge management" at Caterpillar Inc. used to mean buying a colleague a cup of coffee. This "would enable employees to learn anything they needed to know." And for many years, that was adequate.[1] Caterpillar manufactures construction and mining equipment. Most of the company's investment was in the sorts of machines and factories you would associate with a big industrial manufacturing company. Acquiring and sharing knowledge about things like best practices and new ideas was not management's major focus.

Now things are different. Caterpillar's managers saw that all competitors had access to the same manufacturing facilities and machinery. To compete in today's business environment, Caterpillar had to put more emphasis on its intangible, intellectual assets—on things like patents; new, creative ideas; and on world-class best practices in all areas. These best practices include finding out what customers want, delivering better service, producing equipment more efficiently, and better managing its huge workforce. As at most firms, best practices had become the key to Caterpillar's success.

The giant Caterpillar Inc. needed a better way to manage its accumulated corporate knowledge.

In today's business environment, best practices like these now make the difference between success and failure. For Caterpillar, the challenge was that much of the knowledge about best practices was filed away in procedures manuals or hidden away in their employees' minds. How could Caterpillar retrieve and store these millions and millions of ideas and best practices and encourage employees to share what they know? ■

BEHAVIORAL OBJECTIVES

After studying this chapter, you should be able to:

Show that you've learned the chapter's essential information by

- Defining and giving examples of data, information, and knowledge.
- Defining information technology.
- Giving examples of why managers at different levels require different types of information.
- Comparing and contrasting at least four types of information systems.

Show that you can practice what you've learned here by

- Reading the chapter case study and identifying the information system the manager needs.
- Showing how managers in the opening vignette rely on information technology.

Online Study Center
ACE the Test
Managing Now! LIVE

Show that you can apply what you've learned here by

- Viewing the simulation video and identifying if the information is of high quality.

Data, Information, and Knowledge

Online Study Center
ACE the Test
Managing Now! LIVE

The challenge that Caterpillar faced is a challenge that all businesses face today. And it is a challenge that highlights how important managing information has become to companies' success and why information technology is so important.

Information technology is a familiar and inescapable aspect of our lives. We use computers, e-mail, software, cell phones, iPods, fax machines, flash drives, scanners, and BlackBerry© devices to communicate and to assist with our daily chores. We search for travel information on Expedia, download airline tickets prior to trips, wait patiently as voice-mail systems direct our calls, and register for and take college courses online. Computerized diagnostic tools analyze our autos' problems, point-of-sale computers at Target process our credit-card purchases, and computerized traffic-flow systems control our progress to work.

information technology (IT): any processes, practices, or systems that facilitate the processing and transporting of information

information system: the interrelated components working together to collect, process, store, and disseminate information to support decision making, coordination, analysis, and visualization in an organization

What may not be quite so obvious is the vast number of ways in which managers rely on information and information technology. **Information technology (IT)** refers to any processes, practices, or systems that facilitate processing and transporting information. It includes both the hardware (such as computers, iPods, cell phones, and servers) as well as the software systems used to make these devices work. Information systems are more specialized. **Information system** refers to "the interrelated components working together to collect, process, store, and disseminate information to support decision making, coordination, analysis, and visualization in an organization."[2] Managers depend on information technology and systems to manage the vast quantities of ideas, knowledge, and other information that their firms rely on for their success. Like their colleagues at Caterpillar, managers can't manage today without knowing how to manage information.

The Nature of Information

Most information systems transform data into information and knowledge that managers can actually use. *Data* comprise facts, figures, or observations. For example, daily laptop sales figures for Dell computer comprise data. But data—these numbers—are of little use for management decisions—they're just raw data.

Information is data in context. For example, Dell's CEO can review a graph of laptop sales data for a week, and from that glean useful information about whether Dell's sales are trending up or down. Information is data presented in a form that is meaningful to the recipient.[3] "Information," as Peter Drucker said, "is data endowed with relevance and purpose."[4]

All information systems deal with data. Some systems transform data into information, for example, by expressing them in the form of graphs or charts. Thus, Dell's CEO may start each day by viewing on his laptop computerized graphs and charts summarizing the trends for Dell activities such as laptop sales, profit margins, and unit costs.

knowledge: information distilled via study or research and augmented by judgment and experience

Managers combine information like that on Dell's sales graph with what they already know, and with other information (such as competitors' sales for the same period), to create knowledge. **Knowledge** is "information . . . distilled via study or research and augmented by judgment and experience."[5] Managers use knowledge to understand what is happening and to make predictions. The sales graph (information) shows that Dell sales are trending down. Dell's CEO knows that a newly rejuvenated Hewlett-Packard (HP) is selling comparable laptops for 5 percent less cost. This knowledge (Dell sales trending down plus HP selling theirs for 5 percent less) leads Dell's CEO to conclude, based on his previous experience, that HP's laptop sales are undermining Dell's, and that a lower Dell price and more ads are in order.

Consider another example. PepsiCo wants to determine why consumers are not buying its Pepsi Light clear drink. The company's market researchers conduct a survey containing thirty multiple-choice questions, each with five possible choices. They place all these data (all the answers to the thirty questions from the hundreds of people who took the survey) on a DVD. If printed, all these data would appear as streams of unrelated numbers. But then, PepsiCo's market researchers summarize these data using graphs showing average responses by age level and other demographic traits. The result is information. For example, they may find that older people, by and large, don't seem to be purchasing this product. PepsiCo's marketing department can then apply its knowledge to draw meaningful conclusions, such as, in this case, a hypothesis about why older consumers seem less inclined to purchase Pepsi Light than are younger ones.

What Is Information Quality?

Of course, managers don't just want information; they want high-quality information they can use to make good decisions. High-quality information has several characteristics (see Figure 5.1).[6] As in the PepsiCo example, good information must be *pertinent* and related to the problem at hand. It must also be *timely*. For example, the Pepsi Light survey information would be useless if it came rolling in two years after the product was pulled off the shelf. Good information must also be *accurate*, and finally, good information reduces *uncertainty*, which we can define as the absence of information about a particular area of concern.[7] In the PepsiCo example, to meet these last two criteria, the survey information should help the marketing manager answer the question, Why aren't people buying Pepsi Light the way we thought they would?

Yet managers today are, if anything, deluged by information. Having high-quality information is therefore just a start. It's not enough for the company's information systems and technology (all its computer systems, software packages, communication devices, and so on) to generate and transfer more (even high-quality) information. That's often the last thing the manager needs! Those systems

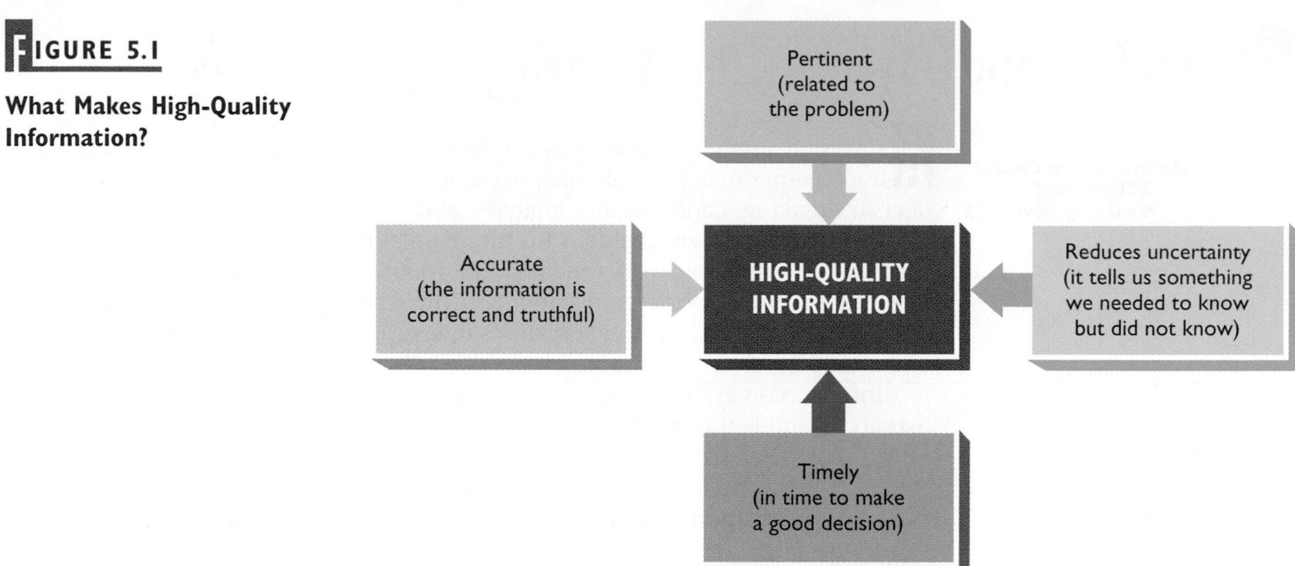

FIGURE 5.1

What Makes High-Quality Information?

must also contribute to the manager's knowledge of what is happening, through analysis, interpretation, and explanation. We'll look at several examples in this chapter, including the following one on data mining.

Managing Now: Data Mining

Data mining is "the set of activities used to find new, hidden, or unexpected patterns in data."[8] Data-mining systems use tools like statistical analysis and so-called intelligent agents to sift through computerized data looking for relationships. Thanks to data mining, the manager can discover patterns that he or she can then use to make predictions. He or she can answer questions such as, Which of our products would this customer be most likely to buy? Which of our customers are making too many returns? What is the likelihood that these customers will respond to our promotional coupons?[9]

Department stores use data mining all the time. For example, Macy's necessarily captures huge amounts of data on its customers—what they buy, when they buy it, how they pay for it, and what day of the week they tend to shop, for instance. Left unanalyzed, all these data are of little use. However, stores like Macy's use data mining to make sense of it. For example, data mining reveals that some customers often come in to redeem 20-percent-off coupons they get in the mail. Furthermore, some customers are much more apt to buy new electronic gadgets with coupons than are other customers. Data mining therefore gives Macy's marketing managers valuable knowledge about which customers should receive which coupons and brochures.

The data Macy's mines come from the firm's data warehouse. The data warehouse is a sort of computerized holding station for Macy's data. The company's operational systems—for instance, its computerized point-of-sale registers and billing systems—are continuously collecting data about customers' purchases. The data warehouse is the location in which the company stores these data. Then Macy's managers can use the sorts of decision support systems we discuss next to mine these data and perform other procedures that help them make better decisions.

Information Systems for Managing Organizations

Online Study Center
ACE the Test
Managing Now! LIVE

As we said, an information system refers to "the interrelated components working together to collect, process, store, and disseminate information to support decision making, coordination, analysis, and visualization in an organization."[10] An information system includes all the people, data, technology, and organizational procedures that work together to retrieve, process, store, and disseminate information to support management. In this book, we'll focus on managerial information systems, which are systems that support managerial decision making and control.

Information systems are more than computers. An information system also usually includes the employees who input data into the system and retrieve its output. Managers are (or should be) part of the information system, since it is designed to serve their specific needs for information, like the PepsiCo managers' need for information about customers' buying patterns. Building an information system usually starts with understanding what information management needs.

Management's Requirement for Information

The information a manager needs generally depends on two basic things—the business department the manager is attached to and the manager's level in the chain of command. Figure 5.2 summarizes this idea.

Business Function Information Needs First, managers in different departments need information that is relevant to their business functions. For example,

FIGURE 5.2

Types of Information Systems

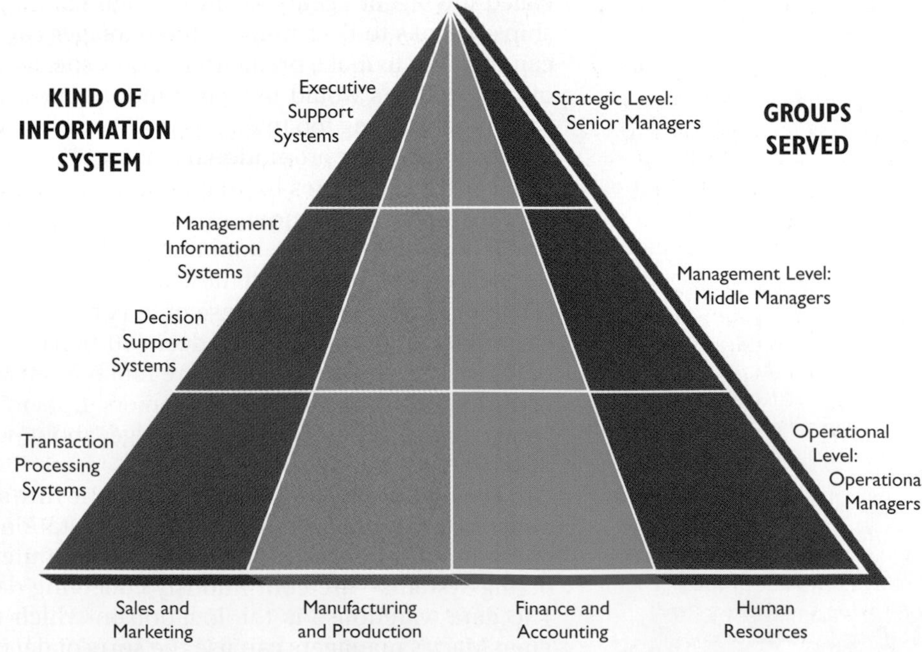

SOURCE: Kenneth C. Laudon and Jane P. Laudon, *Management Information Systems* 9e, © 2006, Prentice Hall, Upper Saddle River, N.J., p. 41.

PepsiCo's marketing managers need marketing information, its production managers need production information, and its human resource (HR) managers need HR-related information on things like turnover and grievances. Therefore, businesses generally have functional information systems, such as sales systems, production systems, finance systems, and HR systems.

● **Business-Level Information Needs** Similarly, managers at different levels in the organization tend to require different types of information.[11] For example, first-line managers (like production supervisors) need a short-term focus. They need to schedule front-desk personnel, supervise accounting departments, and oversee production departments. At this level, the information they need should emphasize operational activities such as production schedules and cash-management information.

Middle managers—who supervise several front-line managers—tend to focus more on broader, intermediate-range issues, like those events that might affect the company in the coming year or so. Therefore, they require information for use in budget analysis (are we meeting our budgets for the year or not?) and in overall factory efficiency.

Top managers, including the CEO and the firm's top vice presidents, focus more on long-range, strategic decisions. They need information that will enable them to make, for example, merger and acquisitions decisions and new-product decisions.

These different information requirements translate into requirements for different types of information systems at each level of the organization.

● **Levels of Information Systems** Thus, different information systems are appropriate to each organizational level.[12] As in Figure 5.2, **executive support systems** provide information for strategic-level decisions on matters such as five-year operating plans. **Management information systems (MISs)** provide middle managers with reports regarding matters such as current versus historical sales levels. **Decision support systems (DSSs)** are information systems that provide middle managers with tools for analyzing and deciding on matters such as which customers would be the best candidates for mailings. **Transaction-processing systems** provide detailed information about the most short-term activities, daily activities such as accounts payables and order status. Within each category, there are information systems serving specific purposes. We'll look more closely at each information system, starting with the most day-to-day systems, transaction-processing systems.

executive support systems: information systems that provide information for strategic-level decisions on matters such as five-year operating plans

management information systems (MISs): information systems that provide middle managers with reports regarding matters such as current versus historical sales levels

decision support systems (DSSs): information systems that provide middle managers with tools for analyzing and deciding on matters such as which customers would be the best candidates for mailings

transaction-processing systems: information systems that provide detailed information about the most short-term activities, daily activities such as accounts payable and order status

Transaction-Processing Systems

A transaction is an event that affects the business. Hiring an employee, selling merchandise, paying an employee, and ordering supplies are transactions. In essence, transaction-processing systems collect and maintain detailed records regarding the organization's transactions. For example, a university must know which students have registered, which have paid fees, which members of the faculty are teaching, and the secretaries that are employed to conduct its business.

The collection and maintenance of such day-to-day transactions were two of the first procedures managers computerized. As is still the case today, early transaction-processing systems automated the collection, maintenance, and processing of mostly repetitive transactions. These include computing withholding taxes and net pay.

Today, transaction-processing systems perform the company's daily operational activities, such as collecting point-of-sale data, maintaining employee records, paying bills, processing orders, and maintaining inventories. They support business activities like tracking responses from the firm's promotional efforts, scheduling orders for production, and billing customers.[13]

Businesses generally have transaction systems for each major business function. Sales and marketing transaction-processing systems do things like enter and process orders. Manufacturing and production systems handle activities like maintaining inventory and scheduling production machines. Finance and accounting systems handle activities such as paying bills, billing customers, and maintaining the company's financial records. Human resource systems help maintain personnel or human resource (HR) records on details such as age, address, and benefits, and track employees' training, skills, and appraisals.

Management Information Systems

Management information systems (MISs) provide decision support for managers by producing standardized, summarized reports on a regular basis.[14] The MIS generally produces reports for longer-term purposes than typical transaction-processing systems.

Management information systems (MISs) aid managers by producing the charts, graphs, and reports they need to understand their departments' or companies' current and past performance.[15] They take data and transform them into information. For example, an MIS may take raw data and show the sales manager the trend of sales for the past two weeks; the production manager a graph of weekly inventory levels; and the CEO a report summarizing the company's revenues, expenses, and profits for the quarter. The MIS thereby helps managers plan, organize, lead, and control.

Decision Support Systems

A decision support system (DSS) is a set of computerized tools that helps managers analyze information and make decisions. The DSS "assist[s] management decision making by combining data, sophisticated analytical models, and user-friendly software into a single powerful system that can support semi-structured or unstructured decision making."[16] (The latter are decisions such as, What are the chances that this new product will succeed?) Decision support systems have five main components: a data management system, a model management system, a knowledge engine, a user interface, and the user (see Figure 5.3):[17]

- The data management component retrieves, stores, and organizes the data, for instance, from point-of-sale cash registers.
- The model management system retrieves, stores, and organizes the quantitative and statistical models that the decision support system uses to analyze the data.

FIGURE 5.3

Five Components of DSS

THE DECISION SUPPORT SYSTEM				
Data Management	Model Management	Knowledge Engine	User Interface	User

For example, Macy's may use a formula to identify customers who make too many returns.

- The knowledge engine does the actual reasoning for the system. For example, the knowledge engine for a commercial bank might use its built-in rules to analyze a loan applicant's credit history, employment history, income level, and debt to arrive at a decision regarding whether that person's credit risk is high or low.
- The user interface consists of the tools (such as the keyboard and screen) the manager uses to interact with the decision support system.
- Finally, the user is the decision maker who is actually using and controlling the decision support system.

When it comes to helping managers make decisions, decision support systems are more powerful than are MISs because of the analytical tools and knowledge engine the DSS contains. Whereas the MIS will dutifully print out preprogrammed sales graphs and reports, the DSS can actually analyze various alternatives. For example, the dean of your school most likely receives weekly MIS-produced reports on enrollments by class. Suppose, however, that your school is facing a faculty strike. Now the dean would turn to a DSS. The dean may want to include in her analysis her estimate of the likelihood that a number of the university's students would move across town to a competing university given the competing university's ability (or inability) to expand its class offerings. Among other things, the dean's DSS could then help the dean estimate the impact on school revenues of having to drop various combinations of classes. Table 5.1 gives some examples of how companies use their DSS systems. The Window on Managing Now feature shows how one small business improved its revenues by installing computerized transactions, MIS, and decision support information systems.

Executive Support Systems

executive support systems (ESSs): information systems that help managers acquire, manipulate, and use the information they need to maintain the overall effectiveness of the company

Executive support systems (ESSs) help top-level executives acquire, manipulate, and use the information they need to maintain the overall effectiveness of the company. Transaction-processing systems, management information systems, and decision support systems rely on internal data, data such as daily sales, weekly profits, and purchases per consumer that the company gathers from its customers and operations.

TABLE 5.1
Examples of Uses for DSS Systems

American Airlines	Price and route selection—how much will we earn if we add or drop this route?
Cornell University	Program selection—should we add a new school of business in China or not?
Donald Trump Realty	Investment evaluation—should we open a new casino in Mississippi or not?
Burger King	Price and promotion selection—if we add this new giant burger, what's the likely impact on our revenues and costs?

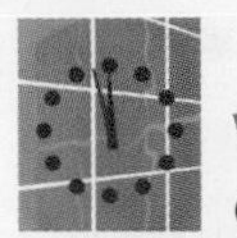

WINDOW ON MANAGING NOW

Computers Add Value at Bissett Nursery

Before it installed its new computer systems, Long Island, New York–based Bissett Nursery could not have handled any more business. Bissett's son Jimmy spent his days sprinting around the shop trying to serve customers, many of whom waited twenty-five minutes for a handwritten invoice. Bookkeeping was a month behind, and inventory control didn't exist.[18]

Both Bissetts knew their company, a wholesaler of nursery materials and lumber, would have to change. The younger Bissett had ideas about expanding the business. He thought the best way to do so would be with the help of brother-in-law Bob Pospischil, an ex–fighter pilot knowledgeable about computer systems and the financial data they could produce. "My goal was not to change the business," says Pospischil, "but to use technology to meet the business needs." The elder Bissett was skeptical. He'd seen competitors go the same route only to find it an expensive mistake, but he relented.

Pospischil spent sixty days getting a handle on buying, sales, shipping, and accounting and then spent $135,000 on the company's first big computer. Order-entry employees took turns visiting the software vendor to learn the new system. After the first thirty minutes of operations, the network crashed. A frantic Jim Bissett insisted everyone return to the old manual system. They ironed out the problem in fifteen minutes, and the elder Bissett gradually became accustomed to the new technology.

One big thing Jim Bissett soon gained from the new system was a better perspective on each phase of his operations. He could now order with precision based on his customers' historical needs. He could easily show small contractors their annual needs for nonperishable goods, enabling them to purchase in bulk and save money. Bissett Nursery's customer base shot from 600 to 7,500. Bob Pospischil was just getting started.

Marketing was costing Bissett $130,000 annually, and better than 60 percent of that budget went to producing ads and catalogs. Pospischil had an easier time selling the elder Bissett on the idea that he needed a desktop publishing system. The price tag was $40,000, but "with the first catalog, we saved enough to pay for the system," says Pospischil.

Landscapers face big barriers with homeowners because they have to sell the aesthetics of their products. It's not easy to get a customer to visualize how a tree would look in the customer's own front yard. That changed when a software company sold Bissett on an imaging system that could produce a rendering of how the planned trees and plants would look in front of the customer's house.

The new technology gave Bissett Nursery a huge competitive edge. More than 95 percent of landscape contractors who bought from Bissett and used Bissett's computer-generated images sold the job and came back to fill orders at the nursery. By 2006, Bissett Nursery had grown to become the largest horticultural distribution center in New York State. Its new computerized information systems helped make Bissett Nursery a huge success.

The information systems that fall under the *executive support systems* umbrella are different. They use internal as well as external data (such as industry sales trends). This is important. For the new CEO of Ford Motor Company, it does little good to know just that Ford sales are up 5 percent. He also needs a comparison with auto industry sales to see that Ford's market share is actually down 2 percent last month. Executive support systems provide that sort of comparison.[19]

● **How Executives Use ESSs** Executives use executive support systems in many ways. Executives such as Dell's Michael Dell use their ESSs to monitor the pulse of their companies. For example, Dell and his top managers have ESS-supported "digital dashboards" on their PCs. These computerized graphs and charts help them to monitor weekly performance, for instance, their progress relative to competitors'. The Window on Managing Now feature presents another example.

Executives also use ESSs to quickly identify and understand evolving situations. A university president could use an ESS to keep tabs on and analyze the following questions:

Is the average student taking fewer courses?

Are costs for maintenance labor substantially higher than they have been in the past?

Is there a significant shift in the Zip Codes from which most of our students come?

An ESS also makes it easy for executives to browse through the data. Says one:

> I like to take a few minutes to review details about our customers, our manufacturers or our financial activities first hand. Having the details flow across the screen gives me a feel for how things are going. I don't look at each record, but will glance at certain elements as they scroll by. If something looks unusual, it will just jump out at me and I can find out more about it. But if nothing is unusual, I will know that, too.[20]

The CEO can also use an ESS to monitor a situation. Thus, a university president can use an ESS to monitor the new dining facilities management firm running the student cafeteria, by reviewing ESS information such as student usage, student complaints, and revenues. Executives also use ESSs to keep track of their competitors. For example, a wealth of information is available in commercial computerized databases, including financial information on tens of thousands of U.S. companies. Executives can use an ESS to tap into such databases and glean competitive data (for instance, regarding last year's sales) regarding other firms in their industry. An ESS can also support analyses. For example, it could enable our university president to create "what if" scenarios that show the likely effects on university revenues of increasing faculty salaries or adding new programs. Finally, an ESS may enable the executive to get at data directly. Using their terminals and personal digital assistants (PDAs), executives can use an executive support system to tap directly into the company's data files and get specific information that may be of interest (such as, What is that manager spending on labor?), without waiting for his or her assistants to assemble it.[21]

CEO Michael Dell, shown here with the president of the Philippines, uses a desktop balanced scorecard with computerized graphs and charts to monitor his company's performance.

expert system: an information system in which computer programs store facts and rules (often called a knowledge base) to replicate the abilities and decisions of true human experts

● **Expert Systems and Artificial Intelligence** An **expert system** is an information system in which computer programs store facts and rules (often called a knowledge base) to replicate the abilities and decisions of true human experts. One early application identified an investment adviser's criteria for recommending investments to clients who were in various demographic and risk-propensity categories. Those criteria were then used to develop a computer program that replicated most of the investment decisions the investment officer (the expert) would have made. Similarly, if you go to a site such as www.vanguard.com, it will compute an ideal investment portfolio for you (in general terms), based on factors such as your risk preferences, current income and savings, and expected future financial needs.

artificial intelligence (AI): a computer's ability to accomplish tasks in a manner that is considered "intelligent" and is characterized by learning and making decisions

computer viruses: programs that can perform destructive actions like erasing data while attached to one of a computer's existing programs

Trojan horses: items that seem innocent, like e-mails from a friend, but that once embedded can contain instructions that enable outsiders to track or manipulate the computer's files

worms: programs that act basically like viruses but can operate independently, without attaching to other programs

spyware: programs that hide themselves in a computer and enable outsiders to keep track of keystrokes

firewalls: hardware/software packages that stand between the company's network and the outside network in order to inhibit unauthorized access

authentication: passwords and similar devices used to verify a user's identity

encryption: coding of messages

The term *artificial intelligence* is often used in association with expert systems because they both are related to replicating human thought processes. However, expert systems are relatively straightforward information systems made up of programs that use decision rules. These decision rules, when combined with the facts of the situation (like the person's age and income level), allow the expert system to mimic the expert's decision-making style.

Artificial intelligence leaps beyond this sort of logical problem solving. **Artificial intelligence (AI)** can be defined as a computer's ability "to accomplish tasks in a manner that is considered 'intelligent' and is characterized by learning and making decisions."[22]

● **Information System Security** Regardless of the type of information system (executive, MIS, or other), managers need to anticipate and prepare for security breaches. Most readers are already somewhat familiar with the sorts of problems that can arise. For example, **computer viruses** are programs that can perform destructive actions like erasing data while attached to one of a computer's existing programs. They're called viruses because they're capable of duplicating and transferring themselves to other linked computers. **Trojan horses** (named after the huge wooden horse of Trojan War fame) seem innocent, like e-mails from a friend, but once embedded, they can enable outsiders to track or manipulate the computer's files. Unlike viruses, Trojan horses can't duplicate themselves. **Worms** basically act like viruses but can operate independently, without attaching to other programs. **Spyware** programs (as the name implies) hide themselves in a computer and enable outsiders to keep track of keystrokes.

Computer security specialists take numerous steps to defend against security breaches. Commercial information systems and those connected to broadband services particularly require **firewalls**, hardware/software packages that stand between the company's network and the outside network in order to inhibit unauthorized access. Systems also use **authentication**, for instance, via passwords, to help protect systems. Various types of software, including antivirus and antispyware programs, help identify and inhibit virus or spyware attacks. Companies also use **encryption**, or coding of messages, to inhibit unauthorized people from reading messages. Companies use several protocols or coding methods to encode data, including *Secure Sockets Layer (SSL)* and the newer *Transport Layer Security (TLS)*. Managers also take other steps to improve computer system security. Indeed, the International Standards Organization has special standards covering security issues.

Enterprise Systems and Knowledge Management

Online Study Center
ACE the Test
Managing Now! LIVE

So far, we have viewed information systems from two perspectives (refer again to Figure 5.2). We looked at systems that cut horizontally across the company's functional departments, systems such as sales, production, finance, and human resource management transaction systems. These serve managers in different departments. We also looked at systems that serve managers depending on their level in the company. These included transaction-processing, management information, decision support, and executive-level systems. A third set of information systems, called enterprise or enterprise resource planning systems, integrates the information from all these horizontal and vertical systems. We discuss these systems next.

What Are Enterprise Systems?

enterprise resource planning (ERP) system: companywide integrated computer systems comprised of compatible software modules for each of the company's separate departments (such as sales, accounting, finance, production, and HR) and designed to communicate with each other and with the central system's database

An **enterprise resource planning (ERP) system** is a companywide integrated computer system comprised of compatible software modules for each of the company's separate departments (such as sales, accounting, finance, production, and HR). Often Internet-based, the ERP modules are designed to communicate with each other and with the central system's database. That way, information from all the departments is readily shared by the ERP system and is available to employees in all the other departments. Activities that formerly required human intervention, such as production telling accounting that it should bill a customer because an order just shipped, now occur automatically. ERP strips away the barriers that typically exist among a company's stand-alone departmental computer systems. The name notwithstanding, enterprise resource planning systems are not primarily planning systems. We'll generally refer to them as enterprise systems in this book.

Enterprise systems help managers coordinate and integrate all the company's functions and processes. By integrating the separate departmental computer modules, enterprise systems can do things for managers that the separate departmental systems (sales, production, finance, and HR) could not do on their own. Here's an example:

> With [ERP], a customer places an order, and the sales order was recorded. The system schedules shipping and works backwards from the shipping date to reserve the materials, to order parts from suppliers, and to schedule manufacturing. The [ERP] [accounting] module checks the customer's credit limit, updates the sales forecast, and creates a bill of materials. The salesperson's commission is updated. Product costs and profitability are calculated. Finally, accounting data is updated, including balance sheets, accounts payable, ledgers, and other financial information.[23]

Software companies like SAS, SAP, and Oracle supply enterprise systems. Sometimes managers start small, by installing one functional module at a time—for instance, first accounting. Then they install sales, production, and human resource management modules at later times. As we'll see in this book, it's hard to be world-class (in controlling operations or costs, for instance) without the benefits that derive from enterprise systems.

● Managing Now: Millipore Corp. For example, Millipore Corp. develops and manufactures technologies for drug companies. Wanting to better integrate its worldwide operations, Millipore installed a Web-based suite of enterprise software products from Oracle Corporation. Now, for example, instead of using different financial packages in thirty countries, the compatible financial modules can communicate with each other and with the systems at Millipore's headquarters. This means top management can get fast feedback on the firm's financial performance around the world. Similarly, Millipore turned to Oracle Corporation to install other compatible modules, including Oracle Order Management and Oracle's financial, warehouse, and distribution systems. Now all these modules can communicate with each other. Orders are processed automatically, production schedules are set, orders are processed, and bills are sent out faster, all automatically, and management can now track orders from entry through delivery.

Three Special Enterprise Systems

In addition to the ERP systems that integrate a company's functional department modules, managers use three other specialized types of integrative enterprise systems: supply chain management, customer relationship management, and knowledge management systems.[24]

Supply Chain Management Systems Supply chain management systems help the company manage its relationship with its suppliers and retailers. They "provide information to help suppliers, purchasing firms, distributors, and logistics companies coordinate, schedule, and control business processes for procurement, production, inventory management, and delivery of products and services."[25] For example, when Dell receives an order for a new personal computer (PC), its supply chain management system automatically notifies Dell's assembly plant to schedule the work; the vendors to send the parts; UPS to pick up the screen, printer, and processor; and Dell's billing department to mail an invoice. Dell's customers follow their orders' progress by logging on to the same system. For many firms today, much of their fame rests on their supply chain management systems. French retailer (and Wal-Mart rival) Carrefour keeps its costs down in part because its point-of-sale computers automatically notify vendors like Levi's and Procter & Gamble (P&G) when it's time to replace merchandise.

Point-of-sale computers like this one enable retailers to keep their suppliers updated in real time about sales and inventory levels of their products.

Customer Relationship Management Systems Customer relationship management systems help the company manage all the processes involved with interacting with customers, such as taking orders, answering technical questions, and sending bills. For example, when a customer calls with a problem, Dell's customer relationship management system shows the technician what system the customer owns and takes the technician through a sequence of diagnostic questions aimed at identifying and solving the problem. Several years ago, to cut costs, Dell started having technicians abroad take and answer customers' calls. When customers complained, Dell largely returned to its domestic system. Its newest technical service system, introduced in 2006, allows the Dell technician (with the customer's okay) to tap into the customer's computer, diagnose it online, and correct the problem.

Knowledge Management Systems In today's competitive business environment, it's usually the company with the best information that's the most successful. As one expert put it, "It is a competitive advantage if your company is learning faster than the competition."[26] As a result, many managers today are embracing knowledge management. **Knowledge management** refers to any efforts aimed at enabling the company's managers and employees to better utilize the information available anywhere in their companies.

knowledge management: any efforts aimed at enabling a company's managers and employees to better utilize the information available anywhere in their companies

Knowledge management is enormously important today. Think of how wasteful it is for an engineer to spend three days writing a quote for a customer, only to discover that her predecessor filed a similar quote last year. One study estimates that *Fortune* 500 companies lose at least $31.5 billion a year by not sharing knowledge internally.[27]

Knowledge management systems focus on organizing and making available important knowledge, wherever and whenever it is needed.[28] Some knowledge management systems focus on accessing, compiling, organizing, and reviewing knowledge that's already written down and stored away in some form in the company. For example, Merck has vast amounts of knowledge stored away in its computers on things like what combinations of drugs they've tested in the past and what the results were. Microsoft's frequently asked questions (FAQ) sections at microsoft.com contain the firm's accumulated knowledge on how to handle various problem issues.

But much of a company's most important knowledge is not written down; it resides in the minds of its employees.[29] For example, think of all the knowledge that must reside in the mind of a company's sales manager as he or she prepares to retire after twenty years on the job. This sales manager knows about each customer's preferences and needs, who to call, the names of those people's spouses, how often they should be contacted, and thousands of similar items of knowledge. The company must have some way to harvest this treasure trove of knowledge before the manager retires.

Types of Knowledge Management Systems

Experts distinguish among four basic types of knowledge management systems: knowledge discovery systems, knowledge capture systems, knowledge sharing systems, and knowledge application systems (see Figure 5.4).[30] *Knowledge discovery systems* help employees create or develop new knowledge. Nontechnical knowledge discovery systems include joint decision-making meetings. Technical

FIGURE 5.4

Types of Knowledge Management Systems

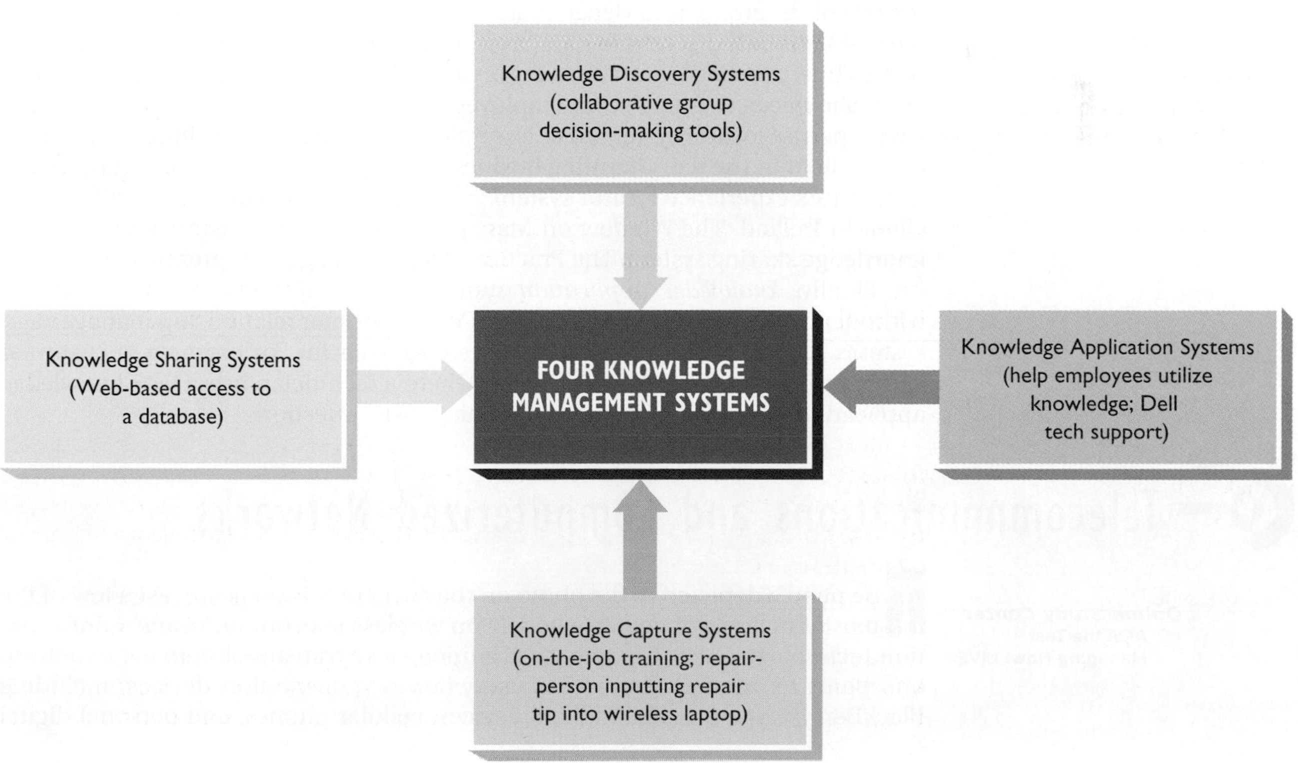

systems include computerized collaborative PC-based group problem-solving systems like those we discuss later in this chapter.

Knowledge capture systems help employees retrieve the knowledge that resides in employees' minds or in some documented form. Organizations have always used at least rudimentary knowledge capture systems, although usually not by that name. When early humans sat telling stories of how to hunt, they were capturing their experience and knowledge for the next generation. Today, on-the-job training and face-to-face meetings are similar ways to let new employees capture their predecessors' knowledge. Companies also use technologies to support knowledge capture.

● **Managing Now: Knowledge Management at Xerox** For example, Xerox has about 23,000 repair technicians around the world fixing copiers at clients' sites. In many cases, the repair solutions exist "only in the heads of experienced technicians, who can solve complex problems faster and more efficiently than less experienced ones."[31] The challenge for Xerox was to find a way to access all that brain-based knowledge and translate it into a usable form. What could Xerox do to give the company's entire 23,000-person worldwide repair force access to this knowledge?

Xerox's solution was to create an intranet-based knowledge-capture communications system named Eureka that was linked to a corporate database. The company encouraged repair technicians around the world to share repair tips by inputting them into the database via Eureka. Xerox gave all technicians laptop computers to facilitate this sharing of knowledge. Soon, more than 5,000 tips were in the database, easily accessible by other service reps around the world.

Knowledge sharing systems help employees share knowledge. For example, Web-based chat groups let people with common interests share knowledge with the rest of the group. Knowledge sharing technologies include giving selected employees Web-based access to databases, where they can find the knowledge they need. Thus, a manager at Dell can log on to the firm's intranet and access the forms he or she needs to appraise an employee. Accenture Consulting uses computerized expertise locator systems. For example, a consultant in the United States with a new client in the dairy-farming business might access information captured in Accenture's experience locator system from an Accenture consultant with a dairy client in Ireland. The Window on Managing Now feature illustrates an IT-based knowledge sharing system. The Practice IT feature (page 132) presents another.

Finally, *knowledge application systems* help employees utilize knowledge without actually learning it themselves. Dell's customer relationship management systems have knowledge application systems built in. For example, a customer with a problem calls Dell tech support, where a technician uses Dell's knowledge application system to follow a series of diagnostic questions.

Telecommunications and Computerized Networks

Online Study Center
ACE the Test
Managing Now! LIVE

The people depicted in the photo on the cover of this book are just a few of the tens of millions of people who rely on wireless telecommunications information technology today. Companies use microwave transmission to get data from one point to another. Employees use wireless transmission devices, including BlackBerry©-type e-mail handheld devices, cellular phones, and personal digital

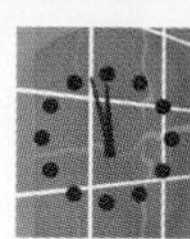

Window on Managing Now

Ryder System's Knowledge Management Center

Ryder Systems Inc. provides logistics and transportation services worldwide. When companies in one country need to coordinate shipments among dozens of suppliers and customers worldwide, they turn to Ryder. Because so much of what Ryder does involves fast-changing, state-of-the-art methods, Ryder's managers recognized how important knowledge management can be. As Gene Tyndall, Ryder's executive vice president of global solutions and e-commerce, put it, "[P]eople, the knowledge they have and the new knowledge they create are the corporate assets that impact Ryder's performance more than any other form of capital."

Ryder's managers therefore also knew that Ryder needed a way for all its employees to share new ideas and to share what they knew about best practices. For Ryder, an online knowledge management solution made the most sense, because its employees needed a simple way to access and share knowledge worldwide.[32]

To build its knowledge management system, Ryder turned to the consulting company Accenture. Ryder wanted its new knowledge management system to serve several purposes: "exchanging best practices, facilitating quick access to experts within Ryder; supplying customized news feeds on key market information; and providing collaborative work areas for project teams."[33]

To meet these goals, Accenture created an online Knowledge Management Center for Ryder. The new system is based in part on Lotus Notes. Lotus Notes is a suite of special collaborative software.[34] For example, features from Lotus Notes that Accenture embedded in the Knowledge Management Center include group calendaring and scheduling, instant messaging (which allows Ryder employees to see each other online and conduct chat sessions), and online instant meetings in which multiple employees can meet to discuss particular issues. The new Knowledge Management Center therefore makes it easy for Ryder employees worldwide to collaborate and to share knowledge.

In creating its new Knowledge Management Center, Ryder recognized that getting employees to use it was crucial. The implementation therefore included special communications from the Knowledge Management Center team to all employees describing the center's purpose and tools, special training, and incentives to encourage employees to use the new system.

assistants to access their firms' computer systems and to communicate. Personal area networks including Bluetooth enable managers to wirelessly link their computers, printers, keyboards, and computers within their homes and offices. When traveling, they seek out Wi-Fi hotspots at airport clubs or Starbucks so they can wirelessly access the Internet with their laptop computers.

Wireless telecommunications and computing have revolutionized customer relationship and supply chain management. UPS has long equipped its delivery personnel with handheld computers to instantaneously communicate pickups and deliveries to the company's central computer systems. Retail firms like Zara use wireless telecommuting to send store sales data to its supply chain management system. Wal-Mart requires that its largest vendors embed small radio frequency identification tags (RFIDs). Wal-Mart and its supply chain partners use these small transponders to keep track of each shipment wirelessly.

Digitizing data—taking data and transforming it into computer-readable forms—enables managers to use information technology. For example, digital imaging makes it easier to retrieve and manage knowledge. Thus, when Select Medical Corp. instituted its new enterprise system, the firm needed a way to process the hard-copy invoices and expense receipts that came in from the firm's hundreds of rehabilitation centers. Employees now fax most of the invoices and

PRACTICE IT
Caterpillar

As a huge manufacturer of construction and mining equipment, Caterpillar's managers knew they needed a way to encourage employees to share their best ideas and to capture what the company already had squirreled away about best practices. Caterpillar engineers began thinking that they wanted to capture what they called lessons learned and thus avoid duplicated efforts. For example, one engineer said, "[W]e found we were repeating the same mistakes and doing the same research multiple times from different business units."[35]

Therefore, about seven years ago, Caterpillar introduced its Knowledge Network, a Web-based system that Caterpillar employees use to collaborate and share knowledge. Caterpillar divided its Knowledge Network into twelve communities. Each community focused on the sorts of issues and challenges that might be of special interest to particular subgroups of Caterpillar employees. One community focused on the best way to bolt together joints, thus enabling the Caterpillar employees who faced this issue to share their best practices and making it easier for them to institute these best practices—in this case, to bolt together and fasten joints on heavy equipment.

The aim of the Knowledge Network is basically to make it easier for Caterpillar employees to share knowledge and record the best way to do things. Using the Knowledge Network, Caterpillar employees can more easily communicate and participate in chatroom-type discussions and post best ideas on community bulletin boards.

Over the past few years, Caterpillar has expanded its Knowledge Network. In August 2002, Caterpillar invited its 7,000 independent dealers to start using the Knowledge Network. Now, dealers can share best practices with each other and with Caterpillar employees. For example, over the years, dealers had lost access to a simple, hands-on aptitude test that some dealers used to hire quality repair technicians. Thanks to the new access to Caterpillar's Knowledge Network, a dealer posted a question about this in the dealer service training community. Another dealer posted a response about a quick and effective selection tool dealers could use. Caterpillar's Knowledge Network means employees and dealers can now share ideas and do things much more productively than they did before.

expense receipts to a central computer server. There, the system automatically transforms these hard-copy receipts into digital images and launches an e-mail-driven invoice and expense approval process. Managers in Select's finance department receive these images, view them, and approve payments (or, if necessary, return the bills unapproved with questions requesting clarification).[36] In the rest of this final section, we'll look more closely at telecommunications and how managers use it.

telecommunications: the electronic transmission of data, text, graphics, voice (audio), or image (video) over any distance

telecommunications system: a set of compatible communications devices that link geographically separated information-processing devices

telecommunications lines: links that provide the medium through which signals are transmitted

terminals: input-output devices that send or receive data

line adapters: devices that modify the signal from the terminal and computer so that it is suitable to be carried on a telecommunications line

Telecommunications Basics

Telecommunications is the electronic transmission of data, text, graphics, voice (audio), or image (video) over any distance.[37] A **telecommunications system** is a set of compatible communications devices that link geographically separated information-processing devices[38] (such as personal computers, telephones, and video displays) for the purpose of exchanging data and information.[39]

As you can see in the simple system shown in Figure 5.5, several common elements exist in any telecommunications system.[40] The **telecommunications lines** or links are the medium through which signals are transmitted. They might be copper wires, coaxial cables, optical fibers, or microwave transmission, for instance. **Terminals** are input-output devices that send or receive data. **Line adapters** modify the signal from the terminal and computer so that it is suitable to be carried on

FIGURE 5.5

A Telecommunications System

A telecommunications system like this one is a set of compatible telecommunications devices like lines, adapters, and computers that link geographically separated devices.

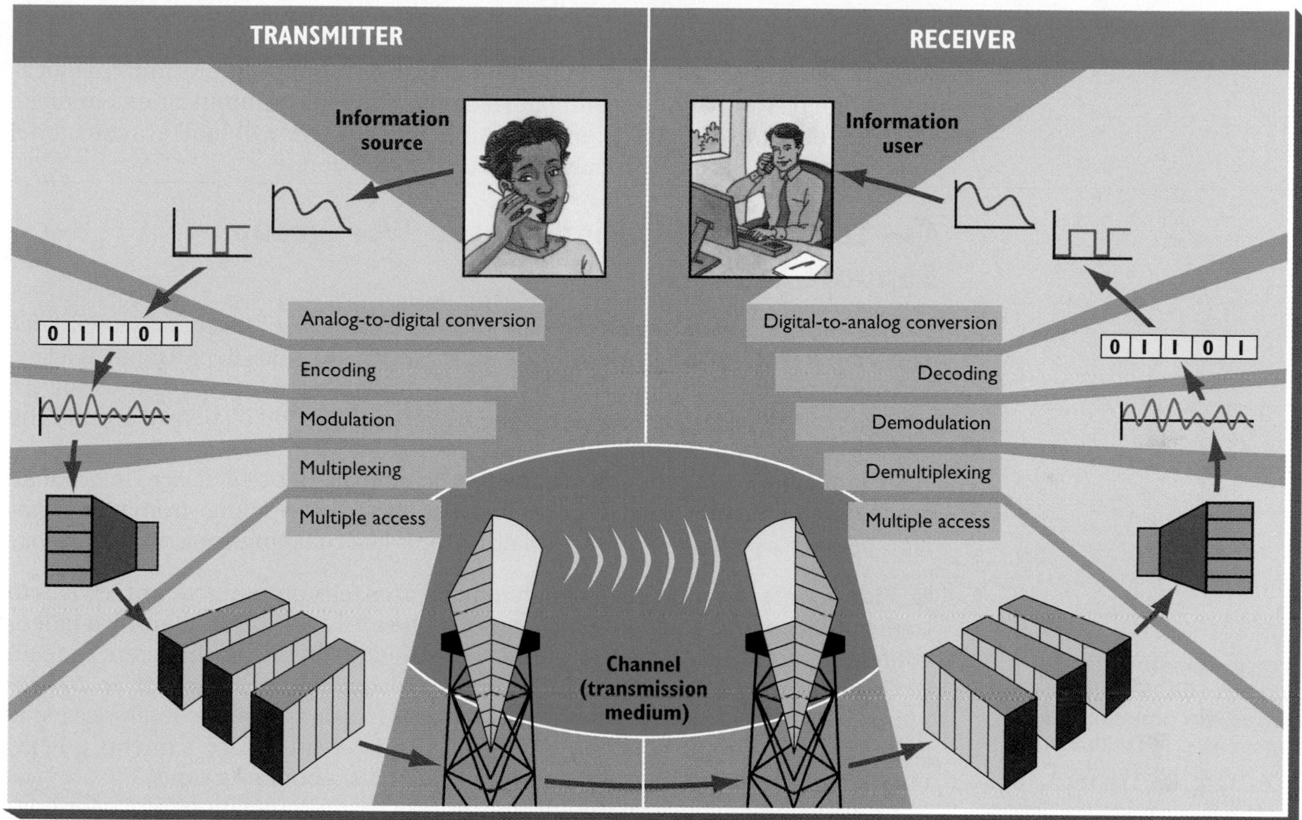

SOURCE: Reprinted with permission from *Encyclopedia Britannica*, © 1999 by Encyclopedia Britannica, Inc.

modem: the most familiar type of line adapter

telecommunications software: the computer program that controls input and output activities and other communications network functions

a telecommunications line. The most familiar line adapter is called a **modem**.[41] Finally, **telecommunications software** is the computer program that controls input and output activities and other communications network functions.

How Managers Use Telecommunications

Few of a company's information systems could function without telecommunications support. For example, apparel manufacturer and retailer Zara uses a sophisticated telecommunications system. The system includes handheld PDAs, which its store staff use to link Zara's own inventory and manufacturing facilities with point-of-sale processing devices at its retail stores. Detailed sales information is transmitted directly to headquarters, where computerized decision-support systems analyze it for trends and buying patterns. Management can then make decisions regarding inventories and production plans. Similarly, retailers such as JCPenney use telecommunications to manage in-store inventories. Its buyers get instant access to sales information from the stores and can modify their purchasing actions accordingly.

The list of ways in which businesses rely on telecommunications to support information transfer and management is endless: Delta Airline's computers automatically e-mail or fax your new reservation to your home or office; radiologists rely on telecommunications to receive digital x-rays, which they can then read from remote locations; your college uses telecommunications to allow you to access library information from your office or home; computer-assisted manufacturing systems use telecommunications to transmit information from one location in the plant to another; and banks depend on telecommunications to make their remote automatic teller machines operational. We will look at managerial applications of telecommunications in this final section.

Telecommunications-Based Workgroup Support Systems

Workgroups and work teams play important roles in just about every company. The team might be a door-assembly team at Saturn, the sales department at a Levi Strauss subsidiary, or a project team set up in a manufacturing plant to solve a quality-control problem. The team's members might all be dispersed around the city or even around the world.

Companies use a variety of telecommunications-supported devices to facilitate group communications and decision making. These devices range from very familiar tools such as e-mail to more specialized tools like collaborative writing systems.

• Videoconferencing Videoconferencing uses telecommunications devices to transmit video and audio among locations. Businesses without their own videoconference equipment can use a local FedEx Kinko's, many of which rent time on their videoconference facilities. Big-screen videoconferencing is not always required. For example, Lotus Notes enables teams of users to videoconference using their PCs, and the introduction of inexpensive PC-based video cameras quickly brought videoconferencing within easy reach of just about everyone.

group decision support system (GDSS): an interactive computer-based system used to facilitate the solution of unstructured problems

Videoconferencing can significantly improve communications and coordination among group members. It thereby helps a workgroup achieve its aims more quickly than the group could otherwise. For example, we saw that the team developing the Boeing 787 made extensive use of videoconferencing for meetings with engine suppliers and key airlines regarding the new aircraft's design.[42]

Videoconferencing is one IT tool that enables even geographically disbursed teams to work together.

• Group Decision Support Systems A **group decision support system (GDSS)** is an interactive computer-based system used to facilitate the solution of unstructured problems (such as, Should we introduce this new product?) by a team of decision makers.[43] The general aim of a GDSS (see Figure 5.6) is to allow a team of decision makers to get together (sometimes in the same room) and facilitate making a decision or completing a task. The GDSS allows team members to interact via their computers and to use a number of software tools aimed at assisting them in their decision making or project completion. Typical GDSS software tools include electronic questionnaires, electronic

FIGURE 5.6

Group Decision Support System

The Ventana Corporation's system demonstrates the features of its GroupSystems for Windows electronic meeting software, which helps people create, share, record, organize, and evaluate ideas in meetings, between offices, or around the world.

brainstorming tools, idea organizers (to help team members synthesize ideas generated during brainstorming), and tools for voting or setting priorities (so recommended solutions can be weighted and prioritized).

Using GDSS helps a workgroup avoid a lot of the group decision-making barriers that often occur in face-to-face groups. For example, there's less likelihood that one assertive person will control the whole meeting, since the computerized GDSS programs govern all the brainstorming and listing of ideas—and the voting.

collaborative writing system: a computerized system that lets a workgroup's members create long written documents (such as proposals) while working simultaneously at one of a number of interconnected or networked computers

group scheduling system: a computerized system that lets each group member put his or her daily schedule into a shared database, which enables group members to identify the most suitable times for meetings to be scheduled or to attend currently scheduled meetings

workflow automation system: a computerized system that uses an e-mail-type process to automate paperwork flow

network: a group of interconnected computers, work stations, or computer devices (such as printers and data storage systems)

● **Other Workgroup Support Systems** Other workgroup support systems are also available. For example, a **collaborative writing system** lets a workgroup's members create long written documents (such as proposals) while working simultaneously at one of a number of interconnected or networked computers. As team members work on different sections of the proposal, each member has automatic access to the rest of the sections and can modify his or her section to be compatible with the rest. A **group scheduling system** lets each group member put his or her daily schedule into a shared database, which enables group members to identify the most suitable times for meetings to be scheduled or to attend currently scheduled meetings. A **workflow automation system** uses an e-mail-type system to automate paperwork flow.[44] For example, if a proposal requires four signatures, it can be sent electronically from mailbox to mailbox for the required signatures.

Figure 5.7 summarizes how a Price Waterhouse (now PricewaterhouseCoopers) team won a consulting job by using groupware.[45] The four Price Waterhouse executives who needed to write the proposal (which was due in three days) were in three different states. But they were able to use their Lotus Notes Groupware to conduct a four-way dialogue on their screens and extract key proposal components from various Price Waterhouse databases. They could pull up résumés of the key Price Waterhouse experts to include in the proposal and borrow passages from similar proposals. The team met the deadline and won the contract.

Networks

For many of these applications, managers rely on telecommunications networks. A **network** "is a group of interconnected computers, work stations, or computer devices (such as printers and data storage systems)."[46] Local area networks (LANs)

FIGURE 5.7

Winning the Job with Groupware

Here's how Price Waterhouse put together a proposal in four days and won a multimillion-dollar consulting contract by using Lotus Notes software for groups. On Thursday a Price Waterhouse executive learned that a major securities firm was out to award a big consulting contract to help develop a complex new trading operation. Price Waterhouse was invited to bid, but there was a hitch: The proposals were due Monday. A Price Waterhouse competitor had been working on its own bid for weeks.

The four Price Waterhouse executives who were needed to write the proposal were in three different states. But they were able to work together using Notes, which allowed them to conduct a four-way dialogue on-screen. They also extracted key components of the proposal from various databases on Notes. From one, they pulled résumés of the Price Waterhouse experts from around the world who could be assigned to the job. From another, they borrowed passages from similar successful proposals. As the draft evolved, each of the four modified it or made comments. Notes kept track of the changes. Other executives looked at the proposal via Notes over the weekend.

The proposal was ready Monday, and Price Waterhouse won the deal. Its competitor didn't even meet the deadline. A year later, the client hired Price Waterhouse to audit the new operation. That contract will probably last for years.

SOURCE: Adapted from David Kirkpatrick, "Groupware Goes Boom," *Fortune*, December 27, 1993, pp. 100–101.

wide area networks (WANs), and distributed networks are three examples of managerial networks.

local area network (LAN): a group of interconnected computers, work stations, or computer devices (such as printers and data storage systems) that spans a limited distance, such as a building or several adjacent buildings

A **local area network (LAN)** spans a limited distance, such as a building or several adjacent buildings, often using the company's own telecommunications links, rather than common-carrier links like those provided by the local phone company's phone lines. At home, many people use LANs such as Bluetooth to link together their telecommunications and computer devices.

Managers generally use LANs for one or more of the following reasons: to distribute information and messages (including e-mail); to drive computer-controlled manufacturing equipment; to distribute documents (such as engineering drawings) from one department to another; to interconnect the LAN's computers with those of a public network such as the Internet; and to make equipment sharing possible (including not just printers but disk storage file servers, for instance).

wide area networks (WANs): networks that serve microcomputers over larger geographic areas, from a few miles to around the globe

distributed processing: a method for handling computerized information that generally uses small local computers (such as point-of-sale systems) to collect, store, and process information, with summary reports and information sent to headquarters as needed

Wide area networks (WANs) are networks that serve microcomputers over larger geographic areas, from a few miles to around the globe. Early WANs utilized common-carrier networks, such as the phone lines of phone companies. However, many firms today own their own wide area networks, which are essentially private, computerized telecommunications systems. For example, Benetton retail stores accumulate sales data during the day and keep them on computer disks. At night, another larger computer at corporate headquarters polls the individual retail stores' computers, accessing data that are then transmitted over telephone lines back to headquarters. Here, the information is processed and a summary of sales trends is forwarded to headquarters and individual store managers.[47]

Benetton's system also relies on distributed processing. **Distributed processing** generally uses small local computers (such as point-of-sale systems) to collect, store, and process information, with summary reports and information sent to headquarters as needed.[48]

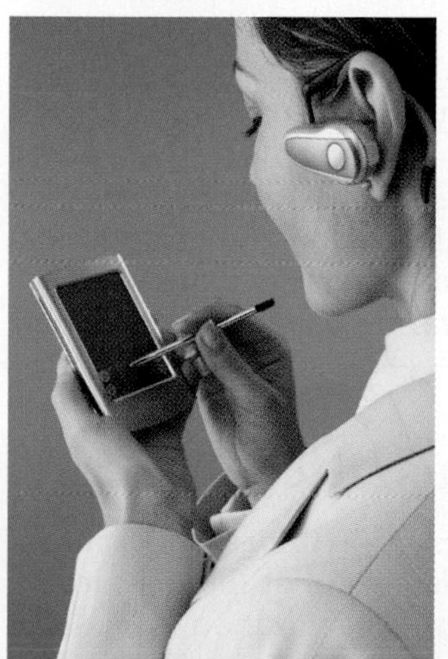

Managers use information technology in the form of computer information systems, cell phones, PDAs, fax machines, and networks to support their activities.

The Internet

Of course, the most familiar telecommunications-based network for most people is the Internet. The value of the Internet lies in its ability to connect easily and inexpensively so many people from so many places and to instantaneously supply information and access to business firms' products and data.

● How Managers Use the Internet We'll see in this book that the Internet supports a vast array of managerial activities. Whirlpool Corporation installed a Web-based supply chain management system. This new system can "talk" directly to a dealer's system for things like transmitting orders, exchanging sales data, and submitting and paying invoices. This cuts the time and cost associated with these transactions and greatly facilitates managing these operations. Just about every company uses the Internet to support the transfer of the encrypted data for their transaction-processing, MIS, decision support, and enterprise information systems, and therefore to better control their operations. Companies can, in a sense, get a free ride on the Internet and thus use it to reduce the cost of their communications. For instance, many use Voice over Internet Protocol (VoIP) in lieu of conventional telephone communications. Using groupware, the Internet makes it easier and less expensive for companies to coordinate and supervise the work of small teams that may, for instance, be opening new markets in isolated places. We will discuss more examples in the following sections.

Managing Now: Managerial Applications of Information Technology

Managers use information technology in the form of computer information systems, cell phones, PDAs, fax machines, and networks to support a vast array of their activities. Indeed, just about all the manager's planning, organizing, leading, and controlling activities rely on information technology today. We'll look at hundreds of specific examples in the following chapters. The following subsections provide an illustrative overview.

Planning: Using Information Technology for Strategic Advantage

From the day that amazon.com first went online and began pushing hundreds of bookstores out of business, managers have known that they need to make information technology part of their strategic, long-term plans. In fact, the most successful companies in their industries owe their success to building their strategic plans around information technology.

UPS is the world's largest air and ground package distribution company, delivering over 3 billion parcels and documents each year in the United States and abroad. Information technology is critical to UPS's success. Its drivers use handheld computers to capture customers' signatures along with pickup, delivery, and time-card information and automatically transmit this information back to headquarters via a wireless telephone network. UPS and its customers can then monitor and control the progress of its packages throughout the delivery process.

Other companies use information technology as part of their strategy to lock in customers so they won't switch to competitors. For example, Baxter Health Care International, Inc., which supplies almost two-thirds of all products used by U.S. hospitals, uses a stockless inventory and ordering system to lock in its hospital customers. Terminals tied to Baxter's own computers are installed in hospitals, which can then easily place an order via direct telecommunications links. The system generates shipping, billing, and inventory information and informs customers via their hospital terminals what their estimated delivery dates will be.[49] Baxter's clever plan makes it much easier for hospitals to use Baxter's products than competitors'.

Organizing: Networking the Organization Structure

Information technology also reorganizes how businesses do things. For example, by linking together employees in different departments and at different levels, group decision-making support tools help "network" the organization structure at many firms. As one New York insurance manager put it, groupware networks the corporate hierarchy "because even non-supervisory office workers plugged into groupware networks have information and intelligence previously available only to their bosses." Similarly, "networks . . . can give the rank and file new access: the ability to join in online discussions with senior executives."[50] This reorganizes things by changing who has authority for what.

For example, when Mary Joe Dirkes, a young insurance firm employee, posted a well-done memo on the network about the firm's worker's compensation efforts, top managers in New York immediately noticed her good work, and her responsibilities were soon broadened. Her message and the network also altered the chain of command, helping make the whole company more responsive:

> She now gets requests for help from around the firm via the network. When a client in Ohio needed someone with experience in cutting workplace injuries in plastics factories, Dirkes clicked into a groupware database to find an expert that could help. "Before, people would have called or sent a memo to my boss, and then he'd assign it to me. . . . Now I do it on my own."[51]

Staffing: Telecommuting

telecommuting: using telecommunications and computers from home, rather than actually commuting to the office, to get one's job done

Millions of people around the world do most of their work at home and "commute" to their employers electronically. **Telecommuting** is using telecommunications and computers from home, rather than actually commuting to the office, to get one's job done.

The typical telecommuter falls into one of three categories. Some are not employees at all but are independent entrepreneurs who work out of their homes—perhaps developing new computer applications for consulting clients, for instance. The second (and largest) group of telecommuters includes professionals and highly skilled people who work at jobs that involve a great deal of independent thought and action. These employees—computer programmers, regional salespersons, textbook editors, or research specialists, for instance—typically work at home most of the time, coming into the office only occasionally, perhaps for monthly meetings.[52] The third telecommuter category involves workers who carry out relatively routine and easily monitored jobs such as data entry or word processing.[53]

When you call American Express (Amex) for travel advice, chances are your travel counselor will not be at Amex headquarters but back home keeping one eye on the kids.[54] For a company that spends over $1 billion annually on information technology, it is probably not surprising that many of Amex's travel counselors have shifted to working at home.

American Express connects its home-workers to its phone lines and data lines for a small one-time expense of about $1,300 each, including hardware. After that, the travel counselors easily bounce information from their homes to the nearest reservation center and check fares and book reservations on their home PCs. Supervisors continue to monitor agents' calls, thus ensuring good control. Home-worker counselors handle 26 percent more calls at home than in the office, resulting in about $30,000 more in annual bookings each. Working at home often means saving three hours a day on commuting and thus translates into having more time with the family.[55]

Leading: Reengineering the Company

Every business performs various processes (sets of activities) to get its work done. Some processes are entirely embedded within some major business function such as sales, finance, manufacturing, or human resources. For example, within manufacturing, one process involves checking and maintaining inventory levels.

Many other business processes are cross-functional because they include activities in two or more departments. For example, a bank's mortgage-approval process typically involves activities in several departments. A loan officer writes up the loan application, the bank's credit department checks the prospective borrower's credit, the real-estate department inspects the property, and the loan-closing department prepares the paperwork and arranges to have its attorney meet with the customer to close the loan. This relay-race approach is not always optimal. Much time may be lost passing the loan from department to department. Customers may be lost to faster-moving rivals.

Reengineering in Practice Managers therefore increasingly reengineer their business processes.[56] In practice, reengineering usually means reorganizing the business processes around small teams of multifunctional specialists, who work together using information technology (such as wireless laptops and MISs) to accomplish the end result. Thus, the bank might have a loan officer receive a mortgage application and type it into her laptop computer, where the bank's new system automatically checks the customer's credit and sends the application to one of several mortgage-processing teams. The team, working together or virtually with wireless devices and group decision support systems, meets to reassess the person's credit, check the property's value, and approve the loan in a fraction of the time the process formerly took. Table 5.2[57] summarizes how some companies applied other reengineering principles.

Most reengineering projects stem from the installation by the company of new information systems. This is because it's usually wasteful to simply superimpose a new information system on the existing way of doing things. For example, why use a new computer system to simplify the bank's old wasteful relay-race approach to approving loans? Instead, the bank's new, reengineered loan improvement system means abolishing the former departments and reorganizing instead around the new mortgage-approval teams. It also means getting these employees to both use the new technology and work together amicably.

TABLE 5.2
Selected Principles of Reengineering Applied

Reengineering Principle	Company	Example
Organize around outcomes, not tasks.	Mutual Benefit Life	A case manager performs and coordinates all underwriting tasks centrally.
Have those who use the output of the process perform the process.	Hewlett-Packard (HP)	Department managers make a note of their own purchases using a shared database of approved vendors.
Link parallel activities during rather than at the end of the process.	Xerox	Concurrent engineering—let production participate in new-product design and engineering.
Treat geographically dispersed resources as if they are centralized.	Hewlett-Packard	Each HP division has access to a shared purchasing database.
Capture information at the source.	Mutual Benefit Life	Customer-service representatives enter application information in a central database.

Source: Adapted from Mary Summer, *Enterprise Resource Planning,* Upper Saddle River, N.J.: Prentice Hall, © 2004, p. 24. Reprinted by permission of Pearson Education, Inc., Upper Saddle River, N.J.

● **The Behavioral Side of Reengineering** Reengineering processes, as at the bank, often succeed, but many efforts fail. Sometimes employees resist the change, deliberately undermining the revised procedures. Often they don't see the advantage to themselves of making the change. As John Champy, a longtime reengineering proponent, has said:

> [Reengineering] . . . is a matter of rearranging the quality of people's attachments—to their work and to each other. These are cultural matters. . . .[58]

What Champy means is that the manager must exercise effective leadership to successfully implement the new technology-based reengineering process. He or she must overcome employees' resistance, for instance. And the manager needs to instill in the employees the values that are consistent with working in a reengineering environment. These values include:

1. To perform up to the highest measure of competence.
2. To take initiatives and risks.
3. To adapt to change.
4. To make decisions.
5. To work cooperatively as a team.
6. To be open, especially with information, knowledge, and news of forthcoming or actual problems.[59]

Controlling

Information technology's impact is particularly notable with respect to managerial control. For example, Hyundai uses wireless handheld scanners to monitor and control the 43,000 cars per year that go through one of its European import centers. The scanners read bar codes on each car. That way, all employees, from accounting to sales to the dealer, can continuously monitor each car's whereabouts.

As another example, with offices in 36 countries, Alltech Inc. (which provides products to the food and feed industries) needed a faster way to get information regarding its order status and finances worldwide. Previously, auditors at each of the company's offices around the world manually entered data onto spreadsheets. Then they sent the spreadsheets to Alltech's headquarters, where accountants compiled all this information into a master spreadsheet. Today, a Web-based software system automatically collects financial information from standardized financial accounting modules in each of the company's offices around the world and feeds this information back to headquarters. As a result, management receives consolidated financial statements in 15 days, instead of 45.

CHAPTER SUMMARY

1. Information is data presented in a form that is meaningful to the recipient. Knowledge, on the other hand, is information distilled via study or research and augmented by judgment and experience. Good-quality information must be pertinent, timely, and accurate and reduce uncertainty.
2. Information technology refers to any processes, practices, and systems that facilitate the processing and transportation of data and information. The increasingly rapid development of information technology in organizations has sped the transformation of many businesses today into

information-based organizations. The role of information technology at work is to contribute to the manager's knowledge of what is happening through analysis, interpretation, and explanation.

3. Managers at different levels in the organization require different types of information. First-line managers tend to focus on short-term, operational decisions and therefore need information that focuses on operational activities. Middle managers tend to concentrate on the intermediate range and so require information for use in tasks such as budget analysis, short-term forecasting, and variance analysis. Top managers make long-range plans and, therefore, require information that will enable them to make better strategic decisions.

4. Information systems are people, data, hardware, and procedures that work together to retrieve, process, store, and disseminate information to support decision making and control. The hierarchy of information systems used in management includes executive support systems, management information and decision support systems, and transaction-processing systems. An expert system uses computer programs to store facts and rules and to replicate the abilities and decisions of human experts. Artificial intelligence may allow computers to accomplish tasks in a manner that is considered intelligent and is characterized by learning and making decisions.

5. Decision support systems have five components: data management, knowledge management, knowledge engine, user interface, and the user.

6. An enterprise resource planning system is a companywide integrated computer system comprised of compatible software modules for each of the company's separate departments. They help managers coordinate and integrate all the functions and processes of the company.

7. Supply chain management systems help the company manage its relationship with its suppliers and retailers. They provide information to help suppliers, purchasing firms, distributors, and logistics companies coordinate, schedule, and control business processes related to supply chain management. Customer relationship management systems help the company manage all the processes involved with interacting with customers, such as taking orders, answering technical questions, and sending bills.

8. Knowledge management refers to any efforts aimed at enabling the company's managers and employees to better utilize the information available anywhere in their companies. There are four basic types of knowledge management systems: knowledge discovery systems, knowledge sharing systems, knowledge capture systems, and knowledge application systems.

9. Telecommunications is the electronic transfer of data, text, graphics, voice, or images over any distance. Telecommunications systems connect geographically separated devices through the use of lines or links, terminals, computers, line adapters, and software. They have fostered the development of numerous new computer systems applications, such as workgroup support systems.

10. Managers use IT in many ways. For example, many firms, such as UPS, design their plans around using information technology and the Internet to obtain a competitive advantage. IT and the Internet also influence how managers organize—for instance, by enabling employees throughout the company to "network" and communicate.

11. Implementing technologically advanced systems requires effective management. For example, reengineering usually involves reorganizing business processes around small teams of multifunctional specialists, who work together using information technology to accomplish the end result. Reorganizations like these typically fail if, due to ineffectual leadership, employees resist using the new equipment or simply refuse to work together cooperatively.

12. Managers at companies such as Hyundai and Alltech use IT to better control their operations. For example, IT facilitates tracking product progress and whereabouts and enables managers at headquarters to obtain, often in real time, information regarding the company's finances.

DISCUSSION QUESTIONS

1. What are the differences among data, information, and knowledge?

2. Is the content of this book information, or is it knowledge? Why?

3. What are ten examples of information technology you use every week?
4. What knowledge management system do you use for this course?
5. What is an enterprise system, and why would a manager use one?
6. What telecommunications networks do you typically use?

EXPERIENTIAL EXERCISES

1. Every morning at 8:30 there is a sixty-minute daily operations review at FedEx. Fifteen to thirty representatives of key departments like Air Operations, Computer Systems, and Meteorology attend in person or participate via conference call. The purpose of the meeting is to see what happened last night and to figure out what needs to be done today to make sure that things run as smoothly as possible. This is so important because customer service is all FedEx offers and is the heart of their strategy. The meeting is designed to ensure that it's reliable. Every weekday at 5 A.M., a recorded recap of the night's performance is made available by voice mail so that participants can check in before the meeting and review any problems they will need to discuss and solve.
   a. What concepts discussed in this chapter is FedEx using, and how do these affect the management of its operations?
   b. How would you describe the way technology has shaped FedEx's strategy and its thinking?
   c. What other examples can you give for how FedEx uses information technology?
2. Form teams with several other students in this class. Your assignment is to list the knowledge management techniques you would use for this class, using only the knowledge management and information technology devices you have with you in class.
3. Form teams with several students in this class. Choose companies you have dealt with (such as Dell Computer), and list the instances in which you believe you came in contact with their customer relationship management systems.

CASE STUDY

Information Technology Wins the Day for KnitMedia

KnitMedia is a company that owns several jazz clubs, including The Knitting Factory in New York. The company went interactive about ten years ago. The Knitting Factory presented what was billed as "the biggest live event the Internet has ever experienced." This festival, called GIG (for Global Internet Gathering), presented interactive virtual live music from London, Tokyo, Cologne, Paris, Toronto, San Francisco, Amsterdam, and Hong Kong. The company used a website linking multiple live musical venues so that, for instance, Steve Lacy in Paris played and interacted visually with a rhythm section in New York. All the KnitMedia clubs, as they go online in the future, will become part of this Internet network. Outlets for these Internet broadcasts already include the Electronic Café in Tokyo, the Café @ Boat Quay in Singapore, and Amsterdam's Paradiso. Michael Dorf, KnitMedia's CEO, knows this is only the start: What he needs are more suggestions about how he and KnitMedia can use information technology to manage its clubs and to bring consumers the music they want to hear.

1. How are music-related companies using information technology today? Compile a list of information technology applications used by KnitMedia's competitors.
2. If you were advising Michael Dorf, how would you suggest he use information technology for improving the performance of KnitMedia and its various businesses?

6 DECISION MAKING NOW

CHAPTER OUTLINE

Fortis Bank

Fortis Bank is the biggest financial institution in Belgium, but that doesn't mean it can rest on its laurels.[1] The bank's managers know that to stay ahead, it's crucial to sign up new customers and get current ones to add new services. Doing so requires a massive marketing effort. Consumers are deluged by offers of credit cards and loans from banks. Spending tens of millions of euros each year reaching out to customers requires a focused approach, or the money will be wasted. Some of the questions the bank's managers face are, for example, Which customers are most likely to purchase this new investment product? How will the market react to a drop in interest rates? Which prospects are most likely to want this new credit card? And which client profile shows the highest risk of not being able to pay back a loan?[2] The challenge facing Fortis managers is how to get answers to these questions so they can make the decisions they must make to properly focus their marketing efforts. ■

Managers at Belgium's Fortis Bank needed to know more about their customers' preferences so they could make the decisions to properly focus their marketing efforts.

BEHAVIORAL OBJECTIVES

After studying this chapter, you should be able to:

Show that you've learned the chapter's essential information by

- ➤ Distinguishing between programmed and nonprogrammed decisions.
- ➤ Listing and describing each step in the decision-making process.
- ➤ Explaining what is meant by *competing on analytics* and *business intelligence*.

Show that you can practice what you've learned here by

- Reading the exercises and explaining what decision support tools you would use.
- Reading the chapter case and identifying what triggered the problem.
- Reading the chapter case and developing a consequences matrix and a decision matrix.

Online Study Center
ACE the Test
Managing Now! LIVE

Show that you can apply what you've learned here by

- Watching the simulation video and determining the decisions made by the manager.

The Basics of Decision Making

Online Study Center
ACE the Test
Managing Now! LIVE

Everyone constantly faces the need to choose—the route to school, the job to accept, or the business strategy to pursue. A **decision** is a choice from among the available alternatives. **Decision making** is the process of developing and analyzing alternatives and making a choice.

decision: a choice made between available alternatives

decision making: the process of developing and analyzing alternatives and choosing from among them

problem: a discrepancy between a desirable and an actual situation

problem solving: the process of developing and analyzing alternatives and making a choice

Why Make Decisions?

Problems prompt most decisions. A **problem** is a discrepancy between a desirable and an actual situation. If you need $50 for a show but can only afford $10, you have a problem. Should you borrow money from a friend? Wait for ticket prices to fall? However, some decisions don't involve problems. Having two job offers to choose from is not a problem, but it still requires a decision. The problem-solving process (the steps one goes through to solve a problem) is the same as the process for making decisions. **Problem solving**, like decision making, is the process of developing and analyzing alternatives and making a choice. Most people, therefore, use the terms *decision making* and *problem solving* interchangeably.

The quality of a decision usually depends more on judgment than on raw IQ. Some smart people have poor judgment. Some less brilliant people have great judgment. *Judgment* refers to the cognitive, or thinking, aspects of the decision-making process.[3] We'll see in this chapter that emotions and biases often influence one's judgment and decisions.

Managers are always making decisions. For example, planning, organizing, leading, and controlling are the basic management functions. However, as we illustrate in Table 6.1, each of these functions calls for decisions—which plan to implement, what goals to choose, which people to hire. Furthermore, managers don't make just planning, organizing, leading, and controlling decisions. They also must make technical, job-related decisions. Table 6.2 illustrates this aspect of managerial decision making. The sales manager decides which sales representatives to use in each region and which advertising agency to use. The production manager decides between alternative suppliers and whether or not to recommend building a new plant.

Types of Decisions

Some decisions are bigger and harder to change (more strategic) than others. Buying a house is more strategic than leasing a car. Some decisions are also more

TABLE 6.1
Everything Managers Do Involves Making Decisions

Management Function	Representative Decisions
Planning	What do we want to achieve? What are our goals? What are the main opportunities and risks we face? What competitive strategy should we pursue?
Organizing	What are the main tasks we have to accomplish? How should we divide the work that needs to be done? Should I make these decisions or let subordinates make them? How should we make sure the work is coordinated?
Leading	What leadership style should I use in this situation? Why is this employee doing what he or she is doing? How should I motivate this employee? How can I get this team to perform better?
Controlling	How am I going to control this activity? Are the goals on which these controls are based out of date? Does this performance deviation merit corrective action?

TABLE 6.2
Decisions Functional Managers Make

Manager	Decisions
Accounting Manager	What accounting firm should we use? Who should process our payroll? Should we give this customer credit?
Finance Manager	What bank should we use? Should we sell bonds or stocks? Should we buy back some of our company's stock?
Human Resource Manager	Where should we recruit for employees? Should we set up a testing program? Should I advise settling the equal-employment complaint?
Production Manager	Which supplier should we use? Should we build the new plant? Should we buy the new machine?
Sales Manager	Which sales rep should we use in this region? Should we use this advertising agency? Should we lower prices in response to our competitor's doing so?

obvious than others. If your car is out of gas, you must fill the tank. The bigger, strategic decisions usually take more thought, as we will see.

Similarly, some decisions are more routine than others. In general, managers try not to have to make the same decision twice. The manager of a Macy's store does not want clerks to check with her every time customers make returns. She wants to focus on the big decisions—for instance, on what to buy for the fall line of clothes. Thus, managers endeavor to premake (or program) as many decisions as they can. Employees can make these decisions more or less automatically.

programmed decision: a decision that is repetitive and routine and can be made by using a definite, systematic procedure

nonprogrammed decision: a decision that is unique and novel

● Programmed and Nonprogrammed Decisions Many (or most) management decisions are therefore programmed. **Programmed decisions** (really, *programmable* decisions) are decisions the manager can set up to be made in advance. Usually, the manager creates rules or policies to help employees make these decisions.[4] Managers want to be able to focus their attention on the big decisions, like how to deal with competitors. Therefore, they write policy, procedure, and rule manuals to help employees make the routine (programmed) decisions on their own.

In contrast, managers usually cannot make **nonprogrammed decisions** in advance. Nonprogrammed (really, *nonprogrammable*) decisions are unique and novel, and they often involve issues of grave importance to the company. For example, strategic decisions (Should we expand overseas?) usually can't be programmed (made) in advance. When the issue arises, the manager needs to analyze the decision carefully and weigh his or her various options and pros and cons. Decisions like these also (given their unpredictability and broad effects) tend to be high risk. Nonprogrammed decisions tend to require intuition, creativity, and judgment and all the information that the manager can muster. Most of the decision-making skills in this chapter aim to improve one's ability to make these nonprogrammed decisions.

Some experts estimate that 90 percent of all management decisions in companies are programmed and so get made more or less automatically.[5] In many state universities, the decision concerning which students to admit is made by mathematically weighing each candidate's test scores and grades. Most firms try to program inventory decisions, such as "reorder ten units of item A when the number of item A in the bin drops to two." When you swipe your credit card at a point of purchase, the computerized card-acceptance decision is a programmed one. The cashier refers the decision to a credit manager only if there's a problem.

Managers distinguish between programmed and nonprogrammed decisions because the manager's time is precious. The more decisions he or she can program or make routine, the less time he or she must devote to them. The manager's subordinates or systems can make these decisions routinely. The *principle of exception*, then, is: bring only exceptions to the (routine) way things should be to the manager's attention.

● Tools for Making Programmed and Nonprogrammed Decisions Table 6.3 compares programmed and nonprogrammed decisions. Making programmed decisions usually involves applying rules, for example, "you may give that person a refund if the jacket is not damaged." Computers are efficient at the automated application of rules. For example, they can compute take-home pay based on tax deductions and other such rules.

Nonprogrammed decisions generally require a very different decision-making methodology because it's difficult to preplan (program) how to respond to problems that are unexpected and unique. One writer says, "[T]hese are the kinds of decisions managers get paid to make."[6] Deciding what career to pursue, which

TABLE 6.3
Comparing Programmed and Nonprogrammed Decisions

	Programmed	Nonprogrammed
Nature of decision	Recurring and predictable; well-defined information and decision criteria	Unpredictable; ambiguous information; shifting decision criteria
Decision-making strategy	Reliance on rules and computation	Reliance on principles, judgment, creative problem-solving processes
Decision-making tools	Policies and rules; capital budgeting; computerized solutions	Judgment; intuition, creativity; computerized decision support systems and modeling

job to take, whether to move across the country, and who to marry are personal nonprogrammed decisions. Deciding whether to buy a $1 million machine or to expand to Asia are nonprogrammed business decisions. These decisions rely heavily on judgment and on access to information. We will spend much of this chapter showing you how to do a better job of making nonprogrammed decisions.

Decision-Making Models: How Do People Make Decisions?

You own a retail store and must decide which of several trucks to buy for deliveries. If you are like most people, you probably assume that you would be quite rational in deciding. For example, wouldn't you size up all your options and their pros and cons? Perhaps. **Decision theory** refers (most broadly) to the body of knowledge concerned with understanding and predicting how people make decisions. We'll see later in his chapter that *decision theory* also refers more narrowly to using quantitative methods to analyze and make decisions. We'll focus next on two widely known and important schools of thought (or theories of decision making) regarding how people make decisions: the classical approach and the administrative approach.

decision theory: the body of knowledge concerned with understanding and predicting how people make decisions

● The Classical Approach The idea that managers are totally rational when making decisions has a long and honorable tradition in economic and management theory. Early classical economists needed a simplified way to explain economic phenomena, such as how demand affects prices. To come up with a workable theory, they accepted a number of simplifying assumptions. Specifically, they assumed that the rational manager:

1. Had complete or "perfect" information about the situation, including the full range of goods and services available on the market and the exact price of each good or service.
2. Could distinguish perfectly between the problem and its symptoms.
3. Could identify all criteria and accurately weigh all the criteria according to his or her preferences.

4. Could accurately calculate and choose the alternative with the highest perceived value.[7]

5. Could, therefore, be expected to make an optimal choice without being confused by irrational thought processes.

bounded rationality: the boundaries on rational decision making imposed by one's values, abilities, and limited capacity for processing information

satisfice: to stop the decision-making process when a satisfactory alternative is found rather than reviewing solutions until the optimal alternative is discovered

● **The Administrative Approach** The assumptions listed above leave something to be desired. For example, does anyone really (even with the Internet) ever have perfect knowledge of all the options?

Herbert Simon and his associates proposed a decision-making model they believe better reflects reality. They agree that decision makers try to be rational. However, they point out that such rationality is, in practice, subject to many constraints: "The number of alternatives [the decision maker] must explore is so great, the information he would need to evaluate them so vast that even an approximation to objective rationality is hard to conceive. . . ."[8]

For example, most people probably would not check out every possible local store before buying a plasma t.v. Experiments support this commonsense notion. In one classic series of studies, participants were required to make decisions based on the amount of information transmitted on a screen. Most people quickly reached a point of information overload and began adjusting in several ways. Some omitted or ignored some of the information; others gave only approximate responses (such as "about 25" instead of "24.6"). Based on a review of other evidence, one expert concluded, "Even the simplest decisions, expressed in the conventional form of a decision tree, rapidly overwhelm human cognitive capabilities."[9]

"So that is unanimous then - nobody has a clue what to do."

Based on realities like these, Simon argues that bounded rationality more accurately represents how managers actually make decisions.[10] **Bounded rationality** means that a manager's decision making is only as rational as his or her unique values, abilities, and limited capacity for processing information permit him or her to be.

There are two main things managers can learn from Simon's administrative approach. One is to always remember that most people can't and don't keep searching until they find the perfect solution—they don't optimize. Optimize means search for the perfect solution. Most people, Simon says, **satisfice**; that is, they search for solutions until they find a satisfactory one. They look for the optimal solution only in exceptional cases.[11]

The second thing managers can learn from Simon is that many cognitive biases and traps lie in wait for unsuspecting managers. Wise managers thus take their own values, biases, abilities, and various other psychological traps into account before making decisions.

How to Make Decisions

Online Study Center
ACE the Test
Managing Now! LIVE

Some assume that good judgment is like a good singing voice—you have it or you don't. However, that's not true. As with singing, it certainly helps to have the raw material. But a conscientious effort at improving decision-making skills can turn anyone into a better decision maker. In this section, we look at the steps in the decision-making process: the steps that a decision maker uses to arrive at a decision. These steps include:

- Define the problem.
- Clarify your objectives.
- Identify alternatives.
- Analyze the consequences.
- Make a choice.

Step 1: Define the Problem[12]

Identifying or defining a problem is trickier than it may appear. People commonly emphasize the obvious and get misled by symptoms.[13] Here is a classic example. Office workers were upset because they had to wait so long for an elevator. Tenants were threatening to move. The owners called in a consulting team and told them the problem was that the elevators were running too slow.

If you agree with defining the problem as "slow-moving elevators," then the potential solutions are all expensive. You could ask the tenants to stagger their work hours, but that request could cause more animosity. Adding more elevators is too expensive.

The point is that the alternatives you identify and the decisions you make reflect how you define the problem. What the consultants did in this case was define the problem as "The tenants are upset because they have to wait for an elevator." The solution they chose was to have full-length mirrors installed by each bank of elevators so the tenants could admire themselves while waiting! The solution was inexpensive and satisfactory: The complaints virtually disappeared. In decision making, **framing** refers to the idea that how the decision maker defines (frames) the problem determines what the solutions will be and thus the quality of the decision. *Never* take the statement of the problem for granted.

framing: the notion that how the decision maker defines the problem determines what the solutions will be and what the quality of the decision will be

How to Define the Problem The consultants' clever solution to the elevator problem described above illustrates the first and most important step in defining problems: always ask, What triggered this problem? Luckily for the owners, the consultants did not jump to any conclusions. They asked themselves, What triggered the problem? The answer, of course, was the tenants' complaints, complaints triggered by frustration at having to wait. The problem then became: How do we reduce or eliminate frustration with having to wait?

There are some useful hints to keep in mind here.[14] Start by writing down your initial assessment of the problem. Then, dissect it. Ask, What triggered this problem (as I've assessed it)? Why am I even thinking about solving this problem? What is the connection between the trigger and the problem? That's how the consultants approached defining the problem—and how you should, too.

Application Example Harold has had his job as marketing manager for Universal Widgets, Inc., for about five years, and he has been happy with his job. However, the recent widget downturn wreaked havoc with the company's business, and it had to cut about 10 percent of the staff. Harold's boss gave him the bad news: "We like the work you've been doing here, but we're closing the New York office. We want you to stay with Universal, though, so we found you a similar position with our plant in Pittsburgh." Harold is thrilled. He tells his parents, "I have to move to Pittsburgh, but at least I still have a job. The problem is, where should I live?" He immediately starts investigating housing possibilities in Pittsburgh. His father thinks Harold may be jumping the gun. What would you do?

Harold's father is right. Harold jumped to the conclusion that his problem now is finding a place to live in Pittsburgh. Is that really the main decision he has to make? Why is Harold even thinking about solving this problem? What triggered this problem? What is the connection between the trigger and the problem? The trigger was his boss's comment that Universal no longer needed his services in New York and that it was, therefore, transferring him to Pittsburgh. What's the real problem Harold must face here? Let us assume that the issue—and the decision Harold really must make—is this: Should I move to Pittsburgh with Universal Widgets? Or should I try to get the best marketing manager job I can, and if so, where?[15]

Step 2: Clarify Your Objectives

Most people are looking to achieve several aims when making a decision. For example, in choosing a location for a new plant, the manager typically wants to achieve several objectives, such as minimize distance from the company's customers, get close to raw materials, and have access to a good labor supply.

● Have More Than One Objective Therefore, few managers would make a decision with just a single objective in mind. (There are exceptions. The great football coach Vince Lombardi once said, "Winning isn't everything. It's the only thing.") However, for most decisions, most people do not have the luxury of focusing like a laser on one single objective. When deciding on a new laptop computer, you may want to get the most memory, portability, and reliability you can for the price. You'd buy the one that, on balance, best satisfied all these objectives. You'd avoid the trap of making your decision as if minimizing price was your only aim.

● How to Clarify Objectives Your objectives should provide an explicit expression of what you really want. If you don't have clear objectives, you will not be able to evaluate your alternatives. For example, if Harold isn't clear about whether or not he wants to stay close to New York, wants at least a 10 percent raise, or wants to stay in the widget industry, how could he possibly decide whether to stay with Universal Widgets or leave—or which of several job offers were best? The answer is, he could not.

How do you decide what you want the decision to accomplish for you? Here is a useful five-step procedure:[16]

1. *Write down all the concerns you hope to address through your decision.* The idea here is to make a comprehensive list of everything you hope to accomplish with your decision. Harold's concerns include the impact of his decision on his long-term career, enjoying what he's doing, living close to a large urban center, and earning more money than he earns now.

2. *Convert your concerns into specific, concrete objectives.* Make your objectives measurable. Harold's concerns translate into these objectives: getting a job that puts him in a position to be marketing director within two years; getting a job with a consumer products company; being within a one-hour drive of a city with a population of at least 1 million people; and earning at least $1,200 per week.

3. *Separate ends from means to establish your fundamental objectives.* This step helps you zero in on what you really want. One way to do this is to ask "why." Harold asks himself, "Why do I want to live within a one-hour drive of a city with a population of at least 1 million people?" Because he wants to make sure he can meet many other people who are his own age and because he enjoys what he sees as big-city benefits such as museums. This helps clarify what Harold really wants. For example, a smaller town might do if the town has the right demographics and cultural attractions.
4. *Clarify what you mean by each objective.* Banish fuzzy thinking. For example, "getting a raise" is a fuzzy objective. Harold, to his credit, wants to earn at least $1,200 per week.
5. *Test your objectives to see if they capture your interests.* This is your reality check. Harold carefully reviews his full list of final objectives to make sure they completely capture what he wants to accomplish with his decision.

Step 3: Identify Alternatives

You must have a choice (in other words, two or more options or alternatives) if you are going to make an effective decision. Wise managers, therefore, usually ask, What are my options? What are my alternatives? Decision-making experts call alternatives the raw material of decision making. They say that alternatives represent "the range of potential choices you'll have for pursuing your objectives."[17]

● How to Identify Alternatives There are several techniques for generating alternatives. Be creative; start by trying to generate alternatives yourself, and then expand your search by checking with other people, including experts. (We'll discuss creativity below.) Also, look at each objective and ask yourself how you could achieve each of them. For example, Harold might ask, "How could I get a position that would lead to a marketing director's job within two years?" One obvious alternative is to take a senior marketing manager's job, a job just a notch below director. However, remember that most managers satisfice. It's rarely productive to spend the time required to find the optimal solution.

● Application Example Through this process, Harold generates several feasible alternatives. He can take the Pittsburgh Universal Widget job, or he can leave the company. If he leaves, his search for alternatives turns up four other possible alternatives: a job with a dot-com as senior manager in New York; a marketing director's job with Ford in Detroit; and two other marketing manager jobs, one with a pet-food company in Newark and one with Nokia in Washington, D.C.

Step 4: Analyze the Consequences

The danger in making decisions is that you make them today, but you feel them tomorrow. Harold decides today to stay with Universal. Then he finds out next year that his prospects of promotion are almost nil because the company already has two Pittsburgh marketing directors. "If only I'd thought of that," Harold says. The manager never wants to have to say, "If only I'd thought of that."

Therefore, the next decision-making step is to analyze (think through) the consequences of choosing each alternative. One expert says, "This is often the most difficult part of the decision-making process, because this is the stage that typically requires forecasting future events."[18] Harold needs a practical way to determine what the consequences of each of his alternatives are. Only then can he decide which option is best.

● **How to Analyze the Consequences** The decision maker's job is to think through, for each alternative, what the consequences of choosing that alternative will be *for each of the objectives*. Here is a basic three-step process to use:[19]

1. *Mentally put yourself in the future.* For example, Harold imagines to himself, here I am one year later in Pittsburgh. Can I get the director's job? No! They already have two directors. Looking into the future is a crucial analytical skill.
2. *Eliminate any clearly inferior alternatives.* For example, if Harold thinks through the consequences of each of his alternatives, it should be obvious that his prospects for promotion to marketing director are virtually nil if he stays with Universal Widgets. Therefore, why should he even continue considering this alternative? He crosses it off.
3. *Organize your remaining alternatives into a consequences table.* A consequences matrix (or table) lists your objectives down the left side of the page and your alternatives along the top. In each box of the matrix, put a brief description that shows the consequences of that alternative for that objective. This provides a concise, bird's-eye view of the consequences of pursuing each alternative.

consequences matrix: in decision making, a grid showing possible alternatives on a vertical axis and one's objectives on a horizontal axis

● **Application Example** Harold started with five alternatives and four basic objectives. Here they are in a **consequences matrix**, along with what he sees as the consequences for each one:

Objective / Alternative	Marketing director in two years	Consumer products company	One-hour drive from major city	Earn at least $1,200 per week
Marketing manager, Universal Widgets, Pittsburgh	Little or no possibility—eliminated this option	NA—eliminated this option	NA—eliminated this option	NA—eliminated this option
Senior manager, dot-com, New York City	High probability—if company survives that long	Consumer-oriented, but does not really sell products	Yes, excellent	$1,250 plus stock options
Marketing manager, Ford, Detroit	Moderate possibility—bigger company, longer climb	Yes, but not as interesting as selling widgets. I may get bored.	Yes	$1,100 plus great benefits (discount on new T-bird)
Marketing manager, pet foods, Newark	High probability—small, growing company with little marketing expertise now	Yes, but not quite as interesting as selling widgets	Yes	$1,200
Marketing manager, Nokia, Washington, D.C.	Fairly high probability—fast-growing company	Yes—exciting industry	Yes—exceptional cultural attractions and demographics	$1,200

Step 5: Make a Choice

Your analysis is useless unless you make the right choice. Under perfect conditions, making the right choice is easy. Review the consequences of each alternative, and choose the alternative that achieves your objectives. But in practice, making a decision—even a simple one like choosing a computer—sometimes can't be done so rationally. Psychology and emotions can drive decisions and make the choice more difficult.[20] And not having all the facts can produce choices that are less than optimal. In today's unforgiving business environment, managers must have the facts so they can make informed decisions.[21] We turn to this topic next.

Managing Now: Technology-Supported Decision Making

Several years ago, Vermont-based Ben & Jerry's Ice Cream had a problem. Dozens of people were suddenly calling its hotline to complain that the company's famous Cherry Garcia ice cream didn't have enough cherries. Ben & Jerry's managers had to make a decision. Should they tell the plant to add more cherries? Ignore the callers? Get more information?

As at Ben & Jerry's, decisions are no better than the information on which they're based. For example, how can Ben & Jerry's possibly identify the problem without getting information from their factory and from other sources? How can they identify alternatives or analyze the consequences of those alternatives without information? They cannot, not without the right information.

Competing on Analytics

When Alan Mulally recently took over as Ford's new CEO, newsapers referred to him as "an engineer's engineer"—meaning that he doesn't make decisions based just on gut feel; he wants to see the data. Some managers still take a laid-back, informal approach to sizing up situations. However, many others, like Al Mulally, compete based on analytics: their decisions are heavily fact-based. They want to make informed decisions.

Author Michael Lewis wrote a best-selling book called *Moneyball.* It describes how the Oakland A's baseball team uses statistical data analysis to improve their performance. Some baseball managers go by their gut in deciding questions like, Who should we put up at bat if we have two outs and runners on first and third, and we are facing a left-handed pitcher? Not the A's. Whether scouting players or deciding how much to raise stadium prices, the A's, and some other teams, rely on data analysis.[22]

Marriott International has a hotel program called Total Hotel Optimization. The team running this program uses knowledge management and decision support software, and statistical analysis. Marriott can now send just the right offerings to frequent customers, for instance, and price the rooms at each hotel at the right level, given the dates and weather conditions.[23] Like the A's, Marriott International competes based on analytics.[24] Figure 6.1 shows some more examples

FIGURE 6.1

How Companies Use Analytics

Analytics competitors make expert use of statistics and modeling to improve a wide variety of functions. Here are some common applications:

Function	How Use Analytics	Exemplars
SUPPLY CHAIN	Simulate and optimize supply chain flows; reduce inventory and stock-outs.	Dell, Wal-Mart, Amazon
CUSTOMER SELECTION, LOYALTY, AND SERVICE	Identify customers with the greatest profit potential; increase likelihood that they will want the product or service offering; retain their loyalty.	Harrah's, Capital One, Barclay's
PRICING	Identify the price that will maximize yield or profit.	Progressive, Marriott
HUMAN CAPITAL	Select the best employees for particular tasks or jobs, at particular compensation levels.	New England Patriots, Oakland A's, Boston Red Sox
PRODUCT AND SERVICE QUALITY	Detect quality problems early and minimize them.	Honda, Intel
FINANCIAL PERFORMANCE	Better understand the drivers of financial performance and the effects of nonfinancial factors.	MCI, Verizon
RESEARCH AND DEVELOPMENT	Improve quality, efficacy, and, where applicable, safety of products and services.	Novartis, Amazon, Yahoo

of how companies use this analytical approach to make better decisions. Analytical companies like Marriott have several attributes, which we discuss next.

● **They Use Quantitative Modeling** A quantitative model is a mathematical representation (like Einstein's famous $E=mc^2$) of some activity. Summarizing the activity in mathematical terms lets the manager study the activity and perform "what if" analyses. Capital One Bank conducts more than 30,000 analyses each year to maximize the likelihood of signing up potential customers who are also good credit risks. To do this, it uses decision support systems and data mining to sift through hundreds of customer variables such as age, address, savings, net worth, and credit history. Then they use models such as, If we send mailings to people with these age, address, savings, net worth, and credit history traits, how likely is it that they'll respond to our offer for a new credit card?" Capital One Bank does not make multimillion-dollar promotional decisions based on intuition. They compete based on analytics.

UPS uses a similar approach. For example, its customer intelligence group uses data mining and modeling to predict customer defections. They track variables like usage patterns and complaints.[25] They know, based on their models, that when customers' usage patterns and complaints change in particular ways, the customers defect to FedEx. So if UPS sees that pattern for a big customer, a UPS salesperson contacts that customer to resolve the problem.

● **They Hire and Develop Analytical People** Companies like Capital One Bank and UPS don't hire just mathematicians and engineers, although that is part of it. They encourage all employees to back up and defend their decisions with facts. And they provide all their employees with the necessary technological support for obtaining the data they need and analyzing it.

● **They Make Extensive Use of Technological Decision-Making Support** Analytical companies rely heavily on information technology to get the information they need. Most have ". . . invested many millions of dollars in systems that snatch data from every conceivable source. Enterprise resource planning, customer relationship management, point-of-sale, and other systems ensure that no transaction or other significant exchange occurs without leaving a mark."[26]

Dell Computer spends hundreds of millions of dollars each year sending special promotions to businesses and consumers via mail, e-mail, and other means. How do they decide who gets what offers? They spent seven years building a database that contains millions of records on the sales results by region for all the company's print, television, and other ads. Dell then uses its computerized decision support systems to retrieve, analyze, and draw conclusions that help it maximize the impact of its marketing dollars.[27] The Window on Managing Now feature shows some important information technology–based analytics support tools.

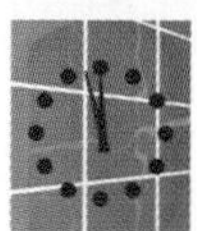

WINDOW ON MANAGING NOW

Analytics Tools

SAS© offers a decision support package called SAS© Analytics, which includes several software tools, listed below. These are the IT-based decision tools managers can use.

- *Statistics.* The *statistics* tool enables the manager to use statistical analysis to analyze relationships and to produce decisions based on facts.
- *Data and text mining.* This software enables the manager to mine or retrieve and to sift through the data in the company's data warehouse (where it holds the data it collects from its day-to-day sales, billing, and other transactions). This helps the manager identify trends and to make predictions and better decisions.
- *Forecasting.* This software takes the data and lets the manager predict outcomes based on historical patterns.
- *Econometrics.* This software enables the manager to apply statistical methods to the data and trends, thus helping him or her to better understand the trends.
- *Quality improvement.* This software enables the manager to identify, monitor, and measure quality processes and trends over time.
- *Operations research.* This software enables the manager to apply mathematical techniques to analyze the data and thus to achieve the best result.[28]

Managing Now: Business Intelligence

Faced with complaints from people claiming that their Cherry Garcia ice cream lacked enough cherries, Ben & Jerry's managers didn't jump to conclusions, for instance, by adding more cherries to the recipe. Instead, they analyzed the information.

Ben & Jerry's decision support software mines all the data that the company collects every day from all its operations, from production and sales to finance and customer service. Then its decision support systems find and retrieve the data its managers need to make their decisions, and then analyze it.[29]

By using their decision support software to review (on desktop computerized charts) the information from all their operations, Ben & Jerry's managers methodically eliminated possible causes. The desktop charts enabled managers to click on particular charts (such as purchase by region) and to drill down and find the underlying data (such as on purchases of Cherry Garcia ice cream by region). It was not a regional problem (complaints came from all over the country). And the factory was adding enough cherries.

What was the problem? Someone had changed the photo on the ice cream carton so that it showed Cherry Garcia frozen yogurt by mistake. Ben & Jerry's Cherry Garcia frozen yogurt is pinker and has more cherries than Cherry Garcia ice cream. So consumers thought they were being shortchanged! Management changed the photo on the box, and complaints stopped.[30] Good information—what many experts call business intelligence—helped Ben & Jerry's define the problem and take corrective action.

business intelligence (BI): synonymous with *decision support system (DSS),* namely, a set of software applications and tools that transform data into a form that managers can use to make better, faster decisions; also, the information (intelligence) itself on which the manager makes his or her decision

● **Business Intelligence** Managers use the phrase **business intelligence (BI)** in two ways. First, they use it more or less synonymously with the phrase *decision support system (DSS)* (discussed in Chapter 5) to refer to a set of software applications and tools that transform data into a form that managers can use to make better, faster decisions.[31] Second, they use the phrase *business intelligence* to refer to the information (intelligence) itself on which the manager makes his or her decision. Thus, the business intelligence Ben & Jerry's got from its analyses helped its managers to decide what to do. It used its business intelligence systems to produce that information.

Business intelligence thus helps managers make better decisions. As a consequence of doing business, companies continuously collect enormous amounts of data from their sales, finance, customer-service, and other systems. This information is of little use if the manager cannot access, manipulate, and analyze it. As we explained earlier in this book, a decision support system is a set of computerized tools that helps managers access and use information to make decisions. Ben & Jerry's managers used the firm's decision support system (DSS) to compile, analyze, and present all these data (from the sales and production departments, for instance) and thus produce the business intelligence its managers needed to make the Cherry Garcia decision.

Recall that decision support systems have five basic components:[32]

- The *data management* component retrieves, stores, and organizes the data.
- The *model management* system retrieves, stores, and organizes the quantitative and statistical models that the decision support system uses to analyze the data and make predictions.
- The *knowledge engine* does the actual reasoning for the system.

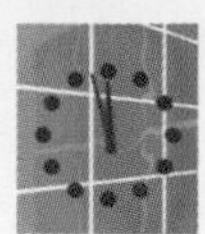

Window on Managing Now
Baylor University

High school seniors shop around like never before to find a college that best fits their needs.[33] As Tom Bohannon, Baylor's assistant vice president of information management and testing services, puts it, "[O]ne of Baylor's primary challenges is managing enrollment while dealing with factors such as the economy, over which we have no control. . . ."[34]

To enable Baylor to compete in such an environment, it uses customer relationship management, data warehousing, and data-mining software packages from SAS. This enables Baylor's administrators to retrieve and analyze student data from all the sources that touch a student, including admissions, academic affairs, and student affairs. For example, they know when each student first makes contact, what information he or she received in the mail, whether that student visited campus, and what his or her major interests are. Baylor's administrators can then follow the students through their application and enrollment process and even see when a student applies for a job or a scholarship.

What all this gives Baylor is the ability to mine a rich trove of data and to get the business intelligence Baylor needs to compete for students. For example, suppose the question is, How should we target our mailings to prospective students? Baylor's information systems use about twenty variables for predicting how Baylor should target its initiatives. The variables include the student prospects' test scores; extracurricular activities; the distance they live from Baylor; whether their parents are alumni; whether they visited the school; and whether Baylor contacted them, or vice versa. Based on such information, Baylor's decision support systems use quantitative models (equations) that can predict, based on past experience, which prospective students are most likely to enroll. So "if a student received a high [likely to enroll] score, he or she would receive an expensive marketing brochure about Baylor."[35] As Bohannon says, "SAS has helped us become more efficient in targeting and streamlining our materials and expenses." Even educational institutions today compete on analytics.

Baylor University relies on information technology to attract, enroll, and provide a top-notch educational experience for its students.

- The *user interface* consists of the tools (such as the keyboard and screen) that the manager uses to interact with the system. The user interface also often includes a computerized video dashboard. For example, Ben & Jerry's manufacturing management dashboard might include (among other things) a bar graph showing fruit ingredients used per pound of ice cream.
- Finally, the *user* is the decision maker who is actually using and controlling the decision support system.

At Ben & Jerry's, the business intelligence effort drew on data from dozens of the company's information systems. For example, it tapped into the company's customer relationship management system to get more information on the actual complaints (who they're coming from, and what the consumers were saying, for instance). It tapped the company's enterprise systems to see if the plant was using too few cherries. It tapped its knowledge management system to see if there had been similar complaints before. And it tapped its supply chain system to see if the plant was purchasing too few cherries. Its managers could access and view all this information on their desktop dashboards and thereby analyze it and determine what the real problem was. The Window on Managing Now feature illustrates business intelligence in action.

How to Make Even Better Decisions

Online Study Center
ACE the Test
Managing Now! LIVE

Experts recommend various techniques to help managers improve the quality of their decisions. We'll discuss several of these techniques in the following sections.

Increase Your Knowledge

"Knowledge is power," someone once said, and that's particularly true in making decisions. Even the simplest decisions—like mapping the route to work each morning—become difficult without basic information, such as the traffic report. To increase your knowledge, ask questions, get experience, use consultants, do research, and use decision support systems.

● Ask Questions Use the six main question words—Who? What? Where? When? Why? How? In buying a used car, for instance, ask the following questions using these question words: *Who* is selling the car, and who previously owned it? *What* do similar cars sell for? *What* is wrong with this car? *Where* did the owner service it? *When* did the owner buy it? *Why* does the owner want to sell? *How* much do you think you could buy it for? Most people could save themselves aggravation by arming themselves with good questions.

● Get Experience For many endeavors, there's no substitute for experience. For example, many students find that interning in a job similar to the occupation they plan to pursue can help in clarifying whether that occupation is right for them. Similarly, multinational corporations with experience in a particular country generally opt for ownership of foreign affiliates. Less-experienced companies tend to establish joint ventures in foreign markets, in part to develop the required expertise.[36]

● Use Consultants Managers use consultants' experience (such as in personnel testing or strategic planning) to supplement their own lack of experience in particular areas. Sometimes, just talking the problem over with other people can help, particularly if they've had experience solving similar problems.

● Do Research Whatever the decision, there's usually a wealth of information you can tap. For example, are you thinking of moving employees from New York City to Washington, D.C.? How do salaries in Washington compare with those in New York? Websites like salary.com can answer that question easily.

● Use Decision Support Systems We saw that using data mining and other decision support system tools is an invaluable way to get the business intelligence a manager needs. The Practice IT feature shows how [illegible] did this.

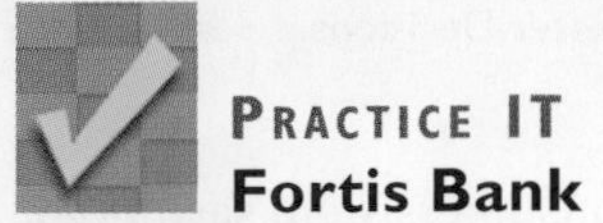

Practice IT
Fortis Bank

Fortis Bank managers had to decide how to target the millions of dollars of marketing programs they offered each year. But to do so, they needed information. The bank already had a relatively untapped customer database. It included an enormous amount of data that the bank's transaction-processing systems collected. These data included facts and figures on each customer such as age, income, savings, other investments, payment patterns, and whether each person responded favorably to a particular bank offering.[37]

Fortis Bank decided to install a new SAS Enterprise Miner decision-support software package. It enables Fortis's marketing analysts to sift through all these data, for instance by income level, age, and credit history. It also enabled them to identify which customers (based on age, address, income, and so on) were historically more likely to respond to particular offerings. That way, Fortis Bank could create models—mathematical equations—that predicted who would best respond to an offering. They could determine, for example, that people with a certain income level, Zip Code, savings level, spending level, credit rating, and so on will more likely want a gold credit card.

SAS Enterprise Miner is Web-based, so the bank's managers can access it wherever they are. Says the bank's commercial analysis manager, "SAS Enterprise Miner gave us a greater understanding of customer motivations. We can now fully exploit the data regarding our customers' buying patterns and behavior."[38] The business intelligence that Fortis Bank thereby derives enables the bank to make fact-based decisions, to compete on analytics.

Use Your Intuition

Several years ago, Malcolm Gladwell published a popular book named *Blink: The Power of Thinking Without Thinking*. His basic point was that people tend to make quick, snap decisions, and to do so based on intuition. Psychiatrist Sigmund Freud made the following similar observation:

> When making a decision of minor importance, I have always found it advantageous to consider all the pros and cons. In vital matters, however, such as the choice of a mate or a profession, the decision should come from the unconscious, from somewhere within ourselves. In the important decisions of our personal life, we should be governed, I think, by the deep inner needs of our nature.[39]

Another expert says you can usually tell when a decision fits your needs because it brings a sense of relief. Good decisions, he says, are the best tranquilizers ever invented; bad ones often increase your anxiety.[40]

intuition: the cognitive process whereby a person instinctively makes a decision based on his or her accumulated knowledge and experience

These experts are talking about intuition. **Intuition** is the cognitive process whereby a person instinctively makes a decision based on his or her accumulated knowledge and experience. Psychologist Gary Klein tells this story to illustrate intuitive decision making. A fire commander and his crew encounter a fire. The commander leads his team into the building. Standing in the living room, they blast water onto the smoke and flames, which appear to be consuming the kitchen, yet the fire roars back. The fire's persistence baffles the commander. His men douse the kitchen fire again, but it flares up again. Suddenly, an uneasy feeling grips the commander. His intuition tells him to order everyone to leave. Just as the crew reaches the street, the living room floor caves in. The fire was in the basement, not the kitchen. Had they been in the house, the men would have plunged into an inferno.[41]

As this story shows, we often reach intuitive decisions by quickly and unthinkingly comparing our present situation to situations we've faced in the past. In his study of firefighters, Klein found they accumulate experiences and "subconsciously categorize fires according to how they should react to them."[42] The fire commander did this: the fire, based on his experience, just didn't make sense. The floor muffled the sounds of the fire and retarded the transfer of heat. The commander, standing with his men in the living room, felt that something was wrong: what he originally thought was a kitchen fire seemed too quiet and too cool. His intuition saved them.

● **Intuition's Limitations** Yet in practice, intuition can also be misleading.[43] For example, studies show that people tend to take higher-than-normal risks when they want to recover a previous loss. (The trap is called escalation of commitment.) Thus, in negotiating a deal after losing out on a previous deal, one might thus foolishly "bet the ranch" with what (they think) is simply an intuitive counteroffer. In fact, the person is overcompensating for losing the previous deal.[44] Intuition without facts and analysis can be deadly.

● **Intuitive People** Some people seem to be more naturally inclined to take an intuitive approach to making decisions. Research shows that systematic decision makers (systematics) take a more logical, step-by-step approach.[45] At the other extreme, intuitive decision makers (intuitives) use a more trial-and-error approach. They disregard much of the information available and bounce from one alternative to another to get a feel for which seems to work best.

One study compared systematics with intuitives. The former systematically searched for information and thoroughly evaluated all alternatives. The latter sought information nonsystematically, and then quickly evaluated just a few favored alternatives. The intuitive approach was usually best.[46] The lesson seems to be that plodding through all the options may be fine if time permits. However, it's sometimes best to follow your instincts.[47] We can measure intuitiveness. The short test in Figure 6.2 provides an approximate reading on whether you are more systematic or more intuitive in your decision making.[48]

Ford decided to close several plants and mortgage several others.

Don't Overstress the Finality of the Decision

In making a decision, remember that few decisions are forever. Some strategic decisions are hard to reverse. When Ford decided in 2006 to close several plants and to mortgage several others, it was a decision it would have to live with for many years. However, the manager can modify most decisions, even bad ones, with time. The manager should not become frozen with an unrealistic fear that a decision can't be changed or modified.[49]

Make Sure the Timing Is Right

"Timing is everything," someone once said, and the same applies to making decisions. With most people, their moods or the pressure they're under affects their

FIGURE 6.2

Are You More Rational or More Intuitive?

WHAT IS MY ORIENTATION?

You can get a rough idea of your relative preferences for the rational and intuitive ways of dealing with situations by rating yourself on four items. For each statement, rank yourself on a six-point scale—from 1 (never), to 2 (once in a while), 3 (sometimes), 4 (quite often), 5 (frequently but not always), or 6 (always)—and place your response in the box to the right of the item:

1. When I have a special job to do, I like to organize it carefully from the start. ☐
2. I feel that a prescribed, step-by-step method is best for solving problems. ☐
3. I prefer people who are imaginative to those who are not. ☐
4. I look at a problem as a whole, approaching it from all sides. ☐

Now add the values for the first two items for one total and for the last two items for another total. Subtract the second total from the first. If your total has a positive value, your preference is *Rational* by that amount, and if your total has a negative value, your preference is *Intuitive* by that amount. Ten represents the maximum possible rational or intuitive score from the equally preferred midpoint (0). Mark your position on the range of possible scores:

Intuitive ◀ | | | | | | | | | | | | | | | | | | | | ▶ **Rational**

-10 -9 -8 -7 -6 -5 -4 -3 -2 -1 0 1 2 3 4 5 6 7 8 9 10

These items are taken from a 30-item Personal Style Inventory (PSI) assessment of preferences for Rational and Intuitive behavior created by William Taggart.

SOURCE: Adapted and reproduced by permission of the publisher, Psychological Assessment Resources, Inc., Odessa, FL 33556, from *The Personal Style Inventory* by William Taggart and Barbara Hausladen.

decisions. Researchers know that when people feel down, their actions tend to be aggressive and destructive. Similarly, people tend to be lenient when they're in good spirits and tough when they are grouchy.

The manager therefore has to do a quick reality check prior to making a decision. Avoid regrettable decisions when moods are extreme, or when you are under duress.

● **Application Exercise: Harold's Choice** So which alternative should Harold choose? He started by doing some research. He learns that there are two marketing directors at the Pittsburgh plant. Because the prospects of a promotion are virtually nil, he discards that option. That leaves four options—the dot-com in New York, Ford in Detroit, the pet food producer in Newark, and Nokia in D.C.

He reviews his consequences matrix. For three of the jobs—the dot-com, Ford, and the pet food producer—his research and intuition suggest that they may lack the direct interaction with consumers and consumer products that he prefers. Promotion to senior director would probably take him more than two years at Ford, which is suffering some reversals. He asks himself where he'll be six months from now if he takes the dot-com job and is dissuaded by the high failure rate of dot-coms. Six months from now, he might be out of a job!

He puts together a decision matrix (shown in Figure 6.3) to summarize all this information. In it, he rates each job on how well it fulfills each of his objectives. First, he weights the importance to him of each of his objectives: 0.50, 0.20, 0.15,

FIGURE 6.3

Harold's Decision Matrix

Harold's Objectives	**How Harold Rates Relative Importance of Each Objective**	**How Harold Rates Senior Manager** DOTCOM • NY **on Satisfying This Objective**	**How Harold Rates Marketing Manager** FORD • DETROIT **on Satisfying This Objective**	**How Harold Rates Marketing Manager** NOKIA • WASH., D.C. **on Satisfying This Objective**	**How Harold Rates Senior Marketing Manager** PET-FOOD PRODUCER • NEWARK **on Satisfying This Objective**
Marketing Director in Two Years	0.50	2 (2 x 0.50 = 1)*	2 (2 x 0.50 = 1)	5 (5 x 0.50 = 2.5)	4 (4 x 0.50 = 2)
Consumer Products Company	0.20	2 (2 x 0.20 = .4)	3 (3 x 0.20 = .6)	3 (3 x 0.20 = .6)	5 (5 x 0.20 = 1)
One-Hour Drive from Major City	0.15	5 (5 x 0.15 = .75)	5 (5 x 0.15 = .75)	5 (5 x 0.15 = .75)	5 (5 x 0.15 = .75)
Earn at least $1,200 per Week	0.15	4 (4 x 0.15 = .6)	3 (3 x 0.15 = .45)	4 (4 x 0.15 = .6)	4 (4 x 0.15 = .6)
Sum	1.00	2.75 (1 + .4 + .75 + .6)	2.80 (1 + .6 + .75 + .45)	4.45 (2.5 + .6 + .75 + .6)	4.35 (2 + 1 + .75 + .6)

*Shows the job's rating (in this case 2) multiplied by the objective's importance weight (in this case 0.50).

and 0.15—they should add up to 1.0. Then he rates (from 5—high to 1—low) the extent to which each job fulfills each of his objectives. Looking over this matrix, Harold sees that the pet-food and Nokia jobs look like the best bets. The pet-food job is a possibility. In terms of senior director, it's a good career move. However, he's a little less enthusiastic about the pet-food business, although it scores close to the Nokia position. Harold has a good feeling about the Nokia job. It satisfies his objectives, and his research suggests that living costs are comparable to New York. He's excited about the cell-phone business. Looking down the road, he sees this industry's fast growth opening many new options for him. He can see himself living in Washington, D.C. He takes the job.

Encourage Creativity

creativity: the process of developing original, novel responses to a problem

To make good decisions, the manager needs to be creative—for instance, in how he or she defines the problem and generates alternatives. **Creativity** is the process of developing original, novel responses to a problem. It is an integral part of making good decisions. We discuss techniques for being more creative in the following sections.

● Create a Culture of Creativity A major airline reportedly spent hundreds of thousands of dollars training its employees to be creative, but the money was largely wasted. After spending several days learning how to be creative, the employees returned to their cubicles, where a bureaucratic environment discouraged them from recommending risky, innovative solutions:

> This was an organization dogged by rules and regulations. What the airline had not realized was that while you can increase the level of creativity by training, the more important element is making sure that the corporate environment allows people to exercise what they've learned.[50]

Management has to be proactive about creating an environment in which creativity can flourish. Recognize (and, if appropriate, reward) innovative ideas. Tolerate failure. If you punish employees for mistakes, they'll tend to avoid creative decisions because creativity involves risk.

● Encourage Brainstorming Meetings called to discuss problems often turn out to be useless. The participants come to the meeting willing and even enthusiastic to define a problem and to provide solutions to it. However, if a participant's suggestion is immediately met with comments like, "That's ridiculous" or "That's impossible," people are unlikely to make innovative suggestions.

brainstorming: a creativity-stimulating technique in which prior judgments and criticisms are specifically forbidden from being expressed in order to encourage the free flow of ideas

Brainstorming is a technique aimed at banishing this problem. It means requiring that all participants withhold any criticism and comments until all suggested alternatives are on the table. One important point here is that people should feel comfortable about making suggestions even if the suggestions seem strange. We saw that group decision-making software can facilitate electronic brainstorming. It enables decision makers to meet in a virtual environment and to type in suggestions and take positions anonymously. The system's computerized decision-making procedure limits premature evaluations of suggestions.

● Suspend Judgment For example, people tend to approach situations by comparing them to similar experiences they've faced in the past. That can constrain their creativity. "Unfortunately, . . . [no] two situations are identical. Many decision makers spot the similarities between situations very quickly but . . . ignore critical differences."[51] Particularly if time permits, some experts suggest suspending judgment. Think through the similarities and differences of the present and former situations before jumping to conclusions.

AOL headquarters in Dulles, Virginia.

● Get More Points of View When it comes to creativity, more points of view are usually better than fewer, and diverse points of view are better than homogeneous ones.

● Provide Physical Support for Creativity The AOL facility in Dulles, Virginia, has a creativity room with leopard-print walls, oversize cartoon murals, and giant paint cans that appear to spill over. The room's creator felt a standard conference room was not casual enough. Similarly, provide plenty of bulletin boards and whiteboards to accommodate the decision-making and creativity process.

● **Encourage Anonymous Input** Even in the most supportive environment, some employees may be too introverted to participate fully. Allowing for anonymous and/or written input can help encourage such people to participate more.[52]

Avoiding Psychological Traps

Online Study Center
ACE the Test
Managing Now! LIVE

As one researcher puts it, "[W]hen we make decisions, we're not always in charge. We can be too impulsive or too deliberate for our own good; one moment we let our emotions get the better of us, and the next we're paralyzed by uncertainty."[53] Let's look at some of the psychological traps that can inhibit good decision making.

Decision-Making Shortcuts

heuristics: rules of thumb or approximations applied as shortcuts to decision making

People making decisions tend to take shortcuts. They do this by using **heuristics**, which are decision-making shortcuts or rules of thumb. For example, mortgage lenders typically abide by the heuristic that "people shouldn't spend more than 28% of their gross monthly income on mortgage payments and other house-related expenses."[54]

Based on 150 interviews with decision makers, one researcher concluded, "Relatively few decisions are made using analytical processes such as generating a variety of options and contrasting their strengths and weaknesses."[55] Instead, most people tend to use cognitive shortcuts, such as rules governing what to do in new situations that are similar to those addressed in the past. Doing so can trap the unsuspecting decision maker when the situation is different.

Anchoring

anchoring: unconsciously giving disproportionate weight to the first information you hear

Anchoring means unconsciously giving too much weight to the first information you hear. It can cause you to define the problem incorrectly.

Assume that you're selling your car, which you know is worth about $10,000. Joe has responded to your classified ad; when he arrives, he offhandedly remarks that the car is worth only about $5,000. What would you do? On the one hand, you know that $5,000 is ridiculous. On the other hand, Joe is the only game in town (one other person called but never showed up). So you start bargaining with Joe. He says $5,000; you say $10,000. Before you know it, you've arrived at a price of $8,000 (for your $10,000 car).

What happened? You just got anchored (to put it mildly). Without realizing it, you gave disproportionate weight to Joe's comment about $5,000, and your decision making (and bargaining) from then on revolved around his price, not yours. What should you have done? One response might have been: "Five thousand dollars? Are you kidding? That's not even in the ballpark!" At least that might have loosened that subliminal anchor so the bargaining could take place on your terms, not his. When negotiating, "think through your position before any negotiation begins in order to avoid being anchored by the other party's initial proposal. At the same time, look for opportunities to use anchors to your own advantage. . . ."[56]

The Status Quo Trap

Decision makers tend to be biased toward alternatives that perpetuate the status quo.[57] Why? Because making a decision that requires a change is fraught with risks. As three experts put it, "[B]reaking from the status quo means taking action, and when we take action, we take responsibility, opening ourselves to criticism and to regret."[58] Years ago, this tendency to stick with the status quo was immortalized in the phrase, "Nobody ever got fired for buying IBM," which came to stand for decisions whose chief rationale was safety.[59]

Managers can take steps to avoid the status quo trap. Don't think of the status quo as the only alternative; instead, force yourself to consider the other options. Don't exaggerate the cost of switching from the status quo. Always keep your objectives in mind, and make sure that they're really best served by the status quo.[60]

Delusions of Success

A rising executive with a *Fortune* 100 manufacturing company led his firm into a disastrous expansion in Asia, in the face of negative evidence. He first discussed the opportunity with his executive staff and consultants; this rational analysis indicated that it was a very risky venture. The market data looked barely favorable, and the political and cultural factors were huge unknowns; yet the executive blundered ahead. His overconfidence led him to assume that his associates really shared his view but that they were being overcautious.[61] He went ahead with his expansion, a decision that proved disastrous.

Overoptimism misleads many decision makers. They have "delusions of success."[62] Overoptimism is something of a built-in trait. Studies show that most people overestimate their own talents. For example, in performance appraisals, about half of all appraisees tend to place themselves in the top 10 percent, and almost all the rest place themselves above the median. Another study asked students to rate themselves on leadership ability; 70 percent said that they were above average. Similarly, people "tend to exaggerate the degree of control we have, discounting the role of luck."[63]

Optimism is laudable, but managers need to guard against uninformed overconfidence. Successful managers compete on analytics. They use business intelligence to make fact-based decisions.

psychological set: the tendency to look at things with a rigid point of view when solving a problem

Psychological Set

Failing to think out of the box is another decision-making trap. The technical term for this is **psychological set**, which means the tendency to look at things with a rigid point of view when solving a problem.[64] Doing so can severely limit a manager's ability to create alternative solutions. Figure 6.4 presents a classic example. Your assignment is to connect all nine dots with no more than four lines running through them, and to do so without lifting your pen from the paper. *Hint:* Don't take a rigid point of view.

FIGURE 6.4

Looking at the Problem in Just One Way

SOURCE: Problem originally appeared in Sam Loyd's 1914 *Cyclopedia of Puzzles*.

To avoid this trap, always question your assumptions. Look again at the problem of the nine dots in Figure 6.4. Your instructions were to connect all nine dots with no more than four lines running through them, and to do so without lifting your pen from the paper. How would you do it? Start by checking your assumptions.

Most people view the nine dots as a square—they're victims of psychological set. Viewing them as a square limits your solutions. There is no way to connect all the dots as long as you assume the dots represent a square. Figure 6.5 shows one solution. The key was checking your assumptions. Now solve the problem in Figure 6.6.

FIGURE 6.5

The Advantage of Not Looking at the Problem in Just One Way

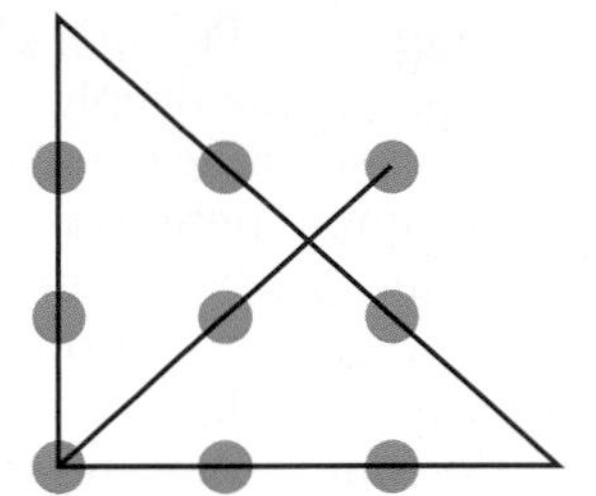

SOURCE: Problem originally appeared in Sam Loyd's 1914 *Cyclopedia of Puzzles*.

FIGURE 6.6

Using Creativity to Find a Solution

How many squares are in the box? Count again. Only sixteen? Take away your preconception of how many squares there are. Now, how many do you find? You should find thirty!

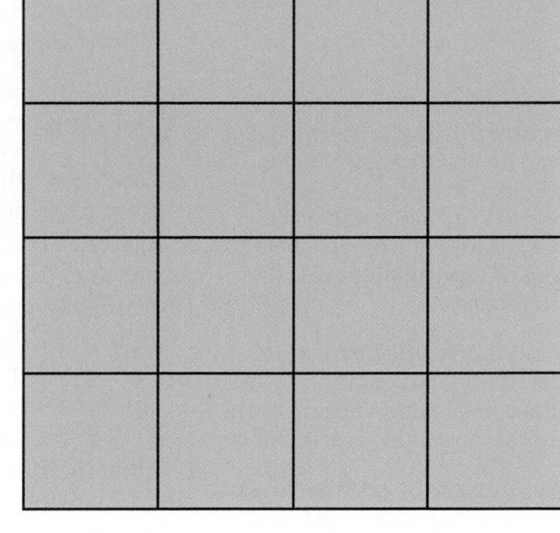

SOURCE: Problem originally appeared in Sam Loyd's *Cyclopedia of Puzzles*.

The psychological-set trap helps explain why many decisions go bad. For example, the owners of the building whose tenants complained about the slow elevators were victims of psychological set. They could see the problem in only one way, and they did not question their assumptions. Luckily, the consultants didn't fall into the same trap.

Perception

perception: the unique way in which each person defines stimuli, depending on the influence of past experiences and the person's present needs and personality

selective perception: choosing, often without thinking about it, the information we're going to see or focus on

The fact that we don't always see things as they really are is another psychological trap. **Perception** is the selection and interpretation of information we receive through our senses, and the meaning we give to the information. Many things, including our individual needs, influence how we perceive stimuli. **Selective perception** means choosing, often without thinking about it, the information we're going to see or focus on. Experiences involving selective perception happen every day. You might be less happy with a B in a course after finding out that your friend, who had about the same test grades, got an A.[65] Similarly, in organizations, prior experiences influence how a person perceives a problem and reacts to it.

A classic study illustrates this point. Researchers asked twenty-three executives, all employed by a large manufacturing firm, to read a business case.[66] Researchers found that a manager's position influenced how he or she defined "the most important problem facing the company." Of six sales executives, five thought the most important problem was a sales problem. Four out of five production executives, but only one sales executive and no accounting executives, mentioned organization problems. The managers looked at the same case, but they drew very different conclusions. Each would probably have taken action based on his or her singular view of the problem.

Selective perception pops up when decision makers selectively ignore critical information. In another study, the researchers told the participants to watch a videotape of two teams passing basketballs and to count the number of times each team passed the ball. The participants concentrated so hard on watching the basketballs that only 21 percent of them noticed a woman walking among the team members with an open umbrella.[67] This finding may seem incredible, but it is not

Most people, when concentrating on a particular issue, can be blind to even the most obvious information. The solution is to work strenuously to step back and view the bigger picture.

Other Psychological Traps

groupthink: the psychological trap in which people deeply engaged in a problem let their desire to go along and reach consensus stifle open debate and full consideration of all the issues

risky shift phenomenon: the notion that groups tend to make riskier decisions than would their individual members

escalation of commitment: an increase in the investment that a person or group has in a decision when faced with negative feedback

Numerous other traps lie in wait for unsuspecting decision makers. Psychologist Irving Janis described the phenomenon of **groupthink**: here, people deeply engaged in a problem let their desire to go along and reach consensus stifle open debate and full consideration of all the issues. The classic example here is when Attorney General Robert Kennedy told one detractor (of the group decision to attack Cuba at the Bay of Pigs), "You may be right and you may be wrong, but President Kennedy has made his decision, so keep your opinions to yourself."[68] The risky shift trap further complicates such a situation. Basically, the **risky shift phenomenon** refers to the fact that groups tend to make riskier decisions than would their individual members. Escalation of commitment can then further aggravate an already bad decision. **Escalation of commitment** occurs when a person or group increases its investment in a decision in the face of negative feedback. In business, for instance, there's a tendency to throw more money at a losing project to make it profitable, although it seems obvious that the original plan was flawed.

CHAPTER SUMMARY

1. A decision is a choice from among available alternatives. Decision making is the process of developing and analyzing alternatives and making a choice.
2. Decisions can be either programmed (repetitive and routine) or nonprogrammed (unique and novel). Nonprogrammed decisions require more intuition and judgment of decision makers.
3. Rational decision making assumes ideal conditions, such as an accurate definition of the problem and complete knowledge about all relevant alternatives and their values. In contrast, decision making in reality is bounded by differences in managers' ability to process information, managers' reliance on heuristics or shortcuts, anchoring, escalation, psychological set, and factors in the organization itself.
4. Defining the problem is crucial. Start by writing down your initial assessment of the problem. Then dissect it. Ask yourself, What triggered this problem (as I've assessed it)? Why am I even thinking about solving this problem? What is the connection between the trigger and the problem?
5. The consequences matrix compares alternatives with objectives. The objectives matrix ranks each alternative's chance of achieving each objective.
6. Although some managers still take an informal, seat-of-the pants approach to getting the facts and information they need, many others now compete based on analytics. In other words, their decisions are heavily fact- and information-based. They do extensive analyses. They want to ensure their big decisions are well informed.
7. Business intelligence (BI) refers to a set of processes (specifically, usually, a set of software applications and technologies) that transform data into a form that managers can use to make better, faster decisions.[69] The phrase *business intelligence* also refers to the actual information these processes produce and on which the manager then bases his or her decision.
8. Suggestions for making better decisions include increase your knowledge, use creativity, use intuition, don't overstress finality, and make sure the timing is right.
9. Psychological traps include decision-making shortcuts, anchoring, status quo traps, psychological set, perception, and ignoring information.

DISCUSSION QUESTIONS

1. List four programmed decisions and four nonprogrammed decisions you typically make.
2. For managers, what are some of the practical implications of Simon's administrative theory?
3. What are the five steps in the decision process?
4. Give one original example of why it is important to define the problem correctly.
5. Explain how you would use a consequences matrix to make a better decision.
6. Give an example of how you have used intuition to make a decision.
7. Explain what you would do to increase the creativity in a workgroup.
8. Give an example of how you use a business-intelligence approach when buying a computer, car, or home.

EXPERIENTIAL EXERCISES

1. Most colleges and universities have grievance procedures to address inappropriate behavior by both students and faculty. Working as a team, obtain the student and/or faculty grievance procedures for your college or university, and answer the following questions: What provision (if any) does the procedure have for allowing the parties to define the student's or faculty member's problem? Assume that a student has accused a faculty member of giving him or her a lower grade than deserved, based on the grading policies laid out in the course syllabus. Propose at least five objectives for the committee that must decide who is right and who is wrong.
2. Working in teams of three to four, choose an article from a recent newspaper about some decision a company or government executive recently made. If the decision is working out well, why do you think that is so, based on what we discussed about decision making in this chapter? If it turned out to be a bad decision, what errors do you think the executive made?
3. In November 2004, retailers were surprised to hear that Kmart was buying Sears. In fact, that was only the latest in a series of events that actually began about three years earlier.

   It began with one decision. Charles Conaway, then Kmart's new CEO, decided to save Kmart by beating Wal-Mart at its own low-cost game. For years, Kmart had attracted customers with circulars in weekly magazines. Conaway's research showed that the circulars accounted for over 10 percent of Kmart's operating expenses (compared with about 2 percent at Target and 1 percent at Wal-Mart).[70] He believed Kmart had to reduce that expense. Conaway and his team thus decided to change their marketing approach. They abolished the circulars, slashed prices on about 40,000 products, and started advertising that "Kmart's prices are lower than Wal-Mart's." Given Wal-Mart's size, those were gutsy decisions.

   They were also disastrous. Wal-Mart's day-to-day operating costs were way below Kmart's, so Wal-Mart simply dropped its own prices even more. Conaway's decisions left Kmart with higher prices and no circulars. Customers stopped showing up. "We made a mistake by cutting too much advertising too fast," is how Conaway put it. In December 2001—typically a retailer's busiest month—Kmart's sales fell 1 percent, while Wal-Mart's rose 8 percent. One month later, Kmart sought bankruptcy protection. Conaway's last big decision was to close 284 stores and fire 22,000 Kmart employees. In March 2002, Conaway left the firm. Investment banker Edward Lampert gained control of Kmart when it emerged from bankruptcy in May 2003. In March 2004, Kmart posted its first profitable quarter in three years. Lampert then went on to merge Sears into Kmart. The whole chain of events started, in a way, with Conaway's circulars decision.

   Working in teams of three or four students, answer this question: Based on what we discussed in this chapter, where did Conaway go wrong? What would you have done differently?

CASE STUDY

Which Routes to Fly?

As an experienced airline executive, JetBlue CEO David Neeleman knows the most important decisions he has to make concern the routes JetBlue will fly. The right decision will maximize ridership and minimize competitive retaliation by offering low-cost flights that competitors aren't now providing. The wrong decision will force Neeleman's fledgling airline to confront fast and sure competitive retaliation, in which case, JetBlue could be out of business before it really takes off.

The first and biggest route decision probably revolved around whether to choose New York's JFK Airport as JetBlue's first major gateway.[71] JFK Airport was once the headquarters for several U.S. airlines, but most moved on to other cities and airports where costs were lower and space was easier to come by. From JetBlue's point of view, JFK had several advantages. It is in the middle of one of the ten busiest air-passenger markets in the United States. New York's political leaders badly wanted a low-cost airline for their state that would help reduce the cost of flying from the New York City area to upper New York State. And while JFK did have heavy delays, it actually was less busy than New York's other major airport, LaGuardia, for the time slots JetBlue was looking at.

Several years ago, Neeleman and his team were considering other airport alternatives. At Boston's Logan Airport, for instance, Neeleman says, "No one would give us gates." In other words, there was so much competition from American Airlines and US Airways that JetBlue couldn't get the gates it needed, even though, according to Neeleman, the gates at Logan were underutilized.

In terms of what he looks for in choosing routes, Neeleman says that one thing his company must watch out for is spreading itself too thin. Spreading his flights among too many destinations runs the risk of lowering the utilization rate of each plane—there would be too much downtime, without enough passengers on each route. As he says, "I just want passengers on the planes." Thus, the basic idea is to go into a few major gateways, like JFK, and to use the traffic and population base around these gateways to fly into smaller cities that are not adequately served by low-cost airlines. For example, he wants to fly passengers from JFK to Buffalo, New York, and Fort Lauderdale (instead of Miami). The question is, Where should JetBlue fly next?

Getting the slots (the permissions to fly in and out at specific times) at a busy airport like JFK is not easy. Neeleman set up a lobbying operation in Washington, D.C., to help convince New York's congressional delegation that New York cities like Buffalo, Syracuse, and Rochester needed JetBlue's low-cost alternative flights from New York City. In turn, New York congressional members will have to work on convincing the Department of Transportation that the needs of New Yorkers (and JetBlue) are important enough to put JetBlue's interest ahead of those of major airlines like American and USAir.

Getting the slots doesn't mean JetBlue is home free. For example, it was able to obtain numerous arrival and departure slots at California's Long Beach airport. However, those slots came with the condition that they must all be utilized within several years. American Airlines is already battling to take over some of those slots; it is lowering prices to Long Beach and increasing incentives (such as adding more frequent-flier miles for those who fly there from JFK).

In addition, Neeleman was considering taking JetBlue abroad—for instance, to Canada and Mexico. Assume you are a consultant to Mr. Neeleman, who is depending on your management expertise to navigate the launch and management of JetBlue. He wants you to complete the following tasks:

1. Accurately spell out what triggered the route-decision problems stated in the case.
2. List at least four ways that Neeleman can identify where JetBlue should fly next and then choose the best alternative.
3. Propose at least five objectives for Neeleman, who must make the decision regarding routes and gateways.
4. Propose at least four alternatives to solve the situation. Develop a consequences matrix for the situation.
5. Develop a decision matrix for the situation.

Note: In May 2007, apparently facing intense pressure from investors and his board stemming from JetBlue's managing of the February 2007 storms that grounded its planes, David Neeleman relinquished the CEO position to his No. 2, Dave Barger. Neeleman remains JetBlue's chairman, however.

CHAPTER 6 APPENDIX

Quantitative Decision-Making Aids

Managers use quantitative analysis to make better decisions. For example, we saw that Fortis Bank's managers use quantitative modeling to express, in an equation, some situation, such as identifying the customers most likely to accept a new gold credit card according to demographic traits like age, address, and so forth. Managers also use quantitative analysis on a more frequent basis. This appendix describes several of the more popular quantitative decision-making aids.

Breakeven Analysis

breakeven analysis: a financial analysis decision-making aid that enables a manager to determine whether a particular volume of sales will result in losses or profits

In financial analysis, the breakeven point is that volume of sales at which revenues just equals expenses, and you have neither a profit nor a loss. **Breakeven analysis** is a decision-making aid that enables a manager to determine whether a particular volume of sales will result in losses or profits.[72]

● **Breakeven Charts** Breakeven analysis makes use of four basic concepts: fixed costs, variable costs, revenues, and profits. Fixed costs (such as for the plant and machinery) are costs that basically do not change with changes in production. In other words, you might use the same machine to produce 10 units, 50 units, or 200 units of a product. Variablc costs (such as for raw material) rise in proportion to volume. Revenue is the total income received from sales of the product. For example, if you sell fifty dolls at \$8 each, then your revenue is \$8 × 50, or \$400. Profit is the money you have left after subtracting fixed and variable costs from revenue.

A breakeven chart, like the one shown in Figure A6.1, is a graph that shows whether a particular volume of sales will result in profits or losses. The fixed costs

FIGURE A6.1

A Breakeven Chart

The breakeven point is the number of units sold at which total revenues just equals total costs.

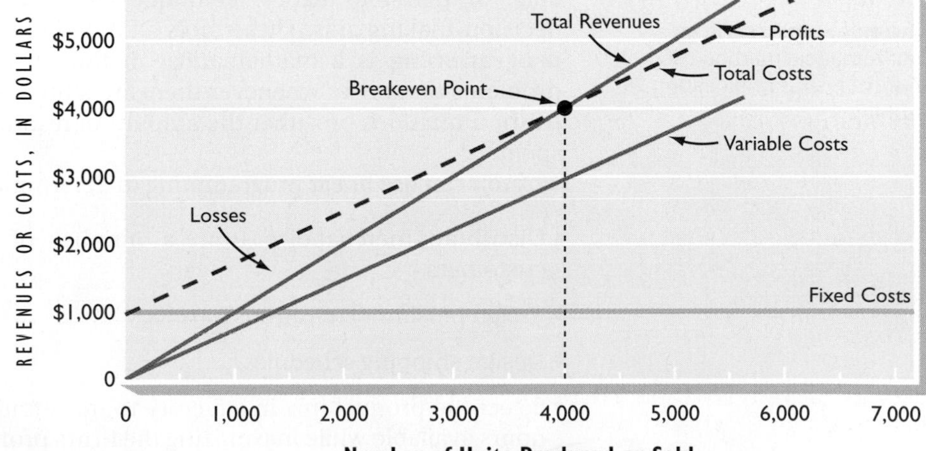

line is horizontal. Variable costs, however, increase in proportion to output and are shown as an upward sloping line. The total costs line is then equal to variable costs plus fixed costs at each level of output. The breakeven point is the point at which the total revenue line crosses the total costs line. Beyond this point (note the shaded area in Figure A6.1), total revenue exceeds total costs. In this example, an output of about 4,000 units is the breakeven point. Above this point, the company can expect to earn a profit. If sales are fewer than 4,000 units, the company can expect a loss.

Breakeven Formula The breakeven chart provides a picture of the relationship between sales volume and profits. However, a chart is not required for determining breakeven points. Instead, you can use the following formula:

$$P(X) = F + V(X)$$

where

F = fixed costs

V = variable costs per unit

X = volume of output (in units)

P = price per unit

We can rearrange this formula and calculate the breakeven point with $F/(P - V)$. In other words, the breakeven point is the volume of sales where total costs just equals total revenues. If, for example, you have a product in which

F = fixed costs = $1,000.00

V = variable costs per unit = $.75

P = price per unit = $1.00 per unit

then the breakeven point is $1,000/($1.00 − $.75) = 4,000 units.

Linear Programming

linear programming: a mathematical method used to solve resource allocation problems

Breakeven analysis is only one of many quantitative techniques. Decision science or decision theory techniques are another category of programmed decision-making aids. These tools all rely on mathematics. For example, **linear programming** is a mathematical method used to solve resource allocation problems that arise "whenever there are a number of activities to be performed, [with] limitations on either the amount of resources or [on] the way they can be spent."[73]

You can use linear programming to determine the best way to:

- Distribute merchandise from a number of warehouses to a number of customers.
- Assign personnel to various jobs.
- Design shipping schedules.
- Select the product mix in a factory to make the best use of machine and labor hours available while maximizing the firm's profit.
- Route production to optimize the use of machinery.

To apply linear programming successfully, the problem must meet certain basic requirements. There must be a stated, quantifiable goal, such as "minimize total shipping costs"; the resources to be utilized must be known (a firm could produce 200 of one item and 300 of another, for instance, or 400 of one or 100 of another); all the necessary relationships must be expressed in the form of mathematical equations or inequalities; and all these relationships must be linear in nature. An example can help illustrate:

> Apex Electronics has five manufacturing plants and twelve warehouses scattered across the country. Each plant is manufacturing the same product and operating at full capacity. Because plant capacity and location do not permit the closest plant to fully support each warehouse, Apex would like to identify the factory that should supply each warehouse and thus minimize total shipping costs.

Applying linear programming techniques to Apex Electronics' problem can provide an optimum shipping schedule.

Waiting-Line/Queuing Techniques

waiting-line/queuing techniques: mathematical techniques used to solve waiting-line problems so that the optimal balance of employees available relative to waiting customers is attained

Waiting-line/queuing techniques are mathematical decision-making techniques for solving waiting-line problems. For example, bank managers need to know how many tellers they should have. If they have too many, they are wasting money on salaries; if they have too few, they may end up with many disgruntled customers. Similar problems arise when selecting the optimal number of airline reservations clerks, warehouse loading docks, highway tollbooths, supermarket checkout registers, and so forth.

Statistical Decision Theory Techniques

statistical decision theory techniques: techniques used to solve problems for which information is incomplete or uncertain

Managers use **statistical decision theory techniques** to solve problems for which information is incomplete or uncertain. Suppose a shopkeeper can stock either brand A or brand B, but not both. She knows how much it will cost to stock her shelves with each brand, and she also knows how much money she would earn (or lose) if each brand turned out to be a success (or failure) with her customers. However, she can only estimate how much of each brand she might sell, so her information is incomplete. Using statistical decision theory, the shopkeeper would assign probabilities (estimates of the likelihood that the brand will sell or not) to each alternative. Then she could determine which alternative—stocking brand A or stocking brand B—would most likely result in the greatest profits.

certainty: the condition of knowing in advance the outcome of a decision

uncertainty: the absence of information about a particular area of concern

● Three Degrees of Uncertainty Statistical decision theory assumes that a manager may face three degrees of uncertainty in making a decision. Managers make some decisions under conditions of **certainty**. Here, the manager knows in advance the outcome of the decision. From a practical point of view, for example, you know that if you buy a $50 U.S. savings bond, the interest rate you will earn to maturity on the bond is, say, 6 percent. Managers rarely make decisions under such conditions.

At the opposite extreme, managers make some decisions under conditions of **uncertainty**. Here, a manager cannot even assign probabilities to the likelihood of

FIGURE A6.2

A Decision Tree

The expected value of each alternative is equal to (1) the chance of success or failure times (2) the expected profit or loss.

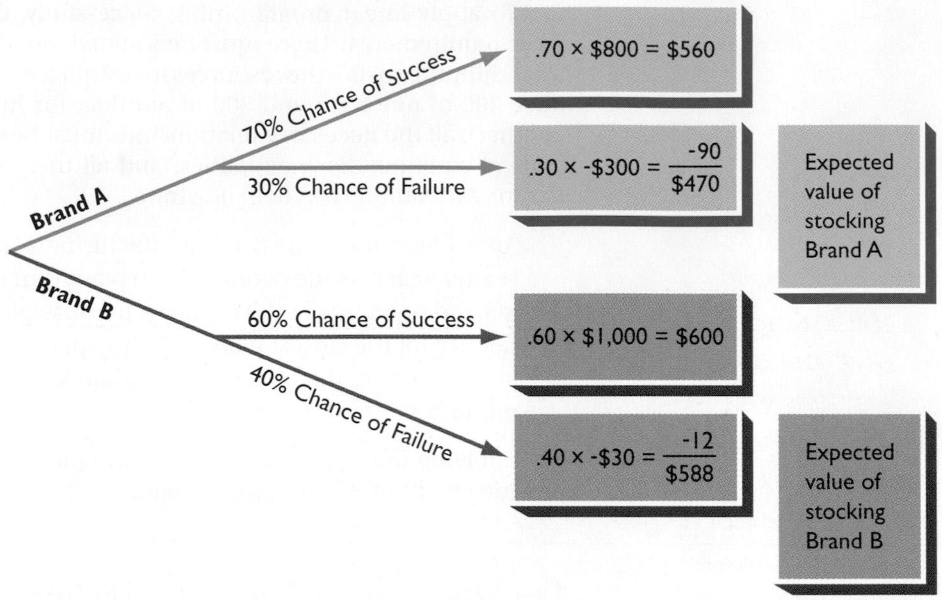

the various outcomes. For example, a shopkeeper may have several new products that could be stocked but not have any idea of the likelihood that one brand will be successful or that another will fail. Conditions of complete uncertainty are also relatively infrequent. Most management decisions are made under conditions of **risk**. Under these conditions, a manager can at least assign probabilities to each outcome. In other words, the manager knows (either from past experience or by making an educated guess) the chance that each possible outcome (such as product A being successful or product B being successful) will occur.

risk: the chance that a particular outcome will or will not occur

decision tree: a technique for facilitating how decisions under conditions of risk are made, whereby an expected value and gain or loss can be applied to each alternative

expected value: a calculated value that equals the probability of the outcome multiplied by the benefit or cost of that outcome

● **Decision Tree** A **decision tree** is one technique for making a decision under conditions of risk. With a decision tree like the one shown in Figure A6.2, an expected value can be calculated for each alternative. **Expected value** equals (1) the probability of the outcome multiplied by (2) the benefit or cost of that outcome.

For example, in Figure A6.2, it pays our shopkeeper to stock brand B rather than brand A. Stocking brand A allows a 70 percent chance of success for an $800 profit, so the shopkeeper has to balance this possible expected $560 profit against the possibility of the $90 loss (.30 × possible loss of $300). The expected value of stocking brand A is thus $470. By stocking brand B, though, the expected value is a relatively high $588.

PLANNING AND STRATEGIC MANAGEMENT

7

Oxford University Press

The managers at Oxford University Press (OUP) knew they had to improve their planning systems. The company publishes over 4,500 new books each year and employs about 4,800 people worldwide.[1] Its education and children's division markets textbooks, dictionaries, children's fiction, and picture books to schools and booksellers. Oxford is one of the top educational publishers in the United Kingdom. However, it competes worldwide with much larger educational publishers.

Publishers need accurate forecasts. It can take from two days to twelve weeks to reprint a title. So if the title's inventory is low and OUP gets a big order, the adopting school may turn to a different book and publisher. On the other hand, stocking too many books ties up cash and space.

Facing global competition, managers at Oxford University Press (OUP) knew they had to improve their planning systems.

OUP's education and children's division relies on traditional forecasting and planning systems. Employees kept track of each book's inventory and sales orders manually, on electronic spreadsheets. Warehouse stock managers can't easily track historical sales patterns for each school or book. This makes it hard to forecast and anticipate future orders and to plan accordingly. "[W]e often have to order rush reprints to fulfill unexpected orders," says one OUP manager. "As a result, we pay higher prices." OUP asks your team to recommend a new forecasting and planning system. You should have a good answer after reading this chapter. ■

CHAPTER OUTLINE

BEHAVIORAL OBJECTIVES

After studying this chapter, you should be able to:

Show that you've learned the chapter's essential information by

- Listing what planning accomplishes.
- Describing each of the steps in the management planning process.
- Briefly explaining what we mean by sales forecasting, marketing research, and competitive intelligence.
- Listing and describing the steps in the strategic management process.
- Giving examples of the various types of strategies.

Show that you can practice what you've learned here by

- Reading the opening vignette about Oxford University Press and suggesting a forecasting and planning system for the company.
- Reading the end-of-chapter exercise and explaining how you would do an environmental scan for your college or university.
- Reading the chapter case study and drawing a strategic map for the company.

Show that you can apply what you've learned here by

- Watching the simulation video and making recommendations to managers with regards to their planning and strategic management processes.

Online Study Center
ACE the Test
Managing Now! LIVE

The Nature and Purpose of Planning

Online Study Center
ACE the Test
Managing Now! LIVE

Planning is something we do every day, often without giving it much thought. For example, most readers of this book are reading it as part of a management course. This course is probably part of their program of studies. The program of studies is a plan. It shows the goal (say, getting a business degree in two years). And it shows how you will get that degree, by listing the courses needed to graduate, the sequence in which to take them, and when.

plans: methods for achieving a desired result

goals: specific results you want to achieve

objectives: specific results you want to achieve

planning: the process of establishing objectives and courses of action

Like the program of studies, **plans** are methods for achieving a desired result. Plans answer the questions, What will we do? When will we do it? Who will do it? and (usually) How much will it cost?[2] Plans always specify (or imply) goals (such as "boost sales by 10 percent") and courses of action (such as "hire a new salesperson and boost advertising by 20 percent"). **Goals**, or **objectives**, are specific results you want to achieve. **Planning** is the process of establishing objectives and courses of action for achieving them.[3] Planning always involves deciding now what to do in the future.

What Planning Accomplishes

The fact that planning "involves deciding now what to do in the future" highlights one of the things that planning accomplishes. Planning lets you *make your decisions ahead of time*, in the comfort of your home (or office), and with the luxury of having the time to research and weigh your options. It also thereby helps you to *anticipate the consequences* of various courses of action, and to think through the practicality and feasibility of each without actually having to commit the resources to carry out each course of action. For example, developing a budget for the year may show the business owner that the move to new, more expensive offices would be unwise.

Planning also provides *direction and a sense of purpose.* For example, someone once said, in reference to career plans, "The world parts and makes a path for the person who knows where he or she is going." Many people find that this sense of purpose—this "knowing where I am going"—pulls them like a magnet through challenges and adversity until they reach their goals.

Planning also helps *avoid piecemeal decision making*—making decisions that are not consistent with the goal or with each other. For example, R. R. Donnelley & Sons Company prints books, magazines, and documents for customers such as investment bankers.[4] Donnelley's planning led its managers to anticipate that, as its customers conducted more business abroad, they would want Donnelley to help service them globally. The company therefore invested in advanced technology and a worldwide digital printing network. It didn't waste money building conventional printing plants in the United States. Now it prints documents simultaneously around the globe. It is also beginning to offer its customers a wider range of services, such as digital content management.[5] Management theorist Peter Drucker says that planning also helps identify potential *opportunities and threats* and reduce long-term risks.[6] For example, R. R. Donnelley's planning process helped identify the opportunity for satellite-based global printing and for expanding its product offerings.

Last but not least, planning *facilitates control.* Control means "ensuring that activities conform to plan." Thus, a company's plan may specify that its profits will double within five years. This goal becomes the standard against which to measure, compare, and control the manager's performance. Planning and control are the twins of the management process. You cannot control if you don't know what your standards are, and it's futile to have a plan if you don't control what you are doing.

The Management Planning Process

The planning process involves five basic steps:

1. *Set an objective.* For example, managers at Ford recently decided to cut about 25 percent of its North American vehicle capacity over five years.

2. *Develop forecasts and planning premises.* Forecasting means making assumptions or premises about the future. Forecasting should help show Ford's managers which plants to cut. Forecasting should reveal, for instance, what oil prices should be, which Ford products should be in highest demand for the next few years, and which countries (like China) should grow the fastest. This is valuable information for a company trying to decide which plants to close and which products to phase out.

3. *Determine what the alternatives are.* Every plan consists of a goal and a course of action for achieving that goal. There are usually several ways to achieve the goal. Ford could cut production costs by closing selected plants or phasing out specific products or product lines.

4. *Evaluate alternatives.* Remember that plans are decisions you make today for what to do tomorrow. Therefore, apply all your decision-making skills (from Chapter 6) to evaluating your alternatives. Think through the consequences of each course of action.

5. *Implement and then evaluate the plan.* Finally, choose the course(s) of action, decide who should do what, and implement the plan. Then periodically check to make sure that actual progress is consistent with the plan.

It hardly matters if you're planning your career or a trip to France, or how you're going to cut costs or market your firm's new product. The basic process always involves setting objectives, forecasting, determining alternative courses of action, evaluating those options, and then choosing and implementing your plan. The process is the same when managers develop plans for their companies, with two small complications.

First, there is usually a hierarchical aspect to managerial planning. Top management approves a long-term or strategic plan. Then each department creates its own budgets and other plans to fit and to contribute to the company's long-term plan.

Second, the process involves much give-and-take among departments. Top management formulates goals and plans partly based on upward feedback from the departments. The departments in turn draw up plans that support top management's plan.

The Planning Hierarchy

As a result, Step 5 in the planning process (implement and then evaluate your plan) is usually not the last step in the businesss planning process. It's often just the start for round 2, because top management's plans and goals become the targets for which lower-level departments then craft derivative plans. The vice president produces a plan for her department. Then her own department heads produce plans for their departments, and so on. In this way, the planning process produces a **hierarchy of plans and goals**.

hierarchy of plans and goals: a set of plans and goals that includes the companywide plan and the derivative plans of subsidiary units required to help achieve the companywide plan

Figure 7.1 summarizes this idea. At the top of the hierarchy, the president and his or her staff set strategic goals (such as "a minimum of 55 percent of sales revenue will come from customized products by 2008"). Lower-level managers (in this case, starting with the vice presidents) then set goals (such as "convert Building C to customized manufacturing operations") that make sense in terms of the goals at the next level up. In this way, the company creates a hierarchy of supporting departmental goals, down to tactical and functional goals and finally short-term operational goals for each employee.

How to Set Objectives

Goals play a central role in what managers do. Managers should always expect to be judged on the extent to which they achieved their units' goals. As Peter Drucker put it, "There has to be something to point to and say, we have not worked in vain."[7]

Effective goals have several characteristics, as summarized by the acronym SMART. They are s*pecific,* and clearly state the desired results. They are *measurable,* and answer the question "How much?" They are *attainable.* They are *relevant* and derive from a crucial organizational need. And they are *timely* and specify deadlines.[8]

Planning expert George Morrisey advises expressing the goal so it addresses four details:

To (1) (action/verb)
(2) the (single measurable result)
by (3) (target date/time span)
(4) at (cost in time and/or energy)

FIGURE 7.1

Hierarchy of Goals

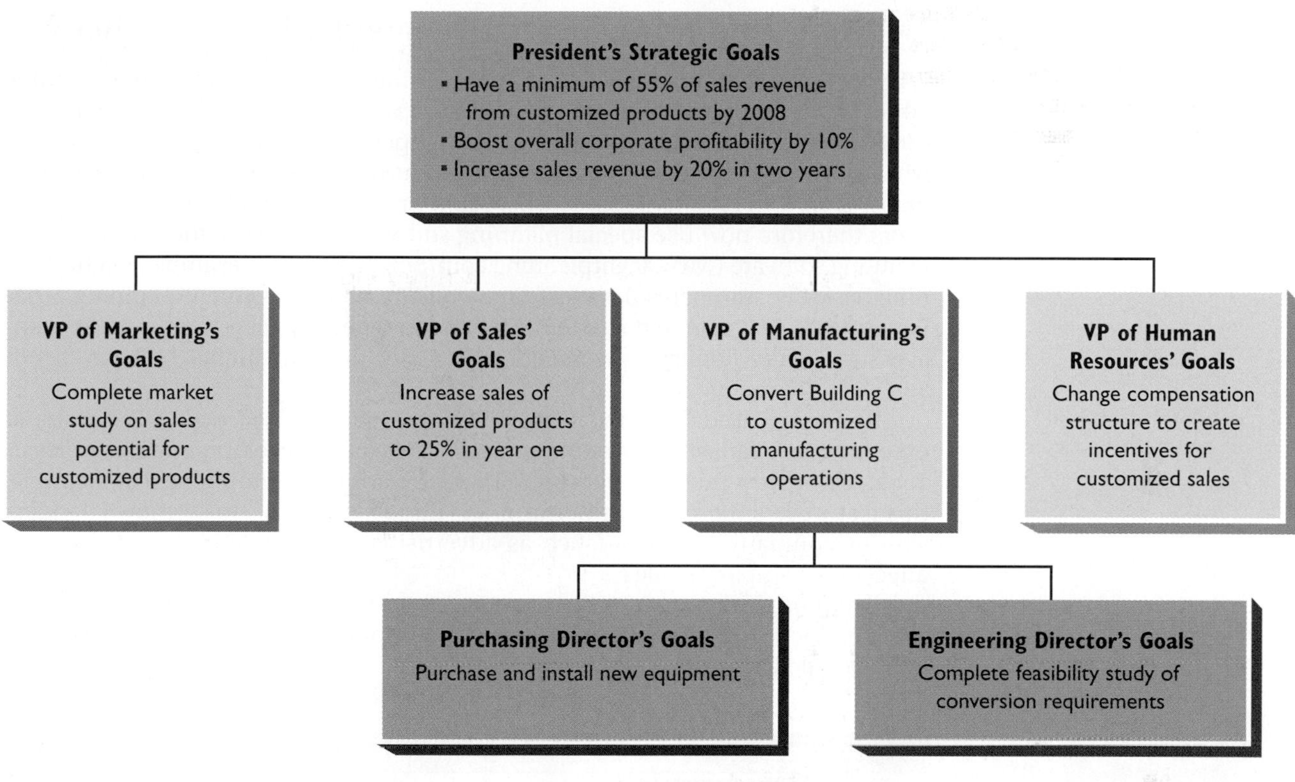

For example, "(1) sell (2) $2 million of product X (3) next year, with (4) the same size sales force."

● **Management by Objectives** Management by objectives (MBO) is a technique in which supervisor and subordinate jointly set goals for the latter and periodically assess progress toward those goals. A manager may engage in a modest MBO program by simply setting goals with his or her subordinates and periodically providing feedback. However, the term *management by objectives* usually refers to a comprehensive organizationwide program for setting goals down the chain of command. The MBO process consists of five steps:

1. *Set organization goals.* Top management sets strategic goals for the company.
2. *Set department goals.* Department heads and their superiors jointly set supporting goals for their departments.
3. *Discuss department goals.* Department heads present department goals and ask all subordinates to develop their own individual goals.
4. *Set individual goals.* Goals are set for each subordinate, and a timetable is assigned for accomplishing those goals.

5. *Give feedback.* The supervisor and subordinate meet periodically to review the subordinate's performance and to monitor and analyze progress toward his or her goals.[9]

Managing Now: The Management Planning Process

Without suitable technological support, planning can be unduly time-consuming. For example, suppose the manager needs to translate revenue forecasts into production and personnel estimates, convert the plan into financial budgets, and see what effect different assumptions about the future might have on the manager's plans. Even with Excel-type spreadsheet support, such tasks take time. Many managers therefore now use special planning software to facilitate these tasks. Alight Planning software (www.alightplanning.com/Software) is one example. Alight Planning basically automates the most time-consuming management planning tasks. For example, its Integrated Financial Statements feature quickly translates the manager's goals into financial statements such as income statements, balance sheets, and cash-flow budgets.

Its Stage Based Planning feature lets the manager see what the results of executing the plan will be over time, at each stage of its development. The Analysis Tools feature lets the manager test and graph various assumptions. For example, this feature lets the manager perform an "impact analysis," to see how changing various company activities (such as advertising expenses and sales-force size) affects the company's sales.

By automating much of the planning process and enabling the manager to more easily test the impact of his or her assumptions, Alight Planning facilitates managerial planning.

SOURCE: www.alightplanning.com (March 9, 2006).

Forecasting

Online Study Center
ACE the Test
Managing Now! LIVE

Managers build their plans on assumptions or premises about the future. Audi expanded to China because it forecast a booming market for high-quality cars in that country. Managers traditionally use several forecasting techniques to produce the premises on which they build their plans. These include sales forecasting, marketing research, and competitive intelligence.

Sales Forecasting Techniques

forecast: estimate or calculate in advance; predict

To **forecast** means to estimate or calculate in advance or to predict. A company's production, personnel, and finance levels usually depend on the company's level of sales. Therefore, business forecasting often starts with predicting the direction and magnitude of sales.

time series: a set of observations taken at specific times, usually at equal intervals

Managers use various quantitative techniques to make sales forecasts. Time-series forecasting is one approach. A **time series** is a set of observations taken at specific times, usually at equal intervals. Examples of time series are a department store's total monthly or yearly sales receipts, and the daily closing prices of a share of stock.[10] The manager uses time-series forecasting to plot and identify basic trends (such as rising sales in China) over time.

Sometimes, just tracking activity over time is not enough. Instead, managers may want to understand the causal relationship between two variables. For example, the sales department at General Motors needs to know the causal relationship between car sales and an indicator of economic activity, like disposable income. Causal forecasting estimates the company factor (such as sales) based on other factors (such as disposable income, or level of unemployment). Managers use statistical techniques such as correlation analysis (which shows how closely the variables are related) to identify the necessary relationships.

Qualitative Forecasting Methods It is true that in developing useful plans, hard data and numbers are always important. However, planning also always involves human judgment. Qualitative forecasting tools emphasize human judgment. They gather, in as logical, unbiased, and systematic a way as possible, all the information and human judgment that a manager can apply to a situation.

jury of executive opinion: a forecasting method that involves asking a group of key executives to forecast sales for, say, the next year

sales force estimation method: the gathering of the opinions of the sales force regarding what they think sales will be in the forthcoming period

The **jury of executive opinion** is one example. It involves asking a group of key executives to forecast sales for, say, the next year. Generally, each executive receives data on forecasted economic levels and anticipated corporate changes. Each executive then makes an independent forecast. They then reconcile their differences. The **sales force estimation method** gathers the opinions of the sales force regarding what they think sales will be in the forthcoming period. Each salesperson estimates his or her next year's sales, usually by product and customer. Sales managers then review each estimate, compare it with the previous year's data, and discuss changes with each salesperson. The sales manager then combines the separate estimates into a sales forecast for the firm.

Necessary though they may be, basing plans just on subjective forecasts can be perilous. Several years ago, Nortel Networks Corp. planned to meet "explosive customer demand" by adding 9,600 jobs.[11] Nortel executives arrived at their "explosive growth" forecast by asking their largest customers for sales estimates. Nortel's CEO later found that some of his largest customers told Nortel to gear up to ship them more equipment, even as their own sales were falling off.

Managing Now Managers today therefore often use software systems to improve their sales forecasting processes. For example, MTN is South Africa's main cellular network. In the past, the company based its forecasts for handsets on salespeople's estimates. Then the company tried a more sophisticated system, but it was still a manual one. Employees manually extracted data on details like inventories of handsets in stores and warehouses and on orders and current sales. That proved to be very time-consuming and still did not provide accurate forecasts.[12]

Management's solution was to turn to several software packages from SAS. Now, MTN's new data warehouse continuously receives information from a variety of sources, including daily sales and handset production lead times. With consultants from SAS, MTN created analytical software tools so its managers could better utilize this information.

The new system enabled management to analyze information from the company's data warehouse. For example, it helps management validate the sales force's forecasts and avoid both loss of sales and overstocking. Combined with two other SAS packages—an Internet application, and a wireless Internet gateway service—the sales force can now use information technology (IT) to interact directly with the data warehouse from anywhere. That gives them a better idea of which handset models sell better, where, and why.

data warehouse: that part of the computer system that collects and stores information on details like sales, inventory, products in transit, and product returns

The following Window on Managing Now and Practice IT features present more illustrations of IT's use in planning.

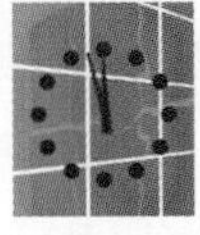

Window on Managing Now
Demand Forecasting at Wal-Mart

As most people know, Wal-Mart has many systems in place whose purpose is to keep costs down. Some of these systems—such as Wal-Mart's policy of paying low wages and of strenuously resisting unions—have understandably elicited the concern and even the anger of many critics. However, not all Wal-Mart's cost-reducing systems directly involve personnel issues. For example, the technology the company uses to monitor and forecast customer preferences helps to keep costs down.

Wal-Mart's forecasting is largely automated thanks to technology. Here, Wal-Mart relies on its data warehouse. A **data warehouse** is that part of the computer system that collects and stores information on details like sales, inventory, products in transit, and product returns, information it gathers from Wal-Mart's computer terminals in 3,000 stores. Software programs then help Wal-Mart's managers to use these data to analyze trends, understand customers, and more effectively manage inventory. As one example, information in its data warehouse tracks the sale by store of about 100,000 Wal-Mart products. Thus, Wal-Mart managers can examine the sales of individual items for individual stores and can also create seasonal profiles for each item. Armed with this information, managers can more accurately plan what items will be needed for each store and when.

Wal-Mart took this a step further. It teamed with suppliers like Warner-Lambert to create an Internet-based collaborative forecasting and replenishment system (Wal-Mart calls it CFAR). We saw that Wal-Mart collects data (on things like sales by product and by store, and seasonal trends) for its sales of Warner-Lambert's (and others') products. Managers at Wal-Mart and Warner-Lambert then collaborated to develop forecasts for sales by store for Warner-Lambert products, such as Listerine. Once Warner-Lambert and Wal-Mart planners decide on mutually acceptable figures, a standard purchase plan is finalized and sent to Warner-Lambert's manufacturing planning system. The supplier then automatically replenishes items. So far, CFAR has helped cut the supply-cycle time for Listerine from twelve weeks to six. That means less inventory, lower costs, and lower prices.[13]

Marketing Research

marketing research: the procedures managers use to develop and analyze customer-related information that helps managers make decisions

secondary data: information collected or published already

primary data: information specifically collected to solve a current problem

Marketing research refers to the procedures managers use to develop and analyze customer-related information that helps managers make decisions.[14] Marketing researchers depend on two main types of information. One source is **secondary data**, or information collected or published already. Good sources of secondary data include the Internet, libraries, trade associations, company files and sales reports, and commercial data (for instance, from companies such as A. C. Nielsen, which tracks television-viewing habits). **Primary data** refer to information specifically collected to solve a current problem. Primary data sources include mail and personal surveys, in-depth and focus-group interviews, and personal observation (watching the reactions of customers who walk into a store).[15]

Competitive Intelligence

Developing useful plans requires knowing as much as possible about what competitors are doing or are planning to do. Competitive intelligence (CI) is a systematic way to obtain and analyze public information about competitors.

PRACTICE IT
Demand Forecasting and Planning at Oxford University Press

Faced with increasing pressure from giant competitors like Pearson and McGraw-Hill, OUP's managers needed a faster way to forecast and estimate textbook demand. Its education and children's division managers wanted to increase market share. To do so, they had to make sure the right quantities of books—not too many and not too few—are in stock when customers need them. The manual system involving sales force estimates and spreadsheets was not working. What would you suggest?

They installed a software package called SAP Demand Planning. Working with the software supplier, OUP employees input into this system details about each title, including its international standard book number, the most economical order quantities, reprint lead times, and three years of historical sales. Each night, data (such as daily sales of each title, current inventory levels, and numbers of books returned) from the education and children's divisions' back-office systems download automatically into the new Demand Planning system. The Demand Planning system then automatically provides OUP's managers with the planning information they need, such as "how many copies of this book will likely be ordered next month?" E-mail or cell-phone text messaging triggers alerts if the system senses a wide discrepancy between historical data for the book and the system's forecast. Stock managers then determine if there's some new factor—such as a huge new adoption—affecting the forecast.

The result has been a dramatic improvement in Oxford University Press's forecasts and plans. Stock managers now have up-to-date information for making reprint decisions. Demand Planning's internal analytical tools do the sales-estimate computations. A graphical digital dashboard user interface (similar to Figure 7.2) makes it easy for managers to see at a glance things like forecasted demand for a book versus historical demand. It also enables them to analyze the most profitable titles, identify why sales forecasts are falling short of target, and track the education and children's divisions' performance against plan. The result is real-time, accurate sales forecasts and plans, and the ability to make corrections quickly, if necessary.

FIGURE 7.2

Balanced Scorecard Digital Dashboard Example

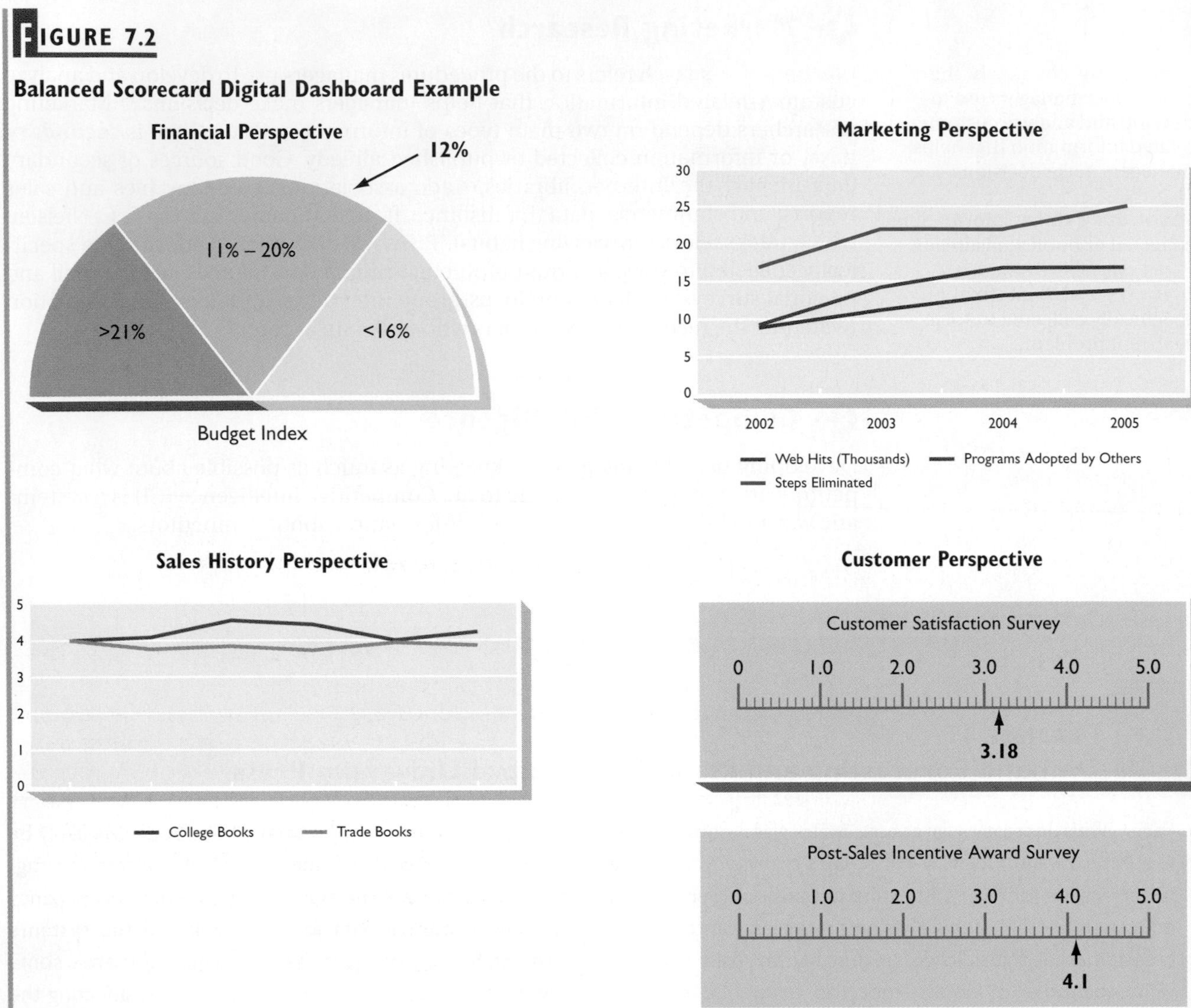

SOURCE: Adapted from www.balancedscorecardsurvival.com/balancedscorecardsample.html (downloaded January 7, 2006).

Companies increased their use of private intelligence services over the past few years. Today, several competitive intelligence companies including Stratfor, Marsh and McClellan's Marsh Kroll subsidiary, and Jane's Information Group also help companies assess terrorism and related risks.[16]

Competitive intelligence practitioners use various tools to discover what their clients' competitors are doing. These tools include having specialists visit their facilities, hiring their workers, and questioning their suppliers and customers. CI firms also do extensive Internet searches to unearth information about competitors, as well as searches like reading stock analysts' reports on the competitors' prospects. CI consulting firms use former prosecutors, business analysts, and FBI and Drug Enforcement Agency (DEA) employees to uncover the sorts of

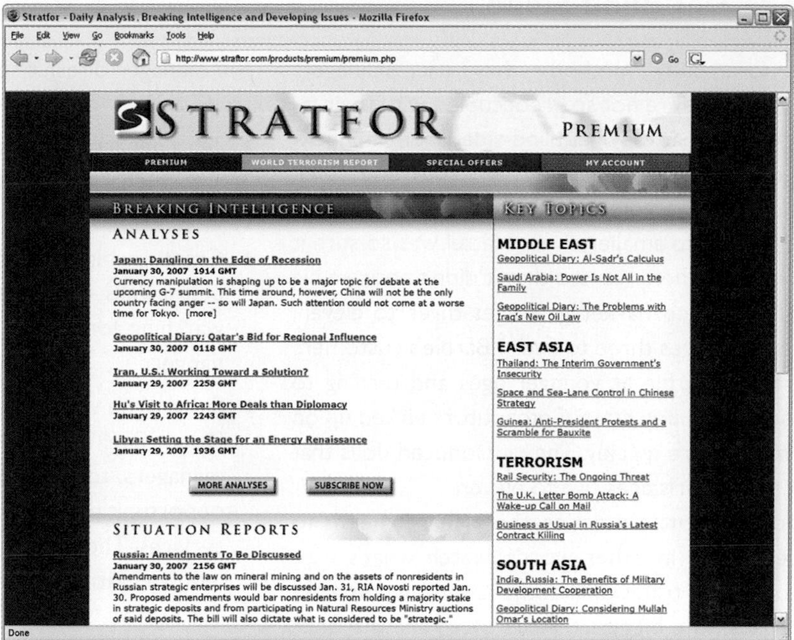

Today, several competitive intelligence companies including Stratfor help companies assess terrorism and related risks.

(Courtesy, Stratfor)

information you might want before entering into an alliance with another company, or before deciding to get into some business.[17]

Using the Internet is a gold mine for competitive intelligence investigations. Amazon.com used this approach to analyze a competitor's new business move. Barnes & Noble had just listed three new-product category tabs on its homepage. Amazon.com hired a competitive intelligence firm to analyze Barnes & Noble's Web activity. They found that only one of the new tabs was popular with shoppers.

Suggestions for unearthing competitors' intelligence over the Web include:[18]

- Use a search engine to get a list of all the webpages your competitor has opened on the Internet by typing in url://companyname.com
- Find all the websites linked to your competitor's site by typing in link://www.companyname.com
- Comb through your competitor's website looking for information on things like the firm's business goals.
- If your competitor is publicly traded, carefully review its investor relations pages. These pages contain public information like quarterly profits reports and unusual expenses.
- On the website, review your competitor's press releases; these may provide insights into potential problems like those indicated by restructuring plans.
- Carefully review your competitor's listed job openings. For example, is one of its product lines listing many new job openings? That might signal a planned expansion.
- Check out message boards and chatrooms dedicated to the company. These often contain customer and/or employee complaints that provide insights into the firm's plans and or weaknesses. The Improving Your *Forecasting* Skills feature presents additional recommendations.

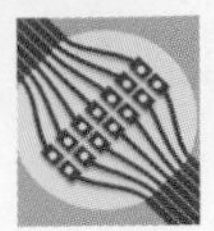

Improving Your *Forecasting* Skills
Don't Get Blind-Sided

Whichever forecasting methods they use, managers should make sure they're not so preoccupied with their familiar competitors that they get blind-sided from an unexpected direction. For example, between 2001 and 2004, Mattel lost about 20 percent of its share of the fashion-doll Barbie-type market to smaller rivals. Mattel was so sure it knew what its customers wanted that it didn't notice a big change: Barbie's target market, girls ages three to eleven, had shrunk to girls ages three to five.[19] Barbie's customers were outgrowing Barbie at younger ages and turning to dolls that looked like pop stars. Competitors picked up on that trend much more quickly. They introduced dolls that better appealed to girls ages five to eleven.

The moral is that, in practice, the manager needs to scan the periphery (in other words, watch what's happening beyond your traditional competitors) when making plans because the biggest threats often are the ones the manager doesn't see coming. There are several ways to do this:

- Tell a department such as market research that they are also in charge of watching out for unexpected events, not just the usual competitors.
- Create a high-level lookout. For example, IBM has a unit it calls Crow's Nest. This team is responsible for watching for new and unexpected opportunities and dangers.
- Start a new initiatives program. For example, Royal Dutch Shell's Game-Changer program encourages its managers to envision and test possibilities for new opportunities beyond the company's core products and services. The program quickly produced 400 ideas and led to creating thirty new technologies and three new businesses.

Types of Plans

descriptive plans: plans that state in words what is to be achieved, by whom, when, and at what cost

budgets: plans stated in financial terms

graphic plans: plans that show what is to be achieved, how, and when, in charts or in graphs

tactical plans: the departmental plans for supporting the business's companywide strategic plan; also known as functional plans

functional plans: (see tactical plans)

operational plans: plans that focus on detailed, day-to-day planning, such as how many machines to use that day

Managers express their plans in a variety of formats. For example, **descriptive plans**, like a student's program of studies, state in words what is to be achieved, by whom, when, and at what cost. **Budgets** are plans stated in financial terms. **Graphic plans** like those in Figure 7.3 show what is to be achieved, how, and when, in charts or in graphs.

Plans also differ in the time span they cover. Top management usually engages in long-term (three- to five-year) business or strategic planning. Middle managers focus on developing midterm tactical plans (of up to two to three years' duration). **Tactical plans** (also sometimes called **functional plans**) pick up where strategic plans leave off: these are your firm's marketing, production, and personnel plans. They show each department's role in helping carry out the company's overall strategic plan. First-line managers focus on short-term **operational plans**. They focus on detailed, day-to-day planning. The Gantt chart (Figure 7.3) is an operational plan.

Finally, some plans are made to be used once, and others, repeatedly. For example, some plans are **programs**. Like a student's program of studies, these present in an orderly fashion all the steps in a major one-time project, used once.

Standing Plans In contrast, managers use *standing plans* repeatedly.[20] Policies, procedures, and rules are examples of standing plans. **Policies** are broad guidelines. For example, it might be the policy at Saks Fifth Avenue that "we sell only high-fashion apparel and top-of-the-line jewelry." This is a plan because it shows

FIGURE 7.3

Gantt Scheduling Chart for Acme Strategic Report Projects, January 1–15, 2007

The Gantt chart helps Acme's managers plan their consultants' time and keep track of each project's progress. Similar Gantt charts help managers in factories plan machine usage for building different products.

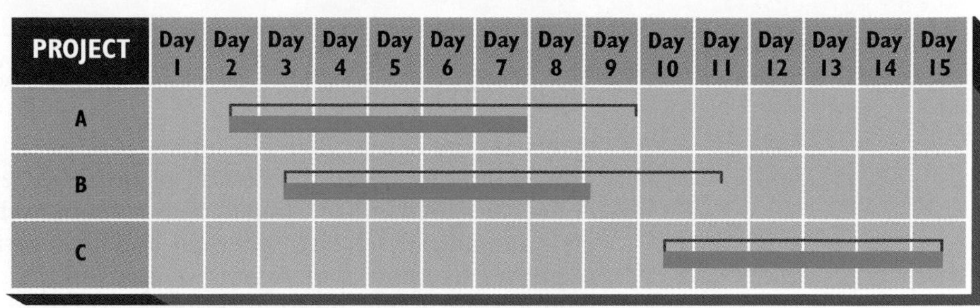

programs: plans that present in an orderly fashion all the steps in a major one-time project

policies: broad guidelines regarding the company's approach to certain major decisions, such as what quality merchandise to offer

procedures: plans that spell out what to do if a specific situation arises

rules: specific guides to day-to-day action

business plan: a plan that provides a comprehensive view of the firm's financial, sales, and business situation today and of its companywide and departmental goals and plans for the next three to five years

marketing plan: a plan that specifies the nature of your product or service (for instance, its variety, quality, design, and features) and the approaches the company plans to take with respect to pricing and promoting the product or service and getting it sold and delivered to the customers

the firm's apparel and jewelry buyers what general course of action they should follow in choosing merchandise to buy for their stores. **Procedures** spell out what to do if a specific situation arises; for example, "Before refunding the customer's purchase price, the salesperson should carefully inspect the garment and then obtain approval for the refund from the floor manager." **Rules** are specific guides to action; for example, "Under no condition will we refund the purchase price after thirty days." In standing plans, the goal or purpose is usually implied but clear.

The Business Plan

The company's **business plan** provides a comprehensive view of the firm's situation today and of its companywide and departmental goals and plans for the next three to five years. Managers most often use the term *business plan* in relation to smaller businesses. It is the sort of plan that investors or lenders want to see before providing money to the firm. However, small businesses don't have monopolies on business plans. Even Dell or Microsoft has a version of a comprehensive plan like this. They often label it their long-term or perhaps strategic plan.

There are no rigid rules regarding what such plans must contain. However, they usually include, at a minimum, (1) a description of the business (including ownership and products or services), (2) the marketing plan, (3) the production plan, (4) the financial plan, and (5) the personnel/human resource plan.

The Marketing Plan To be successful, a business must have customers. And to have customers, it should have a plan for marketing its products or services to them. Acme Business Consulting may have the best consultants. But if the potential clients don't know those consultants exist, Acme's prospects are limited. The **marketing plan** specifies the nature of your product or service (for instance, its variety, quality, design, and features). It also shows the approaches the company plans to take with respect to pricing and promoting the product or service and getting it sold and delivered to the customers. (Marketing managers call these the four P's—product, price, promotion, and place.)

The Production/Operations Plan Implementing the marketing plan necessitates having productive assets. For example, it takes factories and machines to assemble Dell's PCs. Therefore, Dell must plan well in advance for meeting its projected demand for the technology to take orders for, build, and distribute its PCs. The production or operations plan shows how the company will produce the products it plans to sell.

Managing Now The consulting firm Accenture helped Dell install an improved Internet-based production-planning system. This system integrates Dell's entire sales to manufacturing to delivery supply chain. With it, Dell and its suppliers automatically receive real-time updates on sales and production schedules. Suppliers see what components Dell needs where and when. Truckers see what components to pick up from suppliers and where to deliver them and what Dell products to deliver and to whom.[21] The system virtually automates the production-planning process for Dell and its suppliers and truckers.

The Personnel/Human Resource Plan Anything the company does, or plans to do, requires managers and other personnel, and therefore a personnel plan. For example, a consulting company's projected number of clients helps determine how many consultants it needs at each stage of the plan. The personnel plan shows how many of which type of employee the company will need.

The Financial Plan What's the bottom line? is the first question many managers and bankers ask. The question underscores a truism about business and management. At the end of the day, most of a manager's plans and goals and accomplishments end up expressed in financial terms.

The financial plan is the vehicle for doing so. The financial plan translates the manager's sales, production, and personnel plans into financial terms. For example, a projected (or pro forma or planned) profit and loss (P&L) statement shows the revenue, cost, and profit (or loss) implications of a company's marketing, production, and personnel plans.

Business Planning Packages

Several good business planning software packages are available, such as Business Plan Pro from Palo Alto Software. For example, Business Plan Pro contains all the information and planning aids someone would need to create a business plan from beginning to end. It contains thirty sample plans; detailed sample plan outlines; complete, step-by-step instructions (with examples) for creating each part of a plan (executive summary, market analysis, and so on); and financial planning spreadsheets. It also contains easy-to-use tables (for instance, for making sales forecasts) and automatic programs for creating color, three-dimensional (3D) charts for showing facts like monthly sales and yearly profits.

Strategic Planning

Online Study Center
ACE the Test
Managing Now! LIVE

As explained earlier, the planning process usually starts with managers formulating a special type of plan, a strategic plan. A **strategic plan** spells out (1) the desired business or businesses the firm wants to be in, in terms of products, geographic sales area, and competitive advantage, and (2) the major steps it will take to get there, given (3) the company's opportunities and threats and internal strengths and weaknesses. A **strategy** is a course of action. It shows how the enterprise will move from the business it is in now to the business it wants to be in. **Strategic planning** is the process of identifying the firm's business today, its

strategic plan: a plan that spells out (1) the desired business or businesses the firm wants to be in, in terms of products, geographic sales area, and competitive advantage, and (2) the major steps it will take to get there, given (3) the company's opportunities and threats and internal strengths and weaknesses

strategy: a course of action that shows how the enterprise will move from the business it is in now to the business it wants to be in

strategic planning: the process of identifying the firm's business today, its desired future business, and the courses of action it should pursue to get there given its opportunities, threats, strengths, and weaknesses

desired future business, and the courses of action it should pursue to get there given its opportunities, threats, strengths, and weaknesses.

As an example, the Ford Motor Company in 2006 was struggling to compete against stronger, more profitable competitors from abroad. In early 2006, it introduced a new strategic plan, which its managers dubbed Way Forward. It envisioned moving Ford from a loss-making, relatively ponderous company to a leaner, more profitable one. Ford's strategies for moving there include cutting about 25 percent of its North American vehicle capacity and 10 percent of its white-collar workforce and streamlining its purchasing process.[22] (By mid-2006, Ford, facing unexpectedly tough competition, revised its plan to strip even more costs and to do so faster. It then replaced its CEO with a new one.)

The Strategic Management Process

As you can see in Figure 7.4, strategic planning represents the first steps of the strategic management process. The seven-step *strategic management process* includes both strategic planning and strategy implementation and execution.

Step 1: Define the Current Business and Mission Every company must choose the terrain on which it will compete—in particular, what products it will sell, where it will sell them, and how its products or services will differ from its competitors'. Rolex and Seiko are both in the watch business. But Rolex sells a limited product line of high-priced quality watches. Seiko sells a wide variety of

FIGURE 7.4

Strategic Management Process

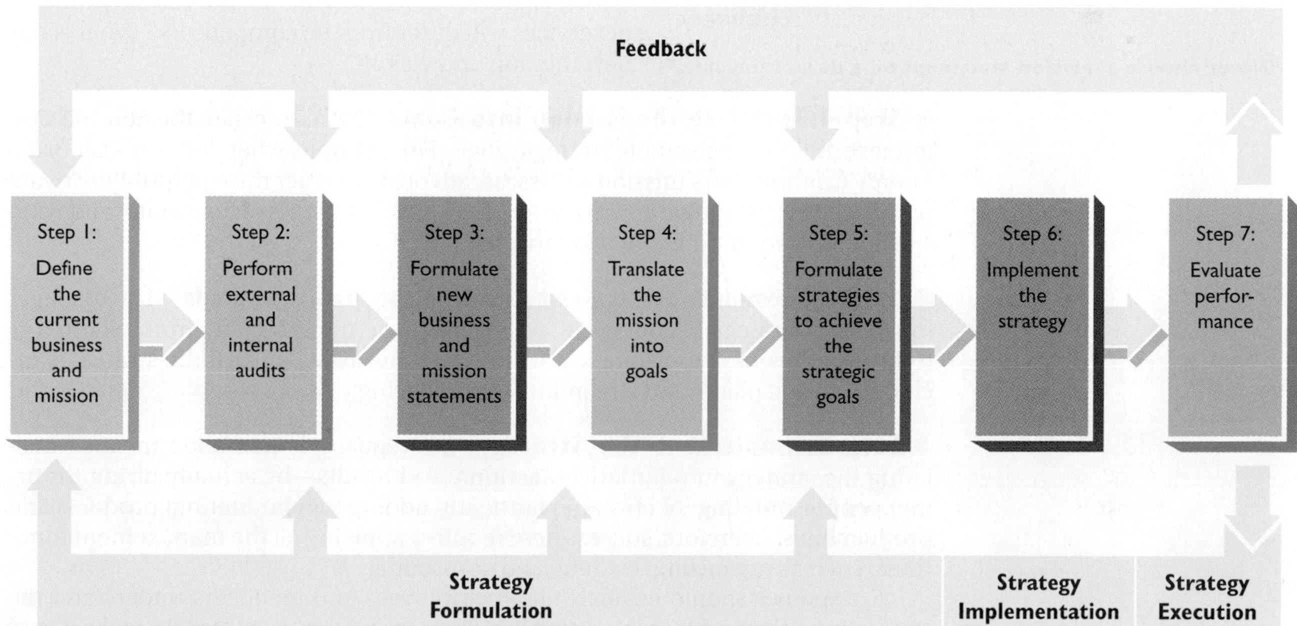

SOURCE: Adapted from Fred David, *Strategic Management* (Upper Saddle River, N.J.: Prentice Hall, 2005), p. 77.

relatively inexpensive but innovative specialty watches with features like compasses and altimeters.

Sometimes, managers use the words *vision* and *mission* to help clarify the businesses in which the company should compete. The manager's vision for the company usually provides a broad overview of where the manager wants the company heading. For example, Rupert Murdoch, chair of News Corporation (which owns the Fox network and many newspapers and satellite TV operations), has a vision of an integrated, global, satellite-based news-gathering, entertainment, and Internet and multimedia firm. WebMD CEO Jeffrey Arnold saw WebMD supplying everything a consumer might want to know about medical-related issues.

The firm's mission statement is usually more specific. Visions show in very broad terms what the business should be tomorrow. The mission describes what it needs to accomplish today. For example, the mission of the California Energy Commission is to "assess, advocate and act through public/private partnerships to improve energy systems that promote a strong economy and a healthy environment."[23]

"Never choose a mission statement on a dark, rainy day."

Step 2: Perform External and Internal Audits Here the manager sizes up the situation. Ideally, the new strategic plan and mission should make sense in terms of the external opportunities and threats the firm faces and in terms of its internal strengths and weaknesses. Managers base their strategic plans on careful analyses of their external and internal situations. We'll discuss strategic analysis tools for doing this later in this chapter.

Step 3: Formulate New Business and Mission Statements Based on the situation analysis, what should our new business be, in terms of what products it will sell, where it will sell them, and how its products or services will differ from its competitors'? What is our new mission and vision?

Step 4: Translate the Mission into Goals Next, translate the new mission into executable, measurable strategic goals. For example, what does the California Energy Commission's mission to "assess, advocate and act through public/private partnerships to improve energy systems . . ." mean in terms of how many and what specific types of partnerships to form, and when?

Step 5: Formulate Strategies to Achieve the Strategic Goals The manager formulates strategies (courses of action) to move the company from where it is today as a business to where it wants to be tomorrow. At Ford, the strategies included closing plants and streamlining purchasing.

Step 6: Implement the Strategy Strategy implementation means translating the strategy into initiatives, actions, and results—by actually hiring (or firing) people, building (or closing) plants, and adding (or eliminating) products and product lines. Therefore, success here requires applying all the management functions, such as organizing, leading, and controlling.

Companies should ensure that all employees and managers understand the strategy and their roles in executing it.[24] Thus, managers usually try to make it easy to communicate the basic principles of their strategies.[25] For example, Dell's strategy boils down to "sell direct."

FIGURE 7.5

Relationships Among Strategies in Multiple-Business Firms

Companies typically formulate three types of strategies: corporate-level strategies, business-level/competitive strategies, and functional-level strategies.

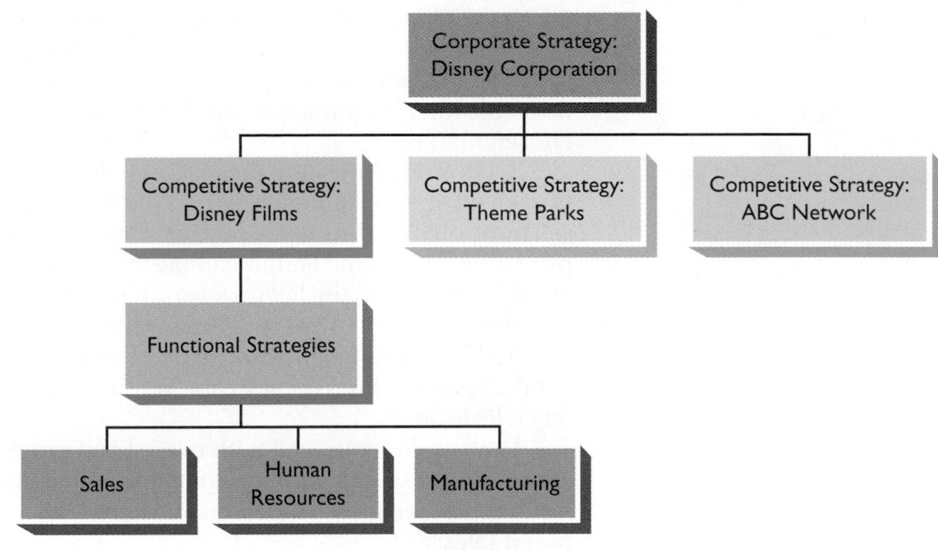

strategic control: the process of assessing the company's progress toward achieving its strategic goals and taking corrective action as needed

● **Step 7: Evaluate Performance** **Strategic control** is the process of assessing the company's progress toward achieving its strategic goals and taking corrective action as needed. Here, management monitors progress and asks why deviations exist. Management simultaneously reviews the firm's strategic situation (competitors, technical advances, customer demographics, and so on) to see if it should make any strategic adjustments.

Strategic plans don't always work out. When General Motors sold the last of its Hughes Electronics assets, it was the end of a plan put in place years earlier. GM had bought both Electronic Data Systems and Hughes Electronics to automate and reinvigorate their automobile production and sales. Many believe that the acquisitions were actually a distraction that helped push GM's market share down.[26]

There are three main types of strategies, corresponding to the level in the company for which you are planning: corporate-level, business-level/competitive, and functional-level strategies. We summarize these strategies in Figure 7.5.

Types of Corporate Strategies

Every company must decide the number of businesses in which it will compete and the relationships that will exist among those businesses. A company's corporate-level strategy describes the variety of products or services the company will sell, the number of businesses in which it will compete, and the relations among those businesses. For example, with a *concentration/single-business* corporate strategy, the company offers one product or product line, usually in one market. Firms with single-business strategies include McDonald's, KFC, and Gerber's. The main advantage here is that the company can specialize, which should allow it to do that one thing better than its competitors. The disadvantage is having all one's eggs in one basket. That's one reason why Harley-Davidson successfully diversified into clothing, restaurants, and finance. There are several other standard or generic corporate strategies managers use.

● **Diversification** Diversification is a strategy of expanding into related or unrelated products or market segments. Diversification helps the firm avoid the problem of having all its eggs in one basket by spreading risk among several products or markets. However, diversification also forces the company's managers to split their attention and resources among several products or markets. Thus, diversification may undermine the firm's ability to compete successfully in its chosen markets.

Related diversification means diversifying into other industries so that a firm's lines of business still possess some kind of fit. For example, Ferrari could probably sell more high-performance cars if it wanted to, but, preferring exclusivity, it limits production. However, Ferrari capitalizes on its exclusive image by diversifying. For example, the company licenses Ferrari designer logo apparel and sponsors weekend trips for Ferrari owners to Napa Valley.[27] In contrast, unrelated or conglomerate diversification means diversifying into products or markets not related to the firm's present businesses or to one another. For example, Getty Oil diversified into pay television.

Amazon.com pursued both related and unrelated diversification. It originally specialized in selling books. It soon diversified into music and electronics. It then formed partnerships with companies like Toys "R" Us to manage their Internet-based sales.[28]

● **Vertical Integration** Vertical integration means owning or controlling the inputs to the firm's processes and/or the channels through which it distributes its products or services. Thus, Shell drills and refines its own oil and also sells it through company-controlled outlets.

Today, firms like Cisco often do not produce the electronic devices (such as cell phones) that bear their names. Instead, vertically integrated manufacturers like Solectron and Flextronics assemble them. These manufacturers (such as Solectron) are continuing to integrate vertically. They are buying up design firms and even shipping firms, because "many are trying to provide cradle to grave services from designing to final ship to customers."[29]

Diversification and integration needn't rely on only internal growth; sometimes the firm can gain similar benefits by partnering with other companies. Strategic alliances or joint ventures are often the strategies of choice here. They are formal agreements between two or more companies that enable the partners to benefit from complementary strengths.

● **Joint Ventures** Joint ventures are companies that involve joint ownership and operation by two or more companies of a business. For example, a small, Florida-based company with a patented industrial pollution–control filter formed a joint venture with a subsidiary of Shell Oil. Here, the joint venture was a separate corporation based in Europe to which each partner contributed funds and other resources. The oil firm got access to a product that could revolutionize its distilling facilities. The filter company got access to the oil firm's vast resources and European marketing network.

Joint ventures are one example of strategic alliances—agreements between actual or potential competitors to achieve some strategic aim. Managers should enter such alliances with care. Several years ago, Bertelsmann's BMG music subsidiary decided to partner with the original Napster, the file-sharing service. Predictably, the other major record labels were soon suing Napster for copyright infringement, and Napster soon suspended its file-sharing service and went bankrupt. Its board then ousted Bertelsmann's CEO, who had masterminded the alliance.[30]

The *virtual corporation* is a modern version of the strategic alliance. It is "a temporary network of independent companies—suppliers, customers, even erstwhile rivals—linked by information technology to share skills, costs, and access to one another's markets."[31] Successful virtual corporations rely on trust and on a sense of codestiny: everyone in these alliances needs to recognize that the fate of each partner and of the alliance as a whole depends on each partner doing its share.

Virtual corporations usually aren't corporations at all in the traditional sense of common ownership or a chain of command. Instead, they are networks of companies. Each lends the virtual corporation/network its special expertise. Information technology enables the virtual corporation's far-flung constituents to communicate and make their contributions.

Managing Now The website eLance (www.elance.com) provides a virtual environment that enables freelance consultants and graphic designers to sell their services to businesses. For example, it allows them to post information about their skills and fees.[32] Denver-based graphic designer Serena Rodriguez gets about 10 percent of her business through that site. She works on projects electronically and long distance, without seeing or being a formal part of client firms like pharmaceuticals manufacturer Merck. Getting a big project often means recruiting other free agents to join your virtual team. For example, says website designer Andrew Keeler, "I work with lots of people here in San Francisco whom I've never even met."[33]

Types of Competitive Strategies

competitive strategy: a plan to establish a profitable and sustainable competitive position against the forces that determine industry competition

Whether a company concentrates on a single business or diversifies into a dozen or more, each of those businesses needs a competitive strategy. Professor Michael Porter defines **competitive strategy** as a plan to establish a profitable and sustainable competitive position against the forces that determine industry competition.[34] The competitive strategy specifies the basis on which the company will compete. For instance, Volvo competes based on safety, and Lexus competes based on high quality. Firms generally pursue one of three competitive strategies: cost leadership, differentiation, or focus.

Cost Leadership Most firms try to hold down costs. A *cost leadership* competitive strategy goes beyond this. A business that pursues this strategy aims to be the low-cost leader in an industry. It usually does this by minimizing costs across the board.

Information technology helps Westdeutsche Bank pursue its low-cost competitive strategy.

Managing Now Managers increasingly use information technology (IT) to drive their cost leadership strategies. Information technology helps Westdeutsche Bank pursue its low-cost competitive strategy. The German bank's mortgage subsidiary's strategic goal is to become the lowest-cost provider of real-estate loans for private customers through its branches in London and Germany.[35] To accomplish this goal, management knew it had to streamline its entire loan-approval process.

Management's solution included installing records-management software from SAP. The new system dramatically reduced the need for paper-based manual tasks, improved the bank's ability to respond quickly to customer inquiries, and improved efficiency. Management estimates their records-management unit is saving at least 2½ hours per employee per week with the new system. That time savings helps the bank achieve its strategic goal of being the low-cost leader in its markets.

Differentiation With a *differentiation strategy*, a firm seeks to be unique in its industry along some dimensions that are valued by buyers.[36] The manager picks one or more attributes of the product or service (such as quality, reliabilty, or high fashion) that buyers (hopefully) perceive as important. The firm then positions itself to meet those needs better than its competitors, for instance, by how it produces, advertises, or sells the product or service.

Companies differentiate in many ways. These range from the product image offered by cosmetics firms (Revlon) to concrete differences such as product durability (Caterpillar), safety (Volvo), usability (Apple Computer), and quality (Lexus).

Focusers Differentiators (like Volvo) and low-cost leaders (like Dell) are generalists when it comes to the market. They aim to sell to all or most potential buyers. Pursuing a *focus competitive strategy* means the company selects a narrow market segment and then builds its business by serving the customers in that niche better or more cheaply than do its generalist competitors. Here, the manager must ask, "By focusing on a narrow niche market, can we provide our target customers with a product or service better or more cheaply than could our generalist competitors?" If the answer is yes (and if the market is big enough), it may pay to focus. A Pea in the Pod, a chain of maternity stores, focuses on selling stylish clothes to pregnant working women. By focusing, the company can provide a wider range of such clothes to its target customers than can generalist competitors like Macy's or JCPenney.

Managers now often make IT-based systems the centerpiece of their competitive strategies. The accompanying Window on Managing Now feature illustrates this.

Functional Strategies

functional strategy: a strategy that lays out a department's basic operating policies, such as where to build plants and what sorts of employees to hire

Finally, functional strategies flow from and depend on the business's competitive strategy. A **functional strategy** lays out a department's basic operating policies. For example, Dell competes as the industry's low-cost leader. To execute this competitive strategy, it formulated departmental functional strategies that support Dell's desired (low-cost leader) position. For example, the customer-service department created a new system that enables Dell advisers to link to customers' computers (with the customers' permission) to efficiently and quickly analyze technical problems. We saw the production department uses special supply chain systems to automatically coordinate production and shipping. The sales department relies almost exclusively on direct telephone or Internet sales to eliminate the costs of intermediaries such as retail stores.

Strategic Planning Tools

Strategic planning involves choosing strategies that will balance (1) the firm's strengths and weaknesses with (2) its external opportunities and threats. Ideally, the manager wants to take advantage of opportunities (such as booming demand in China), while capitalizing on the company's strengths (such as a network of friends and acquaintances in Asia). He or she also wants to anticipate and

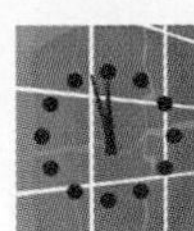

Window on Managing Now
Pella's New Competitive Advantage

Pella Corporation manufactures and sells standard and custom windows and doors through a network of sales branches and sales associates throughout the United States and the world. The company's basic supply chain starts with the customer sale. The chain of events then includes creating the actual order, designing the product, scheduling production, acquiring the raw materials and components (such as locks and hinges), manufacturing it, and delivering it to the customer.

Getting from the initial order to the final delivery is actually quite complex. Doing so involves hundreds of not-so-obvious supporting tasks. These tasks include, for example, creating invoices, computing sales commissions, sending delivery notices to contractors, and generating accounts payable authorizations for paying suppliers. And because Pella produces custom products, there are literally millions of possibilities when it comes to dimensions, window color, and composition. It's also a very expensive process. It used to be filled with costs for manually completing things like orders, production schedules, inventory lists, and delivery notices.

Strategically, Pella is a differentiator. It produces window and doors, with a strong brand image for quality and reliability, at competitive costs. The company's managers believed it could strengthen its differentiation strategy by automating and streamlining the steps in its supply chain process. They did not want just lower costs, although that was important. They wanted to deliver more value to their customers by offering better-designed products faster and with a minimum of hassle.

Working with consultants, Pella installed Oracle E-Business Suite. This enterprise software system included software packages such as Oracle Manufacturing and Oracle Procurement, Sales Online, Order Management, and Marketing. The new system dramatically improved Pella's operations and competitiveness. For example, the Oracle Procurement package helped reduce the number of calls between Pella's purchasing department and suppliers by as much as 95 percent because it processes most of these purchase transactions online automatically. That saved Pella about 20 percent in unplanned overtime labor hours. Pella also now puts bar codes on all its products and components, so it's easier to track them by just scanning the item into Pella's new Oracle system. This change led to about a 20 percent reduction in warehouse receiving labor costs, and means managers can keep closer tabs on inventory.

This Oracle Web-based E-business Suite system provides Pella with a new competitive advantage—delivering accurate orders more quickly and at lower cost. Customers can now get the products they ordered faster and at lower cost than they might otherwise. It thereby helped management strengthen Pella's differentiation strategy. The company can now deliver even more quality and reliability to its customers by offering better-designed products faster, at lower costs.[37]

make accommodations for threats and reduce (or avoid) strategies that might depend on the firm's weaknesses. Managers use SWOT analysis, environmental scanning, portfolio analysis, and the BCG matrix as strategic analyis tools to accomplish this balancing act.

● SWOT Analysis Managers use SWOT analysis to consolidate information regarding their firm's internal strengths and weaknesses and external opportunities and threats. The SWOT analysis matrix (shown in Figure 7.6) supplies illustrative generic strengths, weaknesses, opportunities, and threats (SWOT) to guide the manager's analysis. It also provides a standardized four-quadrant format for compiling the company's strengths, weaknesses, opportunities, and threats.

FIGURE 7.6

SWOT Matrix with Examples of a Company's Strengths, Weaknesses, Opportunities, and Threats

Potential Strengths	**Potential Weaknesses**
• Market leadership • Strong research and development • High-quality products • Cost advantages • Patents	• Large inventories • Excess capacity for market • Management turnover • Weak market image • Lack of management depth
Potential Opportunities	**Potential Threats**
• New overseas markets • Falling trade barriers • Competitors failing • Diversification • Economy rebounding	• Market saturation • Threat of takeover • Low-cost foreign competition • Slower market growth • Growing government regulation

Environmental Scanning Managers traditionally scan or monitor six key areas of the company's environment to identify opportunities and threats for their SWOT analyses. Environmental scanning is the process of gathering and compiling information about six environmental forces that might be relevant to the firm's strategic planners:

1. *Economic trends.* For example, the U.S. government now projects that the country's economic growth through 2014 will be below that of 1995–2005. What opportunities and threats would such a trend imply for businesspeople thinking of expanding in the United States and abroad? (GE recently reached the point where just over half its sales come from abroad.)

2. *Competition trends.* These trends involve actions taken or to be taken by current and potential competitors. For example, Google's emergence as a search powerhouse put Microsoft's search technology at a disadvantage.

3. *Political trends.* For example, most cigarette firms have diversified into other businesses as government regulations became more widespread.

4. *Technological trends.* For example, companies that own chains of movie theaters are irate that Disney wants to introduce new movies simulateously to the theaters and on DVDs.[38]

5. *Social and demographic trends.* These trends reflect the way people live and the nature of the people in a society, including what they value. In the United States, for instance, the proportion of Hispanic people is rising. This prompted GE's NBC division to purchase the Spanish-language network Telemundo.

6. *Geographic trends.* These trends relate to climate, natural resources, and so forth. In Florida, for instance, climate change has reduced the growing area for oranges. Florida growers therefore formed alliances with South American firms, who now supply much of the "Florida oranges."

Portfolio Analysis We saw that diversified firms end up with several businesses in their portfolios. For example, Rupert Murdoch's News Corporation owns

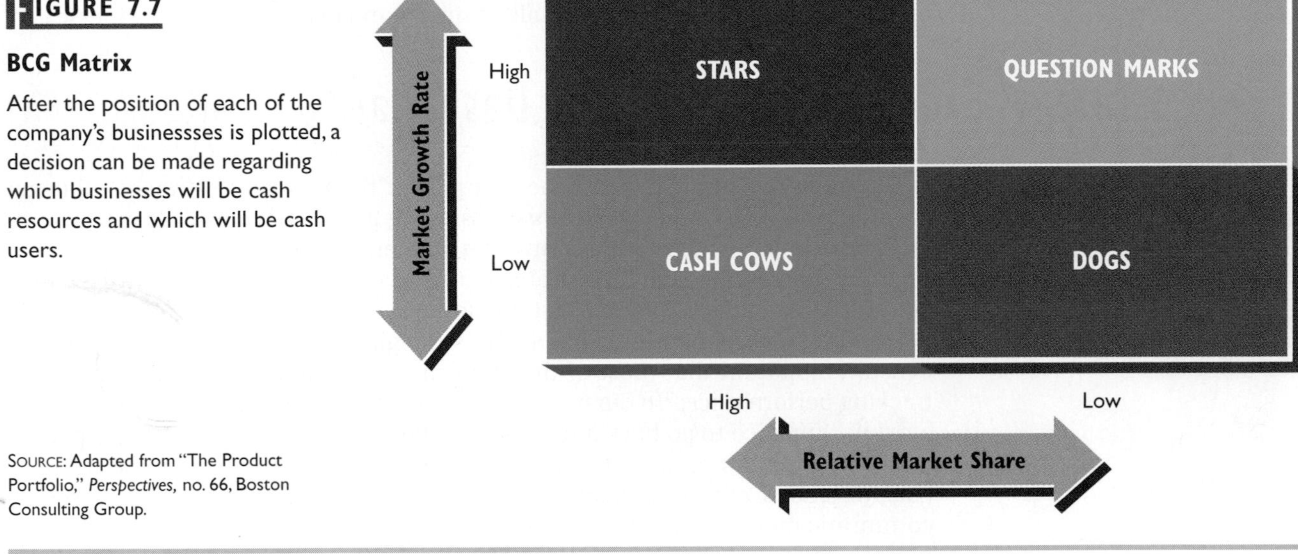

FIGURE 7.7

BCG Matrix

After the position of each of the company's businessses is plotted, a decision can be made regarding which businesses will be cash resources and which will be cash users.

SOURCE: Adapted from "The Product Portfolio," *Perspectives*, no. 66, Boston Consulting Group.

newspapers, television stations (Fox), and movie studios. How does the manager decide which business to keep and which to sell? The BCG matrix is one tool.

● BCG Matrix The BCG matrix, developed by the Boston Consulting Group, helps managers identify the relative attractiveness of each of a firm's businesses. It assumes that a particular business's attractiveness depends on two things—the growth rate of the business and the business's market share. As you can see in Figure 7.7, the manager plots each business on the matrix at the intersection of the business's estimated growth rate and relative competitive position (market share).

This process identifies four types of businesses (see Figure 7.7). *Stars* are businesses in high-growth industries and in which the company has a high relative market share. For example, Apple's iPod business has a high growth rate and a very high market share. Star businesses usually require large infusions of cash to sustain growth. Their strong market positions help them generate the needed cash.

Question marks are businesses in high-growth industries, but the firm has low market shares. The manager here faces a dilemma: the company must either divert cash from its other businesses to boost the question mark's market share or get out of the business.

Cash cows are businesses in low-growth industries (such as cigarettes) that enjoy high relative market shares. Being in a low-growth industry argues against making large cash infusions into these businesses. However, their high market share generally allows them to generate high sales and profits for years, even without much new investment. Cash cows can therefore help drive a firm's future success. For example, Kodak's consumer film unit is still a cash cow: the market is shrinking fast, but Kodak has a big market share. In one recent year, Kodak was able to generate over $1 billion in cash flow from its film business, which helped nurture its digital photography growth business (a star business for Kodak).[39]

Finally, *dogs* are businesses with low market shares in low-growth industries. The low market share puts the business in jeopardy relative to its larger competitors (who can vastly outadvertise it, for instance). As a result, dogs can quickly become cash traps, absorbing cash to support a hopeless low-growth situation. Managers usually sell them to raise cash to build their star and question-mark businesses.

Strategy Execution and Digital Dashboards

Online Study Center
ACE the Test
Managing Now! LIVE

Designing the strategy is just the first part of the manager's strategy management job. The challenge isn't just designing good strategies; it is getting employees to execute them. For example, researchers studied 1,800 large companies. About 90 percent had detailed strategic plans with strategic goals. However, only about one in eight achieved their strategic goals.[40]

Several factors help to explain why strategic goals go unmet. In one study, consultants found that most of the 200 firms they surveyed didn't even bother tracking performance: "In our experience, less than 15 % of the companies make it a regular practice to go back and compare the business's results with the performance forecast for each unit. . . ."[41] Other reasons for not achieving the strategic goals included allocating insufficient resources for executing the plan, poorly communicating the strategy and goals to employees, and not clarifying what employees had to do to execute the strategy or who was in charge of what.

In other words, many managers spend a lot of time formulating strategic plans, but then drop the ball, by not communicating their plans to employees, by not assigning each employee clear goals and responsibilities, and by not monitoring actual progress.

Traditional Methods for Improving Strategy Execution

Therefore, if management expects employees to help execute its strategic plan, it must ask, "Does every employee in the organization understand the business strategy and how he or she can contribute to the success of the strategy?"[42] Three traditional ways for accomplishing this include face-to-face communicating, management by objectives, and executive assignment tables.

Face-to-Face Communications Managers traditionally use face-to-face communications to encourage employees to help execute the managers' plans. CEO Lawrence Bossidy took this approach when he merged Honeywell Corp. and AlliedSignal. In his first two months, "I talked to probably 5,000 employees. I would go to Los Angeles and speak to 500 people, then to Phoenix and talk to another 500. I would stand on a loading dock and speak to people and answer their questions. We talked about what was wrong and what we should do about it."[43]

Management by Objectives (MBO) As we explained earlier, many firms still use management by objectives to communicate and set goals for employees and to monitor their employees' progress in meeting their goals. Department heads meet with their own bosses, and then with their own employees, to work out and assign objectives. The problem is that MBO is time-consuming. It requires numerous meetings among employees and supervisors, and then documenting each person's goals. Then managers typically assess each employee's performance no more than once or twice a year.

Executive Assignment Tables Many managers use an executive assignment table similar to the one shown in Table 7.1 to clarify who is responsible for what

TABLE 7.1

Executive Assignment Action Plan for Achieving a Long-Term Objective*

Long-term goal: have a minimum of 55% of sales revenue from customized products by 2008.

Each Manager's Executive Assignment/Goals	Which Manager Does This, and Who Helps Him or Her?		By When Does the Manager Do This?		Resources Manager Will Require . . .			How Will We Monitor Progress?
	Primary	Supporting	Start	Complete	Capital	Operating	Human Labor	
1. Complete market study on sales potential for customized products	Vice president, marketing	Vice president, sales	Year 1	Year 1		$10,000	500 hrs.	Written progress report
2. Revise sales forecasts for years 1, 2, and 3 to reflect changes	Vice president, sales	Vice president, marketing		Year 1			50 hrs.	Revise forecasts
3. Convert Building C to customized manufacturing operation by 2008	Vice president, manufacturing	Vice president, engineering; vice president, administration	Year 1	Year 2	$500,000	$80,000	1,100 hrs.	Written progress reports
4. Change compensation structure to create better incentives for customized sales	Vice president, human resources	Vice president, sales	Year 1	Year 1		$50,000	100 hrs.	Revised structure report
5. Train sales staff in new technology	Director of training	Vice president, sales	Year 2	Year 2		$50,000	1,000 hrs.	Training plan reports
6. Expand production of customized products	Vice president, manufacturing	Vice president, engineering				Budgeted	Budgeted	Production reports
—to 25%			Year 1	Year 2				
—to 30%				Year 2				
—to 40%				Year 3				
—to 50% to 55%				Year 3				
7. Increase sales of customized products	Vice president, sales	Vice president, marketing						Sales reports
—to 25%			Year 1	Year 2				
—to 30%				Year 2				
—to 40%				Year 3				
—to 55%				Year 3				
8. Revise sales forecasts	Vice president, sales	Vice president, marketing		Year 3				Revised forecasts

*This executive assignment action plan shows the specific executive assignments required to achieve top management's long-term objective: "have a minimum of 55% of sales revenue from customized products by 2008."

Source: Adapted from George Morrisey, *A Guide to Long-Range Planning* (San Francisco: Jossey-Bass, Inc., 1996), pp. 72–73.

aspect of the plan. As you can see, the table lists each manager's assignment in executing the company's strategic plan. In this case, one long-term top-management strategic goal is to "have a minimum of 55% of sales revenue from customized products by 2008." The executive assignment table then lists each department's goals and roles. For example, the vice president of marketing (supported by the sales vice president) should "complete a market study of sales potential for customized products" by the end of year 1.

In summary, managers need tools for communicating strategic goals to subordinates and for monitoring actual progress. Assigment tables provide managers with specific, measurable objectives against which they can measure their performance. However, tables like these are time-consuming to produce. Furthermore, the typical annual or semiannual milestones at best permit periodic, rather than real-time, performance assessments. MBO has much the same delay problem. Managers today need real-time feedback on how they are doing.

Managing Now: Strategy Maps

To get this real-time feedback, managers now often use a performance-management process to communicate goals and responsibilities and to track performance. In this context, *performance management* refers to any system that focuses employees on the goals and initiatives that they must execute for the company to succeed, and that gives managers a timely way to monitor performance and take corrective action. The basic idea of modern performance management is to use information technology to give management a real-time bird's-eye view of how the company is doing in terms of (1) carrying out the tasks required to achieve its strategic goals and (2) actually achieving those goals. This process relies on three information technology–based tools: strategy maps, balanced scorecards, and digital dashboards. Figure 7.8 summarizes this process. It starts with the strategy map.

FIGURE 7.8

Summary of Performance-Management Process

PERFORMANCE MANAGEMENT PROCESS

A system that focuses employees on the goals and initiatives that they must execute for the company to succeed, and that gives managers a timely way to monitor performance and take corrective action.

STRATEGY MAP	BALANCED SCORECARD	DIGITAL DASHBOARD
Graphical tool that summarizes the chain of activities that contribute to a company's success, and so shows employees the "big picture" of how their performance contributes to achieving the company's overall strategic goals.	A process for managing employees' performance and for aligning all employees with key objectives, by assigning financial and non-financial goals, monitoring and assessing performance, and quickly taking corrective action.	Presents the manager with desktop graphs and charts, so he or she gets a picture of where the company has been and where it's going, in terms of each activity in the strategy map.

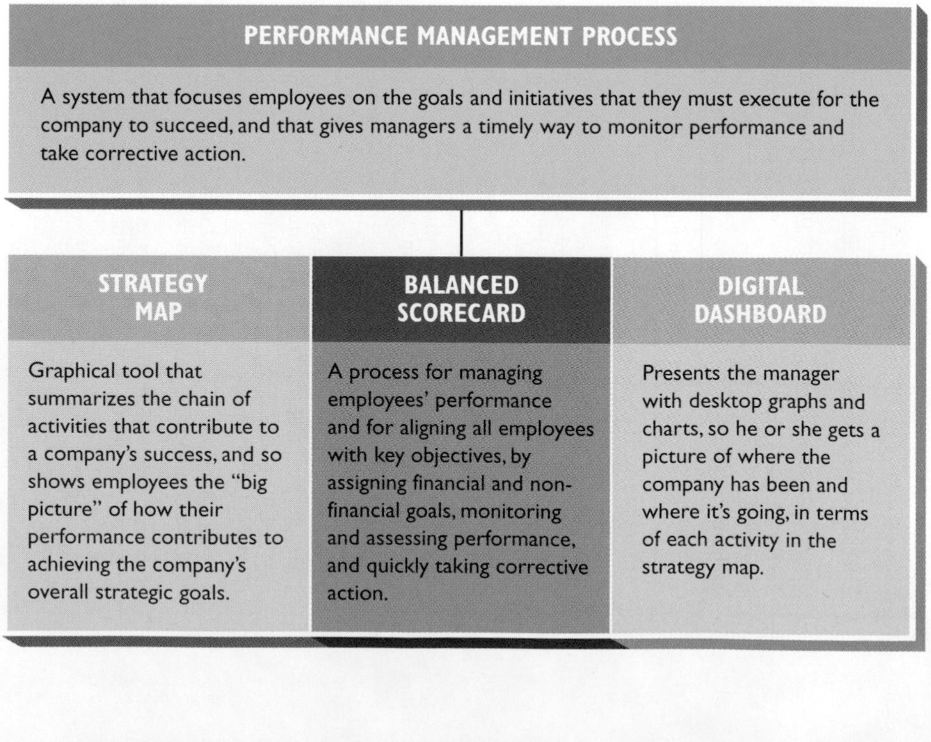

strategy map: a graphical tool that summarizes the chain of activities that contributes to a company's success

The **strategy map** is a graphical tool that summarizes the chain of activities that contributes to a company's success. Thus, it shows the big picture of how each department's or team's performance contributes to achieving the company's overall strategic goals.

Figure 7.9 presents a strategy map for Southwest Airlines. Southwest pursues a low-cost leader competitive strategy. Therefore, it shapes all its activities to

FIGURE 7.9

Strategy Map for Southwest Airlines

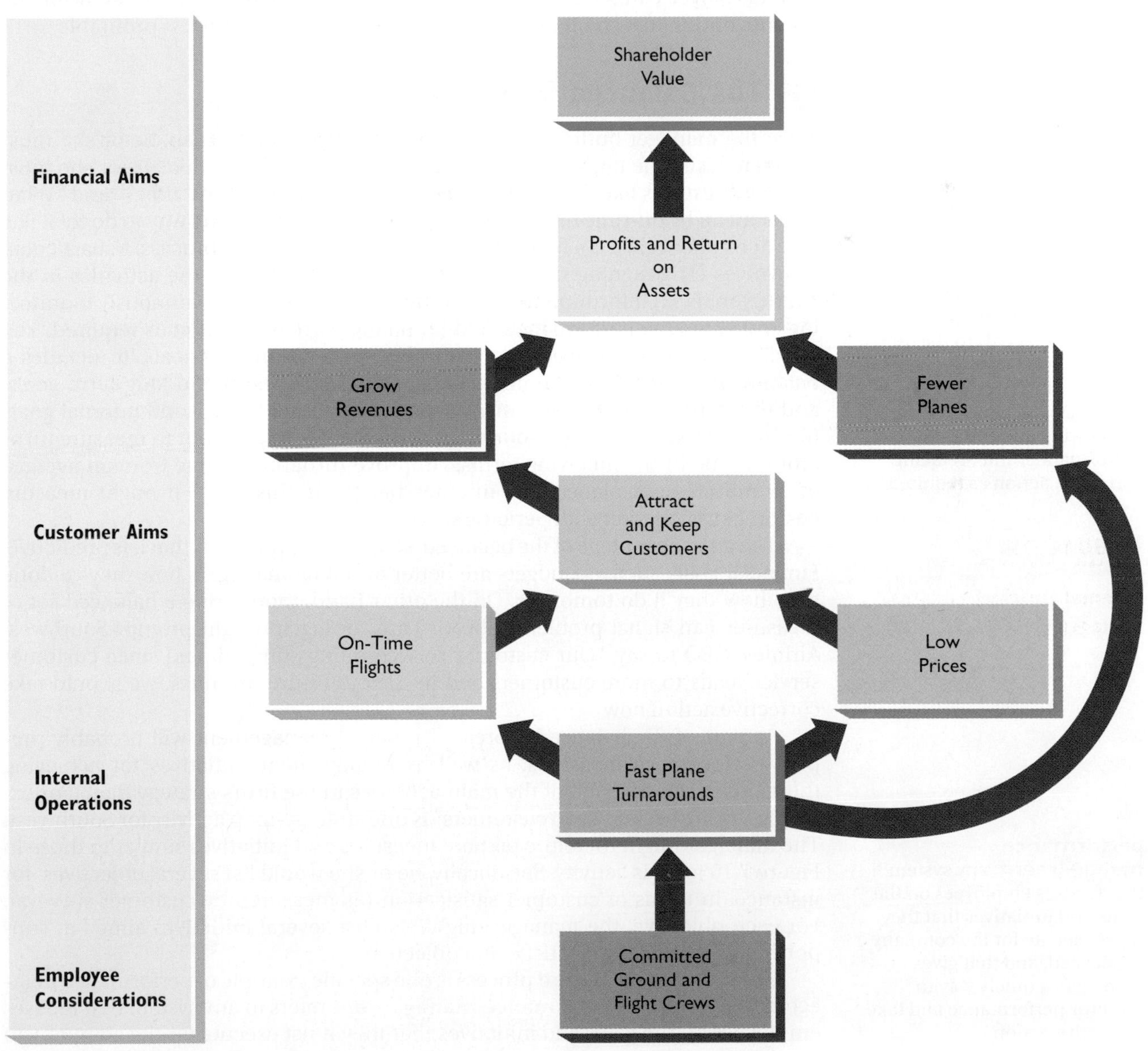

SOURCE: Adapted from Ravi Tangri, "Creating a Strategy Map," www.teamchrysalis.com.

delivering low-cost, convenient service. The strategy map for Southwest succinctly lays out the hierarchy of big activities required for Southwest Airlines to succeed. At the top is achieving companywide, strategic financial goals. The strategy map in Figure 7.9 shows the chain of activities that helps Southwest achieve these goals. To boost revenues and profitability, Southwest needs to fly fewer planes (to keep costs down), attract and keep customers, maintain low prices, and maintain on-time flights. In turn (further down the strategy map), on-time flights and low prices require fast turnaround. And fast turnaround requires motivated, committed ground and flight crews.

The strategy map enables Southwest's management to see in broad terms each of the major activities that contribute to Southwest's success. It also helps employees understand their assignments and roles. For example, each ground-crew employee can see that by working hard to turn planes around fast, he or she is contributing to a chain of activities that helps make Southwest profitable.

The Balanced Scorecard

Once the manager outlines the activities with the strategy map, he or she must attach measurable targets to each of these activities. For example, he or she must answer questions like "What do we mean by faster turnaround time?" and "What do we mean by on-time flights?" The balanced scorecard is one way to do this. The **balanced scorecard** is a type of performance-management process. In particular, it involves (1) assigning financial and nonfinancial goals to the activities in the strategy map, (2) informing all employees of their goals, (3) continuously monitoring and assessing performance, and (4) taking corrective action as required. The word *balanced* in balanced scorecard refers to a balance of goals. It includes a balance of financial and nonfinancial goals, of short-term and long-term goals, and of external goals (for instance, what the customer thinks) and internal goals (for instance, airplane turnaround time). Southwest might want to measure turnaround time in the following terms: "Improve turnaround time from an average of 30 minutes per plane to 26 minutes per plane this year." It might measure customer satisfaction with periodic surveys.

balanced scorecard: a type of performance-management process that involves (1) assigning financial and nonfinancial goals to the activities in the strategy map, (2) informing all employees of their goals, (3) continuously monitoring and assessing performance, and (4) taking corrective action as required

The great advantage of the balanced-scorecard approach is that it is predictive. Financial goals such as budgets are better at telling managers how they've done than how they'll do tomorrow. On the other hand, monitoring a balanced set of measures can signal problems ahead. Thus, doing so might prompt Southwest Airlines' CEO to say, "Our customer-service ratings dipped, and since customer service leads to more customers and in turn to future revenues, we should take corrective action now."

As part of the balanced-scorecard process, management will probably prepare performance measures, as well as management initiatives for achieving these measures, for each of the main activities in the firm's strategy map. For example, "to attract and keep customers" is one strategy-map activity for Southwest. The manager might therefore prepare measures and initiatives similar to those in Figure 7.10 for this activity. Specifically, he or she would list several objectives, for instance, in terms of customer satisfaction (as measured by customer surveys). For each objective, the manager might also list several initiatives aimed at supporting these customer-satisfaction objectives.

performance management: any system that focuses employees on the goals and initiatives that they must execute for the company to succeed, and that gives managers a timely way to monitor performance and take corrective action

The balanced-scorecard process is one specific example of performance management. As noted, **performance management** refers to any system that focuses employees on the goals and initiatives that they must execute for the company to

FIGURE 7.10

Balanced Scorecard: Performance Measures, Performance Targets, and Management Initiatives

ONE BALANCED SCORECARD PERFORMANCE MEASURE AND TARGET*					
BALANCED SCORECARD OBJECTIVE	HOW TO MEASURE OBJECTIVE	OPERATIONAL TARGET	MANAGEMENT INITIATIVES TO IMPROVE PERFORMANCE		
			Project	Manager	Due Date
Customer Satisfaction (Based on customer surveys)	**Timeliness** Extent of customer satisfaction with timeliness of airline boardings, takeoffs, arrivals	**95%** customer satisfaction ratings	Analyze why January 2007 boardings satisfaction ratings dropped to 85%	Janis Smith, customer service manager	March 31, 2007

***Note:** *Customer satisfaction* is one measure of how Southwest Airlines is doing. A company like Southwest might have a table like this addressing each activity in its strategy map, along with specific measurable targets, and (as required) management initiatives for diagnosing and rectifying poor performance. The objectives and measures in this table become the basis for Southwest's performance management process. Specifically, it enables management to monitor how employees are doing with respect to the balanced set of objectives in its strategy map, and thereby makes sure employees are doing what is necessary to achieve the objectives—like customer satisfaction—that Southwest must achieve to be successful.

SOURCE: Adapted from Steve Logan, "Balanced Scorecard 101."

succeed, and that gives managers a timely way to monitor performance and take corrective action. Four features characterize performance management:

1. The aim of any performance-management process is to align the employees' efforts with the company's strategic goals.
2. It provides each employee, from the top to the bottom of the chain of command, with an easy way to visualize and understand his or her role in achieving the company's strategy.
3. Employees receive individual goals that make sense in terms of supporting the company's overall strategic goals.
4. It includes a process for continuously monitoring employees' performance and for taking timely corrective action, usually information technology–based.

Digital Dashboards and Performance-Management Systems

Even a simple strategy map like that for Southwest Airlines may produce dozens of objectives, measures, and initiatives. How is the manager to monitor, integrate, and analyze information on performance for all employees and activities on all these measures—and do so in real time?

Airlines like Southwest and JetBlue use strategy maps to identify the chain of activities that determine their performance.

Managers now use special performance-management software systems to do this. These systems integrate and store information from hundreds or thousands of sources (for instance, feedback from customer surveys, daily airplane turnaround statistics, employee performance measures, and on-time flights). They employ built-in analytical tools to review and analyze all this information and to provide managers with continuous, real-time updates regarding the company's performance. The performance-management systems then generally present the summarized information the managers need in computerized digital dashboards.

digital dashboard: a computer dispay that presents the manager with desktop graphs and charts showing where the company has been and where it's going in terms of each activity in the strategy map

The Digital Dashboard The saying "A picture is worth a thousand words" explains the purpose of the digital dashboard. A **digital dashboard** (like that in Figure 7.2 on page 184) presents the manager with desktop graphs and charts showing where the company has been and where it's going in terms of each activity in the strategy map. The dashboard takes all the results of the number crunching by the company's performance-management software and presents it to the manager in an intelligible form. For example, a top manager's dashboard for Southwest Airlines might display daily trends for strategy-map activities such as fast turnaround, attracting and keeping customers, and on-time flights. This gives the manager time to take corrective action. For example, if ground crews are turning planes around slower today, financial results tomorrow may decline unless the manager takes action.

Like automobile dashboards, these digital dashboards also usually present information so it grabs the manager's attention, such as by a graph blinking red if turnaround time is trending down. For example, SAS software's Strategic Performance Management package is a Web-based system that produces alerts "that call employees to action when performance is not meeting targets."[44]

Software systems like Strategic Performance Management help managers make better decisions. For example, Oracle's Balanced Scorecard package lets management compare their performance (for instance, with respect to airline turnaround time) against industry peers as well as against internal budgets and historical data. From their desktops, managers can also click on any indicator to perform more-detailed analyses. If there are problems, the system enables employees to collaborate online and thus analyze the causes and take corrective action.

With a digital dashboard based on the strategy map, managers can also see how their decisions at each level affect the company's strategy. As the managing director of a Danish mortgage credit organization says, "When I turn on my computer in the morning, our scorecard is the first thing I see. . . . If I discover any deviations of the key figures I contact the person responsible for the specific area. . . ."[45]

CHAPTER SUMMARY

1. Plans are methods for achieving a desired result. Goals or objectives are specific results you want to achieve. Planning is the process of establishing objectives and courses of action, prior to taking action.
2. Planning lets you make your decisions ahead of time, provides direction and a sense of purpose, provides a unifying framework, avoids piecemeal decision making, helps managers identify potential opportunities and threats, and facilitates control.
3. The management process consists of five steps: set the objective, develop forecast and planning premises, determine what the alternatives are, build alternatives, implement and then evaluate the plan.
4. Goals are specific, measurable, attainable, relevant, and timely (SMART).
5. Forecasting is estimating or calculating in advance or predicting. Basic forecasting techniques include time-series forecasting, causal forecasting, and qualitative forecasting. Qualitative methods include jury of executive opinion and the sales force estimation method. Managing now often involves automating the forecasting process by using information technology systems to continuously monitor demand for the company's product and to communicate this information to management.
6. Competitive intelligence is a systematic way to obtain and analyze public information about competitors. The Web is useful for this task, for instance, for finding all the websites linked to the competitor's site and for carefully reviewing its investor relations pages.
7. The steps in the strategic-management process include define the business and its mission, perform external and internal audits, translate the mission into goals, formulate strategies to achieve the strategic goals, implement the strategy, and evaluate performance via strategic control.
8. Examples of strategies include corporate-level strategies (such as concentration and diversification), competitive strategies (such as low-cost, differentiator, and focuser), and functional strategies.
9. A strategy map is a graphical tool that summarizes the chain of activities that contributes to a company's success and shows employees how their performance contributes to achieving the company's overall strategic goals.
10. Performance management refers to any systems that focus employees on the goals and initiatives that they must execute for the company to succeed, and that give managers a timely way to monitor performance and take corrective action. Today, information technology supports the performance-management process, for instance, by using the balanced-scorecard process to apply a balanced set of financial and nonfinancial measures to the activities in the strategy map and then reporting actual performance in real time to management via desktop digital dashboards.

DISCUSSION QUESTIONS

1. What are the advantages of planning?
2. What are the basic steps in the planning process? What are the "two small complications" that occur when managers apply that process in planning for their firms?
3. In what ways are SMART goals smart?
4. What are some advantages and disadvantages of making sales force estimates based on forecasts collected from the sales force?
5. What is competitive intelligence? Do you think that it is an ethical process?
6. What are the basic components of a business plan?
7. What is a strategic plan? What purpose does it serve?
8. What is performance management? What is its relationship to strategy maps, balanced scorecards, and digital dashboards?

EXPERIENTIAL EXERCISES

1. It is probably safe to say that a person's career plan is one of the most important plans he or she creates. Unfortunately, most people never write out such a plan, or they don't realize they need one until it's too late. Using the concepts and techniques in this chapter, develop an outline of a career plan for yourself, one that is sufficiently detailed to provide direction for your career decisions over the next five years. Make sure to include measurable goals and milestones.
2. With three to four other students in the class, form a strategic-management group for your college or university. Your assignment is to develop the outline of a strategic plan for your college or university, including details such as mission and vision statements; strategic goals; corporate, competitive, and functional strategies; and a summary of what business your college or university is in. In preparing your plan, make sure to conduct an environmental scan, collect competitive intelligence, and use a SWOT chart. Draw a strategy map for the college or university.
3. Meet in groups of three or four students and classify local businesses as to whether they appear to be pursuing differentiator, low-cost, or focuser strategies. Explain why you classified the businesses the way you did.

CASE STUDY

The JetBlue Airways Strategy

In the hugely competitive airline industry, a company needs the right strategy, or it may as well close its doors. In the twenty or so years since the U.S. government deregulated the airline industry, dozens of airlines, from Pan Am to Eastern, have gone out of business because they had the wrong strategy or because strategy execution was less than effective, or both.

Therefore, when David Neeleman said he was starting a new airline, there was some skepticism. However, JetBlue has been successful and profitable since its inception, so most of that skepticism has evaporated.

In terms of its corporate-level strategy, JetBlue's plan wasn't that different from the plan followed by other industry start-ups. Its management started small, with several flights from JFK to Fort Lauderdale and from JFK to upper New York State. Gradually, it pursued geographic expansion, starting with a JFK to Long Beach route. For now, contractors at some airports, such as JFK, handle JetBlue's servicing.

JetBlue really distinguished itself with its competitive strategy. Most airlines are differentiator, low-cost leader, or focuser. For example, until recently, American Airlines distinguished itself as a differentiator, providing its passengers with perks like Internet support and a strong frequent-flier program. Southwest Airlines is a low-cost leader. Other airlines, like those specializing in emergency medical evacuation from Europe to the United States, focus on serving very specific niche markets.

In terms of competitive strategy, JetBlue seems to be following a hybrid approach. It seeks to combine the advantages of being a low-cost leader with the kind of quality service you'd expect to find only on major differentiator airlines such as American. JetBlue keeps cost down by flying new, low-maintenance planes; eliminating meals; training teams of employees to turn aircraft around quickly; and flying only one type of aircraft so that all pilots and crew can easily switch from plane to plane. At the same time, JetBlue aims to provide top-notch service. Passengers get leather seats, each with its own TV monitor. JetBlue's Airbus seats are about an inch wider than those on most Boeing economy-class seats. Managers carefully select and train employees to provide upbeat, courteous service. Passengers get reserved seats. And while it doesn't provide meals, JetBlue does provide unlimited snacks.

The competitive strategy has worked until now, but the competition is becoming much more fierce. When JetBlue was not on the radar screens of competitors like American Airlines, it had the low-cost flights from some airports, such as Fort Lauderdale, pretty much to itself. However, its own success has increased the attention it gets from competitors. Most of them, like American, are using JetBlue's playbook, for instance, by cutting out meals to lower costs. Therefore, David Neeleman knows he must monitor events very carefully to make sure that his quality-service/low-cost hybrid competitive strategy keeps JetBlue flying high. A breakdown in JetBlue's systems that left hundreds of passengers stranded on JetBlue planes during a snowstorm in early 2007 made it clear that costs may have already been reduced too much.

You and your team are consultants to Neeleman, who is depending on your management expertise to help navigate the competitive pressures ahead. Here's what he wants to know from you now.

DISCUSSION QUESTIONS

1. Develop a vision and mission statement for JetBlue.
2. On a single sheet of paper, write the outline of a workable strategic plan for JetBlue.
3. Based on newspaper reports and an Internet search, identify JetBlue's current corporate strategies, and list its strategic options.
4. List the strategic planning tools you think JetBlue should use, and why.
5. Draw a strategy map for JetBlue, and give its management team a brief, two-paragraph explanation for why you think JetBlue should institute a digital dashboard performance-management system.

Note: In May 2007, apparently facing intense pressure from investors and his board stemming from JetBlue's managing of the February 2007 storms that grounded its planes, David Neeleman relinquished the CEO position to his No. 2, Dave Barger. Neeleman remains JetBlue's chairman, however.

8 CONTROLLING

Controlling the Cappuccino Makers at Starbucks

With 10,000 company-owned stores around the world doing 34 million customer transactions per week, Starbucks knows that controlling what's happening in those stores is very important.[1] The question is, How do you control a store that's 12,000 miles away?

Starbucks' top managers need a way to control what's happening in their stores, even half a world away, as here in China.

Companies such as Subway or McDonald's don't have Starbucks' problem. They franchise most of their stores, so their top managers can be reasonably sure that the local franchisee will control what's happening in his or her store. If there's a problem like stealing, the local owner should be able to catch it before it gets out of hand.

But Starbucks decided from day one not to franchise. That means Starbucks needs a control system that lets its Seattle-based managers control what's happening in each of those 10,000 stores, even if the store is far away. After reading this chapter, you should be able to recommend a control system for Starbucks. ■

BEHAVIORAL OBJECTIVES

After studying this chapter, you should be able to:

Show that you've learned the chapter's essential information by

- ➤ Describing each step in the basic control process.
- ➤ Giving examples of steering, concurrent, and feedback controls.
- ➤ Briefly explaining personal, traditional, and commitment-based controls.
- ➤ Listing the components of the basic financial management control system.
- ➤ Comparing activity-based and traditional accounting systems.
- ➤ Listing four unintended consequences of controls.

Show that you can practice what you've learned here by

- Reading the chapter-opening vignette about Starbucks and recommending a control system for them.
- Reading the end-of-chapter exercise and recommending specific feedforward, concurrent, and feedback controls the manager could use.
- Reading the chapter case study and explaining the unintended behavioral consequences Ritz-Carlton may experience.

Show that you can apply what you've learned here by

- Watching the simulation video and identifying control tools and systems being used by the company.
- Watching the simulation video and explaining what the managers should do to improve employee commitment.

Online Study Center
ACE the Test
Managing Now! LIVE

The Fundamentals of Effective Control

Online Study Center
ACE the Test
Managing Now! LIVE

As Hurricane Katrina swept through New Orleans several years ago, FEMA officials' control systems signalled that the levees had held and that all were safe. They were soon to find out how mistaken those controls were. Control is the task of ensuring that activities are providing the desired results. As one expert says, "The goal [of the control system] is to have no unpleasant surprises in the future."[2] Controlling involves setting targets, measuring performance, and taking corrective action. Most controls therefore aim to influence employee behavior, which is why controlling someone often has negative overtones. Control also requires that targets, standards, or goals be set. That is why managers often use the word *planning* along with the word *control*. **Control systems** collect, store, and transmit information on profits, sales, or other measures. Starbucks needs a control system to keep track of what's happening in its stores. In Washington, D.C., FEMA needed a contol system to monitor what was happening with those levees in New Orleans, Louisiana.

control systems: devices that collect, store, and transmit information on profits, sales, or other measures

If you could be sure that every plan you made and every task you assigned would be perfectly executed, you really wouldn't need control. There would be no surprises. Unfortunately, events rarely go this smoothly. People vary widely in abilities, motivation, and ethics. Furthermore, plans themselves become outdated, often suddenly. (Think of the scrambling FEMA had to do when the levees broke.)

Many people associate control with large, companywide accounting systems. However, those systems are just part of what control is about. Control actually refers to monitoring every task the manager delegates. Some tasks may be so unimportant or your subordinates so capable that you needn't bother with controls. However, most managers know that abdication like this is risky. Someone once said, "A poor manager delegates nothing, and a mediocre manager delegates everything. An effective manager delegates all that he or she can to subordinates. At the same time, the manager establishes sufficient checkpoints so that he or she knows the work has been performed."

For every task the managers delegates, he or she should ask, How will I keep track of whether this job is done right? We'll see how to do so in this chapter.

The Basic Control Process

As mentioned above, controlling involves setting targets, measuring performance, and taking corrective action. These three steps comprise the basic control process.

Step 1: Set a Standard, Target, or Goal This step shows what the results *ought* to be. Managers express standards in terms of money, time, quantity, or quality (or a combination of these). Thus, a salesperson might have a (money) quota of $8,000 worth of products per month. The editor may give the reporter till June 1 (time) to submit her column. Production supervisors are usually responsible for producing a specified number of units (quantity) of product per week. Lexus speaks glowingly of its few defects per car (quality).

Step 2: Measure Actual Performance Against Standards The next step is to measure and compare actual performance with the standard. Here, the manager can use many tools. These range from personally monitoring how employees are doing to using budgets or information technology–based systems.

Step 3: Take Corrective Action When the manager compares actual with planned performance, he or she should check for any significant deviations. If there are any, the manager takes corrective action.

Three Types of Control Systems

It would surely do Starbucks little good to discover in June that in March, a store manager had run off with $40,000 of a store's receipts. By June, the money might well be lost. Starbucks needs a more responsive control system. Some systems are more responsive than are others. Managers therefore distinguish among three types of control systems. All the controls we'll discuss in this chapter fall into one of these categories.

steering controls: controls that let the manager take corrective action *before* the operation or project is completed; also called feedforward or precontrol

Steering controls (also called feedforward or precontrol) are controls that let the manager take corrective action *before* the operation or project is completed.[3] Steering controls are always preventive in nature. For example, on a flight to Mars, you would not want to find out after the fact that you missed your mark. Engineers therefore track a spacecraft's flight path continuously so they can adjust its trajectory in time to reach the target.

Managers use steering controls all the time. For example, they set intermediate milestones and thus check progress long before the project is complete. They set up procedures to reject defective raw materials and to test and screen out job candidates who may become problem employees. They review budgets on a comparative basis to better identify trends. They monitor aircraft turnaround time on a daily basis, so they can correct any problems before profits start to suffer.

Managing Now Information technology (IT) and the Internet have improved managers' abilities to make timely midcourse corrections. Boeing's use of the Web is a good example. Boeing has an Internet-based network used by 1,000 other companies, including aluminum supplier Alcoa, Inc.[4] To gain access to this network, external users (including most of Boeing's suppliers and customers) receive digital certificates from Boeing, with passwords authorizing them to access the network.

The network allows both Boeing and its suppliers to maintain better, more timely control by, for example, reducing the number of misunderstandings with

Concurrent control: A manager talks to customers at a Cheesecake Factory in California.

suppliers and customers. Access to the e-network means suppliers can continually get real-time updates regarding required delivery dates and schedule changes and can make course corrections if these are required. Boeing also linked its e-commerce system to tracking tools supplied by delivery services such as FedEx. Customers can therefore view the status of their parts orders at any time over the Web, which minimizes delivery surprises.

Boeing's Internet-based system has improved the timeliness of the company's control system in other ways. For example, employees use the system to monitor production lines: "We use the Web to keep track of shortages on airplane production lines so that everyone in the whole organization can know where the hot spots are, not just management."[5] We'll look more closely at IT-based controls later in this chapter.

concurrent (yes/no) controls: controls managers apply at the moment the activity to be controlled takes place

feedback (or postaction) controls: controls the manager uses to compare results to the standard and to take action after the event he or she is controlling has occurred

Concurrent (or yes/no) controls are controls managers apply at the moment the activity to be controlled takes place. They instantly make yes/no decisions about whether the activity can take place. For example, the movie theater clerk makes on-the-spot decisions about whether someone is old enough to see a particular movie. Yes/no controls often involve applying the company's rules and procedures. Ideally, when a situation covered by the rules comes up, the employee will be prepared to say yes or no.

Feedback (or postaction) controls are controls the manager uses to compare results to the standard and to take action after the event he or she is controlling has occurred. The final inspection on a car assembly line is an example. Many other familiar controls fall into this postaction category, including semiannual budgets and the end-of-term grades students receive.

The problem with postaction controls (as with grades) is that you usually can't do much to remedy the situation once the results are in. That's why managers (and professors) try to inject timeliness into their postaction controls. Instead of just a final exam, professors give a midterm, too. Instead of just a midyear budget, the manager prepares monthly budgets, too. The Window on Managing Now feature shows how UPS uses IT to inject an element of timeliness into their postaction controls.

Periodic surveys are another example of postaction controls. For example, twice a year, Siebel Systems (which makes computer systems) has consultants collect data from about 20 percent of its customers. This provides detailed reports on how satisfied the customers are with specific Siebel departments and individuals.[6]

Personal, Traditional, and Commitment-Based Control

Assume you just took over as editor in chief of your college's student paper. What are some of the details you would want to control? A (very) short list would include article length and quality, advertising revenues, operating expenses, article deadlines, article topics, and the format for each issue. How will you make sure all these details stay under control? Any manager has three basic options: you can (1) monitor things personally; (2) rely on traditional control tools, such as budgets; or

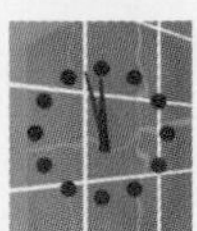

Window on Managing Now
Using Technology to Stay in Control at UPS

UPS is the world's largest air and ground package-distribution company. It delivers close to 3 billion parcels and documents each year in the United States and more than 185 other countries. Critical to its success has been the $1.8 billion UPS invested in information technology. Each UPS driver uses a handheld computer called a delivery information acquisition device (pictured on page 223). This device captures customers' signatures along with pickup, delivery, and time-card information. Then it automatically transmits this information to headquarters via a cellular telephone network.

Through TotalTrack, its automated package-tracking system, UPS can control packages throughout the delivery process. And with its own global communications network called UPSnet, UPS not only tracks its packages but electronically transmits documentation on each shipment directly to customs officials prior to arrival. Shipments are therefore either cleared for shipment or flagged for inspection when they arrive.

UPS uses the Internet to help it and its customers monitor and control the progress of all those billions of packages. For example, the UPS Internet-based tracking system lets a customer store up to twenty-five tracking numbers and then monitor the progress of each package. The system not only lets the customer (and UPS) keep track of each package's progress, it also serves as a value-added feature for the customer. It can easily keep UPS customers informed about the progress of every package.

(3) rely on employees' self-control by appealing to their sense of commitment. (Or, of course, you can use a mixture of all three.)

Personal (or Interactive) Control The editor in chief of a college paper has one big control advantage over the managing editor of the *New York Times.* The college paper is probably small enough so that the editor can continuously talk face-to-face with all the staff. He or she can monitor in real time how everything is going.

personal control: maintaining control by personally monitoring how everyone is doing

Personal control means maintaining control by personally monitoring how everyone is doing. Personal control is the most basic way to stay in control. Even large firms use this approach.[7] For example, firms like Toyota limit their plants to a few hundred employees. In this way, interactions and control in each unit remain more instantaneous and personal.

One simple but effective way to control what's happening is to have people meet and interactively discuss "how we're doing."

In fact, it would be highly unusual for any manager not to rely to some extent on personal interactions as a way to stay in control. Some managers formalize this approach by adhering to the notion of "management by walking around." They stay in control, in part, by literally walking around their facilities to see how things are going.

Others schedule weekly meetings where they discuss results. Senior managers at *USA Today* use this approach.[8] Friday morning they get three weekly reports. This Friday Packet includes information ranging from advertising sales figures to information about particular advertisers. Weekly face-to-face meetings among senior managers and key subordinates help apply this information. Regular topics include advertising volume compared to plan and new business by type of client.

traditional control: controls based on external devices such as budgets and computerized information systems to monitor performance and to report on results

● **Traditional Control** Traditional control uses external devices such as budgets and computerized information systems to monitor performance and to report on results. These methods are what usually spring to mind when most people think of control. Thus, Jeffrey Immelt controls GE in part through a system of (computerized) financial controls and budgets.

● **Self-Control and Commitment-Based Control** Personal observation and traditional controls like budgets get the manager only so far. No control system can anticipate every possible crisis. Employees have many ingenious ways of getting around the system. And in many situations (such as building high-quality cars), you want the employees to *want* to build in quality; you can't really force them to do so. That is why many companies, including Starbucks, work hard to create an environment in which employees want to exercise self-control and do what's best for the firm. Self-control refers to a set of methods managers use to encourage employees to control their own performance.

self-control: a set of methods managers use to encourage employees to control their own performance

We've summarized the three basic control approaches—personal, traditional, and commitment—in Figure 8.1. We'll devote the rest of this chapter to discussing the traditional and the commitment-based systems in detail.

FIGURE 8.1

Three Basic Categories of Control Systems

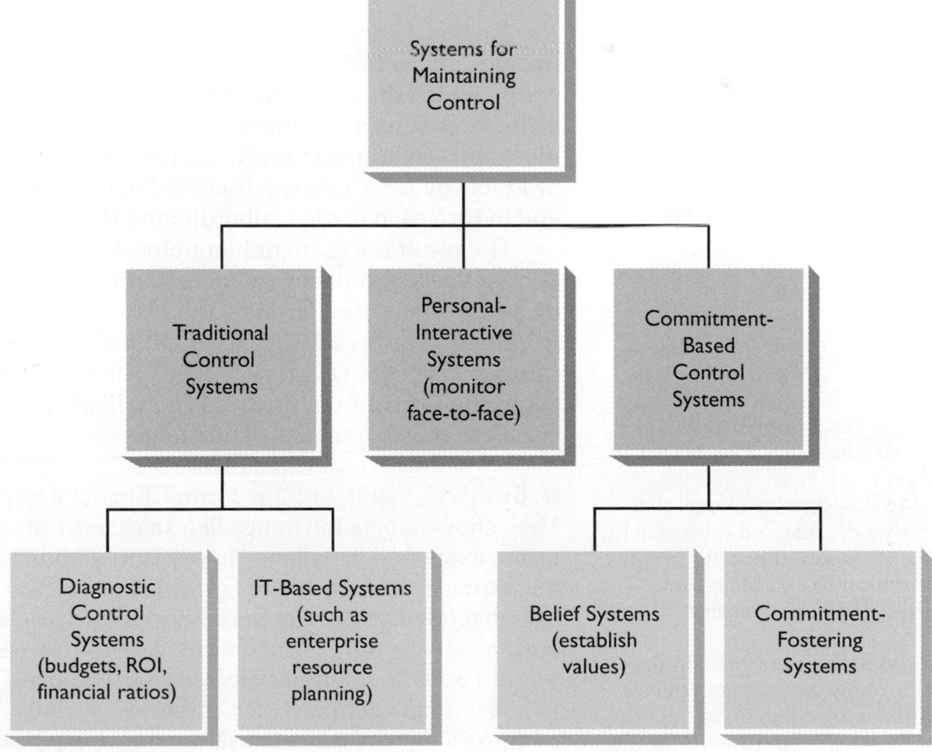

Traditional Controls

traditional controls: formal, preplanned, methodical systems that help managers zero in on discrepancies

Online Study Center
ACE the Test
Managing Now! LIVE

principle of exception: (or management by exception) holds that to conserve managers' time, only significant deviations or exceptions from the standard should be brought to the manager's attention

Traditional controls are formal, preplanned, methodical systems that help managers zero in on discrepancies. Also called diagnostic or budgetary controls, they are the controls most people think of when they think of management control. Budgets and production reports are two examples. These controls reduce the need for managers to continually and personally monitor everything for which they are responsible.[9] Having previously set targets or goals, the manager can (at least in theory) then leave the employees to pursue the goals. Ideally, the manager can be secure in the knowledge that if the goals aren't met, the deviations will show up as red flags in performance reports.

This last idea forms the heart of what managers call the principle of exception. The **principle of exception** (or management by exception) holds that to conserve managers' time, only significant deviations or exceptions from the standard, "both the especially good and bad exceptions," should be brought to the manager's attention.[10]

The Basic Financial Management Control System

Managers—including a student paper's editor in chief—have many nonfinancial details to control. For our editor, these include article deadlines, article length and quality, and the format for each issue. Yet in reality, it's usually the financial aspects—the bottom line—that's first among equals when it comes to control. Financial controls thus form the heart of a company's basic management control system.

Financial controls begin with the firm's planning process. Management formulates an overall strategy and mission for the firm. This provides a framework within which the rest of the planning process can take place. Next, management formulates subsidiary, lower-level plans and a hierarchy of goals. At the top, the president sets strategic goals (such as "have 55% of sales revenue from customized products by 2008"). As we discussed in Chapter 7, each functional vice president, and in turn each of their subordinates, then receives goals.

The result is a chain or hierarchy of departmental goals and short-term operational goals and plans. At each step in this hierarchical process, management invariably translates the goals and plans into financial targets and embodies them in budgets. The president's goal might translate as "$2 million in revenues from the Custom Products Division in 2008." Financial statements and budgets thus become the heart of the firm's basic management control system. Let's look more closely at these statements and budgets.

budgets: formal financial expressions of a manager's plans

sales budget: a budget that shows the planned sales activity for each period (usually in units per month) and the revenue expected from the sales

operating budgets: budgets that show the expected sales and/or expenses for each of the company's departments for the planning period in question

Budgets **Budgets** are formal financial expressions of a manager's plans. They show targets for things like sales, cost of materials, production levels, and profit, expressed in dollars. These planned targets are the standards against which the manager compares and controls the unit's actual performance. The first step in budgeting is generally to develop a sales forecast and sales budget. The **sales budget** shows the planned sales activity for each period (usually in units per month) and the revenue expected from the sales.

The manager can then produce various operating budgets. **Operating budgets** show the expected sales and/or expenses for each of the company's departments for the planning period in question. For example, the production and

FIGURE 8.2

Example of a Budget

OPERATING BUDGET FOR MACHINERY DEPARTMENT, JANUARY 2007	
Budgeted Expenses	**Budget**
Direct Labor	$2,107
Supplies	$3,826
Repairs	$ 402
Overhead (electricity, etc.)	$ 500
TOTAL EXPENSES	$6,835

materials budget (or plan) shows what the company plans to spend for materials, labor, administration, and so forth to fulfill the requirements of the sales budget.

income statement: the profit plan that shows expected sales, expected expenses, and expected income or profit for the year

cash budget: a plan that shows, for each month, the amount of cash the company can expect to receive and the amount it can expect to disperse

balance sheet: a statement that shows managers, owners, and creditors what the company's projected financial picture should be at the end of the year, in terms of assets, liabilities, and net worth

variances: the differences between budgeted and actual amounts (on performance reports)

● **Profit Planning** The next step is to combine all these departmental budgets into a profit plan for the coming year. This profit plan is the budgeted **income statement** or pro forma income statement. It shows expected sales, expected expenses, and expected income or profit for the year. In practice, cash from sales usually doesn't flow into the firm so that it coincides precisely with cash disbursements. (Some customers may take thirty-five days to pay their bills, for instance, but employees expect paychecks every week.) The **cash budget** or plan shows, for each month, the amount of cash the company can expect to receive and the amount it can expect to disperse. The manager can use it to anticipate his or her cash needs and to arrange for short-term loans, if need be.

The company also has a budgeted **balance sheet**. The budgeted balance sheet shows managers, owners, and creditors what the company's projected financial picture should be at the end of the year. It shows assets (such as cash and equipment), liabilities (such as long-term debt), and net worth (the excess of assets over other liabilities).

Budgets are the most widely used control device. Each manager, from first-line supervisor to company president, usually has an operating budget to use as a standard of comparison. Remember, however, that creating the budget (as in Figure 8.2) is just the standard-setting step in the three-step control process. You must still compare the actual and the budgeted figures. And if necessary, you'll need to diagnose any problems and take corrective action.

The firm's accountants compile the financial information and feed it back to the appropriate managers. As in Figure 8.3, the performance report shows budgeted or planned targets. Next to these numbers, it shows the department's actual performance numbers. **Variances** are the differences between budgeted and actual amounts. The report may provide a space for the manager to explain any variances. After reviewing the performance report, management can take corrective action.

FIGURE 8.3

Example of a Performance Report

PERFORMANCE REPORT FOR MACHINERY DEPARTMENT, JANUARY 2007				
	Budget	**Actual**	**Variance**	**Explanation**
Direct Labor	$2,107	$2,480	$373 over	Had to put workers on overtime.
Supplies	$3,826	$4,200	$374 over	Wasted two crates of material.
Repairs	$ 402	$ 150	$252 under	Fewer repairs than planned.
Overhead (electricity, etc.)	$ 500	$ 500	0	
TOTAL	$6,835	$7,330	$495 over	

audit: a systematic process that involves three steps: (1) objectively obtain and evaluate evidence regarding important aspects of the firm's performance; (2) judge the accuracy and validity of the data; and (3) communicate the results to interested users, such as the board of directors and the company's banks

financial ratios: ratios that compare one financial measure on a financial statement to another

strategic ratio: a succinct summary of the crucial measures that the firm must focus on to achieve its strategic aims

The firm's accountants also periodically audit the firm's financial statements. An **audit** is a systematic process that involves three steps: (1) objectively obtain and evaluate evidence regarding important aspects of the firm's performance; (2) judge the accuracy and validity of the data; and (3) communicate the results to interested users, such as the board of directors and the company's banks.[11] The purpose of the audit is to certify that the firm's financial statements accurately reflect its performance.

Ratio Analysis and Return on Investment

Managers also use financial ratio analysis to monitor performance and maintain control. **Financial ratios** compare one financial measure on a financial statement to another. The return on investment (ROI) is one such ratio. ROI equals net profit after taxes divided by total investment. Managers use it as a gauge of overall company performance. Rather than measuring net profit as an absolute figure, it shows profit in relation to the total investment in the business, which is often a more informative figure. For example, a $1 million profit is more impressive with a $10 million investment than it would be with a $100 million investment. Figure 8.4 lists some commonly used financial ratios.

Analyzing financial ratios helps managers analyze their firm's performance. For example (see Figure 8.5), suppose the firm didn't meet its net income target. Ratio analysis shows that low sales or high sales costs may account for this. Similarly, earnings divided by sales (the profit margin) reflects management's success or failure in maintaining satisfactory cost controls. As another example, too much investment may help account for a low ROI. In turn, too much investment might reflect inadequate inventory control, too many accounts receivable, or too much cash.[12]

Strategic Ratios In his book *Good to Great*, Jim Collins studied companies that went from good but average to great. He says that one distinguishing characteristic of companies that went from good to great was that they were able to sum up in one simple ratio what their strategy was all about.[13] A **strategic ratio**

FIGURE 8.4

Widely Used Financial Ratios

NAME OF RATIO	FORMULA	INDUSTRY NORM (AS ILLUSTRATION)
1. Liquidity Ratios (measure the ability of the firm to meet its short-term obligations)		
Current ratio	Current assets / Current liabilities	2.6
Acid-test ratio	Cash and equivalent / Current liability	1.0
Cash velocity	Sales / Cash and equivalent	12 times
Inventory to net working capital	Inventory / (Current assets – Current liabilities)	85%
2. Leverage Ratios (measure the contributions of financing by owners compared with financing provided by creditors)		
Debt to equity	Total debt / Net worth	56%
Coverage of fixed charges	Net profit before fixed charges / Fixed charges	6 times
Current liability to net worth	Current liability / Net worth	32%
Fixed assets to net worth	Fixed assets / Net worth	60%
3. Activities Ratios (measure the effectiveness of the employment of resources)		
Inventory turnover	Sales / Inventory	7 times
Net working capital turnover	Sales / Net working capital	5 times
Fixed-assets turnover	Sales / Fixed assets	6 times
Average collection period	Receivables / Average sales per day	20 days
Equity capital turnover	Sales / Net worth	3 times
Total capital turnover	Sales / Total assets	2 times
4. Profitability Ratios (indicate degree of success in achieving desired profit levels)		
Gross operating margin	Gross operating profit / Sales	30%
Net operating margin	Net operating profit / Sales	6.5%
Sales (profit) margin	Net profit after taxes / Sales	3.2%
Productivity of assets	(Gross income – Taxes) / Total assets	10%
Return on investment	Net profit after taxes / Total investment	7.5%
Net profit on working capital	Net operating profit / Net working capital	14.5%

FIGURE 8.5

Ratio Analysis: Factors Affecting Return on Investment

The firm's overall profitability—its return on total investments—can be better understood by analyzing its components, including earnings as a percentage of sales and turnover.

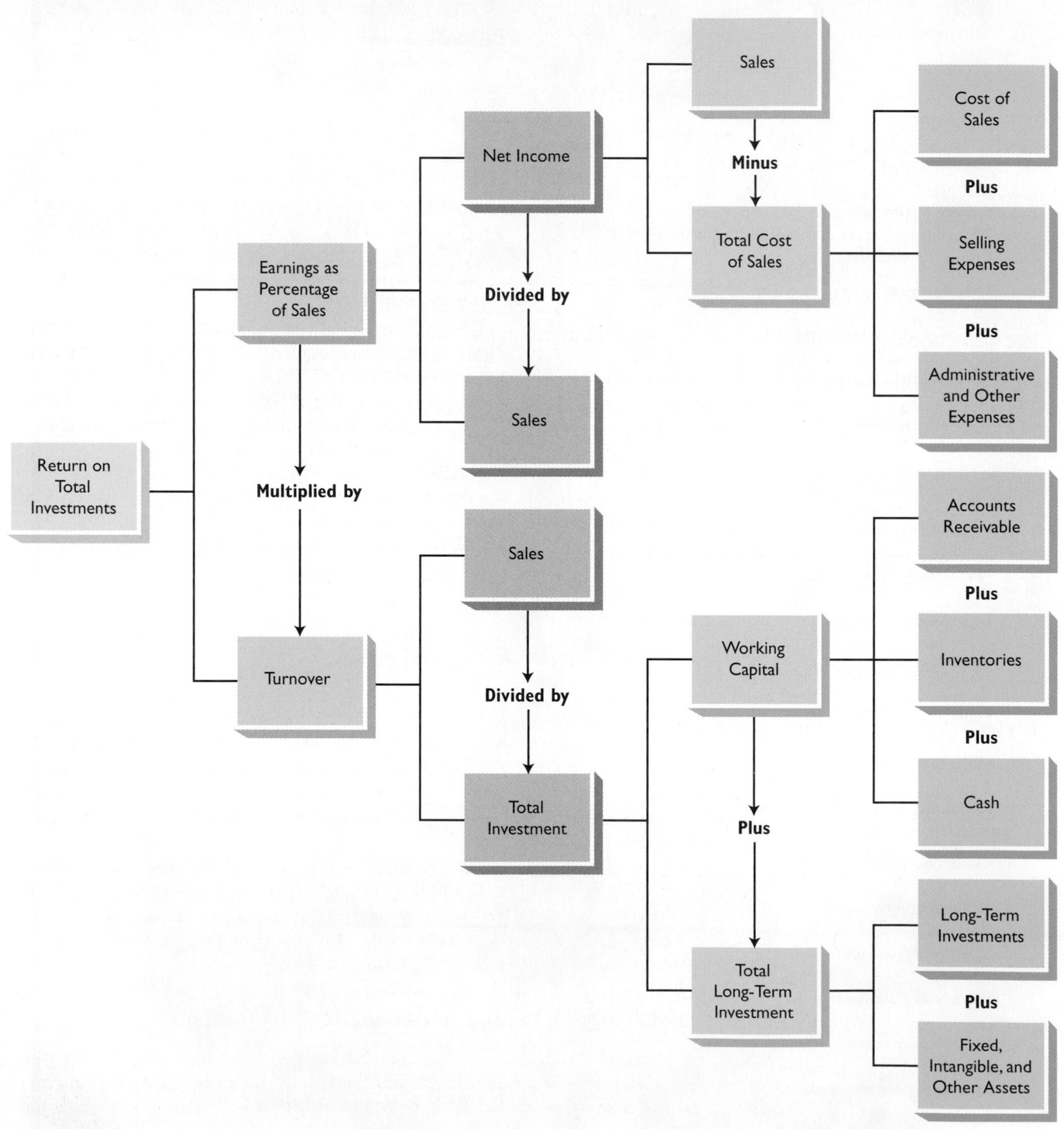

succinctly summarizes the crucial measures that the firm must focus on to achieve its strategic aims. For example, Gillette bases its strategy in part on selling multiple products repeatedly to customers. It therefore focuses on profit per customer rather than profit per division, as other consumer companies do. Walgreen's wants to be "the place to shop," and so it sells a variety of items. It therefore focuses on profit per customer visit rather than profit per store. The grocery firm Kroger wants to dominate in each local market. It therefore focuses on profit per local population instead of profit per store.

Financial Responsibility Centers

financial responsibility centers: organizational units that are responsible for and are measured based on a specific set of financial activities

profit centers: responsibility centers whose managers the company holds accountable for profit

revenue centers: responsibility centers whose managers are responsible for generating a certain level of revenues

cost centers: responsibility centers whose managers are responsible for managing their operations within certain cost constraints

In most firms, certain managers are responsible for achieving specific sets of financial targets. This makes it easier for top management to evaluate these managers' performances. It also makes it easier for each manager to see how the firm will evaluate his or her performance. When the manager has an operating budget tied to specific financial performance targets, we say the manager is in charge of a financial responsibility center. **Financial responsibility centers** are units that are responsible for and are measured based on a specific set of financial activities.

There are several types of financial responsibility centers. **Profit centers** are responsibility centers whose managers the company holds accountable for profit. (Profit is a measure of the difference between the revenues generated and the cost of generating those revenues.[14]) The Allfirst unit of the banking group AIB is a profit center. AIB holds the division's head responsible for the profitability of that division. AIB controls that manager's performance partly by monitoring whether the division "makes its numbers"—in other words, meets its profit goals.

Revenue centers are responsibility centers whose managers are accountable for generating revenues. Thus, firms generally measure sales managers in terms of the sales produced by their revenue center/departments. **Cost centers** are responsibility centers whose managers are accountable for managing their operations—such as factories—within certain cost constraints.

Managing Now: IT-Enabled Control Systems

Hyundai uses wireless handheld scanners to monitor and control the 43,000 cars per year that go through one of its European import centers. The handheld scanners read bar codes on each car. They then automatically send the information directly back to Hyundai's computer systems. That way, all employees along the supply chain, from sales to the dealer, to shipping, can continuously monitor the whereabouts of each car.[15]

As at Hyundai, information technology revolutionized how managers maintain control. We'll look at how this change was achieved in this section, with particular attention to using enterprise resource planning systems, more timely accounting reports, activity-based costing, wireless systems, electronic performance monitoring, and digital dashboards.

Enterprise Resource Planning–Based Control

As we discussed in Chapter 5, enterprise resource planning systems are not primarily planning systems. An enterprise resource planning (ERP) system is a companywide integrated computer system comprised of compatible software modules for each of the company's separate departments, such as sales, accounting, finance, warehousing, production, and human resources (HR). Each department gets its own module or system. Often Internet-based, the ERP modules are designed to communicate with each other and with the central system's database. That way, information from all the departments is readily shared by the ERP system and is available to employees in all the other departments. Activities that formerly required human intervention, such as production telling accounting that it should bill a customer because an order just shipped, now occur automatically. ERP strips away the barriers that typically exist among a company's stand-alone departmental computer systems. With an ERP installed and running, the manager has a platform on which he or she can install IT-based accounting and other controls such as those we discuss in the next sections. This produces better, faster control systems.

More Timely Accounting Reports

Most firms computerized their accounting departments many years ago. The main difference today is that with ERP, all the company's global accounting (and other) departments use compatible accounting modules and share their financial information via a common database.[16] This arrangement gives faster, more timely accounting reports and control. We'll look at several examples.

Managing Now For example, updating and maintaining financial statements was a slow process at NovaCare, a network of over 500 rehabilitation clinics and physical therapy centers. Each clinic and center had its own accounting system. Clinic and center administrators inputted financial data into separate systems for each of their clinics or centers. The process took two to three employees five hours a day.[17] By installing Oracle Financials, the company put all its centers on the same software system. This setup eliminated much of the labor that the financial statement postings previously required. It also made it easy for NovaCare's headquarters staff to run off standardized financial reports for the company. This enables the company to close its books five days faster than it could previously.

With offices in thirty-six countries, Alltech Inc. (which provides products to the food and feed industries) needed a faster way to get information regarding its order status and finances worldwide. Previously, auditors at each of the company's offices around the world manually entered data onto spreadsheets. Then they sent the spreadsheets to Alltech's headquarters, where accountants compiled all this information into a master spreadsheet. The process took about forty-five days to complete.[18]

Today, a Web-based software system automatically collects financial information from standardized financial accounting modules in each of the company's offices around the world. It also feeds this information back to headquarters. As a result, management receives consolidated financial statements in fifteen days, instead of forty-five. This faster feedback means tighter top-management control of global operations. The Window on Managing Now feature provides an in-depth example.

Activity-Based Costing (ABC)

Traditional accounting systems have a problem showing what it actually costs to produce and sell a product or service. Suppose, for example, that an insurance company has a contract to provide insurance to a big client. The insurance firm's president wants to know what the contract costs the company. The traditional

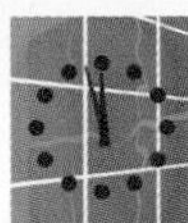

WINDOW ON MANAGING NOW
Millipore Corp. Integrates Its Global Operations with ERP

Millipore Corp. develops and produces the technologies, tools, and services pharmaceuticals companies use to produce new drugs.[19] With about 4,500 employees in facilities in thirty countries, managing and controlling global operations is key to the firm's success. Managers need to know the answers to questions such as, How many employees do we have in each facility? What is the status of a particular order? and What are our sales this month in the European Union?

Their previous systems did not let management answer such questions in a timely manner. Most of Millipore's facilities around the world each used different financial management tools. Compiling information from facilities around the world was therefore a time-consuming process. To better manage its global operations, the company decided to install several integrated software products from Oracle Corp., including the ERP software package components Oracle Financials, Oracle Human Resources, Oracle Self-Service Human Resources, and Oracle Order Management. The components are integrated; for instance, inputting a new order into Order Management automatically informs Oracle Financials that the new order exists. Similarly, when an employee changes his or her pension plan using Self-Service Human Resources, the system automatically "tells" Oracle Financials to deduct the new costs from the employee's paycheck.

The Web-enabled ERP suite of products helped Millipore to control its global operations more effectively. For example, by not using separate financial packages in thirty countries, the standardized financial package means top management can get fast feedback on the firm's financial performance around the world. Similarly, as noted above, Oracle Order Management integrates with Millipore's new Oracle financial, warehouse, and distribution systems. Orders get processed automatically, and management can track and control orders from entry through delivery.

With operations around the world, Millipore also needed to "... get a handle on the number of staff we had at different geographies, what jobs they performed, and what we were paying them."[20] Previously, headquarters managers manually compiled employee spreadsheets each quarter based on data that facilities around the world produced from their own systems. Today, Millipore's facilities all run the same Oracle Human Resource Management system. Thus, executives can now get an accurate picture of how many people the firm employs around the world and an accurate idea of who reports to whom. It also lets managers control an array of new factors. For example, they can easily analyze details like comparative staffing levels versus sales among global departments.

accounting system might show what the company pays out in claims, and perhaps what it paid the salesperson as a commission for getting the client. It might even show (as approximations) what share of the insurance firm's overhead expenses, for things like office lighting and heating, the accounting system is charging to this particular contract.

What the insurance firm's accounting system probably cannot show are all the actual costs of serving this client that are scattered around the insurance company. For example, how much time do this client's employees spend on the phone with the insurance firm's customer-service reps? How much time do the doctors that serve this client's employees spend getting approvals for medical procedures from the insurance company's gatekeepers?

The problem is that traditional accounting systems tend to isolate departments with separate, stand-alone accounting systems. The customer-service department knows what it's spending overall for customer reps. The gatekeeper department knows what it's spending overall for gatekeepers. But the president can't access the insurance company's various departments and determine what each of them is spending on this particular client.

ERP changes that. All departments use compatible software modules. All departments' systems communicate with the central database. By linking together the information from compatible accounting modules in different departments, ERP enables managers to use activity-based costing. **Activity-based costing (ABC)** is a system for allocating costs to products or services that takes all the product's or service's costs into account (including production, marketing, distribution, and sales and follow-up activities) in calculating the actual cost of each product or service.

activity-based costing (ABC): a system for allocating costs to products or services that takes all the product's or service's costs into account (including production, marketing, distribution, and sales and follow-up activities) in calculating the actual cost of each product or service

Activity-based costing is a powerful control tool. With ABC, the manager can access all departments and monitor the costs associated with any activity he or she wants to control. For example, the manager can calculate costs by order, client, project, contract, or business process, rather than by just department or cost center. ERP makes doing so possible.

● Managing Now For example, Montana Blue Cross Blue Shield installed an activity-based management system from SAS. Previously, the company's finance managers controlled costs the traditional way: by computing basic budget variances for the company as a whole and for each department. The new ABC system enabled them to also break out costs by insurance product, and even by individual lines of business and contracts.

For instance, Blue Cross Blue Shield knew it was losing money on one contract with a large client. However, its managers had not been able to track and evaluate all the costs associated with this particular program. With the new SAS ABC system, "We've been able to re-examine the contract and get a good grip on the costs that we're incurring." Then Blue Cross Blue Shield managers took the steps necessary to address the problem costs and began making the contract profitable.[21]

As another example, the check-printing company Deluxe Paper Payment Systems used its ABC system to "get a clearer picture of which of its customers were profitable and which were not."[22] For example, the system helped it discover that orders for checks from banks were much more profitable when they arrived via electronic ordering. Deluxe then launched a campaign to increase electronic ordering—particularly by its 18,000 bank and small-business customers. The number of checks ordered electronically quickly jumped from 48 percent to 62 percent, which dramatically improved profits.

Wireless-Assisted Control

The UPS deliveryperson (see the Window on Managing Now feature on page 212) picks up a package and then uses a delivery information acquisition device to wirelessly communicate the package's whereabouts to UPS's home-base ERP system. The sender of the package, using her laptop to go online wirelessly via a Wi-Fi–enabled hot spot at an airport club before her flight, checks the UPS system. She then uses her cell phone to tell her client that the shipment is on its way.

Control is going wireless. Wireless-assisted control often involves the company's supply chain activities (defined in Chapters 1 and 5). For example, UPS's handheld acquisition devices are part of the firm's supply chain management system. They help UPS control, in real time, the whereabouts of packages in its system. UPS's TotalTrack system (see the Window on Managing Now feature) then enables customers—senders and recipients—to communicate directly with the system to check delivery status. The UPS system, while wireless, depends on employees to use handheld wireless devices to input the data. We'll see next that the trend now is to make the tracking process automatic.

UPS relies on information technology to track and control its package shipments.

● **Managing Now** For example, managers now use radio-frequency identification (RFID) to wirelessly control their materials and products.[23] Basically, each RFID is a computer chip with a tiny antenna. All along the company's supply chain—at the warehouse loading dock, in the inventory stacks, and even at the checkout counter—digital readers scan the RFIDs from a distance and transmit identifying data from the tags to computers. Unlike bar codes that employees must read manually, RFIDs continually transmit an item's location, without human intervention.

A few years ago, Wal-Mart told its 100 top suppliers to start attaching RFID tags to their case and palate shipments. Wal-Mart can now keep better track of inventory as it moves from the warehouse into its distribution centers and, finally, to its stores. For example, it can replenish out-of-stock items three times faster with the RFID technology than it used to.

As another example, remote monitoring devices enable medical equipment manufacturer Beckman Coulture to automate and better control its ordering process. Remote sensors enable Beckman Coulture to automatically monitor the use of blood analyzers by its medical laboratory customers. Then, when the customer's supplies are running low, Beckman Coulture can automatically arrange shipments before the customer runs out. Its Oracle ERP system signals the order department to produce an order, the manufacturing department to get ready to produce it, and the accounting department to produce an invoice.[24]

Electronic Performance Monitoring (EPM)

Managers increasingly use high-tech methods to monitor and control employee performance. As two researchers put it, "As many as 26 million workers in the United States are subject to electronic performance monitoring (EPM)—such as having supervisors monitor through electronic means the amount of computerized data an employee is processing per day—on the job."[25] The supervisors can then take immediate action by speaking with or contacting the errant employee if he or she is not processing enough data. EPM basically means monitoring and controlling employee performance automatically, using electronic means.

● **Managing Now** EPM is not just for monitoring subordinates. It is used for monitoring bosses, too. For example, the Japanese company that controls 7-Eleven is imposing an EPM system on its store managers in Japan and in the United States. Like all 7-Eleven stores, the ones belonging to store manager Michiharu Endo use a point-of-sale computer to let headquarters know each time he makes a sale. With 7-Eleven's new system, headquarters monitors how much time Endo spends using the analytical tools built into the computerized cash register to track product sales and how effective he is at weaning out poor sellers. Headquarters then ranks stores by how often their operators use the computer as a measure of their efficiency. The system has run into particular resistance in the United States. Many 7-Eleven managers thought they escaped the bureaucratic rat race by taking over their own stores. Some are surprised at the degree of control this new EPM system has exposed them to.[26]

Digital Dashboards and Control

All things considered, it is always preferable to find out before things are out of control that a problem exists and must be addressed. That, in essence, is the advantage of using the balanced scorecard and digital dashboard planning and control tools we discussed in Chapter 7. For example, a top manager's dashboard for Southwest Airlines might display daily trends for strategy-map activities such as fast turnaround, attracting and keeping customers, and on-time flights. The manager knows from experience that when these activities start to deteriorate, it's usually not long before profits start deteriorating too. The beauty of the scorecard process is that it gives the manager time to take corrective action. For example, if ground crews are turning planes around more slowly today, financial results tomorrow may decline unless the manager takes action.

Managers monitor their digital dashboards. If there are problems, the display, with its summary graphs and charts for various measures, enables managers to analyze the causes and take corrective action. To quote that Danish mortgage credit managing director again, "When I turn on my computer in the morning, our scorecard is the first thing I see. . . . If I discover any deviations of the key figures I contact the person responsible for the specific area. . . ."[27]

How Do People React to Control?

Online Study Center
ACE the Test
Managing Now! LIVE

Managers can't rely solely on external control tools like budgets, EPM, and digital dashboards to keep employees in line. For one thing, some managers work under an "illusion of control." They believe they can monitor and control everything when in fact they cannot.[28] Even with digital dashboards, it is impossible to have a system that's so comprehensive it can track everything employees say or do. There's no practical way, for instance, to control how a front-desk clerk is greeting guests every minute of every day.

behavioral displacement: a way to evade controls in which the controls encourage behaviors that are inconsistent with what the company wants to accomplish

Second, employees often short-circuit the controls, sometimes with ingenious tactics. These tactics include behavioral displacement, gamesmanship, operating delays, and negative attitudes.[29]

Monitoring just "sales per hour of work" backfired in one store when employees claimed their supervisors were pressuring them to underreport hours on the job.

Behavioral Displacement **Behavioral displacement** occurs when the controls encourage behaviors that are inconsistent with what the company wants to accomplish. A famous management truism is "you get what you measure." This is a double-edged sword. Setting performance targets does focus employees' efforts on those targets. The problem is that the employees may then focus on only what you're measuring and disregard the company's more important goals.

For example, Nordstrom's had a policy of measuring employees in terms of sales per hour of work.[30] Unfortunately, monitoring just "sales per hour of work" backfired. For example, some employees claimed their supervisors were pressuring them to underreport hours on the job. That way they allegedly boosted reported sales per hour and made the supervisors look good. (Nordstrom settled an employee suit about this matter for $15 million.) The moral is: do not focus on just one or two targets.

gamesmanship: management actions that improve the manager's short-term performance but that may harm the firm in the longer run

● **Gamesmanship** Gamesmanship refers to management actions that improve the manager's short-term performance but that may harm the firm in the longer run. For example, one manager overshipped products to distributors at year-end. The aim was to ensure that management would meet its budgeted sales targets. It did, but then it had to deal with excess returns the following year.[31]

● **Operating Delays** Some control processes trigger operating delays and thus unnecessarily slow things down. For example, General Electric's (GE's) former CEO Jack Welch found that it sometimes took a year or more for division managers to get approval to introduce new products. The problem was the long list of yes/no approvals required by GE's control system. Streamlining the approval process solved this problem.

● **Negative Attitudes** Most people react suspiciously, at best, to efforts to control them. Therefore, it's not surprising that controls often trigger negative employee attitudes. One classic study focused on first-line supervisors' reactions to budgets. It found that they saw the budgets as pressure devices. In reaction to this perceived pressure, they formed antimanagement groups. Their own supervisors then reacted by increasing their compliance efforts.[32]

Unintentional Tactics

Sometimes, the behavioral problem is unconscious rather than intentional. For example, as we saw in Chapter 2, corrupt people often have a knack for convincing themselves that the stealing or misreporting that they're engaged in is really okay. This can happen even when the facts seem to be quite clear. For example, most people assume that accounting rules are fairly rigid and that auditors therefore don't have too much leeway in interpreting results. In fact, there's actually much ambiguity. Even apparently obvious questions like What is an expense? and What is an investment? are open to interpretation. For example, asked by *Money* magazine to estimate what a fictitious family owed in income taxes, the accountants' answers ranged from about \$37,000 to \$68,000![33]

That range means that auditors' biases can distort the results. Most auditors who review companies' financial statements are honest. However, they are as susceptible to unconscious bias as other people. For example, the clients themselves hire and fire auditors. So there can be an unconscious bias toward not overturning the client's financial decision, even if that decision is questionable.

Commitment-Based Control Systems

Online Study Center
ACE the Test
Managing Now! LIVE

We've examined several reasons why managers can't rely exclusively on the controls we've discussed in this chapter to keep their companies in line. Employees have many clever ways to evade them. And it's an illusion to think any control system can control everything.

Two other factors complicate employee control. First, companies are increasingly global, and monitoring employees far away is more difficult than if they're next door. Even companies that most people think of as very "controlling" can have problems controlling operations abroad.[34] For example, Wal-Mart recently had to close or sell its facilities in Germany and South Korea because the difficulty of controlling and doing business abroad eroded its profits in [illegible]

Second, controlling the self-managing teams that most companies now rely on can be counterproductive if doing so undermines the employees' sense of empowerment. And for some activities—such as building high-quality cars—you need the employees to want to do an excellent job because you can't force them to do it.

The bottom line is that managers have therefore always endeavored to supplement controls like those in this chapter with efforts to encourage employees to control themselves. Managers use three tools to accomplish this. First, *motivated employees* are more likely to exercise self-control. We will discuss motivation in Chapter 14. We devote the remainder of this chapter to discussing two other tools for encouraging employee self-control: creating *belief systems* and encouraging *employee commitment.*[35]

Creating Belief Systems and Values to Encourage Self-Control

James Collins and Jerry Porras studied firms that had been successful over many years. In their book, *Built to Last,* they explain that firms like Boeing, Disney, GE, Merck, and Motorola are successful in part because they create powerful values for employees to share. Values such as "the customer is always right" help show employees "[w]hat this company stands for."[36] Employees then (hopefully) control themselves by adapting what they do to these values.

For example, at the Toyota plant in Lexington, Kentucky, quality and teamwork are key values. Managers therefore select new employees based on whether they exhibit quality and teamwork during the one-week screening process. Then, Toyota's orientation, training, and appraisal and incentive programs all emphasize quality and teamwork. When employees buy into quality and teamwork, these values guide what they do. Even when there's no one around to supervise them, the employees control themselves.

Johnson & Johnson (J&J) is another company famous for its shared values. It summarizes its corporate values in its famous credo, which is shown in Figure 8.6. The credo contains the firm's guiding values. The first is, "We believe our first responsibility is to the doctors, nurses, and patients . . . who use our products." These guidelines provide the boundaries within which Johnson & Johnson employees work. Selling a product that might be harmful would obviously be out of bounds.

Johnson & Johnson was therefore shocked when armed federal agents briefly closed down its LifeScan unit's headquarters. LifeScan makes a diabetes diagnostic device. Some J&J employees had failed to report that a software glitch made some units show the wrong diagnosis. How could that happen in a company where all 100,000 employees are supposed to adhere to a strong code of ethics? "Mistakes were made in the LifeScan situation. . . . They were errors in judgment. We did too little, too late" is how the firm's CEO put it.[37] Ordinarily, the company's efforts to establish strong values and get employees to stick to them are more successful.

Using Commitment-Building Methods to Foster Self-Control

The U.S. National Weather Service employs highly trained scientists, many making life-or-death forecasts about tornado warnings. Because they are highly trained and their work is vital, one might assume that morale and commitment won't have much effect on the accuracy of their forecasts. However, both do. Tentative results

FIGURE 8.6

Johnson & Johnson Credo

Our Credo

We believe our first responsibility is to the doctors, nurses and patients,
to mothers and fathers and all others who use our products and services.
In meeting their needs, everything we do must be of high quality.
We must constantly strive to reduce our costs
in order to maintain reasonable prices.
Customers' orders must be serviced promptly and accurately.
Our suppliers and distributors must have an opportunity
to make a fair profit.
We are responsible to our employees,
the men and women who work with us throughout the world.
Everyone must be considered as an individual.
We must respect their dignity and recognize their merit.
They must have a sense of security in their jobs.
Compensation must be fair and adequate
and working conditions clean, orderly and safe.
We must be mindful of ways to help our employees fulfill
their family responsibilities.
Employees must feel free to make suggestions and complaints.
There must be equal opportunity for employment, development
and advancement for those qualified.
We must provide competent management,
and their actions must be just and ethical.
We are responsible to the communities in which we live and work
and to the world community as well.
We must be good citizens—support good works and charities
and bear our fair share of taxes.
We must encourage civic improvements and better health and education.
We must maintain in good order
the property we are privileged to use,
protecting the environment and natural resources.
Our final responsibility is to our stockholders.
Business must make a sound profit.
We must experiment with new ideas.
Research must be carried on, innovative programs developed
and mistakes paid for.
New equipment must be purchased, new facilities provided
and new products launched.
Reserves must be created to provide for adverse times.
When we operate according to these principles,
the stockholders should realize a fair return.

Johnson & Johnson

SOURCE: Courtesy of Johnson and Johnson. Reprinted by permission.

from one survey showed that some National Weather Service offices were much more successful than others at predicting potentially destructive storms. Morale and commitment factors seemed to explain much of the difference.[38]

Several years ago, Viacom agreed to sell its publishing operations for about $4.6 billion. In announcing the sale, the publisher's president thanked its employees for their "past hard work and dedication." And he reminded them that during the transition, "[I]t's more important than ever to focus on our individual responsibilities to ensure that our company performs at the highest levels."[39]

These anecdotes illustrate the irony of employee commitment. On the one hand, there is little doubt that employee commitment—employees' identification with and agreement to pursue the company's mission as if it's their own—contributes to organizational success.[40] On the other, the trend in many firms is to take actions that actually undermine commitment. For example, "[T]he trend today is to buy and sell portfolios of businesses, and to downsize and outsource in an attempt to increase short-term profits through cost-cutting."[41]

How to Boost Employee Commitment Managers can take tangible steps to boost employee commitment. After reviewing the research, one writer concludes that the way to do this ". . . is to employ practices that communicate to employees that the organization is supportive of their efforts, that the organization treats its employees fairly, and that the organization is interested in building employees' self-worth and importance"; in other words, that the firm "puts people first."[42] He says that specific practices include improving employment security, selectively hiring employees whose values are consistent with the company's, high compensation tied to organizational performance, extensive training, reduction of status differences among employees, sharing of information between the company and its employees, and pushing authority for decision making down to employees.[43]

In the final subsections below, we will present seven commitment-building practices, summarized as follows: foster people-first values, guarantee organizational justice, build a sense of community, communicate your vision, use value-based hiring, provide financial rewards, and encourage personal development and self-actualization.

Foster People-First Values Managers with "people-first values" characterize high-commitment companies. These managers trust their employees, believe in respecting their employees as individuals and treating them fairly, and are committed to employees' welfare. Here is how one United Auto Workers officer at Saturn's Spring Hill, Tennessee, plant put it: "Our philosophy is, we care about people—and it shows. We involve people in decisions that affect them. . . . Saturn's commitment really comes down to how you feel about people—your attitudes—more than anything, because all the other Saturn programs—the work teams, the extensive training, the way people are paid—all stem from these people attitudes."[44]

Saturn fosters such people-first values. For example, Saturn employees carry a card that lists the firm's values, one of which is:

> Trust and respect for the individual: We have nothing of greater value than our people. We believe that demonstrating respect for the uniqueness of every individual builds a team of confident, creative members possessing a high degree of initiative, self-respect, and self-discipline.[45]

The idea is to apply values like these to every decision. As one JCPenney officer said:

> Our people's high commitment stems from our commitment to them, and that commitment boils down to the fundamental respect for the individual that we all share. That respect goes back to the Penney idea—"To test every act in this wise: Does it square with what is right and just?" As a result, the value of respect for the individual is brought into our management process on a regular basis and is a standard against which we measure each and every decision that we make.[46]

Guarantee Organizational Justice Employee commitment depends in part on developing trust, and this requires treating employees fairly. Managers in firms like Starbucks, Saturn, and FedEx institute programs that guarantee managers treat employees fairly. For example, they have guaranteed-fair-treatment grievance programs for filing grievances, speak-up programs for voicing concerns, periodic surveys for expressing opinions, and top-down programs for keeping employees informed.[47]

Saturn Corp. instituted numerous behavioral methods aimed at fostering Saturn employees' commitment.

Build a Sense of Shared Fate and Community Part of fostering commitment entails making employees feel that "we're all in this together." Professor Rosabeth Moss Kanter found that leaders do this in several ways.[48] They minimize status differences. At Toyota's Camry assembly plant, all employees—from the president on down—shared the same open office space, wore the same uniforms, and ate in the same cafeteria. Others foster a sense of community by encouraging joint effort and communal work. At Saturn, all employees are on teams, and all teams work on projects together. Others bring individual employees into regular contact with the group as a whole.[49] Ben & Jerry's has monthly staff meetings in the receiving bay of its Waterbury, Vermont, plant.

Managing Now Thanks to the Internet, employees don't have to be at the same location to feel that they're part of a close-knit community. Internet-based group communication systems allow companies to build virtual communities by letting employees communicate easily and in real time, even if they are dispersed around the globe.[50] As one expert puts it, "The sales department could hold forums and share information in an interactive community." Said another, "When people interact in a virtual community, there is an exchange of ideas and information, which becomes powerful and generates excitement."[51]

Use Value-Based Hiring Kanter also found that commitment to a cause is higher among employees who share the same basic values. High-commitment firms therefore practice **value-based hiring**. They don't look for just job-related skills in the people they hire. They also look for common experiences and values that may signal the applicant's fit with the firm. Thus, even college grads may start out by cleaning one airline's planes. The idea is that if you don't fit in, you probably won't become committed to the company.

value-based hiring: looking for common experiences and values that may signal the applicant's fit with the firm, rather than hiring based solely on job-related skills

Communicate Your Vision Committed employees need missions to be committed to, preferably missions that they feel are bigger than they are. Employees at organizations like the Salvation Army, Saturn, and Ben & Jerry's become, in effect, soldiers in a crusade. Through their employment, they redefine themselves and their goals in terms of the company's mission. The employee, says Kanter, "finds himself anew in something larger and greater."[52] Employee commitment thus derives in part from the power of the firm's mission and from the manager's ability to crystalize that mission in a few simple values.

Use Financial Rewards and Profit Sharing Although there is more to building commitment than financial rewards, high-commitment firms generally offer above-average pay and incentives. FedEx, for instance, provides a half-dozen types of incentive awards, including a Bravo-Zulu award that a manager can give on the spot.

Encourage Employee Development and Self-Actualization Employees understand that staying loyal to an employer can be risky in an era of continuing mergers and mass layoffs. Earning their commitment therefore requires reciprocity. It requires proof that their employers are committed to them.

One strong signal is to show employees that the company is committed to their personal development. Being the best at what one can be provides the best job security, whether or not the person stays with the firm. Psychologist Abraham Maslow emphasized that people need to self-actualize, "to become . . . everything that one is capable of becoming. [W]hat man can be, he must be. . . ."[53]

Firms can help employees to self-actualize in many ways. They can train employees to expand their skills and to solve problems. They can enrich their jobs and empower them. They can provide career-oriented interviews and help them to continue their education and to grow. The results can be dramatic. Here's how one Saturn assembler put it:

> I'm committed to Saturn in part for what they did for me; for the 300 hours of training in problem solving and leadership that help me expand my personal horizons; for the firm's Excel program that helps me push myself to the limit; and because I know that at Saturn I can go as far as I can go—this company wants its people to be all that they can be.[54]

At FedEx, one manager similarly described his experience:

> At Federal Express, the best I can be is what I can be here. I have been allowed to grow with Federal Express. For the people at Federal Express, it's not the money that draws us to the firm. The biggest benefit is that Federal Express made me a man. It gave me the confidence and self-esteem to become the person I had the potential to become.[55]

The Practice IT feature shows how Starbucks applies this chapter's control concepts.

PRACTICE IT
Controlling the Cappuccino Makers at Starbucks

With about 10,000 stores and 34 million transactions a week, Seattle-based Starbucks Coffee Company's managers must make sure they stay in control of what's happening at each store. Starbucks' solution combines IT with fostering employee commitment. First (in addition to standard traditional control devices such as budgets), Starbucks relies on a global information technology system to monitor transactions in each of its stores. Its XPR system remotely monitors an assortment of metrics at each store. XPR then uses the principle of exception to trigger reports when any of the metrics for a store seems to be moving in unusual ways.[56] For example, the system monitors point-of-sale activities and then triggers reports if a particular register seems to be recording too many free refills. Some employees confess after being confronted with the information; some confessed to stealing as much as $42,000. With much smaller exceptions, the employee gets a letter asking them to explain what's happening. The behavior usually stops after that.

Starbucks does not rely on just external controls. It also works hard to encourage self-control by winning the commitment of its employees. For example, all employees who work at least twenty hours a week receive a full complement of health and other benefits, and they are eligible for the company's stock-option plan. Employees also receive free drinks while on duty. And they get the considerable benefit of working in an environment that some liken to a collegial living room. As a result, committed, engaged Starbucks employees help make sure that things stay under control.

CHAPTER SUMMARY

1. Control is the task of ensuring that activities are providing the desired results. The control process consists of three steps: set goals, measure performance, and take corrective action. Managers distinguish among steering controls, yes/no controls, and postaction controls.
2. Budgets and ratio analysis are among the most widely used diagnostic control tools. Budgets are formal financial expressions of a manager's plan and show targets for yardsticks such as revenues, cost of materials, and profits, usually expressed as dollar amounts. Most managers also achieve control by monitoring various financial ratios.
3. The chapter presented three classes of control methods. Personal, interactive control systems are real-time, usually face-to-face methods of monitoring both a plan's effectiveness and the underlying assumptions on which the plan was built. Traditional control systems like budgets and performance reports are intended to ensure that goals are being achieved and that variances, if any, are explained. Commitment-based control includes using motivation techniques, building value systems, and obtaining employees' commitment.
4. Managers now use IT-based controls, usually based on ERP systems. These include more timely accounting reports, ABC, wireless-based control, electronic performance monitoring, and digital dashboards.
5. A problem with relying on traditional controls is that they can lead to unintended, undesirable, and often harmful employee reactions, such as behavioral displacement, gamesmanship, operating delays, negative attitudes, and reduced empowerment.
6. Steps for improving employee commitment include the following: foster people-first values, guarantee fair treatment, create a shared fate, use values-based hiring, communicate the vision, use rewards, and encourage self-actualization.

DISCUSSION QUESTIONS

1. What are the basic steps in the control process?
2. Give examples of steering, concurrent, and feedback controls that your professor uses in this class.
3. Give examples of personal, traditional, and commitment-based controls that family members use at home.
4. How is activity-based costing different from traditional cost accounting?
5. Discuss why IT-based controls such as ABC, wireless controls, and digital dashboards would be impractical without enterprise resource planning systems.
6. Give examples of the unintended behavioral consequences of controls that the dean of your college might encounter if he or she passed the rule that professors' raises would be based on student ratings only.
7. What do we mean by belief systems and values that encourage self-control?
8. Explain why having committed employees is especially important in today's industrial environment.

EXPERIENTIAL EXERCISES

1. You are one of the founding engineers in your six-month-old firm, and you brought to the firm the values of hard work, quality, teamwork, and excellence. These values have united the original members, but you are concerned that they might change with the addition of fifty new people needed by your fast-growing company. Form teams of four to five students. Each team should answer the following question: What type of control system would you develop to ensure that your values are adhered to, based on the concepts in this chapter?
2. College students deal with professors all the time, but they may not realize how difficult it is for the

college's administrators to control what their faculty members are doing. The typical professor has a number of responsibilities, including teaching classes, writing research articles, and attending curriculum-development committee meetings. The dean also wants to make sure faculty members are conducting themselves professionally, for instance, in terms of how they interact with their students. Knowing that you are a management student, the dean has asked you to develop a control package for the college's business professors. The package is to include, at a minimum, a list of the details that you want to control and a corresponding list showing how you plan to control each detail. Form teams of four to five students. Each team should develop a package for the dean.

3. There is nothing quite like eating in a restaurant where details—from customer service to hygiene—are out of control. Before coming to class, visit one or two local restaurants, and list everything you see that might suggest that (at least in specific areas) details are a bit out of control. Then meet in teams of four to five students, compare notes, and create a checklist for assessing the adequacy of a restaurant's control mechanisms. If time permits and if there is an on-campus cafeteria, evaluate the school cafeteria's controls.

CASE STUDY

Controlling Ritz-Carlton

Many consider business hotels as offering a generic service—a safe, clean, comfortable room in a city away from home. Ritz-Carlton Hotel Company viewed its business differently. Targeting industry executives, meeting and corporate travel planners, and affluent travelers, the Atlanta-based company manages twenty-five luxury hotels that pursue the goal of being the very best in each market. Ritz-Carlton succeeded with more than just its guests. For example, three times it received the U.S. government's Malcom Baldrige National Quality Award. Given its mission of true excellence in service, what types of control systems did Ritz-Carlton need to achieve its goals?

In the presentation of the Baldrige award, the committee commended Ritz-Carlton for a management program that included participatory leadership, thorough information gathering, coordinated planning and execution, and a trained workforce empowered "to move heaven and earth" to satisfy customers. Of all the elements in its system, Ritz-Carlton felt the most important control mechanism was committed employees.

The firm trains all employees in the company's Gold Standards, which set out Ritz-Carlton's service credo and the basics of premium service. The company has translated these basics into twenty Ritz-Carlton Basics. Each employee is to understand and adhere to these standards, which describe processes for solving any problem guests may have.

The corporate motto is "ladies and gentlemen serving ladies and gentlemen." Like many companies, Ritz-Carlton gives new employees an orientation followed by on-the-job training. Unlike other hotel firms, Ritz-Carlton then certifies employees. It reinforces its corporate values continuously by daily lineups; frequent recognition for extraordinary achievement; and a performance appraisal based on expectations explained during the orientation, training, and certification processes.

All workers must act at the first sign of a problem, regardless of the type of problem or customer complaint. Employees are empowered to do whatever it takes to provide what Ritz-Carlton calls instant pacification. Other employees must assist if a coworker requests aid in responding to a guest's complaint or wish. There is never an excuse for not solving a customer problem.

Responsibility for ensuring high-quality guest services and accommodations rests largely with employees. The company surveys all employees annually to determine their understanding of quality standards and their personal satisfaction as a Ritz-Carlton employee. In one case, 96 percent of all employees surveyed named excellence in guest services as the key priority.

DISCUSSION QUESTIONS

1. What actions does Ritz-Carlton take to control the quality of its service?
2. What does Ritz-Carlton do to foster its employees' high level of commitment?
3. How does the company's value system foster employee self-control?

MANAGING OPERATIONS AND SUPPLY CHAINS

9

Will Whirlpool Deliver?

Several years ago, Whirlpool's deliveries were so unreliable that its managers grimly joked that customers ranked Whirlpool "fifth among America's four biggest appliance manufacturers."[1] Whirlpool's salespeople referred to the company's supply chain (the information system Whirlpool used to link together its manufacturing plants, warehouses, distribution partners, and retailers) as "sales disablers."[2] In an industry where getting appliances on time is the consumer's main concern, Whirlpool often missed its dates. Rueben Slone, Whirlpool's new head of supply chain management for America, knew changes were in order. What should he have Whirlpool do now? ■

Several years ago, Whirlpool needed a more effective "supply chain" for getting deliveries of products like these into retailers' stores.

BEHAVIORAL OBJECTIVES

After studying this chapter, you should be able to:

Show that you've learned the chapter's essential information by

- Listing and explaining the basic types of production processes.
- Listing what the manager has to do to minimize the seven wastes.
- Listing the reasons why a company is (and is not) world class.
- Listing and explaining the three A's of supply chain management.

Show that you can practice what you've learned here by

- Reading the opening vignette about Whirlpool and suggesting a supply chain solution for the company.
- Reading the end-of-chapter exercise and evaluating a facility's layout.

CHAPTER OUTLINE

- Reading the end-of-chapter exercise and creating a Gantt chart for a project.
- Reading the end-of-chapter exercise and computing the economic order quantity (EOQ) for an item.

Online Study Center
ACE the Test
Managing Now! LIVE

Show that you can apply what you've learned here by

- Watching the simulation video and identifying how operations management can improve organizational efficiency.

The Basics of Operations Management

Online Study Center
ACE the Test
Managing Now! LIVE

Take a brief walk through a Circuit City or Best Buy. Domestic brands from General Electric (GE) and Whirlpool compete with Miele and Bosch from abroad. In such an environment, only world-class competitors survive. That's why companies like Whirlpool must have operations management systems in place. These systems produce high-quality products at competitive costs and get them to customers on time.

operations management: the process of managing the resources that are needed to produce an organization's goods and services

Operations management is the process of managing the resources required to produce the organization's goods and services.[3] Operations managers particularly focus on managing the "five P's" of the firm's operations: people, plants, parts, processes, and planning and control systems. The *people* include the direct and indirect workforce, such as assembly workers, inventory clerks, and clerical staff. *Plants* are the factories or service branches (like banks) where the firm creates its product or service. *Parts* include the raw materials and other inputs that the firm's operations will transform into finished products or services. *Processes* represent the technology, equipment, and steps required to accomplish production. The *planning and control systems* are the procedures management uses to run the system, such as the methods used to schedule the work and to control quality.[4] Operations managers include, for instance, plant managers, manufacturing managers, purchasing managers, and logistics (or transportation) managers.

Operations management is not important for just manufacturing firms. For example, in the new McDonald's kitchen, computers control production, and sandwiches come off the line in forty-five seconds. American Airlines uses sophisticated operations management planning and scheduling tools to schedule reservations clerks and to adjust flight schedules in the face of rough weather. La Quinta Motor Inns uses operations management tools to analyze variables (such as traffic counts and local purchasing power) to identify preferred locations. Cookie-store managers use special work-scheduling software to chart hourly and daily sales and to tell the manager how many employees he or she will need to staff the store that day.[5]

In this chapter, we'll look at the basic aspects of managing operations, the first of which is managing the production system itself.

Managing the Production System

inputs: resources required for the manufacture of a product or service

The production system is the part of the operations system that actually produces the company's products. Any production system has three main components—inputs, a conversion system, and outputs (see Figure 9.1). **Inputs** are all the resources required to create the product or service. These include raw materials and

FIGURE 9.1

The Basic Production System

The heart of every production system is a conversion process or system, which takes various inputs and converts them into outputs such as products or services.

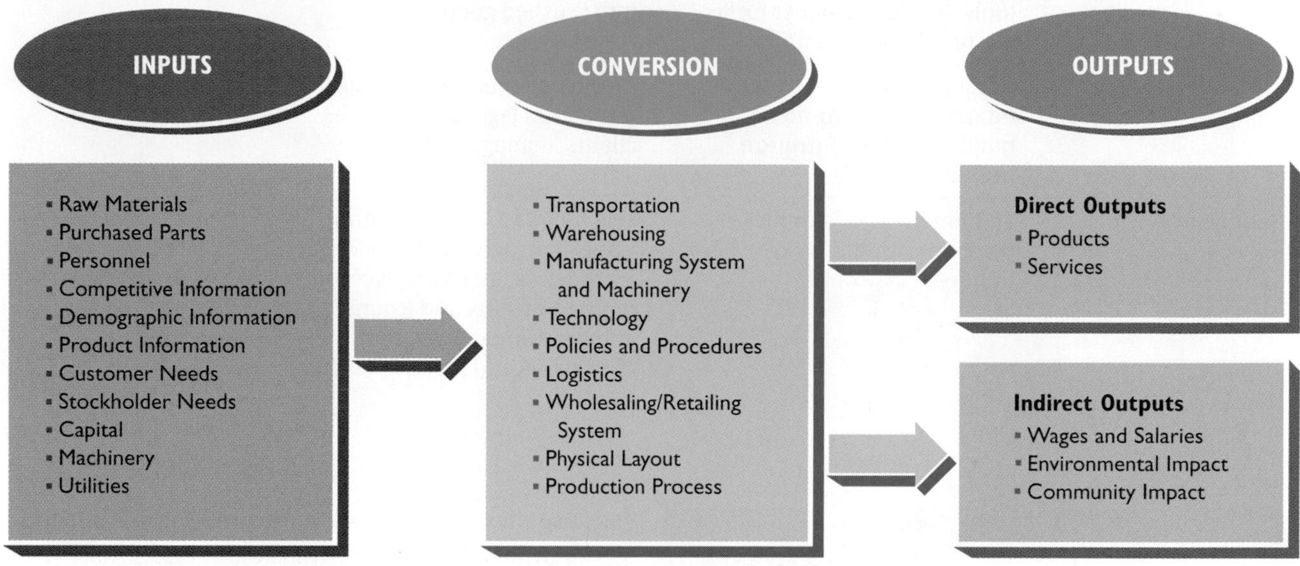

purchased parts, personnel, and capital. Other inputs include data on the competition, the product, and the customer.

conversion system: any production system that converts inputs (material and human resources) into outputs (products or services); sometimes called the production process or technology

output: a direct outcome (actual product or service) or indirect outcome (taxes, wages, salaries) of a production system

Any production system takes inputs and converts them into products or services (outputs). The **conversion system** (also called the production process or technology) has several components, including the production machinery and its physical layout, the transport services that bring in the inputs and deliver the final products to customers, and warehousing services for goods awaiting shipment. The production system's **outputs** include *direct outputs* (the actual products or services) and *indirect outputs* (such as wages and salaries).

The same production system sequence applies to a service business (see Table 9.1).[6] For example, a college's inputs include students, books, professors, and buildings. Its conversion system consists of the lectures, exams, computerized instruction, and so forth. The outputs are educated persons.

Whether you are producing goods or services, designing a production system requires four basic decisions: Where will we locate the facility? What type of production process will we use? What will be the layout of the overall plant or facility? And what will be the layout of the production system itself? We'll look at each.

The Facility Location Decision

Deciding where to locate the facility (plant or store) is crucial. Dry-cleaning businesses try to place their stores near supermarkets to make it convenient for customers. Britain's Marks & Spencer had to close over thirty of its retail stores

TABLE 9.1
Components of Typical Production Systems

Production System	Main Inputs	What Conversion System Does	Main Outputs
1. Cereal factory	Grain, water, sugar, personnel, tools, machines, paper for cartons, buildings, utilities	Converts raw materials into finished goods	Breakfast cereals
2. Law firm	Legal supplies, personnel, information, computers, buildings, office furniture, utilities	Attracts clients, compiles and researches legal data, advises clients, manages billing, etc.	Legal advice, client defenses
3. College	Students, books, supplies, personnel, buildings, utilities	Teaching facts, skills, attitudes, values through various pedagogical devices, including lectures, online learning, and exams, and providing associated counseling and related services	Educated persons

Location, location, location: A dry-cleaning business in a shopping mall allows customers to drop off and pick up clothes on their way to shop for food or other items.

because they were in poor locations. For manufacturers, key factors like transportation costs and labor availability determine plant location.

Managers typically ponder many factors when deciding where to locate a facility. Subjective considerations can include details like the owner's personal preferences, say, for warm weather. More objective criteria include, for instance, government rules and attitudes, cultural issues, availability of labor, taxes, utilities, environmental regulations, government incentives, and proximity to supplies and customers.

Managers ignore location considerations at their peril. In the 1990s, many believed Vietnam was the next great Asian tiger in terms of projected economic growth.[7] But for ten years, the experts were wrong. Until recently, few visitors came. The $64 million Hilton Hanoi Opera Hotel sat nearly empty for years.[8]

Basic Types of Production Processes

Deciding on a production process is a second crucial decision. We can distinguish between two broad types of systems: intermittent production systems and continuous production systems.

intermittent production system: a system in which production is performed on a start-and-stop basis, such as for the manufacture of made-to-order products

Intermittent Systems In an **intermittent production system**, employees work on the product on a start-and-stop basis.[9] Automobile-repair shops, custom-cabinet shops, and construction contractors are examples. Firms like these usually offer made-to-order products. They usually deal with relatively low product volumes and frequent schedule changes and tend to use general-purpose equipment that can make a variety of models or products.

Mass production is a special type of intermittent production process. Here, standardized methods and single-use machines produce long runs of standardized items. Most mass production processes use assembly lines. An assembly line is a fixed sequence of specialized (single-use) machines. In a typical assembly line, the product moves from station to station, where one or more employees and/or specialized machines perform tasks such as inserting bumpers or screwing on doors.

Mass customization is a popular hybrid production process, somewhere between the intermittent and continuous production (discussed below) processes. **Mass customization** means designing, producing, and delivering products so that customers get customized products for at or near the cost and convenience of mass-produced items.[10] Dell's production process exemplifies this approach. Dell customers get customized PCs (they advertise today, "Dell—Purely You") at a price at or below that of mass-produced, standardized machines. Mass customization depends on three factors:[11]

mass customization: designing, producing, and delivering products so that customers get customized products for at or near the cost and convenience of mass-produced items

1. *Modular product design.* Products like Dell's consist of separate modules (each consisting of one or more prewired components) such as modems, DVD drives, and processing chips. Employees can easily assemble these into different forms of the product. Hewlett-Packard (HP) designs its printers to have a separate power supply inserted later. Customers around the globe can get the power supply they need.
2. *Modular process design.* Similarly, the firm designs its production process so that workers can perform different steps in different places. A Dell repairperson may come to your office, just pull out the defective modular component, and replace it.
3. *Agile supply networks.* Mass customization firms design the whole supply chain (from vendors to production to distribution) to be adept at providing a variety of services. For example, IBM designs its products around modules. Vendors supply components and may do some preliminary assembly. IBM factories then assemble these components into modules. IBM distributors then assemble the modules into complete products based on what their customers want.

Mass customization is unique among production processes. Managers in typical intermittent production firms must choose between high-volume mass production and product variety. Mass customization weds high production volume with high product variety.

continuous production system: a production process, such as those used by chemical plants or refineries, that runs for very long periods without the start-and-stop behavior associated with an intermittent production system

● Continuous Production A **continuous production system** runs uninterrupted for very long periods. Chemical plants, paper plants, and petroleum refineries are examples. They may run for months or even years, producing basically the same products (paper, or refined oil, for instance) night and day.

Mass customization is blurring the traditional dividing line between intermittent and continuous production processes. For example, computer-assisted manufacturing processes at Mead Corporation, which produces and sells paper, give the factory the flexibility of intermittent production and the efficiency of continuous production.

FIGURE 9.2

Product Layout

A car wash is an example of an assembly-line product layout. Each special-purpose machine performs its function as the product moves from station to station.

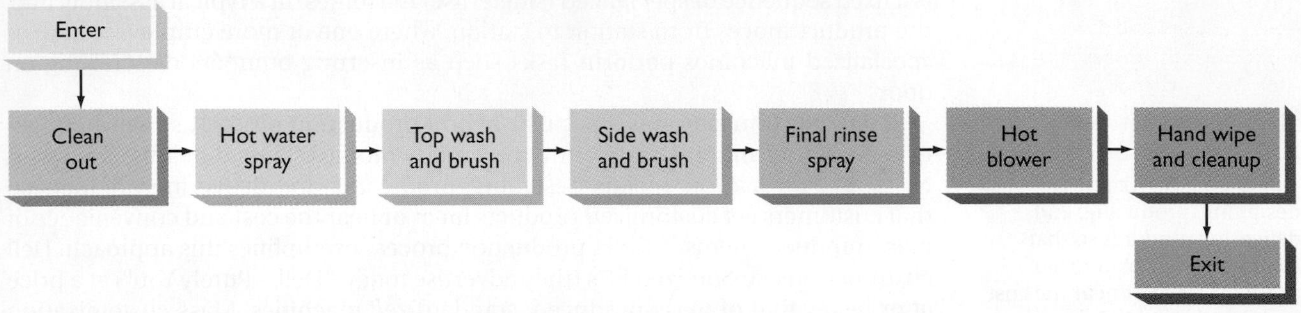

SOURCE: Adapted from Everett Adam, Jr. and Ronald Ebert, *Production and Operations Management* (Upper Saddle River, N.J.: Prentice Hall, 1992), p. 254.

Facility and Production Layout

facility layout: the configuration of all the machines, employee workstations, storage areas, internal walls, and so forth that constitute the facility used to create a firm's product or service

product layout: a production system design in which every item to be produced follows the same sequence of operations from beginning to end, as in an assembly line

process layout: a production system design in which similar machines or functions are grouped together

fixed-position layout: a production system design in which the product being built or produced stays at one location and the machines, workers, and tools required to build the product are brought to that location, as needed, as for the building of ships or other bulky products

cellular manufacturing layout: usually a combination of process and product layouts in which machines and personnel are grouped into cells containing all the tools and operations required to produce a particular product or family of products

Once the manager decides on a production process, he or she can decide how to lay out the plant or facility.

Facility Layout Facility layout refers to the configuration of the total facility—not just the machines, but also the employee workstations, storage areas, internal walls, and so forth. Important objectives here usually include reducing materials-handling costs, providing sufficient capacity, and allowing for safe equipment operation and ease of maintenance.

Facility layout is also important for service firms. Thus, food stores typically put products like meats toward the back; to get to them, customers must pass the other aisles, hopefully prompting them to pick up and buy more products along the way.

Production System Layout Whether in a factory or a service business, there are basically four ways to lay out the production (conversion) system itself. In a product layout, every item produced follows the same sequence from beginning to end. Each item moves from one specialized tool and operation to another. An assembly line is one example. Product layouts are not restricted to manufacturing. For example, automatic car washes use product layouts, as Figure 9.2 illustrates.[12]

In a process layout, the designers group similar machines or processes together. As Figure 9.3 illustrates,[13] service businesses like hospitals are usually organized this way. There are separate locations for departments like pediatrics and for testing and x-ray. In a fixed-position layout, the product stays at one location. The manufacturing machines and workers (or machines) come to that location, as needed. Companies build heavy products like ships and planes this way.

In a cellular manufacturing layout, the company groups machines into cells (small work areas), and each cell contains all the tools required to complete one activity (see Figure 9.4[14]). Thus, a cell may be dedicated to all the grinding and polishing steps required to produce the valves for car engines. The advantage is that cellular layouts reduce the wastes normally associated with moving the items around the plant floor to different workstations.

FIGURE 9.3

Process Layout

In a process layout like this one, each process has its own area. The product (in this case, the patient) is directed to the appropriate processes (such as x-ray and pediatrics).

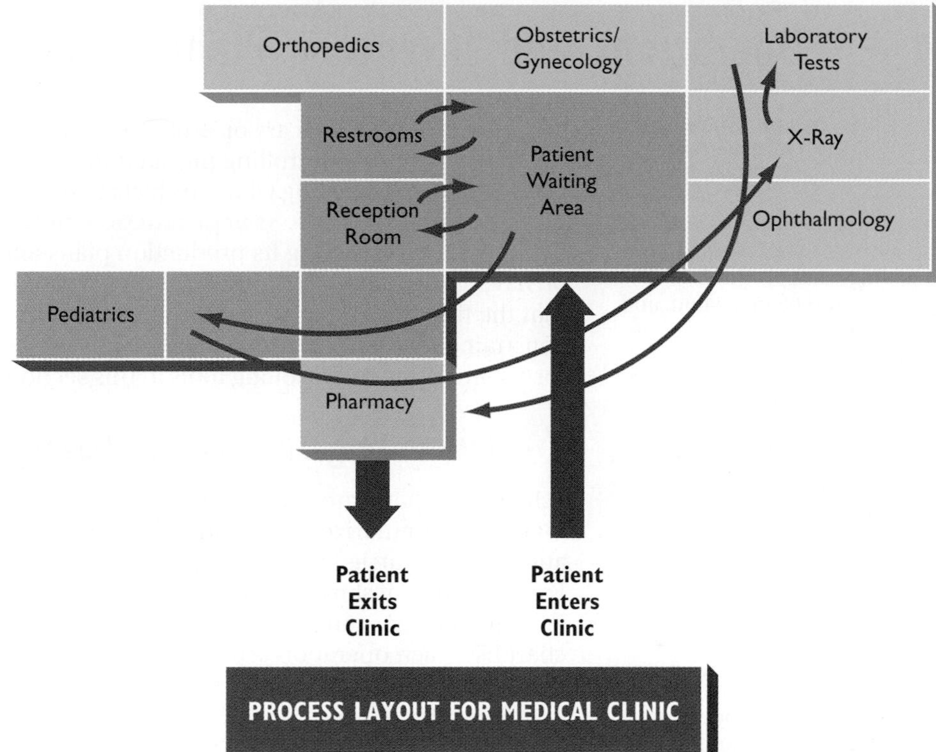

SOURCE: Adapted from Everett Adam, Jr. and Ronald Ebert, *Production and Operations Management* (Upper Saddle River, N.J.: Prentice Hall, 1992), p. 254.

FIGURE 9.4

Improving Layouts by Moving to the Cellular Manufacturing Concept

Note in both (A) and (B) that U-shaped work cells can reduce material and employee movement.

(A)

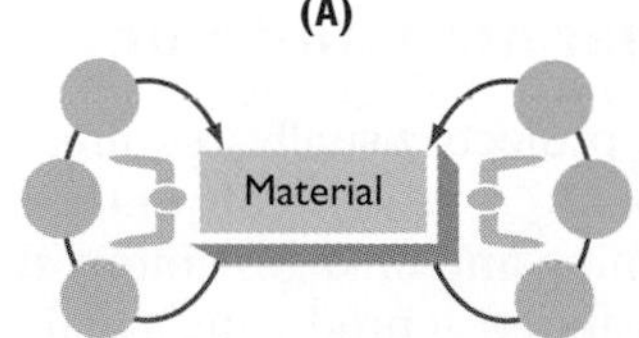

Current layout—workers in small closed areas. Cannot increase output without a third worker.

(B)

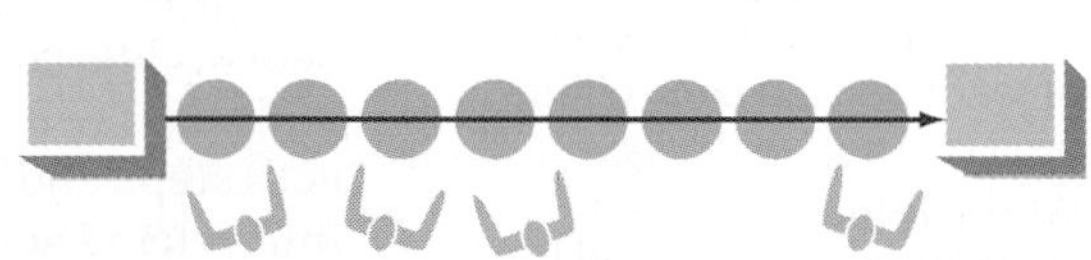

Current layout—straight lines are hard to balance.

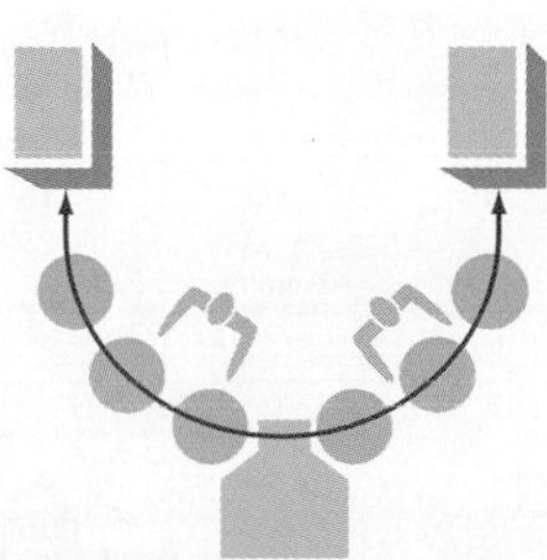

Improved layout—workers can assist each other. May be able to add a third worker.

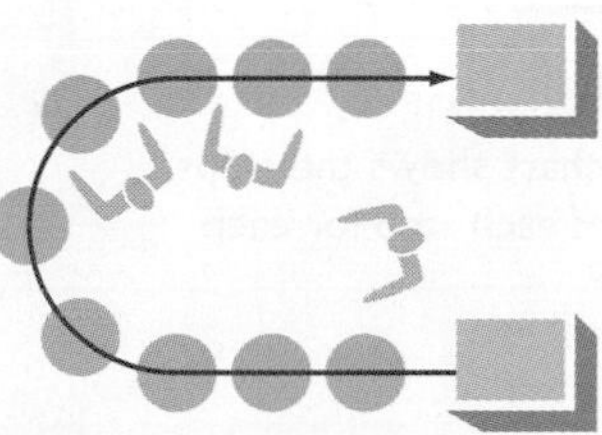

Improved layout—in a U shape, workers have better access. Four workers were reduced to three.

SOURCE: Adapted from Barry Render and Jay Heizer, *Principles of Operations Management*, 2nd ed., © 1997. Reprinted by permission of Prentice Hall, Inc., Upper Saddle River, NJ.

Operations and Inventory Planning and Control

Online Study Center
ACE the Test
Managing Now! LIVE

Whether producing cars or Broadway shows, the manager needs a system for planning and controlling production. **Operations** or **production planning** is the process of deciding what products to produce and where, when, and how to produce them. **Operations** or **production control** is the process of ensuring that the operation is meeting its production plans and schedules. Operations depend on having adequate inventory. **Inventory management** is the process of ensuring that the firm has enough inventories of all required parts and supplies within the constraint of minimizing total inventory costs. We'll look at operations and inventory planning and controlling tools in this section.

operations or **production planning:** the process of deciding what products to produce and where, when, and how to produce them

operations or **production control:** the process of ensuring that the specified production plans and schedules are being adhered to

inventory management: the process of ensuring that the firm has enough inventories of all required parts and supplies within the constraint of minimizing total inventory costs

Gantt chart: a production scheduling chart (named after management pioneer Henry Gantt) that plots time on a horizontal scale and generally shows, for each product or project, the start-and-stop times of each operation

network planning and control methods: ways of planning and controlling projects by graphically representing the projects' steps and the timing and links between those steps

Scheduling and Gantt Charts

Scheduling charts are simple but effective production planning and control tools. Managers summarize their production schedules on charts that show what operations will be carried out and when. The **Gantt chart** in Figure 9.5 is one example. For each order, it shows the start and stop times for each activity. This type of chart lets the manager quickly monitor each order's progress. A second type of Gantt chart lists each operation separately in the left column, one under the other, and the time along the bottom. That Gantt chart helps the manager monitor each operation's progress.

In practice, production schedulers start with the required delivery date. Then they calculate how long each assembly operation will take, how long it will take to obtain raw materials, and so forth. The schedulers can then decide whether the firm can meet its required delivery date and what bottlenecks to unclog.

Network Planning and Control Methods

Scheduling complex projects usually requires computerized network charting tools. **Network planning and control methods** graphically represent the project's steps and the timing and linkages among those steps. A project is a series of interrelated activities aimed at producing a major product (like a new Boeing 787) or a service (like a wedding reception).

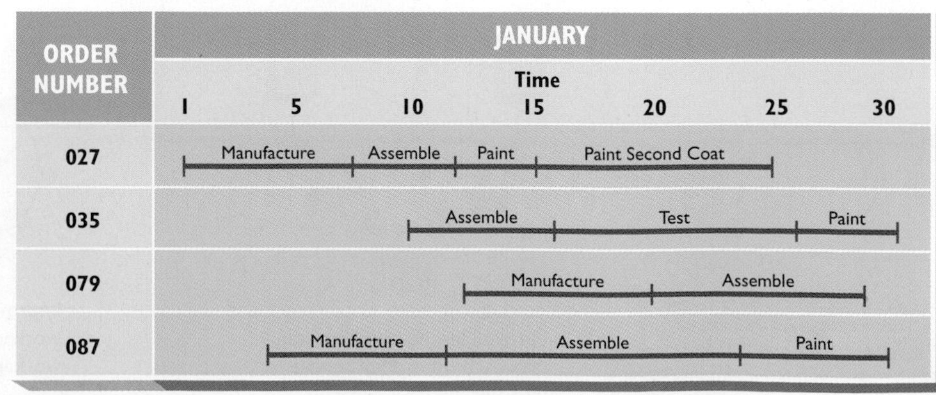

FIGURE 9.5

A Gantt Chart

This Gantt chart shows the steps and timing of each step for each order.

FIGURE 9.6

PERT Chart for Building a House

In a PERT chart like this one, each event is shown in its proper relationship to the other events. The tan circles show the critical—or most time-consuming—path.

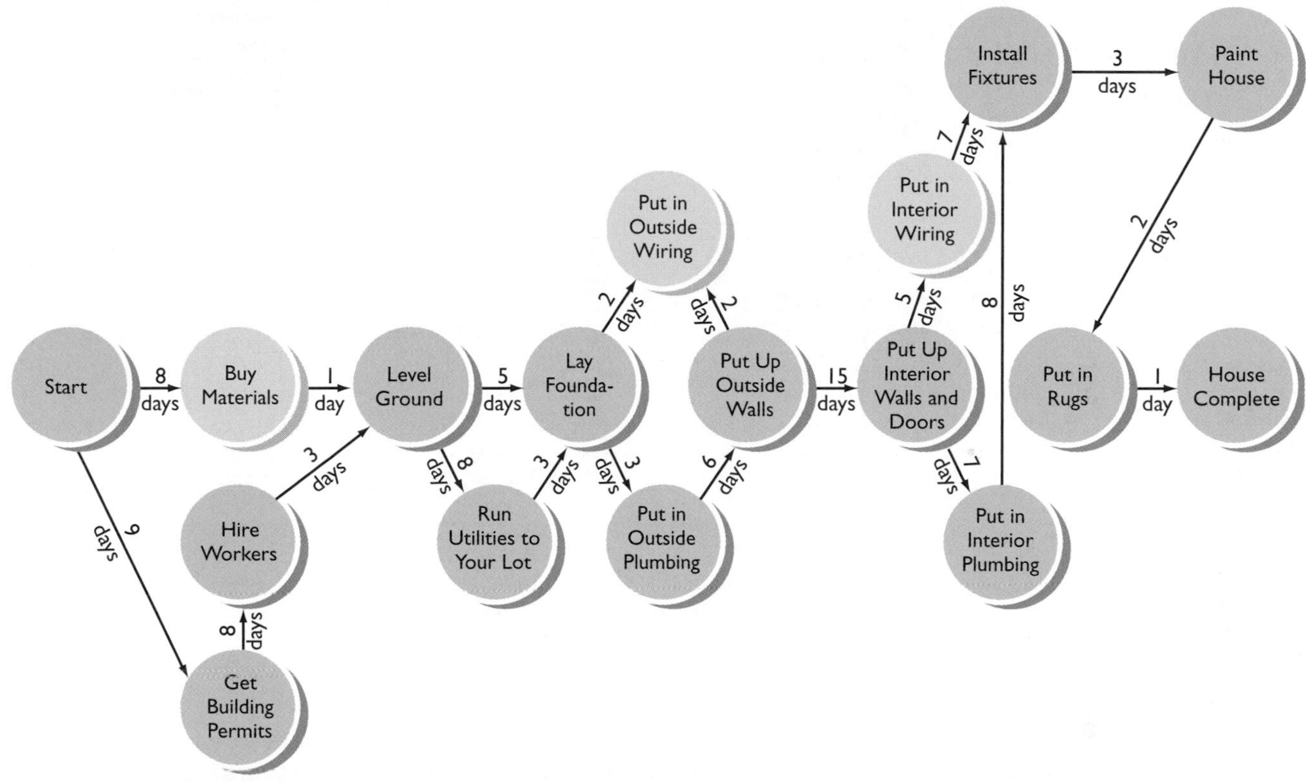

events: the specific accomplishments in a project, represented by circles in a PERT chart

activities: the time-consuming aspects of a project, represented by arrows in a PERT chart

critical path: the sequence of events in a project that, in total, requires the most time to complete

PERT and CPM charts are the two most popular network planning and control methods. PERT (program evaluation review technique) and CPM (critical path method) were invented at about the same time and are similar, although several details (for instance, CPM shows the cost of each step) set PERT apart from CPM.

Events and activities are the two major components of PERT charts. As Figure 9.6 shows, **events**, depicted by circles, represent specific accomplishments, such as "lay foundation." Arrows represent **activities**, which are the time-consuming aspects of the project (like laying the foundation). By studying the PERT chart, the scheduler can determine the **critical path**, the sequence of critical events that, in total, requires the most time to complete.

● Managing Now In practice, managers generally use manual project planning versions of tools like Gantt and PERT for simpler projects. They use computerized versions for more complex projects. Figure 9.7 illustrates a few of such software's benefits. In addition to laying out the network's events and relationships, this software provides pop-up calendars, automatically produces status reports, and makes it easy to link up and communicate project status via the Web. It also helps the manager define project tasks, anticipate obstacles, and print reports.

FIGURE 9.7

Example of a Computerized Project Planning Report

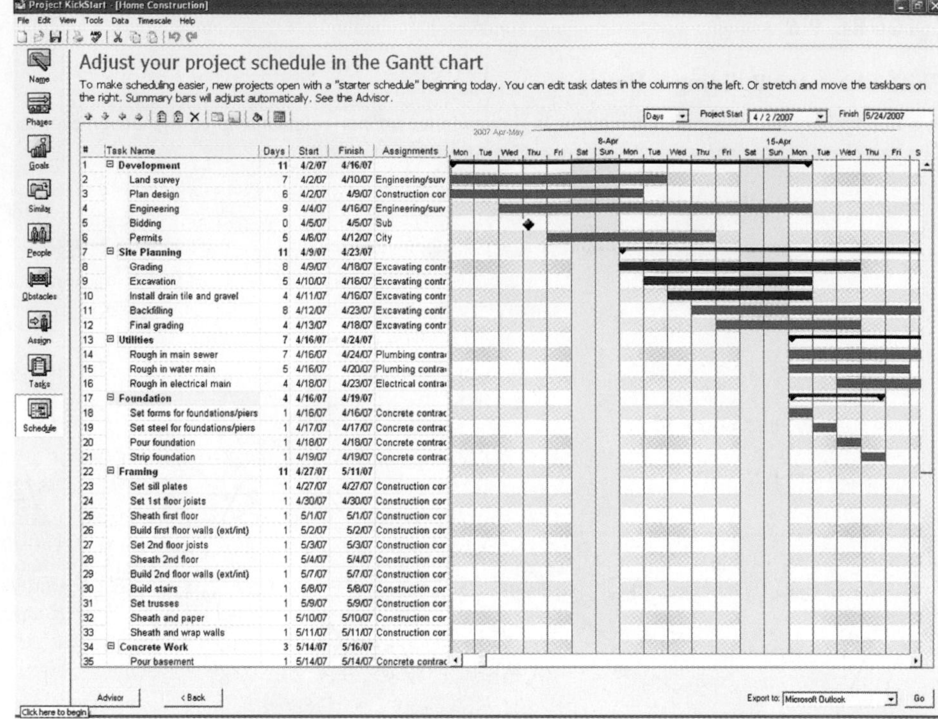

#	Task Name	Days	Start	Finish	Assignments
1	**Development**	11	4/2/07	4/16/07	
2	Land survey	7	4/2/07	4/10/07	Engineering/surv
3	Plan design	6	4/2/07	4/9/07	Construction cor
4	Engineering	9	4/4/07	4/16/07	Engineering/surv
5	Bidding	0	4/5/07	4/5/07	Sub
6	Permits	5	4/6/07	4/12/07	City
7	**Site Planning**	11	4/9/07	4/23/07	
8	Grading	8	4/9/07	4/18/07	Excavating contr
9	Excavation	5	4/10/07	4/16/07	Excavating contr
10	Install drain tile and gravel	4	4/11/07	4/16/07	Excavating contr
11	Backfilling	8	4/12/07	4/23/07	Excavating contr
12	Final grading	4	4/13/07	4/18/07	Excavating contr
13	**Utilities**	7	4/16/07	4/24/07	
14	Rough in main sewer	7	4/16/07	4/24/07	Plumbing contra
15	Rough in water main	5	4/16/07	4/20/07	Plumbing contra
16	Rough in electrical main	4	4/18/07	4/23/07	Electrical contra
17	**Foundation**	4	4/16/07	4/19/07	
18	Set forms for foundations/piers	1	4/16/07	4/16/07	Concrete contrac
19	Set steel for foundations/piers	1	4/17/07	4/17/07	Concrete contrac
20	Pour foundation	1	4/18/07	4/18/07	Concrete contrac
21	Strip foundation	1	4/19/07	4/19/07	Concrete contrac
22	**Framing**	11	4/27/07	5/11/07	
23	Set sill plates	1	4/27/07	4/27/07	Construction cor
24	Set 1st floor joists	1	4/30/07	4/30/07	Construction cor
25	Sheath first floor	1	5/1/07	5/1/07	Construction cor
26	Build first floor walls (ext/int)	1	5/2/07	5/2/07	Construction cor
27	Set 2nd floor joists	1	5/3/07	5/3/07	Construction cor
28	Sheath 2nd floor	1	5/4/07	5/4/07	Construction cor
29	Build 2nd floor walls (ext/int)	1	5/7/07	5/7/07	Construction cor
30	Build stairs	1	5/8/07	5/8/07	Construction cor
31	Set trusses	1	5/9/07	5/9/07	Construction cor
32	Sheath and paper	1	5/10/07	5/10/07	Construction cor
33	Sheath and wrap walls	1	5/11/07	5/11/07	Construction cor
34	**Concrete Work**	3	5/14/07	5/16/07	
35	Pour basement	1	5/14/07	5/14/07	Concrete contrac

Purchasing

Purchasing departments buy all the materials and parts the firm needs to conduct its business, including the raw materials that go into the firm's products as well as machinery, tools, purchased components, and office supplies.

Purchasing is a more important function than many managers realize. Sometimes 60 percent or more of a manufacturer's sales dollars are paid to suppliers for purchased materials.[15] As a rough approximation, a manager might have to boost sales by $3 to $4 to produce the same increase in profits that cutting purchasing costs by $1 would produce. Furthermore, manufacturers striving to maintain quality levels know that the quality of a finished product like a PC can't be any better than the quality of components such as hard drives. Purchasing departments thus affect a firm's cost-effectiveness as well as its reputation. Many firms work closely with suppliers to create better-quality parts. Many firms, such as Ford, send engineers to help suppliers boost their quality management systems.

Purchasing managers traditionally engage in several activities.[16] Of course, they try to minimize the costs of materials and supplies. However, this is usually not their only (or even their main) concern.[17] For many firms, high-quality, reliable, on-time deliveries outweigh costs. Companies like Toyota spend years developing close relationships with favored suppliers, even helping them to improve their own operations.

As we'll see later in this chapter, firms are increasingly automating their purchasing. Suppliers bid for and fulfill their business via the Internet.

The Role of Inventory Management

How much to purchase depends partly on the firm's current inventories. Firms keep inventories of five types of items: raw materials and purchased parts, components, works in process, finished goods, and supplies.[18] Firms obtain raw materials and purchased parts from outside suppliers and hold them for the production of finished products. Components are subassemblies that are awaiting final assembly. Work in process refers to all materials or components on the production floor in various stages of production. Finished goods are final products waiting for purchase or to be sent to customers. Finally, supplies are all items the firm needs that are not part of the finished product, such as paper clips, duplicating machine toner, and tools. **Inventory management** is the process of ensuring that the firm has enough inventories of all required parts and supplies within the constraint of minimizing total inventory costs.

inventory management: the process of ensuring that the firm has adequate inventories of all required parts and supplies within the constraint of minimizing total inventory costs

ordering or **setup costs:** the costs, usually fixed, of placing an order or setting up machines for a production run

acquisition costs: the total costs of all units bought to fill an order, usually varying with the size of the order

inventory-holding or **carrying costs:** all the costs associated with carrying parts or materials in inventory

stockout costs: the costs associated with running out of raw materials, parts, or finished-goods inventory

Inventory Costs In practice, inventory managers must address four types of costs. First, **ordering** or **setup costs** are the costs of placing the order (or of setting up machines for producing the parts, if the parts are being manufactured, not bought). For purchased items, ordering costs might include order-processing costs (such as clerical time for filling out the order) and the cost of inspecting goods when they arrive. For items made in-house, setup costs include the labor involved in setting up the machine and the cost of preparing the paperwork for scheduling the production run. Ordering or setup costs are usually fixed. For example, it costs a clerk about the same to process the paperwork for a big order as for a small order.

Acquisition costs (the total cost of all the units themselves bought to fill an order) vary with the size of the order. For example, ordering parts in larger quantities may reduce each unit's cost thanks to quantity discounts. This, in turn, will lower the total acquisition costs of the order. Ordering smaller quantities may raise the unit cost.

Inventory managers focus on two other inventory costs. **Inventory-holding** or **carrying costs** are all the costs associated with carrying parts or materials in inventory. The biggest specific cost here is usually the firm's cost of capital, which in this case is the value of a unit of the inventory times the length of time it is held times the interest rate at which the firm borrows money.[19] Suppose an item costs $10 and stays in inventory for a year, and the firm must pay its bank 5 percent interest to borrow money. Then it costs the firm $0.50 in finance charges just to hold the item in inventory for a year. **Stockout costs** are the costs associated with running out of raw materials or finished-goods inventory. For example, if a company cannot fill a customer's order, it might lose both the current order and any profits on future sales to this customer.

Inventory managers want to avoid three basic problems. Overinvestment in inventories ties up money and space. Underinvestment leaves the firm unable to fill production orders and discourages customers. Unbalanced inventory means there are some understocked items and some overstocked ones.

Basic Inventory Management Systems

Many quantitative and nonquantitative tools are available for managing inventory. The ABC and EOQ systems are two popular methods.

ABC Inventory Management Most firms find that a small proportion (25 percent to 30 percent) of the parts in their inventory accounts for a large proportion

(70 percent or 80 percent) of their annual dollar volume of inventory use. (Compute a part's annual dollar volume by multiplying its cost per part by the number of parts used in a year.)

When using the ABC system, the manager divides the inventory into three dollar-volume categories—A, B, and C. The A category parts—maybe 5 percent of the total—are the most active. They account for perhaps 40 percent of the annual dollar value of all parts used. The manager concentrates most of his or her surveillance on the A parts. For example, he or she orders them most often but in smaller quantities. In that way, their total number in inventory at any one time is minimized.

At the other extreme, the inventory manager might find that perhaps 50 percent of the parts (the C category parts) in inventory account for, say, 15 percent of all the parts used each year. Why spend as much time closely monitoring all those parts when, in total, they account for only 15 percent of the firm's annual dollar volume of inventory use? They don't tie up that much capital. The idea of ABC is to focus most on the high-annual-dollar-volume A inventory items, to a lesser extent on the B items, and even less on the C items.

economic order quantity (EOQ): an inventory management system based on a simple formula that is used to determine the most economical quantity to order so that the total of inventory and setup costs is minimized

The Economic Order Quantity Inventory Management System The point of the **economic order quantity (EOQ)** system is to determine the most economical quantity to order—in other words, the quantity that will minimize total inventory and setup costs. EOQ is the best-known and probably the oldest inventory system.

Figure 9.8 illustrates the EOQ system. Note that the two major costs, inventory carrying costs and ordering/setup costs, vary inversely with each other. For example, ordering in large quantities (less often) usually allows the firm to reduce average ordering or setup costs (remember, it usually costs about the same in clerical costs to place a big order as a small one). However, it also means higher storage costs. (Ordering less often means placing fewer, bigger orders, so the company has, on average, more inventory in stock.)

In its simplest form the economic order quantity (the most economic quantity to order) is:

$$Q = \sqrt{\frac{2US}{H}}$$

FIGURE 9.8

The Economic Order Quantity Model

When order size goes up, ordering costs per order go down but carrying costs go up because more items are left longer in inventory.

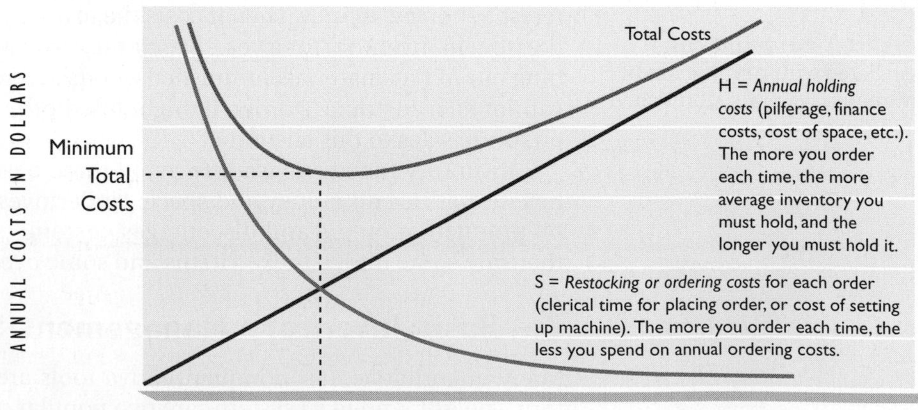

where Q is the economic order quantity (the most economical quantity to order), U is the annual use of the item, S is the restocking or ordering costs, and H is the annual holding cost per unit per year. Suppose a car factory uses 10,000 door handles per year to build its cars; then U for the handles is 10,000. S may refer to either restocking or ordering costs, depending on whether the firm makes or buys the handles. If the car factory orders the handles from a supplier and it costs the factory $200 per order (for forms, clerical support, and so forth) to place the order, then S is $200. Holding (or carrying) costs per unit (H) (in this case, $1.00 per unit) includes such things as pilferage, borrowing costs associated with holding the items in stock, and the costs of the space in which the inventory is held. EOQ would thus be 2000 units.

This EOQ makes some simplifications. For example, it assumes that the same number of units is taken from inventory periodically, such as ten units per day. More sophisticated EOQ versions handle these and other complications.[20]

Controlling for Quality and Productivity

quality: the extent to which a product or service can meet customer needs and expectations

ISO 9000: the quality standards of the International Standards Organization

Quality refers to the totality of features and characteristics of a product or service that bears on its ability to satisfy given needs. Put another way, "[q]uality measures how well a product or service meets customer needs."[21] This quote highlights several things about quality. First, the customer's needs are the basic standard for measuring quality. Thus, many coach flyers understandably consider traveling on JetBlue's wider leather coach seats as high quality compared with the typical coach experience. Second, high quality does not have to mean high price. Again, the basic consideration should be the extent to which the product or service meets the customer's expectations.

It may not be first class, but most passengers rate JetBlue's wide leather coach seats as "high quality."

Quality standards today are international. Doing business often means the firm must show it complies with **ISO 9000**, the quality standards of the International Standards Organization, to which the United States is a signatory. These standards specify practices and procedures for things like how to train employees and how to monitor quality. Complying with ISO 9000 shows potential customers that the products you produce meet international standards. For example, Dell wants its computers to meet international quality standards. Therefore, it must make sure that the companies that supply it with components like hard drives themselves comply with those international standards.

Total Quality Management Programs

total quality management (TQM): a specific organizationwide program that integrates all the functions and related processes of a business so that they are all aimed at maximizing customer satisfaction through ongoing improvements

Total quality management (TQM) programs are companywide programs that integrate all the functions and related processes of a business so that they are all aimed at maximizing customer satisfaction through ongoing improvements. They aim to focus all the company's activities, including design, planning, production, distribution, and field service, on maximizing customer satisfaction. They emphasize management commitment to quality, empowering employees to address quality issues, analyzing quality issues based on data and facts, and continuously improving all aspects of one's operations.[22] Companies like GE that pursue TQM typically train selected employees to become experts in applying TQM principles (GE calls its employee-experts black belts). One team at GE Appliances analyzed the inspection process on one refrigerator line and devised a better system that did not require pulling refrigerators off the line to inspect them. By continually making changes like these in how the company designs, manufactures, and distributes its products, total quality rises, and the savings (for instance, of not having to throw out defective items) boosts profits.

six-sigma: a total quality management program, the aim of which is to reduce errors to about 3.5 defects per million items produced

TQM programs go by many names. Somtimes managers call them continuous improvement, zero defects, six-sigma, or (in Japan) Kaizen programs.[23] **Six-sigma** programs are perhaps the best known. Statisticians use the Greek letter sigma to represent standard deviation. Standard deviation is basically a measure of variation. Suppose we can plot the number of defects our company gets with a normal, or bell-shaped, curve. Then there is a very high probability we will get an average number of defects (say, 10,000 per day), as indicated by the midpoint of the curve. There is less probability we will get more (11,000) or fewer (9,000) defects per day. About two-thirds of all likely defects will be between ± one standard deviation from the average (mean). In the six-sigma system, if a company achieves only one sigma, it's very likely they will get lots of defects. If a company achieves six-sigma, it means it gets very few defects—about 3.5 defects per million items they produce.

Most regard W. Edwards Deming as the intellectual father of TQM. He based his concept of total quality on a fourteen-point system, which he says must be implemented at all organizational levels. To get an idea of his TQM philosophy, we can summarize his points as follows:

1. Create consistency of purpose toward the improvement of product and service.
2. Adopt a philosophy of quality.
3. Cease depending on inspection; instead, build quality into the product from the beginning.
4. Don't choose suppliers based just on price; emphasize loyalty and trust.
5. Improve constantly and forever the production and service system—in other words, aim for continuous improvement.
6. Institute extensive training on the job.
7. Shift your focus from production to quality.
8. Don't do things that make employees fear for their jobs.
9. People in research, design, sales, and production must work as a team to foresee problems.
10. Don't rely on slogans and targets that push for higher quality and productivity, particularly where you don't put in systems for achieving these aims.
11. Eliminate work standards (quotas) on the factory floor.
12. Abolish using tools like annual appraisals; these rob employees of the intrinsic desire to do a great job.
13. Institute a vigorous program of employee training and self-improvement.
14. Make sure all managers push every day for each of the preceding thirteen points.[24]

Deming at first had success converting Japanese, not American, firms to his principles, and Japanese firms still strive hard to win Japan's Deming quality prize.

FIGURE 9.9

Example of a Quality Control Chart

The idea behind any control chart is to track quality trends to ensure that they don't go out of control.

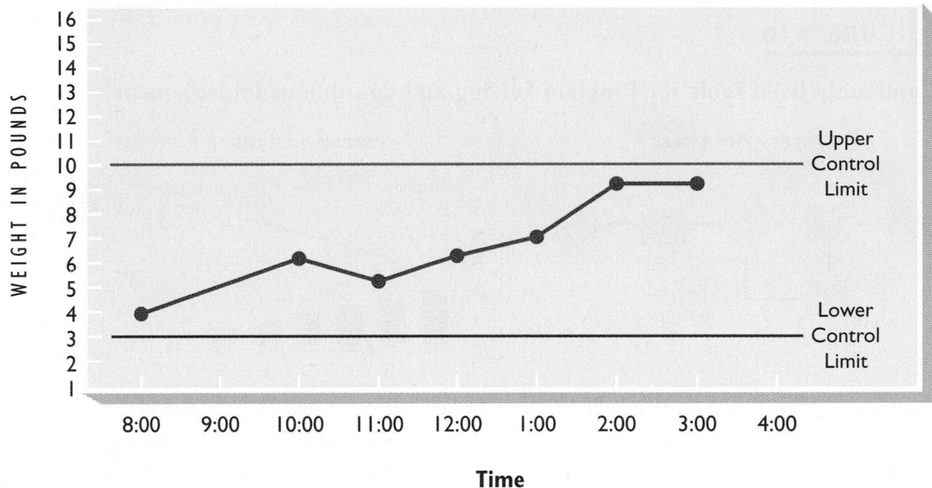

In the United States, the Department of Commerce created the Malcolm Baldrige Award to recognize firms that adhere to Deming-type quality principles. (Baldrige was secretary of commerce around that time.) Most U.S. firms can apply for the award.[25]

Quality Control Methods

acceptance sampling: a method of monitoring product quality that requires the inspection of only a small portion of the produced items

Managers use various tools to control product or service quality. For example, most firms have formal inspection procedures. Sometimes (such as when producing heart pacemakers), 100 percent inspection is typical. More common is **acceptance sampling**. Here, the firm inspects only a portion of the items, perhaps 2 percent or 5 percent.

Firms also use quality control charts like that in Figure 9.9. The manager uses the upper and lower control limits to show the range within which some measurable characteristic should fall. Then employees (or machines) measure the chosen characteristic (such as length or weight). Thus, Kellogg's might want to make sure each box of corn flakes contains no more than 20.2 ounces and no fewer than 19.8 ounces. If the measures begin to move toward the upper or lower control limits, it's time to see what's causing the variation.

● **Managing Now** Modern information technology–based quality control systems enable manufacturers to do more than monitor obvious quality dimensions like size and weight. Firms like Kraft also want to know if the products coming off production lines are chewy, sweet, and/or crunchy.[26] Kraft uses a sensory analysis application from the software company SAS to ensure consistent flavor and appearance of its snack foods. The system includes special electronic sensors and a database of information. These features enable the system to sense whether an item is as chewy, sweet, crunchy, and/or creamy as it's supposed to be.

Inspections and control charts are useful, but Deming pushed for getting the employees themselves to want to produce high-quality products. Modern quality control efforts therefore emphasize getting employee teams involved in monitoring quality and analyzing problems. Employee quality-assurance teams typically use several tools to monitor and analyze quality problems. Figure 9.10 summarizes some of them.[27] For example, a scatter diagram shows the magnitude of one trait (such as the number of defects) versus a second trait (such as time). A

FIGURE 9.10

Commonly Used Tools for Problem Solving and Continuous Improvement

Process Flowchart

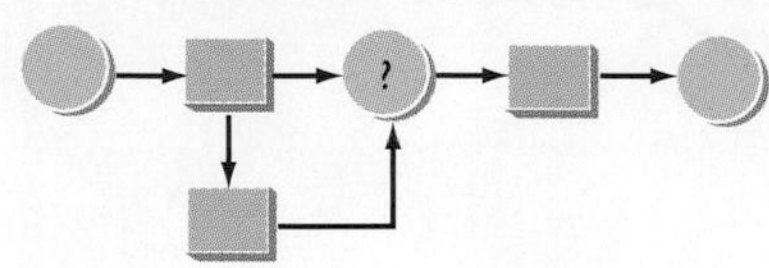

A chart that describes the main steps, branches, and eventual outputs of a process.

Pareto Analysis

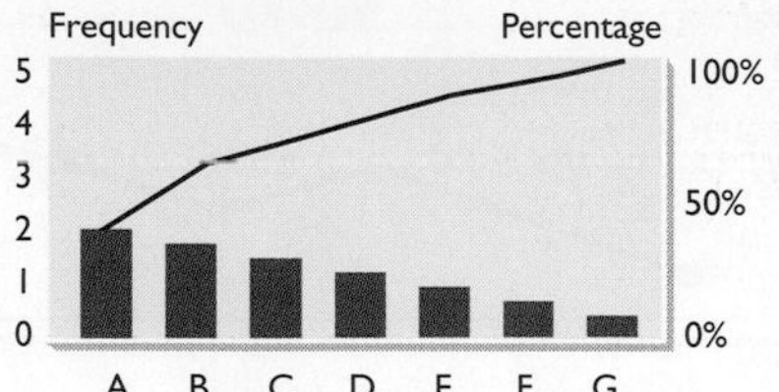

A plot of the frequencies of important error sources. 80/20 rule: 80 percent of problems are due to 20 percent of causes (A, B, etc., are error sources).

Run Chart

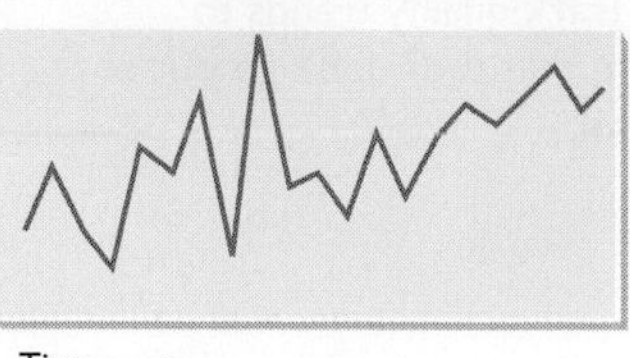

A chart showing plotted values of a characteristic over time.

Histogram

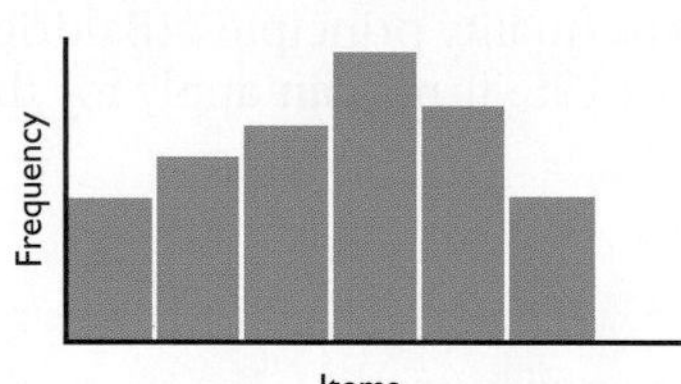

A distribution showing the frequency of occurrences between the high and low range of data.

Scatter Diagram

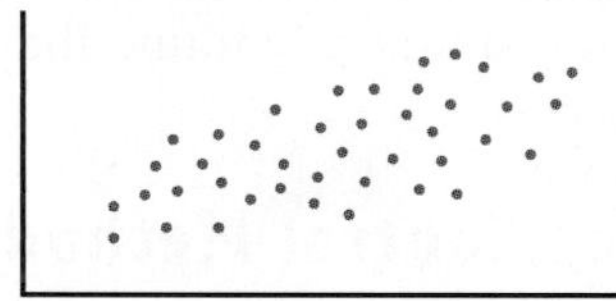

Also known as a correlation chart. A graph of the value of one characteristic versus another characteristic.

Causes-and-Effect Diagram

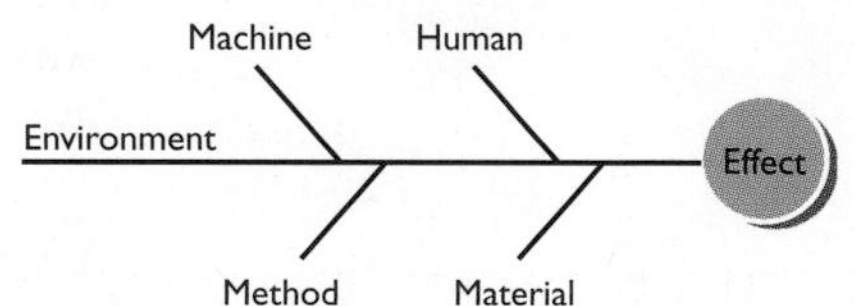

A tool that uses a graphical description to list and analyze potential sources of process variation, classified by machine, human, method, and material.

SOURCE: Adapted from Richard Chase and Nicholas Aquilero, *Production and Operations Management*, 6th ed. (Homewood, Ill.: Irwin, 1992), p. 197.

cause-and-effect, or fishbone, diagram (see Figure 9.11) outlines the four main causes of problems—machines, labor/people, methods, and materials. This kind of diagram gives employees a useful structure they can use to systematically analyze the cause of quality problems.

Design for Manufacturability

designing for manufacturability: designing products with ease of manufacturing and quality in mind

Designing for manufacturability means designing products with ease of high-quality manufacturing in mind.[28] Designing for manufacturability is important: "By the time a product has been designed, only about 8 percent of the total product budget has been spent. But by that point, the design has determined 80 percent of the [eventual] cost of the product!"[29] Experts therefore say, "The design determines the manufacturability."[30] For example, we can see evidence of design for manufacturability in the cars we drive. A few years ago, designers would design new cars just for aesthetics, and the company's assemblers might have to spend hours putting in all of a dashboard's parts. Today, the dashboard

FIGURE 9.11

Cause-and-Effect, or Fishbone, Diagram for Problems with Airline Customer Service

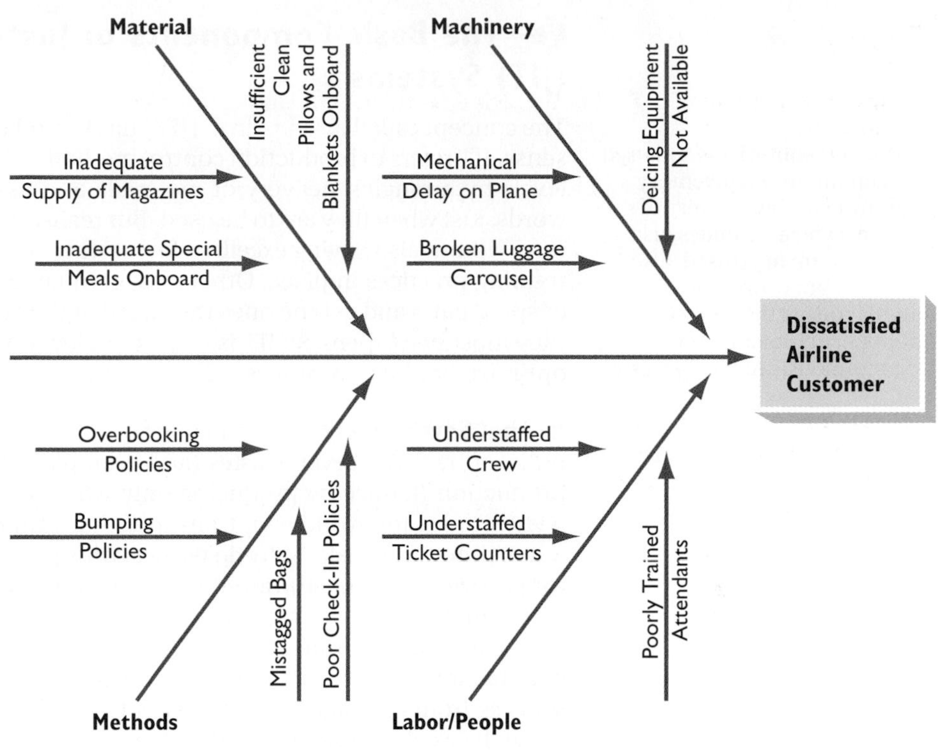

(and headlights, tail lights, and so on) are designed to come to the factory as preassembled modules. This makes assembling the final, high-quality car much simpler.

concurrent engineering: designing products in multidisciplinary teams so that all departments involved in the product's success contribute to its design

Designing for manufacturability often means designing products using multidisciplinary teams. Operations managers call this simultaneous design or **concurrent engineering**. It ensures that all departments involved in the product's success contribute to its design.[31]

World-Class Operations Management Methods

Online Study Center
ACE the Test
Managing Now! LIVE

Competition in almost every industry is global.[32] Thus, firms such as Whirlpool face not just local competitors but foreign ones, like Meile. When competition is global, competition is more intense. Firms everywhere are striving to improve quality, lead time, customer service, and costs in the hope of gaining a stronger hold on their markets. World-class companies are those that can compete based on quality and productivity in an intensely competitive global environment. Firms such as UPS, GE, and Toyota set the performance standards for their industries.

World-class manufacturers are world class in part because they use modern production techniques and management systems to boost productivity, quality, and flexibility. These techniques and systems include TQM (already described), just-in-time manufacturing, computer-aided design and manufacturing, flexible manufacturing systems, computer-integrated manufacturing, supply chain management, and enterprise resource planning. We discuss them next.

The Basic Components of Just-in-Time (JIT) Systems

just-in-time (JIT): a production control method used to attain minimum inventory levels by ensuring delivery of materials and assemblies just when they are to be used; also refers to a philosophy of manufacturing that aims to optimize production processes by continuously reducing waste

The concept called **just-in-time (JIT)** has two related definitions. In the narrowest sense, JIT refers to production control methods used to attain minimum inventory levels by arranging delivery of materials and assemblies just in time—in other words, just when they are to be used. But realistically, one cannot minimize inventory without also having excellent forecasting, assembly, shipping, and employee-training practices in place. Otherwise, companies that keep minimal inventories of spare parts and get the ones they need at the last minute run out of parts when they most need them! So JIT is really a philosophy of manufacturing that aims to optimize production-process efficiency by continuously reducing waste.

The Seven Wastes Reducing seven main wastes is at the heart of the JIT philosophy.[33] The seven wastes (and examples of how to reduce them) are overproduction (reduce by producing only what is needed, as it is needed), waiting (synchronize the workflow), transportation (minimize transport with better layouts), processing (ask, "Why do we need this process at all?"), stock (reduce inventories), motion (reduce wasted employee motions), and defective products (improve quality to reduce rework).

As an example, most firms waste enormous resources waiting—to inspect incoming items, for storing raw materials or work in process, or for moving work in process from one step of the process to another. JIT aims to reduce wastes like these. JIT is also sometimes called **lean** or **value-added manufacturing** (reflecting the fact that any manufacturing activity that does not add value to the product for the customer is wasteful).[34]

lean or **value-added manufacturing:** a management philosophy that assumes that any manufacturing process that does not add value to the product for the customer is wasteful

JIT has its weaknesses. Having minimal inventory and getting parts just in time works great when all is normal. Plants near New Orleans found themselves out of their parts inventory (and out of luck) when Hurricane Katrina shut down UPS and FedEx shipments in 2005.

JIT Characteristics In practice, JIT-based facilities tend to have several characteristics. They tend to be small (less than 100 employees) specialized plants rather than large ones. It is easier to manage small plants, and it is easier to design the workflow and to staff specialized, single-function plants.[35] They tend to be organized around cells, so all the processes required to complete a major part of the product are in one place. One employee can then perform all the processes. Workers tend to be more highly trained and flexible. Each worker also tends to be personally responsible for the quality of the item he or she produces. Thus, quality goes in at the source, when the product is actually made, in turn eliminating a big source of waste.

JIT-based facilities: Toyota inspectors examine a finished car coming off the assembly line in the company's Miyazaki, Japan, factory.

JIT's Human Consequences Manufacturers installing such lean production systems need to consider their potential effects on employees.[36] At firms like Toyota, eliminating waste typically goes hand in hand with increased employee teamwork, participation, and problem solving, and so lean manufacturing seems to boost motivation. However, one recent study shows how one company may have done things wrong. In this study, workers who used to control the pace of their work suddenly found themselves working on an assembly line. Basically, the workers felt that the quality of their jobs had declined and that they were working harder and with less control over what they did than they had previously. The researcher concluded that in this case, lean production "can be damaging to employees."[37] Such a situation is probably the opposite of what Deming had in mind. Deming's principles call for a quality system in which employees take ownership for and pride in their work. Managers instituting quality programs ignore that to their peril.

Computer-Aided Design and Manufacturing

computer-aided design (CAD): a computerized process for designing new products, modifying existing ones, or simulating conditions that may affect the designs

computer-aided manufacturing (CAM): a computerized process for planning and programming production processes and equipment

Technology—not just employee behavior—plays a big role in world-class manufacturing. For example, **computer-aided design (CAD)** is a computerized process for designing new products or modifying existing ones. Designers sketch and modify designs on a computer screen. CAD makes it easier to modify existing designs and lets designers expose their designs to simulated stresses such as wind resistance.

Computer-aided manufacturing (CAM) uses computers to plan and program the production process or equipment. For example, it makes possible computerized control of tool movement and cutting speed. So a machine can carry out several sequential operations on a part, all under the guidance of the computer-assisted system.

Operations managers often use CAD and CAM together. For example, with the design already in place within the CAD system, the computer knows a component's dimensions and specifications and can tell the automated CAM production equipment how to cut and machine it.

Companies use the Internet to expand the usefulness of such computer-based systems. Consider Motorola's plant in Mansfield, Massachusetts. When the plant got approval to produce new cable modems, the plant manager knew he needed a faster and cheaper way to get the engineering documents to the assemblers on the plant floor.[38] The manager and his staff created an internal plant intranet. They used a digital camera to take pictures of each component. They placed these pictures online, along with step-by-step instructions for assembly and testing. This setup eliminated expensive paper engineering drawings. It also helped the plant update its drawings instantaneously.

● **Managing Now** Companies use software applications to create more competitive manufacturing processes. For example, applications like SAP Manufacturing allow production managers to monitor, detect, and resolve production and performance deviations in real time and to improve employee productivity.[39]

Flexible Manufacturing Systems

flexible manufacturing system (FMS): the organization of groups of production machines that are connected by automated materials-handling and transfer machines, and integrated into a computer system for the purpose of combining the benefits of made-to-order flexibility and mass-production efficiency

In many firms today, flexible manufacturing systems are at the heart of their world-class production. Systems like these enable companies to quickly shift production from one product to another, even on the same production line. A **flexible manufacturing system (FMS)** is "a system in which groups of production machines are connected by automated materials-handling and transfer machines, and integrated into a computer system."[40] Computers route parts and components to the appropriate machines, select and load the proper machine tools, and then direct the machines to perform the required operations. Computerized automated guided vehicles (AGVs) then move the items from machine to machine. Often, there is a computer-guided cart system. It picks up and delivers tools and parts to and from multiple workstations. Systems like these depend on automation and robots. **Automation** is the automatic operation of a system, process, or machine. A robot is a programmable machine capable of manipulating items and designed to move materials, parts, or specialized devices through programmed motions.

automation: the automatic operation of a system, process, or machine

Several things contribute to the manufacturing system's flexibility. Computerized manufacturing instructions (CAM) reduce machine setup times. Reduced setup times cut required manufacturing lead times. Automated guided vehicles move parts with relative speed and efficiency. And the firm can respond more quickly to new competing products or changing consumer tastes by using CAD to redesign products and CAM to reprogram its machines. Toshiba's president said the aim of flexible manufacturing "is to push Toshiba's two dozen factories to adapt faster to markets . . . customers wanted choices. They wanted a washing machine or TV set that was precisely right for their needs. We needed variety, not mass production."[41]

Plants like this one owned by Toshiba rely on flexible manufacturing systems.

Flexible manufacturing helps Toshiba combine the advantages of customized, one-at-a-time production with the efficiency of mass production. At the Toshiba plant in Ome, Japan, workers efficiently assemble nine word-processor models on one line and twenty laptop computer models on another.[42] Such flexibility helps Toshiba be responsive to customer requirements. The National Bicycle Industrial Company, a subsidiary of electronics giant Matsushita, is another example.[43] With only twenty employees, National Bicycle's factory can produce more than a million variations of eighteen bicycle models, each custom-made to a customer's unique requirements.

Computer-Integrated Manufacturing

Many firms integrate automation, JIT, flexible manufacturing, and CAD/CAM into one self-regulating production system. **Computer-integrated manufacturing (CIM)** is defined as the total integration of all production-related business activities through the use of computer systems.[44] It gives the firm a competitive advantage based on speed, flexibility, quality, and low cost. Figure 9.12 summarizes this integrative process.

computer-integrated manufacturing (CIM): the total integration of all production-related business activities through the use of computer systems

CIM's advantages usually exceed those of its component parts. For example, CAD reinforces CAM by feeding design changes directly to the machinery tools. Computer-integrated automated guided vehicles facilitate JIT systems by reducing human variability and waiting time in the system.[45] We've also seen that many companies are using the Web to streamline their operations. For example, Boeing's electronic commerce website eliminates the barriers that traditionally separated the company from suppliers and customers. Customers can keep track of their orders. Suppliers can see when Boeing needs their parts. Boeing can see where their parts are. Manufacturing systems are increasingly integrated with customers' and suppliers' systems.[46]

Integration is important. As one Japanese executive put it, "In the past, manufacturing was characterized by large [production run] quantities, with few varieties.

FIGURE 9.12

The Elements of CIM

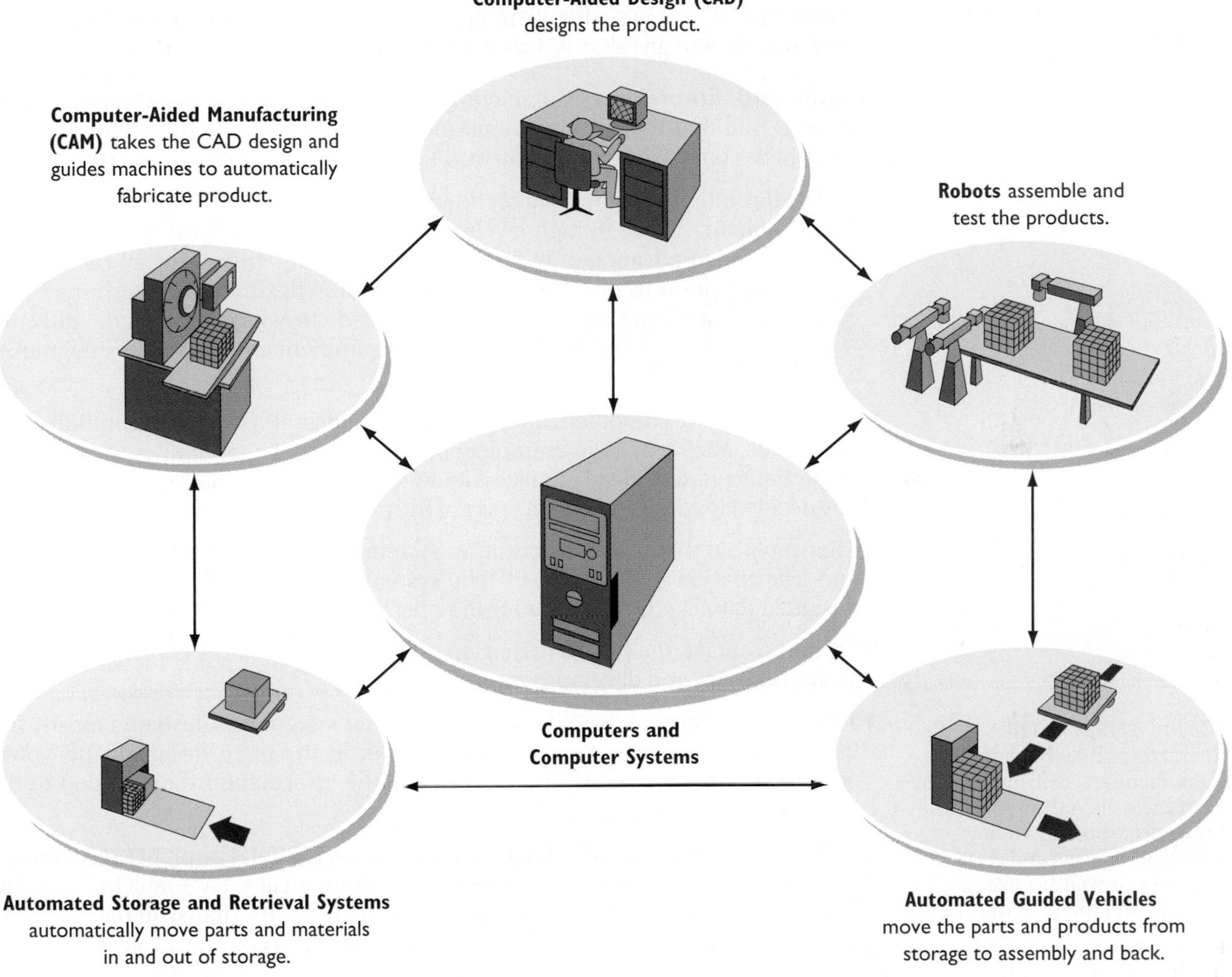

SOURCE: Adapted from Barry Render and Jay Heizer, *Principles of Operations Management*, 2nd ed., p. 179, © 1997. Reprinted by permission of Pearson Education, Inc., Upper Saddle River, N.J.

Today's customers are asking for small quantities in very many varieties. CIM adds flexibility to help make those very short production runs economical."[47]

● **Cook Specialty Company** Cook Specialty Company is a good example of how CIM works. Cook Specialty Company is a small manufacturer of precision metal parts.[48] As its customers trimmed the number of suppliers from whom they purchased parts, Cook needed a way to stay competitive. Somehow, Cook had to combine low-volume production with high variety and low cost. It needed mass-production prices and job-shop flexibility.

Its solution was to switch to being a custom manufacturer, one that not only made the products but helped customers design them. A new CIM system enables Cook to do this. By linking its own computerized manufacturing system with customers' CAD systems, Cook and its customers can now swap drawings and send instructions for final designs directly to Cook's computer-automated machines for manufacture. Cook has a highly integrated system that gives customers a value-added benefit and gives Cook a competitive edge.

CIM and Employees Some companies spend millions installing CIM systems but find that their plants are no more productive or flexible than before. A study sheds some light on why. Harvard Professor David Upton found that:

> The flexibility of the plants depended much more on people than on any technical factor. Although high levels of computer integration can provide critically needed advantages in quality and cost competitiveness, all the data in my study point to one conclusion: operational flexibility is determined primarily by a plant's operators and the extent to which managers cultivate, measure, and communicate with them. Equipment and computer integration are secondary.[49]

The successful computerization of paper manufacturer Mead Corporation's mill in Escanaba, Michigan, is an example.[50] Because some of its machines were already computer integrated, Mead managers knew computerization itself was no panacea. They decided to make the workers part of the plant improvement process:

- They replaced their existing computer systems with a new system called Quality and Information for Decisions.[51] The system (nicknamed QUID) was custom-designed to make things easier for the operators who actually ran the machines.
- From the outset, the plant's managers insisted that operators be involved in the system's design and development.
- The plant managers saw to it that the computer system was designed mostly in-house. The employees at each work function in the plant designed their own computer interface to ensure that they got the information they needed to do their jobs.

supply chain: includes all the interactions between suppliers, manufacturers, distributors, and customers, including specifically transportation, scheduling information, cash and credit transfers, as well as ideas, designs, and material transfers

The new people-friendly program was quite successful. The plant's responsiveness and customer satisfaction measures rose dramatically. Escanaba became the most productive mill in Mead's fine-paper group. Recently, thanks in part to Escanaba's success, Mead sold its entire paper operations to a company called Cerberus.

Supply Chain Management

Online Study Center
ACE the Test
Managing Now! LIVE

Computer-integrated and lean manufacturing aim to eliminate the wastes of unnecessary activities and to help companies respond faster to customers' needs. Supply chain management supports these aims. Indeed, world-class firms like Dell and Toyota are so successful largely due to how they manage their supply chains. A **supply chain** "includes all the interactions between suppliers, manufacturers, distributors, and customers. The chain includes transportation, scheduling information, cash and credit transfers, as well as ideas, designs, and material transfers."[52] **Supply chain management** "is the integration of the activities that procure materials, transform them into intermediate goods and final products, and deliver them to customers."[53] The idea is to build an integrated

supply chain management: the integration of the activities that procure materials, transform them into intermediate goods and final product, and deliver them to customers

FIGURE 9.13

The Supply Chain

The supply chain includes all interactions among suppliers, manufacturers, distributors, and customers. The chain involves transportation, scheduling information, cash and credit transfers, as well as ideas, designs, and material transfers.

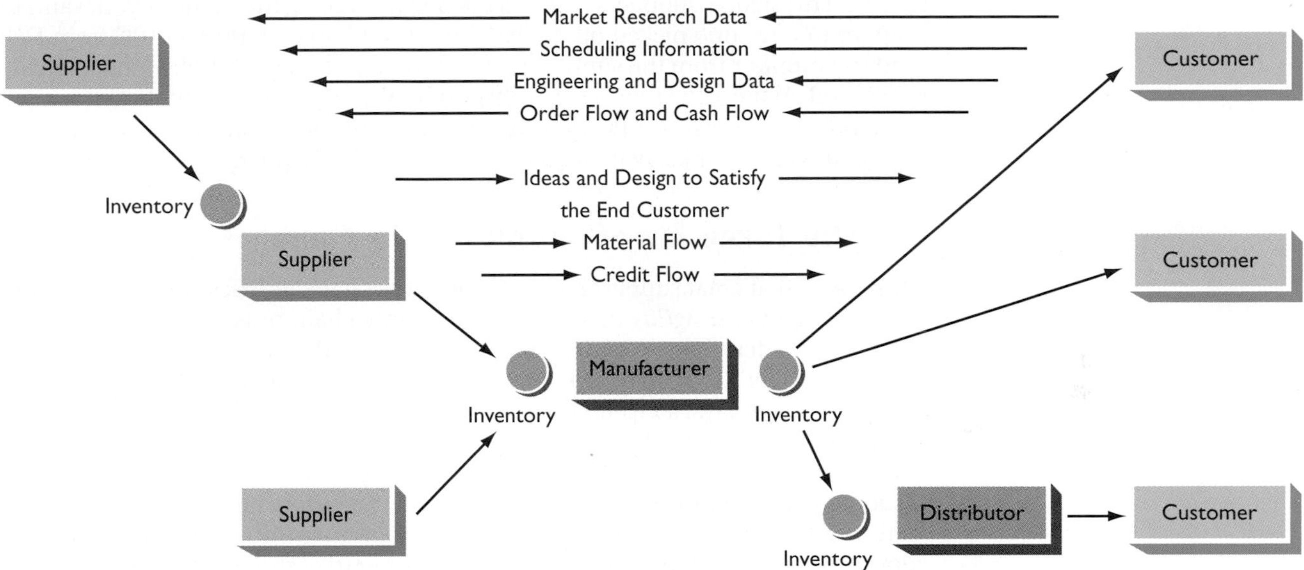

SOURCE: Adapted from Jay Heizer and Barry Render, *Operations Management* (Upper Saddle River, N.J.: Prentice Hall, 2001), p. 434.

chain of suppliers who together focus both on reducing waste and on getting the desired products to the customers as expeditiously as possible.[54] Figure 9.13 summarizes this.

Managing Now: Supply Chain Management Software

Companies usually build their supply chains' interconnectedness around special supply chain management software applications from companies like SAS, SAP, and Oracle. We can get some insights into what these packages do for companies by listing some typical components. For example, Oracle Supply-Chain Management includes components such as: daily business intelligence for purchasing; payables; purchasing; demand planning; e-bill payment; inventory; order promising; manufacturing scheduling; shop floor management; transportation planning; warehouse management; order management; demand consensus; and advanced forecasts modeling.[55]

Supply chain packages like these work together with a company's enterprise resource planning (ERP) software. As we saw, ERP software includes compatible software packages for each department or business function. These business functions include production and materials management, shipping, finance/accounting, and human resources. Add the supply chain software, and the company can also bring in supply chain partners such as distributors, truckers, and suppliers. Now, information from outside the company—say, from and to suppliers and truckers—can also flow from and to the company's inside departments, like production and finance.

For example, what happens when someone places an order for a new Dell PC? Dell's ERP software posts the order and signals manufacturing to plan to produce the PC. It hands off information on the order to Dell's supply chain management system. This signals suppliers (such as the one producing the monitor you want) to prepare to have one picked up. It also notifies UPS to pick up your PC from Dell (and the monitor from the supplier) on a particular day and to deliver it all to you, as ordered. At the same time, Dell's ERP notifies the accounting department to send you a bill, and it lists your PC's specifications on the Dell customer-service system in case you call or link in with a question. And, all this happens automatically.

The Three A's of Supply Chain Management

Experts say that great supply chains exhibit three characteristics: agility, adaptability, and alignment. *Agility* means that the supply chain must be able to respond quickly to sudden changes in markets.[56] For example, thanks to its supply chain system, the retailer Zara can design, manufacture, and ship a new jacket to one of its stores in fifteen days; so when trends change, it can respond quickly. *Adaptability* means being willing to change parts of the supply chain when change is required. For example, Lucent continued to manage its supply chain on the assumption that it should produce its own phones, even after competitors had outsourced manufacturing to highly efficient electronics manufacturing firms like Flextronics. Lucent's failure to adapt helps to explain why it lost market share. Great supply chains also *align* all the supply chain's partners' interests. For example, the incentives are such that each Dell supply chain partner does what's best to support Dell's customers' needs. UPS will do what it needs to get that PC to the customer on time.

PRACTICE IT
Whirlpool Delivers

With Whirlpool's sales force referring to its supply chain as a sales disabler, new supply chain head Reuben Slone took action. Slone and his team began by instituting a new forecasting system called CPFR, which stands for "collaborative planning, forecasting, and replenishment." The basic idea of CPFR is to let all the partners in Whirlpool's supply chain—retailers, truckers, and manufacturing plants, for instance—share information, like how many appliances Whirlpool expects to sell to each retailer (such as Sears). This information enables each supply chain partner to develop its own forecasts and to better prepare for fulfilling their roles in Whirlpool's supply chain. UPS can see when it will have to send trucks to pick up finished appliances. Sears can keep track of when its Whirlpool appliance order will arrive.

Whirlpool's supply chain management team supplemented this system with new Web-based supply chain management tools. For example, they installed a new Web-based tool that lets Whirlpool's system communicate directly with a customer's system for details like transmitting orders, exchanging sales data, and submitting and paying invoices.[57] This cuts the time and costs associated with these transactions. Product availability rose from about 88 percent in 2003 to more than 95 percent today. The number of days the company had to hold finished goods in inventory dropped from about thirty-three days to about twenty-six.

Why Supply Chain Management Is Important

Supply chain management is important because no business today functions alone. The performance of every business depends on the suppliers who supply its parts and on the companies who distribute its products to the ultimate customers. How much the company's products cost, the products' quality and reliability, and the speed and dependability with which the products show up at the customer's door all depend on the company's supply chain partners. For example, when the hard drive on a new Dell PC stops working, the consumer gets upset with Dell, not with the part's manufacturer. When the replacement doesn't arrive on time, he or she gets upset with Dell, not with UPS. Too many supply chain partner slip-ups can doom a company's business. The Practice IT feature shows that Whirlpool, which several years ago suffered from slow deliveries, learned that lesson well.

Managing Now: Reducing Costs with Supply Chain Management Supply chain management helps companies reduce costs. For example, at General Electric's power systems division, the firm's Web-based supply chain management system lets its customers monitor the assembly of the huge turbines they ordered as the turbines move through the production process. These power-generating turbines cost $35 million each and contain thousands of parts. Having customers catch errors early and being able to get suppliers to change designs more expeditiously means big cost savings for GE and the customer.[58]

As another example, Wal-Mart used to order two to four weeks' worth of product for each store. Now, Wal-Mart orders only five days' worth of product. Its supply chain partners (including its suppliers and truckers) are responsible for ensuring that those products show up on time and for consolidating shipments from several suppliers so the delivery trucks are full. Wal-Mart's information technology–based supply chain management system helps make sure the process runs smoothly. It uses radio-frequency sensors, supply chain software, satellites, and digital transmission devices from check-out stations to help suppliers keep track of Wal-Mart's sales and inventory and thus anticipate Wal-Mart's needs.[59]

Basic Building Blocks of Supply Chain Management Systems

In addition to the supply chain management system software and the IT system itself, the four building blocks of supply chain management systems are *supplier partnering, transparency*, *Internet-based purchasing,* and *channel assembly.* **Supplier partnering** means choosing to do business with a limited number of suppliers, with the aim of building relationships that improve quality and reliability rather than just improve costs. Rather than getting competitive bids, the customer-company often decides to work with a few supplier-partners.

supplier partnering: choosing to do business with a limited number of suppliers, with the aim of building relationships that improve quality and reliability rather than just improve costs

Supplier partnering brings many advantages. The customer-buyer company can work with the partner-supplier to ensure a cost-effective design. Firms like Wal-Mart let suppliers literally link into the company's point-of-purchase and inventory systems to learn what products Wal-Mart needs, when. This system reduces inventory costs, improves just-in-time performance, and reduces administrative costs. Supplier partnering reduces the customer-company's administration costs (for instance, fewer purchasing agents are required). It can also improve product quality (for instance, by enabling the customer-company to insist that the supplier be ISO 9000 certified), eliminate waste from the supply chain, and still let the firm push for cost reductions (although, perhaps, not quite so hard).

transparency: giving supply chain partners easy access to information about details like demand, inventory levels, and status of inbound and outbound shipments, usually through a Web-based portal

Most supply chain software applications from companies like SAP, SAS, and Oracle facilitate transparency. **Transparency** basically means giving supply chain partners easy access to information about details like demand, inventory levels, and status of inbound and outbound shipments, usually through a Web-based portal. This information lets supply chain partners (like suppliers and truckers) accurately predict the customer's needs. Transparency requires trust and collaboration. Thus, Dell needs to trust their suppliers to keep proprietary information about Dell's daily sales private. (We address trust and collaboration in Chapter 17). As we said earlier, radio frequency identification (RFID) sensor tags support transparency. Big retailers use these tags to help keep track of inventory as it moves from manufacturer to warehouse to stores.[60]

Managing Now The Safeway supermarket chain in the United Kingdom implemented a supply chain management system that illustrates supplier partnering and transparency. Aiming to improve its service, Safeway did a market research study to find out what customers most disliked about shopping in their stores. "Waiting on line at the checkout counter" topped the list. Safeway responded by installing special scanners; customers can now scan and bag their own items if they choose to. Number 2 on their customers' list was "not being able to buy out of stock items." Safeway therefore reorganized its supply chain. It had been reluctant to share information with suppliers for fear of divulging competitive information. With new point-of-sale computerized registers, Safeway started sharing its real-time sales with its suppliers.[61] In doing so, Safeway turned their suppliers into partners. Their suppliers now get real-time information regarding sales of their products. That gives them the real-time information they need to replenish Safeway's shelves just in time.

Internet-based purchasing is a third building block of supply chain management. For example, companies are creating what amounts to their own eBay-type purchasing websites. They use these sites to enable potential vendors to bid for their business. America's big three automakers—General Motors (GM), Ford, and DaimlerChrysler—created a Web-based purchasing exchange. Every year, these firms make about $250 billion worth of purchases via this exchange.[62]

Internet-based purchasing: making purchasing needs known via the Web, as well as getting orders via the Web and automatically generating and sending the necessary shipping documents and bills electronically; also called e-procurement

However, **Internet-based purchasing** (also called e-procurement) usually means more than just getting orders via the Web. In today's supply chains, supplier partnering and transparency usually mean that favored suppliers (like Levi's) can monitor the real-time sales of customers (like Wal-Mart) and automatically create orders to fulfill the customer's needs. Therefore, Internet-based purchasing also usually means having the system automatically generate the necessary shipping documents and bills.

Managing Now The thousands of orders Dell fills each week translate into millions of component requirements. Dell makes more than 90 percent of its component purchases online.[63] Here's how the system works. Dell's suppliers use the company's special supply chain Internet portal to view Dell's estimated parts requirements and Dell's actual orders and to confirm that they can meet Dell's delivery requirements. Then, as Dell actually receives orders, the online system sends a pull signal to each supplier. This signal triggers the shipment of the parts Dell needs to build current orders. As the head of Dell's supply chain management system says, "[W]e now schedule every line in every factory around the world every two hours, and we only bring into the factory two hours worth of materials."[64] That keeps Dell's inventory to a minimum and helps to explain why its costs are lower than its competitors'.

channel assembly: organizing the product assembly process so that the company doesn't send finished products to its distribution channel partners (such as warehouses, distributors, and retailers), but instead sends the partners components and modules. The partners thus become an extension of the firm's product assembly process

Channel Assembly Finally, some companies also make their suppliers or distributors part of their manufacturing processes. **Channel assembly**, a fourth characteristic of supply chain management, means having a supplier or distributor perform some of the company's manufacturing steps. For example, Hewlett-Packard (HP) doesn't send finished printers to its distributors; it sends components and modules. The distributors thus become an extension of HP's production process. When a retail store asks the distributor for a particular HP printer, the distributor simply plugs together the required components and ships the assembled product.

Many cars are assembled this way. For example, Siemens supplies electronic parts for the Land Rover's dashboard. However, Siemens does more than supply parts. Other Land Rover suppliers send parts to Siemens, which then assembles all these parts into completed dashboards. Siemens then sends these assembled dashboards to the Land Rover plant, ready for installation. Land Rover does not have to put together these components because Siemens has already done it.

The Window on Managing Now feature shows how the retailer Zara used all of these building blocks to create a world-class company.

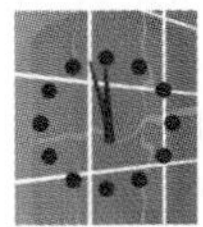

WINDOW ON MANAGING NOW
Zara

Today, the Spanish retailer Zara has more than 650 stores in fifty countries and sales of over $6.5 billion.[65] But the company's founder, Amancio Ortega, still remembers the day, many years ago, when his present company started. A German wholesaler had just canceled a big order, and Ortega thought his clothing company could go bankrupt. He had tied up all his money in the order. How would he get rid of all that merchandise? He opened a shop near his factory in the northwest corner of Spain and sold the goods himself. It was the first Zara shop.[66]

The cancellation of that order taught Ortega a big lesson. As he puts it, to be successful, "You need to have five fingers touching the factory and five touching the customer."[67] In other words, control everything that happens to your product until the customer buys it. That philosophy has driven Ortega to create one of retailing's most efficient supply chains.

Zara runs a very close-knit, mostly company-owned supply chain. Because Ortega still likes to "keep five fingers on the factory and five on the customer," Zara does about half its production in-house. Its communication system quickly transfers both hard data (such as sales from stores' point-of-purchase registers) and anecdotal information from store managers back to designers and production staff in Spain. Zara uses information technology to support its communications. For example, store managers use handheld personal digital assistants (PDAs) to transfer data that augments regular phone conversations between them and Zara's market specialists. In Spain, Zara designers work closely with product and textile engineers to create about 40,000 new designs per year, of which the company selects about 10,000 for production. Keeping design and manufacturing in one place

Zara's state-of-the-art factory in Spain helps ensure that popular items reach Zara's stores in just a few days.

like this makes the whole process run more smoothly and quickly. Once Zara's designers choose a design, its computerized design system translates that design to a final product via computer-aided manufacturing.

Zara store managers throughout most of the world place their orders by 3 P.M. Tuesday and 6 P.M. Friday. The orders then generally ship from Zara's factory within forty-eight hours. Zara tags the items before they reach the stores and ships them hung on special racks. When they arrive, they are ready for display.

Zara's superresponsive supply chain helps to explain the company's success. For example, Zara recently introduced a version of a short, classic women's jacket. When the design proved quite popular, Zara designed, produced, and delivered new variations of that jacket and put them on display in stores worldwide in just fifteen days. Other companies might take months to perfect designs and get them to the stores. By then, the trend may be long gone. As another example, Zara's sends new products to its stores every week, but always in short supply. If a customer finds something that strikes his or her fancy, that customer is inclined to think, "I should buy this now because it's the last one left." Executing that kind of limited supply system means Zara's supply chain must be able to create and quickly replenish small batches of new goods, and fast.

Managing Now: Supply Chain City

Until recently, a quota system in the United States basically required that American clothing manufacturers spread their manufacturing orders around the globe as a way to support fledgling apparel manufacturing industries in countries like Bangladesh. Those quotas ended a few years ago. As a result, apparel manufacturing is quickly consolidating in low-cost, high-efficiency supply chain cities in countries such as China. The supply chain city consolidates in one place product design, engineering, and manufacturing. For example, the supply chain city in Dongguam, in southern China, includes a huge factory, a hotel, dormitory rooms for 4,000 workers, and restaurants.[68]

Apparel maker Liz Claiborne is consolidating all its design, textile engineering, and manufacturing in this supply chain city because it brings together many of the components of Liz Claiborne's supply chain (like design, textile engineering, and manufacturing). The company's designers sit down here with technicians and engineers from textile manufacturers and from the manufacturing facility itself to quickly design and produce new apparel lines.

Liz Claiborne hopes that concentrating all this work in one place will simplify and speed up its whole supply chain process. It used to have 250 suppliers in thirty-five countries. Now, all this work will be done in the supply chain city. With its old system, designs for new items would bounce back and forth from designers in New York to various manufacturing facilities around the world, until the facilities got the designs right. Now, all the design and manufacturing is done in one place. Liz Claiborne hopes to get fast turnaround for new designs. In effect, it has put much of its supply chain partners in one place—in a supply chain city.

CHAPTER SUMMARY

1. Operations management is the process of managing the resources required to produce an organization's goods and services. The direct production resources of a firm are often called the five P's of operations and production management: people, plants, parts, processes, and planning and control systems.
2. Any production system consists of inputs, a conversion system, and outputs. Inputs are the primary resources used in the direct manufacture of the product or service. The conversion system converts those inputs into useful products or services called outputs.

3. The production system is at the heart of the operation. Four production design system decisions include the facility or plant location, the type of production processes that will be used, the layout of the plant or facility, and the layout of the production system itself.
4. Production planning is the process of deciding what products to produce, and where, when, and how to produce them. Production control is the process of ensuring that the specified production plans or schedules are being met.
5. The production schedule is often presented on a chart that shows what operations are to be carried out and when. Network planning and control methods are used to plan and control complex projects. Purchasing departments buy the materials and parts the firm needs to conduct its business.
6. Inventory management ensures that the firm has adequate inventories of all needed parts and supplies within the constraint of minimizing total inventory costs. Many quantitative and nonquantitative systems are available for managing inventory; ABC and EOQ systems are two of the most popular.
7. Quality reflects how well a product or service meets customer needs. Many firms use a process called designing for manufacturability to improve quality. Quality control involves a total, companywide effort. A number of quality control techniques are used to monitor and control product quality, including inspection procedures and acceptance sampling.
8. World-class companies compete based on quality, productivity, and responsiveness in an intensely competitive global environment. World-class manufacturers use modern production techniques and progressive management systems to boost manufacturing productivity, quality, and flexibility. These production techniques and management systems include TQM, JIT, CAD and CAM, FMS, CIM, and mass customization.
9. Supply chain management helps the firm achieve more efficient, integrated operations. Supplier partnering involves choosing a limited number of partners with whom the firm develops closer relationships. Channel assembly means having partners in the supply chain assemble modules to suit their customers' needs.

DISCUSSION QUESTIONS

1. Describe the production system in a dry-cleaning store.
2. What are the basic types of production processes? Which category would a college fit into?
3. What is a PERT chart? What (in outline form) would one look like for buying a car?
4. How could you use ABC inventory control in your pantry?
5. What does *world-class manufacturing* mean to you?
6. What makes a flexible manufacturing system flexible?
7. What is a supply chain?
8. List four types of supply chain partners for your school cafeteria.

EXPERIENTIAL EXERCISES

1. The people managing your school cafeteria (or franchised fast-food restaurant, etc.) have discovered that you know all about laying out a facility to make it more efficient, and they want to use your services. In teams of four or five students, visit your school cafeteria or other restaurant. What type of layout does it use now? Explain how you would change it, and why. Then briefly present your findings to the class.
2. You probably will not want to attempt Experiential Exercise 1 (evaluating your school cafeteria) until you've laid out the schedule for your project. In teams of four or five students, create a Gantt chart for the cafeteria-evaluation project.
3. After you have evaluated the school cafeteria in Experiential Exercise 1, you'll probably identify problems that you want management to address.

Use a fishbone/cause-and-effect diagram to analyze the problems.

4. Your college cafeteria wants to reduce what it spends on its inventory of paper goods by determining the optimal number of paper plates to obtain per order. Its annual demand for paper plates is 50,000. The ordering cost is $10 per order. The holding cost per plate per year is $0.05. Using the EOQ model, how many plates should the cafeteria manager order each time?

CASE STUDY

The Production Process at Wheeled Coach

Wheeled Coach, based in Winter Park, Florida, is the world's largest manufacturer of ambulances; they make about one of every three ambulances you see on the road.[69] Working four ten-hour days, 350 employees make only custom-made ambulances for hospitals, emergency medical teams (EMT), and fire departments. Although they make a full line of vehicles, from small to large, nearly every one is different—one, for instance has a special set of devices to make children more comfortable in it, and most need special compartments in various places for the emergency medical team's equipment. Continuing growth requires large capacity. The LA fire department alone orders about 150 ambulances per year. The firm has two identical factories, one in Kansas, the other in Florida.

Wheeled Coach builds only ambulances and does much of its own fabricating in-house. For example, it builds its own electrical assemblies and seat cushions. Within the factory, computer-assisted machines cut the aluminum for the vehicle's body, and special robotic welders assemble the custom-made doors and weld them to the body. As a focused factory, Wheeled Coach established workcells for every major module (body, doors, and so on). These workcells feed an assembly line, where workers assemble the bodies, electrical-wiring harnesses, interior cabinets, windows, painting, and upholstery into finished vehicles.

Every workcell feeds the assembly line on schedule, just in time for installation. The chassis, usually that of a Ford truck, moves to a station where the aluminum body is mounted. Then the vehicle is moved to painting. Following a custom paint job (usually involving three applications), it is moved to the assembly line, where it will spend seven days. During each of the seven workdays, each workcell delivers its respective module to the appropriate position on the assembly line. During the first day, electrical wiring is installed. On the second day, the unit moves forward to the station where cabinetry is delivered and installed. From there, the unit goes to a window and lighting station, on to upholstery, to fit and finish, to further customizing, and finally to inspection and road testing.

DISCUSSION QUESTIONS

1. Why do you think major auto manufacturers do not build ambulances?
2. What is a possible alternative production process to the assembly line that Wheeled Coach currently uses? Why?
3. Why is it more efficient for the workcells to prepare modules and deliver them to the assembly line than it would be to produce the components (such as the dashboard) as part of the line or have them delivered complete by outside suppliers?
4. What arguments would you make for why Wheeled Coach is a world-class manufacturer?

ORGANIZING 10

Staying in Touch at Millipore

Massachusetts-based Millipore Corp. supplies the technologies, tools, and services that its customers use to produce new drugs.[1] Coordinating the work of all its far-flung units was increasingly challenging for Millipore Corp., with operations and 4,500 employees in more than thirty countries. For example, how could Millipore make sure that what the unit in France was doing for a client made sense in terms of what its Asia unit was doing for that same client? To coordinate their efforts, Millipore's top managers needed information on what each country's subsidiary was doing. The problem was that just about every subsidiary was using a different, incompatible information system. The only way top management could get an overall view of things like sales, inventories, and finances was for employees in the home office to compile and summarize the incoming information from each subsidiary. Doing so took weeks. Bridget Reiss, the firm's chief information officer, knew that to coordinate Millipore's worldwide efforts, it had to make a change. The question was, What should they do? ■

Coordinating the work of all its far-flung units was increasingly challenging for Millipore Corp., with operations and 4,500 employees in more than thirty countries.

BEHAVIORAL OBJECTIVES

After studying this chapter, you should be able to:

Show that you've learned the chapter's essential information by

- Listing and briefly describing five ways to organize departments.
- Listing seven principles of delegating authority.
- Listing and briefly describing three modern organization structures.

CHAPTER OUTLINE

CHAPTER OUTLINE (Continued)

Show that you can practice what you've learned here by

- Reading the chapter-opening vignette and explaining how this company can improve its interdepartmental coordination.
- Reading the chapter case study and developing an organization chart for a company.

Show that you can apply what you've learned here by

- Watching the simulation video scenario and determining ways the company organized its activities to support its overall goals.

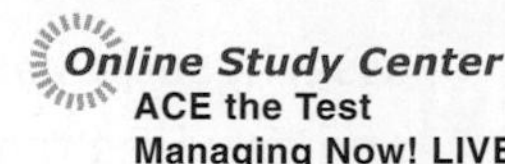

A few years ago, General Motors ran ads in Miami showing people driving Cadillacs through snow. GM's marketing department in Detroit thought the ads would help sell cars, but with temperatures around 80 degrees, the ads were just incongruous. Why run snow ads in Miami? Because, to paraphrase the *Wall Street Journal*, "GM's cumbersome bureaucracy" was so many layers removed from the buyers in Miami that it just lost touch with the market.[2] GM already has many problems (including huge pension obligations). Many people thought that it was bizarre to add a bureaucratic organization structure to its list of ills.

The plans the manager sets need to be transformed into action. The first step in doing so is usually to decide who is responsible for what and for **organizing** the work—to arrange the activities of the enterprise so that they systematically contribute to achieving the enterprise's goals. Organizing may seem to be just common sense, but even some giant companies like GM find it's not so simple.

organizing: arranging the activities of the enterprise so that they systematically contribute to the enterprise's goals

We saw in Chapter 1 that all enterprises—GM, Avon, and dry-cleaning stores, for instance—are organizations. An **organization** consists of people with formally assigned roles who work together to achieve stated goals. Organizations need not be just business firms. The word applies equally well to colleges, local governments, and nonprofits like the Red Cross. In any case, they all must come up with an organization structure such that its people work in unison to achieve the organization's goals.

organization: an entity that consists of people with formally assigned roles who work together to achieve stated goals

Organization Charts

The usual way of depicting an organization's structure is with an **organization chart**. This shows the title of each manager's position and, by means of connecting lines, who is accountable to whom, who has authority for each area, and which people are expected to routinely communicate with each other (see Figure 10.1, page 266). The organization chart also shows the chain of command (sometimes called the scalar chain or the line of authority) between the top of the organization and the lowest positions in the chart. The **chain of command** represents the organization's hierarchy of authority. It shows the path an order should take from the president to employees at the bottom of the organization chart, and the path a comment should take in traveling from employees at the bottom to the top.

organization chart: a chart that shows the structure of the organization including the title of each manager's position and, by means of connecting lines, who is accountable to whom and who has authority for each area

chain of command: the path that a directive and/or answer or request should take through each level of an organization; also called a scalar chain or the line of authority

One thing the organization chart does not show is the **informal organization**. This is the informal, habitual contacts, communications, and ways of doing things that employees develop. When the Avon salesperson, anxious to check on one of her pending orders, calls a friend at Avon's shipping depot instead of asking her own district manager to check, she's illustrating the use of a firm's informal organization. We'll look in this chapter at the basic elements in organizing companies, starting with departmentalization.

informal organization: the informal contacts, communications, and habitual ways of doing things that employees develop

Departmentalization: Creating Departments

Online Study Center
ACE the Test
Managing Now! LIVE

departmentalization: the process through which an organization's activities are grouped together and assigned to managers; the organizationwide division of work

Every enterprise must engage in various activities such as manufacturing, sales, or (in a hospital) radiology in order to accomplish its goals. **Departmentalization** is the process through which the manager groups the enterprise's activities together and assigns them to subordinates; it is the organizationwide division of work. (The groupings of activities go by the names *department, division, unit, section,* or some other similar term.)

The basic question in departmentalization is, Around what activities should we organize departments? For example, in a company, should we organize departments for sales and manufacturing? Or should there be separate departments for industrial and retail customers, each of which then has its own sales and manufacturing units? There are three basic choices.

Three Basic Ways to Departmentalize

In the movie *Gladiator,* each Roman legion, consisting of about 6,000 soldiers, was managed by about sixty centurions, each of whom managed about 100 soldiers. Armies and some other enterprises still organize by simple numbers. In general, however, managers use this approach sparingly. Most business activities (such as sales or human resources) require specialized efforts, so dividing people just by numbers wouldn't make much sense.

Managers therefore traditionally have two realistic choices when it comes to dividing the company's work into departments. They can organize departments around functions, or they can organize departments around self-contained units (often called divisions). For example, the editor in chief of a student newspaper can appoint functional department heads (editors) for editing, production, and sales. Working under the editor in chief, this team publishes all the paper's issues. Or the editor in chief can appoint editors for each of the journal's fall, winter, spring, and summer editions. Each edition here would be self-contained. Each edition's editor gets his or her own editorial, production, and sales editors. Each edition's editor would then control most of the activities required to publish his or her edition.

Creating Departments Around Functions

functional departmentalization: a form of organization that groups a company's activities around functions such as manufacturing, sales, or finance

Functional departmentalization is grouping activities around functions such as manufacturing, sales, and finance. The manager puts subordinates in charge of each of these functions. The local dry-cleaning business organizes like this. It has separate functional departments for things like counter work, spotting, cleaning, and pressing. Figure 10.1 shows the organizational structure for the ABC Car Company. At ABC, management organized each department around a different business function, in this case, sales, finance, and production. Here, the production director reports to the president and manages ABC's production plants. Other directors carry out the sales and finance functions.

This is a simple and obvious way to organize because regardless of how the manager organizes (by functions or by self-contained units), someone must perform these functions if the firm is to survive.

FIGURE 10.1

Functional Departmentalization

This chart shows a functional organization, with departments for basic functions like finance, sales, and production.

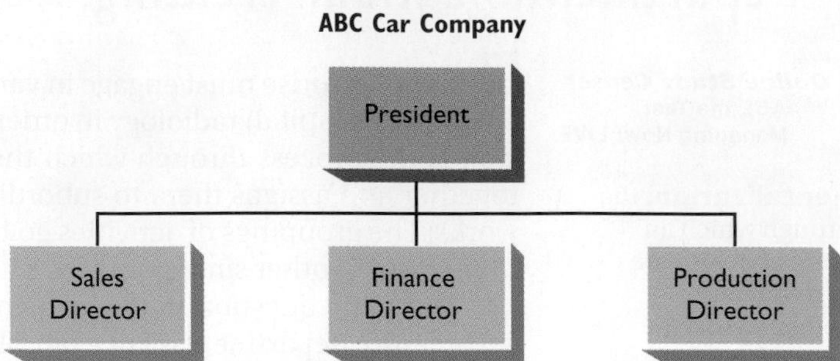

Managers organize departments around three types of functions: business, managerial, and technological. The *business functions* are those the enterprise must engage in to survive. A manufacturing company's business functions include production, sales, and finance. A university's business functions include academic affairs, business affairs, and student affairs. Banks like Chase have business function departments for operations, accounting, and loans. Starbucks needs business function managers for purchasing and sales.

Some managers organize by *managerial functions,* which means putting supervisors in charge of managerial functions like planning, control, and administration. Within production, *technological functions* may include plating, welding, or assembling.

Advantages Organizing by functions has several advantages:

1. *It is simple, obvious, and logical.* The enterprise must perform these functions to survive.
2. *It can promote efficiency for three reasons.* First, functional departments are specialized departments—they focus on doing one thing (such as sales)—and everyone tends to get better with practice. Second, organizing by function means that departments (like sales or production) serve all the firm's products or services. This can mean increased economies of scale (for instance, one large plant and more efficient equipment for manufacturing all the company's products). Third, organizing by function minimizes duplication of effort. For example, there is one production department for all the company's products rather than separate ones for each product.
3. *It can simplify executive hiring and training.* The managers running these departments have specialized jobs (sales manager, for instance). It can be easier to find good specialist managers than general managers, those with the breadth of experience to administer several functions at once.
4. *It can facilitate the top manager's control.* Functional department managers tend to receive information on, and focus on, just the activities that concern their own specialized activities. They usually have to rely on their boss (the top manager) to coordinate their efforts. A functional organization can therefore make it easier for the top manager to control what's happening in the organization.

Disadvantages Organizing by function also has disadvantages:

1. *It increases the coordination workload for the executive to whom the functional department heads report.* Functional departmentalization can increase the top manager's control, but the other side of the coin is that responsibility for coordinating all products and services rests on that person's shoulders. For example, the CEO may be the only one who can coordinate the work of the functional departments. As size and diversity of products increase, the job of coordinating production, sales, and finance for many different products or markets may prove too much for one person.

2. *It may reduce the firm's sensitivity to and service to the customer.* For example, if JCPenney's management decided to organize nationally around the functions of merchandising, purchasing, and personnel, all of its U.S. stores might tend to get the same products to sell, even if customers' tastes in Chicago are different from those in El Paso.

3. *It produces fewer general managers.* A functional organization fosters an emphasis on specialized managers (finance experts, production experts, and so forth). This can make it more difficult to cultivate managers with the breadth of experience required for jobs like CEO.

Often the functional form's disadvantages outweigh its advantages. If so, managers may opt to organize around self-contained units. The four options here are to create departments to focus on different products, customers, marketing channels, or territories.

Creating Departments Around Self-Contained *Product* Units

product departmentalization: a form of departmentalization in which the manager organizes multi-functional departments around the company's products or services (or around each family of products or services)

division: a department that manages all or most of the activities needed to develop, manufacture, and sell a particular product or product line

divisional organization: a form of organization in which the firm's major departments are organized so that each one can manage all or most of the activities needed to develop, manufacture, and sell a particular product or product line

With **product departmentalization**, the manager organizes his or her departments around the company's products or services (or around each family of products or services). For example, GM has product divisions for Cadillac, Buick, Pontiac, and Chevrolet. The editor in chief might organize her paper around separate fall, winter, spring, and summer issues.

The CEO for a pharmaceuticals company (see Figure 10.2) organized the firm's top-level departments so that each contains all the activities required to develop, manufacture, and sell a particular product (skin care, vitamins, drugs). The general manager of each division has functional departments—for production, sales, and personnel—reporting to him or her. Each controls all or most of the resources required to create, produce, and supply its product or products. For example, at Kodak, each division focuses on a product line such as cameras.

Managers often refer to these product departments as business units or **divisions**, and to this type of departmentalization as a **divisional organization**. Divisionalization means the firm's major departments are organized so that each can manage all (or most of) the activities needed to develop, manufacture, and sell a particular product or product line. To the extent that each division head has control of all or most of the resources needed to create, produce, sell, and supply its product or products, each of these product divisions is self-contained. Axa, a large insurance and finance company, recently split its company into divisions with specific product lines such as wealth management, corporate business, and protection.[3]

FIGURE 10.2

Divisional Organization for a Pharmaceuticals Company

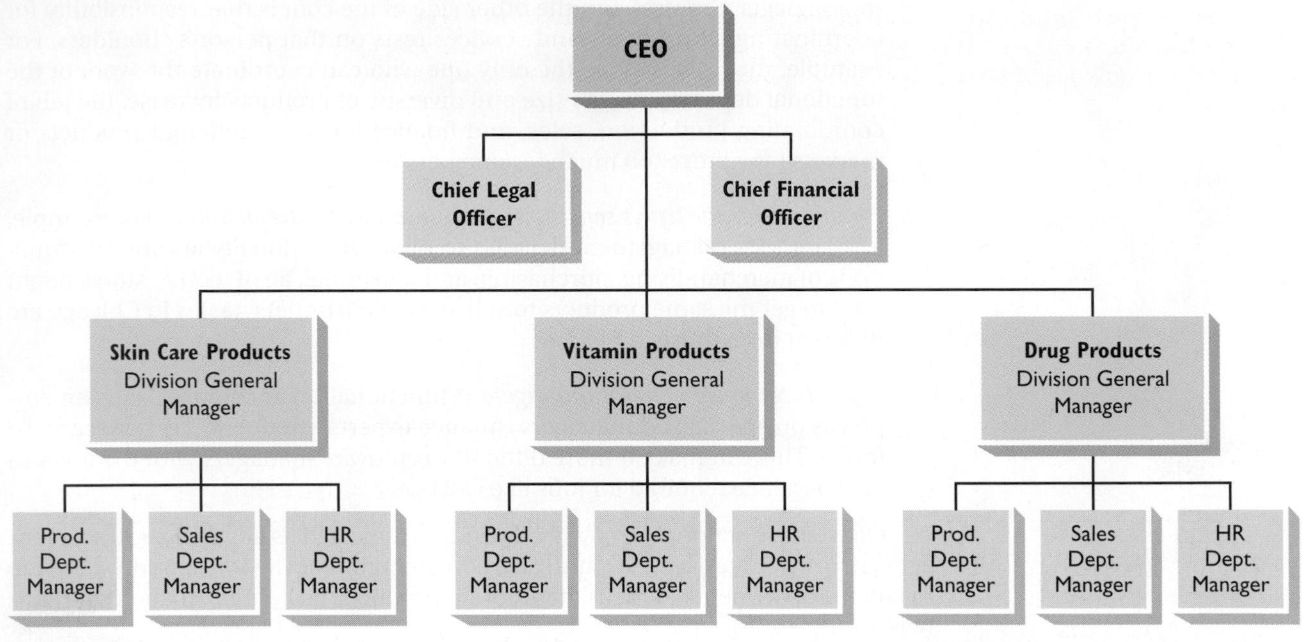

● **Advantages** Organizing by self-contained units such as products has these advantages:

1. *The product or service gets the single-minded attention of its own general manager and unit, and so its customers may get better, more responsive service.* A general manager oversees all the functions required to produce and market each particular product or service. The effect should be that the product or service (and its customers) get focused, more responsive attention with this type of organization than they would in a functional organization (in which, for instance, the same sales manager must address the needs of multiple products).

2. *It's easier to judge performance.* If a division is (or is not) doing well, it is clear who is responsible because one general manager is managing the whole division. This may better motivate the general manager.

3. *It develops general managers.* Divisions can be good training grounds for an enterprise's executives because they are miniature companies that expose managers to a wider range of functional issues.

4. *It reduces the coordination burden for the company's CEO.* In Figure 10.3, the North American division is departmentalized by function, so that the president has to coordinate the tasks of selling, producing, and staffing for each of the company's many products. He or she may thus have to deal with many varied problems. Ideally, the effect of organizing around product divisions is to push the job of coordinating the business units' functional areas down to the business unit heads. The CEO can then focus more on things like strategic planning.

FIGURE 10.3

Divisional Organizations Facilitate Coordination

The top level shows geographic departmentalization. Unless the presidents of the International and North America divisions reorganize by setting up separate divisions for skin care, vitamins, and drugs, they will have to personally coordinate sales, production, and personnel for all three sets of products.

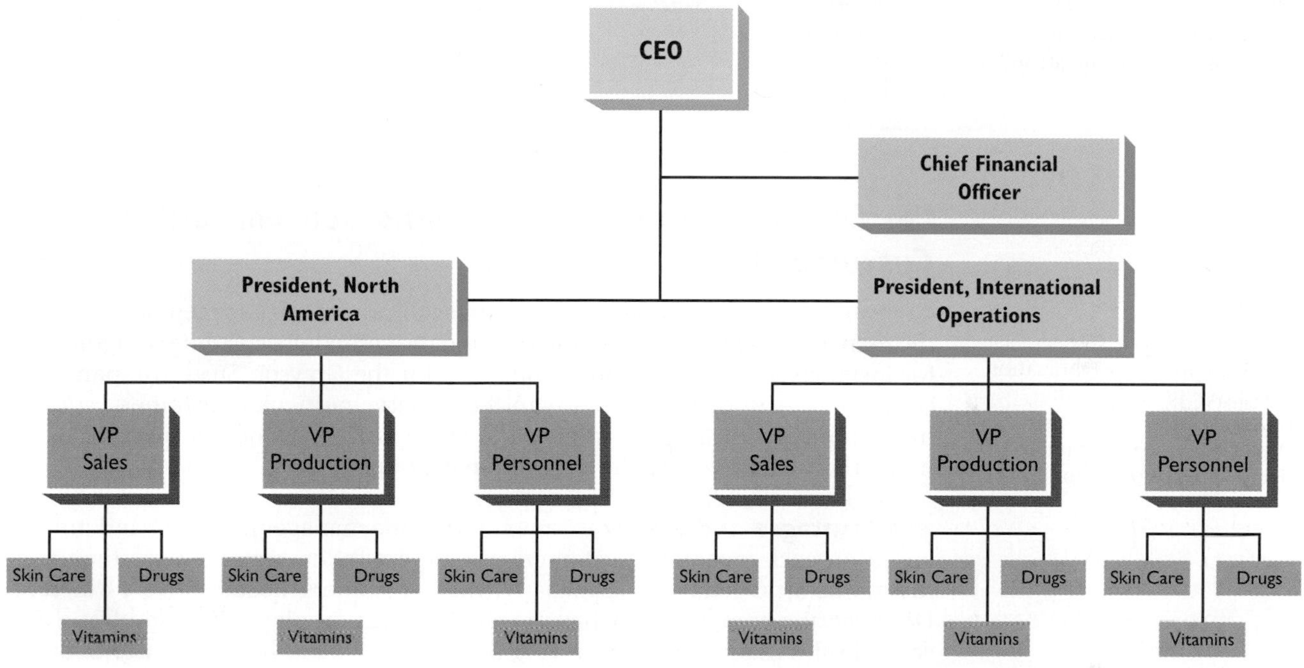

● **Disadvantages** Organizing by self-contained units such as products has these disadvantages:

1. *It creates duplication of effort.* The very fact that each product-oriented unit is self-contained implies that each unit for each product has its own production plants, sales force, and so on.
2. *It reduces opportunities for top management control.* An autonomous division might, for instance, run up excessive expenses before top management discovers there's a problem. Striking a balance between providing each division with enough autonomy while maintaining top-management control is the central issue in organizing in this way.
3. *It requires more managers with general management abilities.* Each product division is, in a sense, a miniature company. This means these firms must work diligently to identify and develop managers with general management potential.
4. *It can encourage compartmentalization.* The managers of the semiautonomous units may be reluctant to pay much attention to the needs of the other divisions. Thus, at toiletries maker Caswell-Massey, CEO Ann Robinson says that her separate divisions were each oblivious to what the others were doing: "The items featured on the catalog's cover were not necessarily in the store window. There was little synergy between brands."[4]

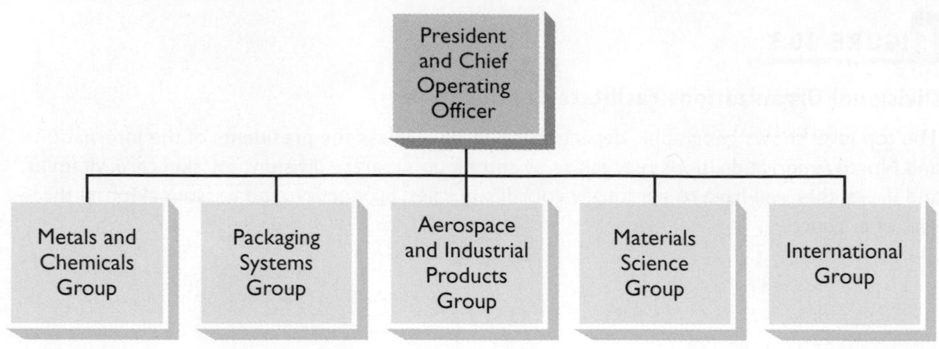

FIGURE 10.4

Customer Departmentalization, Grayson Steel Company

With customer departmentalization, separate departments are organized around customers, such as aerospace as well as metals and chemicals customers.

Creating Departments Around Self-Contained *Customer* Units

customer departmentalization: similar to product organization except that generally self-contained departments are organized to serve the needs of specific groups of customers

Customer departmentalization is similar to product departmentalization, but the manager organizes departments around the company's customers. Figure 10.4, for instance, shows the organization chart for the Grayson Steel Company. The company's main divisions are organized to serve particular customers, such as metals and chemicals customers, packaging systems customers, aerospace and industrial customers, and the international group.

Advantages and Disadvantages With one management team and unit focused on each customer, customers can expect faster, better service than with functional arrangements, particularly when customers' needs are very different. However, the company may have several production plants instead of one and several sales managers, each serving the needs of his or her own customers, instead of one.

Creating Departments Around Self-Contained *Marketing Channel* Units

marketing channel: the conduit through which a manufacturer distributes its products to its ultimate customers

marketing-channel departmentalization: an arrangement in which departments of an organization focus on particular marketing channels, such as drugstores or grocery stores

Many companies, such as Caswell-Massey, sell their products through several marketing channels. A **marketing channel** is the conduit or intermediary (wholesaler, drugstore) through which a manufacturer distributes its products to its ultimate customers. With **marketing-channel departmentalization** (see Figure 10.5), management organizes the departments around each of the firm's marketing channels (instead of products or customers).

Companies departmentalized into marketing-channel departments (like those now used by Caswell-Massey) typically market the same product (such as soap) through two or more channels (such as drugstores and grocery stores). Management here typically chooses one department to manufacture the product for all the marketing-channel departments.

Advantages and Disadvantages Managers use marketing-channel departmentalization when it's important to cater to each marketing channel's unique needs. A department store may want Revlon to supply specially trained salespeople to run concessions in its stores. A discount druggist wants quick delivery.

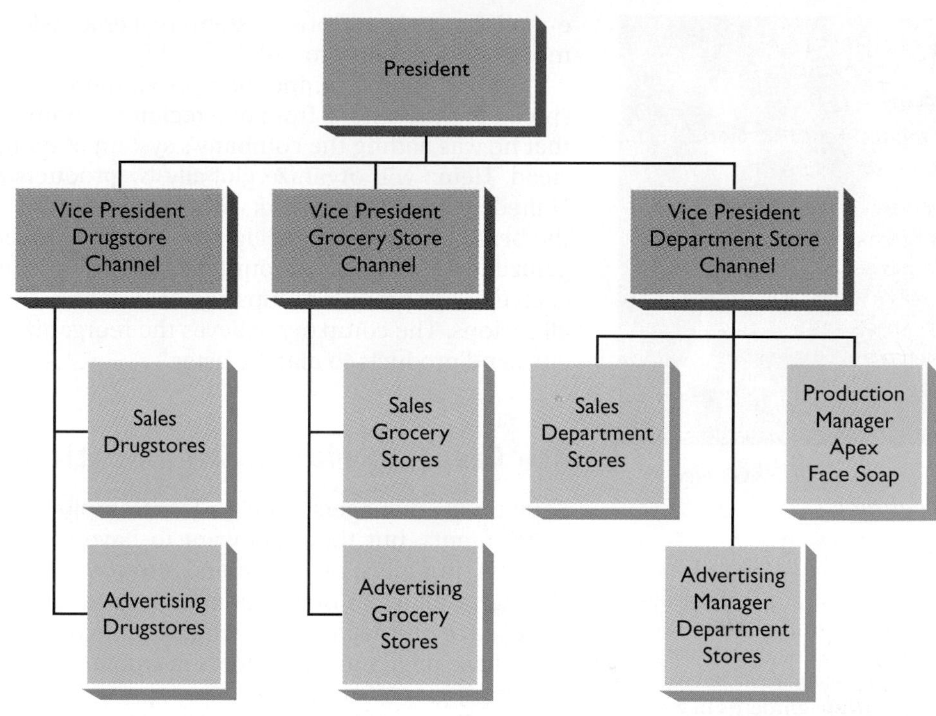

FIGURE 10.5

Marketing Channel Departmentalization

With marketing channels, the main departments are organized to focus on particular marketing channels, such as drugstores and grocery stores. Here, the department store channel produces the soap, and each channel may sell to the same ultimate consumers.

Putting a manager and department in charge of each channel helps ensure that Revlon meets these diverse needs quickly and effectively. As in product and customer departmentalization, the resulting duplication—in this case, of sales forces—is the main disadvantage.

Creating Departments Around Self-Contained *Geographic Area* Units

geographic or **territorial departmentalization:** departmentalization in which the manager organizes separate multifunction departments for each of the territories in which the enterprise does business

With **geographic** or **territorial departmentalization**, the manager organizes separate departments for each of the territories in which the enterprise does business. Each territorial division gets its own management team. Each is often self-contained (with its own production, sales, and personnel activities). We illustrated territorial departmentalization in Figure 10.3 (page 269). At the top level, there are separate presidents for North American and for international operations.

● **Advantages and Disadvantages** As is the case with other divisional-type organizations, the main advantage of territorial departmentalization is that there is one self-contained department dedicated to the needs of each geographic area. Duplication is the main disadvantage. There might be four regional offices to maintain, for instance.

Organizing geographically grew in popularity as firms expanded across national borders. Years ago, when poor communications made it difficult to monitor operations abroad, it made sense to let local managers run regional or country businesses as autonomous companies.

Territorial departmentalization is somewhat less necessary today, for two reasons. First, information technology such as Internet-based videoconferencing,

Susan Arnold, P&G's vice chairman.

e-mail, fax, and enterprise systems makes it easier for an executive in one region to monitor operations around the world.

Second, global competition is so intense that managers can't risk slowing the spread of innovations from one region to another. For example, Heinz's CEO said that he was ending the company's system of managing by country or region.[5] Instead, Heinz will organize globally by products or categories. Managers in the United States will then work with those in Europe, Asia, and other regions to apply the best ideas from one region to another. Similarly, Procter & Gamble's new organization eliminates its four regional business units. Now seven new executives each manage product groups like baby care, beauty, and fabric and home care for all regions. The company believes the reorganization will speed decision making and send products to market faster.[6]

Creating Matrix Organizations

matrix organization: an organization structure in which employees are permanently attached to one department but also simultaneously have ongoing assignments in which they report to project, customer, product, or geographic unit heads. Also known as matrix management

Sometimes, managers want to leave employees in their specialized functional departments, but they also want to have those employees focus on particular projects, products, or customers. A **matrix organization**, also known as matrix management, is an organization structure in which employees are permanently attached to one department (usually a functional department) but also simultaneously have ongoing assignments in which they report to project, customer, product, or geographic unit heads.

We illustrate this in Figure 10.6. Universal Products Company organized the firm's automotive products division functionally, with departments for production, engineering, materials procurement, personnel, and accounting. However, because each of Universal's big customers had special new-product development needs, Universal management also created three project groups. There is one for the Ford project, the Chrysler project, and the GM project. One or more employees from each functional department (like production and engineering) is temporarily assigned to each project. This is thus a matrix organization, with employees each simultaneously housed in functional departments while also (at least temporarily) devoted to particular products. Employees report to both their functional and new-product heads.

J. P. Morgan investment banking uses a matrix structure. Managers around the world answer to two bosses: a J. P. Morgan investment banking manager in Mexico City reports both to her investment banking head back in New York and to the head of J. P. Morgan's Mexico City office. The managing director of advertising agency DBB's Far East subsidiary recently organized using matrix management, to encourage better communications across DBB's diciplines and clients.[7]

Advantages and Disadvantages Ideally, matrix management provides the best of both worlds. It gives the employees the stability and benefits of belonging to permanent specialized departments. And it gives the firm most of the advantages of having units and employees focused on specific projects, products, areas, or customers.

However, the matrix organization also has special drawbacks. Ambiguity is one. Even after years with a matrix structure, GM's chair, when asked who reports to whom, could only reply, "[I]ncreasingly, it depends."[8] Other disadvantages include confusion(from having two bosses),[9] power struggles and conflicts (because authority tends to be more ambiguous), and excessive overhead (due to hiring dual sets of managers, for instance).

FIGURE 10.6

Matrix Organization Departmentalization

With a matrix organization, a self-contained project structure is often superimposed over a functional organization.

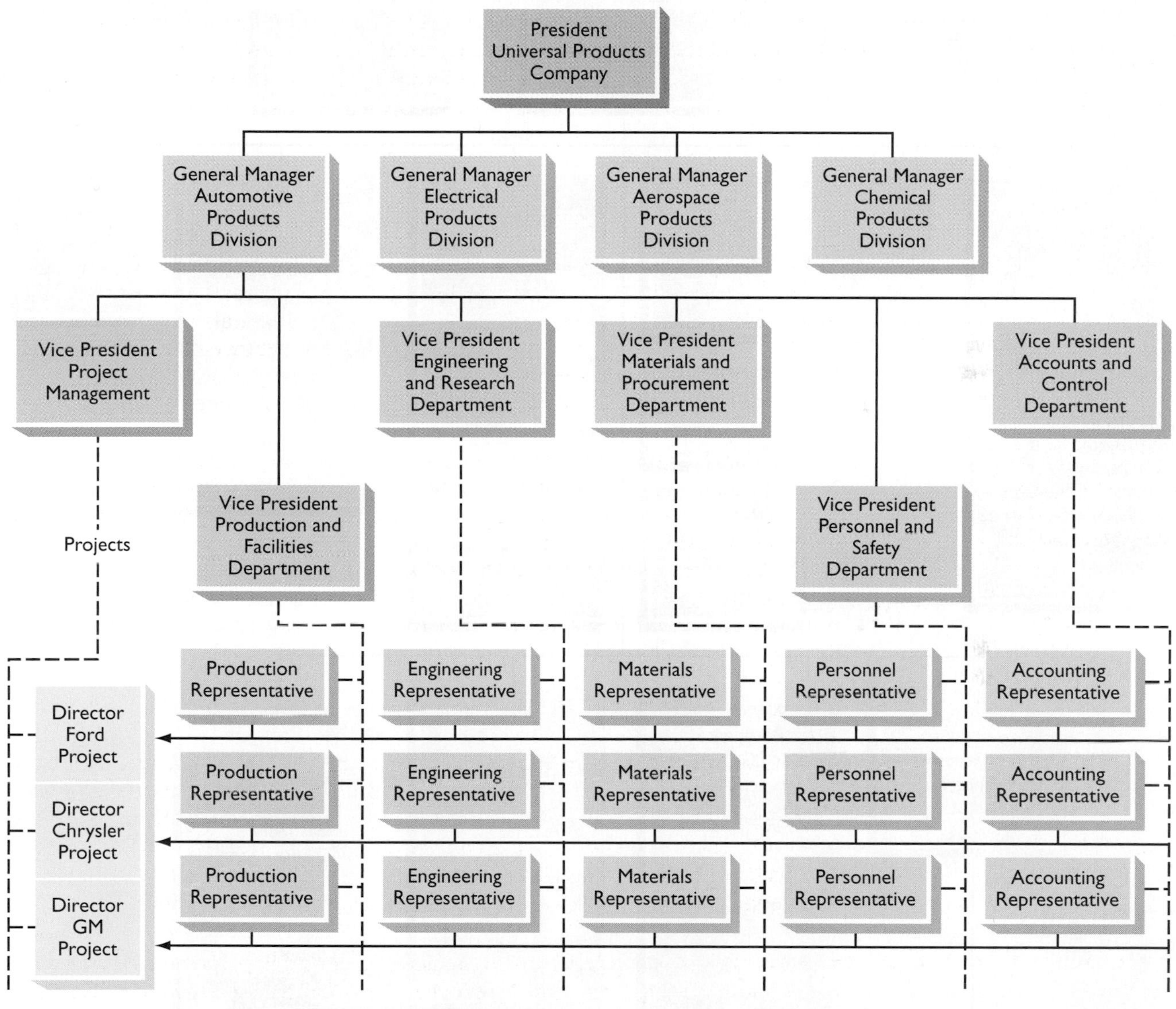

Departmentalization in Practice

All but the smallest firms contain both functional and self-contained departments. Figure 10.7 illustrates this. Within the United States, there are separate product departments for business systems, programming systems, and so forth. Globally, this firm uses territorial departmentalization, with separate officers for the United States, the Americas, Asia/Pacific, and Europe/Middle East/Africa.

FIGURE 10.7

A Hybrid Organization

Particularly in large organizations, several types of departmentalization are typically combined, in this case, fucntional, product, and geographic.

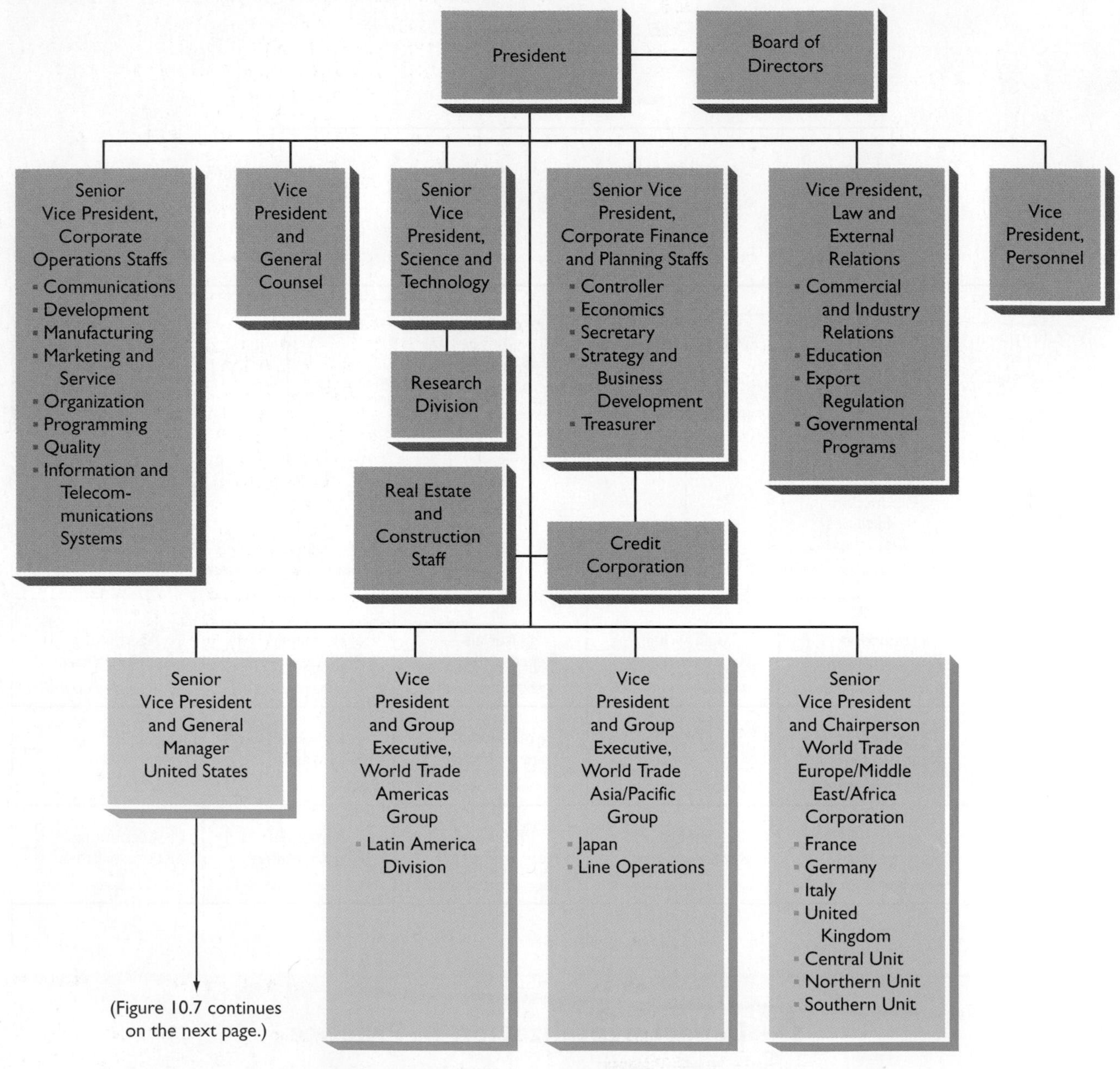

(Figure 10.7 continues on the next page.)

FIGURE 10.7 (*Continued*)

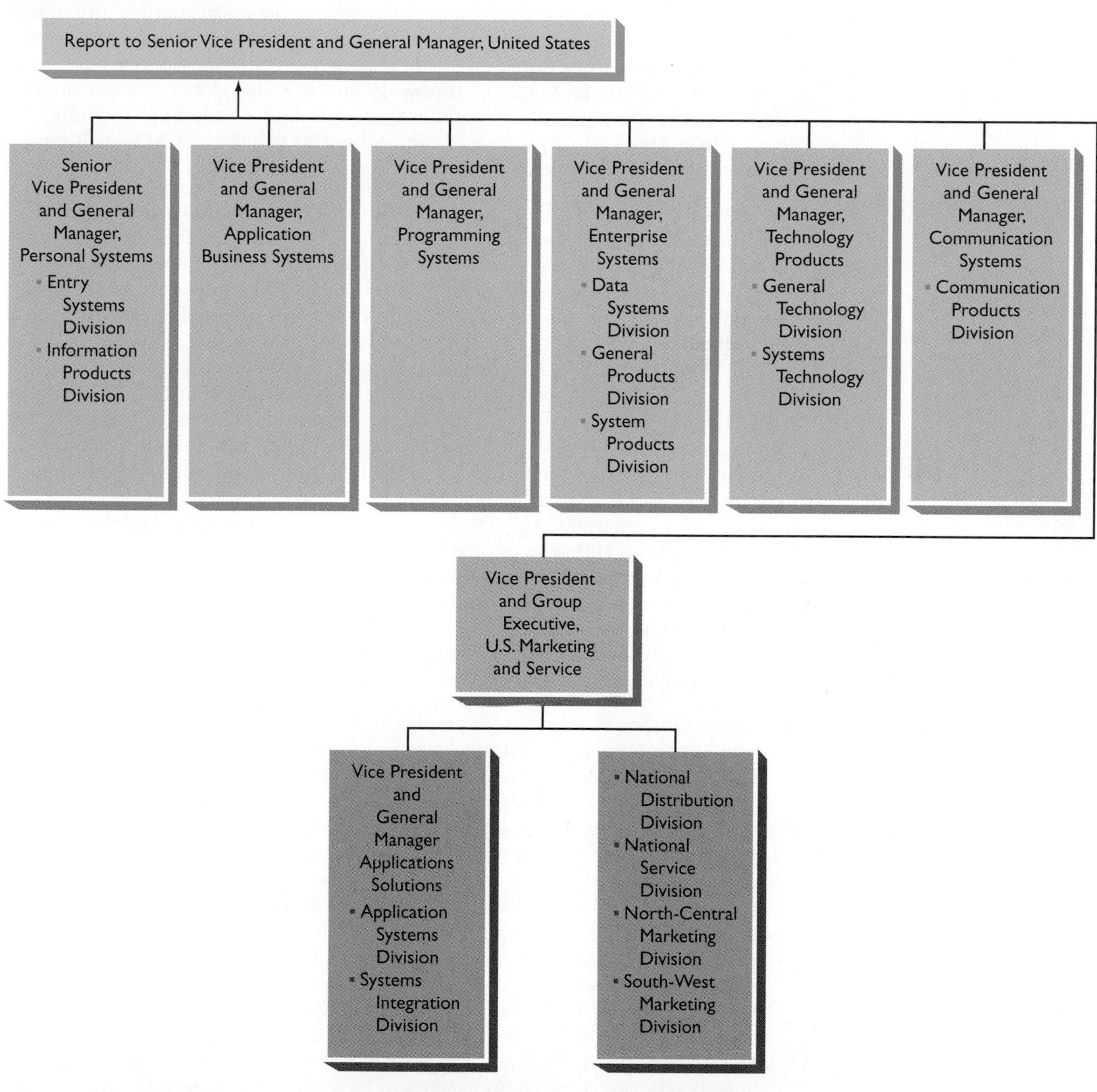

Management organized the headquarters staff around managerial functions (general counsel, finance and planning, and law).

Managers mix the types of departmentalization for three reasons. One is hierarchical considerations: if the top-level departments are based on, say, products, then each product division will probably need subsidiary departments for functions like sales and manufacturing.

The second is efficiency: product, customer, and territorial departments tend to result in duplicate sales, manufacturing, and other functional departments. One way to minimize this source of inefficiency is to have, say, a single production department serving multiple customer departments. For example, after many years of letting each GM brand (like Chevy) design its own cars, GM reorganized its vehicle-design structure in 2005. It now designs vehicles globally rather than by brand. Thus, Germany's Opel leads in designing and developing GM's midsize cars, while other GM subsidiaries design other GM vehicles.[10] GM feels it's more efficient to eliminate duplicate design centers.

Hewlett-Packard's Reorganization However, sometimes, letting business unit heads control all the functions required to produce and sell their products outweighs the inefficiencies of duplication. For example, when he became CEO of Hewlett-Packard (HP), one of the first issues Mark Hurd addressed was the unsatisfactory performance of HP's sales organization. Numerous HP executives and customers described HP's sales effort as underperforming and confused.

At that point (2005), HP consisted of product divisions that focused on businesses such as PCs, servers, and printers, as well as one centralized functional sales department, which served all the business units. The sales force reported through the chain of command to an executive who was separate from and not responsible to the HP product divisions. The heads of the product divisions had to compete within the HP bureaucracy for sales assistance. As a result, customers often had no idea who to call if they wanted to make a purchase. And the division heads lacked the authority to direct a sales effort for their products because the salespeople reported to their own, separate executive.

Hurd decided to abolish the central sales department and redeploy many of the salespeople to the product divisions. This change also enabled Hurd to announce the layoffs of about 10 percent of HP's workforce, many of whom were in administrative or supervisory positions in the old sales division.[11]

Common Sense As these examples illustrate, the third reason to mix departments is common sense. Numerous hard-to-measure factors—including what management plans to achieve and the unique needs of the firm's customers, territories, and products—all influence the departmentalization decision.

Rosenbluth International, a 1,000-office global travel agency, provides an example. CEO Hal Rosenbluth organized it like a farm. "The family farm is the most efficient type of unit I've ever run across, because everybody on the farm has to be fully functional and multifaceted." So Rosenbluth broke his company into more than 100 geographic units, each functioning like a farm. Multitalented agents serve specific regions and clients. Corporate headquarters became what Rosenbluth calls "farm towns." Here, central "stores" like human resources (HR) are available for all the "farms" to use. The firm's computerized Global Distribution Network links each of its travel agents to the company's PCs in Philadelphia. There, centralized data on clients help ensure that the work of all offices is coordinated to serve the clients' needs. The organization seems to have worked. He recently sold Rosenbluth Travel to giant Amex, creating the world's largest travel company.[12]

Achieving Coordination

Online Study Center
ACE the Test
Managing Now! LIVE

It is pointless for a manager to divide work among, say, production, sales, and finance departments and then not provide the means to coordinate these departments' efforts. **Coordination** is the process of achieving unity of action among

coordination: the process of achieving unity of action among interdependent activities

interdependent activities. It is required whenever two or more interdependent individuals, groups, or departments must work together to achieve a common goal.

The more interdependent are the departments, the more coordination they require. Someone must coordinate the work of functional departments, or how can one be sure that the products sold by sales will be produced and financed in sufficient quantities? At the other extreme, the work of semiautonomous product divisions such as GM's Chevrolet, Buick, and Cadillac product divisions require less coordination by the CEO.

Professors Jay Galbraith and Henry Mintzberg, working independently, described the techniques managers use to achieve coordination.[13] We summarize these and other techniques next.

Use Mutual Adjustment

mutual adjustment: achieving coordination through face-to-face interpersonal interaction

Mutual adjustment means achieving coordination by relying on face-to-face interpersonal interaction. For example, two people lifting a heavy log might coordinate by counting "one, two, three, lift," at which point, both people lift the log in unison.

Use Rules and Procedures

Managers use rules and procedures for coordinating routine, recurring activities. Thus, a restaurant manager would have a rule that bussers will clear tables before the waiter returns.

Standardize Goals, Skills, and Values

Firms also achieve coordination by standardizing their employees' goals, skills, values, and operating processes. For example, as long as the sales, finance, and production managers attain their assigned *goals,* the president can be reasonably sure that there will be enough financing and production capacity to meet the sales target. Managers also standardize *skills.* Imagine the chaos if waiters don't know how to take customers' orders and chefs can't cook.

Many companies endeavor to standardize *values* among employees. For example, every year, Unilever gives about 150 of its worldwide managers temporary assignments at corporate headquarters.[14] This gives the visiting managers a strong sense of Unilever's values (such as keeping an open mind and innovating new products; see http://www.unilever.com/ourvalues/).[15] This helps to ensure that wherever they are around the world, Unilever managers' efforts are consistent with Unilever's ethical values and other values.

Managing Now: Standardizing Processes with Enterprise and Supply Chain Systems

Managers also boost coordination by standardizing *processes.* For example, several years ago, the head of Nestlé Corporation's Nordic operations (for Denmark, Finland, Norway, and Sweden) was managing what amounted to four separate companies. The Nestlé subsidiary in each country used its own information system. The top executives responsible for Nestlé Nordic found it relatively difficult to coordinate the four units' operations due to the lack of standardized information on matters such as sales, purchasing, inventory, and billing.

After installing an enterprise system that provided standardized information, two things happened. First, the managers at Nestlé Nordic headquarters had the

Window on Managing Now
LG Electronics

LG Electronics is one of the world's largest consumer-electronics companies, with 66,000 employees in thirty-nine countries. LG produces products ranging from air conditioners to laptops and mobile phones. Several years ago, its sixty-five worldwide offices all used different software systems. Therefore, management had to deal with data and documents on matters such as sales, purchasing, inventory, and finance that were in different formats. The only way top managers could get a unified, coordinated view of what was happening throughout the company was to have employees in the head office merge the information from subsidiaries, often by hand.

Moving to an enterprise system, in this case, from Oracle Corporation, enabled LG to institute standardized information systems across all its global offices. Now they all use compatible software systems. As a result, "communication and cooperation between subsidiaries is expected to improve significantly, enabling different offices to exchange information and resources more easily. Directives from [the] head office can be disseminated via the central system, ensuring all subsidiaries work together to achieve company-wide business goals."[16]

Moving to an enterprise system enabled LG to institute standardized information systems across all its global offices.

information they needed to coordinate the subsidiaries' efforts.[17] Second, standardizing the information systems each subsidiary used for each of its business functions also had the effect of encouraging the units to move more toward standardizing the sales and other processes they used. As at Nestlé, standardizing processes often starts with standardizing a company's software systems. Then, having the way things are done in each subsidiary more standardized makes it easier to coordinate the subsidiaries' efforts.

Supply chain management software systems also help a company's supply chain partners coordinate their efforts. For example, all of a firm's supply chain partners may use a common Internet portal to share information on activities like sales, inventory, and delivery status. This helps to ensure coordinated decision making.[18] The Window on Managing Now feature presents another example.

Exercise Direct Supervision: Use the Chain of Command

Direct supervision achieves coordination by having one person coordinate the work of others, issuing instructions and monitoring results.[19] When problems arise that the rules or procedures don't cover, subordinates bring the problem to the manager. In addition to using rules and mutual adjustment, all managers use the chain of command in this way to achieve coordination.

Divisionalize

As a rule, functional departmentalization creates heavy coordination demands on the CEO because the work of the functional departments (like sales and production) is both specialized and interdependent. (Thus, someone must coordinate the sales, production, and finance departments.) Organizing by product, customer, or geographic divisions reduces interdependence and reduces the coordination burden. The CEO puts each lieutenant in charge of a self-contained operation. The lieutenants coordinate their own operations. The divisions are relatively independent. As noted, the CEO can then coordinate less and strategize more.

Appoint Staff Assistants

The coordinating manager must monitor the activities of the subordinate departments as well as analyze and address questions from lieutenants. Some managers hire staff assistants to help with these tasks. When subordinates bring a problem to the manager, the assistant can compile information about the problem, research it, and offer advice.

Appoint Liaisons

When the volume of contacts between two departments grows, some managers use special liaisons to facilitate coordination. For example, the sales department manager might appoint a salesperson to be his or her liaison with the production department. This liaison stays in the sales department but travels frequently to the factory. When a new order arrives in sales, the sales manager can quickly determine from this liaison what the production schedules are and if the company can deliver the order as promised.

Appoint Committees

Many firms achieve coordination by appointing interdepartmental committees, task forces, or teams composed of representatives of the interdependent departments. They meet periodically to discuss common problems and ensure interdepartmental coordination.

Use Coordination-Supporting Software Packages

Managers use various types of software packages to improve coordination. For example, we saw that Rosenbluth Travel's computerized Global Distribution Network links each of its travel agents to the company's centralized client database, to help ensure that the work of all offices is coordinated to serve that client's needs. San Francisco–based Citadon provides Web-based construction coordination software. By using the Internet and a laptop, everyone involved in a project—from owners and architects to contractors and subcontractors—receives instantaneous updates regarding design changes and construction status. Group decision support systems like Lotus Notes, with tools such as group scheduling and PC-based videoconferencing, make it easier for even remote employees to coordinate their efforts.[20]

independent integrator: an individual or a group that coordinates the activities of several interdependent departments but is independent of them

Organize Independent Integrators

An **independent integrator** is a separate individual or group that coordinates the activities of several interdependent departments.[21] Integrators are independent of the departments they coordinate. They report to the manager who oversees both those departments.

Professors Paul Lawrence and Jay Lorsch studied such departments.[22] In the plastics industry, for instance, developing a new product requires close coordination among the research, engineering, sales, and production departments in a situation where competitors are always introducing new and innovative products. Some firms in the plastics industry thus established new-product development departments. Their role is to coordinate (or integrate) the research, marketing analysis, sales, and production activities needed for developing and introducing a new product. The Window on Managing Now feature shows how managers use information technology (IT) to create such departments.

Authority and the Chain of Command

authority: the right to take action, make decisions, and direct the work of others

No one will generally take orders from someone unless they accept that person's authority to issue those orders. Organizations therefore run on authority. **Authority** refers to a person's legal right or power to take action, make decisions, and direct the work of others. In a corporation, authority stems from the owner/stockholders of the company. They elect a board of directors and authorize the board to represent the owners' interests. The board's main functions are to choose the top executives, approve strategies and long-term plans, and monitor performance to make sure management is protecting the owners' interests. The board and its chairperson then delegate or pass down to the CEO the authority to actually run the company—to develop plans, hire subordinate managers, and enter into agreements. The CEO and each lower manager in turn delegates to or authorizes his or her subordinates to do their jobs.

Line and Staff Authority

line authority: the right (or authority) of a manager to issue orders to other managers or employees, creating a superior-subordinate relationship

Managers need to decide which subordinates will have line authority or staff authority because the company's proper functioning depends on everyone knowing who is in charge of what. Line versus staff authority is basically a question of relationships. **Line authority** gives the manager the right (or authority) to issue orders

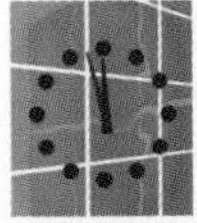

WINDOW ON MANAGING NOW
An IT-Based Independent Integrator at Thales

France-based Thales, an electronics and defense supplier, has three business units: defense, aerospace, and information technology. Each business unit is fairly autonomous.[23] Top management wanted to make sure that the research scientists, engineers, and project managers in each of these three divisions were familiar with each other's projects and that they did not duplicate each other's efforts. Working with consultants from Accenture, Thales created a new, IT-supported independent-integrator-type department called Thales Research & Technology.[24] To support this department's efforts, Thales and its consultants created what they called a knowledge management portal. Thales's business unit engineers and scientists use laptops, PCs, personal digital assistants (PDAs), and the portal to post papers, ask questions, and make suggestions. In this way, each business unit continues to benefit from its own research and engineering teams, but they can also capitalize on each other's knowledge and minimize duplication of effort.

staff authority: the right (or authority) of a manager to advise other managers or employees

line managers: managers who are authorized to issue orders to subordinates down the chain of command

staff managers: managers with authority to assist and advise line managers

functional authority: narrowly limited power to issue orders down the chain of command in a specific functional area such as personnel testing

line-staff conflict: a disagreement between a line manager and the staff manager who is giving him or her advice

to other managers or employees. It creates a superior-subordinate relationship. **Staff authority** gives the manager the right (authority) to advise other managers or employees. It creates an advisory relationship. **Line managers** have line authority. The production vice president is the production manager's boss and can give that person orders. **Staff managers** have staff authority. They generally cannot issue orders down the chain of command (except in their own departments). The HR manager can advise the production manager about who to hire but cannot insist or make the final decision, for instance.

In popular usage, managers associate line managers with managing functions like sales or production that are essential for the company to exist. Staff managers run functions that are generally advisory or supportive, such as purchasing, legal, human resource management, and quality control. This distinction makes sense as long as the staff department is in fact advisory. Strictly speaking, however, it is not the type of department the person is in charge of or its name that determines if the manager in charge is line or staff; it is the nature of the relationship. The line manager can issues orders. The staff manager can advise.

There is one exception. A staff manager may also have functional authority. **Functional authority** means that the staff manager can issue orders down the chain of command within the very narrow limits of his or her functional authority. For example, to protect the company from discrimination claims, the president might give the HR manager functional authority over personnel testing. The latter could order the production manager to use (or not use) a particular test. However, the HR manager would probably want to be diplomatic lest line-staff conflict emerge. **Line-staff conflict** is conflict between line and staff managers and typically arises when line managers feel staff managers are encroaching on their prerogatives.

Some small organizations use only line managers (they are line organizations), but most large ones have staff managers too—they are, therefore, line and staff organizations. Typical line positions include the CEO and the managers for sales and production. Typical staff positions include the managers for marketing research, accounting, security, quality control, legal affairs, and human resource management (HR).

Sources of Authority

One's authority—and the willingness of employees to follow the manager's orders—derives from several sources. First, authority derives in part from a person's rank or position. We saw that in corporations, the owner-stockholders delegate authority first to the board of directors, who then delegate to the CEO. The CEO of software manufacturer Intuit has more authority based on rank than does one of his senior vice presidents.

However, position authority is rarely enough to explain why people follow orders. Some managers have authority because of personal traits, such as intelligence or charisma. People follow their instructions because of the power of their personalities. Others have authority because they are experts in an area or have knowledge that requires others to depend on them.

Some astute management writers argue that, regardless of source, authority always depends on subordinates' acceptance of supervisors' orders. Management guru Chester Barnard was an early proponent of this view. He argued that for orders to be carried out, they must lie within a subordinate's "zone of acceptance"—in other words, they must be viewed as acceptable. Experts often argue that getting employees' acceptance is increasingly important today, given the emphasis on empowered workers and team-based organizations.

Delegating Authority

delegation: the act of passing down authority from supervisor to subordinate

Organizing would be impossible without **delegation**, which is the passing down of authority from supervisor to subordinate. The assignment of responsibility for some department or job traditionally goes hand in hand with the delegation of authority to get the job done.

A well-known management saying is, "You can delegate authority, but you cannot delegate responsibility." The CEO (or other manager) is ultimately responsible for whatever occurs on his or her watch. Because the person doing the delegating always retains the ultimate responsibility, delegation always entails the creation of accountability. Subordinates become accountable—or answerable—to the supervisor for the performance of the tasks assigned to them. The boss may fire or discipline the subordinate who fails to do the job. However, the boss is still responsible for all that goes wrong (or right).

Managers are people who get things done through others, and so knowing how to delegate is a crucial management skill. The Improving Your *Delegating* Skills feature illustrates how to do this.[25]

How to Decentralize

decentralized organization: an organization in which (1) authority for most departmental decisions is delegated to the department heads, while (2) control for major companywide decisions is maintained at headquarters

A **decentralized organization** is one in which (1) authority for most departmental decisions is delegated to the department heads, while (2) control for major companywide decisions is maintained at headquarters. Decentralizing should always represent a shrewd balance between delegated authority and top management's centralized control of essential functions. On the one hand, division managers get the autonomy and resources they need to service their customers. On the other hand, headquarters maintains essential control by centralizing major decisions regarding things like capital appropriations. Achieving this balance is an art. Here is how two famous management writers put this a number of years ago:

> [D]ecentralization cannot mean autonomy; in that it implies establishment of policies to guide decision-making along the desired courses, and in that . . . not being all abdication of responsibility, it must be accompanied by controls designed to ensure that delegated authority is used to further goals and plans. Although the art of authority delegation lies at the base of proper decentralization . . . it is apparent that the mere act of delegation is not enough to ensure decentralization.[26]

Departmentalization and Decentralization Managers most often use the term *decentralized* in conjunction with companies organized around product divisions. Managers of product divisions often run what amount to their own miniature companies (or business units). They have the authority to make most decisions having anything to do with their products, with little or no communication with the firm's CEO. However, the CEO retains authority over major decisions such as building a new plant. Remember, you can't have a properly decentralized company without effective, centralized controls.

Several years ago, accounting firm Arthur Andersen confronted just this sort of problem. Its Houston office wanted to take an aggressive approach to letting the energy trading company Enron account for some transactions. Andersen Worldwide had a special, centralized Professional Standards Group (PSG) at its Chicago headquarters that apparently told local Houston Andersen managers *not* to use the approach. It appears that someone at Andersen Houston may have approved

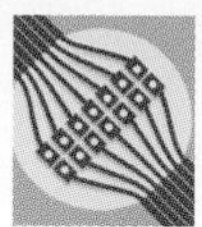

IMPROVING YOUR DELEGATING SKILLS

Suggestions for improving your delegating skills include:

Clarify the Assignment

Make it clear what you want the subordinate to accomplish, what results are expected, and when you want those results.

Delegate, Don't Abdicate

Shortly after assuming the CEO position at Motorola, (former) CEO Chris Galvin sat in on several meetings with the company's Europe mobile phone group. Galvin knew that Europeans preferred light, inexpensive phones, so he asked if the market data supported the idea that the relatively heavy phone they were working on would appeal to customers. The manager said yes, and that's reportedly where Galvin left it. The product subsequently failed.[27] The moral is this: Giving a person a job to do and not following up is abdication, not delegation.

Know What to Delegate

Larry Bossidy, the executive who turned AlliedSignal around and helped it merge with Honeywell, says there is "one job no CEO should delegate—finding and developing great leaders."[28] In Bossidy's case, finding and developing great leaders was the "one job no CEO should delegate." For a manager in a different company and at a different level, there will be other tasks that he or she cannot (or should not) delegate to a subordinate.

Specify the Subordinate's Range of Discretion

The manager can use two guidelines here. First, the manager should give the subordinate enough authority to do the task successfully, but not so much that the person's actions can have adverse effects outside the areas for which the manager has made the person responsible (such as bankrupting the company). Second, the subordinate should know when to check with the manager. One typical set of options the manager can apply is: (1) wait to be told what to do; (2) ask what to do; (3) act, then report results immediately; and (4) take action, and report periodically.

Authority Should Equal Responsibility

A basic principle of management is that authority should equal responsibility. The person should have enough authority to accomplish the task.

Make the Person Accountable for Results

There must be predictable and acceptable measures of results.

Beware of Backward Delegation

A famous *Harvard Business Review* article entitled "Who's Got the Monkey?" explains what happens to an unsuspecting manager whose subordinate comes into his office to discuss a problem. The subordinate says, "I have a problem with the job you gave me to do." After a few minutes of discussion, the manager, pressed for time, says, "I'll handle it." Like a monkey, the job has jumped from the subordinate's to the unsuspecting manager's shoulders. The point is, beware of backward delegation. When your subordinate says the task isn't working out as planned, suggest some solutions or insist that your subordinate take the initiative in solving the problem.

the transaction anyway, with disastrous results for Andersen Worldwide. Managers at Andersen Worldwide had delegated most decisions to its branches, with the understanding that the branches would abide by the PSG's centralized oversight and control. In this case, those controls broke down. Local managers overrode the PSG's decision. Andersen was out of business within two years.

● **Why Decentralize?** In a famous study of how companies grow, historian Alfred Chandler coined the phrase, "Structure follows strategy." He found, for example, that a diversification strategy at firms like General Electric (GE) led to multiple product lines for these firms. This meant that GE's top managers had to manage an increasingly diverse range of products and an increasingly diverse range of customers. Having to deal with so many products and customers made the firm's original functional structures obsolete. At Westinghouse:

> All of the activities of the company were [originally] divided into production, engineering, and sales, each of which was the responsibility of a vice president. The domain of each vice president covered the whole diversified and far-flung operations of the corporation. Such an organization of the corporation's management lacks responsiveness. There was too much delay in the recognition of problems and in the solution of problems after they were recognized.[29]

Chandler found that these companies therefore decentralized. After diversifying, they established product divisions for different product lines like light bulbs, engines, and power plants. The managers of these units then got the authority to run them as self-contained, relatively autonomous units. In practice, most managers decentralize because they want faster decisions.[30]

What to Decentralize The knack is in knowing which decisions to centralize—and which to decentralize. One rule is this: decentralize decisions that will affect just that one division or area and that would take a great deal of time for you to make. Centralize decisions that could adversely affect the entire firm and that you can make yourself fairly quickly and easily.

Cirque du Soleil, producer of international traveling circuses, is a good example of decentralization. Cirque du Soleil's headquarters are in Montreal, with offices in Amsterdam, Las Vegas, and Singapore. Its 2,100 employees worldwide come from forty different countries. Two-thirds of the employees work outside Montreal, in simultaneous, multiple tours.

Cirque du Soleil's 2,100 employees worldwide come from forty different countries.

Each tour is like a separate, small-town circus. Everyone works for Cirque du Soleil, but most of the employees travel with the local, geographic-division tours. Management delegates decisions for matters like human resources to the separate tour managers because employment law, for example, can vary drastically from country to country. It would take days for headquarters managers to make decisions like that. Management centralizes other decisions, for instance, regarding major investments. The company maintains a sense of unity and coordination through its strong culture of shared values. It posts jobs on the Internet, and employees write the company newspaper.

Recentralizing Because information technology in the form of PDAs, cell phones, and enterprise and other software makes it easier for managers to monitor remote operations, there has recently been some movement from decentralizing back to centralizing organizations. Saks Inc. recently centralized its cosmetics-buying functions, which had previously been conducted in three locations.[31] Recently, Home Depot announced it would centralize its three U.S. divisional offices into the firm's Atlanta headquarters. Home Depot's vice presidents and support staff would stay in the firm's Southern, Northern, and Western division locations, but the division presidents relocated to Atlanta.[32] Home Depot's centralization follows a gradual consolidation over the past few years, with Home Depot reducing geographic store division offices from nine to three.[33] China Unicom, the second largest mobile operator in China, recently centralized the management of its international businesses.[34]

By the way, don't let the Home Depot example fool you into thinking that the only way to centralize is to bring far-flung units back to headquarters. Decentralization and centralization are mainly about authority—about where decsions get made. Lots of geographically disbursed companies, like BP and some other giant oil firms, are actually quite centralized. Although they have geographic units spread around the world, their big decisions are made back at headquarters.

Managers often call the centralized departments they create shared-services departments. For example, Warner Music might establish several freestanding music labels, but a single, centralized, shared-services legal affairs department will do all the labels' contracts.

● Managing Now: Recentralizing New information systems make it easier for companies to recentralize. For example, for many years, 7-Eleven decentralized its purchasing. Each regional area used its own software package and made its own purchases. As one 7-Eleven manager said, "[T]here was no consistent process, so different departments used separate access databases and had separate vendor files for each system."[35] Upgrading all the regions to a common Oracle Procurement and Sourcing software package enabled 7-Eleven to centralize its purchasing by giving the central purchasing department real-time information on each store's product needs. The software package even automates the bidding process, thus ensuring that 7-Eleven receives the best bids possible from qualified suppliers.

Delegating authority results in a chain of command. The manager needs to decide whether that chain or hierarchy should be flat or tall. We look at this decision next.

The Span of Control

span of control: the number of subordinates reporting directly to a supervisor

The **span of control** is the number of subordinates reporting directly to a supervisor. In the country-based geographic organization shown in Figure 10.8, the span of control of the country general manager is thirteen: there are six business managers, five directors, one innovation manager, and one manufacturing manager.

The average number of people reporting to a manager determines how many management levels the company will have. For example, if a company with sixty-four workers to supervise has an average span of control of eight, then there will be eight supervisors directing the workers and (because the eight supervisors need their own supervisor) one manager directing the eight supervisors (a flat organization). However, if the span of control were only four, then supervising the same number of workers would require sixteen supervisors. And because every four supervisors needs their own supervisor, the sixteen supervisors would, in turn, be directed by four managers. These four managers would, in turn, be directed by one manager (a tall organization).

Tall Versus Flat Organizations

Classic management theorists said that tall organizational structures (with narrow spans of control) improved performance by guaranteeing close supervision. The thinking was that having six to eight subordinates was ideal. Beyond that it became difficult to closely monitor and control what subordinates do. The counterargument is that flat is better: flat means wide spans, which means less meddling with (and a more motivational experience for) subordinates.

FIGURE 10.8

Spans of Control in Country-Based Organization

In this chart, the span of control of the general manager is thirteen—six business managers, five directors, one innovation manager, and one manufacturing manager.

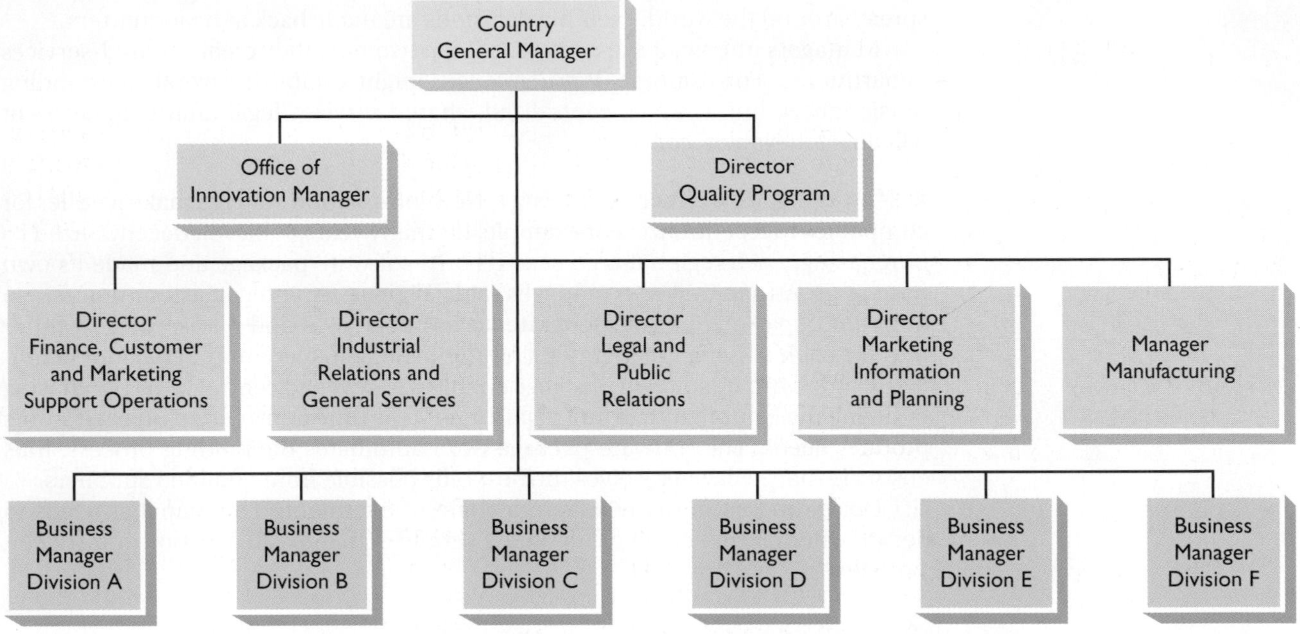

There are other arguments, pro and con. A tall chain of command may also slow decisions by forcing each decision to pass through more people at more levels. Several weeks after the United States began bombing Afghanistan in 2001, reporters asked then-Secretary of Defense Rumsfeld if having several layers of officers making tactical decisions about the ground attacks was slowing the ground forces' responsiveness. (His answer was no.)

The consensus today seems to be that flat is better.[36] For one thing, flattening cuts out levels and managers, and to that extent, it may save the company money and reduce the number of approvals required to make a decision. There is also the belief that eliminating layers pushes the point at which decisions are made closer to the customer because there's less reason to check first with the boss. Having wider spans also implies that the supervisor monitors his or her subordinates less, which makes particular sense today, with the trend toward highly trained and empowered employees.

The classic flattening example occurred some years ago. GE's CEO at the time, Jack Welch, had climbed the ranks and believed GE's chain of command was draining the firm of creativity and responsiveness. Business heads needed approval from the headquarters staff for almost every big decision they made. In one case, the light bulb business managers spent $30,000 producing a video to demonstrate the need for some production equipment they wanted to buy.

First, Welch eliminated redundant organizational levels. Before he took over, "GE's business heads reported to a group head, who reported to a sector head, who reported to the CEO. Each level had its own staff in finance, marketing, and planning, checking and double-checking each business."[37] Welch disbanded the group and the sector levels, thus dramatically flattening the organizational chain of command. When Welch was done, no one stood between the business heads and the CEO's office. He created a leaner, more responsive organization.

Organizing to Manage Change

A recent *BusinessWeek* article said, "[I]f [businesses] are to thrive in this hypercompetitive environment, they must innovate more and faster."[38] And to innovate faster and faster, they need organization structures that enable managers to make decisions faster. So, for example, Microsoft recently reorganized around three core divisions—Platform Products & Services, Business, and Entertainment & Devices—and eliminated several management levels. Microsoft's stated purpose was to "speed decision-making."[39] Also to speed decision making, Home Depot, as we saw, consolidated its divisions, thus reducing store division offices from nine to three, and then centralized its three remaining U.S. divisional offices in Atlanta.[40] If H&M sees a new clothing design is doing well, it can get variations of that style into its stores in three weeks, while traditional retailers typically take ten months. H&M's chief executive says, "Speed is important. You need to have the systems where you can react in a short lead time to [provide] the right products."[41]

To appreciate why rapid change is causing managers to replace traditional structures with more responsive ones, it is useful to understand the factors that influence how companies organize. Two studies help to explain this phenomenon. We briefly look at these, and then turn to modern organizations.

Organization and Environment: The Burns and Stalker Studies

Researchers Tom Burns and G. M. Stalker studied about twenty industrial firms in the United Kingdom a number of years ago. Their purpose was to determine how the nature of the firm's environment affected the way the firm was organized and managed.[42] Their findings continue to provide insight into how managers organize.

Burns and Stalker concluded that to be successful, a rayon manufacturer they studied had to be highly efficient. Its existence therefore depended on keeping unexpected occurrences to a minimum and maintaining steady, high-volume production runs. Burns and Stalker found that the rayon mill's organizational structure reflected this stable, unchanging environment and emphasis on efficiency. The organization was a "pyramid of knowledge": top management made most decisions and communicated them downward. Decision making in the plant was highly centralized. Everyone from the top of the organization to the bottom had a very specialized job to do.[43] Coordination was achieved via the chain of command.

In contrast, Burns and Stalker found that innovation was the big challenge the electronics firms they studied faced. Their survival depended on continually introducing innovative electronic components. They had to be alert and watch for innovations by their competitors. Responsiveness, creativity, and quick learning (rather than efficiency) were paramount here. Here, Burns and Stalker found very different organizational structures. There was a "deliberate attempt to avoid specifying individual tasks."[44] Each worker's job might change daily as employees rushed to respond to the problem of the day. Most important, all employees shared common beliefs and goals, and these common goals (such as "let's make sure we produce only first-rate products") helped ensure they all could work together with little or no guidance. When a problem arose, employees took the initiative to solve it. This often meant bypassing the formal chain of command.

Mechanistic and Organic Organizations Their findings led Burns and Stalker to distinguish between two types of organizations, which they called mechanistic and organic. The rayon firm was typical of mechanistic, classical organizations. The electronics firms were typical of the organic, behavioral ones. In terms of organizational structure, we can summarize the Burns and Stalker findings as follows:

- *Lines of authority.* In mechanistic organizations, the lines of authority are clear, and everyone adheres to the chain of command. In organic organizations, employees' jobs are always changing, and the lines of authority are not so clear. There is less emphasis on sticking to the chain of command in organic organizations. Employees simply speak directly with the person who can answer the problem.
- *Departmentalization.* In mechanistic organizations (with their emphasis on efficiency), functional departmentalization prevails. In organic organizations (where flexibility is the rule), product/divisional departmentalization prevails.
- *Degree of specialization.* In mechanistic organizations, each employee has a highly specialized job. In organic organizations, job enlargement is the rule.
- *Degree of decentralization.* Mechanistic organizations centralize most important decisions. Lower-level employees in organic organizations tend to make more important decisions; these firms are more decentralized.
- *Span of control.* The span of control is narrow in mechanistic organizations, and there is close supervision. Spans are wider in organic organizations, and supervision is more general.
- *Type of coordination.* Managers tend to achieve coordination by sticking to the chain of command in mechanistic organizations. In fast-changing organic organizations, there is more emphasis on committees and cross-functional liaisons. Table 10.1 summarizes the features of mechanistic and organic organizations.

Organization and Technology: The Woodward Studies

British researcher Joan Woodward's contribution lies in her discovery that a firm's production technology (the processes it uses to produce its products or services) affects the way management should organize the firm. Woodward's team analyzed each company's history, size, and policies and procedures.[45] None of these factors explained why some successful firms had classic, mechanistic structures while others had behavioral, organic ones. Finally, Woodward's team decided to classify the companies according to their production technologies, as follows:

1. Unit and small-batch production companies produced one-at-a-time prototypes and specialized custom units made to customers' requirements (like fine pianos). They had to be very responsive to customer needs.

TABLE 10.1
Burns and Stalker's Approach to Organizing

Characteristic	Mechanistic Type of Organization	Organic Type of Organization
Type of environment	Stable	Rapid change
Comparable to . . .	Classical organization	Behavioral organization: emphasis on self-control
Adherence to chain of command	Firm	Flexible—chain of command often bypassed
Type of departmentalization	Functional	Divisional
How specialized are jobs?	Specialized	Jobs change daily, with situation
Degree of decentralization	Decision making centralized	Decision making decentralized
Span of control	Narrow	Wide
Type of coordination and communication	Rules; chain of command	Committees, liaisons, and special integrators; networking

2. Large-batch and mass production companies produced large batches of products on assembly lines (like cars). Here, efficiency was crucial.
3. Process production companies produced products such as paper and petroleum products through continuously running facilities. Here, highly trained technicians had to be ready to respond at a moment's notice to production emergencies, because shutdowns were enormously costly.

Once Woodward classified the firms, it became clear that a different type of organizational structure was appropriate for each type of technology (see Table 10.2). Note that both unit and process production firms tended to have organic structures. Mass production firms usually had mechanistic structures.

In terms of organizational structure, we can summarize the Woodward findings as follows:

- *Lines of authority.* The lines of authority and adherence to the chain of command are rigid in mass production firms, but they are more informal and flexible in unit and process production firms.
- *Departmentalization.* There is a functional departmentalization in mass production firms and a product type of departmentalization in unit and process production firms.
- *Degree of specialization.* Jobs are highly specialized in mass production firms and less so in unit and process production firms.
- *Delegation and decentralization.* Organizations tend to be centralized in mass production firms and decentralized in unit and process production firms.
- *Span of control.* Unit and process production firms have smaller supervisory-level spans of control than do mass production firms.

TABLE 10.2
Summary of Woodward's Research Findings*

Organizational Feature	Unit and Small-Batch Firms (Example: Custom-Built Cars)	Large-Batch and Mass Production (Example: Mass-Produced Cars)	Process Production (Example: Oil Refinery)
Chain of command	Not clear	Clear	Not clear
Span of control	Narrow	Wide	Narrow
Departmentalization	Product	Function	Product
Overall organization	Organic	Mechanistic	Organic
Specialization of jobs	Low	High	Low

*Summary of findings showing how production technology and organizational structure are related.

A Contingency Approach to Organizing

The studies discussed above demonstrate that different organizational structures are appropriate for, or contingent on, different tasks. At one extreme are organizations where efficiency is supreme. Successful organizations here tend to be mechanistic. They stress adherence to rules and to the chain of command; are highly centralized; and have a more specialized, functional departmentalization.

At the other extreme are companies where innovation is supreme. Here, management must emphasize creativity and entrepreneurial activities. To encourage these activities, such organizations tend to be organic. Managers don't encourage employees to stick to the chain of command. Decision making is pushed down closer to the customers (it is more decentralized), and jobs and departments are less specialized.

How Managers Streamline Their Companies

As globalized competition became more pronounced in the 1990s, CEOs began taking steps to streamline their organizations. Their dual aims were to eliminate waste and to boost responsiveness. The effects were twofold: streamlining reduced costs and made the firms more efficient (for instance, by reducing the workforce). And the streamlining made the companies more responsive (for instance, by cutting out management layers). Downsizing was often the method they chose. **Downsizing** means dramatically reducing a company's workforce. This method probably did reduce costs. However, downsizing can and often does have negative consequences, particularly among those employees and their families who end up without a job.

downsizing: dramatically reducing a company's workforce

Other techniques the CEOs used included the following.

Reduce Layers of Management Reducing management layers is one method managers use to streamline and prepare their companies to better respond to change. The assumption, often correct, is that cutting out management layers puts the decision-making employee closer to the customer, where he or she can make a fast decision without having to "check with the boss." The railroad company CSX recently reduced its layers of management from eleven to "no more than eight," in order to create what its CEO called a more responsive, streamlined company.[46]

● **Establish Mini-Units** Many managers split their companies into smaller minicompanies. Intuit broke the company into separate businesses, each with its own general manager and mission. Hal Rosenbluth broke his company into more than 100 farmlike business units, each focused on special regions and clients. In this way, everyone knew everyone else. Layers of management weren't required for approving decisions. Interactions and communications were more frequent.

● **Reassign Support Staff** Many firms also moved headquarters staff (such as industrial engineers) out of headquarters and reassigned them to their business units. For example, candy maker Mars Inc. is a $7 billion company with only a three-person headquarters staff. Mars does have staff employees, but the staff employees are assigned directly to the individual business units. Here, they can help their business units address customer needs rather than act as gatekeepers to check and reject divisional managers' plans.

● **Widen Spans of Control and Empower Employees** Squeezing out management layers results in wider spans of control, as we saw. If the supervisors are not there to supervise, who makes the decisions? The answer is the employees themselves: they are *empowered.* For example, when a new CEO took over at Pratt & Whitney's engine division, airlines were threatening to stop buying Pratt engines unless they got faster responses to their complaints. The new CEO boosted the number of service representatives in the field and then gave them authority to approve multimillion-dollar warranty replacements on the spot. Customers were impressed. Pratt & Whitney quickly turned around.[47]

Modern Organizations

As we saw in Chapter 1, things change fast in business today. After about one year in business, Friendster.com, the social networking site, had about one million unique visitors per month. Introduced a year later, myspace.com went from nothing to fourteen million visitors per month. Amazon (fearing Google's new Froogle shopping site) introduced a new search engine. Then Google introduced Gmail to lure surfers from Yahoo and Microsoft and bought YouTube.

Increasingly today, steps such as downsizing, widening spans of control, or establishing mini-units are not enough. Things are changing too fast, and companies have to be too entrepreneurial. Managers are therefore organizing around *teams, networks,* and *horizontal* and *federal*-type structures to better respond to and manage change. We'll discuss each of these four new structures in this final section. The Improving Your *Boundary-Managing* Skills feature explains one skill managers need when managing these new kinds of organizations.

Building Team-Based Organizations

team: a group of people who work together and share a common objective

Most firms today organize some or all of their activities around self-managing teams. A **team** is a group of people who work together and share a common objective.

For example, at Johnsonville Sausage Company in Wisconsin, the CEO organized most of the plant's activities around self-managing, twelve-person work

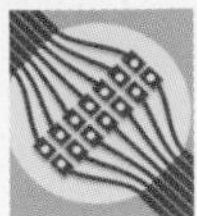

Improving Your *Boundary-Managing* Skills

Finding ways to cut across traditional departmental boundaries is at the heart of the team, network, and federal organizations we discuss in this section. For example, if employees are unwilling or afraid to speak their minds, the open communication that teamwork requires is impossible to obtain.

Traditional departmentalized organizations have four main "boundaries." First, vertically, the chain of command creates *authority* boundaries. The president supervises the vice president, who supervises the managers, and so on. Subordinates are often reluctant to pass bad news on to their bosses. Second are *departmental* boundaries. Each department has its own specialized responsibilities. There is often minimal interdepartmental communication, as if employees work in what amount to separate "silos."[48] Third, each employee tends to focus on doing his or her own narrow job, which creates what some experts call a *task boundary.* An employee might say, "No, that's not my job," for instance.[49] Finally, each department also typically has its own *political* agenda. For example, manufacturing, wanting to boost efficiency, resists last-minute orders, while sales wants to accept them.

These boundaries inhibit communication and decisions and make modern, team-based, networked organizations impossible. A **boundaryless organization** is one in which the widespread use of teams, networks, and similar structures requires that the boundaries that typically separate organizational functions and hierarchical levels be reduced.[50]

Other than being aware of the boundaries, there are no magic bullets for solving them. Reducing authority boundaries requires that managers encourage and welcome honest advice and feedback from subordinates. Reducing departmental and political boundaries requires training and then rewarding employees for putting the company's needs first. Reducing the task ("It's not my job") mentality requires clamping down at the first signs of such behavior and rewarding publicly those who willingly assume additional responsibilities.

teams. Its organization chart would show primarily teams, rather than departments. Some of the teams are responsible for maintaining the firm's packaging equipment, for instance. These self-managing teams are empowered. The employees manage themselves and make fast, on-the-spot decisions. For example, duties of a typical Johnsonville team include:

- Recruit, hire, evaluate, and fire (as necessary)
- Formulate, then track and amend, its own budget
- Handle quality-control inspections, subsequent troubleshooting, and problem solving
- Develop and monitor quantitative standards for productivity and quality
- Suggest and develop prototypes of possible new products and packaging[51]

Part of a twelve-person team at the Johnsonville Sausage plant.

Teams like these bring a double-barreled benefit to the company. Having one team of multitalented workers do all the work required to complete a task eliminates the sorts of error-laden interdepartmental handoffs that normally waste time and cause defects. And empowering team members to supervise themselves can boost efficiency and motivation.

boundaryless organization: an organization in which the widespread use of teams, networks, and similar structures requires that the boundaries that typically separate organizational functions and hierarchical levels be reduced

● **Nature of Team-Based Organizations**[52] Managers traditionally organized their companies with departments as their basic work units. This is evident in a typical organization chart. Such a chart might show, for example, separate boxes for each functional department, down to separate tasks for individual workers at the bottom of the chart.

In team-based organizations, the team is the basic work unit. A typical Toyota plant may have 300 employees and only two or three managers. Each work team is responsible for a body of work such as installing dashboards or maintaining robots. The teams generally supervise themselves.

● **Designing Organizations to Support Teams**[53] Creating a team-based organization requires first instituting the supporting mechanisms that will help the team approach flourish. Experience suggests that these supporting mechanisms include the right philosophy, structure, systems, skills, and policies (see Figure 10.9).

● **Organizational Philosophy** Team-based companies like Saturn and Toyota emphasize values such as "people can be trusted to make important decisions about their work activities." They are characterized by high employee involvement and trust.

● **Organizational Structure** In team-based companies, teams, not departments, are the basic work units. The teams supervise themselves, for instance, scheduling overtime and hiring employees. The organization chart would show primarily teams, rather than departments. These firms have relatively few supervisors and delegate much decision making to the teams.

● **Organizational Systems** Every company depends on standard operating systems or ways of doing things to make things go smoothly. These range from performance appraisal and incentive plans to systems for hiring employees. Organizing around teams requires making the firm's systems and practices compatible with the

FIGURE 10.9

Designing Organizations to Manage Teams

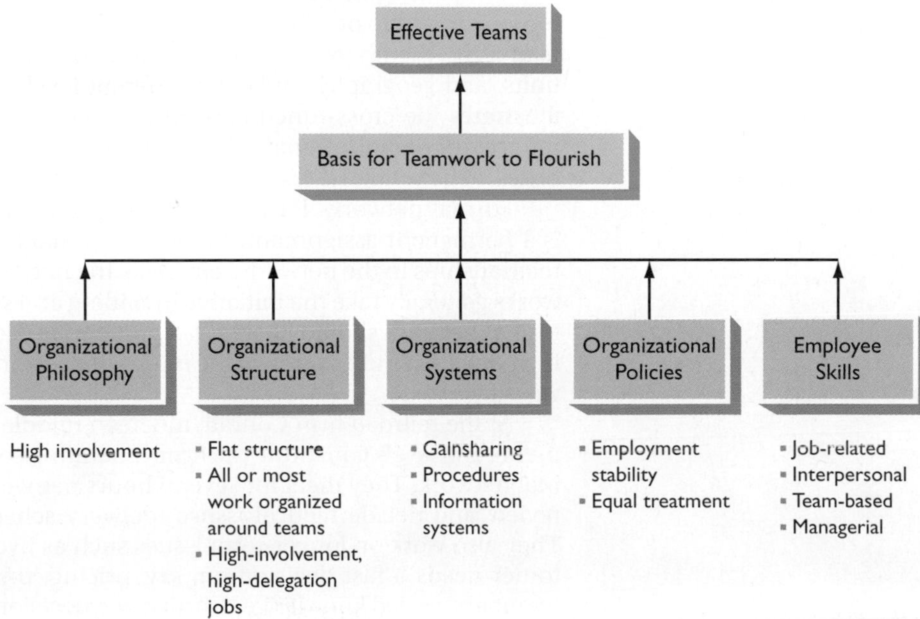

SOURCE: Adapted from James H. Shonk, *Team-Based Organizations* (Homewood, Ill.: Irwin, 1997), p. 36.

team approach. For example, managers often pay financial incentives to the team as a whole rather than to individual employees, to encourage team solidarity.

Organizational Policies Similarly, the company's policies should support the philosophy of empowerment, involvement, and trust that teamwork depends on. For example, in plants like those run by Toyota, equal-treatment policies (such as no reserved parking spaces and minimal status differences in offices and dress) foster a sense of teamwork.

Employee Skills To manage themselves, team members need various decision-making and communications skills.

Network-Based Organizations

organizational network: a system of interconnected or cooperating individuals

Many firms today superimpose organizational networks over their existing structures. An **organizational network** is a system of interconnected or cooperating individuals. Networks enhance the likelihood that the work of even remote units will be carried out promptly and in a coordinated way if quick decisions on some matters must be made.

To put networking's benefits into perspective, consider downloading a song. One option is to methodically check one's friends. Going one by one, we might find our song after seventeen calls. Our other option is to enter one of the new legal variants of the Napster-type online networks. Here, with everyone's record files shared, we instantly find our song. Putting everyone in contact with everyone else expedites solutions.

Whether formal or informal, organizational networks share the same basic idea: to link selected employees from various departments, levels, and geographic areas so that they can communicate quickly and without barriers across normal organizational boundaries. We describe three types of networks: formal organizational networks, informal organizational networks, and electronic information networks.

Formal Organizational Networks A formal organizational network is "a recognized group of managers assembled by the CEO and the senior management team. The members are drawn from across the company's functions, business units, and geography, and from different levels of the hierarchy."[54] Figure 10.10 illustrates the cross-functional, cross-level nature of formal networks. Note the number of organizational levels and the departments represented by the yellow boxes. (The yellow boxes represent the formal network's members.)

Formal networks have several characteristics.[55] First, network membership is a permanent assignment. In fact, each manager's continuing experience and relationships in the network help make the network effective. Second, formal networks generally take the initiative in finding and solving problems. Third, having a formal network should change how the top manager does things.[56] For example, the network handles more of the interunit coordinating that the CEO might otherwise have to do.

At the railroad firm Conrail, nineteen middle managers from various departments and levels constitute the firm's operating committee, which is actually a formal network. They meet for several hours per week, on an as-needed basis. They review and decide tactical issues (delivery schedules and prices, for instance). They also work on longer-term issues such as five-year business plans.[57] If a customer needs a fast decision on, say, pricing, this team can quickly draw on its members' varied knowledge to arrive at a decision.

FIGURE 10.10

How Networks Reshape Organizations

The members of a formal network may be selected from various departments and organizational levels.

SOURCE: From "How Networks Reshape Organziations—For Results," by Ram Charan, *Harvard Business Review*, September–October 1991. Copyright ©1991 by the President and Fellows of Harvard College; all rights reserved. Reprinted by permission of Harvard Business School Publishing.

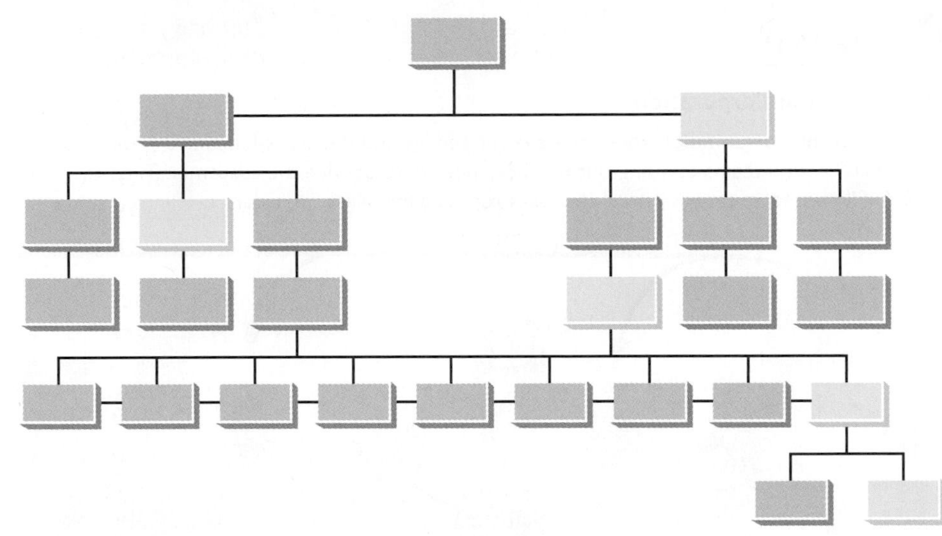

informal organizational networks: networks that consist of cooperating individuals who are interconnected only informally

● **Informal Organizational Networks** Many companies cultivate informal organizational networks. **Informal organizational networks** consist of cooperating individuals who are interconnected only informally. They share information and help solve each other's problems based on their personal knowledge of each other's expertise. The idea is that if a problem arises in one location, the manager can informally network with colleagues at other locations to solve it.

In encouraging informal networks to form, the CEO's main job is to create the conditions that enable managers around the world to meet and to build mutual trust.[58] Executive development programs are one way to do this. For example, both Philips and Shell bring managers from around the world to work together in training centers in New York and London. Moving managers from office to office around the world is another tactic. The transferees can build lasting relationships around the globe. In one firm, for instance:

> [International mobility] has created what one might call a "nervous system" that facilitates both corporate strategic control and the flow of information throughout the firm. Widespread transfers have created an informal information network, a superior degree of communication and mutual understanding between headquarters and subsidiaries and between subsidiaries themselves. . . ."[59]

● **Managing Now: Electronic Networking** Information technology, including the Internet, e-mail, videoconferencing, PDAs, and collaborative computing software, lets companies better utilize formal and informal networks. For example, a new service from Airena, a Web service and mobile phone company, lets users in small companies do group scheduling and organizing via their mobile phones.[60] For larger firms, group decision support systems packages (like Lotus Notes) provide another tool.[61] For example, IBM's Lotus Sametime IM provides instant messaging capabilities to remote network members.[62] The *OneSpace* system is another example. It allows product design teams "to collaborate over the Internet and across firewalls in real-time by working directly on the 3D solid model. . . ."[63] Hewlett-Packard's new life-size Halo Collaboration Studio makes the people "on the other side of the table" at a videoconference look as if they're actually there.

FIGURE 10.11

The Horizontal Corporation

In the horizontal organization, the work is organized around the cross-functional processes, with multifunction teams carrying out the tasks needed to service the customer. Thus, the sales fulfillment team carries out all the tasks required for billing an order.

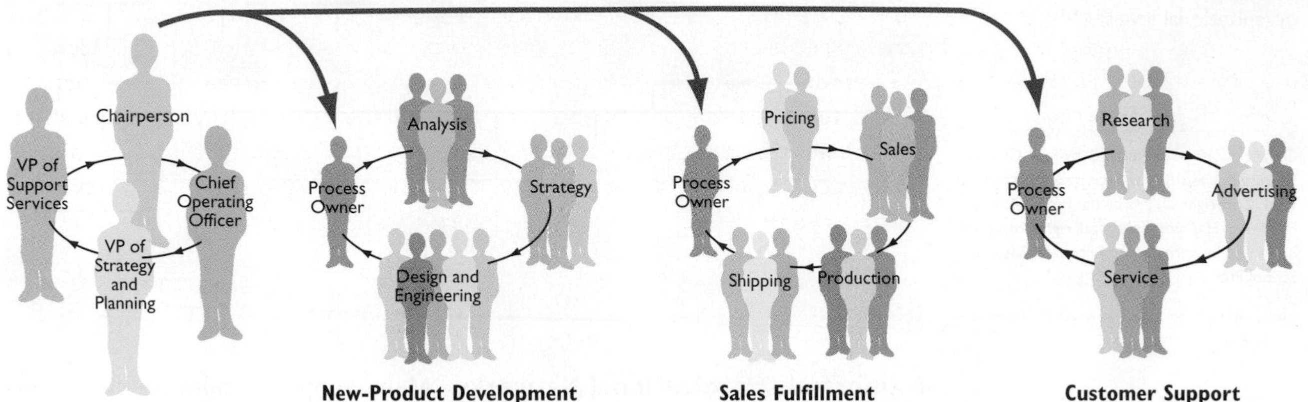

SOURCE: Adapted from John A. Byrne, "The Horizontal Corporation," *BusinessWeek*, 20 December 1993, p. 80.

The Horizontal Organization

horizontal organization: an organization built around multidisciplinary teams, each of which performs a process such as loan approval, sales fulfillment, or customer support; instead of being designed around departments, the processes and the teams performing each process become the basic units of work

The **horizontal organization** is an organization built around multidisciplinary teams, each of which performs a process such as loan approval, sales fulfillment, or customer support. Instead of being designed around departments, the processes and the teams performing each process become the basic units of work. Each team is comprised of several functional specialists. They work together on those teams to carry out the process team's activities (as illustrated in Figure 10.11).[64] Once these process teams are in place and performing, the firm eliminates the departments, levels, and staff that do not directly contribute to the work of the process-oriented teams.

Why Horizontal Organizations? Many firms found that downsizing did not change the way their departments did their work. The firms had fewer employees. However, the work itself was still handled like a relay race. For example, at Ryder Corporation, doing the paperwork for leasing a truck required as many as seventeen handoffs, as the documents made their way from one department to another, such as credit checking, truck valuation, and loan approval. The time and effort wasted were enormous. Errors invariably occurred. So, instead of having the truck-leasing process weave its way through several departments, Ryder created a vehicle-leasing process team. This team combined in one place employees with all the functional specialties needed to approve a lease. That way, this new process-oriented team could quickly approve or reject a lease application.

business process reengineering: redesigning business processes, usually by combining steps so that small multifunction process teams use information technology to do the jobs formerly done by a sequence of departments

Creating horizontal organizations requires *business process reengineering.* **Business process reengineering** means redesigning business processes, usually by combining steps so that small multifunction process teams use information technology to do the jobs formerly done by a sequence of departments. We'll discuss how to do this in Chapter 11, but the Window on Managing Now feature provides one example.

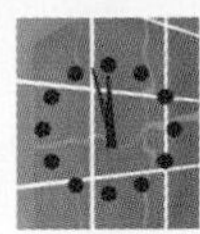

Window on Managing Now
Brady Corp.

Brady Corp., which manufactures identification and safety products, allocated about $50 million to install a new system that will link Brady's suppliers, customers, and distributors over the Internet. However, only about one-third of that money was for the technology. Top management spent the rest on reengineering the firm's organization and processes around team-based horizontal processes.

For example, Brady customer-service employees used to get the orders and pass them on to the firm's production department. The physical orders would then move on to shipping. It was like a relay race. With Brady's new organization, customers with simple orders will send them online directly to manufacturing. In manufacturing, Brady will have a horizontal process. One factory-floor person will oversee the entire production and shipping process for each order. Management expects the new horizontal organization to cut about five steps out of the current fifteen-step sale-manufacturing-shipping process. Brady's new horizontal organization will help it capitalize on its new online, direct customer-to-company information technology system. Without reengineering, Brady would have had its new online ordering system, but the orders would still have been done the old, time-consuming way, from department to department.

Federal Organizations

federal organization: an organization in which power is distributed between a central unit and a number of constituents, but the central unit's authority is intentionally limited

In a **federal organization**, highly autonomous but still company-owned units develop their own products and have the option of collaborating with sister companies under the very loose direction and control of the parent firm's central management.[65] The federal approach lets the parent company tap and hopefully capitalize on the creativity and entrepreneurial spirit of its small, self-managed units.

Some big record labels are run as federal organizations. The parent label, like Sony-EMI, finances people who have successful track records in music to set up their own music labels, and these entrepreneurs then run their firms under the parent firm's umbrella. The parent firm then provides services (such as HR and legal support). The labels are free to work with other labels within Sony-EMI, while the parent firm provides minimal oversight. Virtual organizations, as we describe next, are one modern federal-type example.

Managing Now: Virtual Organizations

virtual organization: a temporary network of independent companies—suppliers, customers, perhaps even rivals—linked by information technology in order to share skills, costs, and access to one another's markets

Sometimes, a company has to marshal resources to accomplish some big project but can't afford the time or expense of acquiring and owning those resources itself. A **virtual organization** is "a temporary network of independent companies—suppliers, customers, perhaps even rivals—linked by information technology to share skills, costs, and access to one another's markets."[66]

Virtual organizations (or virtual corporations) are networks comprised of partner companies. Each company or entity brings to the virtual corporation its special expertise. Information technology—the Internet, cell phones, group decision-making software, and fax, for instance—makes the virtual organization possible by linking each independent entity with the rest.

Some virtual companies are among the biggest in their industries. For example, CorpHQ utilizes a network of professional service providers rather than employees to provide business-consulting services to industry. Its CEO says, "[O]ur virtual organization allows us to utilize the skills and experience of a wide range of business consultants. . . ."[67]

Virtual organizations enable some small businesses to undertake projects they would not otherwise be able to. For example, Indigo Partners (www.indi[illegible]),

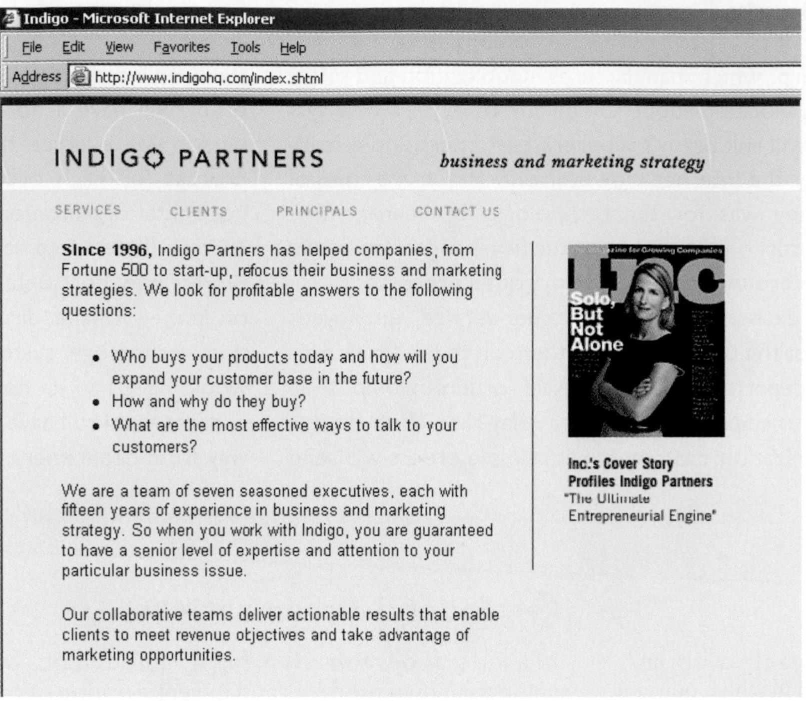
Indigo - Microsoft Internet Explorer
File Edit View Favorites Tools Help
Address http://www.indigohq.com/index.shtml

INDIGO PARTNERS business and marketing strategy

SERVICES CLIENTS PRINCIPALS CONTACT US

Since 1996, Indigo Partners has helped companies, from Fortune 500 to start-up, refocus their business and marketing strategies. We look for profitable answers to the following questions:

- Who buys your products today and how will you expand your customer base in the future?
- How and why do they buy?
- What are the most effective ways to talk to your customers?

We are a team of seven seasoned executives, each with fifteen years of experience in business and marketing strategy. So when you work with Indigo, you are guaranteed to have a senior level of expertise and attention to your particular business issue.

Our collaborative teams deliver actionable results that enable clients to meet revenue objectives and take advantage of marketing opportunities.

Inc.'s Cover Story Profiles Indigo Partners
"The Ultimate Entrepreneurial Engine"

SOURCE: http://www.indigohq.com

begun about ten years ago by Jennifer Overholt, Anne Murguia, and A. C. Ross, is an informal support group for marketing consultants. Indigo's projects range from market analyses for *Fortune* 500 companies to revising business plans for start-ups.[68]

Indigo Partners is a virtual company. It has no headquarters office. The firm's six partners work on projects individually or in small teams. For large projects, they tap online into a pool of specialized freelancers. Thanks to Indigo, these freelancers bid on big jobs, knowing they can tap the sum total of all the other Indigo freelancers' knowledge and expertise. At the same time, the virtual-organization arrangement frees them from having to manage bricks-and-mortar assets like an office.

Learning Organizations

learning organizations: organizations that have the capacity to adapt to unforeseen situations, to learn from their own experiences, to shift their shared mindsets, and to change more quickly

One reason companies downsize, network, and reengineer is so that they can become better at learning what new products competitors are introducing, what new services customers want, and what new technologies may render their own services obsolete.[69] **Learning organizations** are any organizations that have "the capacity to adapt to unforeseen situations, to learn from their own experiences, to shift their shared mindsets, and to change more quickly, broadly, and deeply than ever before."[70] When Microsoft reorganized into three core divisions and eliminated management levels, it did so in part to make sure it remained a learning organization.

If you looked at their organization charts and how they did things, learning organizations generally share the characteristics that we described in the last few pages. To speed up decision making, management starts by downsizing, reducing management layers, and empowering employees. It then creates networks and encourages employees to think outside the boundaries of their own jobs.

However, organizing is not enough to make a company a learning organization. Two more things are required. First, the company provides special knowledge-management tools. For example, Xerox gives its repair personnel laptop computers and encourages them to digitize and share knowledge and ideas for solving repair problems.

Second, management cultivates its employees' "personal mastery." This means management ensures that employees have both the capacity and willingness to learn and to share ideas. Steps here include:

- *Provide continuous learning opportunities.* Learning organizations offer extensive opportunities for on- and off-the-job training to increase personal mastery.
- *Foster inquiry and dialogue.* Learning organizations make sure that all of the company's systems and procedures, as well as all the signals that managers send, encourage open inquiry and dialogue.
- *Establish mechanisms to ensure that the organization is continuously aware of and can interact with its environment.* For example, learning organizations encourage formal and informal environmental scanning activities by employees, to quickly identify opportunities and threats.

Managing Now Companies rely on special software to ensure that their learning management programs stay on track. For example, Aventis Pharmaceuticals recently installed a special learning management system from Saba Software.[71] Programs like these do several things. Most important, they enable Aventis's research scientists to easily access and participate in online training and development courses. In addition, it enables them to register for instructor-led training and lets the company automate the course registration process, deliver tests, track and report student participation, and generate certificates.

Practice IT
Millipore

With subsidiaries in over thirty countries, all operating with different software packages, managers at Millipore's headquarters couldn't effectively coordinate worldwide operations. They had to wait for employees at headquarters to compile and consolidate the information coming in from subsidiaries. The lack of timely information made it difficult for Millipore's top managers to coordinate the subsidiaries' activities.

The company's solution was to install, in phases, a suite of separate but compatible enterprise software packages from Oracle Corporation. Each subsidiary and department got new software such as Oracle Financials, Oracle Self Service Human Resources, and Oracle Purchasing. So, for example, once all the subsidiaries were using the same version of Oracle Financials, coordinating the company's financial operations became relatively simple. It cut in half the time it took to finalize the company's monthly accounting statements. It also reduced the number of employees required for this task and "gave executives better visibility into financial performance across the globe."[72]

Installing this suite of software produced several organizational benefits for Millipore. It improved interdepartmental coordination by providing Millipore managers with standardized information, which they used to compare operations and monitor results. It also eliminated numerous compilation and consolidation activities, thus allowing Millipore to reduce its employee head count. Third, it enabled Millipore to centralize certain shared-services functions, such as human resource management. For example, Oracle HR Self Service reduced the need for local HR staff by enabling employees and supervisors to self-service, via the Web, various activities such as updating personnel forms and completing performance appraisals.

CHAPTER SUMMARY

1. Organizing means arranging an enterprise's activities so that they systematically contribute to the enterprise's goals. An organization consists of people whose specialized tasks are coordinated to contribute to the organization's goals.
2. Departmentalization is the process through which management groups an enterprise's activities together and assigns them to managers. Managers generally group activities by functions, products, customer groups, marketing channels, or geographic areas.
3. Coordination is the process of achieving unity of action among interdependent activities. Techniques for achieving coordination include mutual adjustment; the use of rules; the standardization of targets, skills, values, or processes; direct supervision; coordination software; divisionalizing; and the use of a staff assistant, liaison, committee, and/or independent integrators.
4. Many companies are adopting flatter structures in an effort to eliminate duplication of effort, inspire creativity, and increase responsiveness. The span of control in a company is the number of subordinates reporting directly to a supervisor.
5. Authority is the right to take action, make decisions, and direct the work of others. Managers usually distinguish between line and staff authority.
6. Principles of delegation include delegating authority, not responsibility; clarifying the assignment; delegating, not abdicating; knowing what to delegate; specifying the range of discretion; having authority equal responsibility; making the person accountable for results; and avoiding backward delegation.
7. In practice, a decentralized organization is one in which (1) authority for most departmental decisions is delegated to the department heads, while (2) control for major companywide decisions is maintained at the headquarters office. Managers usually use the term *decentralized* in conjunction with product divisions.
8. Burns and Stalker's findings, as well as Woodward's, show that different organizational structures are appropriate for—and contingent on—different tasks. At one extreme are mechanistic organizations for dealing with predictable, routine tasks. At the other extreme, organic organizations enable companies to respond faster.
9. Managers can institute a number of basic structural changes to make their organizations operate more responsively. Examples of simplifying or reducing structure are reducing layers of management, creating mini-units, reassigning support staff, and widening spans of control.
10. Many firms superimpose organizational networks over existing structures. A network is a system of interconnected or cooperating individuals. It can be formal or informal, or IT-based. Team-based organizations, federal organizations, virtual organizations, and horizontal organizations are other modern organizations.

DISCUSSION QUESTIONS

1. Why do we refer to departmentalization as the organizational division of work?
2. What is the connection among decentralized, divisionalized, and product departmentalization?
3. How does interdependence influence how a company coordinates its operations?
4. Why is decentralization not the same as delegation?
5. What are the pros and cons of matrix management?
6. Do you think a company can flatten its hierarchy without taking steps to prepare its employees for their new roles? Why or why not? What steps would you recommend?
7. How would you use IT to improve coordination?

EXPERIENTIAL EXERCISES

1. Colleges are interesting from an organizational viewpoint because the employees (the faculty) tend to make so many of a college's decisions and run so many of its projects. It's not unusual, for instance, to have the faculty elect a faculty senate, which in turn appoints committees for things like faculty promotions and curricula; the committees then often have a major say in who gets promoted, what programs the college offers, and so on. Similarly, the students elect their own student governments, which in turn decide how the students' fees are spent.

   Some critics say that all of this is a little like "letting the inmates run the asylum." And the pace of criticism has picked up in the past few years. With more colleges and universities going online, students have more educational choices. As a result, tuition fees are under pressure, and universities are scrambling to cut costs and be more efficient. Boards of trustees are reviewing everything about how their colleges do things—from how many courses faculty members teach to how professors are appraised to how to decide which programs to offer or drop. Form teams of four to five students, and answer the following questions:

   a. Draw an organization chart for your college or university. What type(s) of departmentalization does it use? How would you show, on the chart, the authority exercised by the faculty and faculty committees (teams)?
   b. Decentralized structures tend to speed decisions. However, some people think that even though colleges tend to be decentralized, they are still the most bureaucratic organizations they've ever dealt with. To what extent and in what way is your college decentralized? Do you consider it bureaucratic, and, if so, what explains why a decentralized organization produces such bureaucracy?
   c. How would you reorganize the college if streamlining and more efficiency were your goals?

2. In teams of four to five students, spend some time on the Internet or in the library obtaining the organization charts for two companies. Then together answer these questions: What forms of departmentalization can you identify in each chart? Which company would you say is more decentralized? Why do you believe each company organized the way that it did?

3. Because you are in college to learn, it is reasonable to assume that your college (in general) and this management class (in particular) are learning organizations. (After all, your class does have an organizational structure in terms of who does what, whether authority is centralized or dispersed, and so on.) In teams of four to five students, answer these questions: If you were the "manager" taking over this class, what would you say are the main goals you want this class to achieve? Based on these goals, what are the main tasks the class's organization must perform? Draw the organization chart of this class as it is now. Then list five specific things you would do to reorganize this class as a learning organization.

CASE STUDY

Organizing Greenley Communications

Louis Greenley has to make a difficult decision. Greenley Communications was a diversified communications company that operated primarily in the western United States. The firm owned and operated newspapers and radio and television stations. For years, there had been an "invisible wall" between the print operations and radio and television.

Greenley's existing structure was organized by industry: a newspaper division, a radio division, and a television production division. Each division had its own bookkeeping, sales, marketing, operations, and service divisions. Accounting and financial management were handled at the corporate level.

In the newspaper division, a clear distinction existed between the news and the sales/financial sides of the business. Coming from a family of journalists, Greenley was always concerned that the sale of advertising to local clients would influence the paper's coverage of the news—editors might ignore potential stories that reflect negatively on an advertiser.

The vice president of broadcast operations in Greenley's television division proposed a major structural change. The proposal called for organizing Greenley Communications geographically. This reorganization would allow regional managers to have a single sales force that could sell advertising in any form: print, radio, or television. The approach had some appeal. There was significant overlap at Greenley—the company tended to employ multiple sales forces in the same region, for instance, with different salespeople often calling on the same customer. Certainly, there would be savings in personnel because the company would need a far smaller sales staff.

Greenley is not yet persuaded, however. He is trying to decide what to do.

DISCUSSION QUESTIONS

1. Draw Greenley's current organization chart as best you can.
2. What factors should influence Greenley's decision to restructure?
3. What risks does the proposed restructuring create?
4. What are the pros and cons of the vice president's new proposed structure?
5. If you were Greenley, how exactly would you reorganize (if at all), and why?

DESIGNING AND CHANGING ORGANIZATIONS

11

Yellow Transportation

When Bill Zollars became CEO at Yellow Transportation Inc., it had just lost about $30 million, laid off workers, and had a strike. Previously senior vice president at Ryder Corp., Zollars had built Ryder's high-tech logistics unit into a $1.5 billion business. He believed that saving Yellow Transportation would require upgrading the firm's technology. He knew he'd have to get his firm's thousands of truckers, warehouse specialists, and others to change the way they did things and to accept the new technologies. The question was, How should he do this?[1] ■

Bill Zollars, Yellow's new CEO, knew he'd have to get his firm's thousands of employees to change the way they did things and to accept the new technologies the firm required.

BEHAVIORAL OBJECTIVES

After studying this chapter, you should be able to:

Show that you've learned the chapter's essential information by

- Listing and discussing four ways to change an organization.
- Comparing and contrasting reengineering and business process management.
- Explaining how to change an organization's culture.
- Listing and describing at least five ways to resolve a conflict.

CHAPTER OUTLINE

CHAPTER OUTLINE (Continued)

- **Organizational Development and Conflict Management**
  - Human Process Applications
  - Technostructural Applications
  - Human Resource Management Applications
  - Strategic Applications
  - Managing Interpersonal Conflict

Show that you can practice what you've learned here by

- Reading the experiential exercises and explaining how you would reengineer the process.
- Reading the chapter case study and deciding if the company should reorganize and, if so, what the new structure should look like.

Show that you can apply what you've learned here by

- Watching the simulation video and identifying practices used by the company to successfully accomplish change.

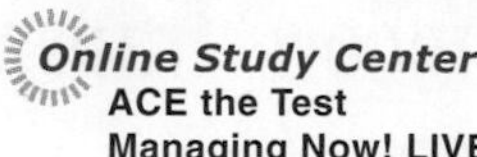

Types of Organizational Change

Online Study Center
ACE the Test
Managing Now! LIVE

You are in management class, and the dean walks in and says that you and some others need to move to a different class because of a fire safety code. How would you feel about that announcement? For a manager, implementing a change almost invariably triggers worry, concern, and resistance.

Several years ago, Nissan was selling 80 percent of its cars at a loss and had lost almost $6 billion in one year alone. The situation facing Carlos Ghosn, the person sent to Japan to fix Nissan, was urgent. He knew the only way to save Nissan was to take some steps that would not normally be considered within Japanese business culture, such as cutting 21,000 jobs.[2] As a French citizen coming to save a Japanese company, how could he lead the required change without prompting vast resistance by Nissan's workers?

The Challenge of Organizational Change

organizational change: a planned, systematic alteration of the company's strategy, structure, technology, and/or people and culture

Faced with the need to respond to competitive pressures, managers like Bill Zollars, Carlos Ghosn, or Avon's Andrea Jung invariably find themselves having to formulate and implement an organizational change. **Organizational change** refers to a planned, systematic alteration of the company's strategy, structure, technology, and/or people and culture. However, no change is ever made in isolation. Thus, a recent decision by Aetna Insurance to change its strategy and downsize also prompted changes in the firm's organization structure and in how Aetna trains its sales force.

Leading an organizational change can be treacherous. The change may require the cooperation of hundreds of managers and employees. Resistance may be extensive, and the company must execute all these changes while still serving its customers. The manager needs to know what to change and how to execute the change. We'll look at what the manager can change in this and the following section, and then turn to how managers actually lead an organizational change.

An Example: Becoming an E-Business

As an example of how one change tends to trigger another, consider becoming an e-business. General Electric (GE) now does most of its purchasing and much of its marketing over the Web. A local jeweler can now attract orders from thousands of miles away with its new associate relationship with Amazon.com. *Fortune* put it this way: "e or be eaten": either get your business on the Web or watch your competitors take your customers.[3]

The problem is that blending old business and e-business is not just about installing new technology.[4] For example, one of the things that torpedoed the AOL-Time Warner merger a few years ago was the fact that their cultures and ways of doing things were so different. Time Warner's more conservative culture clashed with AOL's laid-back entrepreneurial way of doing things.[5]

The chief strategist for one e-business says, "Entering the e-commerce realm is like managing at 90 mph. e-business affects finance, human resources, training, supply-chain management, customer-resource management, and just about every other corporate function."[6] For example, suppose a chain of florist shops decides to expand its sales online. Should they organize the online operation as a separate business unit? Or should they keep the current functional organization (sales, purchasing, marketing, accounting, and human resources) and let each of those department heads also run their parts of the new e-business? It's a dilemma.[7]

Greg Rogers, head of Whirlpool Corporation's e-commerce business, says a new e-business's strategy will have to change too.[8] The company's new strategy will have to reflect the fact that e-commerce is now a big part of the company's plans. Becoming an e-business illustrates a change that requires altering just about everything the company does—its strategy, technology, structure, and people and culture.

● **What's to Come** In the remainder of this first section, we'll look briefly at three types of organizational change (strategy, technology, and culture/people). We'll then look at the fourth type of change, structural change, in the next section of this chapter. Then, in the final two sections of this chapter, we'll turn to the methods that managers use to make their change efforts more successful.

Strategic Change

Many managers face the need to change their companies' strategies. For example, faced with declining profits, Aetna Insurance pulled back from its high-growth strategy. The firm had emphasized adding more policyholders. Its new strategy is to emphasize fewer but more profitable ones. Management reduced policyholders from 22 million to 14.4 million. By focusing on more profitable policyholders, Aetna boosted profits by ten times, to $108 million in one quarter. Andrea Jung decided to change Avon's strategy so that retail stores could also sell Avon products.

strategic change: a change in a firm's corporate and/or competitive strategies

Managers often try to avoid making big strategic changes because **strategic changes** are fraught with peril; it's hard to predict exactly what will happen.

This is especially true when the firm faces "discontinuous change": an unexpected change that triggers a crisis, as when digital photography began crowding Kodak's film off the shelves. Changes like these are usually prompted by things outside of the manager's control.[9] The manager will also probably have to make his or her changes under short time constraints. Strategic changes also tend to have companywide impact. As at Aetna, it's rarely possible to change the firm's strategy without also changing in some way the firm's structure, technology, and people.

Research findings suggest that managers facing strategic changes should keep the following three things in mind:

1. *Strategic changes are usually triggered by factors outside the company.* External threats or challenges, such as deregulation, global competition, and dramatic technological innovations, are usually what prompt managers to embark on companywide, strategic changes.[10]

2. *Strategic changes are often required for survival.* Researchers found that while making a strategic change did not guarantee success, firms that did not change when they should have did not survive. This was especially true when some major change required quick and effective strategic change, but the manager failed to respond. Many neighborhood businesses close if they can't change to compete with a new Wal-Mart.

3. *Strategic changes implemented under crisis conditions are highly risky.* Strategic changes made under crisis conditions and with short time constraints were the riskiest and most prone to fail. Changes like these eventually trigger changes companywide—changes to the firm's structure, technologies, people, and culture and core values. Core values (such as "don't make any risky moves") are especially hard to change.

Technological Change

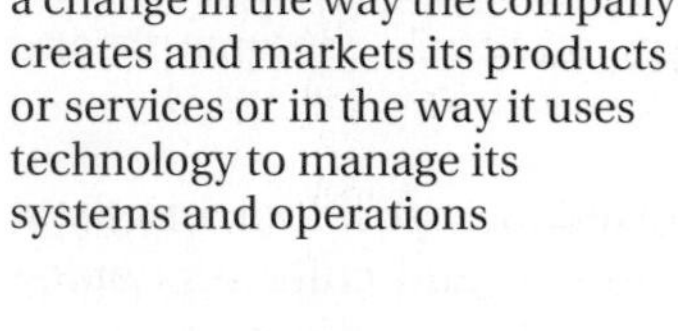
technological change: a change in the way the company creates and markets its products or services or in the way it uses technology to manage its systems and operations

We've seen in this book that many managers increasingly have to implement technological changes. **Technological change** means changing the way the company creates or markets its products or services, or the way it uses technology to manage its systems and operations. For example, the manager might want to improve operations by installing a new supply chain management system or by changing the interface through which the employees (such as UPS delivery people) communicate with their home base. (The Window on Managing Now feature presents one such example.)

Whatever the technological change, managers like Bill Zollars know they must get their employees to accept the change if the change is to be successful. Many of the examples you've read in this book—such as Brady Company installing its new supply chain system—illustrate this. It would make no sense for Brady to have the customers send their orders directly online to the plant floor if the employees there resented having to do the extra work.

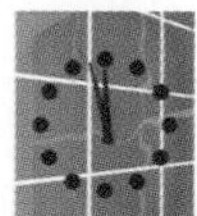

WINDOW ON MANAGING NOW
Baker & McKenzie

The law firm Baker & McKenzie has seventy offices in thirty-eight countries. Many of its clients do business globally. Before accepting a new client, it must ensure that it is not inadvertently creating a conflict, for instance, by agreeing to represent a client that another of its clients is suing. It also needs a process for ensuring that the advice it gives a multinational client complies with laws and regulations (like the U.S.A. Patriot Act) in all the countries in which it does business.[11] Processes like these can be time-consuming if done manually. Baker & McKenzie installed new business intake, conflicts management, and regulatory software systems. These technologies streamlined the firm's former intake and regulatory processes. They enable the firm's lawyers to avoid inadvertently accepting clients that might pose a conflict, and they ensure that all relevant local laws and regulations are being met.

Changing the People and/or the Culture

As at Brady, strategic, technical, and structural changes (which we discuss next) invariably require changes to the behavioral, "people" side of the firm. This includes changing the employees' attitudes, values, or skills, or the firm's culture.

Here, there are several options. If employees don't have the knowledge or skills to do the job, the manager may prescribe *training*. (We discuss training and development in Chapter 12.) At other times, people problems stem from misunderstanding or *conflict*. Here, conflict-resolution efforts (like those discussed at the end of this chapter) may be in order. Sometimes, the manager just needs to overcome resistance to the change by *explaining* the change's true nature. Bill Zollars at Yellow Transportation knew that his new technology would fail if he didn't explain the need for it convincingly.

Sometimes, the manager has to change the company's culture to make his or her broader desired changes work. *Culture* refers to the basic values the employees share and the ways in which these values manifest themselves in behavior. For example, some attribute Motorola's lackluster performance in the early 2000s to the company's culture, which one writer described as "stifling bureaucracy, snail-paced decision making, . . . and internal competition so fierce that [former CEO] Galvin himself has referred to it as a 'culture of warring tribes.'"[12] There were few things Galvin could do to make Motorola succeed in the face of such a culture.

How to Create and Sustain the Right Corporate Culture Alan Mulally, Ford's new CEO, took over late in 2006. Many believe Ford suffered to some extent from a culture of backbiting, bureaucratic behavior, and disdain (while Ford was cutting 30,000 employees, the top executives supposedly still used a fancy executive restaurant at Detroit headquarters). Mulally knew he had to make many changes at Ford to make that company succeed. He could not do that in the face of such a culture.

Alan Mulally, Ford's new CEO, had to change the company's culture.

What steps can a manager like Mulally take to change the company's culture? If, like Mr. Mulally, you wanted to encourage Ford managers to work more like a team, and employees to be more flexible about their pay demands, what would you do? Perhaps close the executive restaurant? Tell managers that from this point on, you will appraise each one on the extent to which he or she was a team player that year?

The essential thing to keep in mind is that it is the manager's behavior, not just what he or she says, that molds what employees come to see as the firm's real culture and values. Experts suggest doing the following to change organizational culture:[13]

1. *Make it clear to your employees what you pay attention to, measure, and control.* For example, at Toyota, quality and teamwork are desirable values. Toyota's selection and training processes therefore focus on the candidate's orientation toward quality and teamwork.
2. *React appropriately to critical incidents and organizational crises.* For example, if you want to emphasize the value that "we're all in this together," don't react to declining profits by saying, "You're all fired."

3. *Use signs, symbols, stories, rites, and ceremonies to signal your values.* JCPenney prides itself on loyalty and tradition. To support this, the firm inducts new management employees into the Penney Partnership. At special conferences they commit to Penney's values of honor, confidence, service, and cooperation.
4. *Deliberately role-model, teach, and coach the values you want to emphasize.* For example, Wal-Mart founder Sam Walton lived the values of hard work, honesty, neighborliness, and thrift. He explained driving a pickup truck by saying, "If I drove a Rolls-Royce, what would I do with my dog?"
5. *Communicate your priorities by how you appraise employees and allocate rewards.* For example, General Foods reoriented its strategy from cost control to diversification and sales growth. It supported these new priorities by linking bonuses to sales volume and new-product development, rather than to just increased earnings.

Lawrence Weinbach, chair and CEO of Unisys, took many steps to change his firm's culture. His basic aim was to focus employees on performance and execution. To do this, he instituted systems that sent the right signals. As he said, "We've moved to a pay-for-performance approach, to make sure that we're properly recognizing the people who are doing things right. . . . [I]n some cases, we've needed to tell people to seek opportunities elsewhere . . . we've invested in training and education and created Unisys University, where employees can find courses and programs on a range of . . . business related topics. We've also spent a lot of time communicating and educating people about the importance of execution."[14]

Managing Now: Reorganizing, Reengineering, and Business Process Management

Online Study Center
ACE the Test
Managing Now! LIVE

We hear on the news that the government had to reorganize the CIA, or that Ford Motor Company laid off 30,000 employees and changed how it organized its car divisions. Often, when we think about "organizational change," it's not strategic, technical, or behavioral change that comes to mind, but reorganizing. In this section, we look at reorganizing and at the closely related topics of reengineering and process management. These are all examples of structural organizational change.

Reorganizing

reorganizing or **structural change:** changing one or more aspects of the company's organizational structure

Reorganizing or **structural change** means changing the company's organizational structure.

Managers reorganize all the time. GE's CEO Jeffrey Immelt reorganized his firm's huge GE Capital division. He broke it into four divisions, with their four managers now reporting directly to him rather than to the former GE Capital head. DaimlerChrysler's U.S. truck maker used to be one part of DaimlerChrysler's commercial vehicles division. DaimlerChrysler recently reorganized its commercial vehicles division. Daimler split it into a new, separate truck group, and into divisions for vans and buses.[15] According to a Daimler spokesperson, having all commercial vehicles in one division created "an artificial layer of administration

DaimlerChrysler recently reorganized its commercial vehicles division by splitting it into a new, separate truck group, and into divisions for vans and buses.

over trucking which will no longer be present" after the reorganization.[16] The reorganization created a "pure truck group." The new organization means that ". . . management can concentrate on the relevant functions [necessary to run the truck business] and further integrate the truck divisions, and to make the truck group comparable for benchmark purposes to other competing truck groups."[17] The other products (vans and buses) that used to be part of Daimler's commercial vehicle division (along with trucks) now constitute one separate division.

Structural changes like these tend to trigger employee resistance. New structures mean new reporting relationships, and some will view the change as demotions. New structures may also mean new tasks and job descriptions (task redesign) for employees. People often have an affinity for predictability and the status quo.

Still, reorganizing is a familiar organizational change technique. For example, after dismissing thousands of employees, Lucent needed a new organizational structure. The former CEO had organized the company around eleven different businesses.[18] His successor argued that the eleven-division structure was too unwieldy and downsized to five and then to two units. One unit, Integrated Network Solutions, handles landline-based businesses, such as optical networks and phone-call switching. Another, Mobility Solutions, focuses on Lucent's wireless products. Today, a revitalized Lucent has merged with France's Alcatel.

● **Two Basic Questions** When contemplating a reorganization, the manager needs to address two basic questions: (1) how effective is our current organizational structure? and (2) if we do restructure, how big a reorganization do we require?

● **Reorganizing Question 1: How Effective Is Our Current Organizational Structure?** The manager begins by determining how effective the current organizational structure is in helping the company achieve its goals. After all, if the current organizational structure works, why change? The manager can apply nine tests here, as follows:[19]

1. ***The market advantage test.*** Does the organizational design make sense in terms of your company's strategy?[20] For example, if the strategy involves expanding overseas, an organizational structure that had no provision for addressing the markets abroad should raise a red flag. The rule of thumb here is this: If a single unit is dedicated to a single segment (to a single market, product, geographic area), the segment is receiving sufficient attention. If no unit has responsibility for the segment, the design is flawed and should be revamped. The DaimlerChrysler reorganization we mentioned earlier, which created the pure truck group, illustrates dedication.

   Similarly, Volkswagen (VW) considered reorganizing its nine brand divisions into three operational divisions—one for premium cars, one for mass-market cars, and one for commercial vehicles.[21] One intent of this reorganization is to enable the firm to better focus on what it sees as VW's three separate market segments: premium brands (Audi, Bugatti, Bentley, and Lamborghini), mass brands (Volkswagen), and commercial vehicles.

2. ***The parenting advantage test.*** Does your current structure help the corporate parent add value to the departments and subsidiaries? For example, investors periodically ask, Would it not be more efficient for each of GE's separate divisions to spin off and run themselves rather than to remain part of GE's overall structure? GE says no. For example, the current GE structure helps ensure that modern management techniques devised in one unit quickly spread to the others.

3. ***The people test.*** Does your design reflect the strengths, weaknesses, and motivations of your people?[22] For example, after PepsiCo purchased Quaker Oats Co., PepsiCo reorganized its business units partly because of the strengths of some executives it inherited with the Quaker purchase. Robert Morrison, Quaker's CEO, quickly assumed responsibility for PepsiCo's Tropicana juice unit, while continuing to oversee Quaker.

4. ***The feasibility test.*** The basic question here is, What could stand in the way of successfully implementing a new organizational structure? For example, 3M Company's new CEO considered not changing that company's structure. He was afraid that 3M was so collegial that making the tough choices required by a reorganization would trigger too much resistance.[23] He decided that the risks of staying with the old structure were too great. He anticipated the potential constraints and dealt with them.

5. ***The specialist culture test.*** Does your design protect departments that need distinct cultures? For example, 3M is known for the number of new products its engineers produce (including Post-it Notes). Its organizational structure needs to support that innovative engineering spirit.[24]

6. ***The difficult-links test.*** Does your structure address the hard-to-coordinate relationships? For example, in Chapter 10, we saw that the product development process in some high-tech firms requires coordination by special new-product development departments. These departments coordinate the research and development (R&D), sales, and manufacturing departments.

7. ***The redundant-hierarchy test.*** Does your organizational structure have too many levels and units? For example, Microsoft recently eliminated several management layers to make sure customers get quicker answers to their inquiries.

8. ***The accountability test.*** Is it clear who is responsible for what? For example, if a problem arose (such as a dramatic sales decline) for a particular product line, could you quickly identify the manager who is responsible? Daimler reorganized its truck division in part to ensure that managers were solely and clearly responsible for truck performance.

9. ***The flexibility test.*** Does your organizational structure foster innovation and responsiveness, or does it stifle it?[25] This is one reason Intuit's CEO breaks his new ventures off into small, self-contained units. Such an approach ensures that their managers can develop their businesses without being stifled waiting for answers from the parent company.

● Reorganizing Question 2: How Big a Reorganization Do We Require? If the current organization is not adequate, the manager may have to reorganize. How big a reorganization is required? Sometimes, the manager can just fine-tune

FIGURE 11.1

Is a New Structure Really Required?

When you identify a problem with your design, first look for ways to fix it without substantially altering it. If that doesn't work, you'll have to make fundamental changes. Here's a step-by-step process for resolving problems:

Steps Not Involving Major Design Change

MODIFY WITHOUT CHANGING THE UNITS.
- Refine the allocation of responsibilities (for example, clarify powers and responsibilities).
- Refine reporting relationships and processes.
- Refine lateral relationships and processes (for example, define coordination mechanisms).
- Refine accountabilities (for example, define more appropriate performance measures).

REDEFINE SKILL REQUIREMENTS AND INCENTIVES.
- Modify criteria for selecting people.
- Redefine skill development needs.
- Develop incentives.

SHAPE INFORMAL CONTEXT.
- Clarify the leadership style needed.
- Define norms of behavior, values, or social context.

Steps Involving Major Design Change

MAKE SUBSTANTIAL CHANGES IN THE UNITS.
- Make major adjustments to unit boundaries.
- Change unit roles (for example, turn functional units into business units or shared services).
- Introduce new units or merge units.

CHANGE THE STRUCTURE.
- Change reporting lines.
- Create new divisions.

NOTE: It may be possible to fix the organizational design without major changes. The first (top) section of this figure shows how the manager can fine-tune the organization and accomplish what needs to be done without making big changes. If these won't work, the manager may have to make the sorts of major changes listed in the figure's second (bottom) section.

If the company does require a major reorganization, the guidelines in Chapter 10 apply, for example, regarding the pros and cons of product versus functional structures and delegating authority. After designing a possible new structure, the manager can then again apply the nine tests described on pages 309–310 to test it and to ensure the new design passes muster.

SOURCE: Adapted from Michael Goold and Andrew Campbell, "Do You Have a Well-Designed Organization?" *Harvard Business Review*, March 2002, p. 124.

the current structure. For example, it might be sufficient to just clarify employees' responsibilities or reporting relationships rather than reorganize the whole company. On the other hand, the situation may require a more dramatic change. At Microsoft, the CEO decided he had to reorganize the entire structure around three core divisions. The checklist in Figure 11.1 helps the manager decide if fine-tuning or a major change is required.

Business Process Reengineering

Today, reorganizing doesn't mean just changing departments from functional to divisional, or delegating more authority. Instead, it can mean reorganizing or reengineering the company's basic business processes. As we saw in Chapter 10, every business uses business processes to get its work done. For example, banks have a loan-approval process. This process consists of activities such as getting loan applications, reviewing creditworthiness, and inspecting the property. One department usually does its part of the task, and then hands the task to the next department, like a relay race. We saw that *business process reengineering* means redesigning business processes, usually by combining steps so that small multifunction process teams use information technology to do the jobs formerly done by a sequence of departments. The basic approach is to:

1. Identify a business process to be redesigned (such as approving a mortgage application).
2. Measure the performance of the existing processes.
3. Identify opportunities to improve these processes.
4. Redesign and implement a new way of doing the work, usually by assigning ownership of formerly separate tasks to an individual or team that uses new computerized systems to support the new arrangement.

We illustrate reengineering in the Window on Managing Now feature.

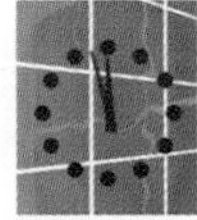

WINDOW ON MANAGING NOW
Reengineering the Loan Process

Here is how one bank reengineered its mortgage-approval process.[26] Previously, a mortgage applicant completed a paper loan application that a bank employee then entered into the bank's computer system. The application then moved through six different departments, where employees such as credit analysts and underwriters performed their tasks. This was too time-consuming for the bank to be competitive. Borrowers wanted quick answers. Squeezing several steps out of a loan-approval process may also save a bank $1,000 or more per loan. The bank reengineered its mortgage-application process so that it required fewer steps and reduced processing time from seventeen days to two. We illustrate the change in Figure 11.2.

As in this example, reengineering often entails having a small team of specially trained employees work together (either in the same physical cell or space, or connected via information technology) to complete a task that the firm formerly did sequentially. This bank reengineered the mortgage-application process by replacing the sequential operation with a cell or multifunction mortgage-approval team. Loan originators in the field now enter the mortgage application directly into wireless laptop computers, where software checks it for completeness. The information then goes electronically to regional production centers. Here, specialists (like credit analysts and loan underwriters) convene electronically, working as a team to review the mortgage together—at once. After they formally close the loan, another team of specialists takes on the task of servicing the loan.

As at this bank, reengineering usually triggers many organizational changes. For example, after creating several loan-approval teams, the bank could eliminate the separate credit-checking, loan-approval, and home-inspecting departments from its organization chart. Reengineering here also required reorganizing some departments and delegating more authority to the loan-approval teams, who now did their jobs with less supervisory oversight. The employees also needed additional training to use the new system. This all could have, but did not, trigger employee resistance. The bank headed that resistance off by dealing with employees' concerns before implementing the change.

FIGURE 11.2

Redesigning the Mortgage-Application Process

By reengineering the mortgage-application process, the bank will be able to handle increased paperwork much more quickly.

BEFORE

Prior to reengineering, the paper loan application went from department to department like a relay race.

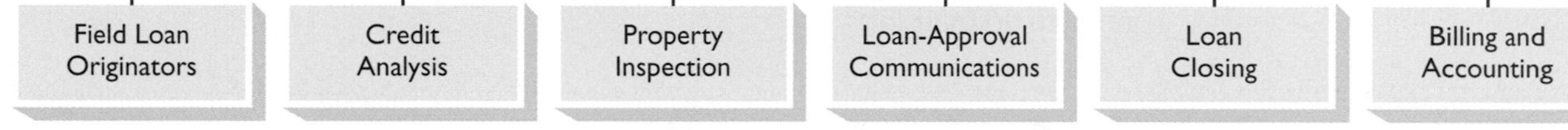

AFTER

After reengineering, the field loan originators took the applications on their laptops, and then electronically transmitted the loans to the loan-processing teams, which met electronically.

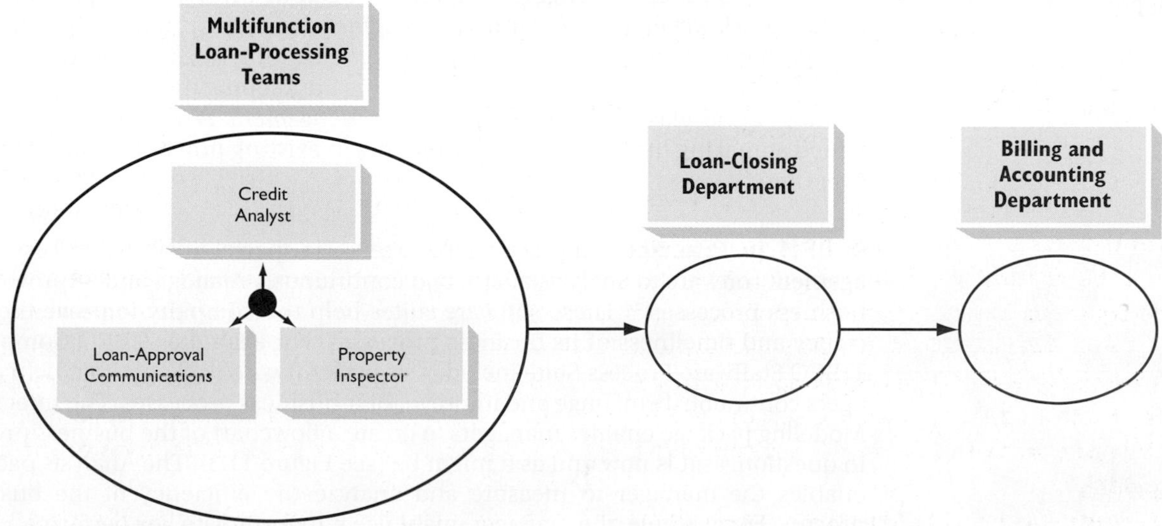

Companies' experiences with reengineering illustrate the importance of overcoming employee resistance. Reengineering failure rates run as high as 70 percent.[27] When reengineering does fail, it is often due to behavioral factors. For example, it would do the bank little good to reengineer its loan process if the field loan originators refuse to take the time to complete the online applications completely. Similarly, reengineering without considering the new loan-approval teams' skill requirements, training, and reporting relationships would have been futile. John Champy, a reengineering expert, says that reengineering is not just about changing processes, but also "... a matter of rearranging the quality of people's attachments—to their work and to each other."[28] The manager must prepare employees for the change, to reduce resistance and also to make sure they have the knowledge, skills, and attitudes they need to do their new jobs.

● **Managing Now** Reengineering also illustrates how managers use information technology (laptops, fax, cell phones, PDAs, software, the Web, and so on) to change management processes. In this case, information technology (IT) makes the bank's new loan-approval process possible. Laptops and special software enable the loan originators in the field to create a complete loan application. The bank's Web portal enables them to send it to the internal loan-processing team. Decision support software and the Web enable even geographically dispersed loan-processing team members to work together virtually to process the loan. And the bank's enterprise systems automatically provide other bank units such as billing, accounting, and top management with the loan-related information they need to do their jobs.

Business Process Management

business process management (BPM): the automation, coordination, and continuous improvement of the many assets and tasks that make up a company's existing business processes

Business process management (BPM) is the automation, coordination, and continuous improvement of the many assets and tasks that make up a company's existing business processes.[29] The assets include, for instance, the employees who make the process work, as well as information technology and physical assets such as trucks and computer equipment.

Business process reengineering and BPM both involve changing business processes. However, business process *reengineering* projects tend to be one-time efforts that aim to produce dramatic reorganizations of the handful of major business processes that management believes are keeping the company from becoming world-class.[30] Business process *management* is an ongoing process aimed at making incremental improvements in existing processes, continuously, over time.[31]

● **BPM in Practice** In practice, managers use special business process management software to analyze, adapt, and continuously manage and improve their business processes.[32] These software suites help the company improve the efficiency and timeliness of its business processes. For example, TIBCO Company's TIBCO Staffware Process Suite includes several software packages that help managers continuously manage and improve their business processes. The Integrated Modeling package enables managers to create a flowchart of the business process in question, as it is now and as it might be (see Figure 11.3). The Analysis package enables the manager to measure and analyze the efficiency of the business process. For example, the manager might use it to formulate key performance indicators (such as "hours required to fulfill an order" and then to continuously

FIGURE 11.3

Creating a Flowchart with Project Software

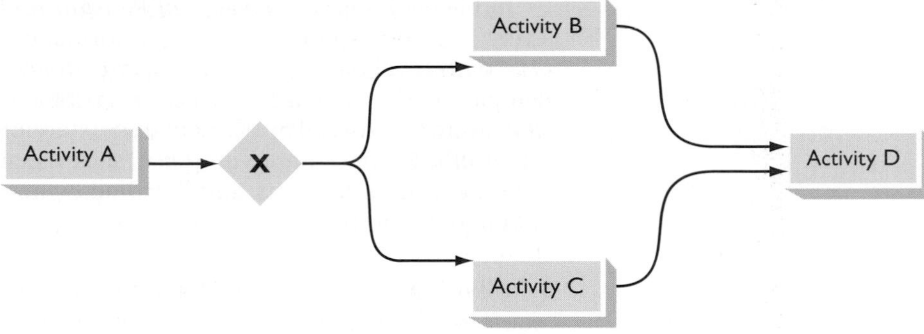

SOURCE: Copyright Tibco Software Inc. All rights reserved. Reprinted by permission.

NOTE: Systems such as TIBCO's process suite help the manager "flowchart" the business process activities and improve the overall process.

monitor the process and improve it.[33] TIBCO's business process management suite also enables the manager to model and simulate changes to the business process, to study what effects a change might have on efficiency.[34]

There is something to say about doing things incrementally. Whereas the results of many large reengineering projects are less than satisfactory, the more incremental BPM seems to raise productivity and lower costs more consistently.[35] Perhaps this is true in part because the incremental approach tends to be less threatening and thus incurs less employee resistance.

Dealing with Resistance to Change

Online Study Center
ACE the Test
Managing Now! LIVE

After deciding *what* to change, the manager must decide how to actually implement the change. The manager's main concern is how to deal with and minimize employee resistance. Here, the manager's options range from unilaterally and authoritatively instituting the change to having the employees themselves decide what to change and how to change it.

Overcoming resistance is often the hardest part of leading a change. Niccolò Machiavelli, a shrewd observer of sixteenth-century Italian politics, put it this way: "There is nothing so difficult to implement as change, since those in favor of the change will often be small in number while those opposing the change will be numerous and enthusiastic in their resistance to change."[36] The fact that a change is advisable or even crucial for the company's survival doesn't mean employees will accept it. Even the company's key people—perhaps including some top and middle managers—may resist it.

Why Do People Resist Change?

Dealing with employee resistance is challenging because the resistance isn't necessarily based on rational factors. Professor Paul Lawrence said that it's usually not the technical aspects of a change employees resist, but its social consequences—"the changes in their human relationships that generally accompany the technical change."[37] Thus, they may see in the change diminished responsibilities for themselves and, therefore, lower status in the organization and less job security.

In his book *Beyond the Wall of Resistance,* consultant Rick Maurer says that Level 1 resistance stems from lack of information or honest disagreement over the facts. With Level 2 resistance, people are afraid—that the change may cost them their jobs, or that they will lose face, for instance. He says treating all resistance as if it were Level 1 (based on a lack of understanding) can undermine the manager's change efforts. For example, don't use "slick visual presentations to explain change with nice neat facts, charts, and time lines, when what people really want to hear is: What does this mean to them?"[38]

Individual Resistance to Change Furthermore, some people are more resistant to change than are others. One study focused on six organizations—two European companies, two Australian banks, a U.S. university, and a Korean manufacturing firm. Three personality traits—tolerance for ambiguity, having a positive self-concept, and being more tolerant of risk—significantly predicted effectiveness in coping with change.[39] Managers with the lowest self-image, the least tolerance for ambiguity, and the least tolerance for risk were the most resistant. Industrial psychologists use tests like the Resistance to Change Scale to measure a person's inclination to resist change. Statements used for measurement include, "I'd rather be bored than surprised," "I generally consider change to be a negative thing," "When I am informed of a change of plans, I tense up a bit," and "I don't change my mind easily."[40]

It's not just employees who may resist the change. For example, when Pirelli, the manufacturer of automobile tires, decided to integrate its customers and dealers into its enterprise systems, Pirelli had to ensure that dealer resistance did not torpedo the change. Pirelli and its Accenture consultants therefore employed numerous initiatives.[41] For example, Pirelli's marketing department produced promotions explaining the new system's benefits to dealers.

Overcoming Resistance to Change

Psychologist Kurt Lewin proposed a famous model to summarize the basic process for implementing a change with minimal resistance. To Lewin, all behavior in organizations was a product of two kinds of forces: those striving to maintain the status quo and those pushing for change. Implementing change thus meant either reducing the forces for the status quo or building up the forces for change. Lewin's process consists of three steps: unfreezing, moving, and refreezing.

unfreezing: a step in psychologist Kurt Lewin's model of change that involves reducing the forces for the status quo, usually by presenting a provocative problem or event to get people to recognize the need for change and to search for new solutions

Unfreezing means reducing the forces pressing for the status quo. The usual way to accomplish this is by presenting a provocative problem or event. The goal is to get employees to recognize the need for change and to search for new solutions. Attitude surveys, interview results, or informational meetings often provide such provocative events. Some managers accomplish this by creating a crisis—such as by suggesting that bankruptcy might be imminent if things don't change fast.

moving: a step in psychologist Kurt Lewin's model of change aimed at using techniques and actually altering the behaviors, values, and attitudes of the individuals in an organization

Having grabbed the employees' attention, the manager leading the change must move them in the desired direction. **Moving** means developing new behaviors, values, and attitudes by applying one or more organizational change techniques (such as having employees participate in a conflict resolution meeting). We discuss organizational change techniques later in this chapter.

Lewin knew that just executing the change is not enough. People tend to revert to their old ways of doing things unless management reinforces the new ways. Whether it's a new diet, a new savings plan, or a new organizational procedure,

refreezing: a step in psychologist Kurt Lewin's model of change aimed at preventing a return to old ways of doing things by instituting new systems and procedures that reinforce the new organizational changes

Lewin knew the manager had to reinforce the change. Lewin called this reinforcement **refreezing**, which means instituting new systems, procedures, and incentives to maintain the changes that were made.

Choosing the Right Method for Overcoming Resistance

Table 11.1 summarizes some methods that managers use to overcome resistance—and when to use them. For example, use education and communication when inaccurate or missing information is contributing to employee resistance. Coercion—forcing through the change—can be a fast way of pushing through a change, particularly when speed is essential. This can work when the manager has the power to force the change. However, it can be risky if it leaves influential employees with the will and ability to undermine the change. The Practice IT feature shows how Bill Zollars overcame resistance at Yellow Transportation.

TABLE 11.1
Six Methods for Dealing with Resistance to Change

Method for Dealing with Resistance	Commonly Used When . . .	Advantages	Drawbacks
Education and communication	There is a lack of information or there is inaccurate information.	Once persuaded, people will often help with implementing the change.	Can be time-consuming.
Participation and involvement	The managers leading the change do not have all the information they need to design the change, or when others have power to resist.	People who participate will be committed to implementing change.	Can be time-consuming, and can backfire if recommendations not accepted.
Facilitation and support	People are resisting because of fear and anxiety.	No other approach works as well when fear is the problem.	Can be time-consuming and expensive, yet still fail.
Negotiation and agreement	Someone or some group will clearly lose out in a change, and that group has power to resist.	Can be a relatively easy way to avoid major resistance.	Can be too expensive if it prompts other groups to negotiate, too.
Manipulation and co-optation	Other tactics won't work or are too time-consuming.	Can be relatively quick and inexpensive.	Can lead to future problems if people feel tricked or manipulated.
Coercion	Speed is essential, and the change initiators possess power.	It is speedy and can overcome any kind of resistance.	Risky if it leaves people angry at the initiators.

Source: Adapted and reprinted by permission of Harvard Business School Publishing. "Six Methods for Dealing with Change," from "Choosing Strategies for Change," by John P. Kotter and Leonard A. Schlesinger, *Harvard Business Review,* March–April 1979.

PRACTICE IT
Bill Zollars

To turn Yellow Transportation around, Bill Zollars knew he had to provide the company and its workers with state-of-the-art technology. He also knew this technology would dramatically change how his employees did things, and that getting their acceptance was therefore vital. The new technology gives the employees the information they need to solve problems for customers quickly. But this also meant that the employees needed additional decision-making authority, as well as training to use the new equipment.

With 25,000 people in hundreds of locations around the country, Zollars spent over a year going from terminal to terminal, standing on loading docks and explaining the changes. Linking employees with the new technology and giving them the authority to make fast, on-the-spot decisions (empowering them) helped to win their commitment and dedication to getting the job done fast.

The change Zollars led was successful. For example, his team equipped each dockworker with a wireless mobile data terminal. Now, even before the truck arrives, the worker can see what's on board and when the truck is pulling into the dock.[42] Managers back at headquarters can monitor progress and send additional employees if help is required.

Soon, Zollars' changes had turned the company around. In 2002 Yellow Freight System Inc. changed its name to Yellow Transportation Inc. to reflect the company's transformation to a full-service global transportation provider. In 2003 Yellow acquired Roadway Corp. to become Yellow Roadway Corp. In 2006 Yellow Roadway Corp. changed its name to YRC Worldwide Inc. to better reflect its capabilities today as a global entity. Bill Zollars is now Chairman of the Board, President, and CEO of YRC Worldwide Inc.

A Process for Leading Organizational Change

Online Study Center
ACE the Test
Managing Now! LIVE

Given the need to deal with resistance to change, experts have proposed many multistep models for leading an organizational change.[43] The following ten-step list provides a useful summary change process for managers:

1. Create a sense of urgency.
2. Decide what to change.
3. Create a guiding coalition and mobilize commitment.
4. Develop and communicate a shared vision.
5. Empower employees to make the change.
6. Implement the change.
7. Generate "short-term wins."
8. Consolidate gains and produce more change.
9. Anchor the new ways of doing things in the company culture.
10. Monitor progress and adjust the vision as required.

Each of the ten steps will be discussed in the following subsections.

Create a Sense of Urgency[44]

Most experienced managers instinctively know that before taking action, they have to unfreeze the old habits. They have to create a sense of urgency.

Creating a sense of urgency has a double-barreled benefit. For those who might want to resist the change, it can convince them of the need for the change. And it may jar those who are neutral (or who simply don't care) out of their complacency. Techniques that managers use to create a sense of urgency include:[45]

- Create a crisis by highlighting a financial loss, or exposing managers to major weaknesses relative to competitors.
- Eliminate examples of excess such as company-owned country club facilities, aircraft, or executive dining rooms.
- Set targets for revenue, income, productivity, and customer satisfaction so high that they can't be reached by those conducting business as usual.
- Send more data about customer satisfaction and financial performance to more employees, especially pinpointing weaknesses relative to competitors.

Decide What to Change

In practice, as we explained earlier, the manager can change the firm's strategy; technology; structure; and/or the culture, attitudes, and skills of its people.

Create a Guiding Coalition and Mobilize Commitment

It is usually imprudent for the owner or top manager to try to lead a change—particularly a major change—him- or herself. People tend to associate major corporate transformations—like what Bill Zollars achieved at YRC Worldwide Inc.—with one leader. Realistically, however, no leader can accomplish a major change alone. Most leaders create a guiding coalition of influential people. They become the missionaries and implementers of change. The coalition should work as a team and should include people with enough power to influence others to buy into the change effort.

The manager must gather political support, and so should ensure he or she has enough key players onboard so that those left out can't easily block progress.[46] The coalition should also have the expertise, credibility, and leadership skills required to explain and implement the change. One option is to create one or more broad, employee-based task forces to diagnose the company's problems. Doing so can produce a shared commitment to what the company can and must improve.

Develop and Communicate a Shared Vision

Beyond the guiding coalition, the firm's other employees also need a vision they can rally around, a signpost on which to focus. As we saw in Chapter 7, a vision is "a general statement of the organization's intended direction that evokes emotional feelings in organization members." When Barry Gibbons became CEO of a struggling Spec's Music retail chain, its employees, owners, and bankers—all of its stakeholders—required a vision around which to rally. Gibbons's vision of a leaner Spec's offering both concerts and retail music helped to provide the needed sense of direction.

When Barry Gibbons became CEO of a struggling Spec's Music retail chain, all of its stakeholders required a vision around which to rally.

Having a vision is useless unless the employees share that vision. Change expert John Kotter says, "The real power of a vision is unleashed only when most of those involved in an enterprise or activity have a common understanding of its goals and direction."[47] Key steps in communicating a vision include:

- *Keep it simple.* For example, "We are going to become faster than anyone else in our industry at satisfying customer needs."
- *Use multiple forums.* Try to use every channel possible—big meetings and small, memos and newspapers, formal and informal interaction—to publicize the vision.
- *Use repetition.* Ideas sink in best after people have heard them many times.
- *Lead by example.* Walk the talk so that your behaviors and decisions are consistent with the vision you advocate.

Empower Employees to Make the Change

In one study of organizational change, the researchers found that employees would not even try to help implement the change unless they believed they had the skills and authority to effect the change.[48] The manager must always ask, Do our employees have the authority and skills to carry out their roles in the change effort? The employees must feel they're empowered to do their new jobs.

Figure 11.4 summarizes typical barriers to such employee empowerment. For example, employees may not have the new skills their new jobs require, and so they couldn't do their new jobs if they wanted to. At Allied Signal (now Honeywell),

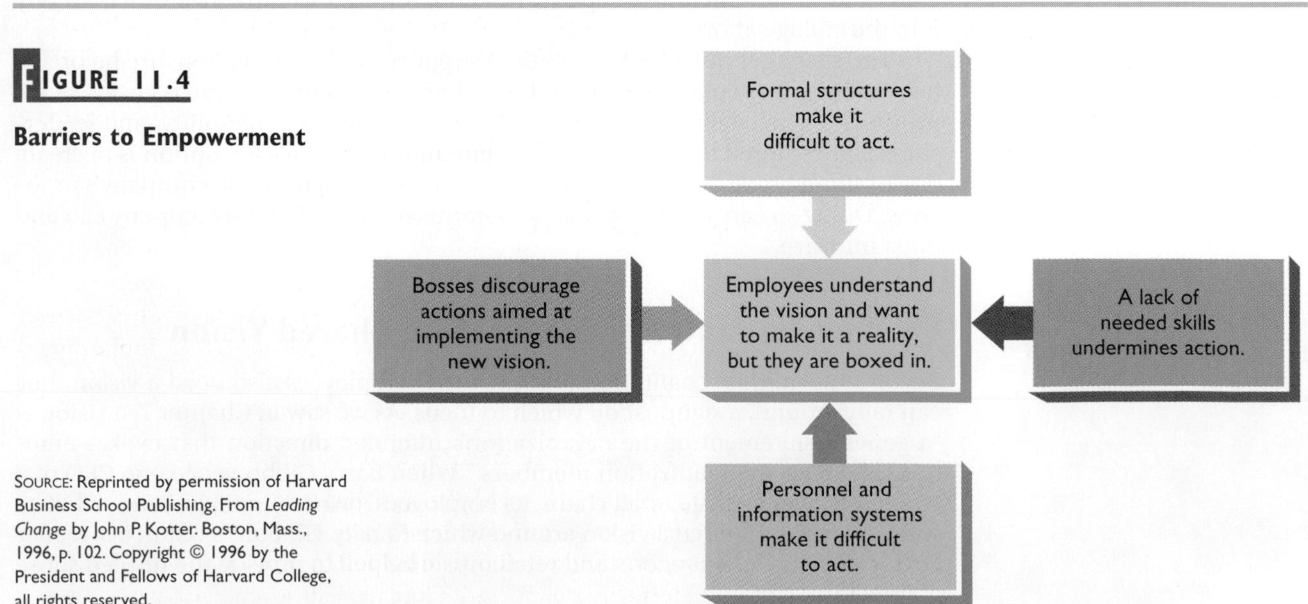

FIGURE 11.4

Barriers to Empowerment

SOURCE: Reprinted by permission of Harvard Business School Publishing. From *Leading Change* by John P. Kotter. Boston, Mass., 1996, p. 102.

CEO Lawrence Bossidy had to create a leaner, more efficient company. He began by putting all of his 80,000 people through quality training. They could then apply this new knowledge to helping Allied improve its quality.[49]

Implement the Change

At about this point, the manager will implement the core features of the change. At Bill Zollars' YRC Worldwide, for instance, the company's technology consultants rolled out the actual new technology the employees were to use. At Microsoft, the CEO implemented the new divisional structure.

Generate "Short-Term Wins"

Employees should not have to wait years before deciding if they're going in the right direction. They need periodic feedback: what change experts call "short-term wins."[50] The coalition guiding the change in one company aimed to produce one particular new product about twenty months after the start of its organizational change effort.[51] It selected the new product in part because it knew that the introduction was doable. Accomplishing it sent a strong signal that the broader, longer-term change was also doable.

Consolidate Gains and Produce More Change

Next, expand and capitalize on the short-term successes by having employees produce more change. To do this, review and change any additional organizational systems, structures, and policies that don't fit well with the company's new direction.

Anchor the New Ways of Doing Things in the Company Culture

The corporate culture must support the changes the manager envisions. He or she must therefore ask, What underlying values and culture does our change imply? For example, he or she might change the bank's reengineered mortgage-approval team's incentive plan to reward the team, rather than individuals, to send the signal that they must work together or their paychecks will suffer.

Monitor Progress and Adjust the Vision as Required

Finally, monitor progress and results of the change effort. One firm administered morale surveys to monitor employees' reactions to the changes. Let's look at what Carlos Ghosn did at Nissan.

Carlos Ghosn Leads a Change at Nissan

The approach used by Carlos Ghosn in his dramatic turnaround of Nissan Motors illustrates how a manager can lead an effective organizational change. When the Renault executive agreed to lead the turnaround at Renault's new strategic partner, Nissan had lost billions of dollars, and it had billions more in debts.[52]

TABLE 11.2
Some of Nissan's Cross-Functional Teams (CFTs)

	Purchasing Team	Manufacturing and Logistics Team	Sales and Marketing Team	Phaseout of Products and Parts Complexity Team	Organization Team
CFT (cross-functional team) Leaders	• Executive VP of purchasing • Executive VP of engineering	• Executive VP of manufacturing • Executive VP of product planning	• Executive VP of overseas sales and marketing • Executive VP of domestic sales and marketing	• Executive VP of domestic sales and marketing • Executive VP of product planning	• Executive VP of finance (CFO) • Executive VP of manufacturing
Day-to-Day CFT Pilot	• General manager of purchasing	• Deputy general manager of manufacturing	• Manager of overseas sales and marketing	• Manager of product planning	• Manager of human resources
Functions Represented on Team	• Purchasing • Engineering • Manufacturing • Finance	• Manufacturing • Logistics • Product planning • Human resources	• Sales and marketing • Purchasing	• Product planning • Sales and marketing • Manufacturing • Engineering • Finance • Purchasing	• Product planning • Sales and marketing • Manufacturing • Engineering • Finance • Purchasing
Team's Focus	• Supplier relationships • Product specifications and standards	• Manufacturing efficiency and cost-effectiveness	• Advertising structure • Distribution structure • Dealer organization • Incentives	• Manufacturing efficiency and cost-effectiveness	• Organizational structure • Employee incentive and pay packages
Team's Objectives, Based on Its Review	• Cut number of suppliers in half • Reduce costs by 20% over three years	• Close three assembly plants in Japan • Close two power-train plants in Japan • Improve capacity utilization in Japan from 53% in 1999 to 82% in 2002	• Move to a single global advertising agency • Reduce SG&A costs by 20% • Reduce distribution subsidiaries by 20% in Japan • Close 10% of retail outlets in Japan	• Reduce number of plants in Japan from 7 to 4 by 2002 • Reduce number of platforms in Japan from 24 to 15 by 2002 • Reduce by 50% the variation in parts (due to differences in engines or cars)	• Create a worldwide corporate headquarters • Create regional management committees • Empower program directors • Implement performance-oriented compensation

Source: Adapted from Carlos Ghosn, "Saving the Business Without Losing the Company," *Harvard Business Review,* January 2002, pp. 40–41.

Carlos Ghosn led a transformational change at Nissan Motors.

Ghosn sized up the external and internal pressures he faced, including the consensus-oriented Japanese culture. As he says, "I knew that if I had tried simply to impose the changes from the top, I would have failed. Instead, I decided to use as the centerpiece of the turnaround effort a set of cross-functional teams."[53]

Table 11.2 summarizes Ghosn's team approach. He organized cross-functional teams, each with responsibilities for the main tasks required for Nissan to have a successful turnaround. (Table 11.2 shows five of the teams.) Each team had several executive leaders, a day-to-day operational "pilot," and specific assignments. Each team consisted of about ten members, all middle managers with line responsibilities (except for the executive leaders).

Based on recent results, the changes designed by and pushed through by Nissan's teams were successful. In 2005, Renault brought Carlos Ghosn back to Paris and awarded him with its presidency. Within a year or two, it was evident more work was required at Nissan. With sales diminishing, even Ghosn's successful turnover required more work.

Organizational Development and Conflict Management

Online Study Center
ACE the Test
Managing Now! LIVE

organizational development (OD): an approach to organizational change in which the employees themselves formulate the change that's required and implement it, usually with the aid of a trained consultant

action research: the process of collecting data from employees about a system in need of change, and then feeding that data back to the employees so that they can analyze it, identify problems, develop solutions, and take action themselves

human process interventions: organizational change techniques aimed at enabling employees to develop a better understanding of their own and others' behaviors for the purpose of improving those behaviors so that the organization benefits

Organizational development (OD) is a special approach to organizational change in which the employees formulate and implement the change, usually with the aid of a trained facilitator. OD has three distinguishing characteristics:

1. It is based on **action research**, which means collecting data about a group, department, or organization, and then feeding that data back to the employees. Then the group members themselves analyze the data and develop hypotheses about what the problems in the unit might be.
2. It applies behavioral science knowledge to improve the organization's effectiveness.
3. It changes the organization in a particular direction—toward improved problem solving, responsiveness, quality of work, and effectiveness.[54]

OD started years ago with **human process interventions**. These interventions aimed to help employees better understand and modify their own and others' attitudes, values, and beliefs—and thereby improve the company.

Today, OD practitioners aren't involved in just changing participants' attitudes, values, and beliefs. However, OD's distinguishing characteristic has stayed the same: to have the employees themselves analyze the situation and develop the solutions. We'll look at the four main types of OD interventions: human process, technostructural, human resource management, and strategic (see Table 11.3).

Human Process Applications

Human process applications aim at improving employees' human relations skills. The goal is to provide employees with the insight and skills they need to analyze

TABLE 11.3
Examples of OD Interventions and the Organizational Levels They Affect

Interventions	Primary Organizational Level Affected		
	Individual	Group	Organization
Human Process			
T-groups	×	×	
Process consultation		×	
Third-party intervention	×	×	
Team building		×	
Organizational confrontation meeting		×	×
Intergroup relations		×	×
Technostructural			
Formal structural change			×
Differentiation and integration			×
Cooperative union-management projects	×	×	×
Quality circles	×	×	
Total quality management		×	×
Work design	×	×	
Human Resource Management			
Goal setting	×	×	
Performance appraisal	×	×	
Reward systems	×	×	×
Career planning and development	×		
Managing workforce diversity	×		
Employee wellness	×		
Strategic			
Integrated strategic management			×
Culture change			×
Strategic change			×
Self-designing organizations		×	×

their own and others' behavior more effectively. With this new insight, they should be able to solve interpersonal and intergroup problems more intelligently. Sensitivity training, team building, and survey research are three classic techniques used in these applications.

Team-building exercises like this one can be effective at building team loyalty and motivation.

Sensitivity training (also known as laboratory or t-group training) was one of the earliest OD techniques. It aims to increase the participant's insight into his or her own behavior and the behavior of others by encouraging an open expression of feelings in the training group. Typically, ten to fifteen people meet, usually away from the job. The focus is on the feelings and interactions of group members. Facilitators encourage participants to portray themselves as they are now, in the group, rather than in terms of past experiences.[55] T-group training is obviously very personal in nature, so it's not surprising that it is controversial. Its use has diminished markedly.[56]

OD's action research emphasis is perhaps most evident in **team building**. This is a special process for improving the effectiveness of a team. The facilitator collects data concerning the team's performance and concerns, and then feeds it back to the members of the team. The participants examine, explain, and analyze the data. Then they develop specific action plans or solutions for solving the team's problems.[57]

Some firms use **survey research** to create a sense of urgency. Here, the facilitator/consultant has employees complete attitude surveys. He or she then feeds back the data to top management and to the appropriate group or groups. The survey data may provide a lucid, comparative, graphic illustration of the fact that the organization has problems.

sensitivity training: the basic aim of this organizational development technique is to increase participants' insight into their own and others' behavior by encouraging an open expression of feelings in a trainer-guided group; also called laboratory or t-group training

team building: the process of improving the effectiveness of a team through action research or other techniques

survey research: the process of collecting data from attitude surveys filled out by employees of an organization, and then feeding the data back to workgroups to provide a basis for problem analysis and action planning

formal structure change program: an intervention technique in which employees collect information on existing formal organizational structures and analyze it for the purpose of redesigning and implementing new organizational structures

Technostructural Applications

OD practitioners are increasingly involved in efforts to change the structures, methods, and job designs of firms. Technostructural interventions include changes such as reorganizing the company and changing the designs of specific jobs. For example, in a **formal structure change program**, employees collect data on existing structures and analyze them. The purpose is to jointly redesign and implement new organizational structures.

Human Resource Management Applications

OD practitioners also use action research to help employees analyze and change personnel practices. Targets of change include the performance appraisal system and reward system. Another typical effort involves using action research to institute workforce diversity programs. These aim to boost cooperation among a firm's diverse employees.

Strategic Applications

Strategic interventions are companywide OD programs aimed at achieving a better fit among a firm's strategy, structure, culture, and strengths and weaknesses. **Integrated strategic management** is one example. Using action research, it involves four steps:

1. *Analyze current strategy and organizational design.* Senior managers and other employees utilize models such as the SWOT matrix (explained in Chapter 5) to analyze the firm's current strategy and organizational design.

strategic intervention: an organizational development application aimed at effecting a suitable fit among a firm's strategy, structure, culture, and external environments

integrated strategic management: an organizational development program to create or change a company's strategy by analyzing the current strategy, choosing a desired strategy, designing a strategic change plan, and implementing the new plan

2. *Choose a desired strategy and organizational design.* Based on the analysis, senior management formulates a strategic vision, objectives, and plan, and an organizational structure for implementing them.
3. *Design a strategic change plan.* The group designs a strategic change plan: "an action plan for moving the organization from its current strategy and organizational design to the desired future strategy and design."[58] It lays out how management will implement the strategic change, including budgets.
4. *Implement the strategic change plan.* The final step is to implement the strategic change plan and then measure and review the results.[59]

● The Global Manager OD practices such as sensitivity training that may be acceptable in one context may be frowned upon in another. Managers thinking of using OD interventions abroad, therefore, need to consider the cultural context. A study of OD usage by U.S., Japanese, and European multinational corporations and local Chinese firms in Hong Kong illustrates this.

There were distinct differences in OD usage between Western and Asian firms. Chinese and Japanese firms generally used OD interventions less frequently than did Western firms. In this study, the researchers also found that the human process types of interventions (like sensitivity training) were least used, even for the American firms, and that the Chinese firms were even less open to individual and personal-level interventions than were European and U.S. firms. The researchers concluded that the Chinese tended to be more skeptical of personal and confrontation-type interventions. On the other hand, local Chinese firms did use HR-type interventions, for instance, to strengthen their reward systems.[60]

Managing Interpersonal Conflict

Few things are potentially as deadly for a company's performance as uncontrolled conflict among employees or departments. Opposing parties put their own aims above those of the organization, and the organization's effectiveness suffers. Time that they could have used productively evaporates when people hide information and jockey for position. Managing conflicts like these is a major part of managers' organizational change responsibilities.

The manager must size up the situation and decide what conflict-resolution approach to use. For example, having the parties meet to confront the facts and hammer out a solution is usually better than pushing problems under a rug. Yet there are times when letting things cool down is advisable. Knowing which conflict-resolution style or approach to use is an art.

● Interpersonal Conflict-Resolution Styles In practice, people usually don't rely on a single conflict-resolution style; they use several simultaneously.[61] A study illustrates this. The researchers studied how supervisors used several conflict-resolution styles, such as confrontation. Table 11.4 summarizes (with definitions) the possible conflict-resolution styles in this study. The researchers' basic question was, "Is using some combination of these styles more effective at resolving conflicts than others?" They analyzed videotapes of 116 police sergeants handling a

TABLE 11.4
Conflict-Resolution Modes

Component	Definition
Forcing	Contending that the adversary do what you say in a direct way
Confronting	Demanding attention to the conflict issue
Process controlling	Dominating the conflict-resolution process to one's own advantage
Problem solving	Reconciling the parties' basic interests
Compromising	Settling through mutual concessions
Accommodating	Giving in to the opponent
Avoiding	Moving away from the conflict issue

Source: Evert Van De Vliert, Martin C. Euwema, and Sipke E. Huismans, "Managing Conflict with a Subordinate or a Superior: Effectiveness of Conglomerated Behavior," *Journal of Applied Psychology*, April 1995, pp. 271–281.

standardized, scripted conflict with either a subordinate or a superior. The possible styles in this study (with examples) included:

- *Confrontation.* Confronting and thrashing around issues head-on, but civilly.
- *Forcing.* "If I am confronted by a roadblock, then I take the decision to somebody higher up."[62]
- *Avoidance.* In general, **avoidance** or **smoothing over** usually won't resolve a conflict. However, some problems do go away by themselves. And avoidance may be your only option if one or both parties are highly emotional.
- *Process controlling.* "We're going to follow my agenda for this meeting and solve this problem my way" is an example of process controlling. **Process controlling** means dominating the conflict-resolution process to one's own advantage.
- *Compromise and collaboration.* **Compromise** means each person gives up something in return for reaching agreement. **Collaboration** means both people work together to achieve agreement.
- *Accommodating.* "Calm down so we can work this out."[63] **Accommodation** means temporarily accommodating the other person, perhaps to calm him or her down.

At least for these police sergeants, using three styles together—*problem solving* while being moderately *accommodating* and still maintaining a strong hand in *controlling* the conflict-resolution process—was an especially effective combination.

Figure 11.5 provides a self-assessment exercise for assessing one's own conflict-resolution style, using a similar list of styles discussed above. Remember that most people are capable of adapting their styles to the situation and using several styles at once.

avoidance: moving away from or refusing to discuss a conflict issue

smoothing over: in conflict management, diminishing or avoiding a conflict issue

process controlling: dominating the conflict-resolution process to one's own advantage

compromise: settling a conflict through mutual concessions

collaboration: a conflict-management style in which both sides work together to achieve agreement

accommodation: temporarily giving in to an opponent in an attempt to end a conflict

FIGURE 11.5

Your Conflict-Resolution Style

Indicate how often you do the following when you differ with someone.

When I Differ with Someone:

	Usually	Sometimes	Seldom
1. I explore our differences, not backing down, but not imposing my view either.	☐	☐	☐
2. I disagree openly, then invite more discussion about our differences.	☐	☐	☐
3. I look for a mutually satisfactory solution.	☐	☐	☐
4. Rather than let the other person make a decision without my input, I make sure that I am heard and that I hear the other out.	☐	☐	☐
5. I agree to a middle ground rather than look for a completely satisfying solution.	☐	☐	☐
6. I admit I am half wrong rather than explore our differences.	☐	☐	☐
7. I have a reputation for meeting a person halfway.	☐	☐	☐
8. I expect to get out about half of what I really want to say.	☐	☐	☐
9. I give in totally rather than try to change another's opinion.	☐	☐	☐
10. I put aside any controversial aspects of an issue.	☐	☐	☐
11. I agree early on rather than argue about a point.	☐	☐	☐
12. I give in as soon as the other party gets emotional about an issue.	☐	☐	☐
13. I try to win the other person over.	☐	☐	☐
14. I work to come out victorious, no matter what.	☐	☐	☐
15. I never back away from a good argument.	☐	☐	☐
16. I would rather win than end up compromising.	☐	☐	☐

Scoring Key and Interpretation

Total your choices as follows: Give yourself 5 points for "Usually"; 3 points for "Sometimes"; and 1 point for "Seldom." Then total them for each set of statements, grouped as follows:

Set A: items 13–16	Set C: items 5–8
Set B: items 9–12	Set D: items 1–4

Treat each set separately.
A score of 17 or above on any set is considered high.
Scores of 8 to 16 are moderate.
Scores of 7 or less are considered low.

Sets A, B, C, and D represent conflict-resolution strategies:
A = Forcing/domination. I win, you lose.
B = Accommodation. I lose, you win.
C = Compromise. Both win some, lose some.
D = Collaboration. I win, you win.

Everyone has a basic or underlying conflict-handling style. Your scores on this exercise indicate the strategies you rely on most.

SOURCE: Adapted from Thomas J. Von de Embse, *Supervision: Managerial Skills for a New Era* (New York: Macmillian Publishing Company, 1987), in Stephen Robbins and Philip Hunsaker, *Training in Interpersonal Skills* (Upper Saddle River, N.J.: Prentice Hall, 1996), pp. 217–219.

CHAPTER SUMMARY

1. The manager's change program can aim to alter one of four basic things: The firm's strategy, technology, structure, and people/behavior/culture. In practice, such changes are rarely compartmentalized. Instead, the manager needs to take a systems view of the change and its implications.
2. Today, reorganizing a company by changing departments and reporting relationships is only part of the manager's organizing responsibilities. Every business consists of various business processes. In a highly competitive global environment, managers can gain a competitive advantage by using information technology to make their processes as efficient and agile as possible.
3. Business process reengineering projects tend to be one-time efforts that aim to produce dramatic reorganizations of the handful of major business processes that management believes are keeping the company from becoming world-class. Business process management is usually an ongoing process aimed at making incremental improvements in processes, continuously, over time.
4. The hardest part of leading a change is overcoming resistance. Resistance stems from several sources: habit, resource limitations, threats to power and influence, fear of the unknown, and altering employees' personal compacts.
5. Methods of dealing with resistance include education and communication, facilitation and support, participation and involvement, negotiation and agreement, manipulation and co-optation, and coercion. Lewin suggests unfreezing the situation, perhaps by using a dramatic event to get people to recognize the need for change.
6. A ten-step process for actually leading organizational change includes creating a sense of urgency, deciding what to change, creating a guiding coalition and mobilizing commitment to change through a joint diagnosis of business problems, developing and then communicating a shared vision, removing barriers to the change and empowering employees, implementing the change, generating short-term wins, consolidating gains and producing more change, anchoring the new ways of doing things in the company's culture, and monitoring progress and adjusting the vision as required.
7. Organizational development (OD) is a special approach to organizational change that basically involves letting the employees themselves formulate and implement the change that's required, often with the assistance of a trained consultant. Types of OD applications include human process applications, technostructural interventions, HR management applications, and strategic applications.

DISCUSSION QUESTIONS

1. Why do we say that no organizational change is ever compartmentalized?
2. List and give examples of the four main things a manager can try to change in his or her organization.
3. How exactly would you go about unfreezing a situation at work?
4. What are the ten steps in the organizational change process? Provide examples of each step.
5. What aspects of the change process did Carlos Ghosn apply at Nissan?
6. Briefly describe the conditions under which you would use education, participation, and coercion to overcome resistance.

EXPERIENTIAL EXERCISES

1. In teams of four to five students, use what you learned about organizational culture in this chapter to describe the organizational culture in this class. List the specific things that you believe contributed to creating that culture and what specifically you would do to fine-tune the culture.
2. Assume that you are the professor in a management class and you have a problem. Classes started last week, and the class did not get off to a good start. You arrived late, were snappy with the students, and gave them the impression that you'd be running a tough, dictatorial classroom. Several

students dropped the course, and most of the others probably stayed only because the other sections were full. You don't want to have a miserable semester. Form teams of four or five students, and write out an outline, using the ten-step change process from page 318, that shows what exactly you would change in your class (if you were the professor) and how you would change it to have a more pleasant and productive class.

3. Working in teams of four to five students, explain specifically how you would apply each of the three steps in Lewin's change process to overcome resistance to change in the following situations: (a) Your brother is 100 pounds overweight. How would you get him to go on a diet? (b) Your professor gave you an A– instead of an A because you compiled a 91.9 average instead of the required 92, and you want the grade changed to an A. (c) You want to go to France on vacation this year, but your significant other is concerned with the risks of flying and of being out of the United States. How can you get your significant other to change his or her mind? (d) You just applied for a job as marketing manager for a local department store. The head of HR says that you seem like a very good candidate but that you don't have quite enough experience. How would you overcome his or her resistance?

4. Your college bookstore has a process for returning and getting credit for used textbooks. In teams of four to five students, visit the bookstore; analyze that process; and explain, complete with a flowchart, how you would reengineer the process.

CASE STUDY

Immelt Splits GE Capital

In his first major reorganization since taking over as CEO of General Electric (GE), Jeffrey Immelt said that he was splitting GE's huge GE capital finance division into four major parts. GE Capital produces about 40 percent of all of GE's earnings, and the heads of its individual insurance, consumer finance, commercial finance, and equipment units formerly reported to GE Capital chief executive Denis Nayden. He, in turn, reported to Jeffrey Immelt, along with the heads of GE's various other businesses, including NBC, appliances, and medical equipment. Under the new organization, Immelt eliminated the position of GE Capital chief executive, and the heads of GE Capital's four main insurance, consumer finance, commercial finance, and equipment units will now report directly to Immelt.

In making the change, Immelt basically said that he wanted more direct day-to-day control over GE Capital's huge financial services businesses. He said, "This will create a clearer line of sight on how our financial services businesses operate and enhance growth." The reorganization will, therefore, give him the same direct control over each of the GE Capital divisions that he now has with respect to GE's other businesses, such as appliances and jet engines. Another benefit of the change, according to GE, is that its "external reporting will mirror this organizational structure, providing greater clarity for investors." In other words, investors will now receive financial reports on each of the four GE Capital businesses rather than on just GE Capital as a whole.

While the reorganization seems to make sense, several observers have criticized it. The range of businesses and the number of people reporting to Immelt are already quite large, and the new organization means he'll have three additional people reporting directly to him. Furthermore, there are some obvious synergies among the four separate GE Capital divisions; therefore, it's now going to be up to Immelt to ensure that he provides the required coordination so that those synergies take place. Others point out that the sorts of improvements that Immelt says he wants—such as giving him a clearer idea of what each of the four divisions is doing—could have been accomplished without a major reorganization. In the past, for instance, GE's former CEO, Jack Welch, personally reviewed major GE Capital transactions. Another analyst pointed out that "... [w]henever a high-level executive [such as Nayden] departs, you have to be a little bit skeptical, and it raises a red flag that perhaps there may be another shoe."[64]

DISCUSSION QUESTIONS

1. Use Figure 11.1 to answer this question: Was this reorganization really necessary? What other knowledge that you have about how to reorganize would you apply to answering this question, and what conclusions do you draw?

2. Use the nine test questions (such as the market advantage test) in this chapter both to analyze the organization that Immelt decided upon and to answer this question: How would you have reorganized GE Capital?

HUMAN RESOURCE MANAGEMENT 12

Sutter Health

Sutter Health is a nonprofit health-care network headquartered in Sacramento, California. The company supports the work of its California health-care affiliates. These affiliates have to fill about 10,000 job openings per year. The company therefore must attract huge numbers of recruits, perhaps 100,000 or more, to fill those 10,000 positions. The job of attracting and keeping track of so many recruits is enormous. Sutter tried putting its job openings online. That produced over 300,000 résumés per year, overwhelming Sutter's human resources (HR) unit. Project manager Keith Vencel had to devise a better recruitment solution. What should he do?[1] ■

Sutter Health needed a way to recruit thousands of applicants per year for its offices around California.

BEHAVIORAL OBJECTIVES

After studying this chapter, you should be able to

Show that you've learned the chapter's essential information by

- ➤ Explaining, with an example, strategic human resource management.
- ➤ Listing techniques managers use to recruit employees.
- ➤ Listing at least five guidelines for disciplining employees.
- ➤ Listing ten examples of how federal equal-employment law affects human resource management decisions.

Show that you can practice what you've learned here by

- ➤ Reading the chapter case study and explaining how this company could improve its interviewing process.
- ➤ Reading the chapter-opening vignette and explaining how to improve the company's recruitment and selection process.
- ➤ Reading the experiential exercises and explaining how to set up the training program.

CHAPTER OUTLINE

CHAPTER OUTLINE (Continued)

- **Appraising and Maintaining Employees**
  - Employee Appraisal
  - Compensation
  - Discipline and Grievances
  - Managing Now: Appraising and Maintaining Employees
  - **Window on Managing Now: GM and NCR**
- **Understanding HR's Legal Framework**
  - Equal-Employment Laws and Affirmative Action
  - Occupational Safety and Health
  - Labor-Management Relations
  - Managing Now: Integrating the Company's Global HR Information Systems

Show that you can apply what you've learned here by

- Watching the video scenario and explaining how you would set up the testing and selection process.
- Watching the simulation video and identifying human resource strategies used by the company to attract and maintain key employees.

Online Study Center
ACE the Test
Managing Now! LIVE

After designing the organization chart, managers turn to staffing their organizations. Staffing, personnel, or (as it is known today) **human resource (HR) management** is the management function devoted to acquiring, training, appraising, paying, and ensuring fairness and safety for the organization's employees. We can view human resource management as a series of steps, starting with identifying the job's requirements, and then recruiting, selecting, training, appraising, and compensating employees while continually attending to the important issues of employee fairness and safety (see Figure 12.1).

human resource (HR) management: the management function devoted to acquiring, training, appraising, paying, and ensuring fairness and safety for the organization's employees

Why study human resource management? Most firms have human resource (HR) departments, so you may reasonably ask, why study human resource management as part of a basic management course?

The answer is that every manager, not just human resource managers, spend much of their day doing HR-type tasks, such as interviewing, appraising, and disciplining employees. Hiring the right people is a prerequisite for managerial success. Hiring dysfunctional employees, experiencing high turnover, not attracting the best candidates, and triggering discrimination charges are some of the human resource management blunders that can torpedo any manager's career. The main purpose of this chapter is to familiarize you with basic staffing skills. The main topics we cover include writing job descriptions, interviewing and selecting employees, and training and appraising the firm's new workers.

Human Resource Management's Strategic Role

Online Study Center
ACE the Test
Managing Now! LIVE

Wisconsin-based Signicast's manufacturing process is very old, although Signicast has improved it dramatically. President Terry Lutz knew that for Signicast to vie with world-class competitors, it needed a new, automated plant. Currently, many of its employees have little formal education. They lacked the mathematical

FIGURE 12.1

The Basic HR Process

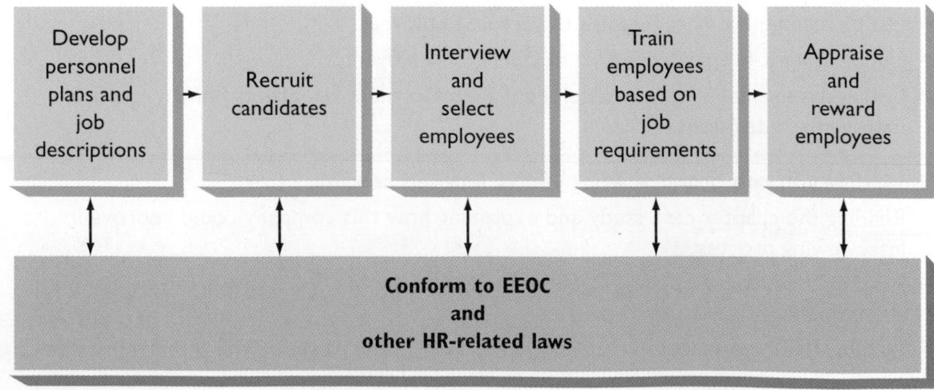

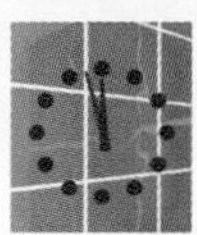

WINDOW ON MANAGING NOW
Signicast

At Signicast, HR's involvement began at the plant design stage. The human resource management group invited current employees to participate in planning and designing the new plant: "Employees would come up with suggestions; we'd implement them, and bring them back to [employees] for confirmation."

HR helped the company execute its new plant expansion strategy in other ways. For example, the new plant would produce parts almost five times faster than the old plant. The employees would therefore need more responsibility and self-control. Selection standards were thus tighter. At the old plant, the only hiring requirements were a high school diploma and a good work ethic. The new plant's employees would require the same high school degree and work ethic, plus team orientation, good trainability, good communication skills, and a willingness to do varied jobs over a twelve-hour shift. Human resources also created a cross-training program so that employees could do each other's jobs and ensure the company's workforce was as flexible as it could be. And a new compensation plan paid workers to learn more about the technical aspects of the plant (such as how to use the new computers). At Signicast, human resources played a strategic role in executing the company's new high-tech plant strategy.

and computer skills the new plant would require.[2] Mr. Lutz's whole strategy for growing his company hinged on finding, attracting, and then hiring and training those new employees, in other words, on human resource management.

What Is Strategic Human Resource Management?

Terry Lutz's experience illustrates why managers say that human resource management is "strategic" today. Computerized machines like Signicast's are useless without the right employees to run them. Building great hotels like Ritz-Carlton is futile without great, service-oriented employees. And Sutter Health will see its growth plans fail if it can't attract enough good employees. We saw (Chapter 7) that strategic planning is the process of identifying the firm's business today, its desired future business, and the courses of action it should pursue to get there given its opportunities, threats, strengths, and weaknesses. **Strategic human resource management** means formulating and executing human resource management policies and practices that produce the employee skills and behaviors that the company needs to achieve its strategic goals.

strategic human resource management: formulating and executing human resource management policies and practices that produce the employee skills and behaviors that the company needs in order to achieve its strategic goals

Many companies use PC-based digital dashboards to track the performance of their human resource management systems. The **HR scorecard** is a process for identifying the employer's essential human resource activities, and the causal links among (1) these activities (such as employee testing), (2) the resulting employee behaviors (such as turnover and productivity), and (3) the resulting contribution to the company (for instance, in terms of improved service and profitability). Thus, it might show that a new policy of testing all applicants seems to have reduced turnover by 80 percent and thus led to an additional profit of $1 million per year. The Window on Managing Now feature shows how Signicast's human resources team made its strategic contribution.

HR scorecard: a process for identifying the employer's essential human resource activities, and the causal links among (1) these activities such as employee testing, and (2) the resulting employee behaviors, such as turnover and productivity, and (3) the resulting contribution to the company, for instance, in terms of improved service and profitability

The Challenges Facing Human Resource Management

As at Signicast, changes are occurring today that are requiring human resources managers to play an increasingly central role in managing companies. These changes or trends include globalization, changes in the nature of work, and technology.

Globalization Trends Globalization is the tendency of firms to extend their sales, ownership, and/or manufacturing to new markets abroad. For managers, more globalization means more competition, and more competition means more pressure to lower costs and to make employees more productive. Both workers and companies therefore have to work harder and smarter than they did without globalization.

Trends in the Nature of Work Technology has had a huge impact on how people work and on the skills and training today's workers need. More and more traditional factory jobs are going high-tech. To paraphrase the U.S. government's Occupational Outlook Quarterly, knowledge-intensive high-tech manufacturing in industries like aerospace and telecommunications are replacing factory jobs in industries like steel and textiles. For managers, this means a growing emphasis on knowledge-based work, and therefore on human capital. *Human capital* refers to the knowledge, education, training, skills, and expertise of a firm's workers.

Labor Force Trends At the same time, workforce demographic trends are making finding and hiring good employees more challenging. Labor force growth is not expected to keep pace with job growth, with an estimated shortfall of about 14 million college-educated workers by 2020.[3] Most notably, the labor force is getting older. As the baby boomers born between 1946 and 1960 start leaving the labor force in the next few years, employers will face a labor shortage.

Trends like the above have had two implications for the human resource manager's job. First, it has become broader and more strategic over time, as it did at Signicast. Second, it now focuses more on productivity and performance.

High-Performance Work Systems Often, in fact, the best-performing companies like Toyota and GE perform so well in part because of their high-performance work systems.[4] A **high-performance work system (HPWS)** is an integrated set of human resource management policies and practices that together produce superior employee performance.

high-performance work system (HPWS): an integrated set of human resource management policies and practices that together produce superior employee performance

While there's no hard and fast rule about what policies and practices comprise high-performance work systems, they tend to include practices such as selective hiring, extensive training, and the use of self-managed teams. In terms of measurable outcomes, high-performance work systems produce, for instance, more qualified applicants per position, more employees hired based on validated selection tests, and more hours of training for new employees.

Managing Now: How Human Resource Managers Use Technology

Human resource managers also use technology to make their companies world-class. You will find specific examples throughout this chapter, but in general, technology improves HR functioning in four main ways: self-service, call centers, operational efficiencies, and outsourcing.[5] For example, Dell Corporation built a special human resources section on its intranet. Its employees can now *self-service* many of their human resources transactions, such as updating personal information and changing benefits allocations. Technology also enabled Dell to create its centralized HR *call center*. Human resources specialists here answer questions from all Dell's far-flung employees, reducing the need for multiple human resources centers at each Dell location.

More firms are installing Internet and computer-based systems for improving the *operational efficiency* of their human resources operations. International Paper Corp.'s "Viking" human resources information system is one example. The goal was to achieve a human resources staff to employee ratio of 1 to 150 (compared with 1 to 100), and a cost per employee of $800 for delivering human resources services.[6] Among other things, Viking includes an intranet employee portal that employees use to self-service certain human resources–related needs (such as updating their personal information).

Finally, technology makes it easier to *outsource* human resources activities to specialist service providers. It does this by enabling outside employee-benefits providers to have real-time Internet-based access to the employer's human resources database. Outsourcing is increasingly popular. About 84 percent of the human resources professionals responding said that their firms outsource the administration of their companies' 401(k) pension plans, and about 68 percent of employers outsource background checks to specialist firms.

In creating a modern human resources system, a logical place to start is by writing job descriptions and instituting an effective recruitment function, topics to which we now turn.

Writing Job Descriptions and Recruiting Employees

Human resource management starts with identifying and actually filling a firm's open positions. As you can see in Figure 12.2, this entire process encompasses job analysis, recruiting, selecting, and training employees.

job analysis: the procedure through which one determines the duties of the jobs and the kinds of people (in terms of skills and experience) to hire for them

Job Analysis and Personnel Planning

Designing an organization chart creates jobs the firm must fill. **Job analysis** is the procedure through which one determines the duties of the jobs and the kinds of

FIGURE 12.2

Steps in the Recruitment and Selection (Staffing) Process

The recruitment and selection process is a series of hurdles aimed at selecting the best candidate for the job.

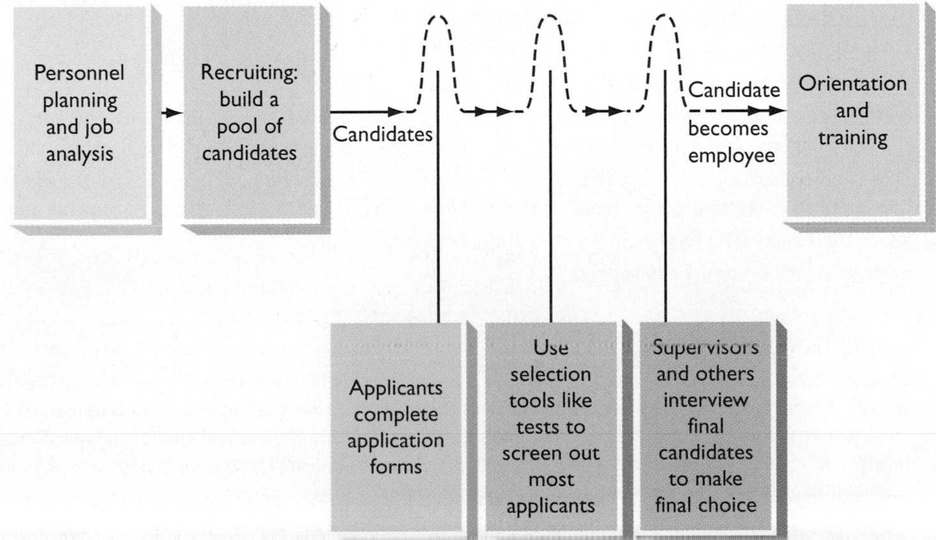

FIGURE 12.3

Sample Job Description

OLEC CORP.
Job Description

Job Title: Marketing Manager
Department: Marketing
Reports To: President
FLSA Status: Non Exempt
Prepared By: Michael George
Prepared Date: April 1, 2007
Approved By: Ian Alexander
Approved Date: April 15, 2007

SUMMARY

Plans, directs, and coordinates the marketing of the organization's products and/or services by performing the following duties personally or through subordinate supervisors.

ESSENTIAL DUTIES AND RESPONSIBILITIES include the following. Other duties may be assigned.

- Establishes marketing goals to ensure share of market and profitability of products and/or services.
- Develops and executes marketing plans and programs, both short and long range, to ensure the profit growth and expansion of company products and/or services.
- Researches, analyzes, and monitors financial, technological, and demographic factors so that market opportunities may be capitalized on and the effects of competitive activity may be minimized.
- Plans and oversees the organization's advertising and promotion activities including print, electronic, and direct mail outlets.
- Communicates with outside advertising agencies on ongoing campaigns.
- Works with writers and artists and oversees copywriting, design, layout, pasteup, and production of promotional materials.
- Develops and recommends pricing strategy for the organization, which will result in the greatest share of the market over the long run.
- Achieves satisfactory profit/loss ratio and share of market performance in relation to preset standards and to general and specific trends within the industry and the economy.
- Ensures effective control of marketing results and that corrective action takes place to be certain that the achievement of marketing objectives are within designated budgets.
- Evaluates market reactions to advertising programs, merchandising policy, and product packaging and formulation to ensure the timely adjustment of marketing strategy and plans to meet changing market and competitive conditions.
- Recommends changes in basic structure and organization of marketing group to ensure the effective fulfillment of objectives assigned to it and to provide the flexibility to move swiftly in relation to marketing problems and opportunities.
- Conducts marketing surveys on current and new product concepts.
- Prepares marketing activity reports.

SUPERVISORY RESPONSIBILITIES

Manages three subordinate supervisors who supervise a total of five employees in the Marketing Department. Is responsible for the overall direction, coordination, and evaluation of this unit. Also directly supervises two non-supervisory employees. Carries out supervisory responsibilities in accordance with the organization's policies and applicable laws. Responsibilities include interviewing, hiring, and training employees; planning, assigning, and directing work; appraising performance; rewarding and disciplining employees; addressing complaints and resolving problems.

FIGURE 12.3 (*Continued*)

QUALIFICATIONS
To perform this job successfully, an individual must be able to perform each essential duty satisfactorily. The requirements listed below are representative of the knowledge, skill, and/or ability required. Reasonable accommodations may be made to enable individuals with disabilities to perform the essential functions.

EDUCATION and/or EXPERIENCE
Master's degree (M.A.) or equivalent; or four to ten years related experience and/or training; or equivalent combination of education and experience.

LANGUAGE SKILLS
Ability to read, analyze, and interpret common scientific and technical journals, financial reports, and legal documents. Ability to respond to common inquiries or complaints from customers, regulatory agencies, or members of the business community. Ability to write speeches and articles for publication that conform to prescribed style and format. Ability to effectively present information to top management, public groups, and/or boards of directors.

MATHEMATICAL SKILLS
Ability to apply advanced mathematical concepts such as exponents, logarithms, quadratic equations, and permutations. Ability to apply mathematical operations to such tasks as frequency distribution, determination of test reliability and validity, analysis of variance, correlation techniques, sampling theory, and factor analysis.

REASONING ABILITY
Ability to define problems, collect data, establish facts, and draw valid conclusions. Ability to interpret an extensive variety of technical instructions in mathematical or diagram form.

people (in terms of skills and experience) to hire for them.[7] Managers then use this information to develop a **job description** (a list of duties showing what each job entails) and a **job specification** (a list of the skills and aptitudes sought in people hired for the job).

job description: a list of duties showing what each job entails

job specification: a list of the skills and aptitudes sought in people hired for a job

The job description, like the one in Figure 12.3, identifies the job, provides a brief job summary, and then lists specific responsibilities and duties. Most descriptions contain sections that cover job identification, job summary, responsibilities and duties, authority of incumbent, working conditions, and job specifications (the human requirements of the job, such as education required).

job analysis questionnaire: a questionnaire used to ascertain a job's duties and responsibilities

Managers can use a **job analysis questionnaire** (see Figure 12.4) to ascertain a job's duties and responsibilities. Employees provide detailed information on what they do. They briefly state their main duties, describe the conditions under which they work, and list any permits or licenses required to their perform duties. Supervisors and/or human resources specialists then review this information.

personnel planning: the process of determining the organization's future personnel needs, as well as the methods to be used to fill those needs

Job analysis is part of personnel planning. **Personnel planning** is the process of determining the organization's future personnel needs, as well as the methods to be used to fill those needs. Here, the manager estimates the company's future personnel needs, for instance, in terms of projected revenues and installing new plants or facilities. Personnel planning also involves deciding ahead of time (planning) where the requisite employees will come from (within or outside the company's employee pool) and how to train them.

FIGURE 12.4

Preliminary Job Description Questionnaire

Use a questionnaire like this one to interview job incumbents, or have them fill it out.

Instructions: Distribute copies of this questionnaire to supervisors, managers, personnel staff members, job analysts, and others who may be involved in writing job descriptions. Ask them to record their answers to these questions in writing.

1. What is the job title? ____________________
2. Summarize the job's more important, regularly performed/duties in a Job Summary.
3. In what department is the job located? ____________________
4. What is the title of the supervisor or manager to whom the jobholder must report?
5. Does the jobholder supervise other employees? If so, give their job titles and a brief description of their responsibilities.

Position Supervised	Responsibilities

6. What essential function duties does the jobholder perform regularly? List them in order of importance.

Duty	Percentage of Time Devoted to This Duty
1.	
2.	
3.	
4.	
5.	
6.	

7. Does the jobholder perform other duties periodically? Infrequently? If so, please list, indicating frequency.
8. What are the working conditions? List such items as noise, heat, outside work, and exposure to bad weather.
9. How much authority does the jobholder have in such matters as training or guiding other people?
10. How much education, experience, and skill are required for satisfactory job performance?
11. At what stage is the jobholder's work reviewed by the supervisor?
12. What machines or equipment is the jobholder responsible for operating?
13. If the jobholder makes a serious mistake or error in performing required duties, what would be the cost to management?

SOURCE: www.HR.BLR.com © 2004 Business and Legal Reports, Inc. Reprinted by permission.

personnel replacement charts: charts that show the present performance and the likelihood of promotion for each potential replacement

Many employers use **personnel replacement charts** (see Figure 12.5) to keep track of inside candidates for important positions. These charts show the present performance and the likelihood of promotion for each potential replacement. Many firms maintain computerized databanks containing information on hundreds of traits (like special skills, product knowledge, work experience, training courses, relocation limitations, and career interests) for each employee.

FIGURE 12.5

Management Personnel Replacement Chart

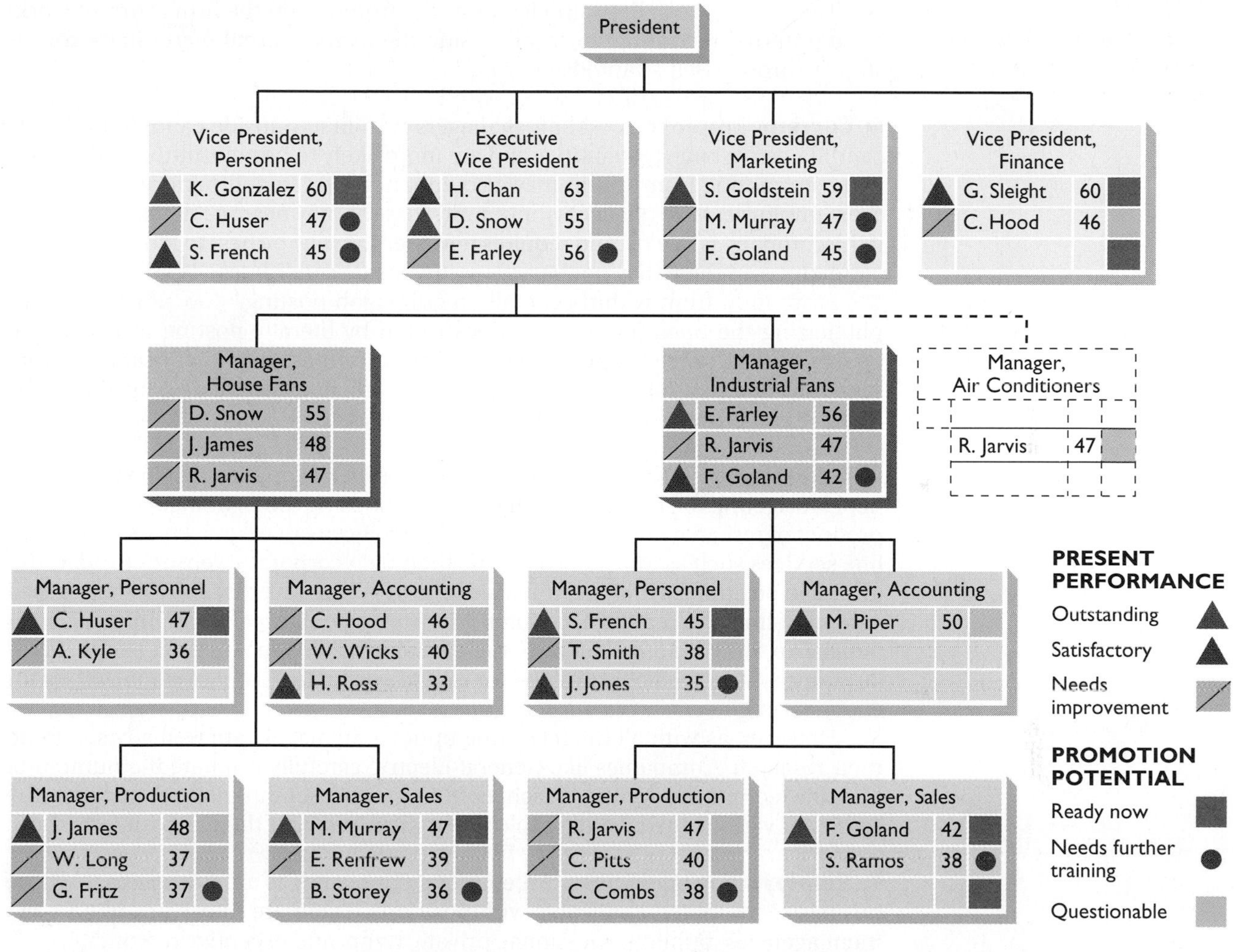

Employee Recruiting

recruiting: attracting a pool of viable job applicants

Once the manager knows the specifics of the jobs to fill, **recruiting**—attracting a pool of viable job applicants—becomes important. Only with a sufficient number of applicants can the manager use techniques like interviews and tests to select the best.

Several things affect a firm's ability to attract candidates. Economic conditions are one: high unemployment tends to make recruiting easier, for instance. The employer's compensation and other personnel policies are also important. For example, hospitals that pay higher salaries find it easier to recruit nurses. The company's reputation is very important. For example, some firms are known for great training programs and for being excellent places to work, for instance, in terms of child-care benefits. Indeed, *BusinessWeek* magazine ran a story on the best places for recent graduates to work, listing firms like Disney, Lockheed Martin, and Goldman Sachs. Some applicants also gravitate toward companies with better growth prospects (perhaps choosing, for instance, Google over a steel company if a choice must be made).

The manager can draw applicants either from within the firm's current workforce (internal recruiting) or from outside the firm (external recruiting)—for instance, through help-wanted ads.

● Current Employees Many managers turn first to inside candidates. Inside candidates are known quantities and are more likely to be committed to the company. Promoting from within may also enhance morale and performance. However, employees who unsuccessfully apply for jobs may become demoralized. And if the company is in a rut and requires new ideas, it may be best to look outside the company. And there may not be any worthy inside candidates.

job posting: publicizing an open job to employees (often by literally posting it on bulletin boards and intranets)

Promotion from within generally requires job posting.[8] **Job posting** means publicizing the open job to employees (often by literally posting it on bulletin boards and intranets) and listing the job's attributes, like qualifications, work schedule, and pay. Job posting can be a good practice, insofar as it facilitates the transfer and promotion of qualified inside candidates.[9]

● Advertising Advertising is a major way to attract applicants. The main issue here is selecting the best advertising media. Choosing the right media should be a product of research and common sense. The majority of employers today use online services such as Monster.com, plus their own corporate websites to advertise available positions. However, it makes little sense to advertise for Chicago-based assembly-line workers in a national Monster-type campaign, or in a business paper like the *Wall Street Journal;* the *Chicago Tribune* makes more sense. Similarly, one would sensibly advertise for executives in the *Wall Street Journal*, or for chemical engineers in *Chemical Engineer.*

However, as with all the recruiting options, managers are well advised to do their research. Companies like General Electric carefully evaluate the number of hireable recruits they get from each recruiting source, comparing, for instance, the results of various media and employment agencies, and then choosing the best.

● Employment Agencies An employment agency is an intermediary whose business is to match applicants with positions. There are four types of employment agencies: public/professional, private, temp, and executive recruiter.

Public Employment Agencies Public employment agencies, often called job-service or unemployment-service agencies, exist in every state. They are good sources of blue-collar and clerical workers, but firms also use them for professional and managerial-level applicants. They also provide applicants with career counseling and job-search training, and they provide employers with counseling in matters such as writing job descriptions. Other employment agencies are associated with *not-for-profit organizations.* For example, most professional and technical societies have units to help members find jobs.

Private Agencies Private agencies charge a fee for each applicant they place. Market conditions determine whether the employer or the candidate pays the fee, but the norm today is for fee-paid jobs, a situation in which the employer pays. These agencies are important sources of clerical, white-collar, and managerial personnel. Even giant companies may use employment agencies because of the specialized work they do in advertising for applicants and winnowing down the applicant pool to an acceptable few. The harried small-business owner may have little choice but to retain one. Points to keep in mind when dealing with employment agencies include:

- Give the agency an accurate and complete job description.
- Make sure that tests, application blanks, and interviews are part of the agency's selection process.
- Periodically review data on candidates accepted or rejected by your firm and by the agency.
- Develop a long-term relationship with one or two agencies.
- Screen the agency: what is its reputation in the community and with the Better Business Bureau?[10]

Contingent Workers and Temporary Help Agencies Employers often supplement their permanent workforce by hiring contingent or temporary workers, often through *temporary help employment agencies.* Also known as part-time or just-in-time workers, they are defined as workers who don't have permanent jobs.[11] It is estimated that 60 percent of the total U.S. temporary payroll is nonclerical and includes "CEOs, human resources directors, computer systems analysts, accountants, doctors, and nurses."[12] When Foster Farms in California found itself falling behind in solving its information technology (IT) problems, it hired an experienced interim chief information officer (CIO).[13]

executive recruiters: agencies retained by employers to look for top management talent, usually in the $70,000 and up category; also called headhunters

Executive Recruiters **Executive recruiters** (also called headhunters) are agencies retained by employers to look for top management talent, usually in the $70,000 and up category. They have extensive contacts and files of potential recruits, and they are adept at contacting qualified employed candidates who aren't looking to change jobs. The recruiter saves employers time by advertising the position and screening what could turn out to be hundreds of applicants. Their ability to research who might be viable and to reach out to them is something of an art that few employers can do themselves.

● Referrals and Walk-Ins Particularly for hourly workers, walk-ins—people who apply directly at the office, perhaps in response to Now Hiring signs—are a major source of applicants. Other firms use employee-referral campaigns to encourage applicants. They may post job openings and requests for referrals in the company's newsletter, on its intranet, or on bulletin boards. Of the firms responding to one survey, 40 percent said that they use employee-referral campaigns and hire about 15 percent of their employees through referrals. A cash award for referring hired candidates is the most common incentive.[14]

● College Recruiting College recruiting—sending employers' representatives to college campuses to prescreen applicants and create an applicant pool from the graduating class—is an important source of management, professional, and technical employees. One study of 251 staffing professionals concluded that firms filled about 38 percent of all externally filled jobs requiring a college degree with new college graduates.[15] They often use the form as presented in Figure 12.6. Traits assessed include motivation, communication skills, education, appearance, and attitude.[16]

College recruiting often involves internships. Here, students may be able to hone business skills, check out potential employers, and learn more about their

FIGURE 12.6

Campus Applicant Interview Report

CAMPUS INTERVIEW REPORT

Name ____________________ Anticipated Graduation Date __________

Current Address ____________________
(if different than on placement form)

Position Applied For ____________________

If Applicable (Use Comment Section if necessary)

Driver's License Yes ____ No ____

Any special considerations affecting your availability for relocation?

____

____

Are you willing to travel? ________ If so, what % of time? ________

EVALUATION	Outstanding	Above Average	Average	Below Average
Education: Courses relevant to job? Does performance in class indicate good potential for work?	____	____	____	____
Appearance: Was applicant neat and dressed appropriately?	____	____	____	____
Communication Skills: Was applicant mentally alert? Did he or she express ideas clearly?	____	____	____	____
Motivation: Does applicant have high energy level? Are his or her interests compatible with job?	____	____	____	____
Attitude: Did applicant appear to be pleasant, people-oriented?	____	____	____	____

COMMENTS: (Use back of sheet if necessary) ____________________

____

Given Application Yes ____ No ____ Received Transcript Release Authorization ____

Recommendations Invite ____ Reject ____

Interviewed by: ____________________ Date: __________

Campus ____________________

SOURCE: Adapted and updated from Joseph J. Famularo, *Handbook of Personnel Forms, Records, and Reports* (New York: McGraw-Hill, 1982), p. 70.

occupational preferences. Employers can use interns to make useful contributions while evaluating them as possible full-time employees. Almost three-quarters of all college students take part in an internship before they graduate, and many get their jobs this way.[17] Some interns are unpaid. On the other hand, it is not unusual

Today, recruiting a diverse workforce isn't just socially responsible; it's a necessity.

for law firms to pay top first-year law students $30,000 or more for a summer internship.

Recruiting a More Diverse Workforce As we discussed in Chapter 2, recruiting a diverse workforce isn't just socially responsible; it's a necessity. Nationwide, minorities already represent over 20 percent of the workforce in 2006 (and much higher percentages in some states, like California).

In this case, recruiting usually involves two special efforts. One is to create job openings that make sense for the women or minorities one wants to attract. For example, knowing that single parents need flexible work hours may suggest creating a flexible work-hour program for the employees. The other issue is ensuring that the people one hires have the job skills they need to get up to speed in the work world. Marriott International hired 600 welfare recipients under its Pathways to Independence program. The program includes a six-week training program that teaches work and life skills.

Managing Now: Job Analysis and Employee Recruitment

Thanks to the Internet, managers now have new ways to analyze jobs and recruit employees. For one thing, the widespread availability of online job-description services makes it easy for any manager to quickly create job descriptions. The site www.jobdescription.com is a good example. Search by alphabetical title, keyword, category, or industry to find the desired job title. This leads you to a generic job description for that title, say, "Computers and EDP systems sales representative." Then use the wizard to add specific information such as job title, department, and preparation date.

The U.S. Department of Labor's occupational information network, called O*NET, is another useful Web tool (you'll find it at www.doleta.gov/programs/onet). From thousands of jobs in its database, the manager can find a specific job's typical duties, as well as its experience, education, and knowledge requirements.

Recruiting on the Internet As mentioned earlier, most employers use the Internet for recruiting. Managing now goes beyond the usual Monster.com-type listings.[18] For example, Unisys Corporation posts Internet-based recruiting fairs. Others search online databases for applicants. Thus, the human resource manager for a hydraulic products company found that one keyword search of the HotJobs database produced fifty-two usable résumés. Newer online recruiting sites capitalize on social networking. For example, users register by supplying their name, location, and the kind of work they do on sites like monsternetworking.com and LinkIn.com. These sites help develop personal relationships for networking, hiring, and employee referrals. The accountants Deloitte & Touche Tohmatsu created a global recruitment site, thus eliminating the need to maintain 35 separate local recruiting websites. Arizona had IBM Global Services create a disability-friendly website, Arizona@YourService, to help link prospective employees and others to various agencies.

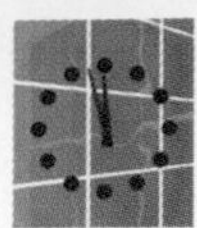

Window on Managing Now
Cisco Systems Inc.

Many employers, including Cisco Systems, use information technology like PC-based video cameras and the Internet to conduct initial screening interviews. Cisco equips its recruiters with PC-based video cameras. The recruiter instructs the applicant to use his or her own PC camera or one at a local FedEx Kinko's. At the appointed time, the candidate calls in and links to the Cisco recruiter via the Web. The process doesn't eliminate face-to-face interviews. However, using it for the initial screening interview reduces travel and recruiting expenses and make things easier for candidates.[19]

Job hunters should know, by the way, that employers are checking candidates' social networking sites' postings. One employer went to Facebook.com and found that a top candidate described his interests as smoking marijuana and shooting people. The student may have been kidding, but he did not get the offer.[20]

The Window on Managing Now feature provides an illustration of how Cisco uses information technology to recruit candidates.

In general, the Web is a relatively cost-effective way to publicize openings. For example, Marsha Wheatley, HR director for the Washington, D.C.–based American Crop Protection Association, no longer runs $400 ads in the *Washington Post* when looking for agricultural engineers. Instead, ads on WashingtonPost.com cost only $200. And "instead of a tiny ad that says, 'ACPA needs an accountant,' I get a whole page to describe the job. . . ."[21]

applicant tracking services: services that compile the employer's online applications, screen the incoming résumés using the employer's standards, and then assist the employer in automatically scheduling interviews for high-potential applicants

● **Managing Now: Applicant Tracking Services** Managers increase the efficiency and effectiveness of their online recruiting efforts by contracting with **applicant tracking services**. These services receive and compile the employer's online applications, automatically screen the incoming résumés using the employer's standards, and then assist the employer in automatically scheduling interviews for high-potential applicants. The Practice IT feature shows how Sutter Health uses this tool.

Practice IT
Sutter Health

With over 300,000 applications per year, online job postings proved to be too much of a good thing for Sutter Health. Project manager Keith Vencel knew he needed a better solution.[22] His solution was to contract with an online applications service provider (ASP) company that supplies an applicant tracking system. Sutter's applicants apply for jobs on what appears to be a Sutter website, but it is really one that the ASP is managing. Applicants fill out applications and answer online questions.

The applicant tracking system first rejects applicants who do not meet the firm's minimum requirements (like willingness to submit to drug tests). Then it scores the applicants' online tests, such as a Web-based skills test in accounting. The applicant tracking system also automatically keeps track of each applicant. For example, it searches for keywords like "MBA" and brings résumés to a hiring manager's attention. It also schedules interviews and reminds supervisors when an applicant is due for an interview.

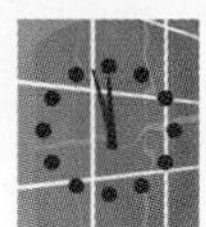

Window on Managing Now
City Garage

Establishing the right screening process can have a decisive effect on a firm's success. For example, City Garage, a 200-employee chain of twenty-five auto-service and -repair shops in Dallas–Fort Worth, Texas, had expanded rapidly. However, its growth was hampered by the problems it was having hiring good managers and employees.[23]

City Garage's original hiring process consisted of a paper-and-pencil application and one interview, immediately followed by a hire–don't hire decision. Local shop managers didn't have the time to evaluate every applicant: "If they had been shorthanded too long, we would hire pretty much anybody who had experience," said training director Rusty Reinhold. City's solution was to purchase the Personality Profile Analysis (PPA) online test from Thompson International USA. Now, after a quick application and background check, candidates take the ten-minute, twenty-four-question PPA. City Garage staff enter the answers into the PPA software system, and employee suitability test results are available in two minutes. As Reinhold says, "[A]t a minimum, we feel like we'll be able to put $500,000 on the bottom line each year, if [the PPA] does what we expect it to in terms of retention and right hiring."

Interviewing and Selecting Employees

Online Study Center
ACE the Test
Managing Now! LIVE

With a pool of applicants, managers turn to assessing the applicants' aptitudes, interests, and backgrounds using various screening techniques. These techniques include application blanks, interviews, tests, and reference checks. From this information, the manager can then choose the best candidate.

Employee selection is important for several reasons. A poor performer drags a manager down, and a good one enhances the manager's and the firms' performance. Hiring applicants is also expensive, so it is best to do it right. The cost of hiring even nonexecutive employees can be $3,000 to $5,000, or more. Effective screening is also important to avoid "negligent hiring" allegations. For example, lawyers sued Wal-Mart, alleging that several of its employees with sexually related convictions had assaulted young girls. Wal-Mart then instituted a program of criminal background checks for otherwise qualified candidates. The Window on Managing Now feature shows how employers use technology to improve their selection processes.

Application Forms

application form: form used in selection; usually includes information about areas such as education, prior work history, and hobbies

For most employers, the **application form** is the first step in the selection process. (Some firms first require a brief prescreening interview.) As you can see in Figure 12.7, it usually includes information about areas such as education, prior work history, and hobbies.

Testing for Employee Selection

test: a sample of a person's behavior

A **test** is a sample of a person's behavior. Employers use tests to predict success on the job. About 45 percent of 1,085 companies surveyed by the American Management Association tested applicants for basic skills (defined as the ability to read

FIGURE 12.7

Employment Application

FEDERAL BUREAU OF INVESTIGATION

Preliminary Application for Special Agent Position (Please Type or Print in Black Ink)

Date: ____________

FIELD OFFICE USE ONLY
Right Thumb Print

Div: Program:

I. PERSONAL HISTORY

Name in Full (Last, First, Middle)

List College Degree(s) Already Received or Pursuing, Major, School, and Month/Year:

Marital Status: ☐ Single ☐ Engaged ☐ Married ☐ Separated ☐ Legally Separated ☐ Widowed ☐ Divorced

Birth Date (Month, Day, Year)
Birth Place:

Social Security Number: (Optional)

Do you understand FBI employment requires availability for assignment anywhere in the U.S.?

Current Address

Street Apt. No.

City State Zip Code

Home Phone: Area Code Number

Work Phone: Area Code Number

Are you: CPA ☐ Yes ☐ No Licensed Driver ☐ Yes ☐ No U. S. Citizen ☐ Yes ☐ No

Have you served on active duty in the U. S. Military? ☐ Yes ☐ No If yes, indicate branch of service and dates (month/year) of active duty. Include military school attendance (month/year):

How did you learn or become interested in FBI employment as a Special Agent?

Have you previously applied for FBI employment? ☐ Yes ☐ No
If yes, location and date:

Do you have a foreign language background? ☐ Yes ☐ No List proficiency for each language on reverse side.

Have you ever been arrested for any crime (include major traffic violations such as Driving Under the Influence or While Intoxicated, etc.)? ☐ Yes ☐ No If so, list all such matters on a continuation sheet, even if not formally charged, or no court appearance or found not guilty, or matter settled by payment of fine or forfeiture of collateral. Include date, place, charge, disposition, details, and police agency on reverse side.

II. EMPLOYMENT HISTORY

Identify your most recent three years FULL-TIME work experience, after high school (excluding summer, part-time and temporary employment).

From Month/Year	To Month/Year	Title of Position and Description of Work	# of hrs. Per week	Name/Location of Employer

III. PERSONAL DECLARATIONS

Persons with a disability who require an accommodation to complete the application process are required to notify the FBI of their need for the accommodation.

Have you used marijuana during the last three years or more than 15 times? ☐ Yes ☐ No

Have you used any illegal drug(s) or combination of illegal drugs, other than marijuana, more than 5 times or during the last 10 years? ☐ Yes ☐ No

All information provided by applicants concerning their drug history will be subject to verification by a preemployment polygraph examination.

Do you understand all prospective FBI employees will be required to submit to an urinalysis for drug abuse prior to employment? ☐ Yes ☐ No

Please do not write below this line.

I am aware that willfully withholding information or making false statements on this application constitutes a violation of Section 1001, Title 18, U.S. Code and if appointed, will be the basis for dismissal from the Federal Bureau of Investigation. I agree to these conditions and I hereby certify that all statements made by me on this application are true and complete, to the best of my knowledge.

Signature of applicant as usually written (Do Not Use Nickname)

FIGURE 12.8

Sample Test

Check Yes or No	Yes	No
1. You like a lot of excitement in your life.	☐	☐
2. An employee who takes it easy at work is cheating on the employer.	☐	☐
3. You are a cautious person.	☐	☐
4. In the past three years, you have found yourself in a shouting match at school or work.	☐	☐
5. You like to drive fast just for fun.	☐	☐

Analysis: According to John Kamp, an industrial psychologist, applicants who answered no, yes, yes, no, no to questions 1, 2, 3, 4, and 5 are statistically likely to be absent less often, to have fewer on-the-job injuries, and, if the job involves driving, to have fewer on-the-job driving accidents. Actual scores on the test are based on answers to 130 questions.

SOURCE: Courtesy of NYT permissions.

instructions, write reports, and do arithmetic at a level adequate to perform common workplace tasks).[24] Another survey concluded that 38.6 percent of companies said that they performed psychological testing on job applicants, ranging from tests of the applicants' cognitive abilities to honesty testing.[25] Try the short test in Figure 12.8 to see how prone you might be to on-the-job accidents.

Tests are not for just low-level workers. For example, consultants McKinsey & Co. flew fifty-four MIT MBA students to Miami for two days of multiple-choice business knowledge tests, case-oriented case studies, and interviews. Barclays Capital gives graduate and undergraduate job candidates aptitude tests instead of first-round interviews.

● Test Reliability and Validity It is useless (and often illegal) to use a test that lacks validity or reliability. Reliability is a test's consistency. Thus, if someone scores 90 on an intelligence test on Monday and 130 on Tuesday, you probably would question the test's reliability. Test validity answers the question, Does this test measure what it is supposed to measure? In practical terms, this usually means, Does performance on the test predict subsequent performance on the job? A test that does not meet that standard is useless. If it also disproportionately screens out minority or female candidates, it might also violate equal-employment laws.

● Types of Tests Many types of tests are available. Employers use intelligence (IQ) tests like the Stanford-Binet or the Wechsler or Wonderlic to measure general intellectual abilities. For some jobs, managers are also interested in testing other abilities. For example, the Bennett Test of Mechanical Comprehension (see Figure 12.9) helps assess an applicant's understanding of basic mechanical principles; it would be useful for predicting success on a job such as machinist or engineer. Other tests measure personality and interests. For example, you probably wouldn't hire someone for an entry-level job as an accounting clerk if he or she had no measurable interest in working with numbers![26] Most of us have had some experience dealing with service people who are obviously not psychologically suited for such jobs. A personality test might have screened them out. Some employers need to

FIGURE 12.9

An Example of the Bennett Test of Mechanical Comprehension

Human resources managers often use personnel tests, like this one, to measure a candidate's skills and aptitudes.

Look at Sample X on this page. It shows two men carrying a weighted object on a plank, and it asks, Which man carries more weight? Because the object is closer to man B than to man A, man B is shouldering more weight; so blacken the circle under B on your answer sheet. Now look at Sample Y and answer it yourself. Fill in the circle under the correct answer on your answer sheet.

A B

A B C

Municipal Busline

X

Which man carries more weight?
(If equal, mark C.)

Examples

	A	B	C
X	○	●	○
Y	○	○	○

Y

Which letter shows the seat where a passenger will get the smoothest ride?

SOURCE: Bennett Mechanical Comprehension Test. "Bennett Mechanical Comprehension Test" and "BMCT" are trademarks of Harcourt Assessment, Inc. registered in the United States of America and/or other jurisdictions.

management assessment center: testing technique in which about a dozen candidates spend two or three days performing realistic management tasks while expert appraisers observe them

test candidates' physical abilities. For example, Dell would want to make sure its assemblers have the finger dexterity to work with tiny objects.

A **management assessment center** is another testing technique. In such centers, about a dozen candidates spend two or three days performing realistic management tasks while expert appraisers observe them. They assess each candidate's potential.[27] The center's activities might include individual presentations, objective tests, interviews, and participation in management games. Participants engage in realistic problem solving, usually as members of two or three simulated companies.

Computerized selection tests like this one are increasingly replacing conventional paper-and-pencil tests.

● Computerized and Online Testing Online tests are increasingly replacing conventional paper-and-pencil tests and manual testing. In one large manufacturing company, experts developed a computerized testing procedure for selecting clerical personnel.[28] For example, for the "travel expense form completion" part of this test, applicants had to access the database file, use some of the information there to compute quarterly expenses, and transfer this information to the travel expense form.

Employers such as 7-Eleven require that applicants responding to ads first answer a series of computerized questions by punching their telephone keypads, or taking a short test online before proceeding (for instance, see www.cia.gov).

Interviews

The interview is the most widely used selection device, and it would be very unusual for a manager to hire a subordinate without at least a brief personal interview.

The problem is that while almost everyone gets a job interview, most interviews don't produce very reliable information. The reasons for this predicament are many. For one thing, research shows that interviewers rather constantly commit blunders such as leaping to conclusions during the first few minutes of the interview or asking for information (like "tell me your main weaknesses") that doesn't really shed much light on what the applicant will actually do on the job. Others are simply uncomfortable asking questions or don't know what to ask.

The manager can boost the usefulness of selection interviews by following procedures such as planning and structuring the interview, establishing rapport, asking questions, delaying the decision, and closing the interview.[29] We review each of these steps next.

Plan the Interview Begin by reviewing the candidate's application and résumé, and note any areas that are vague or may indicate strengths or weaknesses. Review the job specification. Start the interview with a clear picture of the traits of an ideal candidate.

Structure the Interview Most interviews are too informal.[30] The interviewer asks general questions like, "What are your weaknesses?" The preferred approach is to structure the interview by asking questions that relate to performance on the job. Experts call this a behavioral interview. For example, ask the candidate to explain how he or she would handle a hypothetical situation, such as, "If you were a supervisor here, what would you do if one of your subordinates came in consistently late?" If the job calls for making cold calls, ask, "Tell me about a time when you had to make an unsolicited sales call. How did you do it? What was the result?" Interviews based on a structured guide, like the one shown in Figure 12.10 on page 350, usually give better results. Structured interviews are more valid in part because they are more reliable—for example, the same interviewer administers the interview more consistently from candidate to candidate.

Establish Rapport The point of most interviews is to have a productive interchange so that the manager can better estimate how the candidate will perform on the job. Thus, it is usually best to put the candidate at ease and to establish some rapport.

The job interview is the most widely used selection device.

Ask Questions The main issue here, as mentioned above, is to formulate structured questions that provide insight into how the candidate will perform on the job. Figure 12.11 on page 351 presents a list of generic sample questions.

As a rule, when asking questions:

- Avoid questions the candidate can answer with a simple yes or no.
- Don't put words in the applicant's mouth or telegraph the desired answer (for instance, by nodding or smiling in response to the right answer).
- Don't be patronizing, sarcastic, or inattentive.

FIGURE 12.10

Structured Interview Form for College Applicants

CANDIDATE RECORD

NAP 100 (10/77)

CANDIDATE NUMBER I ☐☐☐ U 921 (1–7)

NAME (LAST NAME FIRST) (8–27)

COLLEGE NAME

COLLEGE CODE (28–30)

INTERVIEWER NUMBER ☐☐☐ 0 ☐☐☐☐ (33–40)

INTERVIEWER NAME

SOURCE (41)		RACE (42)		SEX (43)		DEGREE (53)		AVERAGE	CLASS STANDING (59–59)	
Campus	☐ C	White	☐ W	Male	☐ M	Bachelors	☐ B	(A = 4.0)	Top 10%	☐ 10
Walk-in	☐ W	Black	☐ B	Female	☐ F	Masters	☐ M	Overall ☐☐ (54–55)	Top 25%	☐ 25
Intern	☐ I	Asian	☐ A	Init.		Law	☐ L	Acctg. ☐☐ (56–57)	Top Half	☐ 50
Agency	☐ A	Hispanic	☐ H	Cont.	☐☐☐☐☐☐	Majors			Bottom Half	☐ 75
		Native Am.	☐ NA	Date						

CAMPUS INTERVIEW EVALUATIONS

ATTITUDE – MOTIVATION – GOALS

POOR ☐ AVERAGE ☐ GOOD ☐ OUTSTANDING ☐

(POSITIVE, COOPERATIVE, ENERGETIC, MOTIVATED, SUCCESSFUL, GOAL-ORIENTED)

COMMENTS:

COMMUNICATIONS SKILLS – PERSONALITY – SALES ABILITY

POOR ☐ AVERAGE ☐ GOOD ☐ OUTSTANDING ☐

(ARTICULATE, LISTENS, ENTHUSIASTIC, LIKEABLE, POISED, TACTFUL, ACCEPTING, CONVINCING)

COMMENTS:

EXECUTIVE PRESENCE – DEAL WITH TOP PEOPLE

POOR ☐ AVERAGE ☐ GOOD ☐ OUTSTANDING ☐

(IMPRESSIVE, STANDS OUT, A WINNER, REMEMBERED, LEVELHEADED, AT EASE, AWARE)

COMMENTS:

INTELLECTUAL ABILITIES

POOR ☐ AVERAGE ☐ GOOD ☐ OUTSTANDING ☐

(INSIGHTFUL, CREATIVE, CURIOUS, IMAGINATIVE, UNDERSTANDS, REASONS, INTELLIGENT, SCHOLARLY)

COMMENTS:

JUDGMENT – DECISION MAKING ABILITY

POOR ☐ AVERAGE ☐ GOOD ☐ OUTSTANDING ☐

(MATURE, SEASONED, INDEPENDENT, COMMON SENSE, CERTAIN, DETERMINED, LOGICAL)

COMMENTS:

LEADERSHIP

POOR ☐ AVERAGE ☐ GOOD ☐ OUTSTANDING ☐

(SELF-CONFIDENT, TAKES CHARGE, EFFECTIVE, RESPECTED, MANAGEMENT MINDED, GRASPS AUTHORITY)

COMMENTS:

CAMPUS INTERVIEW SUMMARY

INVITE (Circle) Yes No DATE AVAILABLE	AREA OF INTEREST (Circle) AUDIT TAX MCS ABC OTHER	SEMESTER HRS. Acctg. ____ Audit ____ Tax ____	OFFICES PREFERRED: No. 1 ____ No. 2 ____ No. 3 ____	SUMMARY COMMENTS: ____

FIGURE 12.11

Suggested Supplementary Questions for Interviewing Applicants

1. How did you choose this line of work?
2. What did you enjoy most about your last job?
3. What did you like least about your last job?
4. What has been your greatest frustration or disappointment on your present job? Why?
5. What are some of the pluses and minuses of your last job?
6. What were the circumstances surrounding your leaving your last job?
7. Did you give notice?
8. Why should we be hiring you?
9. What do you expect from this employer?
10. What are three things you will not do in your next job?
11. What would your last supervisor say your three weaknesses are?
12. What are your major strengths?
13. How can your supervisor best help you obtain your goals?
14. How did your supervisor rate your job performance?
15. In what ways would you change your last supervisor?
16. What are your career goals during the next 1–3 years? 5–10 years?
17. How will working for this company help you reach those goals?
18. What did you do the last time you received instructions with which you disagreed?
19. What are some of the things about which you and your supervisor disagreed? What did you do?
20. Which do you prefer, working alone or working with groups?
21. What motivated you to do better at your last job?
22. Do you consider your progress on that job representative of your ability? Why?
23. Do you have any questions about the duties of the job for which you have applied?
24. Can you perform the essential functions of the job for which you have applied?

SOURCE: www.HR.BLR.com © 2004 Business and Legal Reports, Inc. Reprinted by permission.

- Don't monopolize the interview or let the applicant dominate the interview.
- Listen to the candidate and encourage him or her to express thoughts fully.
- Don't ask for just general statements about accomplishments; ask for specific examples.[31]
- If the candidate lists specific strengths or weaknesses, follow up with, "What are specific examples that demonstrate each of your strengths?"

Delay the Decision Research shows that interviewers often make snap judgments based on inadequate information. Keep a record of the interview, and then review it before deciding.[32]

Close the Interview End the process courteously. Tell the applicant whether there is an interest, and if so, what the next step will be. Rejections should be diplomatic.

Guidelines for Interviewees

Before managers interview applicants, the managers will have to navigate job interviews themselves—as interviewees. Guidelines here include:

1. *Prepare.* Before the interview, learn all you can about the employer, the job, and the people doing the recruiting.
2. *Make a good first impression.* Bad first impressions are almost impossible to overcome.
3. *Uncover the interviewer's real needs.* Determine what the employer is looking for and what problems he or she needs solved. Sample questions include, Would you mind describing the job for me? and What's the first problem you'd want me to address?
4. *Relate your answers to the interviewer's needs.* For example, say, "One of the problem areas you've said is important to you is similar to a problem I once faced." Then state the problem, describe your solution, and reveal the results.
5. *Think before answering.* Pause to make sure you understand what the interviewer is driving at, think about how to structure your answer, and then speak.
6. *Watch your nonverbal behavior.* Maintain eye contact. Speak with enthusiasm, nod agreement, and remember to take a moment to frame your answer (pause, think, speak) so that you sound articulate and fluent.[33]

Other Selection Techniques

Managers use several other selection techniques to screen applicants, including realistic previews, background investigations and reference checks, honesty testing, and health exams.

● Realistic Previews Sometimes a dose of realism makes the best screening tool. *Realistic previews* provide candid details of what working for the company and on that particular job actually entails. For example, Wal-Mart found that associates who quit within the first ninety days often did so because of conflict in their schedules or because they preferred to work in another geographic area. The firm then began explicitly explaining and asking about work schedules and work preferences.[34]

● Background Investigations and Reference Checks Employers are well advised to verify the applicant's background information and references. As one firm's security director said, "It's not uncommon to find someone who applies and looks good, and then you do a little digging and you start to see all sorts of criminal history."[35]

The most commonly verified background areas are legal eligibility for employment (to comply with immigration laws); dates of prior employment; military service; education; and name, date of birth, and address (see Figure 12.12).[36] Most employers verify current or previous position and salary with the current employer by telephone. Others call to discover more about the person's motivation, technical competence, and ability to work with others. Some employers also get

FIGURE 12.12

Employee Reference Check Form

EMPLOYMENT REFERENCE CHECK FORM

Applicant: 1. Please print out this Reference Check Form.
2. Fill out the top section of the form.
3. Send it to a former employer to complete and return to:

Human Resources Department
Winter Sports, Inc./Big Mountain Ski & Summer Resort
PO Box 1400, Whitefish, MT 59937/or Fax to: 406-862-2955

REFERENCE CHECK FORM Please Type or Print Legibly

To Be Completed by Applicant:

Applicant's Name ______________________________

Name of Reference ______________________________

Business Name ______________________________

I have applied for a position with Winter Sports, Inc. at Big Mountain Ski and Summer Resort. In order to be considered for employment, they have requested information from my previous employers. I would appreciate your cooperation in providing the answers to the following questions. I have been advised this information will be held in confidence by the Winter Sports, Inc. Human Resource Department.

______________________________ __________

Applicant's Signature Date

To be Completed by Employer:

Employed From __________ To __________

Position(s) Held

Reason for Separation: ______ Quit ______ Laid-off ______ Discharged

Other ______________________________

Comments: ______________________________

____

____

As an employee, was this person:

Responsible? _____ YES _____ NO

Able to work well with others? _____ YES _____ NO

Trustworthy? _____ YES _____ NO

Dependable (Attendance)? _____ YES _____ NO

Eligible for rehire? _____ YES _____ NO

A positive customer service representative? (if applies) _____ YES _____ NO

Please comment briefly on "NO" responses: ______________________________

____

____

Additional comments from supervisor, if possible ______________________________

____

____

Signature of person filling out form: ______________________________

Title: ______________________ Date: ______________________

background reports about an applicant's credit standing, indebtedness, reputation, character, and lifestyle. Special preemployment information services such as intellius.com use Internet and computerized databases to access and check information about applicants' compensation histories, credit histories, driving records, and conviction records.

Honesty Testing Many employees work in jobs for which honesty is especially crucial—as bank tellers or cashiers, for instance. With few exceptions, federal law now prohibits employers from using polygraph (lie detector) machines.[37] Paper-and-pencil honesty tests are legal. They ask questions (such as "Have you ever made a personal phone call on company time?") aimed at assessing a person's tendency to be honest. In practice, detecting dishonest candidates involves not just tests but comprehensive antitheft screening procedures. These procedures may include, for instance:

- *Asking blunt questions.*[38] Managers can generally be quite blunt. For example, "Have you recently held jobs other than those listed on your application?" "Have you ever been fired or asked to leave the job?"
- *Doing a credit check.* Have applicants sign an application form declaration saying that the employer is authorized to conduct background checks and credit checks.
- *Carefully checking all employment and personal references.*
- *Using paper-and-pencil honesty tests and psychological tests.*
- *Testing for drugs.* Devise a drug-testing program, and give each applicant a copy of the policy.
- *Establishing a search-and-seizure policy.* The policy should state that all desks and similar property remain the property of the company and may be inspected.[39]

Health Exams Employers use the medical exam to confirm that the applicant qualifies for the physical requirements of the position and to discover any medical limitations they should take into account.

With drug screenings, it is common to test candidates just before they're hired. Many also test current employees when there is reason to believe the person has been using drugs—after a work accident, or in the presence of obvious behavioral symptoms, chronic lateness, or high absenteeism. Some firms routinely administer drug tests on a random or periodic basis.[40]

Managing Now: Interviewing and Selecting Employees

Employers are increasingly using computerized means, often Web-assisted, to conduct interviews. The advantage of using the Web is that it enables employers to integrate the automated Web-based employment interview and test results with applicant tracking capabilities.

A *computerized selection interview* is one in which a job candidate's oral and/or computerized replies are obtained in response to computerized oral, visual, or written questions and/or situations. Most computerized interviews present the applicant with a series of questions regarding his or her background, experience, education, skills, knowledge, and work attitudes that relate to the job. Some (video-based) computerized interviews also confront candidates with realistic scenarios (such as irate customers) to which they must respond. Typical computerized interviews present questions in a multiple-choice format, one at a time; the applicant is expected to respond to the questions on the screen by pressing a key. Pic'n Pay stores, a chain of self-service shoe stores, gives job applicants an 800 number to dial for a computerized interview. The interview contains 100 questions and lasts about ten minutes. Applicants press 1 for *yes* and 0 for *no*. Every applicant then gets a follow-up live telephone interview, from one of the firm's six dedicated interviewers.

Orienting and Training Employees

Online Study Center
ACE the Test
Managing Now! LIVE

Once employees are hired, they must be prepared to do their jobs; this is the purpose of orientation and training. Designing and implementing training programs are essential managerial activities. It is futile to carefully select new employees and then put them on the job with inadequate training.

Orienting Employees

orientation: providing new employees with basic information like work rules and vacation policies

Employee **orientation** means providing new employees with basic information like work rules and vacation policies. In many companies, employees receive a hard-copy or Internet-based handbook containing this information. Orientation aims to familiarize the new employee with the company and his or her coworkers; provide information about working conditions (coffee breaks, overtime policy, and so on); explain how to get on the payroll, how to obtain identification cards, and what the working hours are; and generally reduce the jitters often associated with starting a new job.

Orientation also begins the process of socializing employees into the employer's values and ways of doing things. Here, *socializing* means achieving a fit between the employee's values and way of doing things and those of the firm. For example, the Mayo Clinic recently revised its orientation program. Its new "Heritage and Culture" program now covers matters such as Mayo core principles, history, work atmosphere, teamwork, personal responsibility, innovation, integrity, diversity, customer service, and mutual respect.[41]

Figure 12.13 outlines a typical orientation program.

Training Employees

Orientation usually precedes *training*, which is a set of activities aimed at giving the employee the knowledge and skills to perform the job. Training is one thing that distinguishes superior firms and managers.[42] For example, why does the coffee always taste good at Starbucks? Because "Brewing the Perfect Cup" is one of five classes that all Starbucks employees take during their first six weeks on the job.[43] They learn that they must steam milk at temperatures of at least 157°F, and that coffee should never sit on the hot plate for more than twenty minutes.

FIGURE 12.13

New Employee Departmental Orientation Checklist

SOURCE: UCSDHealthcare. Used with permission.

NEW EMPLOYEE DEPARTMENTAL ORIENTATION CHECKLIST
(Return to Human Resources within 10 days of Hire)

NAME:	HIRE DATE:	SSN:	JOB TITLE:
DEPARTMENT:	NEO DATE:	DEPARTMENTAL ORIENTATION COMPLETED BY:	

TOPIC:	DATE REVIEWED	N/A
1. HUMAN RESOURCES INFORMATION		
a. Departmental Attendance Procedures and UCSD Healthcare Work Time & Attendance Policy	a. ________	❒
b. Job Description Review	b. ________	❒
c. Annual Performance Evaluation and Peer Feedback Process	c. ________	❒
d. Probationary Period Information	d. ________	❒
e. Appearance/Dress Code Requirements	e. ________	❒
f. Annual TB Screening	f. ________	❒
g. License and/or certification Renewals	g. ________	❒
2. DEPARTMENT INFORMATION		
a. Organizational Structure-Department Core Values Orientation	a ________	❒
b. Department/Unit Area Specific Policies & Procedures	b. ________	❒
c. Customer Service Practices	c. ________	❒
d. CQI Effort and Projects	d. ________	❒
e. Tour and Floor Plan	e. ________	❒
f. Equipment/Supplies	f. ________	❒
• Keys issued	________	❒
• Radio Pager issued	________	❒
• Other ________________	________	❒
g. Mail and Recharge Codes	g. ________	❒
3. SAFETY INFORMATION		
a. Departmental Safety Plan	a. ________	❒
b. Employee Safety/Injury Reporting Procedures	b. ________	❒
c. Hazard Communication	c. ________	❒
d. Infection Control/Sharps Disposal	d. ________	❒
e. Attendance at annual Safety Fair (mandatory)	e. ________	❒
4. FACILITIES INFORMATION		
a. Emergency Power	a. ________	❒
b. Mechanical Systems	b. ________	❒
c. Water	c. ________	❒
d. Medical Gases	d. ________	❒
e. Patient Room	e. ________	❒
• Bed	________	❒
• Headwall	________	❒
• Bathroom	________	❒
• Nurse Call System	________	❒
5. SECURITY INFORMATION		
a. Code Triage Assignment	a. ________	❒
b. Code Blue Assignment	b. ________	❒
c. Code Red—Evacuation Procedure	c. ________	❒
d. Code 10—Bomb Threat Procedure	d. ________	❒
e. Departmental Security Measures	e. ________	❒
f. UCSD Emergency Number 6111 or 911	f. ________	❒

This generic checklist may not constitute a complete departmental orientation or assessment. Please attach any additional unit-specific orientation material for placement in the employee's HR file

I have been oriented on the items listed above ________________________________

training programs: program aimed at providing employees with the skills they need to do their jobs

Training programs consist of five steps:

- The first, or needs-analysis, step identifies the specific job performance skills needed; analyzes the skills and needs of the prospective trainees; and develops specific, measurable knowledge and performance objectives.
- In the second step, instructional design, you decide on, compile, and produce the training program content, including workbooks, exercises, and activities.
- There may be a third step, validation, in which the firm works the bugs out of the training program by presenting it to a small representative audience.
- The fourth step is to implement the program by actually training the targeted employee group.
- Fifth is an evaluation and follow-up step to assess the program's effectiveness.

Most managers do not need to create their own training materials because many materials are available on- and offline. For example, the professional development site Click2learn.com offers a wide range of Web-based courses that employees can take online. And many firms, including American Media Inc. of West Des Moines, Iowa, provide packaged training programs on various topics. The programs include a training leader's guide; a self-study book; and a video for improving skills in areas such as customer service, documenting discipline, and appraising performance.

Training Techniques

on-the-job training (OJT): having a person learn a job by actually performing it, usually under guidance of an experienced coworker

Training techniques range from simple to complex. **On-the-job training (OJT)** means having a person learn a job by actually performing it. Just about every employee gets some OJT. It usually involves assigning new employees to experienced workers or supervisors, who then do the actual training.[44] Some employers, like The Men's Wearhouse, do almost all their training via a formal on-the-job training program. This includes providing line managers with detailed manuals explaining how to train employees on the job. At a minimum, employees should get job descriptions and short training manuals that explain their jobs. The Improving Your *Training* Skills feature shows the kinds of information a supervisor should know about using OJT techniques.

Of course, most situations call for using other training techniques as well. For example, instead of sending new rental agents to weeklong, classroom-based training courses, Value Rent-a-Car provides them with interactive, multimedia-based training programs using DVDs. Airlines use simulated learning to train pilots to fly new planes and to react to various emergencies (both situations would be dangerous for training on the job). When steelmaker Dofasco discovered that many of its employees would be retiring in the next few years, it revived its apprenticeship training program. New recruits spend about thirty two months in a training program learning various jobs under the tutelage of experienced employees.[45]

With jobs becoming more technically demanding, literacy training is often required. This often involves bringing in local educators to teach basic literacy skills such as reading, writing, and math.

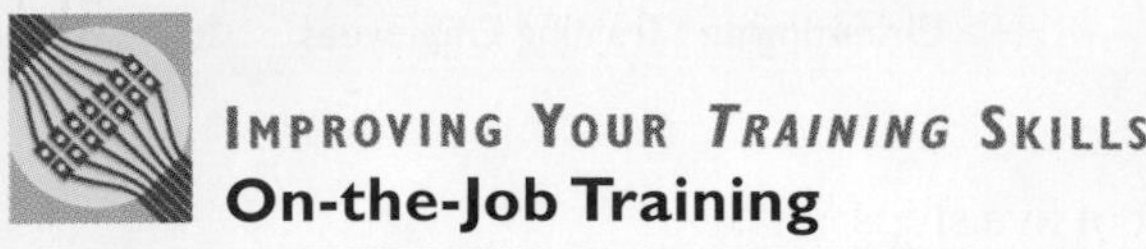

Improving Your *Training* Skills
On-the-Job Training

Step 1: Prepare the Learner

1. Put the learner at ease—relieve tension.
2. Explain why he or she is being taught.
3. Create interest, encourage questions, find out what the learner already knows.
4. Explain the whole job and relate it to some job the worker already knows.
5. Place the learner as close to the normal working position as possible.
6. Familiarize the worker with equipment, materials, tools, and trade terms.

Step 2: Present the Operations

1. Explain quantity and quality requirements.
2. Go through the job at the normal workplace.
3. Go through the job at a slow pace several times, explaining each step.
4. Again go through the job at a slow pace several times; explain the key points.
5. Have the learner explain the steps as you go through the job at a slow pace.

Step 3: Do a Tryout

1. Have the learner go through the job several times, slowly, explaining each step to you.
2. Run the job at the normal pace.
3. Have the learner do the job, gradually building up skill and speed.
4. As soon as the learner demonstrates ability to do the job, let the worker begin, but don't abandon him or her.

Step 4: Follow-Up

1. Designate to whom the learner should go for help.
2. Gradually decrease supervision, checking work from time to time.
3. Correct faulty work patterns before they become a habit.
4. Compliment good work; encourage the worker until he or she is able to meet the quality and quantity standards.[46]

Managing Now: Orientation and Training

Employers use technology in orientation and training. For example, some firms provide incoming managers with preloaded personal digital assistants. These contain information the new managers need to better adjust to their new jobs, such as key contact information, main tasks to undertake, and even digital images of employees the new manager needs to know.[47]

Similarly, just as Web-based courses have changed how college students learn, more employers are moving all or most of their training functions to the Web.

In most cases, the preferred approach is to create Internet-based learning portals for employees, either on the employers' own intranets or on the websites of special online training-content providers. These content providers then offer their training content to the firms' employees via the portal. For example, the U.S. Post Office contracted with Thinq.com to use the latter's online learning management system. Thinq.'s learning management system gives employees access to up-to-date training courses and lets the postal service's managers monitor their employees' training progress.

Increasingly, employers are also integrating their e-learning systems with their overall, enterprise management information systems. Doing so produces several benefits. For example, the employer can more easily combine its online training with its online discussion forums and synchronous meeting tools, thus improving the interactivity of the learning.[48]

Appraising and Maintaining Employees

Online Study Center
ACE the Test
Managing Now! LIVE

Once employees are recruited, hired, oriented, and trained, the manager turns to appraising their performance and to providing for their compensation and working conditions.

Employee Appraisal

performance appraisal: evaluating an employee's performance relative to his or her performance standards

graphic rating scale: appraisal scale that lists several job characteristics (like quality of work) and provides a rating scale (from outstanding to unsatisfactory), along with short definitions of each rating

critical incidents: brief examples of an employee's good or bad performance, used to support the person's appraisal and his or her development needs

ranking: positioning employees at different levels, from low to high, based on their performance

behaviorally anchored rating scales (BARS): scales that combine the benefits of critical incidents and quantified ratings by anchoring each rating from high to low, with illustrative performance examples

forced distribution method: a form of ranking, similar to grading on a curve; the rater places predetermined percentages of ratees into performance categories

Performance appraisal means evaluating an employee's performance relative to his or her performance standards. There are several methods for evaluating employees. Probably the most familiar performance appraisal method involves using a **graphic rating scale**. This scale lists several job characteristics (like quality of work) and provides a rating scale (from outstanding to unsatisfactory), along with short definitions of each rating. Some use the more subjective **critical incidents** method instead. Here, the manager compiles brief examples of the employee's good or bad performance, and then uses these examples to support the person's appraisal and his or her development needs. Some supplement graphic ratings with critical incidents. **Ranking** means positioning employees at different levels, from low to high, based on their performance. **Behaviorally anchored rating scales (BARS)** aim to combine the benefits of critical incidents and quantified ratings by anchoring each rating in the rating scale (from high to low) with illustrative performance examples. The **forced distribution method**, a form of ranking, is similar to grading on a curve. The rater places predetermined percentages of ratees into performance categories, for example, top 10 percent, middle 80 percent, and bottom 10 percent.

Sun Microsystems uses the forced distribution method. Managers appraise employees in groups of about thirty, and the bottom 10 percent of each group gets ninety days to improve. If they're still at the bottom 10 percent in ninety days, they get a chance to resign and take severance pay. Some decide to stay, but if it doesn't work out, the firm fires them without severance.[49] GE still uses forced distribution rankings. Its former CEO, Jack Welch, insisted that managers routinely dismiss their lowest 10 percent–performing employees each year. The current CEO, Jeffrey Immelt, has softened the process by giving bottom 10-percenters more time to improve. About a fourth of *Fortune* 500 companies, including Microsoft, Conoco, and Intel, use versions of forced distribution.[50]

With *360-degree feedback*, performance information is collected via surveys from supervisors, subordinates, peers, and internal or external customers.[51] Based on one study, 29 percent of the responding employers use 360-degree feedback.[52] For managers, surveys might include items such as "returns phone calls promptly" and "my manager keeps me informed."[53] Computerized systems compile the feedback into individualized reports for the ratee.[54] The feedback is generally used for training purposes, not raises.[55]

Performance Management Experts like W. E. Deming argue that forced ranking and even other conventional approaches like rating scales foster fear and are unfair. Their basic argument is that performance is more a product of the quality of management and of the training the person received. Thus, employees shouldn't shoulder all the blame for poor performance. Indeed, in many top companies, including Toyota, you'd be hard-pressed to find any conventional appraisals. Instead, teams and supervisors meet often to review performance issues, analyze them, and figure out how to improve things. Deming recommends, among other things, performance contracts that lay out the steps the worker and company will take to get the employee's performance up to par.

Performance management, which we discussed earlier in this book, plays a role in performance appraisal. As we explained, performance management refers to any system that focuses employees on the goals and initiatives that they must execute for the company to succeed, and that gives managers a timely way to monitor performance and take corrective action. The basic idea of performance management is to give each employee several goals in the context of a strategy map approach—in other words, link the employee's goals and outputs (like good service) directly to what the company needs to do to succeed (like have more guests return more often). The company then uses information technology and digital dashboards to provide employees and managers with a real-time bird's-eye view of how each employee is doing and impacting the company.

Doing this, particularly for larger companies, requires Web-based performance management systems. For example, Seagate Technology uses Enterprise Suite for managing the performance of its 39,000 employees.

The Appraisal Interview An appraisal typically culminates in an appraisal interview. One suggested approach for conducting an appraisal interview includes:

- *Prepare for the interview.* Assemble the data, study the person's job description and performance, and give the person notice to review his or her work.
- *Be direct and specific.* Talk in terms of objective work data, such as absences and quality.
- *Do not get personal.* Try to compare the person's performance to a standard.
- *Encourage the person to talk.* Use expressions such as "go on" or "tell me more."
- *Provide a plan with concrete examples.* Make sure the person leaves with an agreement of remedial steps to take.

Dealing with Common Appraisal Problems Few of the manager's jobs are fraught with more peril than appraising subordinates' performance. Employees in general tend to be overly optimistic about what their ratings should be. They also know that their raises, career progress, and peace of mind may hinge on how you rate them. This alone makes it difficult to rate performance. In addition, managers tend to make one or more common appraisal mistakes when rating subordinates.

The *unclear standards* appraisal problem means that an appraisal scale is too open to interpretation. For example, without clear definitions, each individual supervisor will probably define "good" performance in his or her own way. Rectify this by including descriptive phrases that define each trait and degree of merit.

The *halo effect* problem means that the rating of a subordinate on one trait (such as "gets along with others") influences the way you rate the person on other traits (such as "quantity of work"). Thus, an unfriendly employee might be rated unsatisfactory for all traits rather than just for "gets along with others." Being aware of this problem is a major step toward avoiding it.

Central tendency is the tendency to rate all employees about average. For example, if the rating scale ranges from 1 to 7, a supervisor may tend to rate most of his or her employees from 3 to 5. Ranking employees eliminates this problem.

Leniency or strictness means that some supervisors tend to rate all their subordinates consistently high or low. Again, solutions here include ranking subordinates.

Bias refers to the tendency to let individual differences like age, race, and sex affect the appraisal ratings employees receive. In one study, researchers sought to determine if pregnancy is a source of bias in performance appraisals. Despite having been exposed to otherwise identical behavior by the same female employee, the student raters of this study assigned lower performance ratings to pregnant women than to nonpregnant women months later. Raters must be forewarned of such problems and trained to use objectivity in rating subordinates.

Compensation

employee compensation: all work-related pay or rewards that go to employees

After being appraised, employees expect to be paid. **Employee compensation** refers to all work-related pay or rewards that go to employees. It includes direct financial payments in the form of wages, salaries, incentives, commissions, and bonuses, and indirect payments in the form of financial fringe benefits like employer-paid insurance and vacations. Today, the emphasis is generally on basing the employee's pay at least in part on his or her performance and on his or her skills and competencies. *Competency- or skills-based pay* basically means paying the employees for the range and types of skills they've accumulated.

Salary

However, a fixed salary or an hourly wage is still the centerpiece of most employees' pay. Some employees—managerial, professional, and often secretarial—are salaried. They are paid by the week, month, or year. Other employees typically receive an hourly wage. Under the federal Fair Labor Standards Act, employers must pay certain categories of workers overtime pay if they work more than forty hours per week. Those employees earning under $455 per week are generally nonexempt from the act's overtime provisions and must get overtime pay (at the rate of one and one half times their hourly salary) for each overtime hour worked. Those earning over $100,000 per year are generally exempt.

Companies' boards are clamping down on executive pay.[56] One reason is that investors believe that companies should tie pay more to performance.

financial incentive: any financial reward that is contingent upon performance (some call this pay for performance)

Pay for Performance

A **financial incentive** is any financial reward that is contingent on performance (some call this pay for performance). Salespeople get financial incentives called commissions, generally in proportion to the items or services they sell. Production workers may receive a financial incentive called piecework, which is a standard sum for each item the worker produces.

Today, increasingly, it is common to pay almost all employees, including engineers, secretaries, managers, and college professors, in part based on the extent to which they and/or their companies achieve their goals. For example, in a profit-sharing program, most employees usually receive some small share of the company's profits. Many employees periodically receive merit pay or a merit raise, which is a salary increase awarded to an employee based on individual performance. Merit pay differs from a bonus, which is a one-time financial payment.

employee benefits: pay supplements, such as insurance and vacations

unemployment insurance: a payment made by state agencies to workers who lose their jobs through no fault of their own, and paid for by a tax on the employer's payroll

worker's compensation: a payment aimed at providing sure, prompt income and medical benefits to victims of work-related accidents or their dependents, regardless of fault

● **Benefits** **Employee benefits** are pay supplements. Many benefits are legally mandated. For example, under federal and state law, **unemployment insurance** is available to most employees and is paid by state agencies to workers who lose their jobs through no fault of their own. **Worker's compensation**, another legally mandated benefit, is a payment aimed at providing sure, prompt income and medical benefits to victims of work-related accidents or their dependents, regardless of fault. Social Security is another federally mandated benefit paid for by a tax on an employee's salary or wages. Vacations and holiday days are benefits but are not legally mandated.

In an effort to attract and hold superior employees, employers can differentiate themselves on the basis of the benefits that they offer. For many employees, health and hospitalization benefits are a major determinant of which job to accept. Many other companies such as SAS Institute distinguish themselves with outstanding family-friendly benefits such as child-care facilities, gyms, and flexible work schedules. With the number of employees age sixty and over skyrocketing, many firms are offering early retirement benefits, for instance, allowing those employees to phase into retirement by working half-time until they formally retire.

Discipline and Grievances

Supervisors sometimes discipline subordinates, usually when the latter violate a rule. Prerequisites to discipline include having clear rules (such as "no smoking allowed when dealing with customers"), as well as progressive penalties.

discipline without punishment: disciplinary approach that begins with an oral reminder, then paid time off, and then more punitive measures only if the rules infraction continues

In assessing the need for discipline, some supervisors follow the so-called FRACT model: get the *f*acts, obtain the *r*eason for the infraction, *a*udit the records, pinpoint the *c*onsequences of the infraction, and identify the *t*ype of infraction before taking remedial steps. Some use the **discipline without punishment** approach, where an employee first gets an oral reminder if he or she breaks a rule; then a written reminder if it occurs again; then a paid, one-day decision-making leave if another incident occurs. If he or she breaks the rule again, a dismissal may be in order. Some companies now establish independent ombuds, neutral counselors outside the normal chain of command to whom employees who believe they were treated unfairly can turn for confidential advice.[57] Discipline guidelines include:

- Make sure the evidence supports the charge.
- Protect the employee's due process rights.
- Warn the employee of the disciplinary consequences.
- The rule allegedly violated should be reasonably related to the effective operation of the work environment.
- Investigate the matter.
- Apply rules and penalties evenhandedly.
- Make sure the penalty is reasonably related to the misconduct and to the employee's past work history.

- Don't rob your subordinate of his or her dignity.
- Remember that the burden of proof is on you.
- Don't base your decision on hearsay or a general impression.
- Don't act while angry.

grievance: a complaint an employee lodges against an employer, usually regarding wages, hours, or some condition of employment

A **grievance** is a complaint an employee lodges against an employer, usually regarding wages, hours, or some condition of employment, like supervisory behavior. For example, a terminated employee might file a grievance stating that the supervisor didn't warn her about her impending termination, per the union agreement. Grievance steps typically include discussing the problem with a supervisor, and then referring the matter to the department head, the personnel department, and finally the head of the facility.

Managing Now: Appraising and Maintaining Employees

Appraisal tends to involve extensive documentation. Each employee needs pre-appraisal period goals. And, the appraisal forms may go on for two or three pages, or more.

The Internet is therefore well suited to improving the employee appraisal process. For example, PerformanceReview.com, from KnowledgePoint of Petaluma, California, lets managers evaluate employees online based on their competencies, goals, and development plans. Managers can choose from standard competencies such as communications, or create their own. PerformancePro.net from the Exxceed Company of Chicago, Illinois, is another Internet-based performance review system. It helps the manager and his or her subordinates develop performance objectives for the employee and conduct the annual review.

Benefits Administration The Internet has also revolutionized compensation and benefits administration. For example, benefits administration is a labor-intensive and time-consuming activity for an HR department. Without automation, it can require the employer to devote hundreds or thousands of human resource professionals' hours to transactions such as answering employees' questions about comparative benefits.

When the organization that assists Pennsylvania school districts with their insurance decided to automate their benefits administration, they chose a company called BeneLogic.[58] Its Employee Benefit Electronic Service Tool "lets users manage all aspects of benefits administration, including enrollment, plan descriptions, eligibility, and premium reconciliation, via Microsoft Internet Explorer. . . ."[59] BeneLogic's system provides the school districts with numerous advantages. BeneLogic hosts and maintains the Web support application on its own servers, and it creates customized Web-based applications for each school district. The system facilitates Web-based employee benefits enrollment, provides centralized call center support for benefits-related questions, and even handles benefits-related payroll functions. Each school board's employees access the BeneLogic site via a link on the school board's website and uses it to manage their own accounts.

The Window on Managing Now feature shows how employers use employee portals.

WINDOW ON MANAGING NOW
GM and NCR

Employers now use online employee portals for communicating with employees and for enabling employees to self-service their HR-related tasks.[60] General Motors calls its employee portal mySocrates. It enables employees to keep track of and/or modify details such as their merit awards, pay records, and retirement formulas.[61]

NCR Corporation organized its HR portal into three information areas: benefits and compensation, training and career growth, and NCR values and policies. NCR also has a forms center on the site's title bar. The portal gives NCR employees a shortcut to all the information and forms they need to manage their own tasks, such as updating their personal information. It also helps NCR supervisors carry out day-to-day supervisory tasks such as completing performance appraisal forms.

Understanding HR's Legal Framework

Online Study Center
ACE the Test
Managing Now! LIVE

Thousands of federal, state, and local laws prescribe what companies can and can't do when it comes to employee recruitment and selection, compensation and benefits, and safety on the job.

Equal-Employment Laws and Affirmative Action

A federal court recently ruled that Dial Corp. discriminated against female job applicants at a meatpacking plant by requiring applicants to take a pre-employment strength test.[62] The test screened out disproportionately more women than men, and there appeared to be no compelling need for strength on the job. *Equal-employment opportunity laws* aim to ensure that managers conduct the firm's personnel activities in a nondiscriminatory manner. For example, employers should verify that their selection tests are valid and do not screen out a disproportionate number of women or minorities; interviews should avoid delving into applicants' ethnic, racial, or marital status; and employers usually can't advertise "help wanted—male" or "help wanted—female." The basic idea is that all applicants and employees should be on a level playing field. The manager should not discriminate against an applicant or employee based on that person's age, race, sex, religion, national origin, color, or disability.

Title VII of the 1964 Civil Rights Act bars discrimination because of race, color, religion, sex, or national origin (see Table 12.1). It also created the Equal Employment Opportunity Commission (EEOC), a five-member commission supported by a large staff to enforce these laws. The EEOC receives, investigates, and may file charges regarding job discrimination complaints on behalf of aggrieved individuals. We list other important antidiscrimination laws in Table 12.1.

sexual harassment: unwelcome sexual advances, requests for sexual favors, or other verbal or physical conduct of a sexual nature that occurs under various workplace conditions

Sexual Harassment **Sexual harassment** is a special type of discriminatory behavior. It is:

> . . . unwelcome sexual advances, requests for sexual favors, and other verbal or physical conduct of a sexual nature that occurs under conditions including

TABLE 12.1
Summary of Important Equal Employment Opportunity Legislation and Decisions

Action	What It Does
Title VII of 1964 Civil Rights Act, as amended	Bars discrimination because of race, color, religion, sex, or national origin; instituted EEOC
Executive orders	Prohibit employment discrimination by employers with federal contracts of more than $10,000 (and their subcontractors); establish office of federal compliance; require affirmative action programs
Federal agency guidelines	Used by federal agencies for enforcement of laws barring discrimination based on sex, national origin, and religion, as well as employee selection procedures; for example, they require validation of tests
Supreme Court decisions: *Griggs* v. *Duke Power Co.*, *Albemarie* v. *Moody*	Ruled that job requirements must be related to job success; that discrimination need not be overt to be proved; that the burden of proof is on the employer to prove that the qualification is valid
Equal Pay Act of 1967	Requires equal pay for men and women for performing similar work
Age Discrimination in Employment Act of 1967	Prohibits discriminating against a person 40 years or over in any area of employment because of age
State and local laws	Often cover organizations too small to be covered by federal laws
Vocational Rehabilitation Act of 1973	Requires affirmative action to employ and promote qualified disabled persons and prohibits discrimination against disabled persons
Pregnancy Discrimination Act of 1978	Prohibits discrimination in employment against pregnant women or workers with related conditions
Vietnam Era Veteran's Readjustment Assistance Act of 1974	Requires affirmative action in employment for veterans of the Vietnam War era
Wards Cove v. *Atonio; Patterson* v. *McLean Credit Union*	These Supreme Court decisions made it more difficult to prove a case of unlawful discrimination against an employer
Morton v. *Wilks*	This case allowed consent decrees to be attacked and could have had a chilling effect on certain affirmative action programs
Americans with Disabilities Act of 1990	Strengthens the need for most employers to make reasonable accommodations for disabled employees at work; prohibits discrimination
Civil Rights Act of 1991	Reverses *Wards Cove, Patterson,* and *Morton* decisions; places burden of proof back on employer and permits compensatory and punitive money damages for discrimination

Source: Gray Dessler, *Human Resource Management*, 10th ed. (Upper Saddle River, N.J.: Prentice Hall, 2005), p. 45.

the following: when such conduct is made, either explicitly or implicitly, a term or condition of an individual's employment; when submission to or rejection of such conduct by an individual is used as the basis for employment decisions affecting the individual; or when such conduct has the purpose or effect of unreasonably interfering with an individual's performance or creating an intimidating, hostile, or offensive work environment.

In addition to being unfair and detestable, sexual harassment is also illegal. To comply with the law, managers and employers should:

1. Take all complaints seriously. When confronted with sexual harassment complaints or when sexual conduct is observed in the workplace, "the best reaction is to address the complaint or stop the conduct."[63]
2. Issue a strong policy statement condemning such behavior.
3. Inform all employees about the policy prohibiting sexual harassment and of their rights under the policy.
4. Establish a complaint procedure so that employees understand the chain of command in filing and appealing sexual harassment complaints.
5. Establish a management response system that includes an immediate reaction and investigation by senior management when charges of sexual harassment are made.
6. Hold training sessions with supervisors and increase their awareness of the issues.
7. Discipline managers and employees involved in sexual harassment.

affirmative action: requires employers to make an extra effort to hire and promote those in a protected group (such as women or minorities)

● **Affirmative Action** Whereas equal-employment opportunity aims to ensure equal treatment at work, **affirmative action** requires employers to make an extra effort to hire and promote those in a protected group (such as women or minorities). An example would be setting a goal of promoting more minorities to middle-management jobs.

Occupational Safety and Health

In one recent year, 5,559 U.S. workers died in workplace incidents. There were also over 4.4 million occupational injuries and illnesses resulting from accidents at work. The Occupational Safety and Health Act was passed by Congress "to assure so far as possible every working man and woman in the nation safe and healthful working conditions and to preserve our human resources." It sets safety and health standards that apply to almost all workers in the United States. The Occupational Safety and Health Administration (OSHA), a U.S. government agency, administers these laws. In one recent year, OSHA conducted about 39,000 safety inspections.

Companies take a variety of steps to improve safety and health. One is to reduce unsafe *conditions,* such as slippery floors. For example, the organization Prevent Blindness America estimates that each year, more than 700,000 Americans injure their eyes at work, and that employers could avoid 90 percent of these injuries with safety eyewear.[64] The occupational safety laws address unsafe conditions. A brief checklist like that in Figure 12.14 can be useful for identifying such conditions. Reducing unsafe *acts* is another matter, because careless employees have accidents even where unsafe conditions are minimal. Screening out potentially careless employees, training employees to work carefully, and rewarding those who act properly are some methods employers use to reduce unsafe acts.

● **Managing Now** Employers increasingly turn to the Web to support their safety training programs. For example, www.puresafety.com enables firms to create

FIGURE 12.14

Checklist of Mechanical or Physical Accident-Causing Conditions

I. GENERAL HOUSEKEEPING

- Adequate and wide aisles—no materials protruding into aisles
- Parts and tools stored safely after use—not left in hazardous positions that could cause them to fall
- Even and solid flooring—no defective floors or ramps that could cause falling or tripping accidents
- Waste and trash cans—safely located and not overfilled
- Material piled in safe manner—not too high or too close to sprinkler heads
- All work areas clean and dry
- All exit doors and aisles clear of obstructions
- Aisles kept clear and properly marked; no air lines or electric cords across aisles

II. MATERIAL HANDLING EQUIPMENT AND CONVEYANCES

On all conveyances, electric or hand, check to see that the following items are all in sound working conditions:

- Brakes—properly adjusted
- Not too much play in steering wheel
- Warning device—in place and working
- Wheels—securely in place; properly inflated
- Fuel and oil—enough and right kind
- No loose parts
- Cables, hooks, or chains—not worn or otherwise defective
- Suspended chains or hooks conspicuous
- Safely loaded
- Properly stored

III. LADDERS, SCAFFOLD, BENCHES, STAIRWAYS, ETC.

The following items of major interest to be checked:

- Safety feet on straight ladders
- Guardrails or handrails
- Treads, not slippery
- None splintered, cracked, or rickety
- Properly stored
- Extension ladder ropes in good condition
- Toeboards

IV. POWER TOOLS (STATIONARY)

- Point of operation guarded
- Guards in proper adjustment
- Gears, belts, shafting, counterweights guarded
- Foot pedals guarded
- Brushes provided for cleaning machines
- Adequate lighting
- Properly grounded
- Tool or material rests properly adjusted
- Adequate work space around machines
- Control switch easily accessible
- Safety glasses worn
- Gloves worn by persons handling rough or sharp materials
- No gloves or loose clothing worn by persons operating machines

V. HAND TOOLS AND MISCELLANEOUS

- In good condition—not cracked, worn, or otherwise defective
- Properly stored
- Correct for job
- Goggles, respirators, and other personal protective equipment worn where necessary

VI. ELECTRICITY

- No frayed, cracked, or deteriorated cords
- All portable, as well as fixed, machinery grounded by three-wire connectors
- No dangling wires
- Ground-fault circuit interrupters used in humid conditions

VII. SPRAY PAINTING

- Explosion-proof electrical equipment
- Proper storage of paints and thinners in approved metal cabinets
- Fire extinguishers adequate and suitable; readily accessible
- Minimum storage in work area

VIII. FIRE EXTINGUISHERS

- Properly serviced and tagged
- Readily accessible
- Adequate and suitable for operations involved

SOURCE: Courtesy of the American Insurance Association. From "A Safety Committee Man's Guide," pp.1–64.

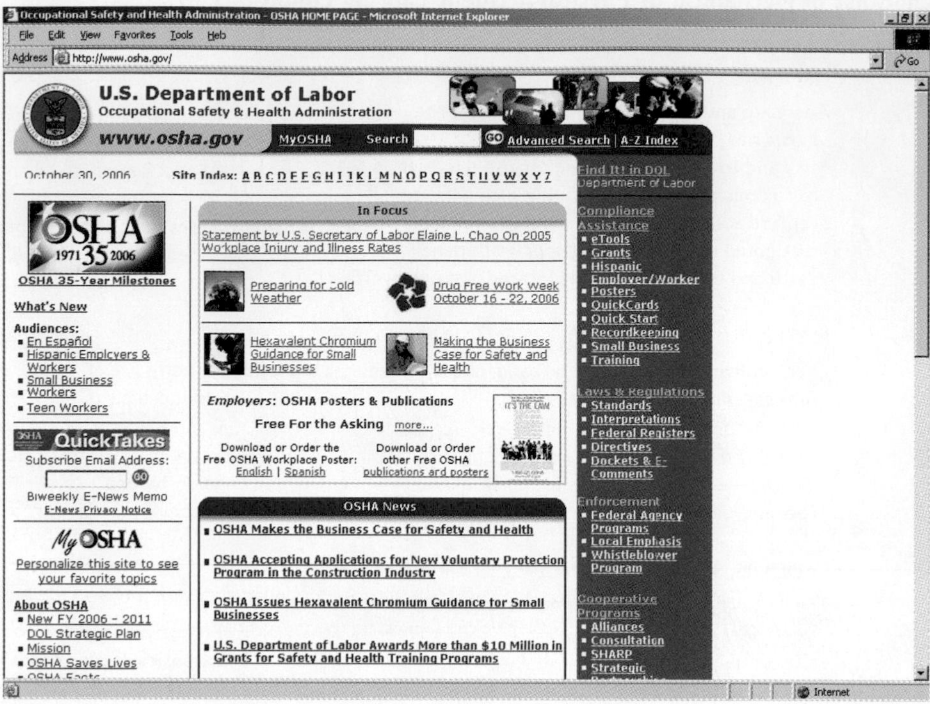

SOURCE: www.osha.gov.

their own training websites, complete with a "message from the safety director." The employer contracts with www.puresafety.com. Puresafety is an applications service provider that creates a website for the employer and populates the site with safety training courses from www.puresafety.com.[65]

Labor-Management Relations

Under the laws of the United States and many other countries, employees may organize into unions. In the United States, the Norris-LaGuardia Act guarantees each employee the right to bargain with employers for union benefits. The Wagner Act outlaws unfair labor practices such as employers interfering with, restraining, or coercing employees who are exercising their legally sanctioned rights of organizing themselves into a union. The Taft-Hartley Act prohibits unfair labor practices by unions against employers (like refusing to bargain with an employer). The Landrum-Griffin Act protects union members from unfair practices perpetrated against them by their unions.

The manager needs to be familiar with a variety of special terms with respect to labor relations. For example, suppose that a union wins, through a special election, the right to represent the company's workers. *Good faith bargaining* means that both the union and management must make reasonable progress toward working out an agreement, by making proposals and counterproposals. If progress is unsatisfactory, the union or management may bring in a third party, such as an *arbitrator* or *mediator*, to help the two sides reach an agreement. The former may have the power to impose an agreement. The latter usually just meets with the parties and tries to get them to agree.

● **Managing Now** Unions' websites are becoming integral parts of many unionization campaigns. Alliance@IBM provides one example. Managed by the Communications Workers of America, Alliance@IBM seeks to encourage IBM employees to join the union. It does so by providing information on a range of issues, such as why IBM employees need a union, questions and concerns about unions, and how employees can join the union and get involved.

Managing Now: Integrating the Company's Global HR Information Systems

human resources information systems (HRISs): interrelated components working together to collect, process, store, and disseminate information to support decision making, coordination, control, analysis, and visualization of an organization's human resource management activities

As a company grows, relying on separate human resources systems (for appraisal, applicant tracking, and so on) becomes unwieldy. Increasingly, the manager wants and needs human resources systems that "talk to each other"—that are integrated. For example, the employer needs a system in which personal data (such as next of kin's name and address) from the applicant tracking system is automatically fed into the benefits system, and completed training courses automatically become part of the employee's appraisal records. More firms are therefore integrating their HR systems into **human resources information systems (HRISs)**. We can define an HRIS as interrelated components working together to collect, process, store, and disseminate information to support decision making, coordination, control, analysis, and visualization of an organization's human resource management activities.

For example, when Buildnet, Inc., decided to integrate its separate human resources systems, it chose a Web-based software package called MyHRIS, from NuView, Inc. (www.nuviewinc.com). This Internet-based system includes human resources and benefits administration, applicant tracking and résumé scanning, training administration, and succession planning and development. With MyHRIS, managers at any of the firm's locations around the world can access and update more than 200 built-in reports such as "termination summary," or "open positions."[66] And the firm's home-office managers can monitor global HR activities on a real-time basis.

Oracle Corp.'s Human Capital Management is another example. A summary of this HRIS system's components helps illustrate what it does for employers. Its components include, for instance, daily business intelligence for human resources, incentive compensation, learning management, self-service human resources, absence management, benefits administration, candidate gateway, pension administration, workforce planning, workforce rewards, and help desk for human resources.[67]

CHAPTER SUMMARY

1. Human resource management is the management function devoted to acquiring, training, appraising, and compensating employees. As workers become more fully empowered, the HR function has grown in importance.

2. Staffing—filling a firm's open positions—starts with job analysis and personnel planning. Recruiting—including the use of internal sources, advertising, the Internet, employment agencies, recruiters, referrals, college recruiting, and recruiting a more diverse workforce—is then used to create a pool of applicants.

3. With a pool of applicants, the employer can turn to screening and selecting and use one or more

techniques—including application blanks, interviews, tests, and reference checks—to assess and investigate an applicant's aptitudes, interests, and background.

4. Once employees have been recruited, screened, and selected, they must be prepared to do their jobs; this is the purpose of employee orientation and training. Orientation means providing new employees with basic information about the employer; training ensures that the new employee has the basic knowledge required to perform the job satisfactorily.

5. Once they've been on the job for some time, employees are appraised.

6. Employee compensation refers to all work-related pay or rewards that go to employees. It includes direct financial payments in the form of wages, salaries, incentives, commissions, and bonuses, as well as indirect payments in the form of financial fringe benefits like employer-paid insurance and vacations.

7. In disciplining employees, managers should be sure they have all the facts and that the discipline is defensible and fair.

8. The HR function is subject to the constraints of numerous federal, state, and local laws. The equal-employment laws prohibiting employment discrimination are among the most important of these personnel laws and include Title VII of the Civil Rights Act, various executive orders, the Equal Pay Act of 1963, and the Americans with Disabilities Act of 1990. The Occupational Safety and Health Act sets safety and health standards that apply to most U.S. workers. Other laws govern union-management relations and include the Wagner Act.

DISCUSSION QUESTIONS

1. Why do we say that HR today is strategic?
2. What are the main elements in a job description?
3. What information would you collect for a job analysis?
4. How would you use JobDescription.com to create a job description?
5. Why is effective employee selection important to the manager?
6. Explain how you would conduct an interview, including the types of questions you would ask.
7. What do the equal-employment laws say managers can and cannot do? Explain briefly.

EXPERIENTIAL EXERCISES

1. Working in teams of four to five students, conduct a job analysis and develop a job description for the instructor of this course. Make sure to include a job summary, as well as a list of job duties and a job specification listing the human requirements of the job.

2. Using the job description that you wrote in Experiential Exercise 1 as a guide, develop a recruiting plan for the job of teaching this course, as well as a list of interview questions your team can use to screen applicants for the job of instructor. Then develop an on-the-job training program for the job or instructor.

3. Working in teams of four to five students, refer to Figure 12.14 and spend thirty minutes assessing the safety of the college building your class meets in.

CASE STUDY

The Out-of-Control Interview

Maria Fernandez is a bright, popular, and well-informed mechanical engineer who graduated with an engineering degree from State University in May 2007. During the spring preceding her graduation, she went out on many job interviews, most of which she thought were courteous. Therefore, she looked forward with great anticipation to an interview with the one firm for which she most wanted to work, Apex Environmental. She had always had a strong interest in cleaning up the environment. The interview, however, was a disaster. When Maria walked into the room, five men, including the president of the company, two vice presidents, the marketing director, and another engineer, began throwing questions at her. The questions ranged from unnecessarily discourteous ("Why would you take a job as a waitress in college if you're such an intelligent person?") to irrelevant and sexist ("Are you planning on settling down and starting a family anytime soon?"). After the interview, she met with two of the men individually (including the president), and the discussions focused almost exclusively on her technical expertise. She thought that these later discussions went fairly well. Given the apparent mean-spiritedness of the panel interview, however, she was astonished when several days later she got a job offer from the firm. The offer forced her to consider several matters. From her point of view, the job itself was perfect—she liked what she would be doing, the industry, and the firm's location. And, in fact, the president had been quite courteous in subsequent discussions, as had the other members of the management team. She was left wondering whether the panel interview had been intentionally tense to see how she'd stand up under pressure and, if so, why the panel members would do such a thing.

DISCUSSION QUESTIONS

1. How would you explain the nature of the interview Maria Fernandez had to endure? Specifically, do you think it reflected a well-thought-out interviewing strategy on the part of the firm or carelessness on the part of the firm's management? If it was carelessness, what would you do to improve the interview process at Apex Environmental?
2. Would you take the job if you were Maria? If you're not sure, is there any additional information that would help you make your decision, and, if so, what is it?
3. The job of applications engineer for which Maria was applying requires (1) excellent technical skills with respect to mechanical engineering, (2) a commitment to working in the area of pollution control, (3) the ability to deal well and confidently with customers who have engineering problems, (4) a willingness to travel worldwide, and (5) a very intelligent and well-balanced personality. What questions would you ask when interviewing applicants for the job?

13 LEADING

CHAPTER OUTLINE

Innovation Leadership at Whirlpool

With stagnating washer and dryer sales, Whirlpool Corporation's former CEO Dave Whitman knew the company needed bold new products. His plan for achieving this was risky and required strong leadership—he would transform Whirpool into a company in which every employee felt driven to come up with new ideas.

Whitman knew that this would require a major leadership effort. Employees had to get the information they needed and have the freedom to develop their ideas. They would need training, and their supervisors would have to learn how to supervise by consensus rather than by command. Whitman's plan meant changing the very nature of what his managers did and how they led. And it meant finding new ways to use information technology (IT) to help employees share information and collaborate. Whirlpool asks your team for advice on two issues: (1) what new leadership styles would you recommend for our managers, and (2) how can we use IT to further our aims?[1] ■

Whirlpool CEO Dave Whitman drove innovation through his effective leadership.

BEHAVIORAL OBJECTIVES

After studying this chapter, you should be able to:

Show that you've learned the chapter's essential information by

- Describing the difference between leadership and management.
- Explaining how leaders can best use different types of power and influence.
- Briefly explaining what traits, skills, and behaviors have been associated with leadership.

CHAPTER OUTLINE (Continued)

- Listing five or more different leadership styles and describing when each is most appropriate.
- Giving examples of factors that influence leaders' effectiveness.

Show that you can practice what you've learned here by

- Reading the Whirlpool chapter-opening vignette and identifying the leadership implications for the organization's change to an innovation democracy.
- Completing the least preferred coworker self-assessment and interpreting your leadership style.
- Reading the chapter case study and identifying what makes Steve Bennett an effective leader.
- Completing the end-of-chapter exercises and analyzing and improving a leader's effectiveness.

Show that you can apply what you've learned here by

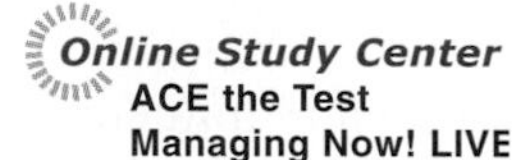

- Watching the video scenario and identifying leadership traits being displayed.
- Watching the video scenario and identifying why the leader is not effective.

Good managers know that information technology, organizational plans, decision-making systems, and supply chains do not make an organization successful by themselves. Even if the right organizational systems and employees are in place, nothing will happen without *leadership*. A leader sets the goals and direction and then influences the employees to work toward achieving those goals. An organization without leadership is like a boat without a captain. Effective leadership taps an organization's potential and converts it into stellar performance. Weak or ineffective leadership drains an organization of its potential and erodes its competitive edge. The administrative debacle in the wake of Hurricane Katrina's impact on the Gulf Coast illustrates what happens without leadership. Mayor Giuliani's leadership in New York City in the wake of the 9/11 attacks illustrates great leadership in a time of crisis.

Leadership involves influencing others, which may require different styles and behaviors in different situations. In this part, Part 5, "Leading Now," we turn our attention to the things managers must do in their leadership roles to enable the company to execute its strategy and meet its goals. Although technology can make some of these behaviors easier, no amount of technology can replace them. Leaders can and must do many things—including motivate, communicate, and build culture, community, and trust. The next five chapters will help you to become a more effective leader and manager. Here's what each covers:

- *Chapter 13, "Leading":* what leaders do; the traits and skills of leadership; situational, process, and contemporary theories of leadership; leadership through technology; and how managers can become better leaders.
- *Chapter 14, "Motivating Employees":* differences among people that help to explain why people behave as they do, and theories that describe how leaders can better motivate employees.

- *Chapter 15, "Improving Communications":* what is communication, what can enhance and impede effective communication, and what a manager should know about communication to lead effectively.
- *Chapter 16, "Building Community, Culture, and Teamwork":* how managers can create an environment in which employees feel committed to the company and its goals, what are important team processes and dynamics, and how leaders can build effective teams.
- *Chapter 17, "Encouraging Sharing, Trust, and Collaboration":* how managers can engage employees in the sharing and collaborative behaviors necessary to establish trust and high performance.

What Is Leadership?

Online Study Center
ACE the Test
Managing Now! LIVE

leadership: setting the direction and inspiring and influencing others to work willingly toward achieving a firm's objectives

Leadership means setting the direction and inspiring and influencing others to work willingly toward achieving a firm's objectives. Leadership can have both positive and negative effects in organizations. At its best, leadership inspires and motivates employees to work hard toward organizational objectives and helps the organization succeed. At its worst, leadership can reduce the performance of individual employees as well as the entire organization, and even result in unethical behavior and an organization's demise.

Are Leadership and Management the Same?

Leadership and management are not the same. Leadership experts Warren Bennis and Burt Nanus put it this way: "Management controls, arranges, does things right; leadership unleashes energy, sets the vision so we do the right thing."[2] Ideally, all managers should be leaders, too (after all, managers plan, organize, lead, and control). Realistically, however, not all managers are leaders. You can probably think of someone, perhaps a former boss, whom you would not describe as being a leader despite his or her managerial authority. Conversely, you can probably also think of someone you would consider a leader, although he or she didn't have formal authority.

Managers establish and implement procedures, processes, and practices that help the firm function smoothly and are responsible for goal attainment.[3] Because of their position in the organization, managers have formal authority to reward and punish while ensuring that what employees do is consistent with the organization's rules and regulations. Leaders can influence the behaviors of others without using rewards or punishment. Leaders help clarify their subordinates' goals and the paths or methods through which they can pursue and achieve those goals, and help them understand their role in implementing those goals. Table 13.1 summarizes the differences between managers and leaders.

Because leadership can help all managers to be more effective, all managers should ideally have excellent leadership skills. The reality is that everyone in an organization, from the CEO to the entry-level employee, can and should exhibit leadership. The leadership displayed by a store employee who inspires her

TABLE 13.1

Management Versus Leadership

Management	Leadership
A function	A relationship
Planning	Selecting and developing talent
Budgeting	Motivating
Evaluating	Coaching
Facilitating	Building trust

Source: Michael Macoby, "Understanding the Difference Between Management and Leadership," *Research & Technology Management*, January–February 2000, pp. 57–59. Reprinted by permission of Research & Technology Management.

coworkers to provide better customer service and the leadership shown by a warehouse supervisor who inspires subordinates to work more safely both have positive consequences for the firm. And leadership does matter—a Hewitt Associates study found that companies with more rigorous leadership development programs tend to outperform their competitors.[4] Successful organizations and leaders develop leadership skills in all of their employees, encouraging employees to set a positive example for their coworkers and continually work toward the accomplishment of the firm's goals.

The next five chapters provide a wealth of information about leadership and behavioral concepts and skills related to effective leadership. After studying them, you should have a variety of tools at your disposal for becoming a better leader.

Studying Leadership

Throughout the ages, Chinese emperors, Egyptian pharaohs, and Indian chiefs must have wondered, "Why are some people more effective leaders than others?"[5] Yet only in the last seventy years or so have behavioral scientists addressed this question. In brief, experts' current thinking is that effective leadership reflects a balance of (1) a leader's traits and skills and (2) a leader's styles or behaviors, (3) combined in a way that best fits the followers and is most appropriate for the situation at hand.[6] Essentially, effective leadership depends on who a person is in terms of their traits and skills, how the person behaves, and the appropriateness of the two given the situation the leader is facing. Followers' perceptions of the leader and their willingness to let the leader influence them further influence leadership effectiveness. No one can be a leader without followers, and only the followers determine whether someone will lead them.

First, we will discuss leadership traits, what leaders do, and what influences a leader's effectiveness. At the end of the chapter, we will review several contemporary approaches to leadership. Let's first look at the Window on Managing Now feature, which illustrates how technology can help new leaders become effective more quickly.

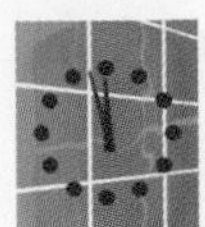

Window on Managing Now
How Can Technology Help New Leaders?

New leaders often have a lot to learn before they can get down to the business of leading. They have to learn what their new goals and responsibilities are and who it is that they are responsible for leading. New and existing leaders also often benefit from training in coaching and leadership skills. Technology can help new leaders get up to speed in a variety of ways.[7]

CD-ROMs

Many companies, like Dell Computer, are putting new-hire and new-leader orientation information on CD-ROMs, including hyperlinks to important company intranet pages; videos featuring corporate leaders and corporate spaces, manufacturing facilities, and product lines; and information about the company's history, mission, and culture. Unlike classroom training programs that require leaders to be in a particular place at a particular time to learn the information, the leader can watch a CD-ROM when he or she has the time to devote to it or when the leader needs the information.

Personal Digital Assistants (PDAs)

Some companies provide incoming leaders with personal digital assistants (PDAs) preloaded with important contact information in the organization, key tasks to complete, and even pictures of staff and others whom the new leader needs to know. Important meeting dates can also be preloaded to help the new leader schedule his or her time.

Web-Based Toolkits

Some companies also create Web-based toolkits or intranet sites that contain information leaders regularly refer to, including information about company ethics, performance management, and other company processes and procedures.

Communities of Practice

Employers encourage leaders and others to visit online chatrooms and bulletin boards to form communities of practice where members ask questions and share answers. These communities can be particularly helpful for a new leader who wants advice on how to handle certain situations or challenges.

Online Leadership Development

Web-based coaches and tools can support leadership development. For example, Boeing's Web-based leadership development tool, called Waypoint, helps leaders develop their leadership and management competence. Waypoint allows leaders to engage in self-directed learning using an interactive website where they can take assessment tests, devise personal development plans, and identify training and developmental assignments. Reading materials and other learning resources facilitate their continued development.[8]

Mixed Modes of Training and Development

Some companies use learning programs that incorporate technology to help leaders learn quickly and develop new skills. For example, Xerox partnered with the Center for Creative Leadership to institute the Emerging Leaders Program, a five-month program that combines Web-based conferencing with face-to-face sessions, along with Web-based learning modules, personal executive coaching, and internal mentoring.[9]

Many organizations use technology to enhance their training and development programs.

What Characteristics Do Leaders Have?

Online Study Center
ACE the Test
Managing Now! LIVE

We'll see in this chapter that a leader's traits, style, and appropriateness for the situation determine his or her leadership effectiveness. But a leader's ability to exercise leadership also depends on that person having the authority or power to influence his or her subordinates. Let's therefore look at this idea first.

Managers typically have formal authority because of their position, which gives them a legitimate right to ask employees to complete tasks that are part of their job descriptions. However, being in a position of authority does not guarantee that employees will fully comply with a manager's requests. For example, employees of an unpopular supervisor may do the minimum amount possible to meet the requirements of their jobs. A manager's ability to influence others to give their all depends on the **power** or capability she or he has to influence other people's behavior or attitudes. Power refers to someone's ability to directly or indirectly control the outcomes of another person in a relationship.[10] Because leadership always involves some sort of power, it is important to understand its use and its consequences.

power: the capability to influence other people's behavior or attitudes and directly or indirectly control the outcomes of another person

Types of Power

Managers' power stems from both organizational authority and personal sources. Organizational authority gives a manager **position power**. For example, the dean of a school has certain authority that comes with this position. However, organizational authority cannot grant a leader all forms of power—some types originate with the person. **Personal power** is based on the characteristics of that individual and stays with him or her regardless of where that person works.

position power: power based on one's position in the organization

personal power: power based on the person's individual characteristics; stays with a person regardless of his or her job or organization

French and Raven[11] identified five sources of power: legitimate, reward, coercive, expert, and referent. Another type of power is informational power. Table 13.2 summarizes these six types of power. We will discuss each of these types of power in more detail next, along with their use and abuse.

legitimate power: a position power based on a person's holding of the managerial position rather than anything the manager is or does as a person

● **Legitimate Power** **Legitimate power** is based on a person's holding of the managerial position rather than anything the manager is or does as a person. Legitimate power is the formal authority the firm gives managers to hire new employees, make work assignments, monitor employees' work, and enforce

TABLE 13.2
Summary of the Six Types of Power

Summary of the Six Types of Power
Legitimate: control because of the position of authority held.
Reward: control over rewards.
Coercive: control over punishments.
Expert: control due to knowledge, skills, and/or expertise.
Referent: control because subordinates respect, admire, and identify with the leader.
Informational: control over information.

organizational rules. Subordinates comply because they believe that holding a managerial position gives the manager the right to make certain requests of them. For example, nurses will show up for their shifts as assigned by a supervisor, even if those shifts are not those preferred by the nurses. Because the scheduling manager has the legitimate power to assign shifts, employees accept the final work schedule.

reward power: a position power that involves the use of rewards to influence and motivate followers

● **Reward Power** **Reward power** is power that involves the use of both tangible (e.g., pay raises or preferred work assignments) and intangible (e.g., praise) rewards to influence and motivate followers. Subordinates comply because they want to receive the rewards. As we discuss further in Chapter 14, rewards are one of the strongest tools used by managers to inspire high performance.

Because rewards are such strong motivators, it is important to monitor the positive and negative impacts they have on employee behavior. For example, the manager of a hair salon wanted to motivate his stylists to sell more hair care products. The manager began offering a monthly prize to the stylist who sold the most. Because one stylist's customers always tended to buy more products than did the other stylists' customers, the other stylists felt that there was no way they could win the prize. Rather than trying harder to sell products, they stopped trying at all and overall product sales and revenues fell. Clearly, if rewards are improperly used, they can decrease the motivation of employees who do not expect to receive them.

coercive power: a position power based on the ability to punish

● **Coercive Power** If a manager has the ability to punish subordinates, she or he can coerce subordinates into complying because people want to avoid punishment. This type of power is **coercive power**. Punishment could be any undesired or negative consequence, including a reduction in work hours, the assignment of undesirable shifts, or a written or verbal reprimand.

Threatening punishment can have negative side effects on employees, including stress, resentment, decreased morale, and retaliation,[12] and can even cost the manager his or her job. Although it can produce behavior change, most managers probably learn early on that it's best to use coercion only when absolutely necessary—for example, if an employee is behaving dangerously.

expert power: a personal power based on an individual's knowledge and/or expertise

● **Expert Power** **Expert power** is based on an individual's expertise in some area. People respond to expert power because of their belief in the person's knowledge, skills, and/or expertise. For example, some sales managers may have specialized knowledge of certain market segments or customers, giving them expert power among other managers and employees.

Because an individual's knowledge is the foundation of expert power, it can exist at any level in an organization. When Jack Welch was the CEO of General Electric (GE), he realized that the Web was going to transform business. He recognized that GE's younger employees had better Internet skills and e-business knowledge than did GE's older and higher-ranking executives. He decided to pair an Internet-savvy employee with each of GE's 600 worldwide executives to share his or her expertise about the new technology. In addition to building the e-business capabilities of his managers, this unique mentoring program made managers at all levels more receptive to influence from people at lower levels of the company who have relevant expertise.[13]

referent power: a personal power based on a manager's charisma and/or attractiveness to others

● **Referent Power** **Referent power** is based on a manager's charisma and/or attractiveness to others. Subordinates refer to the manager as a role model and comply out of respect, admiration, and liking. They behave as the manager does and wants because they seek his or her approval.

Referent power is not limited to high-visibility leaders. All managers can use referent power effectively by displaying respect for subordinates, modeling behaviors consistent with the organization's culture, and being effective role models. By consistently walking the walk and talking the talk, managers can use their referent power to promote the attitudes and behaviors they desire in employees. For example, when Wal-Mart founder Sam Walton was worth more than $25 billion, he still drove an old pickup truck to work and shared budget-hotel rooms with colleagues on business trips. His modeling of frugality permeated the company and promoted the practice of frugality that made Wal-Mart consistently profitable.[14]

informational power: power derived from control over information

● **Informational Power** Control over information is **informational power**. In addition to experts with specialized knowledge, some people in an organization have or are able to control access to important information. These gatekeepers are able to exert power over others by providing or withholding information that others need. For example, managers with extensive personal networks may have access to information few others have. Once the information is shared, however, the informational power that the information provided is lost. Managers who depend on informational power must therefore continually replenish their supply of hard-to-get information.

When Is Each Type of Power Appropriate?

Managers should adjust their use of power to the situation and person they are trying to influence. Because the effects of referent and expert power rely on the employee's internal motivation and voluntary compliance, they are always appropriate. However, these types of power are also the weakest—if they do not motivate employee behavior, then either legitimate or reward organizational power might be appropriate.

Legitimate, reward, and coercive power rely on external motivation and obligatory obedience. Managers often rely on legitimate and reward power, but coercive power is rarely appropriate and should be reserved for only the most extreme situations. Effective leaders tend to rely on expert and referent power more than legitimate, reward, or coercive power.[15]

Abuse of Power

Power in itself is neither good nor bad—what matters is how people use their power or position. Gary Jackson, president of private military contractor and security firm Blackwater USA, preserves his military training company's high-energy culture through his own example of energy and commitment.[16] An important point to make about power is the potential for its abuse. In any firm, the abuse of power is (1) using any type of power to demean, exploit, or take advantage of another or (2) influencing someone to do something they later regret. It is easy to think of news stories where people have abused their power. In addition to financial ruin, the results of the abuse of power may include sexual or racial harassment, abusive behavior, and embarrassed employees.

Unchecked authority can result in the abuse of power. Managers should not have free reign to do whatever they want—a manager's power should match his or her responsibilities. For example, a manager responsible for subordinates' performance should receive some sort of reward power such as performance appraisals or allocating merit-pay awards. Regularly reviewing managers' behaviors and performance and holding them accountable for their actions are important. Even CEOs report to a board of directors, and legislation like the Sarbanes-Oxley Act of 2002 limits the unchecked authority of CEOs.

empowerment: sharing power with employees and giving them the authority to make and implement at least some decisions

● **Empowerment** The degree to which power is shared and an employee has the authority to make and implement at least some decisions is **empowerment.**[17] Empowerment may be organizationwide and embedded in an organization's culture, or it may be something done by individual managers. Empowering employees to improve quality, cut costs, and make their work more efficient is becoming more common in organizations because technologies such as digital dashboards increasingly make it possible for subordinates to lead themselves. If trained employees have important, accurate, and timely information, they can often handle situations and spot opportunities without a manager's intervention. This can increase the flexibility and responsiveness of organizations.

Empowerment is more than mere involvement. Involvement gives subordinates influence in the decision being made; empowerment gives subordinates the ability and authority to make the decision themselves. In today's challenging business environment, empowerment helps free up leaders' time. Leaders can now spend more time running the business rather than micromanaging employees.

Essentially, empowerment requires that managers (1) allow those beneath them to have more power and control over their work and (2) provide training, resources, and coaching to give employees the skills and confidence to act empowered. Just telling an employee that he or she is empowered is not enough. Employees have to have the skills to do what they are empowered to do and believe that they can successfully do it. In one manufacturing facility, newly empowered employee teams had the authority to spend up to $500 to improve their teams' processes without having to consult with a manager. At first, none of the teams was willing to spend anything, fearing that they would make a bad choice. Not until the teams went through a hands-on training program teaching decision-making, communication, and problem-solving skills did they have the confidence to act empowered.

● **Managing Now** Technology can help empower employees to solve problems themselves. For example, knowing that to receive her quarterly bonus she must consistently meet call-volume targets, Pat uses the digital dashboard to check her performance. The color-coded display shows that she is below target. She knows that she's been getting to work on time and that she's productive. So why is her performance below her target?

Pat sees that her call volume has been consistently low for the last month. Further analysis indicates that a dip in her performance occurs at the same time each day—just after lunch. This is the root cause of the problem: her afternoon shift starts at exactly the time her lunch break ends. Although she hurries through lunch, she's getting back from lunch ten minutes after her scheduled start each afternoon. Pat requests a minor schedule change that gives her ten more minutes to get from the cafeteria to her workstation.[18] The digital dashboard helped to empower Pat to solve her performance problem without needing the help of a supervisor, other than approval of the minor schedule change.

Influence

Power does not necessarily translate into influence. Whether a leader's use of power to influence someone will be successful depends on whether the other person allows him- or herself to be influenced. How much formal power or authority a manager has is not as important as the amount of influence the manager has over subordinates. A manager who lacks the respect of subordinates because of unethical behavior or perceptions that the manager is unqualified will not effectively motivate subordinates to work their hardest toward the firm's goals.

In addition to possessing power, leaders can engage in various influence tactics to increase the likelihood that others will respond favorably to their requests. Table 13.3 summarizes some of the influence tactics, along with the possible responses to them. Responses to influence attempts are not always positive.

TABLE 13.3
Influence Tactics and Responses to Them

Effective Influence Tactics
Coalition tactics: engaging the help of others to persuade someone to do something; referring to the support of others to convince someone to agree to a proposal or to change his or her attitude toward something.
Consultation: requesting someone's advice to solve a problem or mutually setting goals to increase a follower's commitment to the leader's decision; being willing to modify the goals or solution based on the person's concerns and suggestions to sustain commitment.
Exchange: offering to exchange something of value now or in the future for someone's cooperation.
Ingratiation: flattering or praising people to put them in a good mood or to make them more likely to want to help (for example, complimenting your manager's outfit before asking for additional project funding).
Inspirational appeals: appealing to someone's aspirations, values, and ideals to gain his or her commitment; increasing the person's confidence that he or she can do something to increase motivation.
Legitimating tactics: enhancing one's formal authority to make a certain request by referring to rules, precedents, or official documents.
Personal appeals: asking someone to do something because of friendship or asking for a personal favor.
Pressure: using coercion or persistent follow-up or reminders to gain influence.
Rational persuasion: using logic and facts to persuade someone.
Responses to Influence Attempts
Commitment: endorsing and becoming an actively involved participant as a result of the influence attempt.
Compliance: just going along with what the influencer wants without being personally committed.
Passive resistance: rejecting the influence attempt but not getting in the way of what the influencer is trying to do.
Active resistance: rejecting the influence attempt and actively trying to stop the influencer from doing what she or he is trying to do or trying to change the influencer's attitudes in return.

Source: Gary Yukl, *Leadership in Organizations*, 4th ed. (Englewood Cliffs, N.J.: Prentice Hall, 1998).
Reprinted by permission of Pearson Education, Inc., Upper Saddle River, N.J.

What Traits and Skills Are Associated with Leadership?

When asked to name people they consider leaders, most people can easily come up with names such as Martin Luther King Jr., Margaret Thatcher, Mahatma Gandhi, and Oprah Winfrey. But why are these people considered leaders? When asked, many people explain that these leaders have charisma, intelligence, a strong vision, and a determination to achieve their goals. But do personality traits or skills really predict who will become a leader?

traits: a person's unchanging characteristics that predispose him or her to act in a certain way

Because people differ in so many ways, it is natural to think that some people have certain unchanging characteristics or special gifts that enhance their abilities to lead. Describing the personal **traits** of leaders is also the way leadership researchers first thought about leaders. The first systematic research studies on leadership investigated individual traits that included intelligence, birth order, socioeconomic status, and child-raising practices.[19] These early attempts to isolate specific leadership traits were generally unsuccessful and led to the conclusion that no single characteristic distinguishes leadership.

Later research on leadership traits and skills had better success in identifying some traits and skills relevant to successful leadership. Leaders seem to have higher energy levels, higher internal control orientation, emotional maturity,[20] intelligence, self-confidence, determination, integrity, and social and interpersonal skills.[21] Table 13.4 describes some important leadership traits and skills.

TABLE 13.4
Some of the Traits and Skills of Leaders

Determination: leaders overcome obstacles and achieve their goals through initiative, drive, dominance, and a motivation to achieve.
Emotional maturity: effective leaders control their emotions rather than letting their emotions control them.
Energy levels: leaders have the energy to work hard toward their goals and can create excitement and enthusiasm in others.
Integrity: leaders who behave honestly and earn the trust of followers are more effective at motivating them.
Intelligence: leaders must scan, interpret, and integrate large amounts of information; identify patterns; and devise courses of action based on the information.
Internal control orientation: leaders tend to believe that they are able to control their environment rather than merely reacting to events around them.
Job-relevant knowledge: leaders make decisions and set appropriate goals and strategies based on their understanding of how their unit and firm works.
Self-confidence: leaders who demonstrate self-confidence and a belief that their chosen course of action is correct develop followers who are more committed.
Social and interpersonal skills: leaders who are good at relating to other people are able to build trusting relationships with followers.

Source: Based on Stephen J. Zaccaro, Cary Kemp, and Paige Bader, "Leader Traits and Attributes," in John Antonakis, Anna T. Cianciolo, and Robert J. Sternberg (eds.), *The Nature of Leadership*, pp. 101–125 (London: Sage, 2004); Peter G. Northouse, *Leadership: Theory and Practice*, 2nd ed. (London: Sage, 2000); and Gary Yukl, *Leadership in Organizations*, 5th ed. (Upper Saddle River, N.J.: Prentice Hall, 2002).

Emotional Intelligence

Emotional intelligence is a person's ability to recognize and manage emotions and relationships. This characteristic gained popularity in the 1990s when psychologists, sociologists, and management consultants claimed that one's emotional quotient (EQ) was twice as important as their intelligence quotient (IQ) or even technical skills when it comes to job performance.[22] One research study found that emotional intelligence accounted for 85 percent of what distinguishes stars from low performers in top leadership positions.[23] Organizations, including American Express, use emotional intelligence programs to improve team and organizational effectiveness.[24] Some of the biggest supporters of emotional intelligence have called the awareness of others' feelings and ability to recognize and control one's own emotions an indispensable ingredient of leadership.[25] Emotional intelligence is composed of five dimensions:

- *Self-awareness:* being aware of what you are feeling.
- *Self-motivation:* persisting in the face of obstacles, setbacks, and failures.
- *Self-management:* managing your own emotions and impulses.
- *Empathy:* sensing how others are feeling.
- *Social skills:* effectively handling the emotions of others.

Part innate and part trainable, emotional intelligence has been receiving increasing attention in leadership development programs. Emotionally intelligent leaders know their own limitations and strengths and have the ability to communicate clearly and convincingly, manage conflicts, build strong personal bonds, and motivate employees and customers.[26] Because leadership involves such a high degree of social interaction, emotional intelligence is likely to enhance leadership effectiveness. In a negotiation setting, Franz Humer, the chairman and CEO of the pharmaceutical firm Roche, tries to switch his entire body, mind, and emotions into "receiving" mode to understand how the other side is reacting and behaving. This increases his sensitivity to how the negotiations are going and how best to negotiate with the other party.[27]

Does Gender Matter?

Despite making up more than 45 percent of the U.S. workforce, women lead less than 2 percent of *Fortune* 1000 companies.[28] Excuses that have been offered as to why so few women reach the top in organizations include women not being in managerial positions long enough, lacking managerial experience, being less suited to demanding jobs, and being insufficiently qualified. Research has not supported these excuses.[29] So why are most women managers having trouble breaking into the top ranks?

One constraint facing women in management may stem from institutional biases, or patterns of preferences inherent in organizations that create barriers. For example, managers often prefer hiring and promoting people who are similar to themselves. Because most managers are male, they tend to prefer that other managers also be male. Whether conscious or unconscious, this type of bias contributes to the glass-ceiling effect by restricting women's access to managerial jobs.

Women leaders often emphasize inaccurate gender stereotypes as a key barrier to their advancement.[30] Stereotypes are generalizations people make to differentiate groups of people, such as believing that men are better leaders than

Carly Fiorina ran into considerable headwinds as HP's CEO, and eventually stepped down.

women. However, men and women are much more similar in personality, communication, ability, and leadership than commonly believed.[31] Several reviews of studies of gender differences in leadership have found many more similarities than differences between males and females,[32] although research does suggest that males tend to punish subordinates more harshly than women do.[33] It is important to note that while males and females may differ with respect to participative management and punishment tendencies, research has found males and females to be equally effective as leaders.

Another problem may be that people frequently compare women to an ideal leadership style that favors autocratic men. It is common for both men and women to view competitive (stereotypically masculine) characteristics as managerial and cooperative and communicative (stereotypically feminine) characteristics as nonmanagerial.[34] Because men are more likely to exhibit the masculine characteristics thought to reflect better managerial and leadership skills, they are more likely than women to be viewed as appropriate leaders.

Research does suggest that many women use a more participative style and can have better interpersonal skills than men.[35] It is interesting to note, however, that a more participative style may actually be more appropriate for today's challenges of managing diversity and leading empowered teams. As Rosabeth Moss Kanter put it, "[W]omen get high ratings on exactly those skills needed to succeed in the global Information Age, where teamwork and partnering are so important."[36] Rather than changing how women lead, it may be more appropriate to change perceptions about what it means to be an effective leader and what characteristics and styles are required to become one.

Communication skills are critical to all managers, regardless of their gender. The Window on Managing Now feature gives you some tips on deciding when technology is an appropriate communication medium.

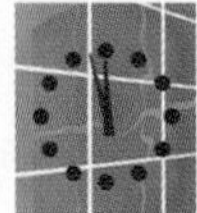

Window on Managing Now

How Does Technology Increase the Importance of Leaders' Communication Skills?

Technology gives managers the opportunity to communicate with employees in a variety of ways. Sometimes technology can enhance a leader's effectiveness, but sometimes it can get in the way. Here are some netiquette tips for deciding when technology is an appropriate medium of communication and for creating appropriate employee expectations about the use of IT:[37]

- Never use e-mail to fire employees or deliver bad news. Because it contains no body language, facial expression, and intonation, e-mail is the worst way to deliver bad news to employees. A one-on-one meeting is better.
- Do not use e-mail to discuss an employee's performance with other managers. Hold these discussions privately.
- Be careful when writing e-mail messages. Like written performance reviews and other documents, e-mails can be subject to discovery and subpoena. Also, e-mail is not always secure, and it sometimes results in unintended readers receiving confidential information.
- Do not rely on e-mail to the exclusion of personal contact. Even in the age of IT, relationship skills are at the heart of long-term business success. Supplement your e-mails with periodic face-to-face staff, customer, and supplier meetings, even if they must occur through videoconferencing.
- Do not use e-mail when there is any chance of the message being misunderstood. Use a telephone call or a face-to-face meeting if a message is complex, technical, or in any danger of being misinterpreted.

What Do Leaders Do?

Online Study Center
ACE the Test
Managing Now! LIVE

If leaders can't always be identified just by their traits, perhaps we can identify leaders by what they do. After the early leadership researchers ran out of steam in their search for traits, attention turned to what leaders did and how they behaved, especially toward followers. This research led to the identification of various leadership behaviors and styles. We now turn our attention to understanding leadership styles and behaviors.

The Ohio State Studies

initiating structure: concern for task accomplishment

consideration: concern for individuals and interpersonal relations

In the 1950s, Ralph Stogdill and his Ohio State University colleagues identified two dimensions of leadership style: **initiating structure** (concern for organizational task accomplishment) and **consideration** (concern for individuals and interpersonal relations). These two dimensions are the Ohio State dimensions of leadership.[38]

- Initiating structure emphasizes the achievement of concrete goals. Leaders look for ways to organize people and activities that will best accomplish these concrete goals. Initiating structure includes planning, organizing, and defining the required tasks, for example, setting goals and clearly communicating them to the group. When Steve Ballmer took the reins at Microsoft, he initiated structure by implementing an online performance appraisal system (previously there had been no formal performance appraisal process).[39]
- Consideration emphasizes the social and emotional needs of individuals, including trust, respect, work satisfaction, and self-esteem, by being respectful and friendly.

The Ohio State team developed the Leader Behavior Description Questionnaire (LBDQ), later refined by others, to measure these two dimensions. One of the major research findings was that effective leaders address both the task and the human aspects of their organizations. Although people tend to be more satisfied when working with considerate leaders,[40] their task performance is not necessarily better.[41] And although leaders high in initiating structure tend to have higher-performing groups, this is not always true. In particular, subordinates of leaders who are very task-oriented can have lower morale unless the leader is also considerate.[42]

The University of Michigan Studies

While the Ohio State studies on leadership styles were being conducted, Rensis Likert and the team at the University of Michigan's Survey Research Center identified two leadership styles[43] that were similar to those resulting from the Ohio State studies:

- Employee-oriented leaders emphasize building good interpersonal relationships with employees and focus on meeting employees' needs.
- Production-oriented leaders focus on the job's technical aspects and on getting the job done.

Consistent with the conclusions of the Ohio State researchers, Likert suggested that leaders must take a balanced approach. He found that the best-performing supervisors focus on the human aspects of their subordinates' problems and on building effective workgroups with high performance goals. Higher-performing managers were also more facilitative than directive, and they used a participative style in making decisions that took recommendations from the team into account.[44]

Blake and Mouton's Managerial Grid

Robert Blake and Jane Mouton[45] developed a two-dimensional managerial grid that has become a classic way to illustrate the behavioral, leadership-style approach to leadership. The grid diagrams leadership styles based on "concern for people" and "concern for task (results)." These two dimensions reflect the Ohio State dimensions of initiating structure and consideration and the University of Michigan dimensions of production orientation and employee orientation.

As Figure 13.1 shows, "concern for people" is on the vertical axis of the grid and "concern for production" (concern for results) is on the horizontal axis. Both have a range of 0 to 9. Each cell of the grid contains a numerical rating reflecting the manager's concern for results *and* for people, which Blake and Mouton say

FIGURE 13.1

Blake and Mouton's Managerial Grid

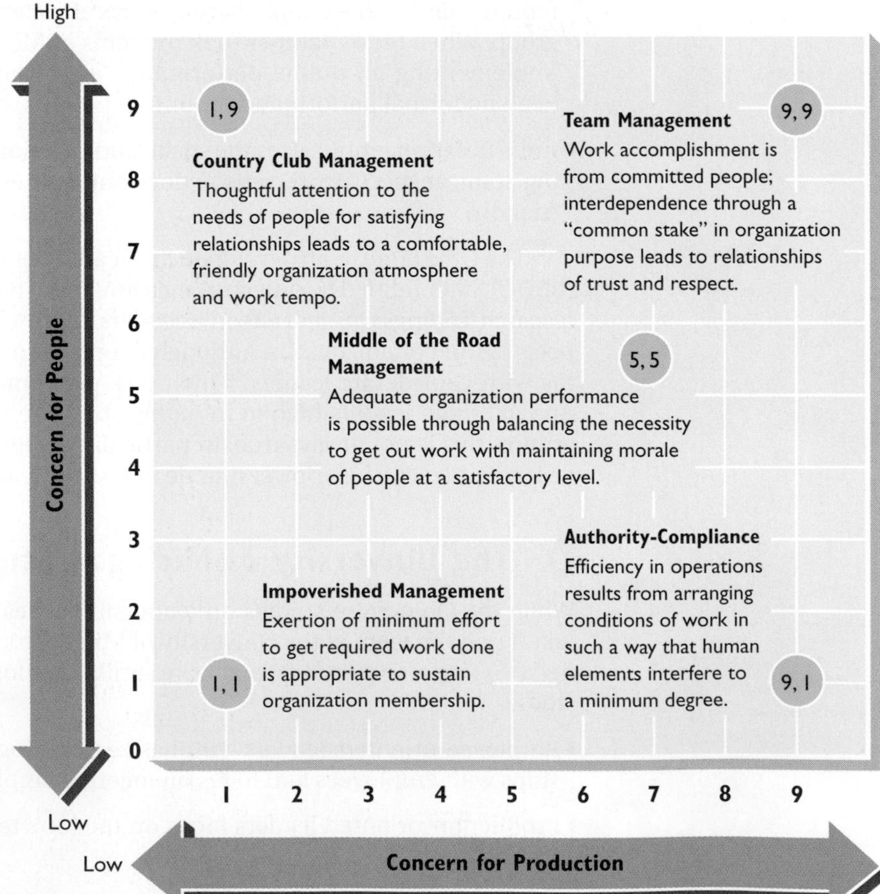

SOURCE: Adapted from Robert R. Blake and Jane S. Mouton, *The Managerial Grid III: The Key to Leadership Excellence*, 3rd ed. (Houston: Gulf Publishing Co., 1985); The Leadership Grid, Grid International, Inc. Online at http://www.gridinternational.com/gridtheory.html. Reprinted with permission from gridinternational.com.

are independent of each other. Although Blake and Mouton considered the ideal to be a 9,9 manager who integrates a high concern for both task and people, there is little evidence to support this style as the most effective in all situations.[46] Effective leadership requires more than the use of a particular style regardless of the context. We'll see that the nature of the followers and the situation are important as well.

University of Iowa Leadership Styles

Kurt Lewin and his colleagues at the University of Iowa[47] explored three types of leadership styles: autocratic, democratic, and laissez-faire. A leader who centralizes authority, makes decisions alone, and expects followers or subordinates simply to follow instructions uses an autocratic leadership style. A leader who shares decision making with others and encourages subordinates to be involved in setting goals uses a democratic leadership style. A democratic leader may be consultative, seeking input from others but making the final decision alone, or participative, giving employees a say in the decision. A laissez-faire leadership style is an extremely hands-off approach. Employees are given discretion to make decisions and perform their work any way they want. A laissez-faire leader exercises little or no control over the group and may not even participate in discussions.

So which of these leadership styles is best? The laissez-faire style of leadership consistently underperforms the democratic and autocratic styles. Although employees' satisfaction is generally higher when working with a democratic leader than an autocratic one,[48] research comparing the two has been inconclusive. Because more employee-centered styles tend to produce higher levels of motivation, decision quality, morale, and teamwork, managers should use them whenever possible.[49]

Many of the early writers on leadership styles argued that greater participation made followers more satisfied. But this idea didn't hold up in practice.[50] There were many inconsistencies from one study to the next, and it was hard to say that any particular style of leadership always enabled groups to work better. Perhaps the biggest problem, though, was one shared with those studies that looked for traits: ignoring the context or setting in which the style was used. We'll see that the same leadership style is not likely to work equally well in a corporate boardroom, on a construction site, and in a hospital emergency room.

Transformational and Transactional Leadership

Another way to consider leadership behavior is to consider what the leader is trying to accomplish. Some leaders focus on making incremental improvements to the status quo. Other leaders focus on making large-scale revolutionary changes to an organization. **Transformational leadership**[51] changes the values and priorities of followers, motivating them to achieve more by doing things in new ways. Transformational leaders inspire followers through a clear mission, optimism, enthusiasm, and emotional appeals. They provide personal support and encouragement, set a personal example, and behave ethically. Followers then connect deeply to the mission and seek ways to improve their performance. John F. Kennedy and Ghandi are good examples of transformational leaders.

transformational leadership: leadership that inspires followers to adopt the values and goals of the leader and put aside their self-interests for the good of the organization

Studies show that transformational leadership affects a wide range of employee outcomes (including motivation, satisfaction, and commitment) and organizational outcomes (including business unit performance).[52] Transformational leaders can influence followers to change their priorities, set new goals, and develop confidence in their abilities by giving subordinates developmental work experiences, inspiring them to do their best, and demonstrating positive behaviors that followers want to emulate.[53]

Transformational leaders are:[54]

- *Inspirational,* and they communicate a future vision of the organization that can be shared with followers. "The leader uses visionary explanations to depict what the employee work group can accomplish."[55]
- *Considerate,* and they treat each employee as an individual rather than simply as a member of the group. A transformational leader tries to bring out the strengths of each employee.
- *Intellectually stimulating,* and they encourage employees to solve problems creatively by approaching old and familiar problems in new ways.[56]
- *Charismatic,*[57] or idealized by followers who develop strong emotional attachments to them. Charismatic leadership during the early stages of a group's life can influence the group's belief that it will be successful, enhancing the likelihood that it will perform well.[58] Although substantial research has found that charismatic leadership spurs high performance and follower satisfaction,[59] it isn't always needed. Charisma appears to be most influential when the environment has a high degree of uncertainty, with accompanying stress, or when the followers' task is ideological in some way.[60]

transactional leadership: leadership based on a reciprocal exchange of something of value

Transactional leadership focuses on a transaction or exchange of something of value that the leader possesses or controls and that the follower wants in return for his or her services. By offering promotions in exchange for work done, or bonuses in exchange for extra effort or good performance, leaders are able to influence and motivate others. With transactional leadership, employees comply because of contingent reinforcement, but with transformational leadership, employees comply because they are personally committed to the leader's goals.

Transformational leadership and transactional leadership complement each other,[61] and the choice of which to use depends on the situation. The best leaders are both transformational and transactional.[62] The transactional style can work well for short-term goals when both leader and led understand and are in agreement about which tasks are important. Because transformational leadership results in employees adopting the leader's mission, vision, and goals as their own, it is more effective for long-term goals and organizational change. Transformational leaders, if unsuccessful in gaining compliance by appealing to the values of the followers or peers, may resort to the transactional style to get things done.[63]

level 5 leadership: a combination of transactional and transformational leadership styles focused on long-term company performance

Level 5 leadership requires a leader to use a combination of transformational and transactional leadership styles and channel his or her ambition into the goal of building a great company.[64] Level 5 leaders are humble and willing to take the blame for failure while simultaneously setting high standards and demonstrating an unwavering resolve to do whatever it takes to produce the best long-term results.

David Maxwell retired after turning financial-services company Fannie Mae around and leading it for nine years. His retirement package, which had grown to be worth $20 million because of Fannie Mae's strong performance, drew the attention of Congress (Fannie Mae operates under a government charter). Maxwell responded by writing a letter to his successor expressing concern that the future of the company could be jeopardized and asked that the remaining $5.5 million balance instead be contributed to the Fannie Mae foundation for low-income housing.[65] Such Level 5 leadership has gained popularity among executives, and some consider it to be the ultimate leadership style.

What Influences a Leader's Effectiveness?

Online Study Center
ACE the Test
Managing Now! LIVE

As we have seen, an effective leader does not rely on a single preferred style. Leadership is more complex—good leaders adapt to the situation, take into account the motivation and capability of followers, evaluate the challenges of the task, and consider the organizational environment. A good manager uses many different leadership styles over the course of a day, depending on the nature of the problem and the people being led. Once researchers realized that leaders can't be differentiated based solely on their personal traits or styles, they began to pursue the idea that leadership needs to change from situation to situation. Researchers began to believe that different contexts required particular types of leadership. This meant that leaders had to develop an ability to work in different ways and to change their style to adapt to the situation and the followers. We will next discuss various **contingency theories of leadership**.

contingency theories of leadership: leadership theories that acknowledge that the appropriateness of any leadership style depends on the nature of the followers and the situation

Hersey-Blanchard Situational Leadership Model

Paul Hersey and Kenneth Blanchard[66] believed that a single best leadership style did not exist, and they developed the situational leadership model to help leaders decide how to adapt their style to a given task or situation. They proposed that leader effectiveness requires successfully diagnosing where subordinates are on a readiness continuum. Because subordinates move back and forth along this continuum, leaders have to adapt. The four leadership styles featured by Hersey and Blanchard are:

"When the boss isn't around to watch us, he loads up this screen saver."

- *Delegating:* letting group members decide what to do.
- *Participating:* asking group members for input but making the final decision alone.
- *Selling:* making the decision alone but explaining to the group the reasons for the decision, then helping followers to complete the task by persuading them and providing opportunities to learn more about the task.
- *Telling:* making the decision and telling the group what to do.

Figure 13.2 summarizes what to look for when choosing which style to use.

- *Delegating:* letting followers make and implement decisions is appropriate when followers are able, willing, and confident. Delegating leaders delegate activities and enhance group effectiveness by providing support and resources and by encouraging autonomy.
- *Participating:* sharing decision-making responsibilities with followers, handling followers' apprehensions and concerns when necessary, and focusing on results

FIGURE 13.2

Using the Situational Leadership Model

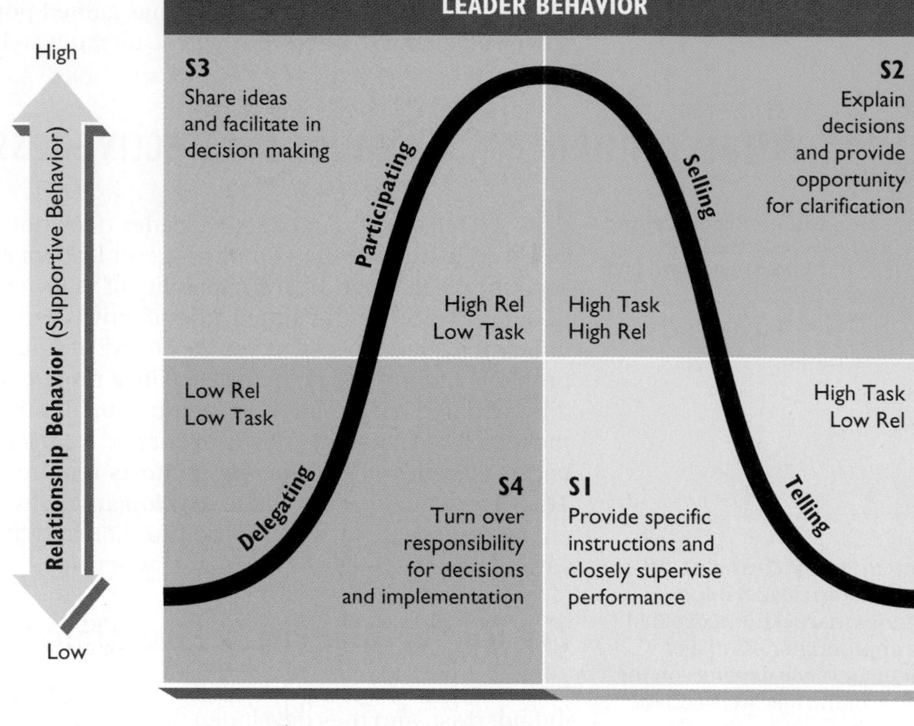

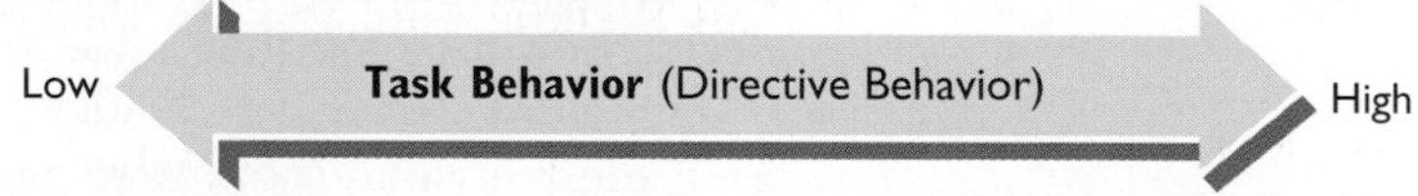

FOLLOWER READINESS (when to use each style)

High	Moderate		Low
S4	S3	S2	S1
Employees able and willing or confident	Employees able but unwilling or insecure	Employees unable but willing or confident	Employees unable and unwilling or insecure

SOURCE: Adapted from Paul Hersey, *Situational Selling* (Escondito, Calif.: Center for Leadership Studies, 1985), p. 19. Reprinted with permission.

works best when followers are somewhat less ready to be led. Participating leaders work well when followers are able but are unwilling or insecure.

- *Selling:* explaining and clarifying decisions is appropriate when followers are even less ready to be led because they are unable but are willing or confident. Here, a leader must persuade followers to buy into the decisions, then the leader must check their understanding of the task, explain why certain actions are taken, encourage questions, and demonstrate how to do the task.

- *Telling:* providing clear directions and closely supervising performance works best when followers are relatively unprepared for the task. The leader provides specific instructions and close supervision and positively reinforces small improvements. Telling leaders work well when followers are unable and are unwilling or insecure.

Fiedler's Leader-Match Model

Fred E. Fiedler[67] argued that leader effectiveness depends on two interacting factors: leadership style and the degree to which the situation gives the leader control and influence. The leader-match model proposes that leadership style is part of who a person is and can't be changed. Fiedler did not believe that leaders can adopt different styles in different situations. Instead, he proposed two ways to make leaders more effective: match them to the situation they are best suited to, or change the context to suit the leader's style. Three factors are important in understanding the context:

- *Leader-follower relations.* Fiedler felt that this was the key: "A leader who is liked, accepted, and trusted by his [or her] members will find it easy to make his [or her] influence felt."[68]

- *Task structure.* If the goals, methods and performance standards of a task are clear, then it is more likely that leaders will be able to exert influence.

- *Position power.* If an organization or group confers powers on the leader to get the job done, then this may well increase the influence of the leader.

According to Fiedler's model, effective leadership is contingent on matching the leader's style to the setting, and certain styles are effective in certain situations. Task-oriented leaders do well when the situation is extremely favorable or extremely unfavorable for the leader (where leader-member relations, task structure, and leader position power are all very high or very low), and relationship-oriented leaders do well in more moderate situations. In favorable situations, the leader can get away with focusing solely on the task, and in unfavorable situations, the leader has no choice but to focus on the task. A more people-oriented leader is appropriate in the middle range where these three contextual factors are mixed.

Fiedler thought of leadership style as a continuum, with task motivation at one end and relationship motivation at the other. He developed the least preferred coworker (LPC) scale to assess a leader's style. Leaders describe their least preferred coworker using a list of adjectives. Leaders who describe their least preferred coworker favorably (pleasant, friendly, enthusiastic) are considered high LPC and are more people-oriented. Leaders who describe their least preferred coworker unfavorably (inefficient, gloomy, uncooperative) are considered low LPC and are more task-oriented. The Improving Your *Leadership* Skills feature provides an opportunity for you to assess your leadership style according to Fiedler's LPC scale. Figure 13.3 on page 393 will help you apply your score to understand where you might be most effective as a leader, according to Fiedler's model.

Researchers have criticized Fiedler's leader-match model because it does not explain why some people are more effective in different situations. It is also not entirely clear what the LPC scale actually measures. For example, some people may have had very different experiences with their LPC than others, and these differences can influence responses to the measure. A fair amount of research has

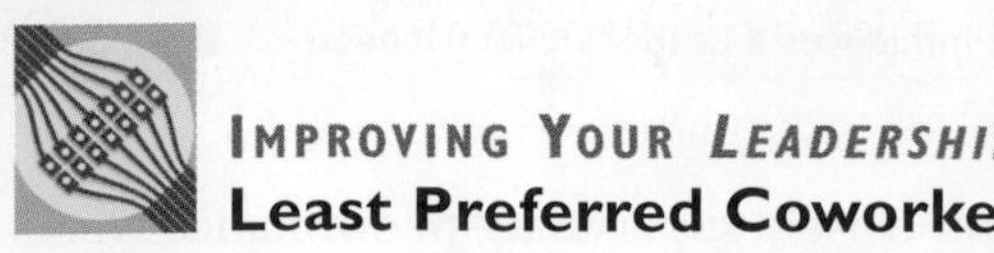

Improving Your *Leadership* Skills
Least Preferred Coworker Scale

Think of the person you work with least well. This may be a person you currently work with or someone you knew in the past. This person is not necessarily the person you like least, but he or she should be the person with whom you had the most difficulty in getting a job done.

The following questionnaire asks you to describe this person as she or he appears to you. Look at the words at both ends of the line before you mark one box with an X. Please remember that there are no right or wrong answers. Work quickly; your first answer is usually the most accurate. Please do not omit any items, and mark only one answer for each item. When you are finished, add up the numbers appearing under each line that you marked with an X. Scoring instructions are at the bottom of the table.

Scores above 78 are considered high LPC and are more people-oriented; scores below 29 are considered low LPC and are more task-oriented.

Pleasant	8	7	6	5	4	3	2	1	**Unpleasant**
Friendly	8	7	6	5	4	3	2	1	**Unfriendly**
Rejecting	1	2	3	4	5	6	7	8	**Accepting**
Helpful	8	7	6	5	4	3	2	1	**Frustrating**
Unenthusiastic	1	2	3	4	5	6	7	8	**Enthusiastic**
Tense	1	2	3	4	5	6	7	8	**Relaxed**
Distant	1	2	3	4	5	6	7	8	**Close**
Cold	1	2	3	4	5	6	7	8	**Warm**
Cooperative	8	7	6	5	4	3	2	1	**Uncooperative**
Supportive	8	7	6	5	4	3	2	1	**Hostile**
Boring	1	2	3	4	5	6	7	8	**Interesting**
Quarrelsome	1	2	3	4	5	6	7	8	**Harmonious**
Self-assured	8	7	6	5	4	3	2	1	**Hesitant**
Efficient	8	7	6	5	4	3	2	1	**Inefficient**
Gloomy	1	2	3	4	5	6	7	8	**Cheerful**
Open	8	7	6	5	4	3	2	1	**Guarded**

Source: Adapted from Fred E. Fiedler, *A Theory of Leadership Effectiveness* (New York: McGraw-Hill, 1967), p. 41.

FIGURE 13.3

Applying Fiedler's Leader-Match Model

High LPC Relationship-Motivated Leaders Perform Better

Low LPC Task-Motivated Leaders Perform Better

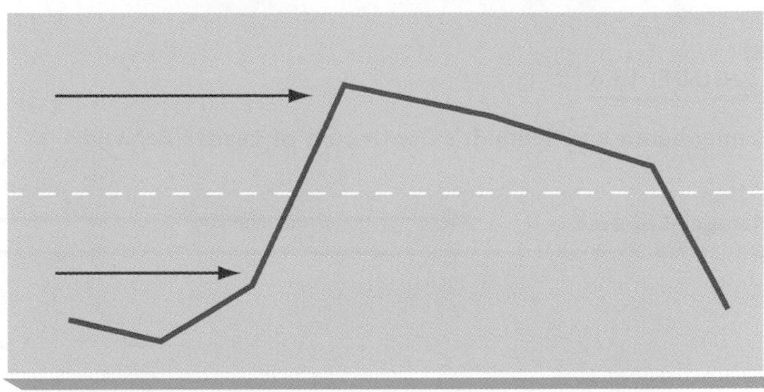

	I	II	III	IV	V	VI	VII	VIII
Leader-Member Relations	Good	Good	Good	Good	Poor	Poor	Poor	Poor
Task Structure	Structured		Unstructured		Structured		Unstructured	
Leader Position Power	Strong	Weak	Strong	Weak	Strong	Weak	Strong	Weak

SOURCE: Adapted and reprinted by permission of the *Harvard Business Review,* "How the Style of Effective Leadership Varies with the Situation" from "Engineer the Job to Fit the Manager" by Fred E. Fiedler, September–October 1965.

produced mixed results. Although popular in management-training programs, the usefulness of the leader-match model, including its more recent variants, is uncertain.[69]

Continuum of Leader Behavior

Tannenbaum and Schmidt[70] presented a simple way to view participation in a group. They identified three forces that influenced the appropriateness of subordinate participation in decision making:[71]

- *Manager factors:* personal values, tolerance for ambiguity, confidence in subordinates, and the leadership behaviors with which the manager is comfortable engaging in.
- *Subordinate factors:* need for independence, willingness to take responsibility, tolerance for ambiguity, problem-solving interest, comprehension of goals and commitment to them, relevant knowledge and experience, expectations about participating.
- *Situation factors:* time constraints, ability of the group to work together, organizational type, nature of problem.

Based on an assessment of these factors, leaders choose a decision-making style along a continuum ranging from autocratic, when the leader makes a decision alone and announces it to the group, to delegative, where the manager permits employees to function autonomously within defined limits. Figure 13.4 illustrates the continuum.

FIGURE 13.4

Tannenbaum and Schmidt's Continuum of Leader Behavior

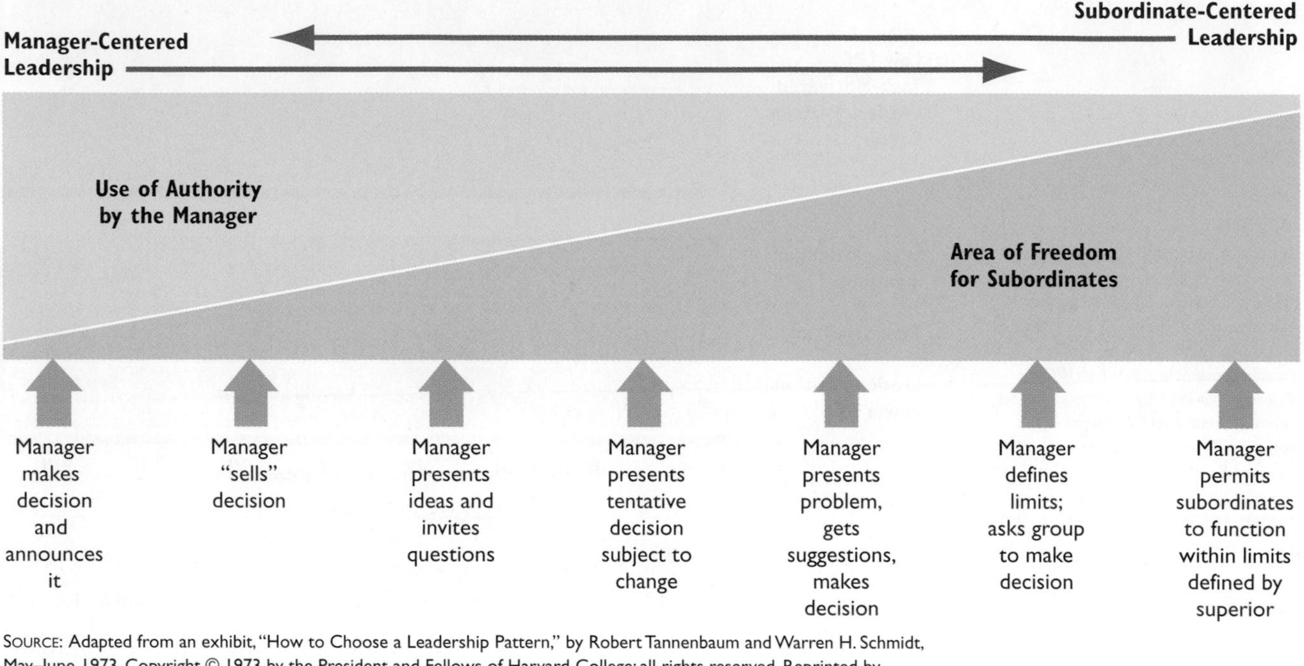

SOURCE: Adapted from an exhibit, "How to Choose a Leadership Pattern," by Robert Tannenbaum and Warren H. Schmidt, May–June 1973.

Tannenbaum and Schmidt stressed to leaders the importance of being honest with subordinates and making clear what kind of leadership behavior is being used. If the manager intends to make a certain decision alone, but group members expect or have the impression that this authority should be delegated to them, considerable confusion and resentment will likely result. They also warned against using a democratic façade to conceal the fact that the leader has already made a decision that she or he hopes the group will accept as its own.[72]

Path-Goal Theory

Respected leadership researcher Robert J. House's[73] path-goal theory emphasizes that the leader's job is to help followers attain their goals and to provide appropriate direction and support to ensure that followers' goals are consistent with those of the group and organization. Path-goal theory is based on the expectancy theory of motivation (see Chapter 14), which proposes that motivation to exert effort is based on a person's belief that (1) he or she has the ability to accomplish a goal, (2) goal accomplishment will lead to rewards, and (3) these rewards are attractive or valued. Path-goal theory reflects the belief that effective leaders increase the personal rewards that subordinates receive for attaining goals, and they clarify the path to these goals by reducing roadblocks. The core assumption is that subordinates will be motivated if they think they can do their work and get a favorable reward or outcome for doing so.

Path-goal theory originally focused on the leadership dimensions of leader consideration and initiating structure.[74] It now focuses on four leadership styles:[75]

- *Directive leadership:* letting subordinates know what the leader expects of them, giving specific guidance about what to do and how to do it, and scheduling the work to be done.
- *Supportive leadership:* being friendly and approachable and showing concern for the status and well-being of subordinates.
- *Participative leadership:* soliciting subordinates' suggestions and input.
- *Achievement-oriented leadership:* setting challenging goals, expecting subordinates to perform at their highest level, continuously seeking improvements in performance, and showing confidence that subordinates will assume responsibility.[76]

The leader's job is to help subordinates reach their goals by providing the guidance, coaching, support, and rewards lacking in the environment that are necessary for effective and satisfying performance.[77] The theory suggests which style is most appropriate for leaders.

Essentially, to be effective, a leader has to structure ambiguous tasks, be supportive and considerate when employees lack confidence or are demoralized, and always clarify how job effort will lead to rewards. The idea is that if employees don't know what to do, think they can't do it, or don't see how effort leads to rewards, they will not be motivated to do the job. Table 13.5 illustrates how to apply the theory.

TABLE 13.5

Fitting the Leadership Style to the Situation: Applying Path-Goal Theory

Leader Behavior	Best for Situations With . . .	Motivational Effects
Directive	Ambiguous, unstructured tasks	Reduces role ambiguity; increases follower beliefs that effort will lead to good performance and that performance will result in an attractive reward
Supportive	Frustrating, routine, stressful, or dissatisfying tasks; employees may lack self-confidence	Increases self-confidence; increases the personal value of job-related effort
Participative	Ambiguous, varied, challenging tasks	Reduces ambiguity, clarifies expectations, increases consistency of subordinate and organizational goals, increases involvement with and commitment to organizational goals
Achievement-oriented	Ambiguous, varied, challenging tasks	Increases subordinate confidence and the personal value of goal-directed effort

Source: Adapted from Jon Howell and Dan Costley, *Understanding Behavior for Effective Leadership* (Upper Saddle River, N.J.: Prentice Hall, 2001), p. 43.

PRACTICE IT

Empowerment Through Technology at Whirlpool[78]

Facing pressure to become more innovative and to build customer loyalty, Whirlpool wanted to empower everyone in the organization to participate in the innovation process. The hardest part was changing the way leaders saw their roles. "Only leaders can change an environment and allow an innovator the freedom to pursue things," says Nancy Snyder, vice president of leadership and competency creation. "Leaders are no longer controlling, managing. Now they're removing barriers, setting up seed funds, interacting." By removing obstacles and genuinely empowering employees, which is consistent with path-goal theory, leaders are helping employees meet their goals.

Technology was critical to empowering employees to innovate. To help with the creative end, Whirlpool built an informal intranet social system called the Innovation E-Space. The homepage links prospective innovators to tools and resources, including innovation templates and I-Mentors. This allows innovators to seek employees with expertise to influence innovations early in the process. On the back end is the I-Pipe, a digital dashboard view of the innovation pipeline adapted from Strategos. By tracking ideas from concept to scale-up, it can provide project details and a view of the big picture. This gives lower-level employees the power to make decisions and changes without having to depend heavily on top management.

The innovation democracy at Whirlpool seems to be working. For example, when a team from marketing played with the idea of appliances for men, it refined the concept into a modular system of garage appliances and storage units. It was so successful that Whirlpool eventually spun off Gladiator Garage Works as a separate brand. Whirlpool now has hundreds of ideas in its innovation pipeline under new CEO Jeff Fettig.

Path-goal theory makes a lot of intuitive sense, but research on the theory has yielded mixed results. Supportive leadership tends to have a positive relationship regardless of the task, and the results for directive leadership generally haven't supported the theory. Research is insufficient to draw conclusions about the situational factors influencing the effectiveness of participative and achievement-oriented leadership.[79]

The Practice IT feature shows how Whirlpool used technology to apply some of these leadership concepts.

Leader-Member Exchange Theory

Managers behave quite differently toward different subordinates, depending on the quality of their interpersonal relationships. Leader-member exchange theory (LMX) describes how leaders develop different relationships with different subordinates over time.[80] Formerly called vertical dyad linkage theory (when it focused on two-person subordinate-supervisor dyads rather than on the leader-group relationship), LMX theory proposes that leaders usually develop a special relationship with a subset of subordinates (the in-group). Members of the in-group serve as trusted advisers and assistants and have greater influence, autonomy, and tangible benefits in exchange. Members of the out-group have less or no input into group decisions and are primarily influenced with position power.

Although the theory does not specify what pattern of leader-member exchange relationships is optimal for effective leadership, research has found that in-group members have greater loyalty and higher performance levels than out-group members.[81] Members of a clear out-group are likely to feel resentment and withdraw effort and participation.[82] The quality of leader-member relations also influences the degree to which managers are willing to empower workers.[83] All organizations have in- and out-groups, and it is not necessary for leaders to treat all subordinates the same; effective leaders relate differently to different people and give them a different amount of influence. But each team member should feel important and respected rather than like a "second-class citizen."[84]

leadership substitutes: factors that make leadership unnecessary

leadership neutralizers: factors that make leadership impossible

Substitutes for Leadership

Leadership substitutes theory[85] proposes that the importance of formal leaders is reduced by aspects of the situation called substitutes and neutralizers. **Leadership substitutes** are factors that make leadership unnecessary, such as empowered employees or highly competent employees. For example, a high-performing call-center team whose members have been together for years may not need a leader to provide instruction or set goals for the team. **Leadership neutralizers** are factors that make leadership impossible, such as a union contract that prohibits a supervisor from giving workers incentives for higher performance. Substitutes for leadership can come from subordinates (i.e., their abilities and need for independence), the task (i.e., if it is routine or intrinsically satisfying), and the organization (i.e., cohesive workgroups or a high degree of formalization or inflexibility). Research has supported the idea. For example, intrinsically satisfying work and task-provided performance feedback diminish a leader's supportive behaviors from making a difference in task performance.[86]

Cross-training of Coast Guard crews allowed them to function after Hurricane Katrina even though their communication was disrupted.

A good example of leadership substitutes occurred in the Coast Guard after Hurricane Katrina in 2005. While Coast Guard employees usually specialize in certain types of operations, they are cross-trained so that they can do other jobs. Cross-training allows teams to form quickly in emergencies, with everyone knowing what each job entails and how it fits into overall operations. After Hurricane Katrina, Coast Guard crews rescued over 33,000 people in Louisiana, Mississippi, and Alabama despite a nearly complete loss of connectivity for extended periods between Air Station New Orleans and the chain of command. The complex operation successfully continued because of the employees' clear objectives, united effort, and flexibility. These factors served as leadership substitutes and reduced the need for centralized leadership.[87]

Leadership Effectiveness in Different Cultures

Much of the leadership literature has a North American bias. However, cultural factors influence the effectiveness of different leadership styles. For example, some cultures are more individualistic and others focus more on preserving group harmony. Different cultures have different norms and expectations about what is appropriate leader behavior and about the use of power and influence. It is important to understand the impact of culture on leadership effectiveness not only because companies are increasingly operating in multiple countries but also because increasing diversity in the workplace means that most Western businesses (even those based in one location) employ people from many cultural backgrounds.[88]

Consider China as an example of how culture influences the exercise of leadership. In China, *Guanxi,* which literally means social relationships or social connections, defines in-group and out-group people. Like LMX, *Guanxi* determines how individuals treat others—in-group people are benefited and protected, while out-group people may be rejected.[89] Followers expect Chinese leaders to have personal contact with subordinates and show their awareness of their subordinates' personal problems and sentiments to gain their loyalty and support.[90] A manager is not only responsible for business success but is also supposed to act as a father figure and take care of employees' personal lives.[91] The effective model for leadership in the Chinese system is thus the wise and loving father, which results in a paternalistic managerial style,[92] in which the leader will take care of subordinates in exchange for responsible behavior and performance. This clearly calls for a different leadership style than would be found in most Western cultures.

A recent large-scale, eleven-year study (the GLOBE study) of global leadership effectiveness investigated the leadership beliefs of people in sixty-two different cultures.[93] One of the goals of the research was to identify the ways in which middle managers worldwide distinguish between effective and ineffective leadership. The GLOBE team identified many leader attributes universally seen as being at least somewhat responsible for a leader's effectiveness or ineffectiveness. They also identified a large number of culturally contingent attributes, whose effects on leadership effectiveness differed from one culture to the next. A summary of the effect of culture on perceptions of leaders' attributes is presented in Table 13.6.

Effective leaders must learn to leverage technology in engaging followers. The next Window on Managing Now feature discusses how to manage the interactions with followers that occur through technology, or e-leadership.

TABLE 13.6

The Effect of Culture on Perceptions of Leaders' Attributes

Some Examples of Universal *Positive* Leader Attributes	**Some Examples of Universal *Negative* Leader Attributes**	**Some Examples of *Culturally Contingent* Leader Attributes**
Trustworthy	Irritable	Cunning
Dependable	Dictatorial	Sensitive
Excellence-oriented	Uncooperative	Evasive
Honest	Ruthless	Risk taker
Motivating	Egocentric	Ruler

Source: Based on Robert J. House, Paul J. Hanges, Mansour Javidan, Peter W. Dorfman, and Vipin Gupta, *Culture, Leadership, and Organizations: The GLOBE Study of 62 Societies* (London: Sage Publications, 2004).

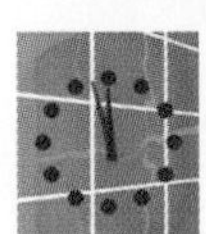

Window on Managing Now
E-Leadership

Technology is rapidly altering how leaders engage followers. Leaders must manage work through telecommuting relationships, communicate with employees through e-mail and Web-based portals, and support virtual teams that may have members around the world. E-leadership addresses the human interactions that now occur through IT. E-leaders use technology to enhance, improve, and refine relationships in an organization's structure and environment. For example, a participative leader may set up chatrooms to solicit input on an important decision. Anonymous commenting during meetings can encourage honest input, and electronic polls can take the pulse of current opinions.[94]

Like traditional leadership, e-leadership can be inspiring and transformative, even if it takes place through website postings, e-mail, or large-scale Web conferencing. So how is e-leadership different from traditional leadership? Emerging trends in leadership and concerns expressed by current mid- and high-level executives provide some clues.[95]

First, e-leaders must use more participative styles to address both global and local demands of decision making. E-leaders must use technology to gather and distribute information around the globe so that others with specific knowledge or expertise can provide insights about emerging issues.

Second, e-leaders must become more comfortable with developing, managing, and maintaining relationships without having direct personal control and oversight. A manager of telecommuting call-center employees must use technology to keep abreast of employee attitudes, maintain effective working relationships, and evaluate current levels of productivity. This requires a different set of skills than those of a leader who has an office inside a call center filled with employees.

Third, e-leaders must become increasingly comfortable using technology to manage, influence, motivate, and inspire others. Although the vast majority of leaders use e-mail to communicate at least once a day, more sophisticated technologies (such as videoconferencing, Web conferencing, instant messaging, chatrooms, blogs, or wikis) are used less frequently. Blogs are Web logs, or online diaries, that can provide information to a particular subscriber audience. Wikis are websites that allow users to add and edit content easily and collaboratively. They are especially well suited for collective writing and collaborative problem solving.

Fourth, e-leaders must be able to communicate with the 'Net generation—people born after 1977 who have grown up with the Internet and technology embedded in the world around them and are very comfortable with new technologies. Attracting, retaining, and motivating people from the 'Net generation requires a departure from traditional hierarchical and autocratic styles of leadership and an appreciation for how one might use technology to motivate and generate commitment to the organization.[96]

Managers must use different techniques when leading face-to-face than when interacting with subordinates through technology.

CHAPTER SUMMARY

1. The difference between leadership and management is that management is a function involving planning, budgeting, evaluating, and facilitating, while leadership is a relationship-based process focused on developing talent, motivating, coaching, and building trust.
2. Leaders can update their knowledge quickly by using technology-based solutions such as CD-ROMs, PDAs, Web-based toolkits, communities of practice, online leadership development, and mixed modes of training and development.
3. Managers have both position power and personal power. Through position power, managers have legitimate, reward, and coercive power by virtue of organizational authority. Effective managers should focus on using personal power that includes expert, referent, and informational power.
4. Leaders can use coalition tactics (consultation, exchange, ingratiation, and inspirational appeals) and legitimating tactics (personal appeals, pressure, and rational persuasion) to influence others. Some of these influence approaches are more effective than others.
5. Traits and skills that tend to identify leaders include determination, emotional maturity, high energy levels, integrity, intelligence, internal control orientation, job-relevant knowledge, self-confidence, sociability, and interpersonal skills.
6. Netiquette is important for effective management in today's world.
7. There are a variety of leadership styles. Coercive leaders make demands and expect results, authoritative/autocratic leaders present workers with clear goals and offer little participation, affiliative leaders focus on human relationships and emotional bonds, democratic leaders encourage employee involvement by being consultative and participative, laissez-faire leaders are extremely hands-off, pace-setting leaders expect high performance from others without telling them what is expected, and coaching leaders develop employees. Transformational leadership is most effective when large-scale change is required. Transactional leadership works well for short-term goals when both leader and led understand and are in agreement about which tasks are important and about when change is smaller in scale.
8. Initiating structure behaviors and production-oriented leaders focus on task accomplishment, i.e., getting the job done. Consideration and employee-oriented leaders focus on employees, their needs, and interpersonal relationships.
9. Path-goal theory emphasizes that the leader's job is to help followers attain their goals. Leaders must provide appropriate direction and support to ensure that followers' goals are consistent with those of the group and organization.
10. Leader-member exchange theory proposes that leaders develop a special relationship with a subset of subordinates (the in-group). Members of the in-group serve as trusted advisers, while members of the out-group are given little opportunity to provide input to group decisions.

DISCUSSION QUESTIONS

1. Do all managers need to be leaders? Why or why not?
2. Can a leader be effective without power? Why or why not?
3. What influence tactics do you believe are most effective? Why?
4. How can emotional intelligence help leaders be more effective?
5. Are men and women equally effective as leaders? Why or why not?
6. When would transactional leadership be preferred to transformational leadership?
7. Which leadership style do you feel is best for managers to use most often? Why?
8. Is it always good to empower workers? Why or why not?

9. How do situational factors influence whether or not leaders will be successful?

10. Do you feel that it is possible for leadership substitutes to be effective? Why or why not?

11. What advice would you give a leader on managing people from the 'Net generation?

EXPERIENTIAL EXERCISES

1. Think of an ineffective leader with whom you are familiar. It could be a manager you've worked with or a public figure. Drawing from the material presented in this chapter, describe what has made this leader ineffective. Then identify three factors that would have made the leader more effective.

2. Habitat for Humanity is a volunteer association whose goal is to eliminate poverty housing and homelessness from the world and to make decent shelter a matter of conscience and action. Habitat invites people of all backgrounds, races, and religions to build houses together in partnership with families in need. Imagine for a moment that you have been asked to lead a Habitat for Humanity team in building a house. Now incorporate information from leader-member exchange theory to describe how you would be effective in this context. Then identify the power and influence tactics you would use to motivate your team.

3. In groups of three or four students, form an executive board and brainstorm the leader characteristics and styles you would look for when hiring a new CEO for a company with which you are all familiar (e.g., Microsoft, Google, McDonald's, GE). From this list, identify the three most important competencies or characteristics for the new CEO and describe why you prioritized them the way you did. Would these competencies and characteristics work equally well in all organizations? Why or why not?

4. *Internet Exercise.* In groups of three or four students, brainstorm three leaders with whom every group member is familiar. As a group, choose one of these leaders to research using the Internet. Write a two-page paper describing the nature of the followers and the situation that the leader faced, the leadership style(s) the leader used, and why the leadership style(s) were or were not appropriate.

CASE STUDY

Steve Bennett of Intuit

When Steve Bennett became president and CEO of Intuit Corporation, the software firm known for Quicken and TurboTax, he became the leader of an organization obsessively devoted to its people but lacking operational rigor. It had focused so intently on its core customers—businesses with fewer than twenty people—that it had not kept up with customers who had outgrown its software.

Bennett had run a variety of business units over the course of two decades and had refined a plan for taking on new challenges. He realized Intuit was an organization with a democratic, employee-centric culture. "We were focused too much on making sure that everybody felt good and not enough on high performance," says Bennett. He adds, "I wanted them to know that a company can be focused on high performance and still be a good place to work."

When he gave his first overview of the company at an analysts' meeting, he did something unthinkable at the time: with the company's founders in the audience, he stood up and said that Intuit was underperforming compared with the opportunity it faced. That message was directed as much to Intuit's employees as it was to the financial markets. He then distributed a document titled "Steve's Dream for Intuit" that mapped his plan for turning the company into a high-performance machine; among his goals: put leaders of business units totally in charge of the end-to-end customer experience, institute zero-based budgeting, standardize equipment as a way of managing costs, and eliminate businesses such as insurance where Intuit couldn't control the critical success factors.

Bennett restructured the organization so that he had eighteen direct reports instead of eight. "I took out some layers so that I could connect directly with more people in order to drive change faster," he says. "If you have that many direct reports, you don't have time to meddle in their business. My job is to conduct the orchestra, not to play all the instruments."

Raymond Stern, Intuit's senior vice president of corporate development and strategy, appreciates the discipline Bennett has introduced. "One of the things that Steve is amazingly good at is getting a crisp understanding of priorities. All of the top-level leaders in this company have a one-page list of priorities. They learned that from him."

Despite all of the new initiatives, including a focus on operational rigor, time management, and the quality-improvement process, Intuit has not lost its small-company feel or its dedication to being a great place to work. Bennett himself now has more time to seek employees' input, and he is often seen in the company cafeteria or around the office talking to employees. He even sends praiseworthy employees handwritten notes.[97]

DISCUSSION QUESTIONS

1. Which traits and characteristics does Steve Bennett possess that make him an effective leader?
2. How would you describe Steve Bennett's leadership style in terms of task and relationship orientation? Is his style appropriate for Intuit? Describe why or why not.
3. Which of the leadership theories covered in this chapter do you think apply to Steve Bennett's leadership at Intuit?
4. If you were the CEO of Intuit, what leadership style and influence tactics would you use to guide Intuit into the future? There is more than one way to be an effective leader; be honest regarding your personal leadership style and beliefs rather than trying to be like Steve Bennett.

MOTIVATING EMPLOYEES 14

Mercury Interactive Corporation

Sunnyvale, California, software company Mercury Interactive Corporation[1] had a problem. The members of their field staff, who maintain and troubleshoot computer systems, were not communicating to managers the sales opportunities they saw while visiting clients. The company realized that if the field staff members could identify weaknesses in existing client systems, they could create sales opportunities. "We asked them to voluntarily jot notes about opportunities they saw when on assignment, but the program was so-so. I thought that if we could create an incentive program we'd generate more interest," says Amit Ronen, vice president of field technical operations.[2] But the program can't cost a lot, and the company wants it to be online. Mercury Interactive asks your team's advice on how to motivate its field staff members to identify and communicate sales leads. ■

Mercury Interactive needed to motivate its computer repair field staff to create new sales opportunities.

BEHAVIORAL OBJECTIVES

After studying this chapter, you should be able to:

Show that you've learned the chapter's essential information by

- Describing the motivation process.
- Listing various ways work can be motivating.
- Briefly explaining the difference between content and process theories of motivation.
- Explaining how valence, instrumentality, and expectancy can influence motivation.
- Listing and describing three ways of being fair.
- Giving examples of when you would use different motivational techniques.

CHAPTER OUTLINE

CHAPTER OUTLINE (Continued)

Show that you can practice what you've learned here by

- Reading the chapter-opening vignette and identifying ways the company can motivate its field staff to identify and report sales opportunities.
- Reading the end-of-chapter exercises and identifying which motivation theories apply to the situation.
- Reading the end-of-chapter exercises and identifying a job's enrichment potential.
- Reading the chapter case study and describing why GM employees' motivation increased.

Show that you can apply what you've learned here by

- Studying the video scenario and recommending what you would do to improve employee motivation in the company.

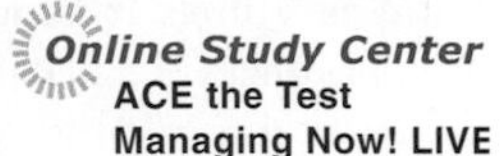

What Is Motivation and Where Does It Come from?

Great managers know that strategizing, planning, and organizing can only lay the foundation for high performance. Managing the motivation of employees is the key to translating strategies, plans, and organizational efforts into action. **Motivation** is the intensity of a person's desire to begin or continue engaging in the pursuit of a goal. Factors from a variety of sources in the individual, job, and work environment arouse, maintain, and channel a person's efforts toward a goal and affect motivation, as shown in Figure 14.1.

motivation: the intensity of a person's desire to begin or continue engaging in the pursuit of a goal

Because people's personal goals are often different from the organization's goals, managers must motivate employees to work toward shared organizational goals.[3] The purpose of this chapter is to show you how to apply different theories of motivation, reinforcement, and rewards to motivate employees and become a more effective leader and manager.

An easy mistake to make when trying to motivate others is to assume that the same things that motivate you also motivate them. Different things motivate different people. It is easy to make incorrect assumptions about the reasons for someone else's behavior if you don't understand what motivates them. People have different abilities, needs, personalities, values, and self-concepts—which psychologists know as the **law of individual differences**. Just as effective leaders change their leadership style to match the followers and the situation, good managers also vary their motivational methods based on what works for a particular employee and situation.[4] We'll see in a moment that three sets of characteristics—in the individual, job, and work environment—influence a manager's ability to motivate his or her subordinates.

law of individual differences: people have different abilities, needs, personalities, values, and self-concepts

FIGURE 14.1

The Basic Motivation Process

Some employees might want money or career advancement from their job, but these things may have relatively little appeal to others. For example, it is clear from the following conversation that what motivates these two workers is quite different.

> Tyler: You're crazy for quitting your old job. The work may have been boring, but it pays better than any other job in the area.
>
> Ryan: You're right about the pay, but the job drove me crazy. Even though I make less money in my new job, I really like it. I do something different every day.

How can work be motivating? Work can be motivating because it:

- Is interesting and satisfying.
- Allows employees to learn new skills.
- Provides needed income.
- Provides needed benefits such as health care.
- Gives status and prestige.
- Gives employees something to do.
- Provides social contact.
- Is a way to give back to society and help others.

Why is motivation important? One reason is that motivated workers are more productive.[5] High performance requires both ability and motivation. Someone who is able to do a task well will do so only if she or he is motivated to do it well. Higher employee motivation can also lead to faster and better-quality work.[6] More motivated employees work more safely,[7] provide suggestions for improvements, and are less likely to quit.[8] Clearly, managers can realize several benefits if they can increase the motivation of their employees.

Characteristics of the Individual

Why does one employee come to work early, stay late, and take on additional work while another does the minimum amount to get by? The answer is because people are not all the same. Personality, values, needs, abilities, and interests are individual characteristics that people bring to their jobs. These individual characteristics motivate people to work harder at some things than at others. Table 14.1 provides examples of individual characteristics that influence people's motivation to do certain things.

People also differ in their perceptions about the nature of other people. After watching how managers interacted with employees, Douglas McGregor proposed that people hold either a generally negative view, called **Theory X**, or a generally positive view, called **Theory Y**, about others.[9] Theory X managers assume that most workers display little ambition and believe that employees dislike work and attempt to avoid it whenever possible. As a result, Theory X managers use coercion and threats to motivate employees to achieve the organization's goals. Theory Y managers, on the other hand, assume that most people enjoy responsibility and can make good decisions. Theory Y managers motivate employees by providing opportunities to develop their skills and abilities.

Theory X: the belief that most people dislike work and will try to avoid it whenever possible

Theory Y: the belief that people can enjoy responsibility and work and can make good decisions and exercise self-direction

TABLE 14.1
Some Individual Characteristics That Influence Motivation

Goals	Needs	Attitudes
To attain a certain quality level	For affiliation	About oneself
To reach a certain performance level	For power	About the job
To complete a task	For the approval of others	About the supervisor
To advance one's career	For achievement	About coworkers

Although McGregor personally subscribed to Theory Y and felt that participatory decision making, challenging and responsible jobs, and good workgroup relations would maximize work motivation, effective managers have held both Theory X and Theory Y views. It is helpful to remember that while some personal characteristics influence our own motivation to accomplish specific goals, our being more aligned with Theory X or Theory Y can also influence how we choose to motivate others.

Characteristics of the Job

Job characteristics refer to the nature of the work. Job characteristics that influence work motivation include the types and variety of tasks done and the amount of feedback a worker gets from the task itself (rather than from a supervisor or someone else). The characteristics of a job that motivate someone to do something are external pull factors because they pull someone to want to exert effort toward a goal. We will discuss a formal theory of job characteristics in more detail later in the chapter.

Characteristics of the Work Environment

The work environment is made up of the rules, management practices and policies, and rewards system of an organization. Things like supportive supervision and a fun work environment can motivate employees. Some organizations create such a positive work environment that employees become passionate about working there. Zingerman's Delicatessen in Ann Arbor, Michigan, is a good example. Zingerman's strong sense of community, deep belief in people, and passion for great food and great service is very motivating to its employees. As one employee put it, "Working here has never felt like a job to me. I'm constantly learning about managing, about food, and about myself."[10]

content theories of motivation: theories of motivation that assume that all individuals possess inner needs and are motivated by the desire to satisfy those needs, and that focus on whether the characteristics of the work environment satisfy the inner needs of the worker

Content Approaches to Motivation

Online Study Center
ACE the Test
Managing Now! LIVE

Motivation theories can be divided into two categories, content and process theories. **Content theories** assume that all individuals possess inner needs and are motivated to satisfy these needs. Content theories therefore address the characteristics jobs should have to satisfy the needs of the worker. Next, we will discuss the four main content theories of motivation.

Maslow's Hierarchy of Needs

Abraham Maslow's hierarchy of needs[11] is one of the most famous content theories of motivation. Maslow suggested that a hierarchy of needs motivate people. Basic physiological needs for food, water, and comfort must be met first, then safety and security needs motivate behavior. We pursue social needs for friendship and belonging next, followed by self-esteem needs for self-respect and respect from others. Eventually, once all the lower-level needs are satisfied, we pursue self-actualization needs, which are desires for self-fulfillment and the realization of our full potential. As one need in the hierarchy is satisfied, it ceases to motivate behavior, and the need at the next level up the hierarchy motivates our behavior. For example, when the basic need for food and clothing is satisfied, we aim for security needs, and so on.

Maslow intended the hierarchy to be a general theory of motivation, but many managerial theorists have enthusiastically adopted it. When jobs are secure, employees will seek ways of satisfying social needs and, if successful, will seek the means to the ultimate end of self-actualization. Although it appeals to managers because it is simple and intuitive, academic research has not supported Maslow's theory.[12] But by identifying the importance of esteem and self-actualization, Maslow helped to increase managers' awareness of the motivating potential of giving employees greater responsibility, challenge, and continuous development, which is consistent with Theory Y. Figure 14.2 illustrates Maslow's needs hierarchy and shows how managers can address each level.

FIGURE 14.2

How Managers Can Address Maslow's Hierarchy of Needs

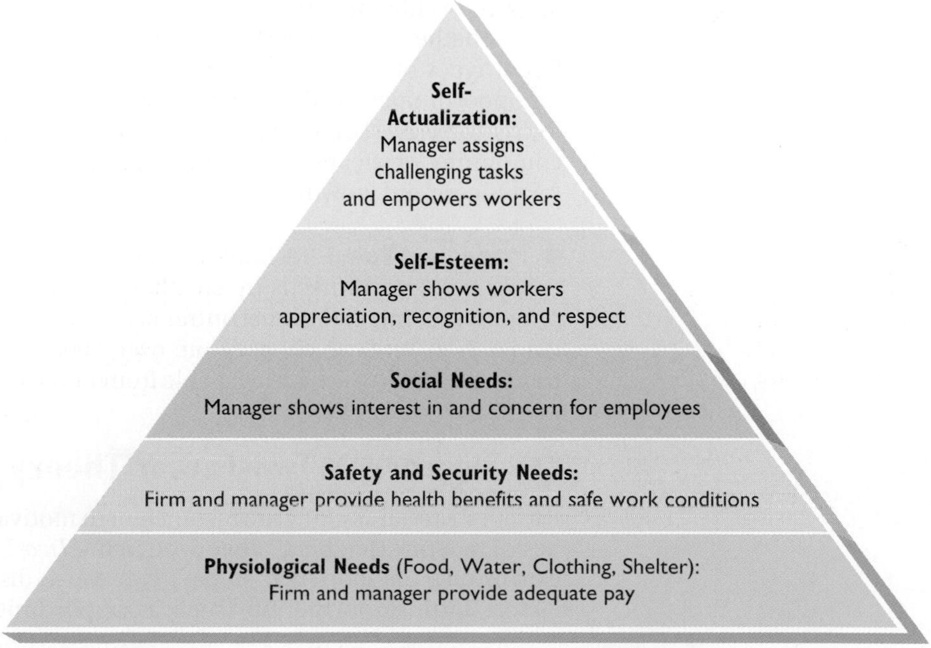

Alderfer's Existence-Relatedness-Growth (ERG) Theory

Clay Alderfer[13] suggested that there are three groups of individual needs:

- *Existence needs* reflect desires for physical and material well-being, including nutritional and material requirements (e.g., pay, benefits, and working conditions).
- *Relatedness needs* reflect desires for respect from and relationships with others.
- *Growth needs* reflect a desire to make useful and productive contributions and to have opportunities for personal development.

Alderfer's existence needs parallel Maslow's physiological and security needs. Similarly, Alderfer's relatedness needs parallel Maslow's social and esteem needs, and his growth needs parallel Maslow's self-actualization needs. Despite these similarities, Alderfer's theory differs from Maslow's in a number of important respects. First, Alderfer argued that it is better to think in terms of a continuum rather than a hierarchy, and he argued that people could move along the continuum in either direction. Maslow proposed that a satisfied need becomes less important, but Alderfer argued that relatedness or growth needs become *more* important when satisfied. This suggests, for instance, that work enriched by organizing employees into teams can continue to motivate employees.

Both Maslow's and Alderfer's theories were developed in the United States, and it is likely that the needs do not fall into the same order in all cultures and countries.[14] It is also likely that the order of the needs differs in one country at different times; during periods of war, for example, security needs may take precedence over physiological needs. Different people are also likely to have different hierarchies when it comes to their own needs, as well as different thresholds for meeting one level's needs. For example, one person may not feel financially secure until he or she has saved $10 million, but another person may feel quite secure with $1 million. These ambiguities make it difficult for managers to base specific actions on either theory.

Nonetheless, it can be helpful for managers to remember that people have different types of needs. Managers can enhance employees' motivation by looking for opportunities to address employees' existence, relatedness, and growth needs in creative ways. For example, some companies sponsor volunteer activities in the community or create mentoring programs with local schools, which can fulfill relatedness and growth needs.

Managing Now Technology and the Internet have helped organizations meet employees' growth needs by enabling the delivery of training and development programs. Using an Internet/intranet training platform, employees at HIP Health Plan of New York can choose from over 2,000 professional business and technical training classes, which are available from home or at work via the Internet.[15]

Herzberg's Two-Factor Theory

Economic rewards alone are insufficient to motivate employees to perform at their best. Frederick Herzberg[16] theorized in his *Two-Factor Theory*[17] that while factors extrinsic to the job (such as pay) can cause dissatisfaction if inadequate, only factors intrinsic to the job (such as opportunities to achieve) could motivate

TABLE 14.2
Herzberg's Motivators and Hygiene Factors

Motivators (Satisfiers)	Hygiene Factors (Maintenance Needs)
Achievement	Pay
Advancement	Supervision
Recognition	Company policies and administration
Growth	Status
Responsibility	Interpersonal relations with colleagues
The work itself	Working conditions

hygiene factors: factors such as pay, status, and working conditions that produce an acceptable work environment and whose absence leads to dissatisfaction

motivators: factors intrinsic to the job that can drive an employee to pursue excellence and whose presence increases satisfaction

behavior. Extrinsic **hygiene factors**, such as pay, status, and working conditions produce an acceptable working environment. Although their presence does not increase satisfaction, their absence causes dissatisfaction. In other words, high pay and good working conditions are generally not enough to make people feel satisfied with their jobs. But if pay or working conditions are poor, then people feel dissatisfied. Hygiene factors correspond to Maslow's lower-level physiological, safety, and social needs and Alderfer's existence and relatedness needs.

Herzberg identified a second set of factors, called satisfiers or **motivators**, that are intrinsic to the job and can drive an employee to pursue excellence. Motivators include recognition, responsibility, and growth.[18] Motivators correspond to Maslow's higher-level needs of esteem and self-actualization and Alderfer's growth need. Table 14.2 lists some examples of motivators and hygiene factors.

As you can see in Figure 14.3, motivator factors can increase satisfaction but do not lead to dissatisfaction, and hygiene factors can reduce dissatisfaction but do not lead to satisfaction or positive motivation. In other words, the opposite of both *satisfaction* and *dissatisfaction* is *no satisfaction*. This differs from the traditional view of motivation that satisfaction is the opposite of dissatisfaction, as summarized in Figure 14.3.

FIGURE 14.3

The Traditional View and Herzberg's View of Motivation

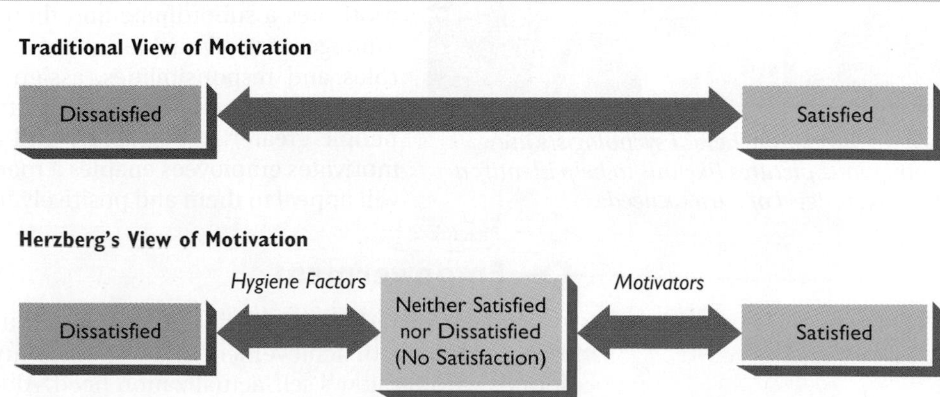

The most important contribution of the two-factor theory is the idea that motivation comes from the intrinsic value and satisfaction the worker gets from the job itself, not from the conditions surrounding the job. Even if pay and benefits are high, a job must also be challenging and interesting, and have opportunities for feelings of achievement, if it is to be motivating. Herzberg's two-factor theory thus draws attention to job design and the role of managers in attending to the motivator factors present in a job.

Although its intuitiveness and simplicity appeals to many managers, many scholars have criticized the two-factor theory.[19] One important issue is the fact that Herzberg talks about satisfiers and dissatisfiers, but satisfaction and motivation aren't necessarily the same. For example, Mary might be satisfied with her pay, but pay may not motivate her to work harder. Despite the criticisms and lack of consistent research support, Herzberg's theory continues to influence management practitioners.[20]

McClelland's Needs for Achievement, Affiliation, and Power

David McClelland[21] divides motivation into three needs that influence both employee and leader performance:[22]

- *Need for affiliation:* The desire to establish and maintain friendly and warm relations with others. People high in need for affiliation tend to be friendly and like to socialize with others, and their interpersonal skills help them to resolve conflicts and facilitate cooperation within and between groups.
- *Need for achievement:* The desire to do something better or more efficiently, to solve problems, or to master complex tasks. People high in need for achievement prefer tasks of moderate difficulty, enjoy pursuing attainable goals, and like to be recognized.
- *Need for power:* The desire to control and influence others, or to be responsible for others. People can express a need for power in ways that improve organizations and societies (a socialized power orientation) or by manipulating and exploiting others (a personalized power orientation). A socialized power orientation motivates by inspiring others.

What's happening here? Psychologists use ambiguous pictures like this to help identify a test taker's level of various needs.

The implication for managers is that they must identify what motivates a subordinate and then create appropriate motivators. Managers can give achievement-motivated workers goals and clear roles and responsibilities, assign affiliation-oriented workers to work with others they know and trust, and give power-motivated people greater responsibility and authority. Understanding what motivates employees enables a manager to choose motivators that will appeal to them and positively influence their behavior.

Empowerment

One theme shared by the four needs or content theories we just discussed is the idea that a sense of achievement and responsibility is motivating. This idea corresponds with Maslow's self-actualization need, Alderfer's growth need, Herzberg's motivators, and McClelland's need for achievement. Empowerment fosters exactly such a sense of achievement. As discussed in Chapter 13, empowerment is the degree to which an employee has the authority to make and implement decisions. Empowerment enables employees to use more of their potential. Workgroups can have empowerment that enhances their performance.[23]

Although some employees are likely to feel more motivated when empowered, increased responsibility will not motivate everyone. Nonetheless, empowerment can be an important management tool to increase the motivation of many employees. Practical ways to empower others include:[24]

- Articulating a clear vision and goals.
- Fostering personal mastery experiences to enhance self-efficacy and build skills.
- Modeling successful behaviors.
- Sending positive messages and arousing positive emotions.
- Connecting employees with the outcomes of their work and giving them feedback.
- Building confidence by showing competence, honesty, and fairness.

● **Managing Now** Technology has helped organizations empower workers by making better and timelier information available to everyone.[25] By empowering workers, technology helps eliminate layers of management and create a flatter organization. Bill Gilmer, owner of Wordsprint Inc. in Wytheville, Virginia, uses technology—such as frequent updates via PDAs—to give his employees the information they need to make decisions without a supervisor. Technology helps monitor employees' productivity and empowers employees to make their own decisions. Gilmer also motivates employees to take responsibility for decisions by basing a substantial portion of their pay on individual, departmental, and company productivity. Cisco uses technology in a different way to help empower workers. When a manager is on vacation or out of the office, he or she electronically delegates various responsibilities by using Cisco's Universal Proxy tool.[26]

Managers who have a clear appreciation for different types of employee needs can design jobs to provide different opportunities to fulfill those needs. Employees can be more empowered or they may have opportunities to engage in autonomous decision making. Always remember, however, that not all employees will be motivated by these and other job characteristics. How can we design more motivating jobs? J. Richard Hackman and Greg R. Oldham developed the job characteristics model to answer this question.

Hackman and Oldham's Job Characteristics Model

job characteristics model: objective characteristics of the job itself, including skill variety, task identity, task significance, autonomy, and task feedback, that lead to job satisfaction for people with a high growth need strength

Hackman and Oldham's **job characteristic model** suggests that objective characteristics of the job lead to motivation.[27] In particular, Hackman and Oldham[28] identified five characteristics on which jobs differ:

- *Skill variety:* The degree to which the job requires a variety of activities, thus enabling the worker to use different skills
- *Task identity:* The degree to which the job requires the worker to complete a whole and identifiable piece of work

- *Task significance:* The degree to which job performance is important and affects the lives or work of others
- *Autonomy:* The degree to which the job gives the worker freedom, discretion, and independence in scheduling the work and determining how to do the work
- *Task feedback:* The degree to which carrying out the job's activities results in direct and clear information about the effectiveness of the worker's performance

These five characteristics together determine the motivating potential of a job.[29] But a high motivating potential score alone does not mean that the job is more motivating for everyone. Not everyone wants more variety, responsibility, and so on—some people just want to do their jobs without having to think much about it. For them, jobs that are stable, less complex, and less demanding (i.e., jobs with a lower motivating potential score) would be more motivating. We look at a person's motivational preferences, such as desire for advancement, to identify the factors that motivate that particular worker. We then compare a job's motivating potential to the person's motivational preferences to identify the job-person match. Ideally, the motivating potential of a job matches the growth needs (such as your achievement) of the individual.

Hackman and Oldham suggest that if there is a good match between the needs of the person and the characteristics of the job, three critical psychological states can occur in employees:

- Experienced meaningfulness of work
- Experienced responsibility for work outcomes
- Knowledge of results of work activities

According to Hackman and Oldham, these psychological states increase work motivation and job satisfaction. Figure 14.4 illustrates the model.

Although research generally supports the existence of a positive relationship between the five job characteristics and job satisfaction and the role of growth need strength,[30] conceptual and methodological difficulties[31] prevent firm conclusions from being drawn.[32] Nonetheless, the job characteristics model highlights the need for managers to be aware of the role of job redesign in addressing worker motivation problems. For example, when a U.S. printing company in the Midwest organized workers into semiautonomous teams to increase worker autonomy, employees put in greater effort, used more skills, and did a better job solving problems.[33]

Managing Now Technology has increased the amount of feedback provided by many jobs. Digital dashboards and other electronic feedback mechanisms help employees continually monitor their performance. According to job characteristics theory, this feedback increases employees' knowledge of work results and increases their motivation, performance, and satisfaction.

Job Enrichment, Job Enlargement, and Job Rotation Related to the notion of motivating potential, enriched and enlarged jobs can increase employee motivation. For many people, enriched, more interesting work tends to be more motivating than simple, repetitive work. Task variety, task significance, and autonomy (characteristics of motivating work proposed by the job characteristics model) are much more likely to exist when a task is complex than when it is simplified.[34]

job enrichment: an approach to job design that increases a job's complexity to give workers greater responsibility and opportunities to feel a sense of achievement

Job enrichment is an approach to job design that increases a job's complexity to give workers a greater sense of responsibility and achievement. Enriched

FIGURE 14.4

The Job Characteristics Model

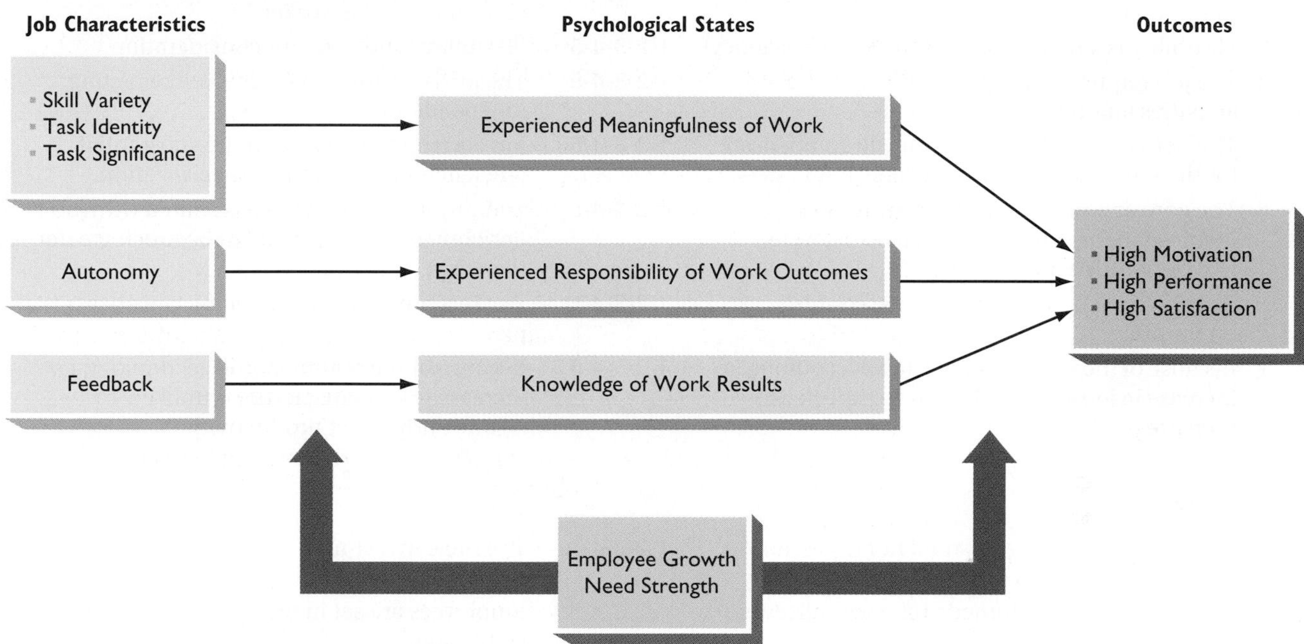

SOURCE: Adapted from J. Richard Hackman and Greg R. Oldham, "Development of the Job Diagnostic Survey," *Journal of Applied Psychology,* 1975, vol. 60, no. 2, pp. 159–170. Reprinted by permission of The American Psychological Association.

jobs are typically expanded vertically—responsibilities previously performed by the supervisor are added to the enriched job. To enrich a job, a supervisor can introduce new or harder tasks, organize work in teams, provide direct feedback from customers, or grant additional authority to employees. Job enrichment gives employees more autonomy and feelings of control, and it can reduce the negative motivational effects of tasks that are repetitive or require little autonomy. Hackman and Oldham's skill variety, task identity, task significance, autonomy, and task feedback are five aspects of the task that determine how enriched it is.

For example, expanding a secretary's job responsibilities to include keeping inventory and ordering office supplies, previously the supervisor's responsibilities, enriches the job. Merely adding more tasks at the same level of responsibility and skill related to an employee's current position (horizontal job expansion) is considered **job enlargement**. When a secretary's job responsibilities of receiving visitors and answering phones expand to include typing correspondence and sorting mail, the job is enlarged. Job enlargement is not the same as job enrichment, although it can help reduce boredom.

job enlargement: adding more tasks at the same level of responsibility and skill related to an employee's current position

Performing a variety of tasks can be motivating, but be careful not to put too much into any one job. When UPS tried to understand the high turnover rate among its drivers, it found that the high turnover was due to requiring drivers to load their own vehicles prior to delivery. UPS responded by redesigning the job: hiring separate workers to handle vehicle loading and allowing drivers to focus on making deliveries.[35]

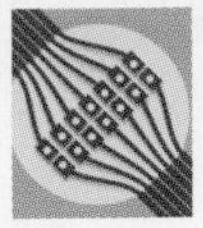

Improving Your *Motivation* Skills
A Job Enrichment Evaluation Form

The Job Itself

1. Quality is important and attributable to the worker.	1-2-3-4-5	Quality is not too important and/or is not controlled by the worker.
2. Flexibility is a major contributor to job efficiency.	1-2-3-4-5	Flexibility is not a major consideration.
3. The job requires the coordination of tasks or activities among several workers.	1-2-3-4-5	The job is performed by one worker acting independently.
4. The benefits of job enrichment will compensate for the efficiencies of task specialization.	1-2-3-4-5	Job enrichment will eliminate substantial efficiencies realized from specialization.
5. The conversion and one-time setup costs involved in job enrichment can be recovered in a reasonable period of time.	1-2-3-4-5	Training and other costs associated with job enrichment are estimated to be much greater than expected results.
6. The wage payment plan is not based solely on output.	1-2-3-4-5	Workers are under a straight piecework wage plan.
7. Because of the worker's ability to affect output, an increase in job satisfaction can be expected to increase productivity.	1-2-3-4-5	Because of the dominance of technology, an increase in job satisfaction is unlikely to significantly affect productivity.

Technology

8. Changes in job content would not necessitate a large investment in equipment and technology.	1-2-3-4-5	The huge investment in equipment and technology overrides all other considerations.
9. Employees are accustomed to change and respond favorably to it.	1-2-3-4-5	Employees are set in their ways and prefer the status quo.
10. Employees feel secure in their jobs; employment has been stable.	1-2-3-4-5	Layoffs are frequent; many employees are concerned about the permanency of employment.
11. Employees are dissatisfied with their jobs and would welcome changes in job content and work relationships.	1-2-3-4-5	Employees are satisfied with their present jobs and general work situation.

job rotation: moving workers through a variety of jobs to increase their interest and motivation

Job rotation occurs when workers are moved through a variety of jobs to increase their interest and motivation. For example, a workgroup of three secretaries may take turns answering the phones, greeting visitors in the reception area, and typing and filing correspondence. Cross-training is usually required to give employees the skills they need to do the different jobs. Because it involves a horizontal rather than vertical expansion of job responsibilities, job rotation is a type of job enlargement rather than job enrichment.

Because some workers actually prefer work with low responsibility, autonomy, and variety to seemingly more stimulating jobs,[36] well-intentioned managers need to be careful when enriching or enlarging the jobs of people who like their jobs just the way they are. Successful job enrichment efforts to improve employee motivation require an understanding of employee and management readiness for proposed changes and an analysis of the job's suitability for enrichment. We can never be certain that job enrichment will work as intended, but the form for evaluating the appropriateness of job enrichment in the Improving Your *Motivation* Skills feature provides a guide. According to the form's creators, "A lower rating (1.0–1.9) indicates that a job is a prime candidate for enrichment; and if properly

12. Employees are highly skilled blue- and white-collar workers, professionals, and supervisors.	1-2-3-4-5	Employees are semi- and unskilled blue- and white-collar workers.
13. Employees are well educated, with most having college degrees.	1-2-3-4-5	The average employee has less than a high school education.
14. Employees are from a small town and rural environment.	1-2-3-4-5	The company is located in a large, highly industrialized metropolitan area.
15. The history of union-management (if no union, worker-management) relations has been one of cooperation and mutual support.	1-2-3-4-5	Union-management (worker-management) relations are strained, and the two parties are antagonistic to one another.

Management

16. Managers are committed to job enrichment and are anxious to implement it.	1-2-3-4-5	Managers show little interest in job enrichment and even less interest in implementing it in their departments.
17. Managers have attended seminars, workshops, and so forth; are quite knowledgeable of the concept; and have had experience in implementing it.	1-2-3-4-5	Managers lack the training and experience necessary to develop and implement job enrichment projects.
18. Management realizes that substantial payoffs from job enrichment usually take one to three years to materialize.	1-2-3-4-5	Management expects immediate results (within six months) from job enrichment projects.

Total Score ___________ ÷ 18 = Job Enrichment Rating

Source: Theodore T. Herbert, *Organizational Behavior: Readings and Cases*, New York: Macmillan Publishing Co., Inc., 1976, pp. 344–345.

implemented, it has a high expected return on investment. A job enrichment rating of 2.0–3.9 identifies jobs that can be enriched that may have a marginal return on investment in terms of productivity measures. A high rating (4.0–5.0) identifies jobs that for all practical purposes cannot be enriched at the present time."[37]

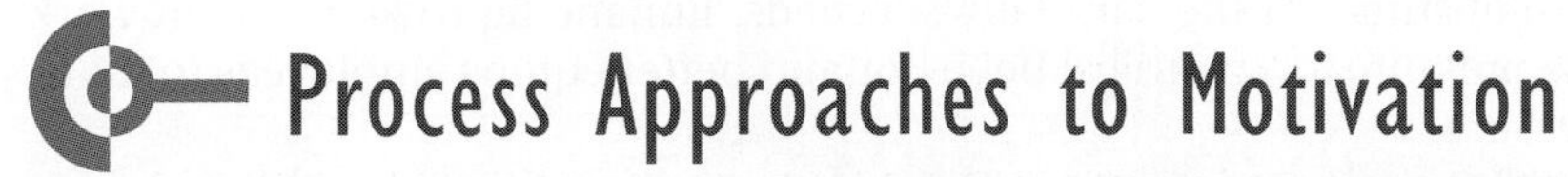

Process Approaches to Motivation

Online Study Center
ACE the Test
Managing Now! LIVE

process theories: theories that address how and why different external factors influence motivation

Process theories of motivation address how and why people choose certain actions to meet their personal goals. In other words, whereas content theories focus on which factors (needs) internal to a person influence motivation, process theories address the process through which different factors external to a person influence motivation. These external influences, such as goals and reinforcement, are often easy for managers to manipulate, making process theories useful in worker motivation.

Goal Setting and Feedback

Edwin Locke and his colleagues[38] developed the goal-setting theory of motivation, which has become perhaps the most consistently supported work motivation theory. Here is a summary of what we know about goal setting:[39]

- Participation in setting goals increases one's sense of control and fairness in the process.
- Performance is enhanced when goals are both difficult (challenging but attainable) and specific (a number rather than a range), for example, selling $1,000 worth of clothing in a shift or assembling fifteen parts per hour.
- A goal is most likely to be attained when people are strongly committed to it and are given feedback showing their progress toward the goal.
- People are most likely to set high goals and be committed to them when they have high self-efficacy (task-specific self-confidence) and believe they can reach the goal.
- Goals affect what people pay attention to, how hard they work, and how long they work, and they motivate people to find and use appropriate task strategies.
- Goals work best on simple tasks that are already learned rather than on complex and novel ones.

Individual goals can sometimes conflict with team or organizational goals. For individual goals to be effective, they must be integrated with team and organizational goals and strategies. Home Depot ensures that all senior store staff work toward the same goals by broadcasting a live twenty-five-minute show called *The Same Page* in stores every Monday. The show emphasizes the week's top priorities so that everyone shares the core goals of the business.[40]

Managers must continually challenge and motivate employees by setting high goals and tight schedules. But in doing this, managers must avoid setting unrealistic targets that may stimulate unethical behavior. People whose performance is falling just short of a goal are the ones most likely to act unethically to collect a reward.[41] In the early 1990s, Sears, Roebuck, and Company set very difficult goals for its automotive service advisers. After a number of complaints, California state regulators found that most of the repairs made were unnecessary. Sears' chairperson, Edward Brennan, later admitted that Sears' "goal setting process for service advisors created an environment where mistakes did occur."[42] To guard against this, managers must create an ethical climate so that employees feel comfortable bringing up conflicts. The pressure to reach high goals is often necessary to ensure that the company succeeds. Enhancing trust and teamwork reduces the pressure for unethical behavior and better equips employees to manage the pressure.

Feeling that goals are important also enhances commitment to them and increases the motivation to do a job well. For example, S. Kenneth Kannappan, CEO of Plantronics, a $560 million maker of headsets and products for the hearing impaired, says, "The way I believe you motivate people is to make it clear not only what goals the company is trying to achieve but also why the goals are important to society. Our products, for example, help people drive safely while talking on mobile phones. That's a societal benefit we want our people to understand."[43] Explaining goal importance also enhances feelings of task significance, which can increase motivation, according to the job characteristics model.

Chick-fil-A employees strive to complete orders within sixty seconds at the counter.

For goal setting to work, people must have feedback about how well they are doing in relation to their goals. It is impossible to know if you need to do anything differently to reach your goal if you don't know you are doing poorly. Some companies have been able to use technology to provide employees with real-time feedback about their performance. For example, employees at fast-food restaurant Chick-fil-A strive to complete orders within ninety seconds in the drive-through window and sixty seconds at the counter. Technology behind the counter gives them constant feedback to help them reach this goal—a timer on the computer monitor flashes yellow if an order is cutting it close, red if it runs over.[44]

● **Managing Now** Information technology (IT) helps to provide timely and accurate feedback to employees. Firms can collect performance information electronically from multiple sources and store it in a centralized data warehouse. Rather than having to check multiple sources to learn how they are doing, employees go to one place, usually the company intranet. For example, Cisco uses IT systems to track individual performance. Cisco employees also have easy access to a variety of performance information, such as sales and customer satisfaction, to get a sense of whether they're accomplishing the goals on which they're measured.[45] In the Window on Managing Now feature below, you will learn more about motivating employees with digital dashboards.

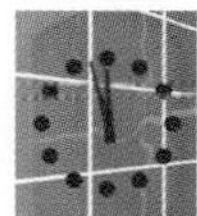

Window on Managing Now
Motivating with Digital Dashboards

As first discussed in Chapter 7, a digital dashboard presents a manager with desktop graphs and charts that paint a picture of performance in terms of various key performance indicators. For example, Johnson & Johnson uses digital dashboards to provide timely and accurate key business indicators to executives.[46] Verizon executives can choose from 300 metrics that reflect company objectives in constructing their dashboards, metrics that include information from broadband sales to wireless subscriber defections.[47] Dashboards can be created that show organization-level performance, workgroup-level performance, or individual performance. Dashboards can provide important feedback to employees about how well they are meeting their individual goals.

Organizations are increasingly using digital dashboards to motivate employees as well as to monitor and control them. Giving employees access to digital dashboards that reflect their own performance regularly reminds employees of their goals and gives them feedback on their performance. Digital dashboards provide personalized information tailored to each user based on his or her organizational role.[48]

Digital dashboards can also stimulate people to help others to reach their goals. For example, Oracle CEO Larry Ellison closely tracks his customers near the end of each financial quarter. "I want to know what our five biggest deals are three days before the quarter closes," he says. "I look at the [dashboard] several times a day. So much of our sales activity gets compressed into a few days." He will then call the companies himself or figure out another way to seal the deal.[49] By reviewing the digital dashboard, Ellison can identify where to best invest his time in closing deals that will help Oracle meet its quarterly goals.

Self-Efficacy

If salespeople did not think that they could sell enough products to meet their quotas, would they be very motivated to try? Because people are motivated in part by what they expect to be able to do, these salespeople would probably not be very motivated. **Self-efficacy** is a person's beliefs in his or her capabilities to do what is required to accomplish a task.[50] Self-efficacy influences an individual's effort and persistence in the face of challenges, potentially aversive situations, and events with high probabilities of failure. Self-efficacy beliefs have three dimensions:

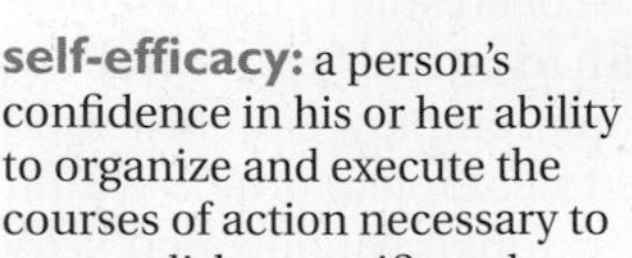

self-efficacy: a person's confidence in his or her ability to organize and execute the courses of action necessary to accomplish a specific task

- *Magnitude:* How difficult is the task to be accomplished?
- *Strength:* How confident is the person that he or she can accomplish the task?
- *Generality:* What is the degree to which he or she can accomplish similar tasks?

"For what it's worth, this is some of the finest substandard mediocrity I've ever seen."

Self-efficacy perceptions are changeable. Good managers enhance subordinates' perceptions of their abilities. Managers can raise self-efficacy through coaching and encouragement. If an employee fails at a task he or she should be able to do, the manager can express confidence in the employee and guide him or her through successful experiences. When an employee is successful, the manager can discuss how the success was due to the employee's skills and effort (rather than to luck) to enhance his or her self-efficacy.

Vroom's Valence, Instrumentality, and Expectancy (VIE) Theory

Valence, instrumentality, and expectancy (VIE) theory resulted from Victor Vroom's[51] research. VIE theory holds that motivation is the product of three key factors: valence, instrumentality, and expectancy. Valence is the perceived value of a given reward or outcome to the person. Instrumentality is a person's belief that performance will result (be instrumental) in obtaining a particular reward. Expectancy is the belief or expectation that effort will lead to performance. Vroom proposed that the perception of a link between effort and reward was crucial to work motivation. A worker must believe that effort will lead to performance (expectancy), that performance will lead to rewards (instrumentality), and that the rewards will be desirable (valence). If the worker perceives valence, instrumentality, or expectancy to be low, then his or her motivation will also be low.

- *Expectancy:* If I work hard and put in a good effort, will I perform well?
- *Instrumentality:* If my performance is good, will I receive any rewards?
- *Valence:* Will the rewards I receive be things that I want?

VIE theory has been criticized.[52] It focuses on only a few variables that are likely to influence motivation. The concept of instrumentality is also ambiguous and difficult to measure.[53] Although support for the theory is mixed, empirical research has shown that the strength of these three factors can influence a worker's effort and performance level.[54] VIE theory is useful to managers because it highlights the role of employee perceptions in the motivation process. Because employees' perceptions determine valences, instrumentalities, and expectancies, managers can influence each of them in the following ways:

- Link rewards to performance (instrumentality) by creating easy-to-understand incentive plans and communicating employees' success stories in earning the rewards.
- Administer rewards that are highly valued (valence) by matching the reward to the worker, or give workers their choice of reward when they meet performance targets.
- Enhance workers' perceptions that they can perform well (expectancy) by ensuring that employees know what they are expected to do; that they know how to do it; and that they believe they can do it through training, coaching, and confidence building.

● **Managing Now** Online incentive programs have made it easier for firms to identify rewards that are highly valued by employees. For example, salesdriver.com offers 1,500 different rewards, including gift certificates, travel, technology, and even motorcycles. This broad selection allows employees to identify rewards that have high valence for them, which increases their motivation. Online incentive programs typically award employees points for engaging in desired behaviors or for reaching goals. Because employees know exactly how many points they need to earn to receive their chosen reward, instrumentality is also high.

What Does It Mean to Be Fair?

How fairly people feel they are being treated influences their motivation.[55] Fairness perceptions affect job performance, satisfaction, organizational commitment, withdrawal behaviors, and counterproductive behaviors such as stealing.[56] Managers have some options for increasing fairness perceptions and reducing negative reactions when people do feel that a situation is unfair. We will discuss the three main ways people perceive situations or results to be fair or unfair next.

● **Distributive Fairness** Distributive fairness is the perception of the fairness of the outcome received. The reality of managerial decision making is that not everyone can get what they want. But how do people react to not getting what they want? Most people feel that positive outcomes are fair and that undesirable outcomes are not fair. But how they react to undesirable outcomes depends on their perceptions of two other types of fairness: procedural fairness and interactional fairness.

● **Procedural Fairness** Procedural fairness is the fairness of the policies and procedures used to determine the outcomes. Does the employee who did not receive the performance bonus feel that the requirements for earning the bonus are fair? Were the methods that determined the bonus awards reasonable? If not, negative outcomes such as lower job performance and withdrawal behaviors like coming to work late or putting in less effort are likely to result. But if procedural fairness is high, negative reactions are much less likely. Consistent with VIE theory, procedural fairness increases instrumentality by helping to reinforce employees' beliefs that if they engage in certain behaviors and perform at a certain level, they will receive rewards.

Interactional Fairness Interactional fairness refers to whether the amount of information about the decision and the process was adequate and whether employees feel that they were treated respectfully during the process. Continuing our example, does the employee who did not receive the performance bonus feel that the supervisor did not adequately explain why she or he did not receive it? When we assess undesirable outcomes, how we are treated can be just as important as the outcomes we receive. If someone treats us rudely, it is hard to feel motivated to do our best for him or her.

Although providing adequate information and treating people respectfully may not sound like powerful tools in work motivation, interactional fairness can reduce negative reactions to undesirable work outcomes.[57] In one case,[58] two plants in the same company announced 15 percent pay cuts for their workers. The CEO gave employees at one plant extensive explanations about why the pay cut was necessary and regretfully and explicitly explained that they would allow the company to avoid layoffs. The second plant heard a short explanation that a pay cut was going to take place to avoid layoffs, but employees received no apology. Interactional fairness was therefore high in the first plant and low in the second plant. After the announcement, theft increased in both plants, but its incidence was significantly higher in the plant that received an inadequate explanation for the pay cuts. Voluntary turnover was also higher in the plant that perceived low interactional fairness.

Managing Fairness A great benefit to understanding how people perceive fairness is that it helps managers identify factors that are not expensive but that can effectively increase employee motivation. Managers can improve fairness perceptions in two ways: (1) change the fairness of the situation or (2) change how employees perceive the fairness of the situation. To change the fairness of the situation, managers can improve distributive fairness by appropriately rewarding employees' contributions. Ensuring that the policies and procedures used in determining employee outcomes are objective and fair improves procedural fairness. Treating employees with respect and giving adequate explanations for why decisions are made can improve interactional fairness.

To change how employees perceive fairness, managers can focus on explaining the procedures and decision-making processes to employees so that they are clear and transparent. Employees should not wonder why some people get bonuses or promotions and others do not—the requirements, procedures, and decision-making processes should be transparent and decisions explained. In addition, managers should always treat employees with sincerity and respect.

Equity Theory

equity theory: the theory that people observe the rewards others are getting and the effort they are putting into their work, and then compare these observations with their own effort and rewards

J. Stacey Adams[59] developed **equity theory** to describe how people arrive at decisions regarding whether a decision was fair. Equity theory proposes that people observe the rewards others are getting and the effort they are putting into their work. They then compare the efforts and rewards of others with their own effort and rewards. If people perceive inequity, especially in comparison to relevant others, they will be dissatisfied and will try to restore equity. Employees' concern for fairness and equity drives this social comparison process. Research has supported this theory, and it has become one of the most useful frameworks for understanding work motivation.

A fair or equitable situation is one in which people with similar inputs experience similar outcomes. Employees will compare their inputs and rewards with the rewards received by others for their inputs. Inputs include effort, ability, experience, and other factors that enable someone to perform the job well. If employees perceive that an inequity exists, they are likely to withhold some of their contributions, either consciously or unconsciously, to bring a situation into better balance. This balance can be expressed as follows:

$$\frac{\text{own inputs}}{\text{own outcomes}} = \frac{\text{others' inputs}}{\text{others' outcomes}}$$

For example, imagine you have a job at which you feel that you work hard for forty hours a week and earn a salary of $50,000. A colleague with the same job and same hours earns a $60,000 salary. Is this fair? In assessing the equity of the situation, you realize that your colleague has advanced training, has worked ten years longer than you have, and is more productive. You decide that, given your colleague's greater job inputs, his or her greater outcome (salary) is fair. You might know of another colleague, however, who has the same effort level, work experience, productivity, and education that you do but who makes $55,000. You may feel that this situation is unfair.

Equality and equity are not the same: equality means that everyone's outcomes are the same; equity means that everyone's outcomes are fair given the nature of their inputs. Equity theory does *not* propose that pay levels (outcomes) need to be equal across employees. Employees generally won't think it's unfair if a comparison employee is receiving more from the organization (such as getting paid more) if he or she also contributes more to the organization (by being a better performer, working more hours, etc.).

If an inequity is perceived, the employee may experience an emotional reaction (such as anger) and try to restore equity. Adams proposed several ways that an individual can try to resolve the inequity. For example, imagine a situation where someone feels that they are underpaid compared to a coworker. To restore feelings of equity, the worker could react by:

- Decreasing inputs (working more slowly or sloppily).
- Increasing outputs from the company (asking for a raise or bonus, or stealing).
- Trying to get the comparison person to work harder (to increase his or her inputs).
- Trying to get the comparison person's outputs from the company reduced.
- Choosing a different comparison person.
- Cognitively distorting the comparison and trying to convince him- or herself that the situation is equitable.
- Quitting.

Employees are more likely to notice being underpaid than being overpaid.[60] When employees perceive that they have been overpaid, they may temporarily increase their productivity to make the situation more equitable, but this effect gradually wears off.[61] It is likely that people reevaluate their inputs to justify the overpayment and convince themselves that they deserve it.

Although equity theory was originally concerned with differences in pay, it is also applicable to other forms of tangible and intangible rewards in the workplace.[62] That is, if any employee input is not balanced with some fair outcome, motivation will be difficult. Managers must manage the perception of fairness in the mind of each employee. If a subordinate thinks that you are treating him or her unfairly, it will be difficult to motivate that employee, even if you disagree with his or her assessment.

Learning and Reinforcement Approaches to Motivation: How Consequences Shape Behavior

Online Study Center
ACE the Test
Managing Now! LIVE

learning: a relatively permanent change in behavior that occurs because of experience

Learning can be thought of as a relatively permanent change in behavior that occurs as a result of experience.[63] Throughout our lives, we learn cause-and-effect relationships both consciously and unconsciously. Children learn appropriate ways to behave as a result of parents' and teachers' smiles and reprimands in response to their actions. Adults learn what their bosses expect through the feedback and rewards received because of their performance. This type of learning tends to happen naturally and instinctively rather than because of deliberate thought. Although several theories exist about how people learn, we will focus our attention on those involving reinforcement. Reinforcement theories address the role of consequences in shaping behavior.

Reinforcing Performance

Reinforcement theory is based on the work of noted psychologist Edward Thorndike and B. F. Skinner.[64] Thorndike discovered three laws:

- *The law of effect:* People tend not to engage in behavior that does not result in a reward.
- *The law of recency:* The most recent consequence of a behavior is likely to govern the recurrence of that behavior.
- *The law of exercise:* Repetition strengthens the association between cause and effect.

The core of reinforcement theory is that behavior that is followed by positive consequences is likely to be repeated. B. F. Skinner expanded on Thorndike's work and found that many behaviors can be controlled using different types of reinforcers.[65] A **reinforcer** is anything that makes a behavior more likely to happen again. Reinforcers work best when they are immediate, sincere, and specific to an activity. There are four types of reinforcers, which are shown in Figure 14.5 and explained more fully below:

reinforcer: anything that makes a behavior more likely to happen again

- *Positive reinforcement:* Use of rewards to increase the likelihood that a behavior will be repeated.
- *Negative reinforcement:* Removal of current or future unpleasant consequences to increase the likelihood that someone will repeat a behavior. In other words, avoidance or removal of something undesirable is motivating.
- *Punishment:* Application of negative outcomes to decrease the likelihood of a behavior.
- *Extinction:* Removal of any reinforcement (positive or negative) following the occurrence of the behavior to be extinguished to decrease the likelihood of that behavior.

For reinforcement to work, the employee must know exactly why he or she is receiving a reward. To best reinforce a behavior, the reward should come as quickly as possible after the behavior. One of the biggest benefits of online incentive

FIGURE 14.5

The Four Types of Reinforcers

		TYPE OF STIMULUS	
		Positive	**Negative**
ACTION	**Present the Stimulus**	Positive Reinforcement *(Increases the Behavior)*	Punishment *(Decreases the Behavior)*
	Remove the Stimulus	Extinction *(Decreases the Behavior)*	Negative Reinforcement *(Increases the Behavior)*

programs is that they immediately reward desired behavior. A reward can be almost anything and does not need to cost a lot of money, but it must be something desired by the employee. Some of the most powerful rewards are symbolic, things like plaques or certificates that cost very little but mean a lot to the people who get them.

The Safety, Environment, Energy and Security Committee (SEES) group at Walt Disney World Resorts created a fun competition using positive and negative reinforcement to motivate Contemporary Hotel employees.[66] SEES hands out a monthly award to the best-performing department as positive reinforcement and a nonaward to the worst-performing department as negative reinforcement in the categories of safety and security, the environment, and energy. If the nonaward-winning department improves within five days, the nonaward is taken away. The general manager ensures that the department managers display the awards in their offices until the following month.

For the category of energy, the award is a nine-inch statue of Sorcerer Mickey. The nonaward is a statue of a burnt-out light bulb. For safety and security, the award is a statue of Donald Duck's uncle, Ludwig Von Drake, and the nonaward depicts a miniature broken crutch. For the environment, the award is a Jiminy Cricket statue, and the nonaward is a clear plastic case containing a noose with a dead rubber chicken. The rubber chicken has been an effective negative reinforcement; because no one wants to have the rubber chicken nonaward in his or her office, environmental performance is often good enough that no department receives it.

Behavior Modification

Behavior modification, based on the work of B. F. Skinner, gives managers a way to apply reinforcement theory to motivate workers. There are two basic issues in using behavior modification: the type of reinforcement (reward or punishment) and the schedule of reinforcement.

Types of Reinforcement Managers must choose from among the four types of reinforcement listed above: positive reinforcement, negative reinforcement, punishment, and extinction. Each is best suited to a different type of situation:

- *Positive reinforcement:* Positive reinforcement motivates more of the desired behavior. For example, when a manufacturing employee wears hearing protection, the manager can praise the employee to increase the likelihood that the employee will wear the hearing protection in the future.

- *Negative reinforcement:* Negative reinforcement is appropriate when an employee perceives something undesirable and the manager wants to increase the frequency of certain types of behaviors. Removing whatever is undesirable motivates the employee to engage in the behavior. For example, when a good employee dislikes her long commute, the manager can allow her to telecommute two days a week as long as her performance exceeds a certain level. Because she wants to avoid the unpleasant commute, the employee is motivated to perform well.
- *Punishment:* Punishment focuses on decreasing the likelihood of undesirable behaviors. It requires giving an employee an unpleasant consequence, such as a suspension, assigning an unpleasant task, or a reprimand. Company policies and procedures usually govern the use of punishment,[67] and it is generally less effective than the other methods of behavior modification.
- *Extinction:* Extinction is appropriate when a manager realizes he or she has been rewarding the wrong action(s) and the manager wants to stop the behavior. For example, a manager used to laugh at an employee's inappropriate comments at meetings but now wants the comments to stop. If the manager begins ignoring the comments, over time, the lack of a positive reaction from the manager reduces the employee's motivation and extinguishes the behavior.

Schedule of Reinforcement Behavior modification also requires attention to the schedule used to apply reinforcement. Research suggests that the fastest way to get someone to learn is to use continuous reinforcement and so reinforce the desired behavior every time it occurs. The downside to this approach is that as soon as the reward is stopped, the desired behavior decreases in frequency.

The most effective schedule for sustaining a behavior is variable reinforcement. This type of schedule requires reinforcing the desired behavior every few times it occurs, around some average number of times, rather than every time it occurs. Because performing the behavior can result in a reward at any time, this approach is a strong motivator of behavior. Slot machines motivate players through variable reinforcement—players know that their machine will eventually pay out but don't know when, so they are motivated to continue playing for a long time, even when they are losing and not being reinforced.

Using Behavior Modification as a Manager To a behavior modification expert, any behavior can be understood as being a result of its consequences. In other words, as a manager, you get whatever behaviors you are reinforcing. For example, if an employee continually comes to work late, it is because you are not providing the right consequences for coming to work on time, the consequences for coming in late are inappropriate, or both. To motivate the right behavior, an expert in behavior modification would identify the desired behaviors and then carefully reinforce them. This process involves five steps:[68]

1. Define the problem—what could be improved?
2. Identify and define the specific behavior(s) you wish to change.
3. Count and record the occurrence of the target behavior.
4. Analyze the current consequences of the behavior and arrange for more appropriate consequences to follow the behavior in the future.
5. Evaluate whether the behavior improved, and by how much.

FIGURE 14.6

Performance Improvement Project Worksheet

1. General Statement of Problem: The accounting department was making many payroll errors, frustrating employees, and increasing costs by taking up managers' time and accounting time.

2. Pinpointed Behaviors: The accounting department counted and recorded the number of payroll errors reported to it by department managers.

3. Count and Record:

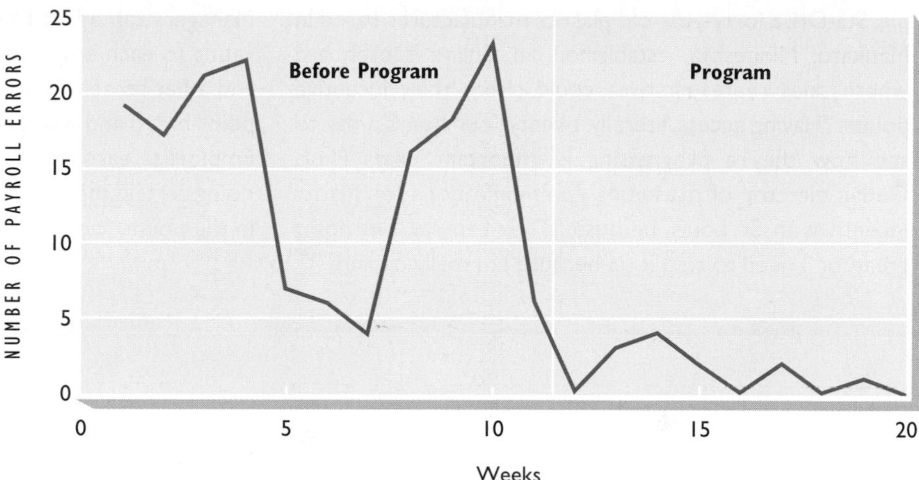

4. Consequences for Behavior Changes: Each bookkeeper in the accounting department started graphing the number of errors for which he or she was responsible. The accounting manager assigned responsibility for each error after discussing it with the bookkeepers. The manager verbally reinforced those bookkeepers who displayed low rates of error to begin with or who showed improvement on their graphs.

5. Evaluate Changes: The number of errors dropped from an average of 11.6 per week to 1.17 per week.

SOURCE: Lawrence Miller, *Behavior Management: The New Science of Managing People at Work* (New York: John Wiley, 1978), p. 18.

Figure 14.6 illustrates an application of the behavior modification approach. In this case, the general problem was the number of payroll errors the accounting department was making. The specific behaviors were the number of payroll errors reported by department managers, which were counted and recorded. The current and desired consequences for payroll accuracy were identified and aligned—in this case, payroll errors reported by the managers were attributed to the appropriate bookkeeper and graphed. The manager verbally reinforced bookkeepers with low error rates and bookkeepers who reduced their error rates, and the number of errors fell.

As you will see in the Window on Managing Now feature on page 426, Internet tools can also be used to motivate employees.

Rewarding Performance

Online Study Center
ACE the Test
Managing Now! LIVE

Rewards are one of the most powerful motivational tools managers have at their disposal. The rewards offered by a job determine not only whether someone is willing to accept a job offer but also how much effort he or she is willing to put

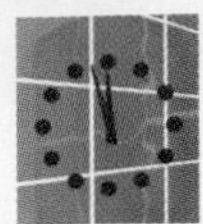

Window on Managing Now
Using Internet Tools to Motivate and Reward Employees

Incentive programs can have a positive impact on employee motivation and performance by providing positive reinforcement.[69] Many companies are using technology to enhance their positive reinforcement programs. For example, Sta-Dri, a forty-year-old plastics manufacturer based in Mankato, Minnesota, established an online scoreboard where sales representatives could check their incentive points. "Having access, literally, twenty-four hours a day to see how they're progressing is important," says Paula Godar, director of marketing communications for Maritz Incentives in St. Louis, because "They can say, 'I'm doing great' or 'I need to step it up because I'm really behind.'"[70]

Many Internet incentive sites exist, including incentivecity.com, emaritz.com, premierchoiceaward.com, salesdriver.com, hinda.com, and loyaltyworks.com. In some cases, employees can specify the rewards they want. Managers can adapt the rewards to be those most motivating to each employee, such as an extra day off for one and a flat-screen TV for another. Many incentive sites are point-based and work like airline frequent-flyer programs. Employees earn points for reaching certain goals or for doing certain things over a set period of time and can cash in the points for a variety of trips and prizes.

forth. In organizations, workers exchange their time and effort for some set of rewards, including pay, benefits, training opportunities, and so forth.

The clearing of the island of Penang illustrates the motivational power of rewards. Before 1786, Penang was covered with jungle and infested with malaria. When English captain Francis Light of the East India Company chose Penang as a new harbor for ships on their way to China to get fresh food and water, he needed his soldiers to clear the thick jungle. The soldiers were understandably not very excited about the job. To motivate them, Light loaded the ship's guns with silver dollars and fired them into the jungle. The work was rapidly finished.

Pay for Performance

Although money motivates people differently, it can be a powerful motivator because it determines the degree to which people will be able to satisfy many of their needs and wants. Employees can be rewarded for their individual performance as well as the performance of their workgroup or even the entire organization.

Merit Pay Merit pay is a salary increase, usually permanent, given because of an individual's past performance. Consistent with VIE theory, employee motivation is enhanced because good performance is expected to result in higher pay. A clear link among effort, job performance, and the reward enhances motivation.

Spot Awards Spot awards are most consistent with reinforcement theory. Spot awards are given on the spot, as soon as a desired behavior is observed.[71] Effective spot reward programs depend on discretion, timely acknowledgments, and clear links between employee actions and recognition. Systems engineering consulting firm Scitor in Sunnyvale, California, has a Be Our Guest program in which employees award bonuses, usually ranging from $100 to $300, to coworkers who go beyond the call of duty at work. If someone feels a coworker has done something worthy, the giver fills out a card indicating the amount of the bonus, and the recipient can spend it as he or she likes through his or her expense account.[72]

Pay for Performance Pay-for-performance programs pay employees based on some specific measure of their performance. The amount employees produce or sell determines their pay—the higher their performance, the more money they make. The clear performance-reward link is consistent with VIE theory.

Several different pay-for-performance programs are popular. Variable pay plans are pay-for-performance plans that put a small amount of base pay at risk, in exchange for the opportunity to earn additional pay. For example, all employees of Chicago-based Ameritech Corp. are compensated using a variable-pay approach. Every Ameritech employee has a set of target incentives ranging from 5 to 35 percent of pay. A portion of the incentive amount (about 60 percent) is based on the performance of the employee's business unit, with the remainder (about 40 percent) based on individual performance.[73] An average of two-thirds of a Nucor steelworker's pay is based on a production bonus, and profit sharing can add even more.[74]

Many companies use stock options to motivate managers.

Stock Options Stock options are an incentive most often given to executives. Stock options motivate managers to increase the company's profitability and therefore its stock price. Stock options allow the purchase of a specific amount of the company's stock at a certain price during a specific period. If the stock price rises above this price, the resulting stock can be sold at a profit. If the stock price decreases below this price, the options are worthless (although organizations have the option of repricing the options to restore their value and motivating potential).

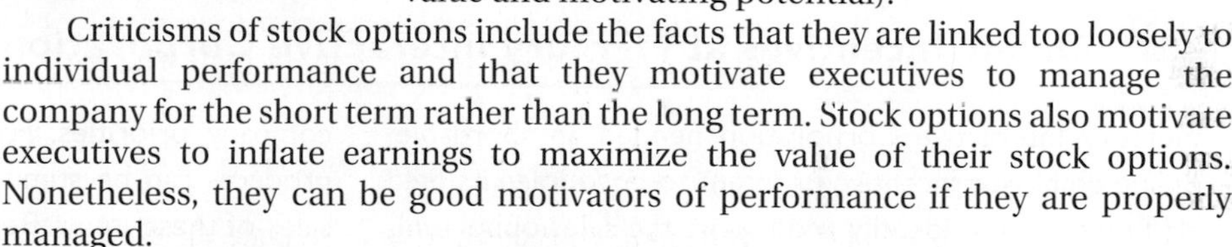

Criticisms of stock options include the facts that they are linked too loosely to individual performance and that they motivate executives to manage the company for the short term rather than the long term. Stock options also motivate executives to inflate earnings to maximize the value of their stock options. Nonetheless, they can be good motivators of performance if they are properly managed.

Gain Sharing Gain sharing is sharing the value of productivity gains with the workforce. For example, if workers come up with ways to increase productivity 10 percent by lowering costs or increasing productivity, they receive some of the value of the 10 percent productivity gain. This clear link between performance and rewards is consistent with VIE theory and can motivate employees to improve productivity because doing so will lead to financial rewards for them. Gain sharing can also increase employees' commitment to organizational goals by focusing their attention on cost and productivity.

Skill-Based Pay Rather than paying employees for the jobs they currently hold, skill-based pay compensates employees for the range and depth of their knowledge and skills.[75] Broader skills make workers more flexible and enable them to contribute to the organization in more ways. When work is organized in teams, skill-based pay can encourage all team members to develop the skills needed to help the team be flexible and perform at its best.

A General Mills plant implemented a skill-based pay plan that paid employees in several types of jobs based on their attained skill levels for their job.[76] Workers could attain three levels of skill in their job: limited ability (ability to perform simple tasks without direction), partial proficiency (ability to apply more advanced principles on the job), and full competence (ability to analyze and solve problems associated with that job). The company periodically tested workers to see if they had attained the next higher skill level on their job. If they had, they received higher pay even though they kept the same job. The program increased employees' overall skill levels and increased managers' ability to move employees from job to job as needed.

Skill-based pay plans are used predominantly in blue-collar environments because of the relative ease of understanding what skills are important to job performance. Competency-based pay is used to evaluate the skills and knowledge of other workers. Using salespeople as an example, the employer first learns what its best salespeople do well. It might be building relationships, tailoring the sales pitch to the client, or possessing technical knowledge about the product. Once the elements that predict sales success are identified, all sales employees would be compensated based on how well they show those competencies.[77]

● **Managing Now** Organizations use IT, the Internet, and their intranets to improve the effectiveness of their incentive and reward programs. When T-Mobile needed to improve the performance of its call-center customer-service professionals, it reinforced its Do More Get More program through in-center TV monitors, e-mail flashes, and an intranet site.[78] A point system awards employees

PRACTICE IT

Online Incentives at Mercury Interactive Corporation

Mercury Interactive Corporation needed an affordable, online employee incentive program to encourage its field staff members to identify and report the sales opportunities they saw while on client assignments. The company implemented an online program in which field staff members receive points for sales leads and even more points for leads that generate new business. "The administration of this would have been way too much if the program wasn't online," a company representative says. "A $7,000 investment has generated more than $600,000 in new business."[79] Setting clear expectations for employees to identify and report sales opportunities and then rewarding these behaviors with points redeemable for valued rewards are consistent with reinforcement theory. Letting employees choose their rewards increases employees' valence, and knowing how many points are required to earn a reward enhances instrumentality, which is consistent with VIE theory.

Online programs also give managers easy access to real-time data and the flexibility to adjust to changing company priorities. For example, sales of slow-moving products can be stimulated by offering bonus points for sales of these items. Because the data in online systems is centralized, firms can continually evaluate the effectiveness of the awards program and ensure that it is making a difference, and they can identify underperformers as well.[80]

An important requirement for online incentive programs is that employees must have Internet access. This requirement is challenging for companies with employees who work on factory floors and at cash registers and thus do not have access to company computers. Many online vendors provide supplemental paper materials for these employees, but other companies find ways to give all employees computer access. By putting its incentive program online, 3M saved enough money that it was able to install computer kiosks so that all employees had access, and it scheduled time on the computer as part of the workday.[81] Incentive programs should also be well promoted and made an integral part of the job.[82]

points based on the achievement of specific goals and performance results. Employees then redeem the points online for rewards ranging from retailer gift certificates to entertainment and travel options. The incentive program has led to improvements in quality, accuracy, and productivity. Employees are more motivated and more satisfied—absenteeism decreased and employee attrition rates fell by 50 percent.[83]

By leveraging technology, online incentive and recognition programs can effectively motivate employees. Program information can be quickly communicated through intranet sites or e-mail, and the speed at which rewards are received strongly reinforces desired behaviors. By running rewards programs online, companies can greatly reduce costs and acquire real-time insight into the program's impact. The Practice IT feature presents another example.

Alternative Rewards

Besides money, employees also value recognition, appreciation, and help in balancing their work and family lives. Recognition and nonmonetary rewards are typically inexpensive, but they can be effective motivators. One study found that financial incentives initially had a greater effect on profit and customer service, but over time, financial and nonfinancial incentives had an equally significant impact.[84] Employee recognition methods include a personal thank-you note, a preferred parking space, public praise, a unique award, company picnics, and management dressing in a crazy outfit if employees meet sales targets.

At Nucor Corporation, the largest steelmaker in the United States, motivation is about focusing on the people on the front line. Managers talk to them, listen to them, and act on their ideas. In exchange for being treated with respect, having real power, and being generously rewarded, Nucor employees put in extraordinary effort.[85]

Sometimes simple gestures can get great results. A Westinghouse sales manager agreed to pay for and cook lunch for all sixteen of the employees who reported directly to him if they met their sales quotas. They subsequently exceeded their goals in eighteen out of nineteen months. Corporate higher-ups volunteered to foot the bill, but the manager refused, saying that the incentive worked because he personally went to the supermarket to buy the steaks with his own money and because employees got a kick out of seeing the boss become a cook and a waiter.[86]

Employees have lives outside work, and facilitating work-life balance can reward and motivate employees. Offering a compressed workweek allows employees to work forty hours in less than five days. Job sharing, which allows two or more people to split a single job, is another option. One person might perform the job on Mondays and Tuesdays, the other person on Thursdays and Fridays, and both on Wednesdays. Or one employee could work in the mornings and the other in the afternoons. This option requires finding compatible pairs of employees who can share the responsibilities of one job successfully, and it can help motivate and retain skilled workers—particularly students, retirees, and parents of young children.

● **Flextime** Flextime is another scheduling option that lets employees decide when to go to work, within certain parameters. Companies typically establish a core set of work hours, say, 9:00 A.M. to 3:00 P.M., during which time all employees need to be at work. Employees have the flexibility of scheduling their other two hours of work either before or after this core period. Flextime can increase the motivation of workers by helping them better match their work schedule to their personal needs and preferences.

● Telecommuting Telecommuting is another way employers can facilitate employees' work-life balance. Telecommuting allows employees to work from home and link to the company's offices via computer. This option eliminates commuting time for employees, increases their ability to meet family demands, and can save the company money by reducing the company's need for office space.[87]

● Lifelong Learning Allowing opportunities for lifelong learning is another way companies can reward employees and help the organization stay competitive at the same time. Lifelong learning is a formal commitment to ensuring that employees have and develop the skills they need to be effective in their jobs today and in the future. Lifelong learning programs include in-house training in basic skills such as English and math, courses on decision making and problem solving, and even tuition reimbursement for relevant college-level coursework. Because it increases employees' self-efficacy and expectancy, and provides an opportunity for employees to feel a sense of achievement and self-actualize, lifelong learning is inherently motivational.

It might not seem like lifelong learning can be an effective tool for motivating employees, but in fact, its motivational impact can be considerable. For many employees, particularly for people working two jobs or with family responsibilities, pursuing educational opportunities outside work can be difficult. Anything learned in these programs—for example, learning to read or improving computer skills—can also enrich employees' personal lives. One study found that "productivity improvements, greater workforce flexibility, reduced material and capital costs, a better motivated workforce, and improved quality of the final product or service are all identified as advantages [of lifelong learning]."[88]

● Managing Now IT makes it easier for organizations to implement lifelong learning programs. For example, Rutgers University instituted a self-paced, computer-based continuous learning program for its facilities and maintenance operations staff by creating a computer room with sixteen terminals. It then developed courses enhancing employees' math, computer literacy, and supervisory skills. The targeted, self-paced approach to training not only improved worker morale, it also raised the skill levels of over 300 workers.[89]

Putting It All Together

This chapter has presented different methods that managers can use to enhance employee motivation. Each motivation method that a manager can use is based on one of the motivation theories we have discussed. Understanding why and how a motivational technique works helps managers match motivational techniques with motivation opportunities and thus enhances the likelihood of success. For example, goal-setting theory and equity theory help to explain why goal setting enhances motivation. Table 14.3 shows the theoretical foundations of ten popular methods of motivating employees. The Window on Managing Now feature on page 432 illustrates how to use technology to retain knowledge workers.

TABLE 14.3
The Motivational Underpinnings of Ten Motivation Methods

Foundations of Behavior and Motivation	Goal Setting	Pay for Performance	Merit Raises	Spot Rewards	Skill-Based Pay	Recognition Awards	Job Redesign	Empower Employees	Positive Reinforcement	Lifelong Learning
Self-Concept: People seek to fulfill their potential.					×	×	×	×		×
Self-Efficacy: People differ in their estimate of how they'll perform on a task: self-efficacy influences setting of goals and effort.	×				×	×		×		×
Maslow's Needs Hierarchy: High-level needs are never totally satisfied and aren't aroused until lower-level needs are fulfilled.			×	×		×	×	×		×
Alderfer: All needs may be active, to some degree, at the same time.			×	×		×	×	×		×
McClelland's Needs (Achievement, Power, Affiliation): Needs for achievement, power, and affiliation are especiallly important in the work setting.					×	×	×	×		×
Herzberg's Two Factors: Extrinsic factors prevent dissatisfactions; intrinsic factors motivate workers.							×	×		×
Vroom's VIE Theory: Motivation is a function of expectancy that effort leads to performance, performance leads to reward, and reward is valued.		×	×	×		×				
Locke's Goal Setting: People are motivated to achieve the goals they consciously set.	×							×		
Adam's Equity Theory: People are motivated to maintain balance between their perceived inputs and outputs.	×	×	×	×		×				
Reinforcement: People will continue behavior that is rewarded and cease behavior that is punished.		×	×	×		×			×	

Source: Adapted from Gary Dessler, Ph.D., 1997.

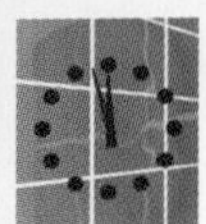

WINDOW ON MANAGING NOW
Using Technology to Retain Knowledge Workers[90]

The challenge in retaining employees often is finding ways to match individuals' passions with the organization's needs. Knowledge workers, who develop or use knowledge in doing their jobs rather than doing production work, are often motivated by doing their work well, building their professional reputations, working on challenging projects that broaden their skills and marketability, and achieving a greater balance between work and their personal lives. Examples of knowledge workers include lawyers, doctors, professors, managers, and bankers. Technology has helped companies better understand the turnover patterns of their knowledge workers so that they can better retain them.

Banca Carige, one of the oldest banks in Italy, uses technology to engage in what it calls employee relationship management. Its first goal was to predict if its best employees were about to leave. Improving employee retention would not only save money (it is cheaper to retain employees than to hire and train new people), it would also help the bank keep its best performers. It wanted a retention model that would help forecast and analyze information and trends, plan proactively for the future, and reduce turnover costs.

To create an employee retention model, Banca Carige used SAS to create an employee data warehouse that contains information about each employee's age, gender, salary, job role, education, and professional information. The retention model analyzes the factors associated with voluntary turnover, builds a model to predict the likelihood of an employee voluntarily leaving, scores all employees based on the model, and delivers reports based on the model's results. The retention model allows the company to answer questions like the following:

- Which employees are at the highest risk of voluntarily leaving the organization?
- What reasons do employees have for wanting to leave?
- Which reasons are the strongest predictors of employees actually leaving?
- What are the profiles of those employees most likely to leave?

While low current turnover is important, it is just as important to keep turnover from increasing, and the retention model from SAS helps with both issues.

CHAPTER SUMMARY

1. Motivation is the intensity of a person's desire to begin or continue engaging in the pursuit of a goal. Motivation is affected by factors that arouse, maintain, and channel a person's efforts toward a goal to fulfill unmet wants or needs.
2. Motivation is affected by characteristics of the individual, job, and work environments.
3. Whereas content theories focus on which factors (needs) internal to a person influence motivation, process theories address how and why different factors external to a person influence motivation.
4. Goal setting is one of the most effective ways of motivating workers. Goal setting is particularly effective if employees participate in setting the goals, are committed to them, and have self-efficacy about reaching the goal. Feedback is necessary to monitor progress toward the goal and to learn if task strategies need to be changed.
5. Digital dashboards help keep employees focused on important goals and provide timely feedback to employees regarding how well they are meeting their goals.
6. According to VIE theory, employees must perceive valence, instrumentality, and expectancy if they are to be motivated. Managers can proactively influence employees' perceptions of all three factors.
7. Employees' fairness perceptions affect their job performance, satisfaction, organizational commitment, withdrawal behaviors, and counterproductive behaviors such as stealing. Fairness perceptions

are determined by the nature of the outcomes received (distributive fairness), the policies and procedures used to determine the outcomes (procedural fairness), and the nature of the information given and interpersonal treatment received during the process.

8. Equity theory proposes that people observe the rewards others are getting and the effort they are putting into their work, and then compare these observations with their own effort and rewards. If inequity is perceived, people are motivated to try to reduce the inequity.

9. Positive reinforcement, negative reinforcement, punishment, and extinction can all be used to encourage or discourage certain behaviors from occurring again, and they are at the core of behavior modification programs.

DISCUSSION QUESTIONS

1. What motivates you at work? What motivates you at school? Are your answers the same? Why or why not?
2. Think about a time when you had a hard time getting motivated to complete a task (a task at work, studying for an exam, etc.). Why did you have a hard time? What could have increased your motivation? How can you use this information to improve your performance in these tasks in the future?
3. Think of a time you felt unfairly treated at work or at school. Now describe why you felt that you were treated unfairly. How do your answers relate to fairness theory? What could have been done differently to make your reactions less negative?
4. Which theory of motivation do you think *best* applies to the workplace? Why? Which theory of motivation do you think *least* applies to the workplace? Why?
5. How can management style and organizational policies affect the motivation levels of employees? Consider both content and process theories in your answer.
6. What suggestions would you give an organization that has little money to spend but wants to motivate its employees to work harder? What would you caution it *not* to do?
7. What can managers do to reward employees for behaving ethically? What are some things that managers should *not* do if they want employees to behave ethically?

EXPERIENTIAL EXERCISES

1. Read the following about motivation and intelligence:

   It can be hard to stay motivated when you do the same thing day after day. Because of this, one town's police department decided that applicants who score too high on a cognitive ability test will not be hired on the premise that they are more likely to feel bored on the job and thus be harder to retain.[91] The test's manual even warns about the cost of replacing high-scoring workers who quit because they become dissatisfied with repetitive work.[92] This premise has proved controversial, however, because the hiring of less intelligent police officers may also reduce their overall performance. And when a gunfight does occur, the consequences of poorer decisions made by less intelligent police officers can clearly be great, including the loss of life. This controversy highlights the importance of understanding the impact of task characteristics on task motivation, as well as the importance of managing jobs to reduce the potential for negative outcomes.

   Now form groups of three or four students, answer the following questions, and share your answers with the class:

   a. Do you agree that candidates high in cognitive ability should not be police officers because they might become bored with the work? Why or why not?

b. What motivation theories best apply to the job of police officer?

c. If you were a police chief, what would you do to increase the motivation of your officers and prevent them from feeling bored?

2. In groups of three or four students, identify a job with which you are all familiar or a job currently held by one of your group members. Use Figure 14.5 to analyze the job's enrichment potential. To what degree is the job enriched now? Why? What would your group recommend to enrich it further?

3. Interview two people about a job they currently hold and try to identify the factors that motivate each person. What are the similarities? What are the differences? Now imagine that you are their manager. Given what you have learned, what recommendations would you make about how best to motivate each of them?

4. Use the Internet to identify a situation where a company leader was effective in motivating employees in some way (i.e., to perform better, to work more safely, etc.). Write a two-page paper describing what made the leader effective, applying material you learned in this chapter.

CASE STUDY

Motivation at General Motors[93]

The 3,500 employees in General Motors' (GM) assembly plant in Wilmington, Delaware, were told by GM executives that the plant would be shut down in five years to reduce costs. They were told that the decision was final. After the executives left, plant manager Ralph Harding spoke passionately to the stunned workers. "There may be nothing we can do to affect this decision, but there is something we can do: We can make them feel really stupid! Because they are going to be closing the best plant in General Motors!"

Motivated by his challenge, employees and managers began working in problem-solving teams to lower costs and tackle quality-control problems. Energized to embarrass GM's top brass, "Be the Best!" became a rallying cry and was printed on posters and sewn onto jackets given to employees. Union leaders and managers worked together more closely than ever to come up with ideas to improve quality and lower costs. Harding kept everyone informed of the plant's weekly progress on quality and costs. And the families of employees were invited to the plant for a luncheon in the spring and for a picnic in the summer. "When your family is engaged, it makes you feel good about what you do," says Harvey G. Thomas, the plant's current manager.

Within two years, the workers made the factory the lowest-cost producer for GM, with the lowest warranty costs as well. The employees succeeded in making the corporation's decision look foolish—and GM reversed itself and kept the plant open.

DISCUSSION QUESTIONS

1. What motivation theories describe why the workers became so motivated to do their best?

2. What might GM have done, rather than announce the plant's closing, to motivate the plant workers to do their best? Would your suggestions have been as effective? Why or why not?

3. Why would involving the workers' families enhance workers' motivation?

IMPROVING COMMUNICATION 15

Communication at Lucent[1]

Lucent Technologies, headquartered in Murray Hill, New Jersey, designs the systems, services, and software that drive next-generation communication networks. With over 30,000 employees located around the globe, communicating with employees is difficult. But in this fast-paced industry, communication is critical to keep employees abreast of company challenges and needs. As a global company, employees live and work in different time zones: work is done somewhere in the world twenty-four hours a day, seven days a week. How can Lucent keep employees abreast of company challenges and needs and use technology to communicate effectively with them? ■

Lucent employees must be able to communicate effectively around the world twenty-four hours a day, seven days a week.

BEHAVIORAL OBJECTIVES

After studying this chapter, you should be able to:

Show that you've learned the chapter's essential information by

- ➤ Describing the communication process.
- ➤ Explaining the difference between formal and informal communication in organizations.
- ➤ Giving examples of different technologies that have influenced organizational communication.
- ➤ Discussing how media richness affects the appropriateness of a medium for different types of messages.
- ➤ Describing active listening and explaining what makes a good listener.
- ➤ Describing how to make an effective presentation.

CHAPTER OUTLINE

Show that you can practice what you've learned here by

- Reading the chapter-opening vignette and identifying how Lucent can use technology to enhance its internal communication.
- Completing the end-of-chapter exercises and practicing the use of appropriate negotiation tactics and nonverbal cues in negotiating a job offer.
- Reading the chapter case study and describing issues related to electronic monitoring at work.

Show that you can apply what you've learned here by

Online Study Center
ACE the Test
Managing Now! LIVE

- Watching the video scenario and determining effective ways of communicating in varying situations.
- Studying the video scenario and identifying the appropriate types of technology that can enhance the communication effectiveness.

Nothing can happen in an organization without communication. Managers can't manage, employees can't work, and decisions can't be made. Communication is the glue that holds organizations together—an organization would cease to exist if communication channels that allow information to flow do not link its employees.

Communication is the means through which firms achieve their strategies, goals, and outcomes. Organizational planning and strategy development require communication among organizational decision makers. Decisions require the communication of information. Managers then communicate these decisions to employees, who communicate among themselves to execute the decision or strategy. Managers also communicate with customers and suppliers, and communication is how people in the firm acquire information about the marketplace and competitors.

To be effective leaders, managers must have good communication skills. In this chapter, we will discuss the communication process, some of the basic issues in interpersonal communication, methods of communication, and how information technology (IT) influences organizational communication. We will also discuss some specific communication skills, present some barriers to effective communication, and consider ways to overcome those barriers. This chapter should give you an understanding of the communication process and help you to become a more effective communicator as a manager.

The Communication Process

Online Study Center
ACE the Test
Managing Now! LIVE

communication: the transmission of information from one person to another to create a shared understanding and feeling

encoding: converting a thought, idea, or fact into a message composed of symbols, pictures, or words

Communication is the transmission of information from one person to another to create a shared understanding and feeling. The word *communication* actually comes from the Latin word *communicare,* which means to share or make common.[2] Figure 15.1 illustrates the communication process. The six parts of the model of the communication process, other than the message sender and message receiver, are defined as follows:

1. **Encoding** is when the message sender converts or encodes a thought, idea, or fact into a message composed of symbols, pictures, or words.

FIGURE 15.1

The Communication Process

When Anita asks David with anticipation, "Is the contract ready yet?" Anita is the *sender* who *encodes* a message using both words and body language *channels* of communication to inquire about the status of a contract. David is the *receiver* who *decodes* her message. Through the noise of ringing phones and the distraction of an urgent e-mail that just came in, his translation of her message is that she is not angry but curious about whether the contract is finished. David sends Anita verbal *feedback* that he understands her message by replying, "Yes, I put it in your mailbox."

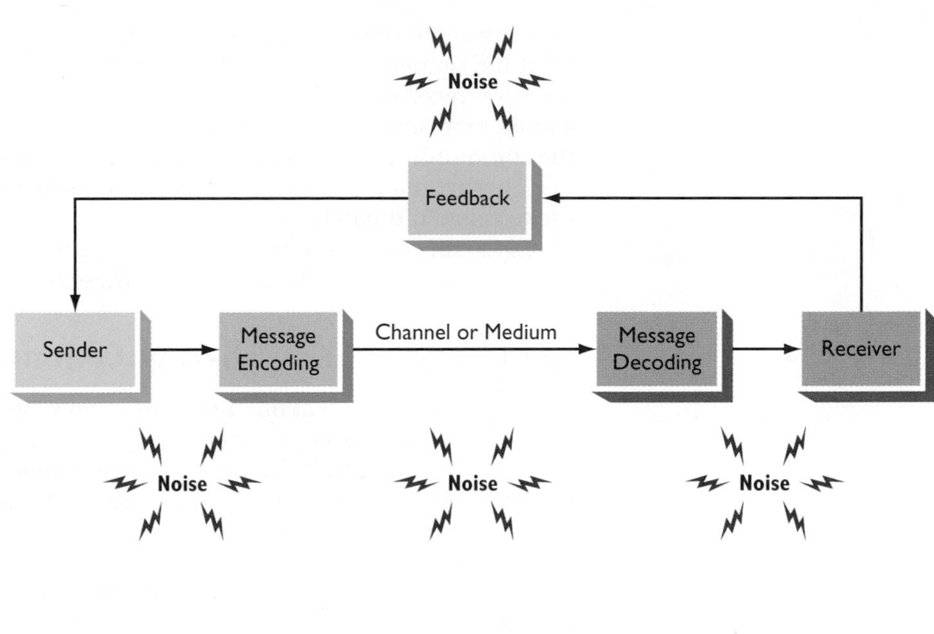

message: the encoded information

2. The **message** is the encoded information that the sender sends. For example, a manager wants to communicate to her new employee Kim that Kim is doing well. The manager encodes that thought into words expressing that Kim's performance has been steadily increasing and that she is performing at 80 percent of her target level. These words are the message. The manager could also create a graph showing Kim's performance pattern and a line representing her target performance level. This graph would then be the message.

channel: the medium used to send the message

3. The **channel** is the medium used to send the message to the receiver, including voice, writing, videos, television, and body language.

decoding: the interpretation and translation of a message back into something that can be understood by the receiver

4. When the message receiver sees, reads, or hears the message, it gets decoded. **Decoding** is the interpretation and translation of the message back into something that can be understood by the receiver. The information resulting from the decoding should be the same as the information the sender intended to communicate.

feedback: a check on the success of the communication

5. **Feedback** is a check on the success of the communication. The message receiver becomes the sender of a new message back to the original sender, and the original sender can assess if the receiver understood the original message as he or she intended. Repeating or paraphrasing the original message, asking for clarification, and asking if your conclusion is correct are examples of feedback.

noise: anything that blocks, distorts, or changes in any way the information the sender intended to communicate

6. **Noise** is anything that blocks, distorts, or changes in any way the information the sender intended to communicate. For example, noise can be something physical in the environment, like machine noise or other people talking, or it can occur because the sender or receiver is distracted by other things and is unable to concentrate on the message being sent or received.

Essentially, in the communication process, the sender translates (encodes) information into words, symbols, or pictures and passes the encoded information to the receiver through some medium (channel). The sender then receives the message and retranslates (decodes) it into a message that is, with luck, the same as what the sender intended. Noise can enter anywhere in the process, making the message received different from the one that the sender intended. Feedback should represent two-way communication that helps to check on the success of the communication and ensure that the received message is accurate.

Throughout the communication process, barriers can make the message that the recipient ultimately receives different from the one sent. These barriers, a form of noise, can come from the sender, the receiver, the organization, or from other forms of noise. We will discuss some of these barriers below.

One-Way and Two-Way Communication

In one-way communication, information flows in only one direction. The sender communicates a message without expecting or getting any feedback from the receiver. For example, if a manager tells an employee to get back to work and the employee does so without saying a word, or if a manager tells an employee that she or he is doing a good job and then leaves before hearing a response, one-way communication has occurred.

When a receiver provides feedback to a sender, the sender and receiver have engaged in two-way communication. If a manager asks an employee to join a client meeting and the employee says, "I'll be right there," two-way communication occurred. Feedback enhances the effectiveness of the communication process by helping to ensure that the intended message is the one received. Have you ever sent an important e-mail and then waited and wondered if the receiver received and understood it? If so, you appreciate the value of two-way communication and feedback.

Communication media can enable synchronous (immediate, like talking to someone face-to-face) or asynchronous (delayed, like leaving a message for someone that she or he receives later) communication. As technology changes, the nature of media can change. For example, telephones originally produced only two-way synchronous communication, but now voice mail allows telephones to provide one-way or asynchronous communication as well. Similarly, e-mail originally generated one- or two-way asynchronous communication, but instant messaging has made it possible to engage in two-way synchronous communication.

Managing Now Information technology (IT) and the Internet have given senders more media channels to choose from than ever before. Managers now regularly use cell phones, voice mail, and instant messaging to communicate. The managers on the cover of this book are using IT devices like wireless laptops, BlackBerries, and cell phones to make two-way communication possible where it has never been possible before.

Communication Barriers

Several potential barriers can prevent effective communication. Table 15.1 summarizes some of the most common barriers that can interfere with the accurate communication of a message.

nonverbal communication: communication that is not spoken or written but that has meaning to others

Nonverbal Communication Our nonverbal behavior and tone is often more important to the meaning of a message than the words we say. **Nonverbal communication** is not spoken or written but has meaning to others. Some of the strongest and most meaningful communication is nonverbal, for example, a smile, or a look of anger on someone's face.

TABLE 15.1
Communications Barriers

Barrier	Description
Body language	Gestures or expressions that carry meaning in themselves, for example, shrugging your shoulders or rolling your eyes.
Verbal intonation	How words are said can affect how they are interpreted.
Selective perception	We select what we are willing to see or hear based on our expectations and beliefs.
Misperception	Messages are not received in the way that they were intended.
Filtering	Information is intentionally withheld, ignored, or distorted to influence the message that is ultimately received.
Information overload	Having so much information that it is impossible to process all of it.
Organizational barriers	The hierarchical structure and culture of an organization can influence who is allowed to communicate what to whom and can limit how messages are sent.
Cultural barriers	Different cultures have different ways of expressing things. For example, a thumbs-up sign does not mean the same thing everywhere in the world.
Noise	Anything that blocks, distorts, or changes the message that the sender intended to communicate. Distractions, the sender's credibility, jargon, and ambiguity are some common sources of noise.

body language: a body movement such as a gesture or expression

The most common nonverbal interpersonal communication involves body language and intonation. **Body language** is a body movement such as a gesture or expression. For example, during a performance appraisal interview, an employee drumming his or her fingers on the table and fidgeting in the chair is communicating anxiety or impatience without saying a word.

The ability to read body language, such as this woman expressing boredom at a meeting, is an important managerial skill.

verbal intonation: the emphasis given to spoken words and phrases

Verbal intonation is the emphasis given to spoken words and phrases. For example, the simple words, "May I speak with you?" can be interpreted very differently if said in a cheery, upbeat tone versus a strong or angry tone. Managers should remember the saying, "It's not what you say that matters but how you say it," every time they communicate. When body language is inconsistent with the spoken message, receivers are more likely to interpret the body language as the "true meaning."[3]

According to noted nonverbal communication researcher Albert Mehrabian, in any face-to-face communication:[4]

- Seven percent of the total message is conveyed by the words.
- Thirty-eight percent of the total message is conveyed by vocal intonation.
- Fifty-five percent of the total message is conveyed by facial and body expressions.

For communication to be effective and meaningful, all three parts of the message need to be similar. If any of the three parts are different, the receiver is receiving conflicting messages.[5]

Consciously controlling our body language is as important a managerial skill as knowing how to interpret others' body language. Managers must control their body signals and tone to ensure that they reinforce their intended message. For example, shifting your eyes and looking away while speaking makes people not trust your message. If you want people to see you as a leader, stand up straight, make eye contact, and smile—those signals project confidence and energy. Walking with slumped shoulders, speaking in a flat tone, and fidgeting will often lead to your being seen as indecisive, negative, or inexperienced.[6] Managers must also be sensitive to how the interpretation of body language varies in different cultures. In some areas of the world, averting your eyes by looking downward is a sign of respect for senior managers, while in others, it is interpreted as a lack of confidence.

selective perception: the tendency to see and hear things according to our beliefs and expectations rather than how they really are

● Misperception People tend not to hear things that they do not want to hear and to hear things that are consistent with what they already believe. **Selective perception** is our tendency to see and hear things according to our beliefs and expectations rather than how they really are. Sometimes people ignore conflicting information and focus on only the information that confirms what they already believe. Selective perception makes a receiver perceive only part of a message because of his or her expectations, needs, motivations, interests, and other personal characteristics.

Managers' functional expertise can influence how they perceive and solve complex problems.[7] Two managers given the same information about a problem may see the problem differently. A manager with a finance background may be more likely to see the problem as financial, while a manager with a production background may be more likely to see it as production-based. Each manager selectively perceives information that is consistent with his or her expertise and expectations and does not pay as much attention to other types of information.

misperception: when a message is not decoded by the receiver in the way the sender intended

Misperception is when a message is not decoded by the receiver in the way the sender intended. A misperception can occur because the sender's body language is inconsistent with the sender's words, and the receiver incorrectly interprets the body language to be the true message. It can also occur if body language or tone is interpreted incorrectly; if the receiver selectively focuses on favorable parts of the sender's message, thus distorting the message's meaning; or if the receiver has poor listening skills.

filtering: less than the full amount of information is received due to withholding, ignoring, or distorting information

● Filtering **Filtering** occurs when people receive less than the full amount of information due to the withholding, ignoring, or distorting of information. Filtering can happen when a sender manipulates information so that the receiver is more likely to perceive it in a favorable way. For example, a manager might tell his or her boss about the things that are going well in the manager's unit and not mention any problems to try to look good during a performance evaluation.

information overload: the amount of information available exceeds a person's ability to process it

● **Information Overload** Filtering can also occur when a receiver has too much information. **Information overload** results when the amount of information available exceeds a person's ability to process it. People faced with too much information have to use some sort of filtering strategy to reduce it to a manageable amount. For example, an executive who starts the day with 500 e-mails in the inbox will apply some sort of filter, such as who sent each e-mail or the urgency conveyed by the sender, to decide which to read and which to delete or save to read later. Filtering is essential to managers because it helps to reduce noise in the communication process. Using technology such as spam filters for e-mail amplifies relevant and accurate information and minimizes the rest.

● **Managing Now** Some companies have used technology to reduce the filtering of messages. For example, Medco Health Solutions wanted to better manage its internal communication and encourage the free flow of information to serve its clients better. Medco built an internal broadcast facility that allows the company to broadcast video with sound to all employee desktop computers in the country. The facility posts taped presentations to the company intranet and hosts real-time interviews and panel discussions with company leaders. Employees can e-mail questions to the people in the studio, who can answer them in real time. This prevents lower-level employees from having to go through the company's hierarchy to get information about company issues. Medco uses polling tools on its intranet and in the broadcast studio to quickly survey employees on important issues.

The broadcast facility has allowed Medco managers to go right to the source to get information that hasn't been filtered as it gets passed around and up the hierarchy. In addition, lower levels of the organization get faster resolution to many of their issues because they can eliminate all of the inefficient filtering and managing that used to take place when the company relied on traditional linear communication channels. An additional benefit of adopting the technology has been greater mutual visibility between the lower and higher levels of the organization, which helps to ensure that everyone shares the same goals and priorities.[8]

Open floor plans facilitate coordination and communication among coworkers.

● **Organizational Barriers** Organizational barriers to communication come from the hierarchical structure and culture of the organization. The hierarchical levels and department specializations within a firm can make communication across levels and departments difficult. Different hierarchical levels typically focus on different types of information, which can interfere with communication. Higher-level executives, for example, typically focus on information related to bigger-picture issues and business strategy, while lower-level employees focus on production issues and deadlines.

Some organizational cultures encourage open communication, while other cultures promote a limited sharing of information. Company spaces can reinforce an organization's communication culture. For example, when music company Muzak moved from

Seattle to Fort Mill, South Carolina, company leaders wanted to take advantage of the move to create more open communication paths. To do this, they designed the new workspace to be completely open, with no cubicle walls. The open environment makes it easy for people to ask questions and offer ideas. This setup facilitates communication and allows the CEO to get ideas from people he previously never would have asked for input.[9]

● **Cultural Barriers** Words and gestures can mean different things in different cultures. For example, in much of the world, the thumbs-up sign means "okay." But in Nigeria, Afghanistan, Iran, and parts of Italy and Greece, it is an obscene insult and carries the same stigmatism as the middle finger does in the United States.

One informal survey of managers from fifteen countries identified lack of cultural understanding as the biggest challenge in communicating with people around the world. Other challenges (in order) were: "being thorough and very careful with interpretations," "careful audience research," "keeping communication simple," "respecting everyone," "using technology as an asset," and "knowing similarities as well as differences."[10]

● **Noise** As we discussed earlier, noise is anything that blocks, distorts, or changes in any way the information that the sender intended to communicate. It can enter anywhere in the communication process and interfere with the successful transmission and reception of a message. We will next discuss some of the most common sources of noise.

Physical barriers that create noise include interruptions, sounds, dim computer screens, or a receiver's headache. Loss of transmission occurs when an Internet connection goes down, phone lines are full of static, or a videoconference link is dropped. Competition from other communication sources, such as employees checking their BlackBerries or whispering to each other during a meeting rather than listening to the speaker, can also create noise.

Ambiguity is another source of noise in communication. Ambiguity of meaning means the receiver isn't sure what the sender meant. (Does "we need to make this happen" mean now or next year?) Ambiguity of intent means the receiver is uncertain about the message's consequences. (What am I supposed to be doing to "make this happen"?) The clearer a message, the less chance ambiguity will cloud its meaning.

Perceptual noise can result from the receiver making unwarranted assumptions and paying more or less attention to what an individual says based on those assumptions. For example, if Rosa assumes that Huan wants to pursue a contract with a vendor, she may erroneously decode his "maybe" as meaning yes and tune out when he describes his concerns.

The sender's credibility can create noise by making the receiver question the accuracy of the message. Jargon, or technical language, can also create ambiguity when the receiver does not understand it. Consider the CEO whose use of jargon prevented audiences from understanding exactly what his company did. He described his company as "a premier developer of intelligent semiconductor intellectual property solutions that dramatically accelerate complex SOC designs while minimizing risk." After some coaching, he more clearly communicated the same information in the statement, "Our technology makes cell phones that are smaller, more powerful, and last longer on a single charge."[11] Effective managers use clear, concrete, and concise language to keep their message simple and understandable.

Semantics are another barrier that introduces noise into communication. Words mean different things to different people. *Soon* might mean "immediately" to one person and "in a few days" or "in a few weeks" to another. Asking for feedback helps the sender ensure that his or her intended meaning is the same as the one ultimately received.

● **Managing Now** Some companies rely on technology to minimize the effect of barriers to effective communication. For example, DreamWorks Animation has three major locations that often need to communicate with one another.[12] However, traditional communication media are ineffective for communicating about animation, and they add noise that distorts messages. CEO Jeffrey Katzenberg says, "We convey stories and ideas and emotions through pictures and words. . . . It's a science and an art, and a lot of it is nonverbal." So DreamWorks created a videoconferencing system to improve productivity and the quality of the company's internal communication.

DreamWorks' custom videoconferencing room resembles a typical corporate boardroom. Meeting participants who are physically present sit on one side of the table, opposite their remote colleagues shown on three giant flat-screen monitors. A fourth screen allows participants to share documents, drawings, and animated sequences. The audio system lets people talk over one another, just as they would in a traditional meeting, rather than waiting for a speaker to finish.

Organizational Communication

Online Study Center
ACE the Test
Managing Now! LIVE

organizational communication: the exchange of information that creates a common basis of understanding and feeling among two or more individuals or groups in an organization

Organizational communication is an exchange of information that creates a common basis of understanding and feeling among two or more individuals or groups in an organization. Organizational communication can move in a variety of directions and can be formal or informal in nature. Figure 15.2 illustrates upward, diagonal, downward, and horizontal communication paths in an organization.

Downward Communication

Downward communication occurs when higher-level employees communicate to those at lower levels in the organization, for example, from a manager to a subordinate. Downward communication typically consists of messages about how to do a job, performance goals, the firm's policies, and how the company is performing.

Management by wandering around is a face-to-face management technique in which managers get out of their offices and spend time talking informally to employees throughout the organization.[13] Being actively engaged in the day-to-day operations of the business gives managers a feel for what is really going on in the company. For example, in the first six months after Gary Kusin became CEO of Kinko's Inc., before it became FedEx Kinko's, he went into each of Kinko's twenty-four markets in the United States, visited over 200 stores, and met with over 2,500 team members to learn what the company needed to do to continue evolving.[14]

● **Managing Now** IT and the Internet have given managers more choices in how to communicate downward, including e-mail, instant messaging, intranets, portals, wikis, blogs, and webcasts, in addition to traditional verbal and written communication. Managers need to fit the medium to the message, use appropriate body language and nonverbal cues, and ensure that subordinates understand

FIGURE 15.2

Communication Paths in an Organization

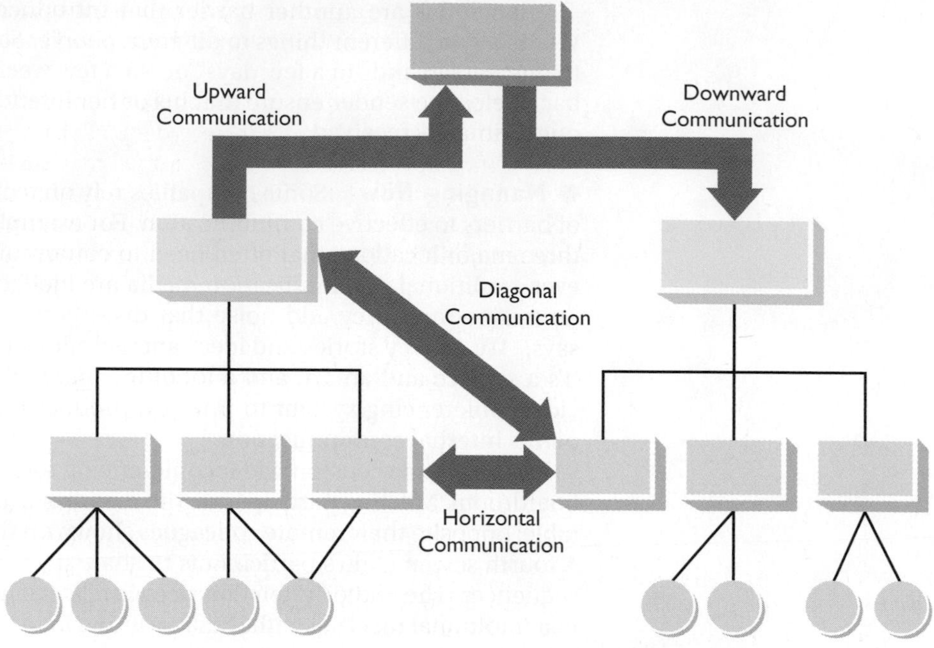

the meaning of the messages sent. As Lucent discovered (see the Practice IT feature on page 447), it is also a good idea to understand how employees like to be communicated with and to seek their feedback about how different communication channels are working.

Upward Communication

Upward communication occurs when lower-level employees communicate with those at higher levels, for example, when a subordinate tells a manager about a problem she or he is having with a customer's request. Encouraging upward communication can help managers check that subordinates understand their goals and instructions, keep managers informed of employee challenges and complaints, and cultivate acceptance and commitment by giving employees the opportunity to express ideas and suggestions.[15]

Despite its potential benefits, getting subordinates to give upward feedback can be challenging. Subordinates often filter bad news, fearing that their bosses do not really want to hear it. A manager who is approachable and accessible and who creates a culture of trust and openness can help subordinates feel more comfortable giving upward feedback. Not overreacting, being defensive, or blameful and respecting confidentiality when a subordinate shares potentially controversial or negative information can help. Attitude surveys, an open-door policy, and regular face-to-face meetings with subordinates can also foster upward communication. One of the best ways to build trust and make subordinates feel comfortable sharing negative information may be sympathetically listening during your daily informal contacts with them in and outside the workplace.[16]

● **Managing Now** Technology tools such as wikis can enhance upward communication in organizations and make all employees part of the brainstorming and problem-solving process. For example, when a manager at an investment bank wanted an analysis of how to double profits on a particular trade, he put the problem on a wiki page where other employees could comment, brainstorm, and edit in real time. In two days, the manager had analytics that would have otherwise taken two weeks.[17]

Technology helps keep managers connected to subordinates in other ways. Old Navy staffers are all connected to the back room via headsets that provide two-way communication so that they can get real-time announcements about out-of-stock items and substitutions as well as real-time responses to customer questions they can't answer.[18] By facilitating both upward and downward communication, this technology helps to improve customer service and boost sales.

Horizontal Communication

Horizontal communication occurs when someone in an organization communicates with others at the same organizational level. Managers often depend on each other to help get the job done, and communication is necessary for them to coordinate resources and workflow. Although horizontal communication occurs between peers, as in all organizational communication, it is important to stay professional and avoid belligerent words and negative body language. Managers can facilitate horizontal or interdepartmental communication by appointing liaison personnel or creating interdepartmental committees or task forces to facilitate communication and coordination and solve common problems.

The Window on Managing Now feature describes how Sperry Marine uses portals to improve horizontal communication and improve project team performance.

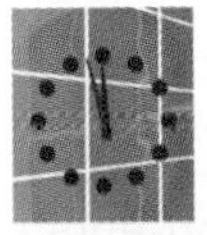

Window on Managing Now
Using Portals to Improve Performance

Portals are pages on a company's intranet that contain links to other sites on the company's intranet. Organizations adopt project management portals to give their executives easy access to the latest project information. Portals also make it easier for their project teams to share information, stay informed of changes, and collaborate. Sperry Marine, a business unit of the global aerospace and defense giant Northrop Grumman, implemented a project management portal to create virtual rooms for collaborating on requests for proposals and resulting projects. The portal also provides a centralized, visible location for coordinated document storage, information, and schedule tracking.

The portal has improved horizontal communication dramatically. "Before using the portal, people had to e-mail back and forth or call to stay informed," says Thea Yancey, proposal manager with Sperry Marine. "The wrong version of a document could be passed to somebody and team members might miss information if they missed meetings. Now everyone gets general information from the portal's home pages, reviews an up-to-date notice board, checks documents in and out, accesses process and risk information, and views live schedule and milestone reports."[19]

Goodrich Aviation Technical Services uses a project management portal, along with a project-scheduling system, to manage the maintenance and repair of Boeing 737 aircraft. With these integrated tools, the company decreased turnaround time from thirty-seven to about twenty-seven days. Goodrich maintenance teams receive real-time work orders and assignments live through the portal. Teams can quickly adjust when a part is missing because that information is communicated instantly on the portal. Mechanics enter progress updates on the shop floor, giving managers the most up-to-the-minute information that allows them to adjust quickly. Decision makers are also able to detect problems earlier because the portal makes schedule status immediately visible and keeps senior managers continually up to date.[20]

Diagonal Communication

When employees communicate across departments *and* levels, they are engaging in diagonal communication. For example, if Lorenzo's subordinate, Amy, contacts Lorenzo's peer in a different department, diagonal communication has occurred. Diagonal communication is common in cross-functional project teams composed of people from different levels drawn from different departments.

Diagonal communication allows employees in different parts of an organization to contribute to creating a new product or solving a problem. Diagonal communication also helps to link groups and spread information around the firm. Almost all successful managers use these informal communication networks to monitor employee communication and to communicate quickly with employees.[21]

IT and the Internet can facilitate horizontal and diagonal communication through the company's intranet, portals, and wikis. By creating a central location where employees can post questions and help solve problems other employees are dealing with, communication can occur among employees who would be unable to communicate without the use of technology. For organizations with multiple locations, IT and the Internet can create employee networks that allow employees located around the world to work together and share knowledge. The Practice IT feature presents another example.

Formal and Informal Communication

Formal communication is official, organization-sanctioned communication. It can be upward, downward, horizontal, or diagonal. Formal communication channels typically involve some sort of written communication that provides a permanent record of the exchange.

Informal communication is communication that is not official. Informal communication includes gossip and answering another employee's question about how to do something. Rumors and the grapevine are also examples of informal communication. The grapevine refers to social networks in organizations that allow employees to exchange information. These informal networks can be helpful because they give employees access to people elsewhere in the company who can help solve problems and get work done. It is often recommended that new employees try to tap into existing social networks to learn how to do their work successfully.[22]

But the grapevine can also promote the spread of gossip or rumors, which can be destructive and interfere with the functioning of the company, particularly if they are untrue.[23] You should not avoid the grapevine, but be sure to evaluate the credibility of the source before you believe what you hear.[24] If the rumor doesn't make sense or is inconsistent with other things you know or have heard, seek more information before reacting.

As a manager, being aware of current office gossip can help to keep you informed of what is on employees' minds and prevent rumors from growing out of control. It is best to prevent rumors from starting by establishing clear communication channels, building trust with your employees, and providing employees adequate facts and information. If a rumor does start to spread, neutralize it by communicating consistently and honestly with employees about the issue. Not making a comment is usually seen by employees as confirmation of a rumor.[25]

PRACTICE IT
Technology-Enabled Communication at Lucent[26]

Lucent relies heavily on IT to facilitate communication with and among employees around the world. Lucent continually uses employee feedback submitted through its intranet to assess which communication methods employees prefer and what is and is not working. Through this feedback, Lucent has learned how best to focus its communication to reach a variety of different audiences. Communication through satellite broadcasts, e-mail messages, and Internet publications helps to share information with employees. Mary Lou Ambrus, Lucent's vice president of group communications, says, "Global communication becomes almost instantaneous when posted to the web site. We can send out an internal press release and ensure that employees are getting accurate information as quickly as possible." When big news hits, audio files are quickly posted to the website so that employees can listen to the leader's message.

Lucent relies on the Internet to make its internal communication entirely Web-based. Bill Price, Lucent's director of corporate communications, and his team researched how to make the site user-friendly and interactive. "Our main Internet homepage, MyLucent, has two weekly feature articles that reinforce the strategic vision and positioning of the company. This prompts weekly employee visits to the MyLucent page, making it easier for us to get important information to employees in a timely fashion." Lucent also distributes a subscriber-based e-mail publication with additional company information.

To ensure that employees share the same organizational goals, once a quarter the CEO and the executive leadership team webcast what the company has done in the prior quarter and what needs to be done in the future. These webcasts are then archived on Lucent's website, making it possible for employees around the world to view the messages at a time that is most convenient for them. Clips of Lucent leaders reflecting on pivotal moments or discussing important topics, such as innovation and taking a risk, are also posted weekly on the MyLucent site. Price says, "Employees want more candor in communications—they want to hear the real voice of what is going on in the business. While we try to reflect this in our written communications, employees often interpret this as 'the company line.' When it's the executive's own voice, the message is given much more credibility." The webcast medium has been so well received by employees that Lucent leaders have begun doing their own webcasts with their teams and archiving them for employees to view when it fits their schedules.

Communication Media

Online Study Center
ACE the Test
Managing Now! LIVE

Information technology has changed the way communication occurs in organizations.[27] Managers now have a variety of communication media available for use. We will discuss some of the most commonly used media next.

The Internet

The Internet has fundamentally changed how many managers communicate. Managers are no longer the filtration system for all information coming into an organization. Now they are responsible for aligning information with business goals, and they act as facilitators by bringing the right people together to solve business problems as a collaborative community. Individuals using the Internet can select only the information they want using information pull.[28] This contrasts with the old broadcast technique of information push, where people receive information just in case they need it.

● **Managing Now: Alpine Access** Sometimes, face-to-face communication simply is not possible. That's true at Alpine Access, a provider of outsourced call-center services based in Golden, Colorado. Nearly all of the company's 7,500 employees work from home and are located around the country—senior executives at the company rarely see them. Hiring, training, day-to-day management, and strategic planning are done electronically or over the phone. "There's no opportunity to look into someone's eyes to make sure they understand what's being said," says cofounder Jim Ball. So the company has developed a number of practices to compensate, and these practices can boost the effectiveness of e-mail at any company.

First, clarity is a priority. Important messages, such as the idea that everyone needs to work harder to meet a monthly target, are checked for everything from grammar to nuance. Second, employees must acknowledge receipt of every e-mail and can immediately ask questions. Managers seek feedback by regularly checking that employees are on track and not missing any critical information. Third, telephone calls are made for truly difficult conversations, such as performance reviews. "You can be just as empathetic over the phone as you would be in person," a company leader insists. "It's more difficult, but it can be done."[29]

Although technology should never replace all human interaction between leaders and subordinates, it can help the communication process by giving leaders more ways to communicate with their employees. For example, e-mail is now an accepted way to communicate with employees and customers. It enables managers to prioritize incoming communications and to catch up while away from work. Key company employees are accessible via e-mail twenty-four hours a day, seven days a week. Work is completed faster because people can e-mail documents to each other and quickly receive feedback. In many organizations, e-mail is a primary and formal means of business correspondence.

Instant messaging enables users to chat with other employees in real time rather than e-mailing and waiting for a response. This method allows employees to get in touch with each other immediately to get input or ask questions. Voice mail is similar to e-mail, but instead of writing, a spoken message is digitized and sent to someone to be retrieved and listened to later. Like e-mails, voice mails can be saved or sent to others.

● **Managing Now: Medco Health Solutions** IT and the Internet have changed some of the skills managers need to be effective communicators. For example, Medco Health Solutions, Inc., is a virtual, real-time, fully networked pharmacy benefit management community. Instant messaging is available companywide and is used constantly to provide high-quality customer service. Most corporate managers are rarely without their wireless laptops. Because meeting customer needs is Medco's priority, managers are even expected to respond to customer-oriented instant messages during meetings. Although this can create some distractions, managers have become good at multitasking and have learned to handle the multiple communication channels open to them at any one time.[30]

Videoconferencing enhances the quality of communication with people in other locations.

Managers are increasingly using cell phone–personal digital assistant hybrids, wireless messaging devices, smart phones, and wireless devices using Internet-based calling systems to communicate with employees. For example, technology distributor Avnet introduced a program that allows executives to make international calls from their laptops using an Internet-based calling system, which yields a savings of more than $1 million annually.[31]

Managers can also use various software tools to meet with staff without being face-to-face. Videoconferencing can enable leaders to communicate effectively with employees and customers. By allowing the parties to see as well as hear each other, videoconferencing can be a very effective form of communication. At the Global Outsourcing Group at Unisys Corporation, leaders regularly use videoconferencing to stay in touch with telecommuting staff. Any employee can schedule a telephone meeting over Unisys's phone system.[32]

● **Managing Now: Telework** Bear Stearns's associate director of corporate marketing, Chris DiFiglia, says, "Bear Stearns first deployed video conferencing . . . because the company was expanding rapidly and needed to stay connected with our branch offices all over the world. Today, video conferencing is an ingrained part of the Bear Stearns culture. It helps us save money on travel, and, even more important, it helps our employees work more effectively and increases productivity."[33] Bear Stearns holds 150 to 200 videoconferences each month, with most calls including three to four different sites. Bear Stearns also uses videoconferencing frequently for hiring, thus saving travel costs on plane tickets and accommodations by interviewing candidates remotely. "While you can't always replace an initial handshake with a video call, many a deal has been closed over video at Bear Stearns," says DiFiglia.[34]

Telework is work conducted in a location other than a central office or production facility, with communication between coworkers and supervisors occurring via electronic communication systems.[35] Immunex, Nortel, and Washington Mutual all use telework. There are four major types of telework:[36]

1. Home-based telecommuting includes people who work at home for some period on a regular basis, but not necessarily every day. Security, the challenge of motivating employees from a distance, and loneliness can be drawbacks to home-based telecommuting.
2. Satellite offices are offices situated to be more convenient for employees and/or customers. These offices are located away from what would normally be the main office location.
3. Neighborhood work centers provide office space for the employees of more than one company to save commuting time to central locations.
4. Mobile work refers to work completed by traveling employees who use technology to communicate with the office as necessary from places such as client offices, airports, cars, hotels, and so forth.

Telecommuting allows organizations to reduce the amount of office space they own or rent, and it decreases employees' need to commute to work. If telecommuting employees sometimes need to work at the company's location, the company can set up a hoteling space for them. This space gives visiting telecommuting employees who don't have dedicated office space at the company's location a cubicle or office in which to set up their laptop computer, log in, and be immediately connected to the company's intranet. They can then work effectively at the company's location when they need to. Deloitte Consulting and Boeing both use hoteling.

Collaboration Software

Computer software such as Microsoft's SharePoint allows members of workgroups and teams to share information to improve their communication, efficiency, and performance. Collaborative software, also called groupware, enhances the collaborative abilities of group or team members by providing an electronic meeting site. It essentially integrates work being done on a single project simultaneously by several employees at different computers located anywhere in the world.[37] General Foods and Seagate Software[38] both use groupware.

Collaborative writing systems allow group members to work simultaneously on written documents through a network of interconnected computers. As team members work on different sections of the document, each member has access to the entire document and can modify his or her section to be compatible with the rest of it. Siemens and IBM use collaborative writing systems.

A group scheduling system lets group members input their daily schedules into a common scheduling database. This system makes it faster and easier to identify the best times for meetings and to schedule them quickly. Both World Family Financial and Bear Stearns use group scheduling systems.

Workflow automation systems use technology to facilitate and speed up work processes. The system sends documents, information, or tasks to the right people or places based on the established procedure. For example, after one person signs a document, the system automatically sends it to the next person for a signature.

Software tools can help groups make more effective decisions.

Group decision support systems are interactive, computer-based systems that help decision-making teams find solutions to unstructured problems that require judgment, evaluation, and insights.[39] Team members can meet in the same room or be located in separate places and interact via their computers. Software tools, including electronic questionnaires, brainstorming tools, idea organizers, and voting tools to weigh and prioritize recommended solutions, help the group make decisions. A group decision support system can reduce the likelihood that one member will dominate the discussion and helps groups avoid many of the barriers that face-to-face groups encounter. The Canadian National Railway System, Pfizer, and Bayer use group decision support systems to improve their decision-making processes.

Intranets

An intranet is a type of centralized information clearinghouse. At its simplest, an intranet is a website stored on a computer that is connected to other company computers by an internal network. Employees reach the intranet site with standard Web-browser software such as Netscape or Microsoft's Internet Explorer. An intranet can be connected to the Internet so that suppliers and customers can visit using company-issued passwords. In such cases, firewall software can be installed to act as a barrier between the internal systems and unauthorized outsiders.

Because they centralize data and provide easy access, intranets are a good idea when a company's employees use several different types of computers and all of the users need to reach the same company information. Intranets give employees controlled access to the information stored on a company's network, which can reduce the need for paper versions of documents such as manuals and company forms. Intranets are not useful if many employees do not use or have access to computers or if no one has the expertise to set up and manage the intranet. Many companies now use intranets, including Intel, Nike, and Safeco Insurance.

● Portals Portals are similar to intranets but tend to be more project-focused rather than providing a wide variety of information like an intranet does. Portals strongly resemble Internet sites like Yahoo.com and AOL.com. Users interact with them with a standard computer browser like Internet Explorer or Netscape, but instead of containing links to news and weather, the links lead employees to sites on the company's private intranet.

Portals can make project status continually visible to managers through real-time reports and visual cues such as red-yellow-green status signals or digital dashboards. Portals allow managers to use their browsers to get high-level summaries of project status at any time. Some portals also provide visual comparisons and metrics between projects within a program.[40]

Project managers use portals to manage schedules and any issues that arise. By centralizing a variety of project information, portals allow managers to track progress and identify any problems early. Managers can also use portals to quickly disseminate information (documents, processes, notices, etc.) to all of their team members, wherever they are located, and solicit input and feedback in a controlled manner.[41]

Portals allow team members to easily share news and ideas, enhancing collaboration and project implementation efficiency. Project managers can delegate responsibilities to individual team members yet still retain control of the project.[42] Portals are often customizable, allowing employees to subscribe to only the information they need.

Portals can be integrated with other applications. For example, one button on a portal might call up yesterday's production charts, another lets employees check their 401(k) balance, and a third lets employees tell colleagues about how they solved important customer problems. Portals also let everyone in a company share databases, documents, calendars, and contact lists. They make it possible to collaborate easily with coworkers in remote locations and even conduct instant employee-opinion polls. By consolidating information and connecting employees with each other, they help companies function as a single unit rather than as individual entities.[43] Companies using portals include EDS, Ford Motor, and Merrill Lynch.

Until recently, portals were strictly for big business. Because they require an intranet, the cost was prohibitive. Their complexity also required a team of computer specialists to set up and administer. But intranets have become more common as software vendors like IBM, Microsoft and Oracle, Plumtree and SAP have developed packaged portal solutions to suit almost every size business and meet almost every business need.[44]

When team members see the big picture of the whole project through a portal, they have a greater appreciation of the impact of their part on the rest of the project. They often feel more involved in the project and want to add to its successful completion. Team members know that progress on their own tasks is visible, too, which also helps motivate productivity.[45] This is consistent with the idea of task identity leading to greater motivation, as we discussed in Chapter 14.

● Managing Now In addition to portals for their employees and customers to use in interacting with the company and employee portals to facilitate work, companies are using specialized portals to meet specific goals. For example, to help control health-care premiums, insurance brokerage firm Keenan & Associates of Torrance, California, created a Web-based portal to encourage employees to eat right and exercise more. The service, KeenanFit, offers customized fitness, nutrition, and self-improvement plans for employees and their families. The portal also allows employees to complete self-assessments to monitor specific health risks.[46]

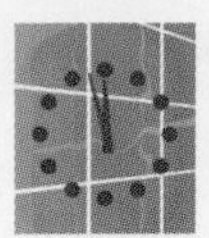

WINDOW ON MANAGING NOW
Building an Intranet

Companies like ExxonMobil recognize that their globally dispersed and increasingly mobile workforce make knowledge management, collaboration, and wireless communication technologies more important to their success than ever.[47] Firms including Boeing, Ford Motor Company, and Sandia National Laboratories are turning to their intranets to address their coordination and communication needs. But how do you start building a company intranet? Here are some recommendations:[48]

1. *Use the intranet as a productivity and communication tool.* First establish what the intranet should contain. What types of information or services would make employees more productive? Needs vary from company to company, but some popular elements include human resources information (the employee handbook, vacation and sick-leave policies, change-of-address forms, etc.), business forms, the ability to book a conference room online, and company news.
2. *Make a single person or group responsible for the intranet.* Depending on your company's size, an employee can manage an intranet in addition to his or her regular role, or one person might manage an entire department responsible for the intranet. Content for the intranet can come from many sources, but to maintain consistency, only one person, or one group, should be responsible for approving the content and setting standards.
3. *Keep pages simple.* All intranet pages should be consistent in format and work in a similar way. Using templates can help ensure simplicity and consistency.
4. *Keep the information updated, trustworthy, and reliable.*
5. *Avoid information overload.* Don't try to cram too much information onto a single page.
6. *The intranet homepage should include company news, easy-to-understand navigation, and a search option.* If it is difficult to use, it won't be used.
7. *Test the usability of your intranet.* Intranet features can't be too complicated, and the links must be clearly labeled, or the intranet won't be used. Before launching an intranet, ask a few employees to use it to solve a problem or locate a form and watch how they do it and how much time it takes. Ask for their feedback about whether the intranet is easy to use and intuitive.
8. *Evaluate the intranet and modify it over time.* An organization's intranet needs change over time, as the company's priorities change and as the ways the intranet can add value change.

Although company intranets can facilitate communication, they require some time and thought to set up. The Window on Managing Now feature gives you some recommendations for setting up a company intranet.

webcasts: live or prerecorded video segments that are broadcast over a company's intranet and archived for employees to view later

Webcasts are live or prerecorded video segments that are broadcast over a company's intranet and archived for employees to view later. They can help higher levels of management communicate with more employees and communicate messages more effectively because the executives can use voice and even video to express the message through intonation and body language. And as Lucent's director of corporate communications said in the Practice IT example, "When it's the executive's own voice, the message is given much more credibility."

wikis: searchable, archiveable websites that allow people to comment on and edit one another's work in real time.

Wikis are searchable, archiveable websites that allow people to comment on and edit one another's work in real time. The name *wiki* is based on the Hawaiian term *wiki,* meaning "fast."[49] Wikis are well suited for collaborative writing because they allow users to quickly and easily add and edit content. Wikis are essentially a simplified system of creating webpages combined with a system that records and catalogs all revisions. This allows entries to be changed to a previous state at any time. A wiki system may also include tools to provide users with an easy way to monitor the constantly changing state of the wiki and a place to discuss and resolve any issues or disagreements over wiki content.[50]

Wikis are easy to use and inexpensive. Because real-time project information is located in one easy-to-access place, project completion times can be greatly reduced. Unlike a portal or intranet, wikis have no inherent structure. Some emerging wiki conventions are an automatically generated list of pages recently changed and an index of all of the wiki's pages.[51] Access can be restricted to a limited group of people and even require passwords. Disney, Kodak, Cingular, and Motorola have all found ways to use wikis successfully.[52]

● **Managing Now** IT and the Internet have made it easier for organizations to communicate with people outside the organization. When Intuit wanted to connect with more tax professionals, it created a free wiki called TaxAlmanac.org, where thousands of professors, authors, and tax attorneys contributed thousands of articles as a tax law resource.[53]

Blogs are individuals' personal accounts of thoughts and interests. Some blogs function as online diaries. A typical blog combines text, images, and links to other blogs, webpages, and other media related to its topic.[54] Companies such as McDonald's, General Motors, Walt Disney, Boeing, Nokia, and Kodak have established blogs to enhance internal communication. In some cases, a CEO will create a blog to communicate more directly with employees and stakeholders. Companies like Sun Microsystems, Google, and Maytag have set up both customer blogs and internal ones, too.[55] A wiki listing the *Fortune* 500 companies that have a blog is on the Internet at http://www.fortune500blogs.com/.

● **Managing Now** When the investment bank Dresdner Kleinwort Wasserstein wanted to make it easier for its employees to collaborate, it used blogs and wikis. Now that its 1,500 employees create, comment, and revise projects in real time, meeting times have been cut in half, and productivity has increased.[56] Boeing even set up blog kiosks at its annual strategy meeting for the company's top 1,000 defense executives. While the CEO and his team discussed hot topics, executives responded via the kiosks. Executives also discussed some of the comments from the blog later in the meeting.[57]

Oral Communication

Despite the speed and convenience of IT message channels, some, like email, tend to promote one-way communication and decrease feedback opportunities. If used improperly, these message channels can increase the chances of miscommunication because the receiver has less opportunity to ask questions or get clarification. They can also decrease the quality of decisions if it is harder for employees to make suggestions or share concerns.

IT and the Internet have changed the ways many managers communicate, but there will always be a need for managers to communicate face-to-face. One expert advises people to use electronic communication only to transmit and confirm simple information and to have actual conversations for anything that could possibly be sensitive.[58] Some companies, like Veritas Software, designate one day a week to be e-mail-free to promote greater in-person communication.

Communicating in person is also important to building credibility and trust. One DreamWorks representative says that despite technological advances, face-to-face conversations are still critical—especially in the early stages of a project. "When you meet someone, there's that instinctive, involuntary chemical reaction, where you decide what you think and whether you trust them."[59]

Media Richness

Communication media can be classified in terms of their richness, or the media's ability to carry nonverbal cues, provide rapid feedback, convey personality traits, and support the use of natural language.[60] The richness of a medium depends on four factors:

1. *Interactivity or the availability of feedback.* Immediate feedback allows senders to adjust their messages—richer media provide faster feedback.
2. *The ability to transmit multiple cues.* Multiple cues include physical presence, voice inflection, nonverbal cues, and pictures. Richer media allow the communication of multiple cues.
3. *Language variety for conveying a broad set of concepts and ideas.* For example, ideas about a new advertising campaign cannot be expressed in as many ways in a letter as they can in a face-to-face conversation. Richer media allow for greater language variety.
4. *The personal focus of the medium.* Personal focus is the degree to which the medium allows the expression of emotions and other social cues.

The more a medium displays these four attributes, the richer it is. Otherwise, it is leaner. Face-to-face interaction is the richest medium because it has the capacity for immediate feedback, carries multiple cues, and uses natural language.

When communicating, managers must choose the medium that best matches the information richness that the task or communication requires.[61] The more ambiguous and uncertain a task is, the richer the medium should be that supports it. For example, text-based computer messaging is a good fit for generating ideas but not for negotiating conflicts. Videoconferencing is a good fit for decision-making tasks, but is often not rich enough for negotiating. Table 15.2 describes how different media compare in terms of their richness.

TABLE 15.2
The Media Richness of Various Managerial Communications

Media	Richness	Feedback Availability	Number of Cues	Language Variety	Personal Focus
Face-to-face interaction	High	High	High	High	High
Videoconferencing	High	High	High	High	High
Telephone	Moderate	Moderate	Moderate	Moderate	High
Instant messaging[62]	Moderate	High	Low	Low	Moderate
E-mail	Moderate	Moderate	Low	Low	Moderate
Personal written correspondence	Low	Low	Low	Low	Low
Formal written correspondence	Low	Low	Low	Low	Low

Interpersonal Communication Skills

Communicating effectively is an important leadership and managerial skill. Many barriers exist to good communication, but improving your communication skills can help to overcome these barriers.

Listening Skills

active listening: becoming actively involved in the process of listening to what others are saying and focusing on the meaning of messages

Listening is not the same as hearing. Hearing is passive, whereas listening is an active search for meaning. **Active listening** plays an important role in communication and is especially important for effective leadership. It requires becoming actively involved in the process of listening to what others are saying and focusing on the meaning of messages. Both parties should engage in active listening until it's clear that each understands the final message.

Being an active listener requires asking (at least to yourself), "What is the sender really saying?" When someone speaks, try to identify any ambiguous words and any discrepancies between the speaker's words and nonverbal cues. Then reflect the message back to the sender, paraphrasing and repeating the message in your own words. The person with whom you are speaking should either confirm your understanding or restate his or her message if there is a misunderstanding. This allows both parties to continue to work toward mutual understanding until you both are sure you understand each other.

Active listening requires the receiver to tune out noise and concentrate on the message. It is harder than it sounds—it can be as difficult to refrain from interrupting a speaker as it can be to keep your mind from wandering while listening to someone else. Ways to be an active listener include asking open-ended questions and sending the other person feedback to check that you understand the message—for example, by saying, "You're really overloaded with work today, I guess." Making eye contact, nodding occasionally, and showing appropriate nonverbal behaviors also show the sender that you are listening. Here is one expert's list of good listening skills:[63]

- Pay close attention to individual inferences, facts, and judgments and make useful and logical connections between what you have heard on multiple occasions.
- Give speakers clear, nonverbal evidence that you are listening attentively, including leaning toward the speaker, maintaining eye contact, and not fidgeting.
- Give speakers clear verbal evidence that you are listening attentively, including giving constructive feedback, paraphrasing, and questioning for clarification and refinement.
- Show the speaker respect by not interrupting and by using an inclusive, friendly, and sharing tone rather than an exclusionary, hostile, and condescending tone.
- Follow up on unusual or inconsistent communication cues from the speaker, such as changes in tone, vocabulary, and body language, to determine the real message that the speaker is trying to send.
- Use what the speaker says or infers to determine his or her motives, self-interest, and expectation(s) of listeners.
- Offer speakers honest, clear, timely, respectful, and relevant acknowledgment of what they have said.

Persuading Skills

Managing often requires persuading others. The manager who wants more resources, the supervisor who wants to keep a key employee from leaving, and the company president who wants to sell her idea to the board of directors all need to be persuasive. Because most people are resistant to altering their habits, managers need to use persuasion skills whenever they need to create change.[64] As we discussed in Chapter 13, persuasion is a more effective way to lead when it gets people to do things differently because they want to, not because they have been ordered to.

Persuasion requires several things: thorough and careful preparation; the compelling framing of arguments; the presentation of vivid supporting evidence; and finding the correct emotional match with the audience. It is much more than a sales skill. As one expert says, "Many businesspeople misunderstand persuasion, and more still underutilize it."[65] Here are some recommendations for being more persuasive:

- Build credibility. Using good posture, an appropriate tone of voice, and showing a sense of confidence increases the chances that others will quickly see you as credible.[66]
- Do not begin with a hard sell. This gives potential opponents something to resist and fight against.[67]
- Search for shared ground. Every audience is different, and it is important not to come across as if you have already made up your mind. Communicate in words easily understood and related to by the audience, incorporate values and beliefs they share, and be willing to compromise.[68]
- Develop compelling positions based on only a few convincing arguments rather than overwhelming people with facts and information.
- Connect with people emotionally rather than relying solely on logical arguments. Appealing to people's needs can better persuade them.
- Create a continuous feedback loop between the audience and yourself. Incorporate the audience's perspective into your own arguments.[69]
- Be patient—people are rarely persuaded on the first try.[70]

"Is that your final answer?"

Negotiating Skills

negotiation: a process in which two or more parties make offers, counteroffers, and concessions to reach an agreement

Negotiation is a process in which two or more parties make offers, counteroffers, and concessions to reach an agreement. Most managers do a lot of negotiating as part of their jobs. Job offers and contracts with customers and suppliers have to be negotiated, resources need to be secured and shared with other departments, and deals have to be cut with bosses and subordinates.

There are two types of negotiation: distributive and integrative. Distributive negotiation (also called competitive negotiation) occurs under zero-sum conditions, where any gain to one party is offset by an equivalent loss to the other party.[71] Distributive negotiation essentially distributes resources among the parties involved. Because distributive negotiation structures the conflict in a win-lose way, it tends to be competitive and adversarial as the parties negotiate who is going to get how much. For example, every dollar one manager gets from the company's total budget is a dollar another manager does not get. Distributive negotiation is a good choice when the relationship with the other person is not important but winning is.

Integrative (or principled) negotiation is a win-win negotiation in which the agreement allows both parties to walk away feeling that they've won.[72] In general, integrative negotiation is better than distributive negotiation because neither party feels that it has lost when it is over. Integrative negotiation helps to build good long-term relationships and minimizes grudges between the parties. This is particularly beneficial when the parties have to work together on an ongoing basis once the negotiations are finished.

The classic example of integrative negotiation involves a dispute over an orange. Two people say that they want the whole orange. In a simple distributive negotiation decision, the mediator might simply give each person half of the orange. However, if the parties' interests were considered, there could have been a different, win-win outcome. One person wanted to eat the meat of the orange, but the other wanted just the peel to use in a recipe. If the mediator had understood their interests, they both could have gotten all of what they wanted rather than just half.[73]

The four fundamental principles of integrative negotiation are:[74]

- *Separate the people from the problem.* Separate relationship issues (or "people problems" such as emotions, misperceptions, or communication issues) from substantive issues, and deal with them independently.
- *Focus on interests, not positions.* Negotiate about issues that people really want and need, not what they say they want or need.
- *Invent options for mutual gain.* Look for new solutions to the problem that will allow both sides to win rather than fight over the original positions that assume one side must lose for one to win.
- *Insist on objective criteria.* Outside, objective fairness criteria (like the terms of another company's union-management contract) for the negotiated agreement are ideal, if they exist.

When negotiating, it is helpful to research and understand the individual with whom you will be negotiating. Try to begin with a positive exchange, create an open and trusting environment, and emphasize win-win situations. Be sure to prepare well, listen actively, and think through your alternatives. The more options you feel you have, the better your negotiating position.[75] Here are one expert's suggestions for being an effective negotiator:[76]

- *Do not look at a deal as an either/or proposition.* Negotiating is about compromise.
- *Identify what you can and cannot part with.* Identify the details most important to you and those details that are less important. Act like everything is important and grudgingly concede ground on the details that matter less to you. The other party will count these concessions as victories and might yield on issues you value more.
- *Try to identify and use sources of leverage.* Leverage consists of anything that can help or hinder a party in a bargaining situation. For example, a seller who must sell is at a disadvantage, and if the other party needs to move quickly, you might be able to make a tougher offer. Competing offers can also increase the leverage one party has over another.

- *Show the other side that you understand her or his position.* Help the other person to see you as an ally by mirroring their emotions. If the other person appears frustrated, let him or her know that you recognize he or she is frustrated. They may respond with, "You're right I'm frustrated!" and now you're agreeing on something. By empathizing with the other party, you stand a better chance of preserving a cordial and productive atmosphere.
- *Suppress your emotions.* Negotiations can become tense and stir emotions. Constantly reminding yourself of your goal can help you keep an appropriate level of detachment and continue to see the deal clearly. Stay rationally focused on the issue being negotiated, and take a break if emotions start to flare up. Also, be careful not to show too much desire for something, or your bargaining power will be reduced.
- *Know your BATNA.* BATNA is an acronym for "best alternative to a negotiated agreement." It is what you could have done had no negotiation taken place, or what you will do if you can't reach an agreement with the other party. The purpose of negotiations is to see if you can meet your needs better by negotiating an agreement with the other party, compared to this best alternative. If the BATNA is not compared to the agreement being negotiated, negotiators can make agreements that are worse than not making an agreement at all.[77] If negotiations stall, letting the other side know that you're prepared to proceed with your backup plan can also help to get the process started again.

Conflict-Resolution Skills

We all regularly deal with conflict at home, at work, and with friends. Whenever two or more parties want different things, the potential for conflict exists. Eventually, all managers have to deal with conflicts between coworkers and/or between themselves and employees. Good managers take action to resolve a conflict before it interferes with productivity or performance.

In managing conflict between others, sometimes conflict resolution can be as easy as directing the disputing parties to leave their disagreements at the door. More frequently, however, managers have to get more directly involved by ordering the disputants to behave in a certain way (arbitrarily settling the argument for them) or by mediating the conflict (helping the parties find their own settlement or solution). Arbitrarily imposing a solution seldom works, however, and often backfires. Mediating the conflict usually has the most positive and lasting effects, but it requires skills that don't come naturally to many managers.

Conflict Management Skills The good news is that almost everyone can learn to develop effective conflict-management skills. Professionals in conflict-resolution training suggest four areas of skill development: listening, questioning, communicating nonverbally, and mediating.[78] Listening skills include making eye contact, rephrasing, and summarizing what each side tells you to show them that you understand their positions. Also reflect back the feelings you observe them expressing (anger, frustration, disappointment, etc.).

Ask open rather than loaded or leading questions, and use nonverbal cues to show both parties that you are listening respectfully and are sincerely trying to help. Read both parties' nonverbal cues to learn additional information. Mediation skills include being open-minded, staying nonjudgmental and calm, demonstrating empathy and sensitivity, remaining neutral, respecting confidentiality, and showing flexibility and resiliency.[79]

TABLE 15.3
Best and Worst Conflict-Resolution Behaviors for Career Advancement

Best Conflict-Resolution Behaviors

- *Perspective taking:* trying to put yourself in the other person's position and trying to understand her or his point of view.
- *Creating solutions:* brainstorming with the other person, asking questions, and trying to create solutions to the problem.
- *Expressing emotions:* talking honestly with the other person and expressing one's thoughts and feelings.
- *Reaching out:* reaching out to the other person, making the first move and trying to make amends.

Worst Conflict-Resolution Behaviors

- *Avoidance:* avoiding or ignoring the other person and acting distant and aloof.
- *Winning at all costs:* arguing vigorously for your own opinion, refusing to consider changing your position, and trying to win regardless of the interpersonal costs.
- *Displaying anger:* expressing anger; raising your voice and using harsh, angry words.
- *Demeaning others:* laughing at the other person, ridiculing the other's ideas and using sarcasm.
- *Retaliating:* obstructing the other person, retaliating against the other person and trying to get revenge.

Source: Martin Delahoussaye, "Don't Get Mad, Get Promoted," *Training*, June 2002, vol. 39, no. 6, p. 20.
Reprinted by permission of *Training* magazine.

One study found a strong link between a person's ability to resolve conflict and his or her perceived effectiveness as a leader.[80] Managers with poor conflict-management skills encountered a promotional ceiling much earlier in their careers. The study revealed strong relationships between certain conflict-resolution behaviors and perceived suitability for promotion. These conflict-resolution behaviors are summarized in Table 15.3.

Nonverbal Communication Skills

As we discussed earlier, your body language and other nonverbal cues can communicate a greater part of your message than the words you say. Sending appropriate nonverbal cues can make us better communicators. The information in the Improving Your *Communication* Skills box on page 460 will help you to use the right body language in two important managerial situations: negotiating and conducting job interviews.

Writing Skills

From memos and business letters to e-mails, managers frequently need to communicate in writing. Effective business writing isn't about just grammar and punctuation; the style and tone also have to be appropriate for the audience.[81] The style of business writing also needs to be professional and direct, and it often needs to be persuasive. Here are some guidelines for effective business writing:[82]

1. *Make sense.* Express ideas in an organized and logical way. Provide transitions between ideas.
2. *Back up your assertions.* Support your points with statistics, examples, citation of authorities, and anecdotes.

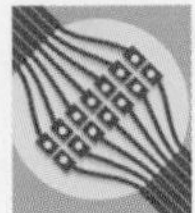

Improving Your *Communication* Skills[83]

When Negotiating

Do:

- Prepare well
- Control the environment
- Offer a warm greeting
- Understand your position
- Have an upright, confident posture
- Use open body language (relaxed, not stiff)
- Build rapport
- Maintain good eye contact
- Ask high-quality, open questions
- Speak in a clear, measured manner
- Show empathy
- Display controlled energy

Do not:

- Constantly make eye contact
- Ignore members of the group
- Inject coldness or harshness in your voice
- Display closed body language (arms folded, head down, avoiding eye contact)

When Conducting Interviews

Do:

- Use open body language
- Present a straight, relaxed, confident posture
- Maintain good eye contact so that you look pleasant and engaged
- Take charge
- Express interest in the other person and his or her experience
- Offer a firm handshake
- Show sincerity in voice tone
- Speak at a suitable pace
- Explain expectations
- Ask framed, contextualized questions
- Listen attentively and nod occasionally

Do not:

- Give a flimsy or a bone-crushing handshake
- Sit across a table
- Stand too close on arrival
- Invade personal space
- Say, "Tell me about yourself"

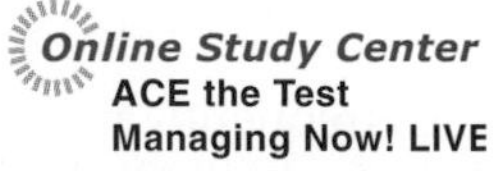

3. *Write for your audience.* Ensure that your language, length, and evidence suit your audience.
4. *Edit and revise.* Correct grammar and spelling errors, and stay focused.
5. *Format for readability.* Make documents attractive and easy to read.
6. *Write to express, not to impress.* Get to the point.
7. *Use common language rather than jargon or difficult verbiage.* For example, Mark Twain vowed never to write *metropolis* when paid the same for writing *city*.[84]
8. *Acknowledge your sources.* Cite any ideas, phrases, sentences, and terms that are not your own.

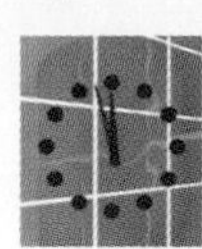

Window on Managing Now
E-Mail Tips

Composing effective electronic communication can be challenging. Because e-mail is not an interactive conversation, the rules for phone conversations aren't appropriate. Neither are the rules for written correspondence, which is more formal and not instantaneous. Because e-mail falls in between a phone call and a letter, e-mail etiquette can be difficult. Here are some suggestions for using e-mail at work effectively:[85]

1. Deliver important personal information in person or by telephone rather than via e-mail.
2. Read your e-mails before sending them to check for clarity and readability.
3. Have clear company policies about what is acceptable and what is not acceptable to send in e-mails; for example, salary and layoff information may not be appropriate.
4. Write concise and informative subject lines; for example, "We're meeting Tuesday morning at 10" sends a message without employees even needing to open the e-mail.
5. Don't criticize employees via e-mail. Their inability to respond can make them feel that you have not shown them respect.
6. Don't use your in-box as a catchall folder. After reading an incoming item, answer immediately, delete it, or move it to a project-specific folder.
7. Agree on company acronyms for subject lines, such as AR for "action required" or MFR for "monthly financial report." This saves time and prevents confusion.
8. Send group mail only when the message is useful to all recipients. Use "reply all" and "cc" sparingly.
9. When traveling, unsubscribe from e-mail distribution lists (e.g., listservs), use the out-of-office feature to let people know that you may not be able to respond quickly.
10. Because they are slow to download, avoid sending large attachments and graphics to people who are traveling unless it is necessary. Post large attachments on a wiki or portal instead.
11. Be specific and helpful in letting the recipient know what is important. If you send a twenty-five-page attachment, highlight critical information.
12. Consolidate your messages in one organized e-mail rather than sending one message per thought.
13. Respond to e-mails quickly, preferably by the end of the same day.

Training in using all forms of electronic communication, including e-mail, instant messaging, blogs, and wikis, can help managers and employees reduce misunderstandings and enhance communication efficiency. For example, the New Jersey Hospital Association (NJHA) in Princeton, New Jersey, gives all new hires e-mail etiquette training, which covers the basics including how to communicate quickly but with courtesy, what not to put in writing, and the importance of proofreading e-mails before sending them.

9. *Use graphic aids and pictures where appropriate to highlight and express ideas.*
10. *Write with energy and conviction.*

Knowing when and how to use e-mail to communicate is another important managerial skill. The Window on Managing Now feature gives you some tips for effectively using e-mail at work.

Speech and Presentation Skills

Do you ever get the jitters when you are about to make a presentation? It is perfectly normal to feel nervous before speaking in front of a group, even if you have a lot of experience. Fortunately, the jitters tend to improve with practice, and it is even possible to take courses on public speaking. Managers need effective presentation skills to present proposals to supervisors and to communicate with other managers and groups of subordinates.

When giving a speech, be sure to organize your talk so that you first present an overview of the material you will cover, then the body of your material, then a summary at the end. It is best to restrict yourself to only three to five key points to prevent information overload, and to monitor the audience's body language for feedback that they understand your message.

Here are some suggestions for making effective presentations:[86]

1. *Speak up and speak clearly.*
2. *Quickly achieve rapport.* In the first few moments, show audience members that you feel comfortable with them.
3. *Look at your audience.*
4. *Use gestures to express your ideas.*
5. *Move freely and naturally without pacing.*
6. *Try not to fidget or use vocalized pauses.* Channel your energy into your talk and nervous behaviors. Try to avoid saying "um" or "uh" or "you know" or other similar vocalized pauses.
7. *Minimize notes and use them unobtrusively.* Notes work best as thought triggers.
8. *Highlight key ideas.* Use voice volume, graphic aids, pauses, and headlining (telling the audience that a point is particularly important).
9. *Channel nervous energy into an enthusiastic delivery.*
10. *Don't focus on any errors or problems in your delivery.* Keep going, even if something throws you off.
11. *Watch the audience for signs of comprehension or misunderstanding.* Tilted heads and furrowed brows can signal a need for clarification and review.
12. *End with a bang.* Your concluding words should be memorable.

Meeting Skills

Because they lead groups and teams, another way that managers often have to communicate is through meetings. In addition to wasting time and money, poorly led meetings are often a source of frustration. One international survey found that employee well-being in meetings was related to whether meeting time was well spent, not to the amount of meeting time or number of meetings attended. Meeting effectiveness may be improved when people come to meetings prepared, an agenda is used, meetings are punctual (start and end on time), purposes are clear, and there is widespread participation.[87]

Leading meetings requires skills in organizing, eliciting input from meeting participants, and conflict management. Here are some suggestions for running effective meetings:[88]

- Have a good reason to meet in the first place, or do not meet.
- Distribute an agenda in advance that clearly states the purpose of the meeting and the key steps to satisfying that purpose by the end of the meeting. Require that participants know what you expect of them and to come prepared for the meeting.

- State a time frame at the beginning of the meeting and stick to it.
- Keep participants focused on the agenda items and quickly manage any interpersonal issues so that the meeting stays productive. Record additional issues that arise so that they can be attended to later.
- Before adjourning, decide what needs to be done next and assign tasks, responsibilities, and time lines accordingly.

CHAPTER SUMMARY

1. In the communication process, the sender encodes information into words, symbols, or pictures and passes it to the receiver through a channel. The sender then receives the message and decodes it into a message that is, with luck, the same as what the sender intended.
2. The message carried by nonverbal communications, such as body language and verbal intonation, can carry more meaning than a spoken message.
3. There are numerous barriers to effective communication, including body language, verbal intonation, selective perception, misperception, filtering, overload, noise, organizational barriers, and cultural barriers. Noise can enter anywhere in the communication process, making the message received different from the one that the sender intended.
4. Formal communication is official and organization-sanctioned. Informal communication is anything that is not official. Informal communication occurs via informal networks, gossip, or the grapevine. Employees rely on both formal and informal communication to communicate effectively.
5. E-mail, instant messaging, teleconferencing, telecommuting, wikis, blogs, portals, and collaboration software are all ways IT and the Internet have changed organizational communication.
6. The richness of a medium, or its ability to carry nonverbal cues, provide rapid feedback, convey personality traits, and support the use of natural language, affects its appropriateness for different types of messages.
7. Active listening requires becoming actively involved in the process of listening to what others are saying and clarifying the meaning of messages. It requires the sender to tune out noise and focus on the message being sent.
8. Distributive negotiation means that one side's gain is the other side's loss. Integrative negotiation is win-win negotiation that focuses on meeting each party's needs.
9. Making a good presentation requires speaking loudly and clearly, achieving a good rapport with the audience, minimizing notes, looking at the audience, highlighting key ideas, and taking cues from the audience to assess any misunderstandings.

DISCUSSION QUESTIONS

1. How is communication important in helping managers be effective leaders?
2. Think about a time when someone's nonverbal cues overrode their spoken words in communicating a message. What about their behavior made you question what they were saying?
3. When do you think formal communication is best in an organization? When is informal communication best?
4. How have IT and the Internet changed organizational communication? Do you think each of these changes is for the better, or have any of them made organizational communication more difficult? Why?
5. What are some of the negative consequences if media richness is not matched to the message being sent?
6. What do you think are the most important communication skills for managers?

7. Think about a time when you listened to a speaker you thought was very effective. What did she or he do that made them so good?

8. Think about a time you were at a poorly run meeting. What could have been done to make the meeting more effective?

EXPERIENTIAL EXERCISES

1. Pair up with another student. One student should be the job candidate, and the other should be the company representative negotiating a job offer for an entry-level management position. Assume that the company typically pays similar new hires in the range of $30,000 to $40,000, with the dollar amount depending on the new hire's background and relevant work experience. Health and dental benefits are included, as are a $2,500 relocation package, two weeks paid vacation that increases to three weeks after one year of service, and the opportunity to earn up to 15 percent of base salary as an annual bonus depending on individual and organizational performance. The recruit's start date is flexible.

   Using the material presented in this chapter, negotiate a compensation package. The company representative should assume that the company would really like to hire this person, but it is important not to offer a package that is out of line with what current employees are receiving. You should be creative in meeting the recruit's needs and try to keep the candidate enthusiastic about joining your company, even if you can't give him or her everything requested.

   The job candidate should try to negotiate the best compensation package possible. You would really like to take this job, but you want the best starting salary and compensation package you can get. Both parties should give each other feedback on their negotiation tactics and use of nonverbal cues. When you have finished, switch roles and negotiate again.

2. Form groups of four to five students and appoint one member as the group's spokesperson. As a group, brainstorm ways that IT and the Internet can make managers *more* effective in their roles as leaders. From this list, identify what your group thinks are the best three ways managers can leverage IT and the Internet to lead better.

   Now brainstorm ways that IT and the Internet can make managers *less* effective in their roles as leaders. From this list, identify the three most important of which managers should be aware. Share your answers with the class.

3. It is midterm week. You have four exams scheduled in two days and are concerned that you won't be able to do your best on the exam in this class. In groups of four to five students, use what you learned in this chapter to persuade the instructor to reschedule the midterm for this class to the following week. A spokesperson for the group should briefly present the message to the class, and the instructor will identify the most persuasive one.

4. Working alone or in small groups, use the Internet to research different ways two different companies are using webcasts to communicate. Write a two-page paper comparing and contrasting how the two different companies are using the technology, and provide recommendations for how each company could use webcasts as a communication tool. The material you learned in this chapter should inform your evaluation and suggestions for improvement.

CASE STUDY

Electronic Monitoring

Although employers are increasingly using technology to monitor employees at work,[89] a workplace privacy survey found a huge discrepancy between how organizations and employees view electronic monitoring. Employees think that their bosses monitor them to check their productivity levels and job performance, and because management does not trust them. Human resources (HR) professionals, on the other hand, say that the reasons organizations monitor employee behavior are to prevent computer viruses, keep hackers and others from interfering with business operations, and protect the organization's proprietary information.[90] Employees have become more cautious about Internet usage while at work because they believe that their behavior may be monitored by their organizations. More companies are starting to block instant messaging and employee access to personal e-mail accounts to protect proprietary information.[91]

The survey found that HR professionals were more likely than employees to agree that organizations have the right to monitor the use of cell phones in the workplace (76 percent compared with 52 percent, respectively), and that organizations have the right to search employee desks and offices (49 percent compared with 23 percent), although overall, both groups tended to oppose these searches. HR professionals and employees agreed that organizations should not read employee postal mail, listen to employee telephone conversations, and search employee desks and offices without cause.[92] Many states have enacted laws prohibiting e-mail or computer-use monitoring unless employees have been informed of the monitoring.[93]

DISCUSSION QUESTIONS

1. What forms of electronic monitoring would you be in favor of at work? What forms of electronic monitoring would you be opposed to? What could your manager do to make you feel more comfortable with being electronically monitored?
2. Do you think that organizations have the right to monitor employees electronically? Are there any situations in which you think organizations should not be allowed to monitor employees electronically?
3. How do you think electronic monitoring affects employees' morale?
4. What can managers do to effectively communicate to employees why they are being electronically monitored and make them more comfortable with the monitoring?

16 BUILDING TEAMWORK, COMMUNITY, AND CULTURE

CHAPTER OUTLINE

Customer-Service Representatives at Medco

Medco Health Solutions, Inc., a *Fortune* 50 company headquartered in Franklin Lakes, New Jersey, is a leader in managing prescription-drug benefit programs in the United States. Meeting client needs safely and effectively is a priority at Medco, and it is important that its customer-service representatives provide high-quality service. A large part of their work involves answering benefits questions and addressing client needs over the telephone. Because the work is largely telephone-based, Medco felt that it could improve efficiency and increase employee satisfaction by allowing some of its customer-service representatives to work from home. Challenges remained. How can these work-at-home employees be integrated into Medco's culture and feel part of the Medco community? What would your team suggest to Medco to prevent the representatives from feeling disconnected from the rest of the company?[1] ■

Working at home can make employees more efficient and satisfied.

BEHAVIORAL OBJECTIVES

After studying this chapter, you should be able to:

Show that you've learned the chapter's essential information by

- Explaining the difference between groups and teams.
- Describing the stages of team development and explaining what happens to teams during each stage.
- Explaining why shared goals, values, and rules help to create organizational community.

- Explaining why organizational culture is important.
- Discussing how intranets can be used to reinforce organizational culture.

Show that you can practice what you've learned here by

- Reading the chapter-opening vignette and identifying how the company can help its work-from-home employees stay connected with the company's community and culture.
- Reading the end-of-chapter exercises and identifying ways to enhance feelings of community and commitment among members of a geographically distributed team.
- Completing the chapter case study and identifying ways to reinforce Barclay's teamwork culture.

Show that you can apply what you've learned here by

Online Study Center
ACE the Test
Managing Now! LIVE

- Watching the video scenario and identifying characteristics of effective teams being exhibited by team members.
- Watching the video scenario and identifying how the organization's culture influenced the employee's behaviors and ability to work together as a team.

Some of the most important things managers do in their leadership roles are building a sense of community, creating a strong and positive culture, and organizing effective teams. As a manager, you will definitely be working in and will probably also need to lead teams. In the first part of this chapter, you will learn how to make your teams more effective. Later, you will learn how to build a strong culture and sense of community among employees.

Basics of Teamwork

Online Study Center
ACE the Test
Managing Now! LIVE

Of the many trends in business, perhaps the best documented has been the increased use of teams in organizations.[2] One reason why organizations have increasingly relied on teams is the belief that they can be more creative, responsive, productive, and efficient than individuals working alone. Although few managers seem to question the potential benefits of work teams,[3] the fact remains that teams often fail.[4] Good teams are not the result of luck—they are a product of careful planning, effective leadership, and support from the broader organization. Companies like Hewlett-Packard use information technology (IT) to promote effective teamwork by making it easy to express information visually and to share files and data freely, and by promoting communication.[5]

Groups Versus Teams

teams: interdependent collections of at least two individuals who share a common goal and responsibility for specific outcomes

What are teams? The definition that we will use is that **teams** are interdependent collections of at least two individuals who share a common goal and responsibility for specific outcomes.[6] A key part of this definition is that team members are *interdependent* with respect to information, resources, and skills. As tasks become more complex, they require greater coordination among team members. Team members' roles become interdependent, increasing the need for teamwork, reciprocal communication, and feedback. Communication and collaboration demands also increase dramatically.[7] A **group**, on the other hand, is simply two or more people interacting so that each influences the other.

group: two or more people interacting so that each influences the other

Companies have long used groups at work—workgroups—to help get work done. GM uses groups of employees to install dashboard parts in new cars or to unload trucks at the loading dock. However, such groups differ from today's work teams in several ways (as Table 16.1 summarizes). In general, workgroups tend to be simply clusters of people who find themselves working together, whereas teams tend to be more premeditated, pre-designed, self-directing, and self-contained. In particular, *group* members tend to continue to focus on their own individual goals, while *team* members subordinate their goals to those of the team. Team members' efforts tend to be highly interdependent, while group members can do their jobs more independently. Group members tend to be more individually accountable for their results, while team members are jointly responsible for the team's performance. Group members need only their individual technical skills, while team members also need team-supporting social skills (such as in interpersonal communications and problem solving) to make the team function effectively. Group decisions tend to be made by an appointed leader, while team decisions tend to be self-directed and shared. Today's teams thus "bring to the table" a set of advantages that most employers work hard to capitalize on.

Types of Teams

There are many different types of teams.

functional teams: teams whose members come from the same department or functional area

● **Functional Teams** The members of **functional teams** come from the same department or functional area. A team of marketing employees and a team of finance employees are examples of functional teams.

cross-functional teams: teams whose members come from different departments or functional areas

● **Cross-Functional Teams** **Cross-functional teams** have members from different departments or functional areas. This is one of the most common types

TABLE 16.1
Differences Between Workgroups and Work Teams

Workgroups	Characteristic	Work Teams
Low	*Interdependence*	High
Individual	*Goals*	Shared
Individual	*Accountability*	Individual and group
Task	*Competencies*	Task and social
Individual/leader	*Decision making*	Shared
Fixed	*Leadership*	Shared or rotated

Team members at Rodel, Inc., a Delaware manufacturing firm, after completing a rigorous leadership-training program aimed at building trust, teamwork, and leadership.

of work teams. An example of a cross-functional team is a top management team with members representing different functions or units of the organization. Some organizations are structured so that work is done in cross-functional teams.

For example, IDEO, a product innovation and design company, believes that interdisciplinary teamwork boosts innovation and creativity.[8] Teams share and improve ideas, building on their members' skills and providing more opportunities for problem solving. Steelcase; IDEO; Hammel, Green, and Abrahamson, Inc.; and the Mayo Clinic formed a cross-functional team that worked together to integrate technology to improve patient care at the Mayo Clinic.[9]

quality circles: teams created to solve problems and make improvements

● **Quality Circles** **Quality circles**, or work councils, are teams established to solve problems and make improvements at work. Because employees are the ones actually doing the work, they usually know the job best. Putting employees on teams responsible for solving problems puts this expertise to work. Quality circles at the Paul Revere Insurance Group use computers to log, track, and share ideas with each other.[10]

Suggestion teams are teams that meet to address a specific work issue such as productivity or safety improvements. For example, Colgate-Palmolive and JM Huber, a raw materials supplier, assembled a multidisciplinary team to identify ways to reduce costs. The team ultimately realized savings of hundreds of thousands of dollars.[11] Unlike quality circles that can exist for long periods, suggestion teams are short-lived and assembled to address specific issues.

self-directed teams: teams that set their own goals and pursue them in ways defined by the team

● **Self-Directed Teams** **Self-directed teams** set their own goals and pursue them in ways defined by the team. Team members are responsible for tasks typically reserved for team leaders or managers, including scheduling work and vacations, ordering supplies, and evaluating their performance. At 3M, self-directed work teams have made improvements in products, services, and processes while increasing customer responsiveness, lowering operating costs, increasing productivity, and decreasing cycle times. Warner-Lambert, FedEx, and Silicon Graphics also use self-directed teams.[12]

The General Electric (GE) plant in Durham, North Carolina, that assembles engines for the Boeing 777 is a good example of self-directed teams.[13] The plant has one manager and 170 employees. The only company mandate for each of the nine teams is the day their next engine must be finished. Teams make the schedule, assign tasks, and deal with underperforming teammates. Teams also send members to a work council that deals with supplier problems, computer systems, and other issues. The manager's job is listening, informing, focusing the teams on costs, and representing the factory within GE and to customers.[14]

venture teams: teams that operate semiautonomously to create and develop new products, processes, or businesses

● **Venture Teams** **Venture teams** are teams that operate semiautonomously to create and develop new products (product development teams), processes (process design teams), or businesses (venture teams).[15] Separating a team from the formal structure of the rest of the organization can enhance its innovativeness and speed up cycle time. The classic example is the IBM team created to develop IBM's first personal computer (PC).[16] The team had its own budgets and leader and the freedom to make decisions without the constraints of many of the typical IBM rules and policies.

IBM's experience illustrates the pros and cons of venture teams. The team successfully developed the new PC and brought it to market in less than two years—much faster than it would have taken with IBM's usual hierarchical, check-with-me-first, product development approach. However, the team's autonomy also let it avoid IBM's traditional requirement of using only IBM parts. The team instead used Microsoft for the computer's disk operation system and Intel for its processor. This allowed Microsoft and Intel to sell these same parts to any PC manufacturer, leading to increased competition from low-priced IBM clones.[17] Team autonomy can clearly have advantages, but appropriate controls should hold it in check.

virtual teams: teams whose members are linked by technology

● **Virtual Teams** **Virtual teams** are teams of geographically and/or organizationally dispersed coworkers who communicate using telecommunications and information technologies.[18] Some virtual team members may never see each other face-to-face. Many organizations use virtual teams to accomplish a variety of goals. For example, PricewaterhouseCoopers, one of the world's largest accounting firms with over 130,000 employees in 148 countries, uses virtual teams to bring employees from around the globe "together" for a week or two to prepare work for a particular client. Whirlpool Corporation used a virtual team composed of experts from the United States, Brazil, and Italy during a two-year project to develop a chlorofluorocarbon-free refrigerator.[19] You will learn more about leading virtual teams later in this chapter.

● **Managing Now** Virtual teams rely on IT to communicate. Bausch & Lomb uses Documentum's eRoom collaboration tool to bring together globally dispersed teams to develop new products. Each team member has immediate access to every type of document and information in a common virtual workspace, and project leaders and team members communicate during e-meetings via audioconference calls. The service provides capabilities for group edits, whiteboard sessions, real-time discussions, and one-to-many presentations. In addition, users can share their desktops and let other meeting participants access applications on them remotely. A team's guests can even attend meetings via a secure URL.[20]

global teams: face-to-face or virtual teams whose members are from different countries

● **Global Teams** **Global teams** consist of members from different countries. Global teams can be virtual or they can meet face-to-face. Procter & Gamble (P&G), a multinational manufacturer of family, personal, and household care products, uses global teams to allow employees at its Cincinnati headquarters to collaborate with employees and suppliers all over the world. Bosch und Siemens Hausgeräte GmbH (BSH) is a global company that operates thirty-one production sites and forty-three factories in fifteen countries in Europe, Asia, the United States, and Latin America. The company sells household appliances under brand names including Bosch and Siemens and uses global teams of employees from Spain, China, and Latin America to develop technologies and concepts for new products.

How Groups Become Teams

All groups progress through a series of developmental stages before performing effectively as a team. Many models of team development exist, but most are a

TABLE 16.2
How Groups Become Teams

Forming: team members learn about each other and the team's purpose, goals, and lifespan and begin to identify each member's strengths and potential contribution to the team.
Storming: team members begin establishing goals, work processes, and individual roles, and they test how the team will respond to differences among team members and to conflict.
Norming: the team becomes more cohesive and clarifies members' roles and responsibilities and team goals; team processes and members' expectations of each other are established.
Performing: the team is cohesive and productive and makes progress toward its goals; cohesiveness and goal commitment are high.
Adjourning: the team disbands.

variation of the basic five-stage model developed by Bruce W. Tuckman in the 1960s and refined in the 1970s.[21] Teams vary in how they proceed through the stages, but Tuckman's stages, summarized in Table 16.2, are useful guideposts for leaders and team members.

forming: first stage of team development in which members learn about each other and the team's goals, purpose, and lifespan

During the first stage, **forming**, team members get to know each other; learn the team's purpose, goals, and lifespan and begin to identify each member's strengths and potential contribution to the team. Members typically ask the leader questions about the team's purpose and goals, try to establish their identity in the team, and test what types of behaviors are acceptable. The purpose of the forming stage of team development is to create a team with a clear structure, goals, and roles so that members begin to trust each other and feel like a team. Managers can facilitate this process by providing a good orientation to the team, clarifying the team's mission and goals, and establishing expectations about the team's process and outcomes.

storming: stage of team development in which team members begin establishing goals, work processes, and individual roles

The **storming** stage is characterized by conflict as team members begin establishing goals, work processes, and individual roles and test how the team will respond to differences among team members and to conflict. *Cognitive conflict* focuses on work goals and processes, and *affective conflict* focuses on personalities and conflicts between individual group members. Cognitive conflict is a positive type of conflict, and, by addressing it, the team identifies the goals and processes that will best work for it. Affective conflict fosters distrust and cynicism and can undermine team effectiveness. The team leader needs to keep team members focused on their goals, roles, and tasks to avoid members' becoming distracted by the frustrations and conflicts developing among the team members. At the end of the storming stage, team goals and leadership are clear.

norming: stage of team development in which the team becomes more cohesive and clarifies members' roles and responsibilities, team goals, and team processes

During the **norming** stage, the team clarifies roles and responsibilities and reaches agreement about team goals and processes. The team develops cohesiveness as members accept their teammates' differences and recognize that the diversity of member opinions and perspectives strengthens the team. Goal commitment is strong. At the end of the norming stage, team processes and members' expectations of each other are established.

performing: stage of team development in which the team is cohesive, productive, and makes progress toward its goals

During the fourth stage of team development, **performing**, the team has a shared understanding of why it is doing what it is doing; it is cohesive and productive, and makes progress toward its goals. Disagreements in the team are resolved positively, and the focus is on goal achievement. Team members are also able to attend to relationship and process issues that arise. As team members master their roles, team roles may become more flexible, with members taking on various roles and responsibilities as needed. Cohesiveness and goal commitment are high, and the team makes significant progress toward its goals.

The performing stage is where teams hopefully become high-performing. Even when a team has reached this stage, however, it is not the end of the team's development. The team needs to be able to adapt to any changes in its environment or goals. The team also needs to address membership changes—each new member requires the team to cycle back to an earlier stage to incorporate the new member and find ways to fill the roles left by the departing member. A team that does not take the time to socialize a new member and modify the team's roles and processes does not allow the newcomer to contribute maximally to the team. If membership and environmental changes are recognized and addressed, teams can remain in this stage indefinitely.

● **Managing Now** Technology can facilitate and speed up the integration of new team members. By keeping everything a new team member needs to know on a website, Deloitte Consulting says that it can bring a new team member up to speed on a project in a day or two, compared to three weeks without it.[22]

adjourning: fifth stage of team development, when the team disbands

The fifth stage of team development is **adjourning**, or the breakup of the team. This stage is less relevant to managing and developing a team, but it is important to members who have formed an attachment to the team. Ideally, the team is ending because it has accomplished goals and everyone feels good about what the team has achieved. If members of the team have become friends and enjoyed the team experience, it can be beneficial to recognize their sense of loss and give them a sense of closure. It is also a good idea to address members' anxiety over the uncertainty of their next assignment in the organization. This is also the time to evaluate what the team did well and what it did poorly to learn how to make future teams more effective.

Holding a closing celebration that acknowledges the contributions of each team member and the accomplishments of the team as a whole formally ends the team's existence. It is also a good time to evaluate the team's processes and outcomes to identify lessons learned that can be passed on to other team leaders.

Closing celebrations are important to members who have formed an attachment to the team.

It is important to note that the amount of time teams spend in each stage can differ considerably. Some teams never get out of the storming stage, while others are able to advance rapidly to the performing stage. Some teams may also be able to perform effectively at the storming and norming stages, depending on the nature of the task and the team members.

Although research has supported the idea that teams tend to develop in this five-stage sequence, not all teams do. Teams develop in different ways and at their own speeds. It is best to consider Tuckman's sequence as a general framework and not hold teams rigidly to each stage.

Building Teamwork

Enhancing Team Effectiveness

We can define "team effectiveness" in terms of three outcomes: (1) a team product acceptable to clients, (2) growth in team capability (the team enhances its ability to work together effectively in the future), and (3) a team experience that is meaningful and satisfying for its members.[23] Teams that deliver on all three of these components are the most effective.

It is the leader's job to create the conditions needed for a team to be successful. Noted team expert J. Richard Hackman believes that teams perform best when leaders create five conditions that allow teams to manage themselves effectively. The five conditions he has identified as necessary for effective teams are as follows:[24]

1. *The team must be a real team, rather than a team in name only.* The team needs to have a real team task requiring interdependence, rather than being merely a group of individual workers. The team task must be neither too large nor too small for the team to accomplish and find energizing. Teams need to have the authority to manage their own work processes, and membership needs to be stable over a reasonable period. If team members are frequently reassigned or quit, the team's effectiveness is compromised.
2. *The team has compelling direction.* Setting direction for the team means that the team's leadership is insistent about the team's goals but does not specify how the team should go about achieving those goals. Creativity and innovation are enhanced when team goals are clear, but appropriately trained team members are allowed to decide the means.
3. *It has an enabling structure that facilitates teamwork.* Consistent with the job characteristics model of motivation that you learned about in Chapter 14, a team's work should provide meaningfulness, responsibility, and knowledge of results to maximize team members' motivation. In addition, the team needs to develop appropriate norms. Teams should also be an appropriate size and have an appropriate mix of skills, and team members should possess the interpersonal skills required for effective teamwork. Hackman refers to these characteristics of the team structure as "the shell of the team . . . the shaping structure within which (the team) comes to life."[25] He states, "[T]hose who create teams have two quite different but equally important responsibilities: to make sure that a team has the best structure that can be provided, and to help members move into that structure and competently launch themselves onto a course of their own."[26]
4. *It operates within a supportive organizational context.* The rest of the organization's policies and practices need to be designed to support teamwork. For example, a reward system that recognizes and rewards individual performance rather than team excellence is not supportive of work teams. Information systems must provide teams with the necessary information, at the appropriate time and in the appropriate format. Leaders must also ensure that team members receive the training and technical assistance to acquire needed technical and interpersonal skills. The extent to which these systems are supportive of team efforts reflects the extent to which an organization's culture truly supports a team-based approach to effective operations. Without cultural support for teams, team efforts are not likely to be successful.

5. *It has effective teamwork coaching.* Acquiring teamwork skills often takes some coaching. Leaders can promote team effectiveness by helping team members develop the skills required to work interdependently with others. Coaching with well-timed suggestions can influence team members' motivation and effort, the levels of knowledge and skills that team members can apply to team tasks, and teams' performance strategies. Coaching efforts should reflect the team's stage of activity, with special opportunities for coaching activities available at the beginning, midpoint, and end of task cycles.

Creating Effective Teams

In creating an effective work team, employers need to strive to do several things, starting with creating synergy.

● Create Synergy Overall, the goal is to create synergy, which means to make sure that the sum of the team members' individual outputs is greater than what any one individual's effect would be. *Process gain* refers to the performance improvements that occur because people work together rather than independently. Process gain is the goal of teamwork—people working together doing more and doing it better than would be possible by working alone. IT helps teams accomplish synergy despite the increased communication and coordination requirements of team-based work. Bausch & Lomb found that a Web-based collaboration tool increased synergy by decreasing the number of meetings, giving people more free work time to get things done.[27]

Unfortunately, many teams do not realize process gain and instead experience process loss. *Process loss* occurs when a team of people working together performs worse than the individual members would have if they had worked alone. Process loss can be reduced by clarifying role and task requirements and not tolerating free riders. Free riders don't contribute because they rely on the work of others. Making team roles and expectations clear helps to reduce process loss.

● Develop Cohesiveness Cohesiveness refers to the degree to which members are attracted to and how loyal they are to the team and to each other. Members of a highly cohesive team are motivated to stay in the team, contribute as much as they can, and conform to team norms. Because members of teams that lack cohesiveness are not strongly committed to the team or its goals and do not contribute up to their full potential, team performance is compromised.[28] Even high cohesiveness can interfere with team effectiveness if it encourages the wrong norms and goals. For example, a highly cohesive team that pursues its own goals for having fun and socializing rather than accomplishing the organization's goals can actually backfire on the employer. Factors that promote cohesiveness include a smaller team size, the experience of team success, and the effective management of conflict. Friendly competition with other teams can also build cohesiveness.

● Create Trust Trust is someone's confidence that another person will honor her or his commitments, especially when it is difficult to monitor or observe the other person's behavior.[29] Teams build trust through repeated positive experiences, commitment to shared goals, and an understanding of team members' needs, motives, and ideas. Because the lack of trust in a team can undermine any team activity, building trust is one of managers' most important tasks.

Mutual trust is the foundation of the entire team strategy of Team EcoInternet, an adventure racing team. The team can progress only as fast as its current weakest member, and because the grueling race lasts several days, every team member will be the weakest link at one point. Team founder Robert Nagle says, "If one of us stumbles for the second time in 10 minutes, there's no question about what needs to be done: Somebody reaches into that person's pack and takes out some weight, and then we all just move on."[30] Team members don't feel heroic for helping each other, nor do they feel like they're letting the team down if they need help. Team members trust their teammates and know that in a while, the person whose stuff they are carrying is likely to be carrying theirs.

● **Prevent Social Loafing** Social loafing occurs when people put less effort into a task when working with a team than they do when working alone.[31] Research has supported the existence of social loafing,[32] particularly for trivial to moderately important tasks. Social loafing is less common with very important tasks[33] and with smaller teams.[34] Social loafing occurs because team members feel that their individual contributions will not be evaluated or because team members expect others in the team to do tasks, so they choose not to. An opposite behavior occurs when people actually work harder and are more motivated when others are present than when they are working alone. This *social facilitation* effect happens when people are motivated to look good to others and want to maintain a positive self-image.

Keeping team size small, clarifying what the team expects each member to do, and clarifying individual contributions to the team can help reduce social loafing.[35] Letting team members choose which tasks they will be responsible for can also increase their motivation for getting them done.

roles: the behaviors and tasks team members are expected to perform because of their positions

● **Establish Clear Roles** **Roles** define the behaviors and tasks each team member is expected to perform because of the position he or she holds. One of the primary outcomes of the forming, storming, norming, and performing process of team development is the establishment of clear roles in the team. Understanding what teammates expect you to do and what you can expect your teammates to do reduces conflict and enables smooth team performance.

Two types of roles must be performed in any team.[36] The *task specialist* role keeps the team moving toward goal accomplishment and is played by people with more advanced job-related skills and abilities. The *team maintenance* role creates and maintains team harmony. Team maintenance specialists boost morale, show concern for members' well-being, and provide support and humor. You may notice that these roles parallel the concern for people and concern for production leadership behaviors that you learned about in Chapter 13. Any member of the team can perform these roles, and over time, different team members are likely to play both roles.

groupthink: the situation that occurs when decision-making groups do not consider all alternatives and value unanimity rather than quality decisions

● **Prevent Groupthink** Irving L. Janis coined the term *groupthink* to explain a type of faulty decision making that he observed in groups. **Groupthink** occurs when decision-making groups do not consider all alternatives, and value unanimity rather than quality decisions.[37] Janis said that groupthink can be found whenever institutions make difficult decisions, and that it reflects the triumph of agreement over good sense and authority over expertise. The escalation of the Vietnam War, the debacle at the Bay of Pigs,[38] and the space shuttle Columbia disaster[39] have all been used as examples of groupthink. The three conditions Janis identified as antecedents of groupthink are (1) high group cohesiveness, (2) leader preference for a particular decision, and (3) group insulation from outside opinions.[40]

Symptoms of groupthink include the group believing it is invulnerable, group members pressuring other group members to conform, rationalizing poor decisions, and maintaining an illusion of unanimity.[41] Self-appointed "mindguards" who protect the group and its leader from negative information are an additional symptom of groupthink. The Abilene paradox is a classic example of groupthink in action:[42]

> In a small town near Abilene, Texas, a couple and the wife's parents are sitting on a porch in 104-degree heat. They are engaging in as little motion as possible, drinking lemonade, and occasionally playing dominoes. At some point, the wife's father suggests they drive to Abilene to eat. The son-in-law thinks this is a crazy idea but doesn't see any need to upset the apple cart, so he goes along with it, as do the two women. They get in their non-air-conditioned Buick and drive 53 miles through a dust storm to Abilene. They eat a mediocre lunch at a cafeteria and return exhausted, hot, and generally unhappy with the experience. It is not until they return home that they learn that none of them really wanted to go to Abilene—they were just going along because they thought the others were eager to go.

Social pressures often create pressure to conform to group opinions rather than expressing a different opinion and risking conflict. Using outside experts, having a group member play devil's advocate to question the group's assumptions and ideas, making it clear that all opinions are welcome, and not punishing anyone for speaking up can help to discourage groupthink.

norms: shared rules, standards, or guidelines for team member behavior and performance

● Establish Positive Norms **Norms** are shared rules, standards, or guidelines for team member behavior and performance. By helping team members know what to expect from each other, norms help to ensure high performance. An example of a positive team norm is arriving to meetings prepared and on time and participating fully. Team members comply with team norms (1) to avoid punishments and receive rewards, (2) to imitate team members who they like and admire, and (3) because they have internalized the norm and believe it is the appropriate way to behave.[43]

Team norms can also be negative, such as not producing more than is required to meet the team's quota, not thoroughly checking product quality to save time, or not wearing safety equipment. As team leaders, managers are influential in setting and reinforcing team norms. Managers can help to establish positive team norms by leading discussions about how the team can best function to achieve both the team's and the team members' objectives. Clear and mutually agreed-upon norms, work processes, and rules are important for effective teams. When a problem arises, effective teams have an open discussion and find a solution.[44]

● Create Shared Team Goals High-performing teams have clear and challenging goals that all team members are committed to, and they create subgoals and milestones against which they measure themselves. If performance is lagging, the team quickly adjusts its behavior and processes to reach its goals.[45]

● Provide Appropriate Rewards Team rewards motivate effective teamwork behaviors. Tying team rewards to team performance motivates team members to pursue team goals rather than individual goals.[46] Teams require firms to shift the emphasis of their compensation and rewards programs from individual to team rewards. Any remaining individual rewards should acknowledge people who are effective team players—people who freely share their expertise and their help when needed, and challenge their teams to improve. A system that rewards only individual performance undermines team effectiveness. Some individual rewards may be appropriate for rewarding particularly critical individual contributions to the team, but the bulk of the rewards need to be made at the team level.

Southwest Airlines is an example of a company that relies heavily on cross-functional teams and uses collective rewards such as profit sharing and stock ownership to promote teamwork.[47] At Men's Wearhouse, CEO George Zimmer rewards team selling because shoppers want to have a positive total store experience. To encourage collaboration, Men's Wearhouse tracks the sales performance of each so-called wardrobe consultant. Having substantially more sales than one's coworkers is taken as a sign that the person is hogging rather than sharing customers. Team selling is taken so seriously that the company even terminated one of its most successful salespeople because he refused to conform to the firm's cultural values. After the salesperson was fired, no one matched his individual sales figures but the store's total sales volume still increased significantly.[48]

● **Use an Appropriate Team Size** Jeff Bezos of Amazon.com feels that if you can't feed a team with two pizzas, it's too big and will be hindered by bureaucracy.[49] The insight that teams can get bogged down if they are too big is a good one. Although larger teams technically have more resources available, members of smaller teams are better able to interact and share information, tend to be more motivated and satisfied, and can more clearly identify their contributions to the team. Imagine working on a project or exercise for this class on a team of twenty-five people versus a team of five people. It would be difficult for everyone to participate fully and communicate effectively with each other on such a large team. A team should be only large enough to contain the expertise it needs to get its work done without compromising individual and team productivity. Teams should have fifteen or fewer members, and the ideal number is about seven.

● **Integrate New Team Members** Over time, some team members may leave the team or be reassigned, and the team may need additional team members to work effectively and meet its goals. As replacement team members are introduced, they need to be integrated and socialized.[50] Leaders are critical to this newcomer integration and socialization process. New team member integration involves promoting shared goal commitment, creating positive feelings toward the team, and shaping team processes. Team socialization creates effective bonds that connect members to the team and its mission and helps build trust and a sense of community. If new members are not incorporated into the fabric of the team, the team will be less cohesive, and new members will not be able to contribute to their full potential and will likely be less committed to the team.

● **Acquire Emotional Intelligence** Another characteristic that is important for team members and team leaders to have is **emotional intelligence**, or the ability to understand and manage one's own emotions and moods and those of other people.[51] The team leader establishes norms and maximizes collaboration to ensure that the team benefits from the best talents of each member. He or she does this by setting a positive emotional tone; modeling appropriate behavior; and using positive images, optimistic interpretations, and culture-building norms and leadership styles.[52] Setting the right ground rules for a team requires an emotionally intelligent leader. The best leaders pay attention and act on their sense of what's going on in the team. This helps teams naturally develop positive norms and

emotional intelligence: the ability to understand and manage one's own emotions and moods and those of other people

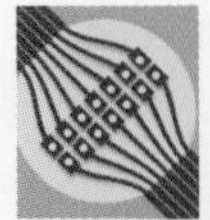

IMPROVING YOUR *TEAMWORK* SKILLS
Are You Emotionally Intelligent?[53]

Being an effective team leader or team member requires emotional intelligence. The following sixteen questions will help you to assess yourself on four aspects of emotional intelligence. Answer each question honestly using the following scale. Write the number from 1 to 7 that corresponds to your answer in the space to the left of each item number.

1	2	3	4	5	6	7
Strongly Disagree	**Disagree**	**Slightly Disagree**	**Neither Agree nor Disagree**	**Slightly Agree**	**Agree**	**Strongly Agree**

____ 1. I have a good sense of why I have certain feelings most of the time.

____ 2. I have a good understanding of my own emotions.

____ 3. I really understand what I feel.

____ 4. I always know whether or not I am happy.

____ 5. I always know my friends' emotions from their behavior.

____ 6. I am a good observer of others' emotions.

____ 7. I am sensitive to the feelings and emotions of others.

____ 8. I have a good understanding of the emotions of people around me.

____ 9. I always set goals for myself and then try my best to achieve them.

____10. I always tell myself I am a competent person.

____11. I am a self-motivating person.

____12. I would always encourage myself to try my best.

____13. I am able to control my temper so that I can handle difficulties rationally.

____14. I am quite capable of controlling my own emotions.

____15. I can always calm down quickly when I am very angry.

____16. I have good control of my own emotions.

Scoring: Add up your scores for statements 1 to 4. A score above 23 reflects high self-emotion appraisal and means that you have a good understanding of your own emotions. Add up your scores for statements 5 to 8. A score above 22 reflects high others' emotion appraisal and means that you are sensitive to what others are feeling. Add up your scores for statements 9 to 12. A score above 22 reflects high use of emotion and means that you are able to use your emotions to drive positive behavior. Add up your scores for statements 13 to 16. A score above 23 reflects high regulation of emotion and means that you control your emotions effectively.

Source: Reprinted by permission of *The Leadership Quarterly,* a publication of Elsevier Science.

expectations about how to work with each other.[54] The U.S. Air Force and L'Oréal use emotional intelligence to improve team performance. The Improving Your *Teamwork* Skills feature will help you to evaluate and understand your emotional intelligence. Table 16.3 contains diagnostic questions that you can use to see if you are doing what is necessary to address some of the critical factors for team success.

Managing Now: Leading Virtual Teams

Managing virtual teams is one of the most difficult leadership challenges. It's hard enough to lead teams who see each other and whose members share a common language and culture. The challenges multiply when teams go virtual and communicate via technology and when team members have different cultures and life experiences.[55]

Virtual teams allow organizations to access the most qualified individuals for a particular job regardless of their location, respond faster to increased competition, and provide greater flexibility to individuals working from home or on the road. In some cases, some members of the team may be free agents or alliance partners rather than employees of the organization. In some teams, members may never

TABLE 16.3
Diagnosing a Team[56]

1. **Clear Direction**	Can team members articulate a clear direction, shared by all members, of the basic purpose that the team has been organized to achieve?
2. **A Real Team Task**	Is the team assigned collective responsibility for all of the team's customers and major outputs? Is the team required to make collective decisions about work strategies (rather than leaving it to individuals)? Are members cross-trained and able to help each other? Does the team get team-level data and feedback about its performance? Is the team required to meet frequently, and does it do so?
3. **Team Rewards**	Counting all reward dollars available, are more than 80 percent of those dollars available to teams only and not to individuals?
4. **Basic Material Resources**	Does the team have its own meeting space? Can the team get basic materials needed for the work easily?
5. **Authority to Manage the Work**	Do the team members have the authority to decide the following (without first receiving special authorization)? • How to meet client demands • Which actions to take, and when • Whether to change their work strategies when they deem necessary
6. **Team Goals**	Can the team members articulate specific goals? Do these goals stretch their performance? Do they specify a time by which they intend to accomplish these goals?
7. **Strategy Norms**	Do team members encourage each other to detect problems without the leader's intervention? Do team members openly discuss differences in what members have to contribute to the team? Do team members encourage experimentation with new ways of operating? Does the team actively seek to learn from other teams?

Source: Ruth Wageman, *Organizational Dynamics.* Copyright © 1997 by Elsevier Science & Technology Journals. Reproduced with permission of Elsevier Science & Technology Journals in the format Textbook via Copyright Clearance Center.

even meet face-to-face. Many virtual teams operate within a particular organization, but increasingly they cross organizational boundaries as well.[57] Hewlett-Packard, Motorola, and Bank of Boston rely on virtual teams to execute their strategies.[58]

● **Virtual Team Leadership Skills** The effective management and leadership of teams whose members are linked by technology and whose members often don't see each other require unique skills and behaviors compared to managing and leading teams located in the same place.[59] Working from different locations introduces challenges with communication, collaboration, and integration of the team members with the rest of the team and the broader organization. When team members rarely see each other or other employees, it can be difficult for them to feel like part of the team and organizational community. One expert identified five categories of important leadership skills in virtual project team or distance management situations:[60]

1. *Communicating effectively and matching technology to the situation.* Collaborative online tools help virtual teams manage files, meetings, and task assignments.

2. *Building community among team members based on mutual trust, respect, affiliation, and fairness.* Effective leaders solicit and value the contributions of all team members and consistently treat all team members with respect and fairness.

3. *Establishing a clear and motivating shared vision, team purpose, goals, and expectations.* Subtle messages, such as quietly reminding someone not to attack ideas during a brainstorming session, are powerful tools in shaping virtual team norms.

4. *Leading by example and focusing on measurable results.* Effective virtual leaders set clear goals and make clear task assignments. The leaders then hold team members accountable for them.

5. *Coordinating and collaborating across organizational boundaries.* Virtual team leaders need to work effectively with people in multiple organizations and with free agents and alliance partners who are not employees of the leader's organization.

● **Leader Behaviors** The lack of face-to-face contact with virtual team members makes it difficult for leaders to monitor team member performance and to implement solutions to work problems. It is also difficult for virtual team leaders to perform typical mentoring, coaching, and developmental functions. The challenges for virtual team leaders are that these tasks must be accomplished without being physically present and finding ways to empower the team to perform these functions itself.[61]

For example, members of virtual teams are usually chosen for their expertise and competence and for their prior virtual team experience. They are expected to have the technical knowledge, skills, abilities, and other attributes to be able to contribute to team effectiveness and to operate effectively in a virtual environment. Thus, the need for virtual team leaders to monitor or develop team members may not be as crucial. In addition, it is important for virtual team leaders to distribute aspects of these functions to the team itself, in effect, making it more of a self-managing team.[62]

Virtual team leaders need to provide a clear, engaging direction for the team,[63] along with specific individual goals. Clear direction and goals allow team members to monitor and evaluate their own performance.[64] Although this kind of clarity is relevant in all teams, virtual team leaders need to be more proactive about structuring direction and goals. Virtual team leaders need to develop team processes that become the way the team naturally behaves.

One way virtual team leaders can provide this structure is by developing appropriate routines and procedures early in the team's life cycle.[65] Routines create consistent patterns of behavior that occur even in the leader's absence. Leaders can establish routines by defining desired standard operating procedures, training members in them, and providing motivational incentives sufficient to ensure compliance with them. Leaders can also establish rules and guidelines that specify appropriate team member behavior. For example, computer-mediated communication tends to lead to more uninhibited individual behavior, such as strong and inflammatory expressions.[66] Therefore, virtual team leaders may need to develop standard operating procedures that specify appropriate and inappropriate computer-mediated communication. Because virtual team members are more detached from the overall team environment, it is important for leaders to monitor the environment and inform team members of any important changes.[67]

● Groupware and Group Decision Support Systems Synchronous and asynchronous information technologies support members of virtual teams.[68] Synchronous technologies such as videoconferencing, instant messaging, and even conference calls allow real-time communication and interaction. Asynchronous technologies such as e-mail, wikis, and some electronic meetings delay the communication of the message. Many virtual teams rely on both types of information technology and use the one best suited to the message being communicated and the task being performed.

Many team meetings are poorly run, take too long, and accomplish too little. Meeting-management software can facilitate meetings by creating a record of ideas presented, comments made, votes taken, and action items identified. It allows people to meet while sitting at their own desks, wherever they are in the world, thus eliminating travel expense and wasted time. Meeting-management software allows people to contribute ideas, view other people's ideas anonymously, and comment and vote on them. Everybody can see everything, but because contributions can be anonymous, it can promote greater participation and idea sharing.

Effective communication is critical for virtual teams to function well. Because communication occurs largely through technology, team members have to diagnose both the verbal and nonverbal elements of team communications. Technology can facilitate communication among virtual team members, and it can support team decision making as well. Electronic whiteboards and collaborative document editors allow members located anywhere in the world to see where others are pointing in a document. Revisions and comments appear on all users' screens at the same time, and changes are tracked and saved automatically. Document-management systems provide indexing and search-engine capabilities to prevent companies from being overwhelmed by the proliferation of messages created by groupware.

Instant poll capabilities allow teams to assess member opinions quickly.[69] Instant messaging allows for fast, personal communication. The company intranet can also contain discussion threads and a place to store shared documents. Videoconferencing gives team members a richer medium through which to communicate when necessary. Technology-based meeting aids include a silent-voting function to assess consensus among meeting participants and a raise-hands function for asking questions during a virtual presentation.

● Managing Now Using group support systems can take some getting used to. In one hospital, teams developing plans to improve customer service tried using group support systems instead of their usual face-to-face meetings. When they found the technology-based meeting process uncomfortable, they reverted to their traditional, verbal, discussion-based process. They then found the traditional processes also to be uncomfortable after their experience with the technology and went back to using more electronic communication-based processes.[70]

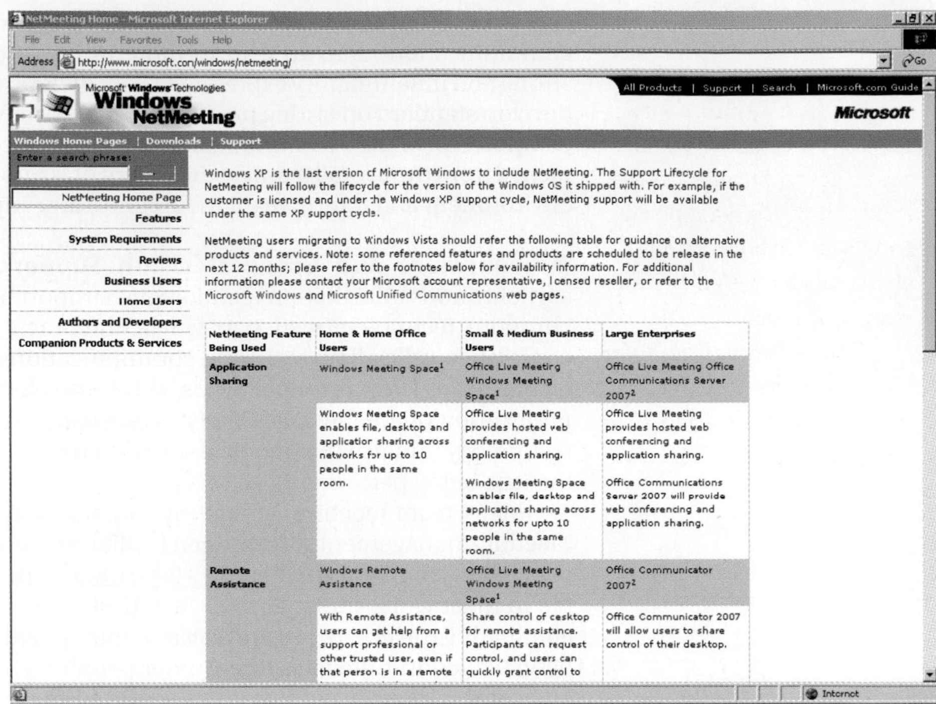

SOURCE: Reprinted by permission of Microsoft Corporation, Inc.

Videoconferencing is also an important component of groupware. Group video can link meeting rooms in multiple locations, and participants can see who is in each room, who is talking, and who has entered or left the meeting. Thus, group video provides a virtual meeting space.

For collaboration to work well, it has to be between people, not just machines. Management experts say that digital workspaces can't completely replace more traditional interactions, especially in the creative process. In-person communication can be important for training and building relationships. For example, Land O' Lakes builds trust and helps virtual teams resolve their problems by requiring face-to-face meetings every quarter.[71]

● Managing Now The goal of the World Health Organization's (WHO) Health InterNetwork is to improve global public health by providing health professionals, researchers, and policy makers in developing countries access to high-quality, relevant, and timely health information using the Internet.[72] WHO's challenge is to keep its worldwide project teams both productive and on track, while minimizing the expense and time associated with coordinating such a global effort.

To coordinate and support its widely dispersed project teams, WHO uses Project.net to facilitate the teams' global collaboration. WHO invites relevant experts and consultants worldwide to participate in the project, and they then work together in a Web-based virtual forum. Team members can participate at times and places convenient to them; the software helps manage processes and documentation and provides tools to track and archive completed work. Using Project.net, WHO now works with health experts in more than twenty countries on this important health initiative for the world's underserved populations. The Window on Managing Now feature describes virtual team technology at Steelcase.

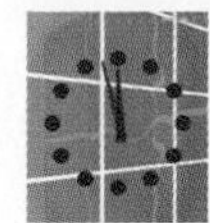

Window on Managing Now
Virtual Team Technology at Steelcase

The right technology is critical to making virtual teams work. Office furniture maker Steelcase relies on its cross-functional, cross-office, and even cross-company virtual teams to do business every day.[73] To reduce travel costs and to increase team productivity and efficiency, the company uses Groove Virtual Office software to support its virtual teams and enable them to work together as if they were in the same location.[74]

The collaboration software connects virtual teams with members in locations around the world and helps structure the meeting process. Teams can share files, manage projects, and coordinate business processes by marking up documents and showing PowerPoint presentations within secure workspaces synchronized across all team members' personal computers (PCs). Team members communicate via instant messaging, chatrooms, or voice over Internet protocol using the virtual meeting tool. A meeting wizard facilitates the process of creating a meeting and inviting team members. Once a meeting is created, any participant can easily add agenda topics, create action items, attach files, and record minutes. The ease of using the e-meeting software system and its many features helped to promote user acceptance.[75]

Building Community

Online Study Center
ACE the Test
Managing Now! LIVE

organizational community: employees' shared sense of personal connection to the mission of the organization and to their business unit

One of the most challenging aspects of managing now is maintaining a balance between integrating technology into jobs for maximum efficiency and keeping employees engaged and connected to the organizational community. A sense of **organizational community** develops when employees have a strong sense of personal connection to the mission of the organization and to their business unit. How can community be enhanced in an organization in which employees are linked by technology and spend less time talking face-to-face?

Establishing Shared Goals, Values, and Rules

Despite working near each other, these customer-service call-center employees spend most of their day interacting with customers through technology.

Some jobs require people to spend much if not all of their workday interacting with technology. For example, customer-service representatives may take orders and answer customer questions over the Internet or over the phone and may have face-to-face conversations with other employees only during breaks from work. Decreasing human contact during the workday can create feelings of detachment from work and from the organization, leading to lower commitment and even burnout.

What can managers do to keep employees engaged and help them feel like part of the company's community? Maintaining continuous communication and holding occasional face-to-face meetings to share information and reinforce the employee's personal connection to the firm can help. In the case of telecommuters, the benefits of having a shorter commute and being better able to take care of family or other needs might offset the loss of human contact at work. Holding community events like company picnics and parties serves a ritualistic as well as a practical purpose. At such events, people can physically experience being part of the community and be reminded of the company's culture and values. Recognition and awards given during these events also reinforce the behaviors the company expects from its employees and help keep them connected to the company and to their coworkers.

One of the best ways to create and maintain a sense of community is for leaders to establish core sets of values that link employees to the broader organization and work rules that ensure that all employees feel valued and respected. Firms can help employees feel connected to the broader organization by clearly identifying, stating, and discussing the organization's values. Holding employees accountable for behaving consistently with those values is also important. For example, Johnson & Johnson is a widely distributed organization with over thirty-five global affiliates and over 200 different operating units. Each operating unit is highly autonomous and accountable for its individual performance. Employees' shared values and consistent adherence to the company's credo help to unify these separate units and connect them with the broader organization.[76]

What should managers do to build community? One expert suggests the following:[77]

- Modeling the behaviors you want from all members by consistently demonstrating openness, respect, and trust.
- Maintaining members' self-esteem and self-confidence by demonstrating respect for all employees and their opinions and encouraging everyone to participate fully.
- Confronting issues directly and taking the initiative for improvement.
- Maintaining constructive relationships by respecting what is told in confidence, keeping commitments, and admitting mistakes.
- Using technology such as bulletin boards, the company intranet, blogs, and wikis to build a sense of community among dispersed employees.

Communities of Practice

communities of practice: groups of people whose shared expertise and interest in a joint enterprise informally binds them together

Communities of practice are groups of people whose shared expertise and interest in a joint enterprise informally binds them together. Examples include consultants who specialize in designing training systems, or environmental engineers willing to share their knowledge and insights with other environmental engineers. A community of practice may or may not meet regularly or even in person. The people involved in a community of practice share their knowledge and experiences in open, creative ways that can create new solutions and approaches to problems.[78] The company intranet can cultivate a sense of community and employee loyalty.

For example, The St. Paul Companies is a global organization providing insurance products and services. It understands that its success depends on the expertise of its people. Because it is a global company, it needs extensive knowledge-sharing activities to ensure that employee expertise is consistent around the world. Through their intranet site, called the Knowledge Exchange, employees use a variety of tools and processes for online virtual communities. These communities allow The St. Paul Companies' employees to network with each other and to share their expertise to solve work problems.[79] The Practice IT feature presents another example.

PRACTICE IT
Using Technology to Build Community at Medco[80]

Medco Health Solutions needs to ensure that its work-at-home customer-service representatives (CSRs) do not feel disconnected from the Medco community and culture. The CSRs are given a preconfigured workstation to use in their home offices. Medco uses various tools and technology to ensure that its CSRs can do their jobs effectively and still feel part of Medco's community. For instance, CSRs have e-mail and instant-messaging capability and can also talk with their supervisor via phone or webcam. Also, some of Medco's CSRs can participate in virtual meetings using Internet and webcam technology. Karin Princivalle, Medco's senior vice president of human resources, says, "We're always conscious of the fact that they're working alone, and we want to make sure they feel part of Medco and our culture."

Medco places an especially high priority on keeping work-at-home CSRs connected to their supervisors and the corporate resources needed to perform their jobs. For example, if a CSR needs assistance, he or she can quickly instant message or videoconference with a supervisor or technical support staff member and receive an answer while the client is still on the phone. Time is also scheduled for CSRs to watch videotaped presentations about company issues via the company intranet.

CSRs may work from home, but they are far from isolated. Managers can see the work-at-home CSRs through a video camera on top of each computer, and they can monitor what CSRs type on their keyboards and discuss with customers. Managers then use this information to give CSRs performance feedback. Managers also take great care to stay in touch with their staff by including them in communications and celebrations. Team meetings are also held that require the work-at-home CSRs to come onsite, see each other face-to-face, and learn what is happening in the business.

Rather than feeling disconnected from the rest of the company, technology has helped the work-at-home CSRs actually feel more committed to the company. Kenny Klepper, Medco's president and chief operating officer, says, "Never before have I done something that delivered such employee satisfaction and business results. The work-at-home CSRs are more productive than our on-site CSRs and have a lower attrition rate." Medco's surveys of its CSRs have found no sense of disconnection with the rest of the company. In fact, in focus-group discussions, employees report feeling less stressed, healthier, and even more committed to the company. The work-at-home program has been so successful that soon more than half of Medco's over 2,500 customer-service representatives will work from home.

Successful managers cultivate communities of practice by identifying and bringing the right people together, building trust among community members, and providing an infrastructure that meets the group's needs.[81] The heart of a community of practice is the web of relationships among community members, and much of the communication occurs in one-on-one exchanges. Every phone call, wiki posting, and e-mail exchange strengthens members' relationships and builds the community.

As a manager, how would you create the conditions that enable communities of practice to flourish? Here are some experts' tips:[82]

1. *Start with a clear area of business need.* Think about how communities of practice can help the company. Build communities that help the company work more effectively. For example, Hewlett-Packard's Work Innovation Networks are a means of focusing effort on developing a creative approach to a current problem.[83]

2. *Start small.* Test ideas and try several formats to see what employees like and what works best. For example, any Hewlett-Packard business can create a network. A business announces itself as the host for a series of presentations, conferences, and seminars on a topic it is currently striving to understand. An invitation is broadcast to the rest of the company, and if employees respond, then the subject area takes on a life of its own in a community of practice.[84]

3. *Recruit management involvement.* If lower-level employees see their bosses actively participating in the community, they are more likely to participate as well.

4. *Use technology that supports the community's needs and that community members are comfortable using.* Manufacturing employees who do not have computer access will be unable to participate in a technologically mediated community of practice, even if they would like to. Providing computer kiosks, installing computer workstations in break rooms or lunchrooms, and scheduling computer time for employees allow them to participate. Some training in using wikis, portals, or other technologies may also be necessary. Some companies, including Ford Motor Company and Delta Airlines, have even provided home computers and Internet connections for employees for a very low price.

5. *Respect and build on informal employee initiatives already under way.* Employees may have already created a type of community of practice to help them do their jobs better. Understand what is already in place and working, and build on it. Employees will already be somewhat familiar with the processes and practices of the community and thus will be more willing to use it.

6. *Celebrate contributions and build on small successes.* Building a community of practice takes time and requires employees to behave in new ways. Highlight on the company intranet or in the company newsletter ways that the community has solved business problems, and recognize employees who have meaningfully contributed.

● **Managing Now** Communities of practice can be located in a single company or span companies. Technology is critical in facilitating communities of practice that involve people who work for multiple firms. Community homepages on the Internet can link to forums and electronic communities where employees can share ideas, news, and documents with like-minded colleagues. These pages can then link to other discussion forums, technical libraries, and other resources.

One example of a non-company-specific community of practice is IEE Networks for Engineers (http://www.iee.org/oncomms/sector/index.cfm), which describes itself as "[a] community for the growth and exchange of knowledge in engineering and technology." Their website contains various communities in electronics and electrical engineering, discussion forums, an online library, and article archives.

A key driver for investing in communities of practice is their ability to transfer knowledge among people—organizations such as IBM, HP, and Unisys even prefer to call them knowledge networks. In the knowledge economy, organizations need their employees to become knowledge workers who constantly draw on their

expertise to respond to a rapidly changing market. Employees need to be able to participate in a flow of knowledge that consists of not only written and online information sources but also the active exchange of ideas with others who have related experience and skills.[85] The Window on Managing Now feature describes how technology enables communities of practice.

communities of interest: groups that bring together stakeholders from different communities of practice to solve a common problem

Communities of interest bring together stakeholders from different communities of practice to solve a common problem. They can be thought of as communities of communities or a community of representatives of communities.[86]

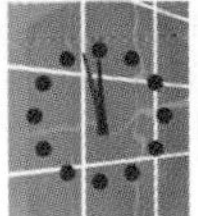

WINDOW ON MANAGING NOW
How Technology Enables Communities of Practice

IT helps companies improve the flow of information through communities of practice. For example, Ericsson Canada pools the talent of its geographically dispersed employees by using a Web system. Employees can ask questions and quickly get answers over the company's intranet. The company is experimenting with six communities of practice—four in face-to-face meetings and two online.[87]

Schlumberger oilfield services engineers can quickly reach out to other Schlumberger employees for answers to questions and help with problems by using their InTouch system. Peter Day, InTouch program manager, credits the program with "$200 million in cost savings and revenue in 2001, along with a 95 percent reduction in the time required to solve difficult operational problems and a 75 percent decrease in the time necessary to update engineering modifications."[88] Technology helps communities of practice become valuable resources for real-time help and information.

TABLE 16.4
Communities of Practice, Formal Workgroups, Project Teams, and Informal Networks[89]

	What's the Purpose?	Who Belongs?	What Holds It Together?	How Long Does It Last?
Community of Practice	To develop members' capabilities; to build and exchange knowledge	Members who join the community by their own decision	Passion, commitment, and identification with the group's expertise	As long as there is interest in maintaining the group
Formal Workgroup	To deliver a product or service	Everyone who reports to the group's manager	Job requirements and common goals	Until the next reorganization
Project Team	To accomplish a specified task	Employees assigned by senior management	The project's milestones and goals	Until the project has been completed
Informal Network	To collect and pass on business information	Friends and business acquaintances	Mutual needs	As long as people have a reason to connect

Source: Reprinted by permission of *The Harvard Business Review.*

An example of a community of interest is a group of citizens and experts in environmental health who are interested in cleaning a polluted river. Communities of interest are characterized by their shared interest in the framing and resolution of a specific problem, and as a result, they are more temporary than are communities of practice. Once the project they came together to do is finished, the community of interest dissolves. For example, the Linux community set up a new kind of work model in which a temporary, self-managed group of diverse individuals created a new computer operating system.

By bringing together people from across an organization and even outside it who are able to contribute to a problem or project, organizations can both perform better and enhance the feeling of community among employees. Members of a community of practice or a community of interest expand their network of relationships in the organization by participating in the community. Those relationships continue even after a project has ended and a community of interest has disbanded. Table 16.4 summarizes the characteristics of communities of practice, formal workgroups, project teams, and informal networks.

Building Culture

Online Study Center
ACE the Test
Managing Now! LIVE

organizational culture: a system of shared values and norms that guide members' attitudes and behaviors

Organizational culture is a system of shared values and norms that guide members' attitudes and behaviors.[90] Common organizational culture themes or emphases include innovation, stability, being casual or formal, having a people orientation, having an orientation toward outcomes or results, valuing attention to detail, and having a collaborative or team orientation.[91] An organization's culture is reflected in how it gets work done and how employees interact with each other. In many ways, culture is like the organization's personality because it influences the way employees behave. If a company's culture is inconsistent with its business strategy, the culture will win no matter how great the strategy is.[92]

Does Culture Matter?

Noted culture researcher Edgar Schein states, "Organizational culture is the key to organizational excellence . . . and the function of leadership is the creation and management of culture."[93] Research has shown that by actively managing culture, an organization and its employees will be more likely to deliver on the organization's strategic objectives over the long run. In particular, culture boosts organizational performance when it (1) is strategically relevant, (2) is strong, and (3) emphasizes innovation and change.[94]

A company's culture should reinforce its business strategy. A good example is seen in the way Acadian Ambulance Service in New Orleans responded after Hurricane Katrina hit in the fall of 2005. Employees from medics to mechanics, some of whom had lost their homes, quickly began delivering supplies, cooking, and keeping generators working. By the weekend, over 5,000 patients and about 11,000 hospital staff and family members were evacuated. Ross Judice, M.D., Acadian Ambulance Service's medical director said, "Acadian's culture has always been to 'Get the job done' . . . Things happen because you have good people wanting to do good things who have the leadership and the motivation to do it. We saw a need and stepped up. That happened over and over again."[95]

Organizational cultures can be strong and highly determinant of employees' performance, or weak. Strong cultures can enhance organizational performance in two ways. First, they improve performance by energizing employees—appealing to their higher ideals and values and rallying them around a set of meaningful, unified goals. Because they are engaging, these cultures stimulate employee commitment and effort.[96]

At Quicken Loans, CEO Bill Emerson believes that "[g]reat companies create a culture where everyone believes we're all in this together and together we can accomplish anything." He and chair and founder Dan Gilbert spend an entire day of new employees' orientation discussing the company's culture and philosophies.[97]

Second, strong cultures improve performance by coordinating employees' behavior. Shared values and norms focus employees' attention on company priorities and goals that then guide their behavior and decision making without impinging, as formal control systems do, on employee autonomy. This makes strong cultures particularly helpful for dealing with changing environments.[98]

Cultures can reinforce both positive and negative norms. When a culture is strong, it pushes employees to engage in behaviors that reinforce the firm's values and culture, whether good or bad. What ruined Enron? Accounting shenanigans is the easy answer. But underlying many of its problems was a culture that pushed for visible results and individual performance above all. An emphasis on consistent earnings growth and individual initiative, combined with the absence of the usual corporate checks and balances, tipped the culture to one that reinforced unethical corner cutting.[99]

Most managers' training prepares them well to set the business strategy and ensure that the organization's capabilities are in line. Changing an organization's culture is harder to learn in school and takes personal involvement. The leader has to define the culture to support the strategy, consistently behave in ways that demonstrate the culture, explain the culture to employees so they understand why it is critical, and then hold him- or herself and others accountable for maintaining

TABLE 16.5
Evaluating an Organization's Culture[100]

1. *Observe the physical surroundings.* Pay attention to how employees are dressed, how open the offices are, what type of furniture is used, and what is displayed on the walls. Signs warning of prohibited activities can also provide information.
2. *Sit in on a team meeting.* Observe how employees treat each other and how open the conversation is. Are there obvious differences in how different employees are treated?
3. *Listen to the language.* Do you hear a lot of talk about customer service and ethics? Or do you hear more emphasis on meeting targets and making the numbers?
4. *Note to whom you are introduced and how they act.* Is the person formal or casual, serious or laid back? Do you feel you're being introduced to everyone in the unit or only to a few select employees?
5. *Get the views of outsiders, including vendors, customers, and former employees.* Do these sources of information describe the organization as bureaucratic and frustrating to deal with or open and flexible and a positive and engaging place to work?

it. It can be very time-consuming to create and maintain a strong organizational culture. Nevertheless, organizations like GE, Nordstrom, Southwest Airlines, and Google didn't earn their success by letting their cultures happen accidentally.

How Leaders Create Culture

Changes in strategy, technology, and organizational structure all trigger a need for changes in employees' attitudes, behaviors, values, and skills. These changes can require changes in the organization's culture to reinforce these new employee behaviors and values. The first step in changing a firm's culture is to understand its current culture. Table 16.5 can help you assess an organization's culture.

Managers can shape culture. Steelmaker Nucor Corporation uses symbolic gestures to build and reinforce their strong culture. For example, every single employee's name is listed on the front cover of the company's annual report.[101]

How can leaders create, maintain, and/or change an organization's culture? Here are some tactics several experts recommend:[102]

- Develop a clear sense of mission and values about what the company should be, and communicate it to employees through what you pay attention to, measure, and control.
- Select employees who can share, express, and reinforce the desired values and thus help build the desired culture. Steelmaker Nucor Corporation protects its culture by making cultural compatibility a key issue in acquiring other companies. In visiting companies it is interested in acquiring, Nucor pays careful attention to how plant managers and employees interact.[103]
- Use daily routines and concrete actions and behaviors to demonstrate and exemplify appropriate values and beliefs. For example, Wal-Mart employees are

constantly reminded of the company's cost-control culture. A Wal-Mart vice president responsible for billions of dollars' worth of business even has his visitors sit in mismatched, cast-off lawn chairs likely left behind as free samples during a sales call.[104]

- Consistently role-model behaviors that reinforce the culture. For example, Wal-Mart CEO Lee Scott and chief financial officer Tom Schoewe each earn millions of dollars a year. But on business trips, the two regularly share a modest hotel room. "Sharing rooms is a very symbolic part of what we do," Scott says. "It's also an equalizer. If I'm asking the district managers to share a room, but I won't share a room with Schoewe, then what am I saying? There are two different standards here? The customer is the most important thing for all of you, but for me I think I'll run a different standard."[105] Leaders set the culture, and employees learn what behaviors and attitudes are appropriate from their leaders' behaviors.
- Make your human resource management procedures and criteria consistent with the desired values and culture. Communicate your priorities in the way you reward employees. Linking raises and promotions to specific behaviors communicates leaders' priorities. When Lou Gerstner became chair and CEO of IBM, he reinforced his performance focus with new performance appraisal and compensation systems. Toyota, a company whose culture values teamwork and high quality, has selection and training processes that emphasize employee teamwork and quality orientations.
- Nurture traditions and rituals that express, define, and reinforce the culture. Awards and recognition ceremonies, having the CEO address new employees during their orientations, and reciting stories of past company successes can all define and reinforce a firm's culture.

● **Managing Now** Business research firm Dun & Bradstreet's formal telework program requires employees to put in at least three to six months in an office before embarking on a remote work program. Time in the office for the Murray Hill, New Jersey–based company lets managers assess employees' strengths, weaknesses, and work habits in person. Employees also experience the company's unique corporate culture and work ethic firsthand. Working in the same place also allows team members to get to know one another before embarking on an e-mail and phone-based relationship.[106]

Using Intranets to Build and Maintain Culture

Being virtual challenges an organization's identity and culture, particularly when the company relies on free agents or alliances with other firms that have their own cultures. It is hard for virtual employees to become familiar with an organization's culture. It is also harder for the organization to reinforce its cultural values. This situation has important implications for employee identification with the organization and for the ability of managers to manage organizational identities.[107]

By building and fostering a sense of community among employees, intranets can help reinforce an organization's culture. An organization's culture can vary across divisions and even across managers. Ask people who work in different parts of a large company to describe its culture and you may well get different answers. Intranet-based web pages can help to foster more consistency. Because workgroups develop their own subcultures, intranets help to build a common cultural foundation that can help unify employees in different units and locations around common company values. This keeps people connected to the broader organization and also promotes consistency in how employees behave and make decisions.

The key issue for organizations is not about using the latest information technologies but about leveraging the right technologies for creating and maintaining a culture of trust, openness, relationship building, and information sharing. An organization's intranet strongly reflects its culture. Intranets can reflect and influence a firm's culture through:

1. *Their scope.* Intranets with a narrow scope can reinforce a culture of secrecy and information hoarding. Intranets that contain information on a variety of topics and links to other useful sites such as human resources, company news, industry news, blogs, wikis, bulletin boards, interviews with company leaders, and performance indicators reflect a culture of openness and teamwork.
2. *Their openness to employee feedback and contributions.* Intranets that contain feedback tools, ways of easily communicating feedback on the intranet that will actually be considered, and features that allow employees to contribute reflect a participative culture that values employee contributions. A more centralized, heavily edited and filtered site reflects a culture in which information flows less freely and employee contributions are less valued.
3. *The frequency with which they are updated.* Intranets that are rarely updated are not likely to influence the company's culture and can reflect a culture that does not value employee contributions, does not value individual contributions, and has poor attention to detail. Lucent updates its intranet multiple times a day, if appropriate. It also posts two weekly feature articles that reinforce the strategic vision and positioning of the company to entice employees to visit multiple times each week.
4. *The number of intranets.* Does the company have one intranet or several, each serving different groups of employees? For example, some organizations have one intranet for its sales force and another, completely different one for its research and development (R&D) group.
5. *The use of symbols, stories, and ceremonies.* Because symbols, stories, and ceremonies express a company's culture, intranets can convey news of events affecting the organization, messages from CEOs, and announcements of employees' awards programs.

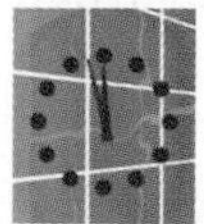

WINDOW ON MANAGING NOW
Technology-Assisted Culture at Xerox

Creating a culture that supports sharing and helping other employees can have big business results. Technology can make that type of culture possible. For example, Xerox gave 25,000 field-service engineers access to a knowledge-sharing system that engineers can consult during sales calls. The system led to a nearly 10 percent savings on parts and labor, worth $15 to $20 million per year. Dan Holtshouse, director of knowledge initiatives, talks about "the 50,000 solution tips that have been entered into the knowledge base, all on a purely voluntary basis, in exchange for contributors' being recognized. What we have learned is the importance of creating a work environment with a culture and incentives that are conducive to sharing, and to support that environment with improved work processes and strong technology."[108]

Each intranet design reflects a different type of organizational culture, and in turn reinforces the firm's culture by controlling the flow of information and establishing norms of behavior. The Window on Managing Now describes how Xerox uses technology to reinforce its knowledge-sharing culture.

CHAPTER SUMMARY

1. Groups and teams differ in terms of members' competencies, interdependence, and accountability; the degree to which goals and decision-making responsibilities are shared; and whether leadership is fixed or shared.
2. Organizations use different types of teams to accomplish different goals. Some teams meet face-to-face, some are virtual, and some are comprised of members from around the world.
3. The five stages of team development are storming, forming, norming, performing, and adjourning.
4. Team effectiveness is influenced by team members' trust, cohesiveness, shared goals, and team rewards.
5. Synergy can be realized when the team as a whole performs better than its individual members would have performed working separately. Synergy is reduced by process loss, social loafing, and avoiding conflict resolution.
6. It is the leader's job to create the five conditions needed for a team to be successful.
7. Leading virtual teams requires different skills and behaviors than does leading face-to-face teams.
8. Shared goals, values, and rules help to create organizational community.
9. Communities of practice can help organizations build a sense of community among employees and help the organization leverage the knowledge of all of its employees.
10. Strong, positive organizational cultures can enhance organizational performance by energizing employees and helping to coordinate their behavior.
11. Leaders play an important role in creating and maintaining organizational culture. Intranets can also be used to reinforce an organizational culture.

DISCUSSION QUESTIONS

1. Think about a time you were on a high-performing team. What made the team function so well? Link your answers to the material you learned in this chapter.
2. Think about a time you were on a team that performed poorly. What could have been different that would have allowed the team to perform better? Link your answers to the material you learned in this chapter.
3. What do you think are the three biggest threats to team performance? Why?
4. What do you think are the most important skills for leading a team? Why?
5. Think about a time when you interacted with a team leader who you thought was very effective. What did she or he do that made the team so effective? Link your answers to the material you learned in this chapter.
6. What might you do differently as a leader of a virtual versus a face-to-face team?
7. How do you think that working on a virtual product development team would be different from working on a face-to-face team? Do you think that the characteristics you identified would help or hurt the team's performance? Why?
8. Do you think that it is important for employees to feel a sense of community at work? Why or why not?
9. Why is organizational culture important to organizations? What would happen if a company let its culture develop on its own and did not try to proactively shape or influence it?
10. Do you think that the increasing use of IT and the Internet strengthens or weakens organizational culture? Why?

EXPERIENTIAL EXERCISES

1. Working alone or in a group of three to five students, read the following description of work teams at IDEO, the Palo Alto, California, industrial design company that helped create the Swiffer Quick Flick, Apple mouse, and Palm V handheld computer. Then answer the following questions. Be prepared to share your answers with the class.

    Teamwork is the name of the game at IDEO, with over 350 employees located around the world. The company has built its success on getting employees to work in teams, to share ideas, and to build on them. Employees at each location are broken down into "studios" with their own names and themes. IDEO promotes the establishment of group identity by holding outside retreats, and uses a bonus system based on company performance, the studio, and the individual to reinforce teamwork. Studios adopt their own names and themes, including a "Lost Horizon" theme that has the studio nestled under a DC-3 wing and another made to look like a supper club complete with velvet curtains. A project often starts with a brainstorming session to encourage the free flow of ideas. Project team members then develop extensive prototypes to test and refine their ideas.[109]

    a. If you were a manager in charge of facilitating teamwork at IDEO, what would you do to help the teams work even more effectively?

    b. What types of managerial skills do you think are most important for IDEO teams?

    c. How has IDEO created both an organizational culture and a sense of community among members of smaller workgroups?

2. Assume that members of your group of three to five students are each business strategy consultants who know each other from college. You have decided to form an alliance to better serve each of your clients and increase business. You each work in different towns in the same state but are at least an hour's drive from each other. How will your group create a sense of community among each of your members so that you each feel like committed members of your team? How might technology help you create a sense of community and enhance your ability to work as a team?

3. Imagine that you are about to start working on a semester-long class project in a team of five students. What can your team do to ensure that it performs well? What should your team watch out for as signs that the team might be underperforming? Think about what you learned from reading this chapter and your past experiences working in teams as you develop your answers.

4. This exercise should be completed out of class in groups of three to five students. Your assignment is use the Internet to research the values and culture of an organization chosen by your group. Then write a two-page report describing two aspects of the organization's culture that you feel are positive and two aspects that are negative. Then identify what you would do to improve the culture if you were the company's top management team. Be prepared to share your answers with the class.

CASE STUDY

Improving Teamwork at Novartis

Novartis is a global pharmaceutical and consumer health company headquartered in Basel, Switzerland, employing over 75,000 employees in over 140 countries.[110] Feedback from associates to management at Novartis showed that performance was being compromised by poor communication and a lack of cooperation within teams. Annette Schirmer, global account manager within Pharmaceutical Development Training for Novartis's Clinical Development & Medical Affairs division, states, "In an organization the size of Novartis, everything relies on communication."[111] Members of the clinical teams responsible for testing new products are located around the world, and cultural and language barriers are only part of the teamwork challenge. Because insufficient information was flowing through the teams, the teams were having trouble identifying priorities, planning, and making timely decisions. This resulted in critical issues not being addressed. The lack of face-to-face contact in some of the global teams required skills that team members lacked.

Novartis knew that team synergy was critical to its short- and long-term success and wanted to take action. One of the first things Novartis did was create a team-building training program. The training topics included remote and virtual team building, cultural diversity, matrix organizations, global talent, and global structure in large organizations. A variety of team-building exercises required good leadership and teamwork and simulated real pressure.[112]

The program was a success. Teamwork was enhanced, communication was improved, and team member interactions were friendly and more common, even for team members located around the world. The improved communication and work processes in the teams have led to faster problem solving, smoother decision making, and faster product development times.[113]

DISCUSSION QUESTIONS

1. What were the main issues compromising team effectiveness at Novartis?
2. Besides training, what should Novartis do to improve teamwork in these teams?
3. If you were the leader of a team at Novartis, what would you do to maximize the effectiveness of your own team? Be sure to take into account your own leadership and teamwork styles and preferences.

17 MANAGING TRUST AND COLLABORATION

CHAPTER OUTLINE

Online Study Center
ACE the Test
Managing Now! LIVE

Saturn Corp.

Saturn has always built its reputation on giving car buyers an outstanding service experience. Part of that experience means making sure that when customers bring their cars in for service, the dealer has the required parts in stock. The problem is that most retailers aren't great at inventory planning.[1] But if the parts aren't there, it's Saturn, not just the dealer, who the customers blame. The question is, What can Saturn and its dealers do to make sure the parts are definitely on hand when customers need them? ■

Saturn and its dealers needed some way to make sure the parts their customers required were definitely on hand when customers needed them.

BEHAVIORAL OBJECTIVES

After studying this chapter, you should be able to:

Show that you've learned the chapter's essential information by

- Explaining, with examples, why using information technology often depends on trust.
- Using examples to define *collaboration* and *collaboration technology*.
- Explaining why supply chains rely on collaboration and trust.
- Listing and giving examples of the seven C's of collaboration.
- Listing at least five trusting behaviors.

Show that you can practice what you've learned here by

- Reading the end-of-chapter exercises and explaining how to promote collaboration.
- Reading the chapter case study and explaining why the employees need to collaborate and how you would go about developing trust in that situation.

Show that you can apply what you've learned here by

- Watching the video scenario and making recommendations on ways to improve trust and collaboration in the company.
- Watching the video scenario and identifying appropriate types of collaborative technology to maximize the opportunities for collaboration.

Building Trust and Collaboration

Online Study Center
ACE the Test
Managing Now! LIVE

A new website service, Yodlee, recently went online. Yodlee lets users store all their financial information online, on its website. This gives users a sort of one-stop shop for keeping track of and accessing everything financial—all their credit-card balances, frequent-flyer miles, checking accounts, and stock investments, for instance. Want to check that Visa bill from last June? Just open the Yodlee website, access your account, and all the details are there. The site is easy to navigate and use, and, perhaps best of all, it's free.[2]

What's the catch? Nothing, except that to make this site work, you need to give it all your financial information, including checking and savings account numbers, credit-card numbers, mutual fund accounts, and frequent-flyer accounts—as well as all the passwords for each. That way, Yodlee automatically and continually accesses all those accounts to compile the information you can then use on the Yodlee website.

Information Technology, Collaboration, and Trust

As with much of the information technology–based world today, using Yodlee depends on trust. When we type our credit-card information into Amazon's website to make a purchase, we trust that Amazon's system will keep this information secure. When we buy a car with a GPS navigation system like General Motors's OnStar, we trust that someone in the company is not tracking our every move. When we make phone calls using our digital phones, we trust AT&T and the others not to share the details of our conversations with the government. And when we type search terms into Google, we trust Google not to tell the government what we were searching for. E-commerce, as we know it, as well as just about every information technology (IT) device we use depends on trust.

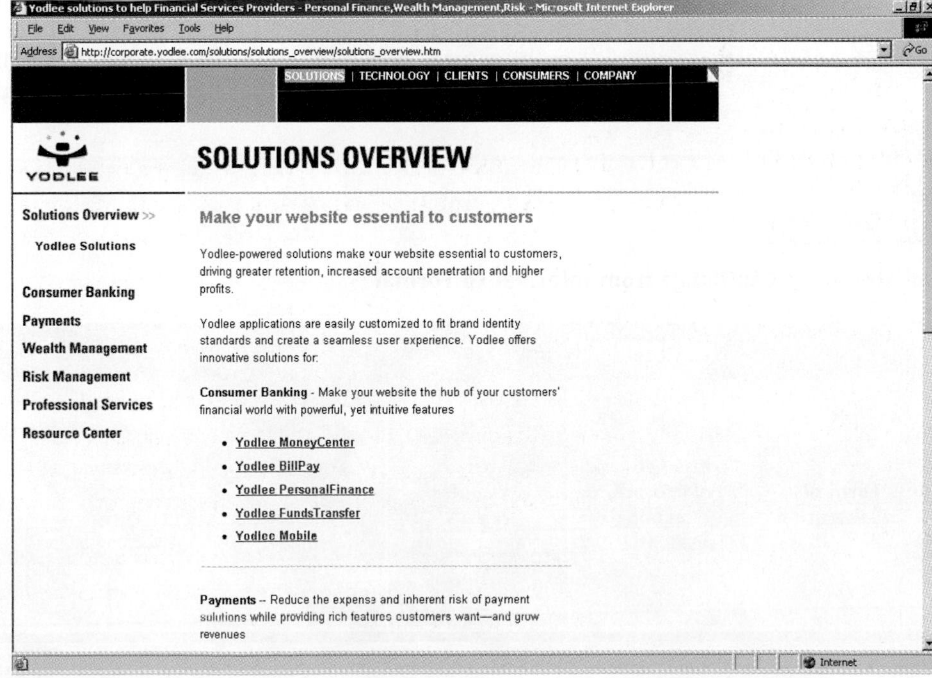

SOURCE: © 2006 Yodlee, Inc. All rights reserved.

Similarly, when retailers such as Target enter into collaborative supply chain relationships with Levi's and Procter & Gamble (P&G), each partner needs to trust the other, for instance, with the confidential details of their stores' demand for various products. When Xerox Corp. asks its repair personnel to input their repair experience into its new knowledge database, the repair personnel need to trust that Xerox won't use this information to phase out these same employees. When Boeing formed an alliance with suppliers and others to collaborate online in designing its 787, it trusted those alliance partners to keep the plane's details confidential. Trust and collaboration underpin almost everything companies do today.

Nonprofit organizations and governments also rely on collaboration. For example, Microsoft Corp. recently donated $41 million in technology and cash to several humanitarian agencies to foster collaboration and communication.[3] The aim is to help these agencies use technological solutions to collaborate more effectively in responding to tragedies. Thus, the online Guatemalan Humanitarian Center now provides a central clearinghouse for the agencies involved in the relief efforts after mudslides in that country.

The American Management Association polled 461 of its members and customers about the executives' main concerns. Sixty percent of the executives cited lack of collaboration as their main leadership challenge. Balancing priorities (56 percent) and motivating workers (40 percent) ranked second and third, respectively.[4] In this chapter, we'll focus on how managers improve collaboration and trust.

What Is Collaboration?

collaboration: working together cooperatively to achieve some aim in an atmosphere of teamwork, group effort, trust, and goodwill

Collaboration means working together cooperatively to achieve some aim in an atmosphere of teamwork, group effort, trust, and goodwill. Collaboration is not an either/or situation; instead, collaboration can range from informal, loose, ad hoc relationships to formal arrangements. Figure 17.1 illustrates this. The informal networks we discussed in Chapter 10 cut across the company's hierarchical and horizontal boundaries and achieve, through collaboration, what the company might not achieve as well in another way. Three small contracting, design, and architecture firms might informally agree to collaborate and to submit a proposal for a new building. When the client accepts their design, the three formalize their

FIGURE 17.1

Collaboration Can Range from Informal to Formal

	INFORMAL →					FORMAL
Form of Collaboration	Loose network of informal, ad hoc relationships	Limited agreement to share information	Agreement to undertake activities jointly	Agreement to constitute formal governing body	Creation of federal structure in which participating bodies agree to devolve upward some of their autonomy	Merger of participating bodies into single organization

SOURCE: Adapted from Helen Sullivan and Chris Skelcher, *Working Across Boundaries* (New York: Pelgrave, 2002), p. 43. Reprinted by permission.

collaborative arrangement with a partnership agreement and perhaps choose one or two people from each of their firms to lead the effort.[5]

However, collaboration in business today often blurs the distinctions among things like contractual, networked, and partnership approaches to collaborating. For example, Toyota creates its supply chain using a relatively few trusted suppliers. Price is not the sole or even the main concern. Other factors, including the partners' abilities to deliver quality products on time under continuous improvement requirements, are more important. Supply chains like these rely on several types of collaboration. For example, legal agreements lay out certain requirements. Networked employees throughout the supply chain informally interact to keep the supply chain humming. And gluing all this effort together is a sense of cooperatively working together to achieve some aim in an environment of teamwork, group effort, trust, and goodwill.[6]

Why Collaborate?

Individuals or companies collaborate when they see that they can't achieve their objectives with their own resources. Collaboration "aims to secure the delivery of benefits or added value which could not have been provided by any single [entity] acting alone or through the employment of others."[7]

Companies collaborate more today because of the complexity of doing business in a world that depends on systems like supply chains. As one expert on collaborative efforts summarizes, "We are living at a time when organizations cannot succeed on their own."[8] Collaboration is a recognition of the fact that the challenges facing companies, communities, and even countries today are so "complex in scope and scale as to require the involvement of a range of actors with complementary perspectives, expertise and resources."[9]

NUMMI automobile factory in Fremont, California.

Sometimes, even competitors need to collaborate. Ford, General Motors, and DaimlerChrysler created a joint purchasing website where suppliers come to match their products to America's big three auto companies' needs.

New United Motor Manufacturing Incorporated (NUMMI) is a classic example of competitive collaboration. A number of years ago, General Motors and Toyota collaborated in managing an automobile factory in California. The factory, in Fremont, California, was formerly one of GM's worst in terms of grievances and productivity. GM wanted to find out more about the Toyota way of manufacturing. Toyota wanted to learn more about marketing cars in the United States. NUMMI helped these competitors work together to achieve what neither could do as well alone.

Sometimes companies collaborate to share risk, for example, in undertaking a project that may be too large for either partner to handle. Efficiency is another reason. Companies like Dell use their supply chains to squeeze more efficiency from their suppliers and transportation systems. They do this by making the transactions among the participants digital and seamless: ". . . in the current digital economy, organizations gain competitive advantage through *collaborative commerce* (C-Commerce) and by sharing information and synchronizing transactions in the collaborative network of value chain partners."[10] And in such situations, sharing information and knowledge, and therefore trust, between trading partners is a necessity.[11]

Examples of Collaborative Efforts

Online Study Center
ACE the Test
Managing Now! LIVE

In this section, we'll review a sampling of the modern techniques we discussed earlier in this book that rely on collaboration and trust. These techniques include supply chains, strategic alliances, and virtual teams.

Supply Chain Management

Supply chains grind to a halt without collaboration and trust, since they rely on the partners' willingness to share information, knowledge, and decision making. For example, companies like Dell must be comfortable exchanging *information* such as demand forecasts and sales data with its supply chain partners. This enables those partners to make their plans and to ensure that they'll have the components Dell needs, when it needs them. Supply chain partners also exchange *knowledge*. For example, Toyota routinely shares its knowledge about improving manufacturing processes with its supply chain partners, on the assumption that all the partners gain when any of them improves. Supply chain partners must also be willing to exchange the right to make *decisions*. For example, Levi's tracks jeans sales in each Target store through supply chain systems tied to each store's point-of-sale computer. Levi's then makes the restock decision for each store itself, a process supply chain managers call vendor-managed inventory.[12]

Supply chain partners must also be willing to exchange the right to make decisions. For example, Levi's tracks jeans sales in each Target store through systems tied to each store's point-of-sale computer.

Creating successful supply chains therefore requires building deep supplier relationships. The basic requirement for doing so is to learn as much as possible about suppliers and to share best-practice knowledge with them. The following quote provides an example: "Unlike most companies we know, Toyota and Honda take the trouble to learn all they can about their suppliers. They believe they can create the foundations for partnerships only if they know as much about their vendors as the vendors know about themselves."[13] Figure 17.2 summarizes six rules for building such relationships. These rules include engaging in joint improvement activities, sharing information, and exchanging best practices with suppliers. The rules assume an atmosphere of collaboration and trust.

Alliances

alliance: a relationship between separate companies that involves joint contributions and shared ownership and control

An **alliance** "is a relationship between separate companies that involves joint contributions and shared ownership and control."[14] (We discussed strategic alliances in Chapters 3 and 7.) Companies enter into alliances when they believe that doing so beats the other two basic options. One option is simply to enter into a legally binding agreement. The problem here is that legal agreements usually don't, by themselves, provide enough incentives for the sort of collaborative innovation that a fast-changing situation may require.[15] The other option is a merger or acquisition to obtain the required resources. However, the permanence here may be too expensive or too risky.

Strategic alliances have three characteristics.[16] First, "All alliances are agreements between two or more separate firms that involve ongoing resource

FIGURE 17.2

Rules for Supplier Partnering

THE SUPPLIER-PARTNERING HIERARCHY

Conduct Joint Improvement Activities
- Exchange best practices with suppliers.
- Initiate *kaizen* projects at suppliers' facilities.
- Set up supplier study groups.

Share Information Intensively but Selectively
- Set specific times, places, and agendas for meetings.
- Use rigid formats for sharing information.
- Insist on accurate data collection.
- Share information in a structured fashion.

Develop Suppliers' Technical Capabilities
- Build suppliers' problem-solving skills.
- Develop a common lexicon.
- Hone core suppliers' innovation capabilities.

Supervise Your Suppliers
- Send monthly report cards to core suppliers.
- Provide immediate and constant feedback.
- Get senior managers involved in solving problems.

Turn Supplier Rivalry into Opportunity
- Source each component from two or three vendors.
- Create compatible production philosophies and systems.
- Set up joint ventures with existing suppliers to transfer knowledge and maintain control.

Understand How Your Suppliers Work
- Learn about suppliers' businesses.
- Go see how suppliers work.
- Respect suppliers' capabilities.
- Commit to coprosperity.

SOURCE: Jeffrey Liker and Thomas Choi, "Building Deep Supplier Relationships," *Harvard Business Review,* December 2004, p. 108. Reprinted by permission of *The Harvard Business Review.*

contributions from each to create joint value."[17] Contributions include, for instance, technology, staff, capital, and customers. Second, the nature of most alliances is that the parties cannot completely specify and agree to all the details of their relationship in advance. As a result, all alliances have a third characteristic, namely, "joint decision-making to manage the business and share the value."

● **Ten Suggestions for Creating Alliances** Based on one study of strategic alliances, two researchers make the following suggestions for creating successful alliances:[18]

1. Don't do it unless you have to. Working with other organizations is inherently difficult and resource consuming. Unless you can see the potential for real collaborative advantage (that is, you can achieve something really worthwhile that you couldn't otherwise achieve), it's more efficient to do it on your own.
2. Budget a great deal more time for the collaborative activities than you would normally need.

3. Don't set up an alliance and then delegate the task of making it work to junior staff. Alliances need to be continually nurtured by you or your most able and committed staff.
4. Remember that the other organizations involved are unlikely to want to achieve exactly the same goal(s) as you. Be prepared to compromise.
5. Try to begin by setting yourselves some small, achievable tasks. Build up mutual trust gradually through achieving mutual small wins.
6. Pay attention to communication. Beware of your own company jargon and professional jargon and try to find clear ways to express yourself to others who do not share your daily world. If partners speak in ways that do not make sense, don't be afraid to seek clarification.
7. Don't expect other organizations to do things the same way you do. Tasks that may be easy to do in your organization may require major political maneuvering in another.
8. Ensure that those who have to manage the alliance are sufficiently briefed so that they can act with a high degree of autonomy. They need to be able to react quickly and contingently without having to check back with the parent organizations.
9. Recognize that power plays are often a part of the negotiation process. Understanding your own source of power and ensuring that your partners do not feel vulnerable is a valuable part of building trust.
10. In summary: always be sensitive to the needs of, and constraints on, your partner(s). Then, with commitment, determination, and stamina, you can achieve the advantages that derive from collaboration.[19]

Virtual Teams

As we explained in Chapter 3, virtual teams are groups of people who work together interdependently, using information technology to communicate and collaborate over long distances. Developing trust in virtual teams is no easy matter. In teams that meet face-to-face, members can build trust by spending time with each other and by "sharing meals, discussing personal matters, and socializing outside work."[20] Given the distances involved and the limited opportunities for face-to-face interaction, building trust in virtual teams presents some special challenges. The problems can be especially challenging when people from different cultures comprise, for instance, a global virtual team. For example, many people in Asia are more comfortable with rich, face-to-face communications where they can see the context of what is being said, while many Americans are comfortable simply zipping orders and suggestions around the world by e-mail. Based on the virtual teams used by one successful online company, we can draw the following conclusions about establishing trust in virtual teams:

1. Establish trust based on performance consistency (doing what you are supposed to do, when you are supposed to do it) rather than on social bonds.
2. Remember that rapid responses to virtual teammates foster trust.
3. Establishing norms for acceptable communication patterns is key. For instance, each party should know how to contact each other, when to expect the response, and so on.
4. Team leaders need to play important roles in reinforcing timeliness and consistency of team interaction.[21]

Collaboration Technology

Everyone collaborates today thanks to information technology. We use instant messaging via cell phones to plan and organize meetings, file-sharing websites to share and download music, and e-bulletin boards to work on team projects for school. At work, management makes extensive use of collaboration technology to help their companies compete more effectively. Companies use videoconferencing to facilitate communications of geographically dispersed members of work teams. For example, we saw that the team that developed the Boeing 787 made extensive use of videoconferencing for meetings with engine suppliers and airlines around the world to discuss the new aircraft's design. Hewlett-Packard's new life-size Halo Collaboration Studio makes videoconferencing so clear that talking to meeting participants via this technology makes it look as if they're actually there. Collaborative writing systems let group members create long written documents (such as proposals) interactively, while working separately at interconnected computers.

Hewlett-Packard's new life-size Halo Collaboration Studio makes videoconferencing so clear that talking to meeting participants makes it look as if they're in the room with you.

The Internet powers much of the new collaborative technology. For example, a typical $100 million building project produces about 150,000 technical drawings, legal contracts, and other such documents. These documents can run up millions of dollars in reproduction, storage, and shipping costs.[22] By using online collaborative software from Citadon Corp., everyone involved in a project, including owners, contractors, and architects, can receive instantaneous updates on design changes and construction status.

Types of Collaboration Technology

collaboration technology: any technology, such as instant messaging and e-bulletin boards, that supports collaboration by facilitating several types of collaborative tasks

Collaboration technology is "all types of information and communication technologies that enable collaboration at various levels, from two persons co-authoring a document to inter-organizational collaboration, where several companies are engaged in common tasks."[23] Examples include desktop conferencing, knowledge-management databases, online meeting scheduling systems, and the devices that support virtual teamwork. Business information technology experts refer to these technologies collectively as collaborative commerce or c-commerce.

Figure 17.3 on page 504 shows one way to classify types of collaboration technology. For example, employees meeting at the same place and at the same time can use electronic meeting systems to improve group problem solving. Those meeting at the same place (say, within the same building) but interacting at different times can use e-mail and electronic bulletin boards. Virtual teams working from different locations but at the same time can use videoconferencing. Those same people working at different times can use e-mail, calendar and scheduling systems, and electronic bulletin boards.

Why Use Collaboration Technology?

Collaboration technology supports collaboration by facilitating several types of collaborative tasks. Collaboration requires communication, and these devices enable interpersonal communication through audio, video, or textual means. Collaboration requires information sharing, and technologies such as e-bulletin

FIGURE 17.3

Classifying Collaboration Technology

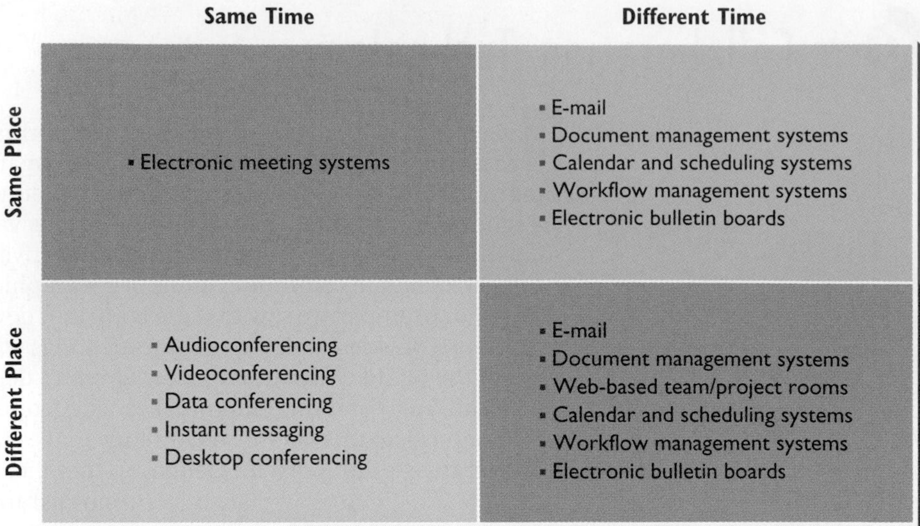

SOURCE: Bjorn Munkvold, *Implementing Collaboration Technologies in Industry* (London, England: Springer, 2002), p. 9. Reprinted by permission of Springer-Verlag.

boards make it easier to create and manipulate shared information. Collaboration also requires coordination (for instance, arranging to have everyone online at the same time for a virtual meeting), and these technologies facilitate coordination (via online calendaring, for example).[24]

Figure 17.4 summarizes collaboration technology tools by purpose. Most of these tools are self-descriptive. "Shared information space technologies" (like document-management systems and electronic bulletin boards) support collaborative work by making it easier to produce and manipulate information such as documents and drawings.[25] Workflow-management systems help automate work processes by routing information among project employees according to a predetermined sequence; the idea is to make sure each person has the right information at the right time. For example, when Banc One reengineered its mortgage approval loan process, the new teams used a workflow-management system to move

FIGURE 17.4

Categories of Collaboration Technology, by Purpose

Main Categories	Examples of Technologies
Communication technologies	E-mail Instant messaging Audio- and videoconferencing
Shared information space technologies	Document management systems Web-based team/project rooms Data conferencing/application sharing Electronic bulletin boards
Meeting support technologies	Electronic meeting systems
Coordination technologies	Workflow management systems Calendar and scheduling systems
Integrated products	Collaboration product suites, integrated team support technologies, e-learning technologies

SOURCE: Bjorn Munkvold, *Implementing Collaboration Technologies in Industry* (London, England: Springer, 2002), p. 10. Reprinted by permission of Springer-Verlag.

applications from loan approval to loan processing to credit approval. Integrated collaborative technology products like Lotus Notes provide several collaboration supporting services (such as communication, shared information, and virtual meeting support) simultaneously.

Challenges in Implementing Collaboration Technology

Installing collaboration technology and getting employees to use it are two different things. Gaining employees' acceptance of the new systems is crucial. However, managers face several challenges in doing so, challenges that would not normally arise when installing noncollaborative, single-user systems such as e-mail. (In fact, failure to gain employees' acceptance to the new technology is one reason why about half of all business process reengineering projects fail to produce the expected results.) It's not necessarily that installing systems like Lotus Notes didn't produce some gains; it did, but often there was no corresponding improvement in interpersonal or organizational collaboration.[26]

Figure 17.5 summarizes the challenges in implementing collaborative systems. For example, groupware applications (like Lotus Notes) can require extra effort. Employees may have to invest extra time in reporting and maintaining information for use by other team members. Collaborative systems can also disrupt existing social processes. For example, they cut across department lines and so can suffer from interdepartmental infighting.[27]

Managers can take steps to avoid the problems and thereby improve the chances for successful implementation. The following are indicative of the conditions under which these technologies are most likely to fail:[28]

- There is no clear need for improved collaboration.
- The implementers do not define a clear need for collaboration before implementing the system.

FIGURE 17.5

Challenges in Designing and Implementing Collaboration Technology and Groupware Systems

1. **Disparity between work and benefit:** Groupware applications often require additional work from individuals, who do not perceive a direct benefit from the use of the application.
2. **The critical-mass problem:** If the groupware doesn't attract the critical mass (number) of users required to be useful, the system won't achieve its aims.
3. **Disruption of social processes:** Groupware can lead to activity that violates social taboos and threatens existing political structures or in some other way motivates users who are critical of or threatened by its success.
4. **Exception handling:** The groupware may not accommodate the wide range of exceptions and improvisations that a particular group's activity requires.
5. **Difficulty of evaluation:** It is difficult to meaningfully evaluate the improvements in collaboration that the new system produces, which in turn could detract from its acceptability.
6. **The adoption process:** Groupware can require more careful implementation and/or introduction in the workplace than other types of computer-based systems, given the additional challenges of getting teams of people to use it to work together collaboratively.

SOURCE: Adapted from Bjorn Munkvold, *Implementing Collaboration Technologies in Industry* (London, England: Springer, 2002), p. 32. Reprinted by permission of Springer-Verlag.

FIGURE 17.6

Suggestions for Implementing Colloboration Technology

1. Clearly identify communication problems.
2. Effectively match computer system solutions to existing problems.
3. Provide education that demonstrates a positive impact on the employees' workday.
4. Provide step-by-step training on unfamiliar features.
5. Encourage top management to use the new system.
6. Provide follow-up support to encourage system use.
7. Troubleshoot system problems quickly to avoid premature rejection.

SOURCE: Bjorn Munkvold, *Implementing Collaboration Technologies in Industry* (London, England: Springer, 2002), p. 38. Reprinted by permission of Springer-Verlag.

- Users do not understand the new technology.
- Sufficient training in the underlying collaborative technology is not provided.
- The organizational culture does not support collaboration.
- Limited information is available to the users prior to the implementation, resulting in confusion and uncertainty about how to use the technology.
- Taking a top-down approach to implementing the new system, rather than getting the participants involved, alienates the employees who are supposed to use it.

Figure 17.6 lists suggestions for implementing collaboration technology. These suggestions include clearly identifying the communication problems ahead of time, providing education and training that demonstrate a positive impact on the workday, and troubleshooting the systems' problems quickly to avoid premature rejection by the users.

How to Improve Collaboration

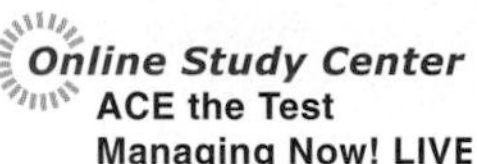

Managers can take several steps to build and maintain collaboration. We will discuss these steps next.

Factors in Promoting Collaboration

Research shows that building and maintaining collaboration depends on several factors. Collaboration usually does not emerge spontaneously. Therefore, it requires, first, having *people* who are adept at seeing the linkages that need to be made and at bringing people together, for instance, by acting as catalysts to build relationships and to convene meetings.[29] *Trust* is an essential ingredient. A basic level of trust between the parties is "essential both to begin a collaborative venture and to sustain and deepen the collaboration over time."[30] Collaboration also requires *leadership:* "the ability to develop and communicate a persuasive vision of the future and a strategy for achieving that [collaborative] vision."[31]

Building collaborative relationships also means overcoming some very real *impediments* to collaboration. For example, in agreeing to collaborate, the participants

"No decision. They're still sleeping on it."

necessarily lose some of their independence; they must also invest the time and effort in building the collaboration, with no guarantee that the investment will pay off.[32] Overcoming these obstacles requires, as one expert says, creating a "normative environment for collaboration." In other words, don't try to adopt collaborative tools or kick off a project that requires collaboration unless the people who'll have to collaborate share cultural values like trust, openness, and communication.[33]

Collaboration also depends on having the right *attitudes* and inclinations toward dealing with people and conflicts. Figure 17.7 summarizes these factors. For example, when the employees involved in the collaboration have open minds, respect for the other's position, and commitment to carrying out the solution, conflict is less likely to arise. Conversely, hidden agendas, emotions, and a "me only" mentality will trigger conflict, not collaboration.

Guidelines for Collaborating Successfully

One series of collaboration studies focused on strategic alliances between nonprofit organizations and corporations. The researcher concluded that building and maintaining effective collaboration depends on what he calls the seven C's of collaboration, shown in the following checklist:[34]

- Connect purpose and people
  - — To what extent are the individuals personally and emotionally connected to the purpose of the collaboration?
  - — What level and what quality of interaction exist among senior leaders?
  - — To what extent do personal connections and interactions occur at other levels across the organizations?
  - — How strong are interpersonal bonds?

FIGURE 17.7

Attitudes and Behaviors During Conflict

Open	Closed
• Open minds	• Hidden agendas
• Respect for the other's position	• Emotions
• Defining the problem up front	• "Me only" attitude
• Cooperation	• Assumptions
• Commitment to a solution	• Fixed conclusions
• Willingness to meet others' needs	• Positionalism
• Compromise	• Personal attacks
• Win-win possibility	• Lack of communication
• Commitment to excellence	• Lack of information
• Objective	• Lack of listening
• Better rapport	• Misstating facts
• No personalization	• Personality conflicts
• Lots of listening and communication, plenty of information	• Defensiveness
	• Old history comes into play

SOURCE: John Glaser, *Leading Through Collaboration* (Thousand Oaks, Calif.: Corwin Press, 2005), p. 24. Reprinted by permission of Corwin Press.

- Clarity of purpose
  - What is the purpose of the collaboration?
  - Do both partners have written collaboration purpose statements?
- Congruency of mission, strategy, and values
  - How well does each partner understand the other's business?
  - What are the missions, strategies, and values of each partner?
  - What are the areas of current and potential overlap?
  - How can each partner help the other accomplish its mission?
  - To what extent is the collaboration a strategic tool for each partner?
  - Have the partners engaged in shared visioning about future fit?
- Creation of value
  - What resources of each partner are of value to the other?
  - What specific benefits will accrue to each partner from the collaboration?
  - Do benefits outweigh costs and risks?
  - What new resources, capabilities, and benefits can be created by the collaboration?
  - Are benefits equitably balanced between the partners?
  - Is it time to end the collaboration?
- Communication between partners
  - What level of respect and trust exists between the partners?
  - Is communication open and frank, and is critical communication constructive?
  - How is communication between the partners managed?
  - Does each partner have a partner relationship manager?
  - What channels and vehicles are used to communicate internally?
  - Are there potential dissenters, and can they be converted?
  - How does the alliance communicate externally?
  - Do the partners have a coordinated external communication strategy and program?
- Continual learning
  - What has each partner learned from the collaboration about how to work with another organization more effectively and how to create greater partner and social value?
  - How has this learning been incorporated into the collaboration?
  - Is there a process for routinely assessing learning from the collaboration?
  - Is complacency stifling innovation?
- Commitment to the partnership
  - What is the level of organizational commitment to the partnership, and how is this commitment demonstrated?

— What is the trend in investments (personal, financial, institutional) in the partnership?

— Are the partners' expectations of each other high?

— Are partner expectations and commitments commensurate with execution capabilities?

The Window on Managing Now feature shows how one alliance applied these ideas.

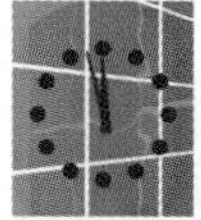

WINDOW ON MANAGING NOW
Solectron Corp.

Solectron Corp. is a leading example of supply chain integration.[35] The company started out as a contract manufacturer, handling the manufacturing overflow from companies such as Hewlett-Packard and Sony. During the 1990s, as companies began outsourcing more of the activities in which they did not have a core, strategic competence, Solectron was well placed to take on more of this work. It was already providing world-class manufacturing and had twice won the Malcolm Baldrige award for quality in manufacturing.

Solectron gradually took on more and more of their customers' design, manufacturing, and distribution responsibilities. Soon, it became what some referred to as a global supply chain facilitator, "that is, a company that can manage the entire supply chain."[36] As such, Solectron now handles "all the actions, processes, and relationships necessary to turn a great idea into a product—and to keep it in great working condition for the end-user . . . [f]rom the time a product is conceived all the way through repair and end-of-life."[37] Today, when you get a new Motorola or other cell phone, chances are Solectron (or one of its competitors, such as Flextronics) made it.

To make their systems work, supply chain facilitators like Solectron must collaborate closely with their suppliers. Furthermore, they must do this in an increasingly competitive industrial environment, with changing business conditions across countries and cultures. Solectron follows several rules in building the sorts of strong, collaborative supply chain relationships it requires. Its rules underscore the fact that in collaborative efforts, trust is often heavily based on satisfying measurable performance criteria. These rules include:

- *Base relationships on a foundation of performance metrics, information, and formal contracts.* Otherwise, collaborators' styles, approaches, and relationships will tend to vary widely, and performance will be unpredictable.[38]
- *Use a supplier scorecard.* Every quarter, Solectron evaluates 100 of its most important, preferred suppliers on a number of metrics, including price, terms and conditions, quality, and on-time delivery.[39] Solectron sends a copy of this review to the supplier and then holds meetings with the suppliers to identify and discuss any issues they need to address.
- *Formalize relationships.* While supply chain relationships rely on trust and collaboration, Solectron does not do business based solely on handshakes. Solectron reduces informal agreements to formal contracts, even though "every day things get negotiated outside a contract. Life is compromise and negotiation."[40]
- *Offer suppliers several ways to provide feedback, so that the review process is not one way.* For example, Solectron has a supplier council, whose purpose is to enable suppliers to provide their perspective on emerging trends and best practices to Solectron and to other suppliers.
- *Encourage the use of standardized processes and practices.* This "helps make suppliers' jobs easier and improves the effectiveness of Solectron's procurement processes . . . ."[41]

FIGURE 17.8

Building Trust and Collaboration at Selectron Corporation

Phase	Action Step

PHASE I:
Setting the Stage
	▪ Promote a strategic vision of supply chain collaboration through written and spoken words and actions.
	▪ Develop an organizationwide infrastructure that supports collaboration through:
	  ▪ Information systems and metrics
	  ▪ Contracts
	  ▪ Standardized practices

PHASE II:
Getting Started with Specific Projects
	▪ Find partners with compatible performance-based cultures.
	▪ Management actively and visibly supports projects by:
	  ▪ Developing trust and taking visible risks
	  ▪ Providing autonomy to participants
	▪ Put the right people in the right place:
	  ▪ Create liaison roles
	  ▪ Link the liaisons in collaborative pairs
	  ▪ Fill liaison roles with people who have good lateral skills (that is, people who can communicate across geographical and functional cultures, provide customer service and more, demonstrate integrity, and inspire trust)

PHASE III: Creating the Infrastructure	▪ Adapt preexisting governance and management practices to specific projects (for example, by creating an account management team and providing lots of autonomy to on-site participants). ▪ Develop and use performance metrics for strategic and political purposes (for example, as early indicators of success to build support).
PHASE IV: Doing the Work	▪ Establish norms for communicating across cultures and organizations by using liaisons to establish and teach norms and by sharing information. ▪ Build relationships through travel and face-to-face interaction. ▪ Learn from doing. ▪ Go for early wins.

SOURCE: Don Mankin and Susan Cohen, *Business Without Boundaries* (San Francisco, Calif.: John Wiley and Sons, 2004), pp. 136–137. Copyright © 2004. Reprinted by permission of John Wiley & Sons.

Figure 17.8 summarizes what the Solectron way of doing things tells managers about how to build collaboration across the supply chain and in other, similar situations. For example, Solectron set the stage for effective collaboration by investing the time in promoting a strategic vision and culture that support collaboration across the boundaries between Solectron and its suppliers and customers. Solectron not only made it clear what its strategic vision as a supply chain facilitator was; it also created a culture that helped make collaboration possible (including values such as consistency, metrics, and systems) and developed an infrastructure that supports collaboration, for instance, in terms of its supply chain systems and performance metrics.

Building Trust

Online Study Center
ACE the Test
Managing Now! LIVE

Several years ago, the *Harvard Business Review* brought together a panel of supply chain management experts. Most agreed that while information systems and technology are important for supply chain management, supply chain effectiveness actually depends on more subjective considerations. One participant said:

> [T]rust is the basis of agility, of flexibility. Yet it's an incredible challenge to establish trust, and maybe even harder to maintain it . . . But it's important. As the world gets more complicated, when I sell a product, I may be selling a solution that requires input from 45 companies. How do they get along with each other? If suppliers don't trust each other, the customer will be whipsawed. Also, trust enables you to make fast decisions, which lets you be more innovative and get rid of unproductive work. Trust is a competitive advantage.[42]

trust: a person's belief and confidence in the goodwill of others, and the conviction that their actions will be consistent with the group's goals

Trust is a person's belief and confidence in the goodwill of others, and the conviction that their actions will be consistent with the group's goals.[43] As one researcher says, trust "is the essential intangible aspect of the effect of alliances, the interpersonal webbing that ties organizations together and facilitates considered action."[44] The Practice IT feature illustrates this concept at Saturn Corp.

Trusting Behaviors

Research sheds light on the specific behaviors people need to exhibit to build trust. These behaviors include:

- *Integrity*—honesty and truthfulness.[45]
- *Competence*—technical and interpersonal knowledge and skills.

PRACTICE IT
Saturn's Technology Aids Its Customers and Dealers

Having the right part in stock was a big factor in a car buyer's customer experience. Knowing that, Saturn and its dealers came up with an innovative, collaborative solution. Saturn, with its dealers' agreement, took over the entire dealership inventory planning and forecasting job. Saturn installed its own supply chain system to track the inventory at every dealer.

Letting Saturn implement that solution took considerable trust on the dealer's part. Inventory is a very expensive and profitable category for all dealers: stock too much and profits go down; don't stock enough and you upset customers. Saturn won its dealers' trust for its collaborative inventory system in two ways. First, it showed them over time how effective it could be. For example, the average Saturn dealer now turns over or utilizes its inventory about 7.5 times per year, versus the industry average of 2.5 times. That means a lot more profit from each dollar invested in inventory for Saturn dealers. Second, Saturn won its dealers' trust by assuming part of the risk. If a customer wants a part and it's not available, Saturn gets the part from another dealer and has it delivered overnight. At Saturn Corp., trust and collaboration meant superior customer service and better profitability for both the dealers and for Saturn.[46]

- *Consistency*—reliability, predictability, and good judgment in handling situations.
- *Loyalty*—willingness to protect and save face for a person.
- *Openness*—willingness to share ideas and information freely.[47]
- *Community*—willingly offer materials and resources to help the team move ahead.
- *Respect*—recognize the strengths and abilities of others.[48]
- *Cooperation*—behave cooperatively, and put oneself in the other person's position.
- *Dependability*—partners "promise cautiously, and then keep their promises."

The Trust-Building Process

Although collaboration requires trust, the parties' initial position may well be one of suspicion rather than trust.[49] Trust building therefore generally involves starting small and following a process, such as the process shown in Figure 17.9. First, the parties need to have enough trust to be willing to take the first, initial steps in collaborating. They start working together, aiming for realistic but initially modest outcomes. Their success then reinforces mutual trust. These new attitudes then encourage the participants to pursue more ambitious, collaborative projects. The Window on Managing Now feature helps to illustrate this concept.

FIGURE 17.9

The Trust-Building Loop

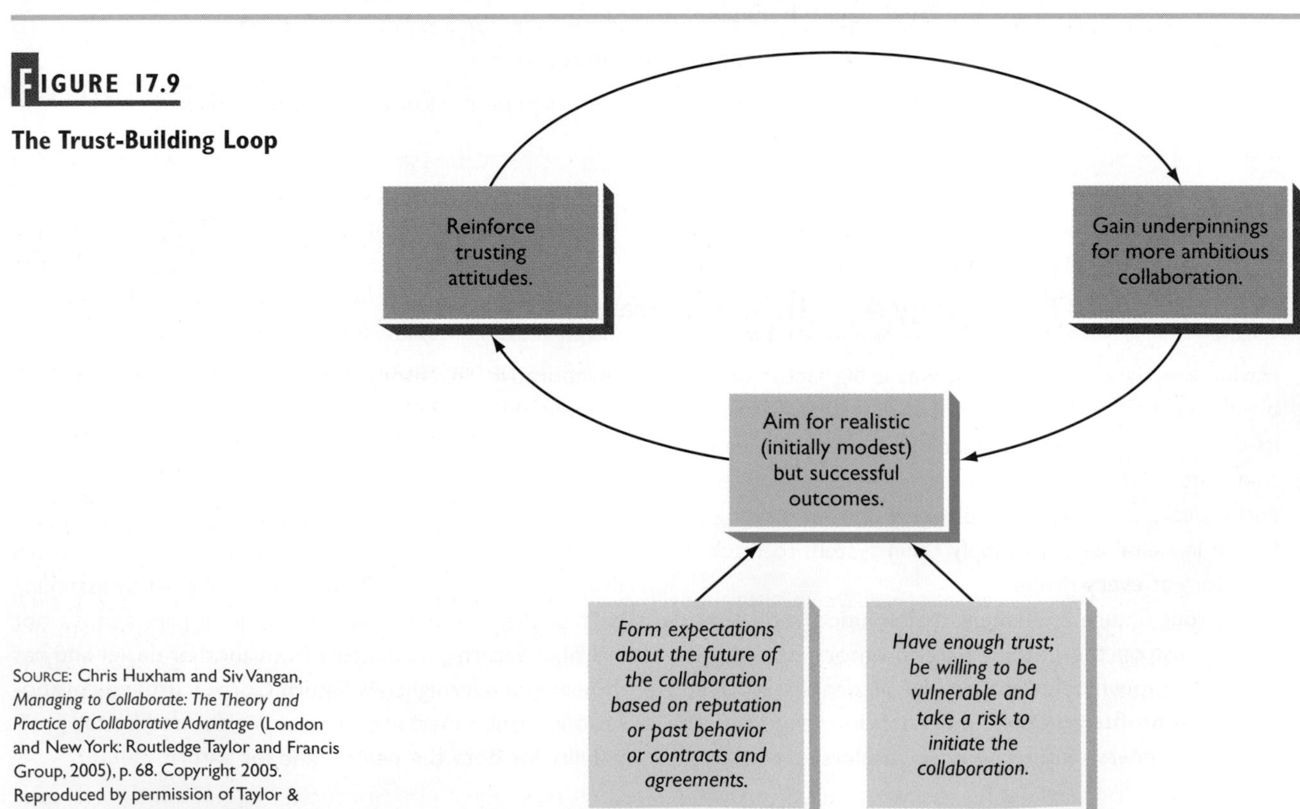

SOURCE: Chris Huxham and Siv Vangan, *Managing to Collaborate: The Theory and Practice of Collaborative Advantage* (London and New York: Routledge Taylor and Francis Group, 2005), p. 68. Copyright 2005. Reproduced by permission of Taylor & Francis, Inc., http://www.routledge-ny.com.

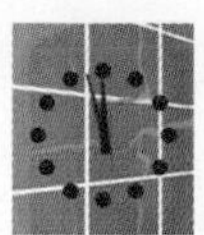

Window on Managing Now
Customer Relationship Management Collaboration at Audi[50]

We saw in Chapter 5 that *customer relationship management* (CRM) systems help the company manage all the processes involved with interacting with customers, such as taking orders, answering technical questions, and sending bills. For example, when a customer calls with a problem, Dell's customer relationship management system shows the technician what system the customer owns.

Audi is using its customer relationship management systems and effective management practices to collaborate with its dealers and thereby improve the Audi customer's experience. The National Auto Dealer Association estimates that 50 to 70 percent of the approximately 22,000 car dealerships in the United States engage in some form of customer relationship management. However, the potential collaboration between manufacturer and dealer still faces several challenges. For example, even with CRM, manufacturers like Audi often don't have full access to their dealers' customers' data. So even though firms like Audi have sophisticated decision support systems that could use this data for predicting things like local marketing program effectiveness, the manufacturers and dealers can't fully get at or utilize the data.

Audi is working effectively with its dealers to overcome this. For one thing, it is building trust among the dealers in its network by showing them the long-term benefits of sharing customer data with Audi. As the head of Audi's customer and dealer systems put it, "[I]n using CRM, our goal is to help facilitate more relevant interactions between dealer and customer, to help dealers sell more cars." For example, Audi showed its dealers how they could create more complete customer profiles and thereby generate more effective marketing. Audi is also building trust by emphasizing customer data privacy and security. With the new system, "consumers specify to the dealer at the point-of-sale whether or not they want their information used, and whether the dealer, Audi, or both can have access." Audi also outlines its formal data privacy policies in its contracts with consumers and dealers, and Audi does not sell its consumer list.

The bottom line is that by building trust based on integrity and competence, Audi AG built a collaborative relationship with its dealers, one that enables both sets of partners to compete more effectively.

CHAPTER SUMMARY

1. Using most types of information technology devices requires trust. Similarly, collaborative supply chains require that each partner trust each other, for instance, with the details of their stores' demand for various products.
2. Collaboration means working together cooperatively to achieve some aim in an atmosphere of teamwork, group effort, trust, and goodwill. Collaboration is not an either/or situation, but instead can range from informal, ad hoc relationships to formal arrangements.
3. Modern collaborative supply chain relationships blur the distinctions between types and levels of collaboration because they depend on a range of collaborative behaviors, from informal, ad hoc day-to-day interactions to formal, contractual agreements.
4. Individuals or companies collaborate when they see they can't achieve their objectives with their own resources. Collaboration "aims to secure the delivery of benefits or added value which could not have been provided by any single entity acting alone or through the employment of others."
5. Many of the modern techniques we discussed in this book rely on collaboration and trust. Supply chains rely on collaboration and trust because the partners must feel comfortable to exchange information, knowledge, and their right to make decisions, as in vendor-managed inventory situations.
6. An alliance is a relationship between separate companies that involves joint contributions and shared ownership and control. Companies enter into alliances when they believe simple legal agreements don't provide enough incentive for the required collaborative innovation and when they believe a merger or acquisition is too expensive or risky.
7. Ten suggestions for creating alliances include: don't do it unless you have to; budget sufficient

time; don't delegate work to junior staff; be prepared to compromise; begin with small tasks; pay attention to communication; don't expect others to do things the same way you do; ensure that those managing the alliance have the required knowledge and autonomy; recognize that power plays may be a part of the negotiation process; and, in summary, always be sensitive to the needs of, and constraints on, your partner.

8. Virtual teams are groups of people who work together interdependently using information technology to communicate and collaborate over long distances. Developing trust and virtual teams is not easy because, by their nature, they lack the opportunities for day-to-day social interactions that traditional teams have. Virtual teams build trust by relying on performance consistency, quickly responding to virtual teammates, establishing norms for acceptable communication patterns, and having the right team leaders.

9. Collaboration technology includes all types of information and communication technologies that enable collaboration at various levels, from collaboration between two persons to organizational collaboration, where several companies are engaged in common tasks. Examples of collaboration technology include desktop videoconferencing, knowledge-management databases, online meeting scheduling systems, and the devices that support virtual teamwork.

10. Collaborative technology supports collaboration by facilitating several types of collaborative tasks, including communication, information sharing, and coordination.

11. There are many challenges to implementing collaborative systems, including the fact that employees may have to invest extra time in maintaining information for use by other team members. Conditions under which these technologies are most likely to fail include instances when there is no clear need for improved collaboration, users do not understand the new technology, or the organizational culture does not support collaboration.

12. Building and maintaining collaboration depends on several factors. These factors include having people who are adept at seeing the linkages that need to be made and then bringing people together, plus trust and leadership. Furthermore, participants may lose some of their independence, and they must invest time and effort in building collaboration with no guarantee of success. Thus, a normative environment for collaboration should already exist, which means that the people involved share cultural values like trust, openness, and communication. The seven C's of collaboration include connect purpose and people; clarity of purpose; congruency of mission, strategy, and values; creation of value; communication between partners; continual learning; and commitment to partnership.

13. Successful supply chains require collaboration. Solectron's rules for supply chain success include basing relationships on a foundation of performance metrics, using a supplier scorecard, formalizing relationships, offering suppliers several ways to provide feedback, and encouraging the use of standardized processes and practices. Trust depends on cultural and behavioral issues but also on proving one is trustworthy by meeting agreed-to performance standards.

14. Supply chains (and all other collaborative efforts) also depend heavily on trust. Trust is a person's belief and confidence in the goodwill of others and the conviction that their actions will be consistent with the group's goals. Trusting behaviors include integrity, competence, consistency, loyalty, openness, community, respect, cooperation, and dependability. The trust-building process generally involves starting small and gradually building trust by successfully collaborating and achieving successes.

DISCUSSION QUESTIONS

1. List five reasons supply chains can't function without trust.
2. What are the main types of collaborative technologies, and what situations are they most suitable for?
3. What does building and maintaining collaboration depend on?
4. What virtual teams do you participate in, and what types of technology does your virtual team rely on?
5. What role do measurable performance goals play in building collaboration and trust?

EXPERIENTIAL EXERCISES

1. We've all probably met, at one time or another, people we did not trust. In groups of three or four students, pick (without mentioning names) one or two people who each student did not trust. Make a list of what those people did—in terms of their actual behaviors—that made them untrustworthy. How does your list compare with the trusting behaviors discussed in this chapter? If time permits, write the untrustworthy behaviors on the board and compare them in class.

2. Just about everyone uses information technology systems and devices today, and many of these systems and devices support collaborative activities. In teams of three or four students, list at least ten information technology systems and/or devices that you typically use, and next to each one, itemize the ways in which you either do or could use these systems and devices to improve collaboration.

CASE STUDY

AT&T

Prior to its recent merger with SBC, AT&T provided data and voice-service communications to businesses and consumers worldwide. The company employed about 100,000 employees, half of whom telecommute, either full- or part-time. AT&T had long promoted telework, which means encouraging its employees to work at home or in other nontraditional locations during regular business hours.[51]

AT&T began seriously promoting telework when management decided that, henceforth, all its information systems salespeople would work out in the field 100 percent of the time. AT&T took away their offices and cubicles, and AT&T's new era of telework was born. Of the 50,000 or so employees who telecommute, about 15,000 are managerial personnel. AT&T gives the typical teleworker a laptop, external keyboard and monitor, router, and an allowance of about $100 to purchase a telephone (AT&T is also rolling out Voice over Internet Protocol phones).

One chronic drawback to telework (or telecommuting) in many firms is that the remote workers sometimes take on a second-class status. After all, they frequently don't have offices, and they usually aren't around to socialize with the other office employees for lunch or after work. Even AT&T's own studies show that these factors can be a problem. For example, about 68 percent of its teleworkers cited reduced visibility in the office, and 68 percent cited a need to interact with people live. Another drawback to telecommuting involves the larger issue of encouraging and facilitating collaboration among employees (both among the telecommuters and between telecommuters and office personnel). AT&T doesn't view itself as having two separate sets of employees: office workers and telecommuters. Instead, the company understandably expects all its employees to collaborate and network together.

AT&T has installed several tools to connect its telecommuters—which it now refers to as its remote knowledge workers—to each other. For example, its InfoCenter portal supplies basic information like organization charts and personnel details, so even employees outside the office should not have a problem finding out who to go to if they have a question.

Even so, encouraging collaboration remains a challenge. AT&T needs to decide what additional information systems and collaborative technology it can supply to its employees to encourage collaboration. And it must try to anticipate the problems that it may encounter by trying to get its employees to use these new technologies.

DISCUSSION QUESTIONS

1. Specifically, what types of collaborative technology would you recommend that AT&T provide to its telecommuters and office staff now to maximize the opportunities for collaboration? Why did you suggest these types of technology?

2. Assume that AT&T's managers have accepted your recommendations. Now, provide ATA&T with a short report itemizing the problems it can anticipate in getting employees to use these collaborative devices and how you suggest it can overcome those problems.

PHOTO CREDITS

CHAPTER 1
p. 1: AP Photo/Marco Jose Sanchez; p. 10: Jack Plunkett/Bloomberg News/Landov; p. 13: Underwood & Underwood/Corbis; p. 15: Debra DeBoise; p. 18: PicturePress/Getty Images; p. 20: AP Photo/Suzanne Plunkett

CHAPTER 2
p. 29: Chris Kleponis/Bloomberg News/Landov; p. 33: Courtesy of Air-Trak; p. 38: AP Photo/John Cogill; p. 48: AP Photo/Dmitry Lovetsky; p. 50: Hugh Siegenthaler/Bloomberg News/Landov; p. 52: Alan Levenson

CHAPTER 3
p. 59: Courtesy, Congressman Todd Tiahrt's Office; p. 61: Money Sharma/epa/Corbis; p. 65: Kevin Lee/Bloomberg News/Landov; p. 71: Andrew T. Malana/Bloomberg News/Landov; p. 75: Christopher Farina/Corbis; p. 76: AP Photo/Richard Drew

CHAPTER 4
p. 89: Tannen Maury/Bloomberg News/Landov; p. 97: Courtesy, Freestyle Audio; p. 102: AP Photo/Wilfredo Lee; p. 103: © David Redferns/Redferns; p. 109: AP Photo/Denis Poroy

CHAPTER 5
p. 116: AP Photo/Toby Talbot; p. 125: Joel Nito/AFP/Getty Images; p. 128: Bill Aron/PhotoEdit; p. 134: Comstock/Corbis; p. 135: Courtesy FacilitatePro.; p. 137: Image100/Jupiter Images

CHAPTER 6
p. 144: Thierry Roge/Reuters/Landov; p. 149 (cartoon): Morris/Cartoonstock.com; p. 158: AP Photo/Roy Aydelotte; p. 161: AP Photo/The Plain Dealer/Joshua Gunter; p. 164: Steve Barrett/Bloomberg News/Landov

CHAPTER 7
p. 175: Shangara Singh/Alamy; p. 190 (cartoon): Randy Glasbergen; p. 193: AP Photo/Edgard R.; p. 204: David Butow/Corbis/SABA

CHAPTER 8
p. 208: © Reuters/Corbis; p. 211: Spencer Grant/PhotoEdit; p. 212: Banana Stock/Jupiter Images; p. 223: David R. Frazier Photography, Inc./Alamy; p. 224: Photodisc Red/Getty Royalty Free; p. 229: AP Photo/Mark Humphrey

CHAPTER 9
p. 233: © David Young Wolff/PhotoEdit; p. 236: Jim Whitmer Photography; p. 245: Courtesy, JetBlue; p. 250: Michael S. Yamashita/Corbis; p. 252: © TWPhoto/Corbis; p. 259: Miguel Vidal/Reuters/Landov

CHAPTER 10
p. 263: Courtesy, Millipore Corporation; p. 272: CHIP EAST/Reuters/Landov; p. 278: Reuters/You Sung-ho; p. 284: Christinne Muschi/Reuters/Landov; p. 292: Johnsonville

CHAPTER 11
p. 303: YRC Worldwide Inc.; p. 307: AP Photo/Carlos Osorio; p. 309: AP Photo/Koji Sasahara; p. 320: Jeff Greenberg/PhotoEdit; p. 323: Joern Wolter/vario images Gmb & Co. KG/Alamy; p. 325: Jason Smalley/Wildscape/Alamy

CHAPTER 12
p. 331: Elena Rooraid/PhotoEdit; p. 343: Purestock/Getty Royalty Free; p. 348: Susan Van Etten/PhotoEdit; p. 349: Creatas/Jupiter Images

CHAPTER 13
p. 372: Kevin Horan/Time&Life Pictures/Getty Images; p. 376: Fisher/Thatcher/Stone/Getty Images; p. 384: Doug Kanter/AFP/Getty Images; p. 389 (cartoon): Randy Glasbergen; p. 397: Robert Galbraith/Reuters; p. 399: © Fredrik Renander/Alamy

CHAPTER 14
p. 403: Michael Newman/PhotoEdit; p. 410: Prentice Hall; p. 417: Robin Nelson/PhotoEdit; p. 418 (cartoon): Randy Glasbergen; p. 427: AP Photo

CHAPTER 15
p. 435: AP Photo/Jeff Zelevansky; p. 439: Image100/Jupiter Images; p. 441: Mark Richards/PhotoEdit; p. 448: Thinkstock/Jupiter Images; p. 450: Purestock/Getty Royalty Free; p. 456 (cartoon): © LaughingStock Licensing Inc. All rights reserved.

CHAPTER 16
p. 466: Tony Freeman/PhotoEdit; p. 469: James Wasserman Photography; p. 472: Digital Vision/Getty Royalty Free; p. 483: Image Source/Jupiter Royalty Free

CHAPTER 17
p. 496: AP Photo/General Motors/Joe Polimeni; p. 499: © NOAH Berger/Bloomberg News/Landov; p. 500: AP Photo/Ann Heisenfelt; p. 503: Courtesy, Hewlett Packard; p. 507 (cartoon): © The New Yorker Collection 1988 Bernard Schoenbaum from cartoonbank.com. All rights reserved.

ENDNOTES

CHAPTER 1

1. Katrina Brooker, "It Took a Lady to Save Avon," *Fortune*, October 15, 2001, pp. 203–208; Emily Nelson, "Avon Calls on Good-Looking Research," *Wall Street Journal*, May 23, 2002, p. B6. "Avon Sees China Operation as a Sole Business Unit," *SinoCast China Business Daily News*, December 13, 2005, p. 1; and "Avon, The Net, and Glass Ceilings," *BusinessWeek*, New York, February 6, 2005, p. 104.
2. Brooker, op. cit., p. 203.
3. Ibid., p. 204.
4. Molly Prior, "Slimming Down at Avon: Company Restructures to Become More Nimble," WWD, December 8.
5. http://www.supplychainplanet.com/e_article00030547.cfm
6. Ibid., p. 208.
7. Devin Leonard, "The Only Lifeline Was the Wal-Mart," *Fortune*, October 3, 2005, pp. 74–80.
8. In G. Hanson, "Determinants of Firm Performance: An Integration of Economic and Organizational Factors," unpublished doctoral dissertation, University of Michigan Business School, 1986.
9. M. A. Huselid, "The Impact of Human Resource Management Practices on Turnover, Productivity, and Corporate Financial Performance," *Academy of Management Journal*, 1995, p. 647; J. Pfeffer and J. Vega, "Putting People First for Organizational Success," *Academy of Management Executive*, 1999, pp. 37–48.
10. Peter Drucker, *An Introductory View of Management* (New York: Harper's College Press, 1977), p. 15.
11. Adam Lshimsky, "Meg and a Machine," *Fortune*, September 1, 2003, pp. 68–76.
12. Katie Hafner, "For eBay, Departures Underscore a Risky Time," *New York Times*, July 10, 2006, p. C1.
13. These are based on Henry Mintzberg, "The Manager's Job: Folklore and Fact," *Harvard Business Review*, July–August 1975, pp. 489–561.
14. Sumantra Ghoshal and Christopher Bartlett, "Changing the Role of Top Management: Beyond Structure to Processes," *Harvard Business Review*, January–February 1995, pp. 86–96.
15. Ibid., p. 89.
16. Ibid., p. 91.
17. Ibid., p. 96.
18. Ibid., p. 94.
19. Liz Simpson, "Fostering Creativity," *Training*, December 2001, vol. 38, no. 12, pp. 54–57.
20. Mintzberg, op. cit., pp. 489–561.
21. See, for example, ibid.; and George Copeman, *The Chief Executive* (London: Leviathan House, 1971), p. 271. See also George Weathersby, "Facing Today's Sea Changes," *Management Review*, June 1999, p. 5; David Kirkpatrick, "The Second Coming of Apple," *Fortune*, November 9, 1998, pp. 86–104; and Jenny McCune, "The Changemakers," *Management Review*, May 1999, pp. 16–22.
22. For information on employment prospects for managers, see "The 2004–14 Job Outlook in Brief," *Occupational Outlook Quarterly*, Spring 2006, pp. 7–11.
23. John Holland, *Making Vocational Choices: A Theory of Careers* (Upper Saddle River, N.J.: Prentice Hall, 1973). See also John Holland, *Assessment Booklet: A Guide to Educational and Career Planning* (Odessa, Fla.: Psychological Assessment Resources, Inc., 1990).
24. Edgar Schein, *Career Dynamics: Matching Individual and Organizational Needs* (Reading, Mass.: Addison-Wesley, 1978), pp. 128–129.
25. A. Howard and D. W. Bray, *Managerial Lives in Transition: Advancing Age and Changing Times* (New York: Guilford, 1988); discussed in Dwayne Schultz and Sydney Ellen Schultz, *Psychology and Work Today* (New York: Macmillan Publishing Co., 1994), pp. 103–104.
26. Ibid., Schultz and Schultz, p. 104.
27. Ibid.
28. Unless otherwise noted, the following discussion is based on Gary Yukl, *Leadership in Organizations* (Upper Saddle River, N.J.: Prentice Hall, 1998), pp. 251–255.
29. Joan Lloyd, "Derailing Your Career," *Baltimore Business Journal*, October 19, 2000, pp. 21, 33.
30. Yukl, op. cit., p. 252.
31. Shelley Kirkpatrick and Edwin Locke, "Leadership: Do Traits Matter?" *Academy of Management Executive*, May 1991, p. 49.
32. Yukl, op. cit., p. 253.
33. Quoted in William Holstein, "Why Big Ideas Often Fall Flat," *New York Times*, May 26, 2002, p. B5. See also Judith Chapman, "The Work of Managers in New Organizational Context," *Journal of Management Development*, January 2001, vol. 20, no. 1, p. 55.
34. Claude George, *The History of Management Thought* (Upper Saddle River, N.J.: Prentice Hall, 1968), p. 6.
35. Ibid., p. 7.
36. Alfred Chandler, *Strategy and Structure* (Cambridge, Mass.: MIT Press, 1962). See also Daniel Wren, *The Evolution of Management Thought* (New York: John Wiley, 1979).
37. D. S. Pugh, *Organization Theory* (Baltimore: Penguin, 1971), pp. 126–127.
38. Claude George Jr., *The History of Management Thought* (Upper Saddle River, N.J.: Prentice Hall, 1972), pp. 99–101.
39. Richard Hopeman, *Production* (Columbus, Ohio: Charles Merrill, 1965), pp. 478–485.
40. Henri Fayol, *General and Industrial Management*, transl. Constance Storrs (London: Sir Isaac Pitman, 1949), pp. 42–43.
41. Based on Richard Hall, "Intra-Organizational Structural Variation: Application of the Bureaucratic Model," *Administrative Science Quarterly*, December 1962, pp. 295–308.
42. William Scott, *Organization Theory* (Homewood, Ill.: Richard D. Irwin, 1967).
43. F. L. Roethlisberger and William Dickson, *Management and the Worker* (Boston, Mass.: Harvard University Graduate School of Business, 1947), p. 21.
44. Douglas McGregor, "The Human Side of Enterprise," eds. Edward Deci, B. Von Haller Gilmer, and Harry Kairn, *Readings in Industrial and Organizational Psychology* (New York: McGraw-Hill, 1972), p. 123.
45. R. Likert, *New Patterns of Management* (New York: McGraw-Hill, 1961), p. 6.
46. Ibid., p. 100.
47. Chris Argyris, *Integrating the Individual and the Organization* (New York: John Wiley, 1964).
48. Chester Barnard, *The Functions of the Executive* (Cambridge, Mass.: Harvard University Press, 1968), p. 84.
49. Ibid., p. 167.
50. Herbert A. Simon, *Administrative Behavior* (New York: Free Press, 1976), p. 11.

51. C. West Churchman, Russell Ackoff, and E. Leonard Arnoff, *Introduction to Operations Research* (New York: John Wiley. 1957), p. 18.
52. Daniel Wren, *The Evolution of Management Thought* (New York: John Wiley, 1979), p. 512.
53. Fred Vogelstein, "No Love Lost for Google," *Fortune*, August 23, 2004, pp. 19–20.
54. "10 on the Spot: These CEOs Are Facing Herculean Challenges," *Fortune*, February 20, 2006, vol. 153, no. 3, p. 81.
55. *The World Almanac and Book of Facts*, 1998 (Mahwah, N.J.: K-III Reference Corporation, 1998), p. 207.
56. Ibid., p. 9. See also "The Impact of Globalization on HR," *Workplace Visions*, Society for Human Resource Management, 2000, no. 5, pp. 1–8.
57. Bryan O'Reilly, "Your New Global Workforce," *Fortune*, December 14, 1992, pp. 52–66.
58. Robert Hof, "The Power of Us," *BusinessWeek*, June 20, 2005, pp. 75–81.
59. Kevin Werbach, "Using VOIP to Compete," *Harvard Business Review*, September 2005, pp. 140–147.
60. www.knowledge.wharton.upe.edu, "Human Resources Wharton," downloaded January 8, 2006. See also Richard Crawford, *In the Era of Human Capital* (New York: Harper Business, 1991), p. 10.
61. This discussion is based on Gary Dessler, *Management Fundamentals* (Reston, Va.: Reston, 1977), p. 2. See also William Berliner and William McClarney, *Management Practice and Training* (Burr Ridge, Ill.: McGraw-Hill, 1974), p. 11.
62. Rachel Moskowitz and Drew Warwick, "The 1994–2005 Job Outlook in Brief," *Occupational Outlook Quarterly*, Spring 1996, vol. 40, no. 1, pp. 2–41. See also Mahlon Apgar IV, "The Alternative Workplace: Changing Where and How People Work," *Harvard Business Review,* May–June 1998, pp. 121–136.
63. Crawford, op. cit., p. 26.
64. Peter Drucker, "The Coming of the New Organization," *Harvard Business Review*, January–February 1988, p. 45. For a good discussion, see also Thomas Davenport, *Thinking for a Living: How to Get Better Performance and Results from Knowledge Workers* (Boston, Mass.: Harvard Business School Press, 2006).
65. Thomas Peters and Robert Waterman Jr., "In Search of Excellence," eds. Jon Pierce and John Nestrom, *The Manager's Bookshelf* (Upper Saddle River, N.J.: Prentice Hall, 2000), p. 45.
66. Rosabeth Moss Kanter, *When Giants Learn to Dance* (New York: Touchstone, 1989).
67. James Brian Quinn, *Intelligent Enterprises* (New York: The Free Press, 1992).
68. Peter Senge, *The Fifth Discipline* (New York: Currency Doubleday, 1994), p. 3.
69. Tom Peters, *Liberation Management* (New York: Alfred Knopf, 1992), p. 9.
70. Bryan Dumaine, "What the Leaders of Tomorrow See," *Fortune*, July 3, 1989, p. 58. See also Weathersby, op. cit., p. 5; and Gary Hamel and Jeff Sampler, "The eCorp.: Building a New Industrial," *Fortune*, December 7, 1998, pp. 80–112.
71. Bryan Dumaine, "What the Leaders of Tomorrow See," *Fortune*, July 3, 1989, p. 51.
72. Rosabeth Moss Kanter, "The New Managerial Work," *Harvard Business Review*, November–December 1989, p. 88.
73. Drucker, "The Coming of the New Organization," p. 45.
74. Bryan Dumaine, "The New Non-Managers," *Fortune*, February 22, 1993, p. 81. See also David Kirkpatrick, "IBM: From Big Blue Dinosaur to e-Business Animal," *Fortune*, April 26, 1999, pp. 116–127. See also McCune, pp. 16–22; and Brent Schlender, "Larry Ellison: Oracle at Web Speed," *Fortune*, May 24, 1999, pp. 128–137.
75. Peter Drucker, "The Coming of the New Organization," p. 43.
76. Stratford Sherman, "A Master Class in Radical Change," *Fortune*, December 13, 1993, p. 82. See also McCune, pp. 16–22.
77. Some argue that with IT so widely available and used, it doesn't matter—unless you don't use it. See Nicholas Carr, "IT Doesn't Matter," *Harvard Business Review*, May 2003, pp. 41–49.
78. Kasra Ferdows et al., "Rapid Fire Fulfillment," *Harvard Business Review*, November 2004, pp. 104–110.
79. Ibid., p. 167.
80. "J. Crew Enhances Business Agility with ERP Solution," www.stores.org, downloaded July 8, 2006; "J. Crew Starts Fast in Trading Debut," Anne D'Innocenzio, www.techNewsworld.com, downloaded July 8, 2006; www.Forbes.com, downloaded July 8, 2006.
81. Joan Magretta, "The Power of a Virtual Integration: An Interview with Dell Computer's Michael Dell," *Harvard Business Review*, March–April 1998, p. 73.
82. Ibid., p. 76.
83. See, for example, Darrel Rigby and Dianne Ledingham, "CRM Done Right," *Harvard Business Review*, November 2004, pp. 118–127.
84. Pamela Babcock, "Shedding Light on Knowledge Management," *HR Magazine*, May 2004, pp. 47–50.
85. Ibid.

CHAPTER 2

1. Janet Adams et al., "Code of Ethics as Signals for Ethical Behavior," *Journal of Business Ethics*, February 2001, vol. 29, no. 3, pp. 199–211. See also Michael Burr, "Corporate Governance: Embracing Sarbanes-Oxley," *Public Utilities Fortnightly*, October 15, 2003, vol. 141, no. 19, pp. 20–22.
2. Ibid. See also Max Rexroad and Joyce Ostrosky, "Sarbanes-Oxley: What It Means to the Marketplace," *Journal of Accountancy*, February 2004, vol. 197, no. 2, pp. 43–48.
3. Adam Liptak, "Privacy Not the Issue in Google Case," *International Herald Tribune*, January 27, 2006, p. 22.
4. Manuel Velasquez, *Business Ethics: Concepts and Cases* (Upper Saddle River, N.J.: Prentice-Hall, 1992), p. 9; Kate Walter, "Ethics Hot Lines Tap into More Than Wrongdoing," *HR Magazine*, September 1995, pp. 79–85. See also Skip Kaltenheuser, "Bribery Is Being Outlawed Virtually Worldwide," *Business Ethics*, May 1998, p. 11.
5. S. Morris Engel, *The Study of Philosophy*, San Diego, Calif.: Collegiate Press, 1987, p. 52.
6. Richard Osborne, "A Matter of Ethics," *Industry Week*, September 4, 2000, vol. 49, no. 14, pp. 41–42.
7. Michael Boylon, *Business Ethics* (Upper Saddle River, N.J.: Prentice-Hall, 2001), pp. 37–38.
8. Ibid., p. 119.
9. Rachel Zimmerman, "Sites Ordered Shut-In Spam Case," *Wall Street Journal*, May 12, 2005, p. A35.
10. See, for example, Bonnie A. Osif, "Computer and Internet Ethics, Part 2," *Library Administration and Management*, Summer 2005, vol. 19, no. 3, pp. 149–153.
11. "Patent Granted for Groundbreaking Information Privacy Technology," Internet Wire, October 4, 2005.
12. Lee Freeman and A. Graham Peace, "Information Ethics: Privacy and Intellectual Property," *Information Management*, Spring 2005, vol. 18, no. 1/2, pp. 17, 31.
13. Brian Morrisey, "Cookies Are Seen as Privacy Threat," Adweek Online, December 5, 2005.
14. Ibid.
15. Darren Charters, "Electronic Monitoring and Privacy Issues in Business Marketing: The Ethics of the Double-Click Experience," *Journal of Business Ethics*, February 15, 2002, vol. 35, no. 4, pp. 243–255.

16. Janice Sipior et al., "Ethics of Collecting and Using Consumer Internet Data," *Information Systems Management*, Winter 2004, vol. 21, no. 1, pp. 58–67.
17. See, for example, Abbie Maliniak and Lynsey Mitchel, "Overview of the Current State of HIPAA Enforcement: Three Useful Tips for Avoiding Civil Penalties," *Journal of Health Care Compliance*, November–December 2006, vol. 8, no. 6, pp. 23–26.
18. "Do You Know Where Your Workers Are? GPS Units Aid Efficiency, Raise Privacy Issues," *BNA Bulletin to Management*, July 22, 2004, p. 233.
19. "Time Clocks Go High Touch, High-Tech to Keep Workers from Gaining the System," *BNA Bulletin to Management*, March 25, 2004, p. 97.
20. D. Leonard and Angela France, "Workplace Monitoring: Balancing Business Interests with Employee Privacy Rights," *Society for Human Resource Management Legal Report*, May–June 2003, pp. 3–6.
21. "You've Got Mail and the Boss Knows: Survey by Bentley's Center for Business Ethics Reveals Nine out of Ten Companies Monitor Their Employee's E-mail, Internet Use at Work," Europe Intelligence Wire, October 7, 2003.
22. See also Ravi Sarathy and Christopher Robertson, "Strategic and Ethical Considerations in Managing Digital Privacy," *Journal of Business Ethics*, August 15, 2003, vol. 46, no. 2, pp. 111–127.
23. "Workers Sharing Music, Movies at Work Violate Copyrights, Trigger Employer Fines," *BNA Bulletin to Management*, June 19, 2003, vol. 54, no. 25, p. 193.
24. "Privacy Breeds for Australian Stock Exchange Web Site," *Asia Pulse News*, July 22, 2004.
25. Thomas Watkins, "Malpractice Issues in the Technology Sector," *The Computer and Internet Lawyer*, August 2004, vol. 21, no. 8, pp. 14–22.
26. Norman E. Bowie, "Digital Rights and Wrongs: Intellectual Property in the Information Age," *Business and Society Review*, Spring 2005, vol. 110, no. 1, pp. 77–96.
27. "Former CEO Joins WorldCom's Indicted," *Miami Herald*, March 3, 2004, p. 4C.
28. Janet Adams et al., "Code of Ethics as Signals for Ethical Behavior," *Journal of Business Ethics*, February 2001, vol. 29, no. 3, pp. 199–211.
29. Sara Morris et al., "A Test of Environmental, Situational, and Personal Influences on the Ethical Intentions of CEOs," Business and Society, August 1995, pp. 119–147.
30. Justin Longnecker, Joseph McKinney, and Carlos Moore, "The Generation Gap in Business Ethics," *Business Horizons*, September–October 1989, pp. 9–14.
31. Vincent Calluzzo and Charles Cante, "Ethics in Informational Technology and Software Use," *Journal of Business Ethics*, May 15, 2004, vol. 15, no. 3, pp. 301–313.
32. Susan Winter et al., "Individual Differences in the Acceptability of Unethical Information Technology Practices: The Case of Machiavellianism and Ethical Ideology," *Journal of Business Ethics*, October 15, 2004, vol. 54, no. 3, pp. 303–326.
33. Vikas Anand et al., "Business as Usual: The Acceptance and Perpetuation of Corruption in Organizations," *Academy of Management Executive*, 2004, vol. 18, no. 2, pp. 40–41.
34. Ibid., p. 40.
35. Ibid., p. 41.
36. Floyd Norris and Diana Henriques, "Three Admit Guilty and Falsifying CUC's Books," *New York Times*, June 15, 2000, p. C1.
37. Stanley Milgram, "Behavioral Study of Obedience," *Journal of Abnormal and Social Psychology*, 1963, vol. 67, pp. 371–378.
38. Discussed in Samuel Greengard, "Cheating and Stealing," *Workforce*, October 1997, pp. 45–53.
39. For a discussion, see Steen Brener and Earl Molander, "Is the Ethics of Business Changing?" *Harvard Business Review*, January–February 1977, pp. 57–71; Robert Jackyll, "Moral Mazes: Bureaucracy and Managerial Work," *Harvard Business Review*, September–October 1983, pp. 118–130. See also Ishmael P. Akaah, "The Influence of Organization Rank and Role of Marketing Professionals' Ethical Judgments," *Journal of Business Ethics*, June 1996, pp. 605–614.
40. Jennifer Schramm, "Perceptions on Ethics," *HR Magazine*, November 2004, p. 176.
41. From Guy Bromback, "Managing Above the Bottom Line of Ethics," *Supervisory Management*, December 1993, p. 12.
42. Tom Horton, "Tone at the Top," *Directors and Boards*, Summer 2002, vol. 26, no. 4, pp. 8–9. See also Terry Thomas et al., "Strategic Leadership of Ethical Behavior in Business," *Academy of Management Executive*, 2004, vol. 17, no. 2, pp. 56–66.
43. Julian Barnes, "Unilever Once P&G Placed Under Monitor and Spikes," *New York Times*, September 1, 2001, p. B1.
44. Marcia Miceli and Janet Near, "Ethical Issues in the Management of Human Resources," *Human Resource Management Review*, vol. 11, no. 1, pp. 1–10.
45. Deon Nel, Leyland Pitt, and Richard Watson, "Business Ethics: Defining the Twilight Zone," *Journal of Business Ethics*, 1989, vol. 8, p. 781; Brenner and Molander, "Is the Ethics of Business Changing?" See also Daniel Glasner, "Past Mistakes Make Present Future Challenges," *Workforce*, May 1998, p. 117.
46. Rochelle Kelin, "Ethnic Versus Organizational Cultures: The Bureaucratic Alternatives," *International Journal of Public Administration*, March 1996, pp. 323–344.
47. Tom Beauchamp and Norman Bowie, *Ethical Theory and Business* (Upper Saddle River, N.J.: Prentice Hall, 2001), p. 109.
48. Lynne Paine et al., "Up to Code: Does Your Company's Conduct Meet World-Class Standards?" *Harvard Business Review*, December 2005, pp. 122–133.
49. Ibid., p. 123.
50. Amy Zuckerman, "Managing Business Ethics in a World of Pay All," *World Trade*, December 2001, vol. 14, no. 12, pp. 38–39.
51. These eight items are quoted from Lynne Paine, op. cit., p. 123.
52. Marcia Miceli and Janet Near, "Ethical Issues in the Management of Human Resources," *Human Resource Management Review*, vol. 11, no. 1, pp. 1–10.
53. James Kunen, "Enron Division (and Values) Thing," *New York Times*, January 19, 2002, p. A19.
54. Adams et al., op. cit.
55. Ibid.
56. Ibid.
57. For a discussion, see, for example, Alan Rowe et al., *Strategic Management: A Methodological Approach* (Reading, Mass.: Addison-Wesley Publishing Co., 1994), p. 101.
58. Dale Buss, "Corporate Compasses," *HR Magazine*, June 2004, pp. 127–132.
59. Miceli and Near, op. cit., p. 9.
60. Sandra Gray, "Audit Your Ethics," *Association Management*, September 1996, p. 188.
61. Richard Beatty et al., "HR's Role in Corporate Governance: Present and Prospective," *Human Resource Management*, Fall 2003, vol. 42, no. 3, p. 268.
62. Michael McCarthy, "Now the Boss Knows Where You're Clicking," *Wall Street Journal*, October 21, 1999, p. B1.
63. www.sap.com/solutions, January 9, 2005.
64. www.sap.com, January 13, 2006.
65. www.sap.com, January 13, 2006.
66. www.sas.com, January 10, 2006.
67. Tammy Joyner, "Big Boss Is Watching," *Atlanta Constitution*, July 25, 2001, p. D1.
68. Michael J. McCarthy, "How One Firm Attracts Ethics Electronically," *Wall Street Journal*, October 21, 1999, p. B1.
69. Adams et al., op. cit.

70. Ibid.
71. "A Lean, Clean Electric Machine," *Economist*, December 10, 2005, pp. 77–79.
72. S. A. Moorehead et al., "Corporate Citizenship in the New Century: Accountability, Transparency, and Global Stakeholder Engagement," New York: The Conference Board Inc., 2002, quoted in Nancy Lockwood, "Corporate Social Responsibility: HR's Leading Role," *The Society for Human Resource Management*, 2004, p. 2.
73. Lockwood, op. cit., p. 3.
74. Dennis Patton, "Give or Take on the Internet: An Examination of the Disclosure Practices of Insurance Firm Web Innovators," *Journal of Business Ethics*, March 15, 2002, vol. 36, no. 3, pp. 247–260.
75. See also Deborah Doan, "Beyond Corporate Social Responsibility: Minnows, Myths and Markets," *Futures*, March–April 2005, vol. 37, no. 2–3, pp. 215–230.
76. Beauchamp and Bowie, op. cit., p. 45.
77. Milton Friedman, *Capitalism and Freedom* (Chicago: University of Chicago Press, 1962), p. 133. See also Charles Handy, "A Better Capitalism," *Across the Board*, April 1998, pp. 16–22. See also Robert Reich, "The New Meaning of Corporate Social Responsibility," *California Management Review*, Winter 1998, pp. 8–17. Reich also believes that because of pressure from investors, nonowner stakeholders are being neglected and that the government should step in to protect them.
78. Beauchamp and Bowie, op. cit., pp. 49–52. See also Marjorie Kelly, "Do Stockholders 'Own' Corporations?" *Business Ethics*, June 1999, pp. 4–5.
79. Beauchamp and Bowie, op. cit., p. 79.
80. Ibid., p. 60.
81. Ibid., p. 54.
82. John Simon, Charles Powers, and John Gunnerman, "The Responsibilities of Corporations and Their Owners," *The Ethical Investor: Universities and Corporate Responsibilities* (New Haven, Conn.: Yale University Press, 1972); reprinted in Beauchamp and Bowie, pp. 60–65. See also Roger Kaufman et al., "The Changing Corporate Mind: Organizations, Vision, Missions, Purposes, and Indicators on the Move Toward Societal Payoffs," *Performance Improvement Quarterly*, 1998, vol. 11, no. 3, pp. 32–44.
83. Alexander Harney, "Falsified Records Highlight Flaw in the Social Audit Culture Standards," *Financial Times*, November 28, 2005, p. 4.
84. Charles Hess and Kenneth Hey, "Good Doesn't Always Mean Right," *Across the Board*, July/August 2001, vol. 38, no. 4, pp. 61–64.
85. Simon Zadek, "The Path to Corporate Responsibility," *Harvard Business Review*, December 2004, p. 127.
86. Jo-Ann Johnston, "Social Auditors: The New Breed of Expert," *Business Ethics*, March 1996, p. 27.
87. Harney, op. cit., p. 4.
88. Karen Paul and Steven Ludenberg, "Applications of Corporate Social Monitoring Systems: Types, Dimensions and Goals," *Journal of Business Ethics*, 1992, vol. 11, pp. 1–10.
89. Karen Paul, "Corporate Social Monitoring in South Africa: A Decade of Achievement, An Uncertain Future," *Journal of Business Ethics*, 1989, vol. 8, p. 464. See also Bernadette Ruf et al., "The Development of a Systematic, Aggregate Measure of Corporate Social Performance," *Journal of Management*, 1998, vol. 24, no. 1, pp. 119–133.
90. Ibid. See also John S. North, "Living Under a Social Code of Ethics: Eli Lilly in South Africa Operating Under the Sullivan Principles," *Business and the Contemporary World*, 1996, vol. 8, no. 1, pp. 168–180; and S. Prakash Sethi, "Working with International Codes of Conduct: Experience of U.S. Companies Operating in South Africa Under the Sullivan Principles," *Business and the Contemporary World*, 1996, vol. 8, no. 1, pp. 129–150. Standards similar to the international quality standards that have been used for some time have been put in place for social accountability areas such as child labor and health and safety. See Ruth Thaler-Carter, "Social Accountability 8000: A Social Guide for Companies or Another Layer of Bureaucracy?" *HR Magazine*, June 1999, pp. 106–108. In the 1990s, Sullivan proposed a new code for companies returning to South Africa after apartheid had ended, stressing the protection of equal rights and the promotion of education and job training.
91. Philip Berkowitz, "Sarbanes-Oxley Whistleblower Claims: The Meaning of Fraud Against Shareholders," *Society for Human Resource Management Legal Report*, July–August 2005.
92. Janet Near, "Whistle-Blowing: Encourage It!" *Business Horizons*, January–February, 1989, p. 5. See also Robert J. Paul and James B. Townsend, "Don't Kill the Messenger! Whistle-Blowing in America: A Review with Recommendations," *Employee Responsibilities and Rights*, June 1996, pp. 149–161. Nick Perry, "Indecent Exposures: Theorizing Whistle Blowing," *Organization Studies*, 1998, vol. 19, no. 2, pp. 235–257.
93. Near, op. cit., p. 5. See also Fraser Younson, "Spilling the Beans," *People Management*, June 11, 1998, pp. 25–26.
94. Near, op. cit., p. 6. See also David Lewis, "Whistleblowing at Work: Ingredients for an Effective Procedure," *Human Resource Management Journal*, 1997, vol. 7, no. 4, pp. 5–11.
95. "The Importance of Business Ethics," *HR Focus*, July 2001, vol. 78, no. 7, pp. 1, 13.
96. Jeffery Unerman and Mark Bennett, "Increased Stakeholder Dialog and the Internet: Towards Greater Corporate Accountability or Reinforcing Capitalist Enemy Economy in the Company Accounting," *Organizations and Society*, October 2004, vol. 29, no. 7, pp. 685–718.
97. Cox, op. cit., p. 11.
98. Carol Heimowitz, "The New Diversity," *Wall Street Journal*, November 14, 2005, p. R1.
99. Ibid., p. R3.
100. Patricia Digh, "Creating a New Balance Sheet: The Need for Better Diversity Metrics," *Mosaics*, Society for Human Resource Management, September–October 1999, p. 1.
101. Michael Carrell, Daniel Jennings, and Christina Heavrin, *Fundamentals of Organizational Behavior* (Upper Saddle River, N.J.: Prentice-Hall, 1997), pp. 282–283.
102. George Kronenberger, "Out of the Closet," *Personnel Journal*, June 1991, pp. 40–44.
103. Cox, op. cit., p. 88.
104. Ibid., p. 89.
105. J. H. Greenhaus and S. Parasuraman, "Job Performance Attributions and Career Advancement Prospects: An Examination of Gender and Race Effects," *Organizational Behavior and Human Decision Processes*, July 1993, vol. 55, pp. 273–298.
106. Adapted from Cox, op. cit., p. 64.
107. Ibid., pp. 179–180.
108. Madeleine Heilmann and Lewis Saruwatari, "When Beauty Is Beastly: The Effects of Appearance and Sex on Evaluation of Job Applicants for Managerial and Nonmanagerial Jobs," *Organizational Behavior and Human Performance*, June 1979, pp. 360–372; see also Tracy McDonald and Milton Hakel, "Effects of Applicant Race, Sex, Suitability, and Answers on Interviewer's Questioning Strategy and Ratings," *Personnel Psychology*, Summer 1985, pp. 321–334.
109. Francis Milliken and Luis Martins, "Searching for Common Threads: Understanding the Multiple Effects of Diversity in

Organizational Groups," *Academy of Management Review*, 1996, vol. 21, no. 2, p. 415; see also Patricia Nemetz and Sandra Christensen, "The Challenge of Cultural Diversity: Harnessing a Diversity of Views to Understand Multiculturalism," *Academy of Management Review*, July 21, 1996, pp. 434–462.

110. Patricia Digh, "Coming to Terms with Diversity," *HR Magazine*, November 1998, p. 119.
111. Jeremy Kahn, "Diversity Trumps the Downturn," *Fortune*, July 9, 2001, vol. 144, no. 1, pp. 114–116.
112. Cox, op. cit., p. 236.
113. Digh, op. cit., p. 119.
114. K. Kram, *Mentoring at Work* (Glenview, Ill.: Scott Foresman, 1985); Cox, op. cit., p. 198. See also Ian Cunningham and Linda Honold, "Everyone Can Be a Coach," *HR Magazine*, June 1998, pp. 63–66.
115. See, for example, G. F. Dreher and R. A. Ash, "A Comparative Study of Mentoring Among Men and Women in Managerial, Professional, and Technical Positions," *Journal of Applied Psychology*, 1990, vol. 75, no. 5, pp. 1–8.
116. Michelle Conlon and Wendy Zellner, "Is Wal-Mart Hostile to Women?" *BusinessWeek*, July 16, 2001, pp. 58–59.

CHAPTER 3

1. Andrew Schneider, "Small Business Going Global to Tap Markets," *Kiplinger Business Forecasts*, June 8, 2005, vol. 1, no. 2, p. 2.
2. Matthew Boyle, "Why FedEx Is Flying High," *Fortune*, November 1, 2003, pp. 145–152.
3. Moon Ihlwan, "Mom and Pop Outfits Are Embracing a Government Sponsored Effort to Get Them Online—Fast," *BusinessWeek Online*, August 27, 2003; Sagren Moodley, "E-Commerce and Export Markets," *Journal of Small Business Management*, July 2003, vol. 41, no. 3, pp. 31–39; Susannah Cahalan, "Small Businesses Find Success Melding the Local and the Global," *International Herald Tribune*, August 25, 2006, p. 10.
4. Schneider, op. cit.
5. Steven Zeitchik, "Global Face for MySpace," *Daily Variety*, June 21, 2006, vol. 291, no. 157, pp. 1–2.
6. Michael Tobin, "Debunking the Five Myths of Global Expansion," *Financial Executive*, March 2006, vol. 22, no. 2, pp. 57–60.
7. "Forrester's Study Pumps Up Estimated Increase in Offshoring Over Next Two Years," *BNA Bulletin to Management*, May 27, 2004, p. 171.
8. Lara Sowinski, "The Global Market," *World Trade*, August 2005, vol. 18, no. 8, pp. 28–32.
9. Charles Hill, *International Business* (Boston, Mass.: Irwin-McGraw Hill, 2001), p. 484.
10. Margaret Allen, "Technology Spawned Changes in Exporting," *Dallas Business Journal*, September 7, 2001, p. 22; Jan Quintrall, "It Pays to Know the Nuts and Bolts of E-Exporting," *Wenatchee Business Journal*, October 2005, p. C7.
11. See, for example, John Daniels and Lee Radebaugh, *International Business* (Reading, Mass.: Addison-Wesley, 1994), p. 544.
12. Michael Czinkota, Pietra Rivoli, and Ilka Tonkinen, *International Business* (Fort Worth, Tex.: The Dryden Press, 1992), p. 278.
13. Aaron Lucchetti, "Pioneer Group Blazes Trail After Purchase by Milan Bank," *Wall Street Journal*, July 9, 2001, p. 1.
14. Hill, op. cit., p. 492.
15. Barry James, "Air France and Delta Pave the Way for the Third Alliance," *International Herald Tribune*, June 23, 1999, p. 1.
16. John Daniels and Lee Radebaugh, *International Business* (Upper Saddle River, N.J.: Prentice Hall, 2001) p. 12.
17. "Shanghai General Motors Co.," www.sap.com, downloaded March 2006.
18. Czinkota et al., op. cit., p. 320.
19. Saritha Rai, "India Company Reaches Deal with AOL for Programming," *New York Times*, December 14, 2001, p. W1.
20. Gregory White, "In Asia, GM Pins Hope on a Delicate Web of Alliances," *Wall Street Journal*, October 23, 2001, p. A23; Alex Taylor III, "Shanghai Auto Wants to Be the World's Next Great Car Company," *Fortune*, October 4, 2004, pp. 103–110.
21. Wilfred Vanhonacker, "Entering China: An Unconventional Approach," *Harvard Business Review*, March–April 1997, pp. 130–40.
22. James Bamford et al., "Launching a World-Class Joint Venture," *Harvard Business Review*, February 2004, pp. 91–100.
23. For a discussion, see, for example, Arvind Phatak, *International Dimensions of Management* (Boston, Mass.: PWS-Kent, 1989), p. 2.
24. Note that there are few, if any, pure market economies or command economies anymore. For example, some of the French banking system is still under government control.
25. David Kemme, "The World Economic Outlook for 1999," *Business Perspectives*, January 1999, pp. 6–9.
26. Daniels and Radebaugh, op. cit., p. 138.
27. Czinkota et al., op. cit., p. 640.
28. For a discussion, see, for example, ibid., Chapter 2; and James Flanigan, "Asian Crisis Could Bring New Threat: Protectionism," *Los Angeles Times*, February 3, 1999, p. N1.
29. Czinkota et al., op. cit., p. 116.
30. Daniels and Radebaugh, op. cit., 1994, p. 409.
31. Molly O'Meara, "Riding the Dragon," *World Watch*, March/April 1997, pp. 8–18.
32. This is based on John Daniels and Lee Radebaugh, *International Business* (Upper Saddle River, N.J.: Prentice Hall, 2001), pp. 217–219.
33. Ibid., p. 218.
34. Karby Leggett, "Beijing Allows New York Life, Met Life, Nippon to sell in China," *Wall Street Journal*, December 12, 2001, p. A8.
35. Andrew Tanzer, "Chinese Walls," *Forbes*, November 12, 2001, vol. 168, pp. 74–75.
36. Mitch Betts, "Navigating Global IT," *Computer World*, July 18, 2005, vol. 40, no. 8, p. 23.
37. Mary Pratt, "Global Gotchas: How to Avoid Hidden Tracks in International Laws," *Computer World*, vol. 40, February 20, 2006, pp. 32–34.
38. Laura Pincus and James Belohlav, "Legal Issues in Multinational Business Strategy: To Play the Game, You Have to Know the Rules," *Academy of Management Executive*, November 1996, pp. 52–61.
39. Ibid., pp. 53–54.
40. Ibid., p. 53.
41. Richard Behar, "China's Phony War on Fakes," *Fortune*, October 30, 2000, p. 206. See also Derek Dessler, "China's Intellectual Property Protection: Prospects for Achieving International Standards," *Fordham International Law Journal*, 1995, 181.
42. Steve Levine and Betsy McKay, "Coke Finds Mixing Marriage and Businesses Tricky in Tashkent," *Wall Street Journal*, August 21, 2001, p. A1.
43. "Site Allows Owners to Assess Global Risk," *Indianapolis Business Journal*, September 29, 2003, vol. 24, no. 29, p. 38A.
44. Catherine Tinsley, "Models of Conflict Resolution in Japanese, German, and American Cultures," *Journal of Applied Psychology*, April 1998, pp. 316–322.
45. In John Tagliabue, "In the French Factory, Culture Is a Two-Way Street," *New York Times*, February 25, 2001, p. BU4.

46. Ken Belson, "As Starbucks Grows, Japan, Too, Is Awash," *New York Times*, October 21, 2001, p. BU5.
47. United Nations, "Draft International Code of Conduct on the Transfer of Technology" (New York: United Nations, 1981), p. 3; quoted in Michael Czinkota et al., op. cit., p. 313.
48. Ibid., p. 314.
49. Alex Taylor III, "Shanghai Auto Wants to Be the World's Next Great Car Company," *Fortune*, October 4, 2004, p. 110.
50. David Kirkpatrick, "Groupware Goes Boom," *Fortune*, December 27, 1993, pp. 99–100.
51. Paula Caproni, *The Practical Coach* (Upper Saddle River, N.J.: Prentice Hall, 2001), pp. 106–108; "In Brief: Office Workers Want Instant E-mail Responses," *New Media Age*, March 16, 2006, p. 13.
52. Paul Saffo, "The Future of Travel," *Fortune*, Autumn 1993, p. 119; Michael Miller, "Halo: Videoconferencing Done Right," *PC Magazine*, March 7, 2006, vol. 25, no. 4, p. 22.
53. Stephen Loudermilk, "Desktop Video Conferencing Getting Prime Time," *PC Week*, October 19, 1992, p. 81. See also Alan Weiner, "Face-to-Face Communication: Is It Really Necessary in a Digitizing World?" *Business Horizons*, May–June 2005, vol. 48, no. 3, pp. 247–254.
54. Kenneth Laudon and Jane Laudon, *Essentials of Management Information Systems* (Upper Saddle River, N.J.: Prentice Hall, 1997), p. 413; Simon Lam and John Schaubroeck, "Improving Group Decisions by Better Pooling Information: A Comparative Advantage of Group Decision Support Systems," *Journal of Applied Psychology*, August 2000, vol. 85, no. 4, p. 565.
55. David Kroenke and Richard Hatch, *Management Information Systems* (New York: McGraw-Hill, 1994), p. 359.
56. "Project Collaboration," www.oracle.com, downloaded January 15, 2006.
57. Elizabeth Roman, "Parents Shown Internet Dangers," *Telegram & Gazette*, January 8, 2006, p. B1; www.myspace.com, downloaded March 24, 2006.
58. "Virtual Communities," Asia Africa Intelligence Wire, July 2, 2005.
59. Jennifer Rowley, "Online Communities: Stabilizing E-Business," *Global Business & Economics Review*, February 7, 2005, vol. 1, no. 1, p. 84.
60. Laudon and Laudon, op. cit., p. 348.
61. Ibid., p. 384.
62. Philip Harris and Robert Moran, *Managing Cultural Differences* (Houston, Tex.: Gulf Publishing Company, 1979), p. 1.
63. Richard Siklos, "Sony's Unlikely Mogul, at the Crossroads," *New York Times*, September 18, 2005, p. BU5.
64. Gail Dutton, "Building a Global Brain," *Management Review*, May 1999, pp. 34–38.
65. Ibid., p. 35.
66. Gretchen Spreitzer, Morgan McCall Jr., and Joan Mahoney, "Early Identification of International Executive Potential," *Journal of Applied Psychology*, February 1997, pp. 6–29.
67. Lisa Bannon et al., "Mattel Hits Big by Marketing Same Toys Around the Globe," *Wall Street Journal*, April 29, 2003, p. A1.
68. Richard Tomlinson, "Who's Afraid of Wal-Mart?" *Fortune*, June 26, 2000, p. 196.
69. Ibid.
70. Darrell Rigby and Vijay Vishwanath, "Localization: The Revolution in Consumer Markets," *Harvard Business Review*, April 2006, pp. 82–92.
71. See, for example, S. M. Davis, "Managing and Organizing Multinational Corporations," eds. C. A. Bartlett and S. Ghoshal, *Transnational Management* (Homewood, Ill.: Irwin, 1992).
72. "Porsche Optimizes Its Global Parts Management Using Set Supply Chain Management," www.sap.com, downloaded March 2006.
73. Discussed in Kamel Fatehi, *International Management* (Upper Saddle River, N.J.: Prentice Hall, 1996), p. 123.
74. Ibid.
75. Ken Siegmann, "Workforce," *Profit*, November 1999, p. 47.
76. "Dräger Safety Re-Engineers Global Supply Chain, Builds Centralized Logistics and IT Infrastructure Yielding Three-Year ROI of 193%," www.oracle.com, downloaded March 2006.
77. Daniels and Radebaugh, op. cit., p. 529.
78. Fatehi, op. cit., p. 129.
79. See, for example, ibid., p. 230.
80. Ibid.
81. Geert Hofstede, "Cultural Dimensions in People Management," eds. Vladimir Pucik, Noel Tichy, and Carole Barnett, *Globalizing Management* (New York: John Wiley & Sons, Inc., 1992), pp. 139–158.
82. Ibid., p. 143.
83. Ibid.
84. Ibid., p. 147.
85. Geert Hofstede, "Cultural Constraints and Management Theories," *Academy of Management Review*, 1993, vol. 7, no. 1, pp. 81–93; reprinted in Joyce Osland, David Kolb, and Irwin Rubin, *The Organizational Behavior Reader* (Upper Saddle River, N.J.: Prentice Hall, 2001), pp. 345–356.
86. Fatehi, op. cit., p. 279.
87. Discussed in Helen Deresky, *International Management* (Reading, Mass.: Addison-Wesley, 1997), pp. 401–402.
88. Kevin Lowe et al., "International Compensation Practices: A Ten-Country Comparative Analysis," *Human Resource Management*, Spring 2002, pp. 45–66.
89. Christopher Earley and Elaine Mosakowski, "Cultural Intelligence," *Harvard Business Review*, October 2004, pp. 139–146.

CHAPTER 4

1. Gary Anthes, "Innovation Inside Out: IT Is Helping Visionary Companies Harness Outside Talent to Boost Innovation While Minimizing Costs and Risks," *Computerworld*, September 13, 2004, vol. 38, no. 37, pp. 49–51.
2. Kerk Phillips and Jeff Wrase, "Is Schumpeterian 'Creative Destruction' a Plausible Source of Endogenous Real Business Cycle Shocks?" *Journal of Economic Dynamics & Control*, November 2006, vol. 30, no. 11, pp. 1885–1914.
3. For example, see Mary Coulter, *Entrepreneurship in Action* (Upper Saddle River, N.J.: Prentice Hall, 2001), pp. 3–5.
4. Ibid.
5. Jeffrey Timmons, "The Entrepreneurial Mind," *Success*, April 1994, p. 48.
6. Ibid.
7. This is based on Marc Dollinger, *Entrepreneurship: Strategies and Resources* (Upper Saddle River, N.J.: Prentice Hall, 2003), pp. 7–8.
8. U.S. Patent and Trademark Office, "Issues and Patent Numbers," April 1999 (www.uspto.gov).
9. W. Gartner, "The Conceptual Framework for Describing the Phenomenon of New Venture Creation," *Academy of Management Review*, 1985, vol. 10, pp. 696–706, as cited in Dollinger, op. cit., p. 19.
10. "Small Business Economic Indicators 2000," Office of Advocacy, U.S. Small Business Administration, Washington, D.C., 2001, p. 5. See also "Small Business Laid Foundation for Job Gains," www.sba.gov/advo, downloaded March 9, 2006.
11. This data comes from "Small Business: A Report of the President," 1998, www.sba.gov/advo/stats. See also "Statistics of U.S. Businesses and Non-employer Status," www.sba.gov/advo/research/data.html, downloaded March 9, 2006.
12. R. J. Arend, "The Emergence of Entrepreneurs Following Exogenous Technological Change," *Strategic Management*

Journal, 1999, vol. 20, no. 1, pp. 31–47; discussed in Mary Coulter, *Entrepreneurship in Action* (Upper Saddle River, N.J.: Prentice Hall, 2001), p. 4.

13. Coulter, op. cit., p. 18.
14. C. R. Brockhaus, "The Psychology of the Entrepreneur," eds. C. Kent, D. Sexton, and K. Verspers, *Encyclopedia of Entrepreneurship* (Upper Saddle River, N.J.: Prentice Hall, 1982), pp. 39–71; discussed in Dollinger, op. cit., p. 38. See also Robert Baum and Edwin Locke, "The Relationship of Entrepreneurial Traits, Skill, and Motivation to Subsequent Venture Growth," *Journal of Applied Psychology*, August 2004, vol. 89, no. 4, pp. 587–599.
15. Richard Becherer and John Maurer, "The Proactive Personality Disposition and Entrepreneurial Behavior Among Small Company Presidents," *Journal of Small Business Management*, January 1999, vol. 37, no. 1, pp. 28–37.
16. Ibid.
17. Jill Kickul and Lisa Gundry, "Prospective for Strategic Advantage: The Proactive Entrepreneurial Personality and Small Firm Innovation," *Journal of Small Business Management*, April 2002, vol. 40, no. 2, pp. 85–98.
18. S. D. McKenna, "The Darker Side of the Entrepreneur," *Leadership and Organization Development Journal*, November 1996, vol. 17, no. 6, pp. 41–46. See also Richard Hendrickson, "Ingredients of Success," *Inside Business*, August 2002, vol. 4, no. 8, pp. 3–7.
19. Ibid.
20. Arlene Weintraub, "Can Boingo Wireless, from the Founder of EarthLink, Turn Hot Spots into Money?" *BusinessWeek*, April 29, 2002, no. 3780, p. 106.
21. From "The U.S. Small Business Administration's Small Business Start-Up Kit," downloaded May 12, 2002, www.sba.gov/starting/ask.html.
22. A. Bhide, "How Entrepreneurs Craft Strategies That Work," *Harvard Business Review*, March–April 1994, pp. 150–161; John Case, "The Origins of Entrepreneurship," *Inc.*, June 1989, pp. 51–62.
23. Peggy Lambing and Charles Kuehl, *Entrepreneurship* (Upper Saddle River, N.J.: Prentice Hall, 2000), p. 90.
24. Ibid., p. 91. See also Lora Kolodny, "The Problem: Lance Fried Planned to Sell His Waterproof MP3 Players in Surf Shops. But Could He Really Say No to the Big-Box Retailers?" *Inc*, April 2005.
25. Norman Scarborough and Thomas Zimmerer, *Effective Small Business Management* (Upper Saddle River, N.J.: Prentice Hall, 2002), p. 21.
26. Lambing and Kuehl, op. cit., p. 35.
27. Quoted in ibid.
28. Barbara Marsh, "When Owners of Family Businesses Die, Survivors Often Feel Unsuited to Fill the Void," *Wall Street Journal*, May 7, 1990, pp. B1–B2; discussed in William Schoell, Gary Dessler, and John Reinecke, *Introduction to Business* (Boston, Mass.: Allyn & Bacon, 1993), p. 173.
29. Lambing and Kuehl, op. cit., p. 38.
30. Steps 1 to 4 from Small Business Administration, "First Steps: How to Start a Small Business," downloaded May 12, 2002, www.sba.gov/starting/indexsteps.html. See also Nichole Torres, "Diary of a Startup," *Entrepreneur*, March 2006, vol. 34, no. 3, p. 94.
31. Schoell, Dessler, and Reinecke, op. cit., pp. 178–179. See also "All You Need to Know About Franchising," *Entrepreneur*, January 2006, vol. 34, no. 18, p. 8.
32. Laverne Urlacher, *Small Business Entrepreneurship: An Ethics and Human Relations Perspective* (Upper Saddle River, N.J.: Prentice Hall, 1999), pp. 114–119.
33. This section is based on Schoell, Dessler, and Reinecke, op. cit., pp. 132–42.
34. John Vinturella, *The Entrepreneur's Field Book* (Upper Saddle River, N.J.: Prentice Hall, 1999), pp. 109–110.
35. Cara Buckley, "A Long-Awaited Debut," *Miami Herald*, May 15, 2002, p. C1.
36. Dollinger, op. cit., pp. 314–333.
37. U.S. Small Business Administration, "Small Business Frequently Asked Questions," downloaded May 12, 2002, www.sba.gov/addl/stats/spfaq.txt.
38. Bill Friskics-Warren, "Tapping an Audience with an Ear to the Ground," *New York Times*, March 17, 2002, pp. 2, 33.
39. Ibid.
40. Ibid.
41. Ibid.
42. Ibid.
43. Ibid.
44. Ibid.
45. Ross Kerber, "dotcoms May Be Dead, But Small Businesses Are Still Using the Internet," *Boston Globe*, April 15, 2002, p. C1.
46. W. Keith Schilit, *The Entrepreneurs' Guide to Preparing a Winning Business Plan and Raising Venture Capital* (Upper Saddle River, N.J.: Prentice Hall, 1990), pp. 4–6.
47. Ibid., p. 5.
48. For a discussion, see Peter Wright, Mark Kroll, and John Parnell, *Strategic Management Concepts* (Upper Saddle River, N.J.: Prentice Hall, 1996), pp. 224–225.
49. See, for example, Paul Horn, "The Changing Nature of Innovation: R&D Management Needs to Enhance Collaboration and Integrate with Its Ecosystem of Suppliers," *Research-Technology Management*, November–December 2005, vol. 48, no. 6, pp. 28–34.
50. Horn, op. cit.
51. Mary Brandel, "Jumpstart Innovation," *Computerworld*, March 6, 2006, p. 44.
52. This is based on Philip Kotler and Gary Armstrong, *Principles of Marketing* (Upper Saddle River, N.J.: Prentice Hall, 2001), pp. 336–352.
53. Dollinger, op. cit., p. 335.
54. Adapted from R. Nielsen, M. Peters, and R. Hisrich, "Intrapreneurship Strategy for Internal Markets: Corporate, Nonprofit Anti-Government Institution Cases," *Strategic Management Journal*, April–June 1985, no. 6, pp. 181–89, quoted in Dollinger, op. cit., p. 333.
55. This is based on Dean Takahashi, "Reinventing the Intrapreneur," *Red Herring*, September 2000, pp. 189–196.
56. "Big Lessons from Little Divisions: Intrapreneurship 101," The Americas Intelligence Wire, March 23, 2006.
57. Ibid.
58. See, for example, Rosa Grimaldi and Alessandro Grandi, "Business Incubators and New-Venture Creation: An Assessment of Incubating Models," *Technovation*, February 2005, vol. 25, no. 2, pp. 111–122.
59. For a discussion of this, see Bahman Edrahimi et al., "The Success Factors in New-Product Development," *International Journal of Management and Decision-Making*, March 6, 2006, vol. 7, no. 2/3, p. 313.
60. See also "Three New Features of Innovation Brought About by Information and Communication," *International Journal of Information Technology and Management*, July 7, 2004, vol. 3, no. 1, p. 3.
61. "Kraft Looks Outside the Box for Inspiration," *Wall Street Journal*, June 2, 2006, p. 815.
62. "IBM Turns Inside Out to Usher in the Innovation Age," *Asia Pulse News*, March 14, 2006.
63. Mary Brandel, "Jumpstart Innovation," *Computer World*, March 6, 2006, p. 48.
64. John Carreyou and Barbara Martinez, "Research Chief Stirs Up Merck by Seeking Help of Others," *Wall Street Journal*, June 7, 2006, pp. A1, A12.

65. Anthes, op. cit.
66. See, for example, Hock-Hai Teo et al., "Organizational Learning Capacity and Attitude Toward Complex Technological Innovations: An Empirical Study," *Journal of the American Society for Information Science and Technology*, January 15, 2006, vol. 57, no. 2, pp. 265–279.
67. Morgan Swink, "Building Collaborative Innovation Capability: The Central Challenge of New-Product Development Is to Integrate and Address Dependencies That Span Customer Needs/Values, Product Specs and Supply-Chain Capabilities," *Research-Technology Management*, March–April 2006, vol. 49, no. 2, pp. 37–48.
68. Anthes, op. cit.
69. See also George Farris et al., "Web-Enabled Innovation in New-Product Development," *Research-Technology Management*, November–December 2003, vol. 46, no. 6, pp. 24–36.
70. Robert Rycroft and Don Kash, "Self Organizing Innovation Networks: Implications for Globalization," *Technovation*, March 2004, vol. 24, no. 3, pp. 187–198; see also Emmanuel Amadides and Nikos Karacapildes, "Information Technology Support for Knowledge and Social Processes of Innovation Management," *Technovation*, January 2006, vol. 26, no. 1, pp. 50–60.
71. See, for example, Andi Gray, "Exploring Product Lifecycle," *Fairfield County Business Journal*, June 20, 2005, vol. 44, no. 25, p. 9.
72. "Better by Design," *Economist*, September 17, 2005, vol. 376, no. 1444, p. 28.
73. Ibid.
74. This case is quoted from Dollinger, op. cit., p. 37, and it is adapted from Meera Louis, "Pooled Savings Help Jamaicans Build Business," *Wall Street Journal*, October 17, 2000, pp. B1–B2.

CHAPTER 5

1. Vicki Powers, "Virtual Communities at Caterpillar Foster Knowledge Sharing," *Training and Development*, June 2004, p. 41.
2. Kenneth C. Laudon and Jane P. Laudon, *Management Information Systems,* 9th ed. (Upper Saddle River, N.J.: Pearson Education, 2006), p. G7.
3. James Senn, *Information Systems in Management* (Belmont, Calif.: Wadsworth Publishing, 1990), p. 58.
4. Peter F. Drucker, "The Coming of the New Organization," *Harvard Business Review,* January–February 1988, p. 45.
5. Carroll Frenzel, *Management of Information Technology* (Boston, Mass.: Boyd & Fraser, 1992), p. 10.
6. See, for example, David Kroenke and Richard Hatch, *Management Information Systems* (New York: McGraw-Hill, 1994), p. 20.
7. Senn, op cit., p. 58.
8. George Marakas, *Decision Support Systems* (Upper Saddle River, N.J.: Prentice-Hall, 2003), p. 326.
9. Ibid.
10. Laudon and Laudon, op. cit., p. G7.
11. Frenzel, op. cit., p. 11.
12. Laudon and Laudon, op. cit., Chapter 2.
13. Laudon and Laudon, op. cit., pp. 43–44. See also Maracas, op. cit., p. 176, and, for an example, see "Mitek's QuickStrokes Recognition Tool," *Bank Systems & Technology,* January 2005, p. 42.
14. See, for example, Kroenke and Hatch, op. cit., p. 51.
15. Laudon and Laudon, op. cit., pp. 44–45.
16. Kenneth Laudon and Jane Laudon, *Essentials of Management Information Systems (*Upper Saddle River, N.J.: Prentice Hall, 1997), p. 405. See also Marakas, op. cit., pp. 3–5.
17. Marakas, op. cit., pp. 8–22.
18. Donna Fenn, "Picture the Image," *Inc.*, February 1994, pp. 66–71; http://www.bissettnursery.com/ (accessed September 10, 2006).
19. Larry Long and Nancy Long, *Computers* (Upper Saddle River, N.J.: Prentice-Hall, 1996), p. 18.
20. Senn, op. cit., p. 576.
21. This discussion is based on Senn, op. cit., pp. 576–577.
22. Senn, op. cit., p. A11.
23. Mary Sumner, *Enterprise Resource Planning* (Upper Saddle River, N.J.: Pearson Education, 2005), p. 63.
24. Laudon and Laudon, *Management Information Systems,* pp. 54–62. See also Sumner, op. cit., pp. 63–65, and Irma Becerra-Fernandez et al., *Knowledge Management* (Upper Saddle River, N.J.: Pearson Education, 2004), pp. 2–3.
25. Laudon and Laudon, ibid., pp. 57–59. See also "Dell: Build-To-Order Manufacturing," www.accenture.com (accessed January 9, 2006).
26. Michael Hickins, "Xerox Shares Its Knowledge," *Management Review*, September 1999, p. 42; http://www.darwinmagazine.com/read/020101/share.html (accessed September 10, 2006).
27. Pamela Babcock, "Shedding Light on Knowledge Management," *HR Magazine*, May 2004, pp. 47–50.
28. Irma Becerra-Fernandez et al., op. cit., p. 3.
29. Ibid.
30. Ibid., pp. 37–39.
31. Michael Hickins, op. cit., p. 42.
32. "Ryder Systems," Accenture.com, 2003. Accessed March 2, 2006.
33. Ibid.
34. http://www-306.ibm.com/software/lotus/ (accessed September 13, 2006).
35. Vicki Powers, op. cit., p. 42.
36. "Select Medical Corp Implements Oracle E-Business Week for 79 Long-Term Acute-Care Hospitals and 790 Outpatient Clinics," Oracle.com. Accessed March 2, 2006.
37. For the definition of *telecommunications*, see G. Michael Ashmore, "Telecommunications Opens New Strategic Business," *Journal of Business Strategy,* March–April 1990, p. 58.
38. Laudon and Laudon, *Management Information Systems*, pp. 262–268.
39. Frenzel, op. cit., pp. 159–160.
40. Ibid., p. 160.
41. The term *modem* is derived from the functions of modulation and demodulation. A modem's function is to modulate or superimpose on the telephone line's analog signal the digital information form the computer input device. See, for example, Frenzel, op. cit., p. 162.
42. Marakas, op. cit., p. 29.
43. Laudon and Laudon, *Essentials*, p. 413.
44. Kroenke and Hatch, op. cit., p. 359.
45. David Kirkpatrick, "Groupware Goes Boom," *Fortune*, December 27, 1993, pp. 100–101. For a discussion of group decision support systems, see also Marakas, op. cit., pp. 153–154.
46. Senn, op. cit., p. 415.
47. See, for example, Senn, op. cit., p. 418.
48. Ibid., p. 427.
49. Laudon and Laudon, *Management Information Systems,* p. 54.
50. John Wilke, "Computer Links Erode Hierarchical Nature of Workplace Culture," *Wall Street Journal*, December 9, 1993, p. A7.
51. Ibid.
52. See, for example, Laudon and Laudon, *Essentials,* pp. 413–416, and Tom Williams, "Virgin Holidays to Set Up 600 Homeworkers," *Travel Trade Gazette UK & Ireland,* November 17, 2006, p. 3.
53. See Sandra Atchison, "The Care and Feeding of Loan Eagles," *BusinessWeek*, November 15, 1993, p. 58; William Van Winkle, "Your Away-from-Home Office," *Home Office Computing,* January 2001, vol. 19, no. 1, p. 54; and Williams, op. cit., p. 3.

54. Atchison, op. cit., pp. 24–25.
55. Ibid., p. 28.
56. Mary Sumner, op. cit., p. 8.
57. Ibid., p. 24.
58. John Champy, *Reengineering Management: The Mandate for New Leadership* (New York: Harper Business, 1995), pp. 78–79.
59. Ibid., p. 79.

CHAPTER 6

1. "Fortis Bank Marketing Campaigns Gain in Efficiency," www.sas.com (downloaded March 4, 2006).
2. Ibid.
3. Max Bazerman, *Judgment in Managerial Decision Making* (New York: Wiley, 1994), p. 3.
4. See, for example, Herbert Simon, *The New Science of Management Decision* (Upper Saddle River, N.J.: Prentice Hall, 1971), pp. 45–47.
5. Larry Long and Nancy Long, *Computers* (Upper Saddle River, N.J.: Prentice Hall, 1996), p. M7.
6. Mairead Browne, *Organizational Decision Making and Information* (Norwood, N.J.: Ablex Publishing Corporation, 1993), p. 6.
7. Bazerman, op. cit., p. 5.
8. Herbert Simon, *Administrative Behavior* (New York: Free Press, 1977).
9. George Lowenstein, "The Creative Destruction of Decision Research," *Journal of Consumer Research*, December 2001, vol. 38, no. 4, pp. 499–505. See also Leigh Buchanan and Andrew O'Connell, "A Brief History of Decision Making," *Harvard Business Review*, January 2006, vol. 84, no. 1, pp. 32–42.
10. See, for example, Bazerman, op. cit., p. 5. Recent research addresses the question of how decision makers faced with severe uncertainty should deal with the problem; one study concluded that the decision maker needs to avoid demanding more information than is usable. See, for example, Yakov Ben-Haim, *Information Gap Decision Theory: Decisions Under Severe Uncertainty* (New York: Academic Press, 2001).
11. James March and Herbert Simon, *Organizations* (New York: Wiley, 1958), pp. 140–141.
12. For a discussion, see, for example, Bazerman, op. cit., pp. 4–5.
13. Ibid., p. 4.
14. John Hammond, Ralph Keeney, and Howard Raiffa, *Smart Choices* (Boston, Mass.: Harvard Business School Press, 1999), pp. 19–30.
15. Of course, this also assumes that Harold wants to stay in marketing.
16. Except as noted, the titles of the steps and the ideas for this section are based on Hammond et al., op cit., pp. 35–41.
17. Ibid., p. 47. See also Paul Nutt, "Expanding the Search for Alternatives During Strategic Decision-Making," *Academy of Management Executive*, 2004, vol. 18, no. 4, pp. 13–28.
18. Bazerman, op. cit., p. 4. See also Max H. Bazerman and Dolly Chugh, "Decisions Without Blinders," *Harvard Business Review*, January 2006, vol. 84, no. 1, pp. 88–98.
19. Based on Hammond et al., op. cit, pp. 67–72.
20. See, for example, Ram Charan, "Conquering a Culture of Indecision," *Harvard Business Review*, January 2006, pp. 108–116.
21. See, for example, Lisa Sayegh et. al, "Managerial Decision Making Under Crisis: The Role of Emotion in an Intuitive Decision Process," *Human Resource Management Review*, 2004, vol. 14, pp. 179–199; and Jeffrey Pfeffer and Robert Sutton, "Evidence Based Management," *Harvard Business Review*, January 2006, pp. 66–74.
22. Thomas Davenport, "Competing on Analytics," *Harvard Business Review*, January 2006, pp. 99–107.
23. Ibid., p. 100.
24. Ibid., p. 105.
25. Ibid., p. 102.
26. Ibid., p. 106.
27. Ibid.
28. "Analytics," sas.com (downloaded March 4, 2006).
29. Julie Schlosser, "Looking for Intelligence in Ice Cream," *Fortune*, March 17, 2003, p. 120.
30. Ibid.
31. See, for example, www.oracle.com/applications/cpm/intelligence.html (downloaded September 15, 2006).
32. George Marakas, *Decision Support Systems* (Upper Saddle River, N.J.: Pearson, 2003), pp. 8–22.
33. "Baylor Relies on SAS for Cost-Saving Strategic Enrollment Management," sas.com/Baylor (downloaded January 10, 2006).
34. Ibid.
35. Ibid.
36. Prased Padmanabhan, "Decision Specific Experience in Foreign Ownership and Establishment Strategies: Evidence from Japanese Firms," *Journal of International Studies*, Spring 1999, pp. 25–27. For further discussion of the usefulness of experience, see, for example, Michael McDonald and James Westphal, "Getting by with the Advice of Their Friends: CEOs' Advice Networks and Firms' Strategic Responses to Poor Performance," *Administrative Science Quarterly*, March 2003, vol. 48, no. 1, pp. 1–32.
37. "Fortis Bank Marketing Campaigns Gain in Efficiency," sas.com (accessed March 4, 2006).
38. Ibid.
39. Quoted in Robert L. Heilbroner, "How to Make an Intelligent Decision," *Think*, December 1990, pp. 2–4.
40. Ibid. See also Theodore Rubin, *Overcoming Indecisiveness: The Eight Stages of Effective Decision Making* (New York: Avon Books, 1985); John Hammond et al., op. cit.; and J. Frank Yates, "Decision Management: How to Assure Better Decisions in Your Company," *Global Cosmetic Industry*, February 2006, vol. 174, no. 2, p. 33(1).
41. This anecdote is quoted and paraphrased from Bill Breen, "What's Your Intuition?" *Fast Company*, September 2000, pp. 294–295.
42. Ibid., p. 296.
43. Alden Hayashi, "When to Trust Your Gut," *Harvard Business Review*, February 2001, p. 64. See also David A. Garvin, "All the Wrong Moves," *Harvard Business Review*, January 2006, vol. 84, no. 1, pp. 18–27.
44. J. Wesley Hutchinson and Joseph Alba, "When Business Is a Confidence Game," *Harvard Business Review*, June 2001, pp. 20–21. For an additional perspective, see, for example, John Middlebrook and Peter Tobia, "Decision-Making in the Digital Age," *USA Today*, September 2001, vol. 130, no. 2676, p. 50; and Linda Freeman, "Disney Exec Suggests Matrix for Decision-Making," *Credit Union Journal*, September 3, 2001, vol. 5, no. 35, p. 7.
45. Kenneth Laudon and Jane Price Laudon, *Management Information Systems* (Upper Saddle River, N.J.: Prentice Hall, 1996), p. 125. See also Bob F. Holder, "Intuitive Decision Making," *CMA*, October 1995, p. 6.
46. Joan Johnston et al., "Vigilant and Hypervigilant Decision Making," *Journal of Applied Psychology*, August 1997, vol. 82, no. 4, pp. 614–622.
47. Studies indicate that you can adjust your style and that decision styles are more like preferences and are not set in stone. See Dorothy Leonard and Susan Straus, "Putting Your Company's Whole Brain to Work," *Harvard Business Review*, July–August 1997, pp. 111–121.
48. See, for example, William Taggart and Enzo Valenzi, "Assessing Rational and Intuitive Styles: A Human Information Processing Metaphor," *Journal of Management Studies*, March 1990, pp. 1501–1571; and Christopher W. Allinson and John Hayes, "The Cognitive Style Index: A Measure of Intuition—Anaylsis for Organizational Research," *Journal of Management Studies*, January 1996, pp. 119–135.

49. This and the following guidelines are from Heilbroner, op. cit.
50. These techniques are based on Monica Elliott, "Breakthrough Thinking," *IIE Solutions*, October 2001, vol. 33, no. 10, p. 22; Curtis Sittenfeld, "The Most Creative Man in Silicon Valley," *Fast Company*, June 2000, pp. 275–290; Joy Caldwell, "Beyond Brainstorming: How Managers Can Cultivate Creativity and Creative Problem Solving Skills in Employees," *Supervision*, August 2001, pp. 6–9; "Creativity Rooms Help Brainstormers Become Rainmakers at America Online," *BNA Bulletin to Management*, June 24, 1999, p. 193; and Max Messner, "Encouraging Employee Creativity," *Strategic Finance*, December 2001, vol. 83, no. 6, pp. 16–18.
51. As discussed in Michael Roberto, "Making Difficult Decisions in Turbulent Times," *Ivey Business Journal*, January/February 2002, vol. 66, no. 3, pp. 14–20.
52. For an additional perspective, see, for example; Ruth Weiss, "How to Foster Creativity at Work," *Training & Development*, February 2001, pp. 61–67; A. Muoio, "Where Do Great Ideas Come From?" *Fast Company*, January–February 2000, pp. 149–164; Charles Fishman, "Creative Tension," *Fast Company*, November 2000, pp. 359–368; Andrew Hargadon and Robert Sutton, "Building an Innovation Factory," *Harvard Business Review*, May–June 2000, pp. 157–166; Michael Michalko, "Jumpstart Your Company's Creativity," *Supervision*, January 2001, vol. 62, no. 1, p. 14; and Liz Sampson, "Fostering Creativity: Companies Enhance the Bottom Line by Building Corporate Cultures That Encourage Employee Innovation," *Training*, December 2001, vol. 38, no. 12, pp. 54–58.
53. Gardiner Morse, "Decisions and Desire," *Harvard Business Review*, January 2006, p. 42.
54. Bazerman, op. cit., pp. 6–8; Roberto, op. cit., pp. 14–20.
55. Lowenstein, op. cit., pp. 499–505.
56. John Hammond et. al., "The Hidden Traps in Decision-Making," *Harvard Business Review*, January 2006, p. 121.
57. Ibid.
58. Ibid.
59. Leigh Buchanan and Andrew O'Connell, "A Brief History of Decision-Making," *Harvard Business Review*, January 2006, p. 40.
60. Hammond et al., op. cit.
61. Robert Cross and Susan Brodt, "How Assumptions of Consensus Undermined Decision-Making," *MIT Sloan Management Review*, Winter 2001, vol. 42, no. 2, p. 86.
62. Dan Lovallo and Daniel Kahneman, "Delusions of Success," *Harvard Business Review*, July 2003, pp. 56–64.
63. Ibid., p. 59.
64. Lester Letton and Laura Valvatne, *Mastering Psychology* (Boston, Mass.: Allyn & Bacon, 1992), pp. 248–249. See also Daphne Main and Joyce Lambert, "Improving Your Decision Making," *Business and Economic Review*, April 1998, pp. 9–12; and John Hammond, Ralph L. Keeney, and Howard Raiffa, "The Hidden Traps in Decision Making, *Harvard Business Review*, January 2006, vol. 84, no. 1, pp. 118–126.
65. See, for example, Janice Beyer et al., "The Selective Perception of Managers Revisited," *Academy of Management Journal*, June 1997, pp. 716–737.
66. Dewitt Dearborn and Herbert A. Simon, "Selective Perception: A Note on the Departmental Identification of Executives," *Sociometry*, 1958, vol. 21, pp. 140–144. For a recent study of this phenomenon, see Mary Waller, George Huber, and William Glick, "Functional Background as a Determinant of Executives' Selective Perception," *Academy of Management Journal*, August 1995, pp. 943–994. While not completely supporting the Dearborn findings, these researchers did also conclude that managers' functional backgrounds affected how they perceived organizational changes. See also Paul Gamble and Duncan Gibson, "Executive Values and Decision Making: The Relationship of Culture and Information Flows," *Journal of Management Studies*, March 1999, pp. 217–240.
67. Max Bazerman and Dolly Chugh, "Decisions Without Blinders," *Harvard Business Review*, January 2006, pp. 88–97.
68. Irving Janis, *Groupthink: Psychological Studies of Policy Decisions and Fiascos*, 2d ed. (Boston, Mass.: Houghton Mifflin, 1982). See also James Esser, "Alive and Well After 25 Years: A Review of Group Think Research," *Organizational Behavior and Human Performance*, February–March 1998, pp. 116–142.
69. See, for example, www.oracle.com/applications/cpm/intelligennce.html (downloaded September 15, 2006).
70. Amy Merrick, "Expensive Circulars Help Precipitate Kmart President's Departure," *Wall Street Journal*, January 18, 2002, p. B1; "Kmart to Acquire Sears in $11 Billion Deal," http://www.msnbc.com/id/6509683/. Downloaded March 9, 2006.
71. This discussion is based on Joan Feldman, "JetBlue Loves New York," *Air Transport World*, June 2001, vol. 38, no. 6, p. 78.
72. The breakeven point is also sometimes defined more technically as the quantity of output or sales that will result in a zero level of earnings before interest or taxes. See, for example, J. William Petty et al., *Basic Financial Management* (Upper Saddle River, N.J.: Prentice Hall, 1993), p. 932.
73. Jay Heizer and Barry Render, *Production and Operations Management* (Upper Saddle River, N.J.: Prentice Hall, 1996), pp. 240–250. For a good treatment of statistical decision theory, see, for example, Simon French and David Rios, *Statistical Decision Theory* (New York: Oxford University Press, 2000).

CHAPTER 7

1. Oxford University Press, www.sap.com. Downloaded January 9, 2006.
2. George L. Morrisey, *A Guide to Tactical Planning* (San Francisco: Jossey-Bass, 1996), p. 61; Fred David, *Strategic Management* (Upper Saddle River, N.J.: Pearson, 2005), pp. 123–124.
3. Fred David, ibid.
4. R. R. Donnelley and Sons Company website, www.rrdonnelley.com.
5. Ronald Henkoff, "How to Plan for 1995," *Fortune*, December 31, 1990, p. 74; and "RR Donnelley Paying $1.3 Billion for Banta," UPI NewsTrack, November 1, 2006, p. NA.
6. Peter Drucker, "Long Range Planning," *Management Science*, 1959, vol. 5, pp. 238–249. See also Bristol Voss, "Cover to Cover Drucker," *Journal of Business Strategy*, May–June 1999, pp. 1–9.
7. Peter F. Drucker, *The Effective Executive* (New York: Harper & Row, 1966); quoted in Keith Curtis, *From Management Goal Setting to Organizational Results* (Westport, Conn.: Quorum Books, 1994), p. 101.
8. "Setting Departmental Goals You Can Actually Achieve," *Info-Tech Advisor Newsletter*, January 22, 2002.
9. Steven Carroll and Henry Tosi, *Management by Objectives* (New York: Macmillan, 1973); see also Conny Antoni, "Management by Objectives: An Effective Tool for Teamwork," *International Journal of Human Resource Management*, February 2005, vol. 16, no. 2, pp. 174–185.
10. Other examples of time series include daily average temperatures in Chicago, daily average aircraft turnaround time for Southwest Airlines, and monthly customer service satisfaction ratings.
11. Dennis Berman, "Lousy Sales Forecasts Helped Fuel the Telecom Mess," *Wall Street Journal*, July 9, 2001, p. B1.
12. "First Too Few, Then Too Many . . . and Finally a Spot On!" sas.com (accessed January 10, 2006).
13. Kenneth Laudon and Jane Laudon, *Management Information Systems* (Upper Saddle River, N.J.: Prentice Hall), p. 598; and "Wal-Mart to Triple Size of a Warehouse," TechWeb,

http://192.215.17.45/newsflash/nf617/0210—st6.htm (accessed February 10, 1999).
14. Philip Kotler, *Marketing Management* (Upper Saddle River, N.J.: Prentice Hall, 1997), p. 113.
15. Phillip Kotler and Gary Armstrong, *Principles of Marketing,* (Upper Saddle River, N.J.: Pearson, 2001), pp. G7–8.
16. "Companies Turn to Private Spies," *Fortune*, August 23, 2004, p. 24.
17. For a tool that helps managers more clearly understand environmental trends, see Sarsha Drafi and Paul Kampas, "How to Identify Your Enemies Before They Destroy You," *Harvard Business Review*, November 2002, pp. 115–120.
18. Susan Warren, "I-Spy: Getting the Lowdown on Your Competition Is Just a Few Clicks Away," *Wall Street Journal*, January 14, 2002, p. 14.
19. George Day and Paul Shoemaker, "Scanning the Periphery," *Harvard Business Review*, November 2005, pp. 135–148.
20. Harvey Kahalas, "A Look at Planning and Its Components," *Managerial Planning*, January–February 1982, pp. 13–16; reprinted in Phillip DuBose, *Readings in Management* (Upper Saddle River, N.J.: Prentice Hall, 1988), pp. 49–50. For a discussion of a modern technique for evaluating management policies and procedures, see Salwa Ammar and Ronald Wright, "Characteristics and Features of a Performance Evaluation Model Using a Multilevel Fuzzy Rule-Based System," *International Journal of Technology, Policy and Management,* May 10, 2004, vol. 3, no. 2, p. 301.
21. "Annual Report, 2001. Feature Stories, Dell," Accenture.com (accessed January 9, 2006).
22. Jeffrey McCracken, "'Way Forward' Requires Culture Shift at Ford," *Wall Street Journal*, January 23, 2006, p. B1.
23. Fred David, *Strategic Management* (Upper Saddle River, N.J.: Prentice Hall, 2001), p. 54.
24. David Pringle, "Nokia's CEO, Marking a Decade, Faces Struggling, Quickly Changing Industry," *Wall Street Journal*, January 23, 2002, p. B70.
25. Orit Gadiesh and James Gilbert, "Transforming Corner Office Strategy into Front-Line Action," *Harvard Business Review*, May 2000, p. 74.
26. Danny Hakim, "With Huge Sale, GM Buries a Discarded Strategy," *New York Times*, October 30, 2001, p. C8.
27. Joseph Weitz, "How Ferarri Toils in the Nirvana of Carmakers," *Wall Street Journal*, January 24, 2006, p. B2.
28. Mylene Mangalindian, "How Amazon's Dream Alliance with Toys 'R' Us Went So Sour," *Wall Street Journal*, January 23, 2006, p. A1.
29. Jim Carbone, "Contract Manufacture Is Moved to Vertical Integration," *Purchasing*, October 18, 2001, vol. 130, no. 20, pp. 33–35.
30. "Killer App," *Fortune*, September 1, 2003, pp. 111–116.
31. John Byrne et al., "The Virtual Corporation," *BusinessWeek*, Feburary 8, 1993, p. 99; see also Keith Hammonds, "This Virtual Agency Has Big Ideas," *Fast Company*, November 1999, pp. 70–74.
32. Gary Latham and J. James Baldes, "The Practical Significance of Locke's Theory of Goal Setting," *Journal of Applied Psychology*, February 1975, pp. 605–612. See also Gary Latham, "The Effects of Proximal and Distal Goals on Performance of a Moderately Complex Task," *Journal of Organizational Behavior*, July 1999, pp. 421–430.
33. Katherin Mieszkowski, "The E Lance Economy," *Fast Company*, November 1999, pp. 66–68. See also www.elance.com/ (accessed January 5, 2007).
34. Michael Porter, *Competitive Advantage* (New York: Free Press, 1980).
35. "Westdeutsche Bank," www.sap.com (accessed January 9, 2006).
36. Michael Porter, op. cit.
37. "Pella Corp. Streamlines Business Processes to Cut Costs and Boost Productivity with Oracle E-Business Suite," Oracle.com (January 9, 2006).
38. Laura Holson and John Markoff, "With One Click of the Mouse," *New York Times*, January 23, 2006, p. C1.
39. Adrienne Carter, "Kodak's Promising Development," *Money*, Feburary 2002, vol. 31, no. 2, p. 39.
40. Robert Kaplan and David Norton, "The Office of Strategy Management," *Harvard Business Review*, October 2005, pp. 72–80.
41. Michael Mankin and Richard Steele, "Turning Great Strategy into Great Performance," *Harvard Business Review*, July/August 2005, pp. 65–72.
42. Laura Ponticello, "Scorecard: Linking Strategy to Performance Objectives," www.ISIXSIGMA.com (accessed January 21, 2006).
43. Noel Tichy and the RAM Charan, "The CEO as Coach: An Interview with Allied Signal's Lawrence Bossidy," *Harvard Business Reivew*, March–April 1995, pp. 69–78.
44. www.sas.com (accessed January 9, 2006).
45. www.sas.com/success (accessed January 10, 2006).

CHAPTER 8

1. Ron Ruggles, "Transaction Monitoring Boosts Safety, Perks Up Coffee Chain Profits," *Nation's Restaurant News*, November 28, 2005, vol. 39, no. 58, p. 35.
2. Kenneth Merchant, "The Control Function of Management," *Sloan Management Review*, Summer 1982, p. 44.
3. This section is based on William Newman, *Constructive Control* (Upper Saddle River, N.J.: Prentice Hall, 1995), pp. 6–9.
4. Kristina Sullivant, "Boeing Achieves Internet Liftoff," *PC Week*, May 10, 1999, p. 67.
5. Ibid.
6. Melanie Warner, "Confessions of a Control Freak," *Fortune*, September 4, 2000, pp. 130–140.
7. These characteristics are based on Robert Simons, *Levers of Control, How Managers Use Innovative Control Systems to Drive Strategic Renewal* (Boston, Mass.: Harvard Business School Press, 1995), p. 87.
8. This discussion is based on Simons, op. cit., pp. 87–88.
9. For an example, see Simons, op. cit., p. 82.
10. Daniel Wren, *The Evolution of Management Thought* (New York: John Wiley & Sons, 1994), p. 115.
11. Based on Kenneth Merchant, *Modern Management Control Systems* (Upper Saddle River, N.J.: Prentice Hall, 1998), p. 642.
12. For a discussion, see ibid., pp. 542–545.
13. Biff Motely, "Picking the Right Ratio to Measure Performance," *Bank Marketing*, January/February 2002, vol. 34, no. 1, p. 44.
14. Merchant, *Modern Management Control Systems,* p. 304.
15. Arif Mohammed, "Hyundai Boosts Network Access and Control," *Computer Weekly*, February 22, 2005, p. 44.
16. Mary Sumner, *Enterprise Resource Planning* (Upper Saddle River, N.J.: Pearson Education, 2005).
17. "Select Medical Corp Implements Oracle E-Business Suite for 79 Long-Term Acute-Care Hospitals and 790 Outpatient Clinics," www.oracle.com (accessed January 10, 2006).
18. "Midsize Company Turns to Process-Driven ERP System; Biotech Firm Rolls Out ERP System from Exact Software in 18 Months to 48 Offices Worldwide," *InformationWeek*, December 23, 2004, no. 9750-6874.
19. "Millipore Goes Global with Oracle," www.oracle.com (accessed January 9, 2006).
20. Ibid.
21. "Healthcare Insurer Fit for Success," www.sas.com (accessed January 10, 2006).
22. Matt Hicks, "Tuning to the Big Picture for a Better Business," *PC Week*, July 15, 1999, p. 69.

23. "RFID: Technology Tracks Goods, Now People," Knight-Ridder Tribune Business News (accessed January 20, 2006).
24. Jennifer Maselli and Beth Batcheldor, "Remote-Control Businesses: Integrating Real-Time Remote Diagnostic Data with CRM and ERP Systems to Boost Sales and Improve Service," *InformationWeek*, September 3, 2001, vol. 18, p. NA.
25. Jeffrey Stanton and Janet Barnes-Farrell, "Effects of Electronic Performance Monitoring on Personal Control, Task Satisfaction, and Task Performance," *Journal of Applied Psychology*, December 1996, p. 738; and Paul Greenlaw, "The Impact of Federal Legislation to Limit Electronic Monitoring," *Public Personnel Management*, Summer 1997, pp. 227–245.
26. Norihiko Shirouzu and Jon Bigness, "7-Elevens' Operators Resist System to Monitor Managers," *Wall Street Journal*, June 16, 1997, pp. B1–B6.
27. www.sas.com/success (accessed January 10, 2006).
28. Joseph Rosanas and Manuel Nevilla, "The Ethics of Management Control Systems: Developing Technical and Moral Values," *Journal of Business Ethics*, March 2005, vol. 57, no. 1, pp. 83–97.
29. The following, except as noted, is based on Kenneth Merchant, *Control in Business Organizations* (Boston, Mass.: Pitman, 1985), pp. 71–120. See also Robert Kaplan, "New Systems for Measurement and Control," *The Engineering Economist*, Spring 1991, pp. 201–218.
30. This is based on Simons, op. cit., pp. 81–82.
31. "Did Warner-Lambert Make a $468 Million Mistake?" *BusinessWeek*, November 21, 1983, p. 123; quoted in Merchant, *Control in Business Organizations,* pp. 98–99.
32. Chris Argyris, "Human Problems with Budgets," *Harvard Business Review*, January–February 1953, pp. 97–110.
33. "Why Good Accountants Do Bad Audits," *Harvard Business Review*, November 2002, pp. 97–102.
34. "Wal-Mart Takes Reigns at Seiyu," *MMR*, December 12, 2005, vol. 22, no. 20, p. 103.
35. See also Eric Krell, "Greener Pastures," *Training*, November 2001, vol. 38, no. 11, pp. 54–59.
36. Tom Burns and G. M. Stalker, *The Management of Innovation* (London: Tavistock, 1961), p. 119.
37. Jeffrey Seglin, "A Company Credo, as Applied or Not," *New York Times*, July 15, 2001, pp. 3–4.
38. David Pollitt, "Satisfied Employees Keep Better Track of Tornadoes at the US National Weather Service," *Human Resource Management International Digest*, 2005, vol. 13, no. 1, pp. 15–18.
39. J. Newcomb, 1998 letter to employees, May 17, 1999.
40. J. Pfeffer and J. Veiga, "Putting People First for Organizational Success," *Academy of Management Executive*, 1999, vol. 13, pp. 37–48.
41. See also John Myer, "Employee Commitment and Motivation: A Conceptual Analysis and Integrative Model," *Journal of Applied Psychology*, December 2004, vol. 89, no. 6, pp. 191–206.
42. James McElroy, "Managing Workplace Commitment by Putting People First," *Human Resource Management Review*, 2001, vol. 11, pp. 329–334.
43. See also Rene Schalk and Wim Van Dijk, "Quality Management and Employee Commitment Illustrated with Examples from Dutch Healthcare," *International Journal of Healthcare Quality Assurance*, 2005, vol. 18, nos. 2–3, pp. 170–178.
44. Personal interview. See Gary Dessler, *Winning Commitment: How to Build and Keep a Competitive Work Force* (New York: McGraw-Hill, 1993), pp. 27–28.
45. Ibid., p. 28.
46. Ibid., p. 30.
47. See, for example, Gerald Fryxell et al., "The Role of Trustworthiness in Maintaining Employee Commitment During Restructuring in China," *Asia Pacific Journal of Management*, 2004, vol. 21, pp. 515–533.
48. Rosabeth Moss Kanter, *Commitment and Community* (Cambridge, Mass.: Harvard University Press, 1972), pp. 24–25.
49. See Dessler, op. cit., p. 64.
50. JoAnn Davy, "Online at the Office: Virtual Communities Go to Work," *Managing Office Technology*, July–August 1998, pp. 9–11.
51. Ibid.
52. Dessler, op. cit., p. 69.
53. Abraham Maslow, *Motivation and Personality* (New York: Harper & Row, 1954), p. 336.
54. Interview with assembler Dan Dise, March 1992.
55. Personal interview, March 1992.
56. Ron Ruggles, op. cit., p. 35.

CHAPTER 9

1. Reuben Slone, "Leading a Supply-Chain Turnaround," *Harvard Business Review*, October 2004, pp. 114–121.
2. Ibid., p. 114.
3. Richard Chase and Nicholas Aquilero, *Production and Operations Management*, 6th ed. (Homewood, Ill.: Irwin, 1992), p. 5.
4. Ibid., p. 5.
5. Based on Jay Heizer and Barry Render, *Operations Management,* 6th ed. (Upper Saddle River, N.J.: Prentice Hall, 2001), p. 181.
6. Norman Gaither, *Production and Operations Management*, 5th ed. (Fort Worth, Tex.: The Dryden Press, 1992), p. 22.
7. "Goodnight, Vietnam," *Economist*, January 8, 2000, p. 65.
8. Ibid., p. 65.
9. Gaither, op. cit., pp. 132–133.
10. See, for example, James Gilmore and Joseph Pine II, "The Four Faces of Mass Customization," *Harvard Business Review*, January–February 1997, pp. 91–101; and Mark Willoughby, "SOA: Enabler of Mass Customization," *Computerworld*, November 20, 2006, p. 30.
11. For a discussion of how other companies apply these concepts, see, for example, Edward Feitzinger and Jan Lee, "Mass Customization and Hewlett-Packard: The Power of Postponement," *Harvard Business Review*, January–February 1997, pp. 116–121; and Frank Piller and Ashok Kumar, "For Each, Their Own: The Strategic Imperative of Mass Customization," *Industrial Engineer*, September 2006, pp. 40–46.
12. Everett Adam Jr. and Ronald Ebert, *Production and Operations Management* (Upper Saddle River, N.J.: Prentice Hall, 1992), p. 254.
13. Ibid.
14. Gaither, op. cit., p. 135. See also Nancy Hyer, "The Discipline of Real Cells," *Journal of Operations Management*, August 1999, pp. 557–559; and Tom Dassenbach, "Cellular Manufacturing Part 1—What's in It for You?" *Wood & Wood Products*, November 2005, pp. 29–33.
15. Barry Render and Jay Heizer, *Principles of Operations Management* (Upper Saddle River, N.J.: Prentice Hall, 1997), p. 551.
16. Ibid., pp. 551–553.
17. Jack Robertson, "Sony Centralizes Procurement," *EBN*, January 28, 2002, p. 1.
18. James Evans et al., *Applied Production and Operations Management* (St. Paul, Minn.: West Publishing Co., 1984), pp. 500–501.
19. Ibid., p. 511.
20. See, for example, T. C. E. Cheng, "An EOQ Model with Learning Effect on Set-Ups," *Production and Inventory Management Journal*, First Quarter 1991, pp. 83–84.
21. Evans et al., op. cit., p. 39.
22. Joel E. Ross, *Total Quality Management: Text, Cases and Readings* (Delray Beach, Fla.: St. Lucie Press, 1993), p. 1. See also James Gaskin, "Bonner Bets on Total Quality Management," *Internet Week*, September 6, 1999, p. 43.

23. Render and Heizer, op. cit., p. 96. See also, Chip Caldwell, "Lean-Six Sigma: Tools for Rapid Cost Reduction: Have You Ever Conducted a "Manager Quality Waste Walk"? If Not, Read On." *Healthcare Financial Management,* October 2006, pp. 96–99.
24. Discussed in Ross, op. cit., pp. 2–3, 35–36.
25. In Richard Hodgetts, *Blueprints for Continuous Improvement: Lessons from the Baldrige Winners* (New York: American Management Association, 1993), p. 19. See also www.quality.nist.gov/Business_Criteria.htm (accessed November 8, 2006).
26. "How Creamy? How Crunchy? Kraft Foods Discovers the True Measure of SAS," www.sas.com (accessed January 10, 2006).
27. Chase and Aquilero, op. cit., p. 197.
28. These traits are quoted from David Anderson, *Design for Manufacturability* (Lafayette, Calif.: CI Press, 1990), p. 9.
29. Ibid., p. 16.
30. Ibid., p. 15. See also F. Robert Jacobs and Vincent Mabert, *Production Planning, Scheduling, and Inventory Control* (Norcross, Ga.: Industrial Engineering and Management Press, 1986), pp. 96–100; and Otis Port, Zachary Shiller, Gregory Miles, and Amy Schulman, "Smart Factories, America's Turn," *BusinessWeek,* May 8, 1989, pp. 142–148.
31. See, for example, Joseph Martinich, *Production and Operations Management* (New York: Wiley, 1997), pp. 215–216.
32. Valerie Reitman, "Global Money Trends Rattle Shop Windows in Heartland America," *Wall Street Journal,* November 26, 1993, p. A1. See also Derek Korn, "Surviving Global Competition Through Aggressive Business Practices," *Modern Machine Shop,* August 2005, vol. 78, no. 3, pp. 72–74.
33. These elements are based on Kenneth Wantuck, *The Japanese Approach to Productivity* (Southfield, Mich.: Bendix Corporation, 1983). See also Chase and Aquilero, op. cit., pp. 261–272; Adam and Ebert, op. cit., p. 568; Carla Kalogeridis, Gary Witzenburg, and John Peter, "A Decade of Tech," *Automotive Industries,* January 2005, vol. 185, no. 1, pp. 34–36; and John McClenahen, "JIT Tops Management Practices," *Industry Week,* December 2006, p. 13.
34. See, for example, Mike Kaye, "Continuous Improvement: Ten Essential Criteria," *International Journal of Quality & Reliability Management,* April–May 1999, pp. 485–487; and David Blanchard, "What's Working for U.S. Manufacturers: The Latest Census of Manufacturers Reveals That Lean Is Still the Most Popular Improvement Method," *Industry Week,* October 2006, pp. 49–52.
35. Chase and Aquilero, op. cit., p. 261. See also "Flexibility Critical for Auto Sector to Succeed," *M P & P, Metal-Working Production & Purchasing,* June 2005, vol. 32, no. 4, p. 17.
36. Sharon Parker, "Longitudinal Effects of Lean Production on Employee Outcomes and the Mediating Role of Work Characteristics," *Journal of Applied Psychology,* 2004, vol. 88, no. 4, pp. 620–634.
37. Ibid., p. 631.
38. Mary Cronin, "Intranets Reach the Factory Floor," *Fortune,* August 18, 1997, p. 208.
39. "SAP Manufacturing: Drive Manufacturing at the Speed of Business," www.sap.com (downloaded January 12, 2006).
40. Adapted from Gaither, op. cit., pp. 6–8. See also Mike Brezonick, "New Vickers Plant Focuses on Flexibility," *Diesel Progress,* North American Edition, January 1999, pp. 32–35; Millan Yeung, "The Future Looks Like Flexible Automation," *DPN: Design Product News,* May 2005, vol. 33, no. 3, p. 4; and "Chrysler Shifting to Japanese Method of 'Flexible Manufacturing,'" *Machine Design,* September 2005, vol. 77, no. 17, p. 49.
41. Thomas Stewart, "Brace for Japan's Hot New Strategy," *Fortune,* September 21, 1992, p. 64. See also Bobby Ray Inman, "Are You Implementing a Pull System by Putting the Cart Before the Horse?" *Production & Inventory Management Journal,* Spring 1999, pp. 67–72.
42. Ibid., p. 64.
43. Susan Moffat, "Japan's New Personalized Production," *Fortune,* October 22, 1990, pp. 132–135. See also Richard Truett, "Chrysler Robots Are Boon to Plant Flexibility," *Automotive News,* August 2005, vol. 79, no. 6160, p. 16.
44. Mark Vonderem and Gregory White, *Operations Management* (St. Paul, Minn.: West Publishing, 1988), pp. 44–45. For more information on computer-integrated manufacturing, see Michael Baudin, *Manufacturing Systems Analysis* (Upper Saddle River, N.J.: Prentice Hall, 1990), pp. 2–5. See also Bob Trebilcock, "Synching up Production Lines," *Modern Materials Handling,* May 2005, vol. 60, no. 5, p. 31.
45. For additional information, see, for example, Alan Luber, "Living in the Real World of Computer Interfaced Manufacturing," *Production & Inventory Management,* September 1991, pp. 10–11; and Jeremy Main, "Computers of the World, Unite!" *Fortune,* September 24, 1990, pp. 115–122. See also John Teresko, "Japan's New Idea," *Industry Week,* September 3, 1990, pp. 62–66; and David Bak, "Shared Intelligence Guides Control System," *Design News,* October 18, 1999, p. 97.
46. Kristina Sullivan, "Boeing Achieves Liftoff," *PC Week,* May 10, 1999, p. 67.
47. John Teresko, "Manufacturing in Japan," *Industry Week,* September 4, 1989, p. 35–48. See also Richard Jensen, "How to Be Nimble, How to Be Quick," *CMA Management,* October 1999, pp. 34–38.
48. Brian McWilliams, "Re-Engineering of the Small Factory," *Inc. Technology,* March 19, 1996, pp. 44–47, reprinted in Roberta Russell and Bernard Taylor, *Operations Management* (Upper Saddle River, N.J.: Prentice Hall), p. 260.
49. David Upton, "What Really Makes Factories Flexible?" *Harvard Business Review,* July–August 1995, p. 75.
50. Ibid., pp. 80–81.
51. Ibid., p. 80; Lisa Gewirtz, "Cerberus Buying Mead Paper Unit," TheDeal.com, January 18, 2005, p. 1.
52. Heizer and Render, op. cit., p. 434.
53. Ibid.
54. Ibid.
55. "Oracle Supply-Chain Management," www.oracle.com (downloaded January 15, 2006).
56. Hau Lee, "The Triple-A Supply Chain," *Harvard Business Review,* October 2004, pp. 102–110.
57. Reuben Slone, "Leading a Supply-Chain Turnaround," *Harvard Business Review,* October 2004, p. 120.
58. "In the Room," *BusinessWeek,* February 14, 2000, p. 116.
59. William Cassidy, "At Wal-Mart, Less Is More," *Journal of Commerce,* November 7, 2005, vol. 6, no. 45, pp. 29–31.
60. "RFID: Technology Tracks Goods, Now People," Knight-Ridder Tribune Business News, January 20, 2006 (accessed February 20, 2006).
61. Janet Perna, "Reinventing How We Do Business," *Vital Speeches of the Day,* July 15, 2001, vol. 67, no. 19, pp. 587–591.
62. Robert Simison et al., "Big Three Carmakers Plan Net Exchange," *Wall Street Journal,* February 28, 2000, p. A3.
63. "Dell: Build-To-Order Manufacturing," www.accenture.com (downloaded January 9, 2006).
64. Ibid.
65. Kasra Ferdows et al., "Rapid-Fire Fulfillment," *Harvard Business Review,* November 2004, pp. 104–110.
66. Ibid., p. 104.
67. Ibid., p. 106.
68. Gabriel Kahn, "Making Labels for Less," *Wall Street Journal,* August 13, 2004, p. B1.

69. Heizer and Render, op. cit., p. 277; "Wheeled Coach Ambulances Dominate The Market," *Fire Apparatus*, October 2004, vol. 9, no. 10, pp. 1–6; www.wheeledcoach.com/ (accessed December 10, 2006).

CHAPTER 10

1. "Millipore Goes Global with Oracle," www.oracle.com (accessed January 12, 2006).
2. Lee Hawkins Jr., "Lost in Transmission: Behind GM's Slide: Bosses Misjudged New Urban Tastes," *Wall Street Journal*, March 8, 2006, p. A1.
3. "Reshuffle Sees Axa Split into Product Divisions," *Money Management*, December 7, 2006, p. 12.
4. Mark Dale Franco, "Synergies 250 Years in the Making," *Catalog Age*, March 15, 2001, vol. 18, no. 4, pp. 47–38. See also "Caswell-Massey Forges Ahead with Aggressive Growth Plan," *Cosmetics International*, September 9, 2005, p. 2.
5. Rekha Back, "Heinz's Johnson to Divest Operations, Scrap Management of Firm by Region," *Wall Street Journal*, December 8, 1997, pp. B10, B12. See also "HJ Heinz: Restructuring Plan Announced by HJ Heinz," *The Economist*, February 20, 1999, p. 7.
6. Jana Parker-Pope and Joann Lublin, "P&G Will Make Jager CEO Ahead of Schedule," *Wall Street Journal*, September 10, 1998, pp. B1, B8.
7. John Barham, "The Morgan Matrix," *Latin Finance*, April 2001, no. 126, p. 18; and "Thailand: Ad Agency Far East DDB Applies Matrix Management," *Thai Press Reports*, September 20, 2006, p. NA.
8. Lee Hawkins Jr., op. cit., p. A1.
9. John Hunt, "Is Matrix Management a Recipe for Chaos?" *Financial Times*, January 1998, p. 14.
10. "Germany: Opel Takes Over Key Role in Development of Saturn Cars," just-auto.com, February 21, 2005 (downloaded March 20, 2006).
11. Pui Tam, "Hurd's Big Challenge at HP: Overhauling Corporate Sales," *Wall Street Journal*, April 3, 2006, pp. A1, A13.
12. Rob Walker, "Down on the Farm," *Fast Company*, February–March 1997, pp. 112–122; and "Amex acquires Rosenbluth," *Travel Trade Gazette UK & Ireland*, July 21, 2003, p. 3.
13. Jay Galbraith, "Organizational Design: An Information Processing View," *Interfaces*, 1974, vol. 4, no. 3, pp. 28–36; and Jay Galbraith, *Organizational Design* (Reading, Mass.: Addison-Wesley, 1977). See also Ranjay Gulati, "The Architecture of Cooperation: Managing Coordination Costs and Appropriation Concerns in Strategic Alliances," *Administrative Science Quarterly*, December 1998, pp. 781–784; Henry Mintzberg, *Structures in Fives: Designing Effective Organizations* (Upper Saddle River, N.J.: Prentice Hall, 1983), pp. 4–9; and Cliff McGoon, "Cutting-Edge Companies Use Integrated Marketing Communication," *Communication World*, December 1998, pp. 15–20.
14. Christopher A. Bartlett and Sumantra Ghoshal, "Matrix Management: Not a Structure, a Frame of Mind," *Harvard Business Review*, July–August 1990, pp. 138–145. See also K. Simon-Elorz, "Information Technology for Organizational Systems: Some Evidence with Case Studies," *International Journal of Information Management*, February 1999, p. 75; and Alexander Gerybadz, "Globalization of R&D: Recent Changes in the Management of Innovation in Transnational Corporations," *Research Policy*, March 1999, pp. 251–253.
15. Bartlett and Ghoshal, ibid., pp. 143–144.
16. "LG Electronics Maximizes Efficiency of Global Business with Centralized Oracle Platform," www.oracle.com (accessed January 12, 2006).
17. "My SAP CRM Unites Nestle Nordic," mysap.com (downloaded January 9, 2006).
18. "Visibility with mySAP Supply-Chain Management," mysap.com (downloaded January 4, 2006).
19. Mintzberg, op. cit., p. 4.
20. Delia Craven, "Click and Mortar," *Red Herring*, November 1999, p. 208; Steven Thompson et al., "Improving Disastor Response Efforts with Decision Support Systems," *International Journal of Emergency Management*, November 14, 2006, p. 250; and www.citadon.com/ (accessed December 18, 2006).
21. Paul Lawrence and Jay Lorsch, *Organization and Environment* (Cambridge, Mass.: Harvard University Press, 1967). See also Frank Mueller and Romano Dyerson, "Expert Humans or Expert Organizations?" *Organization Studies*, 1999, vol. 20, no. 2, pp. 225–256. Some companies today practice concurrent engineering to improve production coordination, which basically means having all the departments—design, production, and marketing, for instance—work together to develop the product so that its production and marketing are more easily coordinated once the item goes into production. See Hassan Abdalla, "Concurrent Engineering for Global Manufacturing," *International Journal of Production Economics*, April 20, 1999, p. 251.
22. Paul Lawrence and Jay Lorsch, *Organization and Environment* (Boston, Mass.: Division of Research, Graduate School of Business Administration, Harvard University, 1967), p. 1.
23. This is based on "Thales: Knowledge Management and Worker Transformation," www.accenture.com (downloaded January 9, 2006).
24. Ibid.
25. These principles are based on Stephen Robbins and Philip Hunsaker, *Training in Interpersonal Skills* (Upper Saddle River, N.J.: Prentice Hall, 1996), pp. 91–95; and David Whetter and Kim Cameron, *Developing Management Skills* (Upper Saddle River, N.J.: Prentice Hall, 2002), p. 435.
26. Harold Koontz and Cyril O'Donnell, *The Principles of Management* (New York: McGraw-Hill, 1964), p. 335.
27. Roger Crockett, "Can Chris Galvin Save His Family's Legacy?" *BusinessWeek*, July 16, 2001, pp. 72–78.
28. Larry Bossidy, "The Job No CEO Should Delegate," *Harvard Business Review*, March 2001, pp. 47–49.
29. The foundation study for this conclusion is Alfred Chandler, *Strategy and Structure* (Cambridge, Mass.: MIT Press, 1962).
30. James Murdock, "Management Matters: To Centralize or Decentralize?" *Commercial Property News*, April 16, 2005, vol. 19, no. A, p. 20.
31. "Saks, Inc. Will Centralize," *Chain Store Age*, September 2004, vol. 80, no. 9, p. 26.
32. "Home Depot to Centralize in Atlanta," *Display and Design Ideas*, May 2005, vol. 17, no. 5, p. 6.
33. "Home Depot to Centralize Store Teams," *Do-It-Yourself Retailing*, May 2005, vol. 188, no. 5, p. 14.
34. "China Unicom to Set Up International Department to Centralize Business Management," *China Business News*, February 6, 2006.
35. "7-Eleven Maximizes Savings with Complete Sourcing, Procurement, and Financial Solution," www.oracle.com (downloaded January 9, 2006).
36. For a discussion of the contingencies affecting span of control (task uncertainty, professionalism, and interdependence), see, for example, Daniel Robey, *Designing Organizations*, 3rd ed. (Homewood, Ill.: Irwin, 1991), pp. 258–259.
37. Judith H. Dobrzynski, "Jack Welch: How Good a Manager?" *BusinessWeek*, December 14, 1987, p. 94. See also Thomas Stewart, "Brain Power," *Fortune*, March 17, 1997, pp. 105–110.

38. Steve Hamm, "Speed Demons," *BusinessWeek*, March 27, 2006, pp. 69–70.
39. Robert Guth, "Microsoft to Restructure Business," *Wall Street Journal*, September 21, 2005, p. A3.
40. "Home Depot to Centralize in Atlanta," *Display and Design Ideas*, May 2005, vol. 17, no. 5, p. 6; "Home Depot to Centralize Divisional Store Teams," *Do-It-Yourself Retailing Telling*, May 2005, vol. 188, no. 5, p. 14.
41. Steve Hamm, "Speed Demons," op. cit., pp. 69–70.
42. Tom Burns and G. M. Stalker, *The Management of Innovation* (London: Tavistock, 1961), p. 1.
43. Ibid., p. 80.
44. Ibid., p. 92.
45. Joan Woodward, *Industrial Organization: Theory and Practice* (London: Tavistock Publications, 1965).
46. "CSX Cutting Three Layers of Management," *Railway Age*, December 2003, p. 15.
47. Peters, *Liberation Management*, p. 238.
48. Marianne Devanna and Noel Tichy, "Creating the Competitive Organization of the 21st Century: The Boundaryless Corporation," *Human Resource Management*, Winter 1990, vol. 29, no. 4, pp. 455–471; and Ron Ashkenas et al., *The Boundaryless Organization* (San Fransisco: Jossey-Bass, 2002).
49. Except as noted, the remainder of this section is based on Larry Hirschhorn and Thomas Gilmore, "The New Boundaries of the Boundaryless Company," *Harvard Business Review*, May–June 1992, pp. 107–108. For a contrary view of "boundarylessness," see Victoria Sharpe, "The Myth of the Boundaryless Organization," *Technical Communication*, May 2002, p. 262.
50. This is based on Hirschhorn and Gilmore, op. cit., pp. 104–108.
51. Peters, *Liberation Management*, p. 238.
52. This section is based on James Shonk, *Team-Based Organizations* (Chicago, Ill.: Irwin, 1997).
53. Ibid., pp. 35–38. See also Susanne Scott and Walter Einstein, "Strategic Performance Appraisal in Team-Based Organizations: One Size Does Not Fit All," *The Academy of Management Executive*, May 2001, pp. 107–117.
54. Ram Charan, "How Networks Reshape Organizations—For Results," *Harvard Business Review*, September–October 1991, pp. 14–15.
55. Ibid., pp. 16–17.
56. Ibid., p. 106.
57. Ibid., p. 108.
58. Christopher Bartlett and Sumantra Ghoshal, "What Is a Global Manager?" *Harvard Business Review*, September–October 1992, pp. 62–74.
59. Paul Evan, Yves Doz, and Andre Laurent, *Human Resource Management in International Firms* (London: Macmillan, 1989), p. 123. See also Carla Mahieu, "Management Development in Royal Dutch/Shell," *Journal of Management Development*, February 2001, p. NA.
60. "Groupware Service Turns Mobile Phones into Smartphones," *Product News Network*, December 21, 2005, p. NA.
61. "Enterprise E-Mail and IM, the Linux Way," *eWeek*, August 14, 2006, p. NA.
62. Ibid.
63. Douglas Johnson, "Discuss Changing Models in Real Time," *Design News*, May 3, 1999, p. 96; and www.onespace.com/ (accessed December 15, 2006).
64. Except as noted, this section is based on John Byrn, "The Horizontal Corporation," *BusinessWeek*, December 20, 1993, vol. 20, pp. 76–81. See also Frank Ostroff, *The Horizontal Organization* (London: Oxford University Press, 1999).
65. As in a federal government–type arrangement, the parent firm need not necessarily "own" the autonomous units. The important thing is that they agree to abide by its rules.
66. John Byrne, Richard Brandt, and Otis Port, "The Virtual Corporation," *BusinessWeek*, February 8, 1992, p. 99.
67. "The Americas' Intelligence Wire," September 21, 2005 (downloaded March 20, 2006).
68. Julie Bick, "The New Fact of Self-Employment," *Inc. Magazine*, November 2001, vol. 23, no. 5, pp. 87–89.
69. Peter Senge, *The Fifth Discipline: The Art and Practice of the Learning Organizations* (New York: Currency Doubleday, 1994), p. 3. See also Hershey Friedman et al., "Transforming a University from a Teaching Organization to a Learning Organization," *Review of Business*, Fall 2005, vol. 26, no. 3, pp. 31–36.
70. Robert Rowden, "The Learning Organization and Strategic Change," *SAM Advanced Management Journal*, Summer 2001, vol. 66, no. 1, p. 11. See also "Pull Virtual Teams Together," *Investors Business Daily*, January 30, 2006, p. 88.
71. K. Martin et al., "Implementing a Learning Management System Globally: An Innovative Change Management Approach," *IBM Systems Journal*, March 2005, vol. 44, no. 1, pp. 125–144.
72. "Millipore Goes Global with Oracle," www.oracle.com (downloaded January 9, 2006).

CHAPTER 11

1. Chuck Salter, "On the Road Again," *Fast Company*, January 2002, pp. 51–58; "Trucking Getting Global," *Traffic World*, December 19, 2005, vol. 269, no. 51, p. 34.
2. Roger Schreffler, "Revivalist Art," *Ward's Auto World*, November 2001, vol. 37, no. 11, pp. 38–39; and Bruce Crumley, "Speeding Up Renault: Carlos Ghosn, Nissan's Savior, Is Pushing the French Automaker to Get into Gear," *Time*, March 27, 2006, vol. 167, no. 13, p. A15.
3. Erin Brown, "Big Business Meets the E World," *Fortune*, November 8, 1999, p. 88.
4. Ibid., p. 91.
5. Ibid.
6. David Baum, "Running the Rapids," *Profit Magazine*, November 1999, p. 54.
7. Ibid.
8. Stewart Alsop, "E or Be Eaten," *Fortune*, November 8, 1999, pp. 94–95.
9. Based on David Nadler and Michael Tushman, "Beyond the Charismatic Leader: Leadership and Organizational Change," *California Management Review*, Winter 1990, p. 80; and Alfred Marcus, "Responses to Externally Induced Innovation: Their Effects on Organizational Performance," *Strategic Management Journal*, 1988, vol. 9, pp. 194–202. See also Steve Crom, "Change Leadership: The Virtues of Obedience," *Leadership & Organization Development Journal*, March–June 1999, pp. 162–168; and Omar S. Khan, "The Case for Real Change," *Strategy & Leadership*, January–February 2006, vol. 34, no. 1, pp. 32–36.
10. Nadler and Tushman, op. cit., p. 80. See also "The Art and Process of Strategy Development and Deployment," *Journal for Quality and Participation*, Winter 2005, vol. 28, no. 4, pp. 10–18; and Marc H. Meyer, Mark Anzani, and George Walsh, "Organizational Change for Enterprise Growth: IBM Had to Change Its Organization and Development Processes to Survive the 1990s," *Research-Technology Management*, November–December 2005, vol. 48, no. 6, pp. 48–57.
11. "Baker and McKenzie Selects Hummingbird LegalKEY®," CNW Group, January 31, 2006 (downloaded April 28, 2006).
12. John Kador, "Shall We Dance?" *Electronic Business*, February 2002, vol. 28, no. 2, p. 56.
13. Edgar Schein, *Organizational Culture and Leadership* (San Francisco: Jossey-Bass, 1985), pp. 224–237; Peter Wright, Mark Kroll, and John Parnell, *Strategic Management Concepts*

(Upper Saddle River, N.J.: Prentice Hall, 1996), pp. 233–236; and Benjamin Schneider et al., "Creating a Climate and Culture for Sustainable Organizational Change," *Organizational Dynamics*, 1996, vol. 24, no. 4, pp. 7–19. See also John S. Oakland and Steve J. Tanner, "Quality Management in the 21st Century: Implementing Successful Change," *International Journal of Productivity and Quality Management*, December 12, 2005, vol. 1, no. 1/2, p. 69.

14. Peter N. Haapaniemi, "How Companies Transformed Themselves," *Chief Executive*, November 2001, pp. 2–5. See also "Unisys to Get New CEO," *Client Server News*, November 1, 2004, p. NA.
15. Daniel Guido, "Daimler to Reorganize Commercial Vehicle Unit," *Transport Topics*, January 30, 2005, issue 3675, pp. 3–5.
16. Ibid.
17. Ibid.
18. Dennis Berman, "Lucent's Latest Revamp to Split Five Businesses into Two Units," *Wall Street Journal*, July 11, 2001, p. B7.
19. Michael Goold and Andrew Campbell, "Do You Have a Well-Designed Organization?" *Harvard Business Review*, March 2002, pp. 117–124.
20. Ibid., p. 118.
21. Scott Miller, "Volkswagen Is Considering a Reorganization into Three Divisions," *Wall Street Journal*, June 26, 2001, p. 18.
22. Goold and Campbell, op. cit., p. 120.
23. Carol Hymowitz, "How a Leader at 3M Got His Employees to Back Big Changes," *Wall Street Journal*, April 23, 2002, p. B1.
24. Ibid., p. B1.
25. Goold and Campbell, op. cit., p. 123.
26. Gary Dessler, *Winning Commitment: How to Build and Keep a Competitive Work Force* (New York: McGraw-Hill, 1993), p. 85.
27. Ibid. See also Varun Grover, "From Business Reengineering to Business Process Change Management: A Longitudinal Study of Trends and Practices," *IEEE Transactions on Engineering Management*, February 1999, p. 36.
28. Daniel Denison, *Corporate Culture and Organizational Effectiveness* (Hoboken, N.J.: John Wiley & Sons, 1990), p. 12. See also Daniel Denison, "What Is the Difference Between Organizational Culture and Organizational Climate? A Native's Point of View on a Decade of Paradigm Wars," *Academy of Management Review*, July 1996, pp. 619–654.
29. "Business Process Management," www.TIBCO.com (downloaded April 28, 2006).
30. Bruce Silver, "The ABCs of BPM," *InfoWorld*, February 20, 2006, vol. 28, no. A, p. 8.
31. See also "Evolve Business Processes, Don't Reengineer Them," *Internet Week*, November 11, 2004.
32. "Independent Research Company Ranks TIBCO Leader Among Business Process Management Suites' Vendors," PR Newswire (April 13, 2006).
33. "TIBCO Staffware Process Suites," www.TIBCO.com (accessed April 28, 2006).
34. www.TIBCO.com (April 28, 2006).
35. Based on one independent survey of twenty-two companies reported by TIBCO. "TIBCO Staffware Process Suites," www.TIBCO.com (downloaded April 28, 2006).
36. Niccolò Machiavelli, *The Prince*, trans. W. K. Marriott (London: J. M. Dent & Sons, Ltd., 1958).
37. Paul Lawrence, "How to Deal with Resistance to Change," *Harvard Business Review*, May–June, 1954. See also Andrew W. Schwartz, "Eight Guidelines for Managing Change," *Supervisory Management*, July 1994, pp. 3–5; Thomas J. Werner and Robert F. Lynch, "Challenges of a Change Agent," *Journal for Quality and Participation*, June 1994, pp. 50–54; Larry Reynolds, "Understand Employees' Resistance to Change," *HR Focus*, June 1994, pp. 17–18; Kenneth E. Hultman, "Scaling the Wall of Resistance," *Training & Development Journal*, October 1995, pp. 15–18; Eric Dent, "Challenging Resistance to Change," *Journal of Applied Behavioral Science*, March 1999, p. 25; and "The Key to Innovation: Overcoming Resistance," *CIO*, October 15, 2005, vol. 19, no. 2, pp. 34–38. See also Tina Kiefer, "Feeling Bad: Antecedents and Consequences of Negative Emotions in Ongoing Change," *Journal of Organizational Behavior*, December 2005, vol. 26, no. 8, pp. 875–898.
38. John Mariotti, "The Challenge of Change," *Industry Week*, April 6, 1998, p. 140. See also Jim Folaron, "The Human Side of Change Leadership," *Quality Progress*, April 2005, vol. 38, no. 4, pp. 39–44; and Tina Kiefer, op. cit.
39. Timothy Judge et al., "Managerial Coping with Organizational Change: A Dispositional Perspective," *Journal of Applied Psychology*, 1999, vol. 84, no. 1, pp. 107–122.
40. Shaul Oreg, "Resistance to Change: Developing an Individual Differences Measure," *Journal of Applied Psychology*, 2003, vol. 88, no. 4, p. 682.
41. "Pirelli: Enterprise Integration," www.accenture.com (downloaded January 9, 2006).
42. Salter, op. cit., p. 56.
43. Wendell French and Cecil Bell Jr., *Organization Development*, 6th ed. (Upper Saddle River, N.J.: Prentice Hall, 1999), pp. 74–82.
44. John R. Kotter, *Leading Change* (Boston, Mass.: Harvard Business School Press, 1996), pp. 40–41. See also Gary Hamel, "Waking up IBM," *Harvard Business Review*, July–August 2000, pp. 137–146. See also "Mapping an Effective Change Programme," *Marketing Strategy*, October 2005, p. NA.
45. Kotter, op. cit., p. 44.
46. Ibid., p. 57.
47. Ibid., pp. 90–91.
48. Richard Pascale et al., "Changing the Way We Change," *Harvard Business Review*, November–December 1997, p. 129.
49. Noel Tichy and Ram Charan, "The CEO as Coach: An Interview with Allied Signal's Lawrence A. Bossidy," *Harvard Business Review*, March–April 1995, p. 77.
50. This is based on Kotter, op. cit., pp. 61–66.
51. Ibid., p. 65.
52. This subsection is based on Carlos Ghosn, "Saving the Business Without Losing the Company," *Harvard Business Review*, January 2002, pp. 37–45; and Bruce Crumley, op. cit.
53. Ghosn, op. cit., p. 41.
54. Thomas Cummings and Christopher Worley, *Organization Development and Change* (Minneapolis, Minn.: West Publishing Company, 1993), p. 3.
55. Based on J. T. Campbell and M. D. Dunnette, "Effectiveness of T-Group Experiences in Managerial Training and Development," *Psychological Bulletin*, 1968, vol. 7, pp. 73–104, reprinted in W. E. Scott and L. L. Cummings, *Readings in Organizational Behavior and Human Performance* (Homewood, Ill.: Irwin, 1973), p. 571.
56. Robert J. House, *Management Development* (Ann Arbor, Mich.: Bureau of Industrial Relations, University of Michigan, 1967), p. 71; Louis White and Kevin Wooten, "Ethical Dilemmas in Various Stages of Organizational Development," *Academy of Management Review*, 1983, vol. 8, no. 4, pp. 690–697.
57. Wendell French and Cecil Bell Jr., *Organization Development* (Upper Saddle River, N.J.: Prentice Hall, 1995), pp. 171–193.
58. Cummings and Worley, op. cit., p. 501.
59. For a description of how to make OD a part of organizational strategy, see Aubrey Mendelow and S. Jay Liebowitz, "Difficulties in Making OD a Part of Organizational Strategy," *Human Resource Planning*, 1995, vol. 12, no. 4, pp. 317–329.
60. Chung-Ming Lau and Hang-Yue Ngo, "Organizational Development and Firm Performance: A Comparison of

Multinational and Local Firms," *Journal of International Business Studies*, Spring 2001, vol. 32, no. 1, p. 95.

61. This section is based on Evert Van De Vliert, Martin C. Euwema, and Sipke E. Huismans, "Managing Conflict with a Subordinate or a Superior: Effectiveness of Conglomerated Behavior," *Journal of Applied Psychology*, April 1995, pp. 271–281. See also Claire Murphy, "Change Management: Motivation vs. Manipulation," *Marketing*, October 19, 2005, p. 36.
62. Paul Lawrence and Jay Lorsch, *Organization and Environment* (Boston, Mass.: Harvard University, Graduate School of Business Administration, Division of Research, 1967), pp. 74–75.
63. Kenneth Thomas, "Conflict and Conflict Management," in Marvin Dunnette, *Handbook of Industrial and Organizational Psychology* (Chicago, Ill.: Rand McNally, 1976), pp. 900–902; and Michael Carrell, Daniel Jennings, and Christina Heavrin, *Fundamentals of Organizational Behavior* (Upper Saddle River, N.J.: Prentice Hall, 1997), pp. 505–509.
64. "One into Four," *The Economist*, August 1, 2002, www.economist.com. See also Philip Klein, "GE Capital to Split into Four," July 26, 2002, biz.yahoo.com.

CHAPTER 12

1. Gilbert Nicholson, "Automated Assessments for Better Hires," *Workforce*, December 2000, pp. 102–104.
2. Ben Nagler, "Recasting Employees into Teams," *Workforce*, January 1998, pp. 101–106.
3. Tony Carneval, "The Coming Labor and Skills Shortage," *Training & Development*, January 2005, p. 39.
4. Brian Becker, Mark Huselid, and David Ulrich, *The HR Scorecard: Linking People, Strategy, and Performance* (Boston, Mass.: Harvard Business School Press, 2001).
5. "The Future of HR," *Workplace Visions*, Society for Human Resource Management, 2001, no. 6, pp. 3–4.
6. Bill Robert, "Process First, Technology Second," *HR Magazine*, June 2002, pp. 40–46.
7. See also James Clifford, "Manage Work Better to Better Manage Human Resources: A Comparative Study of Two Approaches to Job Analysis," *Public Personnel Management*, Spring 1996, pp. 89–103.
8. Arthur R. Pell, *Recruiting and Selecting Personnel* (New York: Regents, 1969), pp. 10–12. See also Katherine Tyler, "Employees Can Help Recruit New Talent," *HR Magazine*, September 1996, pp. 57–61; and Martha Frase-Blunt, "Make a Good First Impression," *HR Magazine*, April 2004, pp. 81–86.
9. Arthur R. Pell, ibid., p. 11.
10. Gary Dessler, *Human Resource Management*, 10th ed. (Upper Saddle River, N.J.: Prentice-Hall, 2005), pp. 114–129.
11. Allison Thompson, "The Contingent Workforce," *Occupational Outlook Quarterly*, Spring 2005, pp. 28–34.
12. Brenda Palk Sunoo, "From Santa to CEO—Can Display All Roles," *Personnel Journal*, April 1996, pp. 4034–4044.
13. Gretchen Weber, "Tempts at the Top," *Workforce Management*, August 2004, pp. 35–38.
14. "High-Stakes Recruiting in High-Tech," *BNA Bulletin to Management*, February 12, 1998, p. 48.
15. Sara Rynes, Marc Orlitzky, and Robert Bretz Jr., "Experienced Hiring Versus College Recruiting: Practices and Emerging Trends," *Personnel Psychology*, 1997, vol. 50, pp. 309–339.
16. See, for example, Richard Becker, "Ten Common Mistakes in College Recruiting—How to Try Without Really Succeeding," *Personnel*, March–April 1975, pp. 19–28. See also Sara Ryne and John Bordreau, "College Recruiting in Large Organizations: Practice, Evaluation, and Research Implications," *Personnel Psychology*, Winter 1986, pp. 729–757.
17. "Internships Provide Workplace Snapshot," *BNA Bulletin to Management*, May 22, 1997, p. 168.
18. For a discussion of these and others, see Eric Krell, "Recruiting Outlook: Creative HR for 2003," *Workforce*, December 2002; Jennifer Berkshire, "Social Network Recruiting", *HR Magazine*, April 2005, pp. 95–98; Joe Mullich, "Hiring Without Limits," *Workforce Management*, June 2004, pp. 52–58; and Jessica Marquez, "A Global Recruiting Site Helps Far-Flung Managers at the Professional Services Company Acquire the Talent They Need—and Saves One Half-Million Dollars a Year," *Workforce Management*, March 13, 2006, p. 22.
19. Gary Dessler, *Human Resource Management*, 10th ed. (Upper Saddle River, N.J.: Prentice-Hall, 2005), p. 245.
20. Alan Finder, "When a Risque Online Persona Undermines a Chance for a Job," *New York Times*, June 11, 2006, p. 1.
21. Sarah Gale, "Internet Recruiting: Better, Cheaper, Faster," *Workforce*, December 2001, p. 75.
22. Gilbert Nicholson, "Automated Assessments for Better Hires," *Workforce*, December 2000, pp. 102–104.
23. Ibid.
24. "Workforce Testing and Monitoring," *Management Review*, October 1998, pp. 31–42.
25. Ibid.
26. Mel Kleiman, "Employee Testing Essential to Hiring Effectively in the '90s," *Houston Business Journal*, February 8, 1993, p. 31; and Gerald L. Borofsky, "Pre-Employment Psychological Screening," *Risk Management*, January 1993, p. 47. See also Christina Ronquist, "Pre-Employment Testing: Making It Work for You," *Occupational Hazards*, December 1997, pp. 38–40.
27. Louis Olivas, "Using Assessment Centers for Individual and Organizational Development," *Personnel*, May–June 1980, pp. 63–67; Tim Payne, Neil Anderson, and Tom Smith, "Assessment Centers, Selection Systems and Cost-Effectiveness: An Evaluative Study," *Personnel Review*, Fall 1992, p. 48; Roger Mottram, "Assessment Centers Are Not Only for Selection: The Assessment Center as a Development Workshop," *Journal of Managerial Psychology*, January 1992, p. A1; and Charles Woodruffe, "Going Back a Generation," *People Management*, February 20, 1997, pp. 32–35.
28. Neal Schmitt et al., "Computer-Based Testing Applied to Selection of Secretarial Candidates," *Personnel Psychology*, November 1991, vol. 46, no. 19, pp. 149–165.
29. For a full discussion of interviewing, see, for example, Gary Dessler, *Human Resource Management*, 10th ed. (Upper Saddle River, N.J.: Prentice-Hall, 2005), Chapter 7.
30. The research on interviewing is extensive. See, for example, R. E. Carlson, "Selective Interview Decisions: The Effects of Interviewer Experience, Relative Quota Situation, and Applicant Sample on Interview Decisions," *Personnel Psychology*, 1967, vol. 20, pp. 259–280; Linda Thornburgh, "Computer-Assisted Interviewing Shortens Hiring Cycle," *HR Magazine*, February 1998, pp. 73–76; Chad Higgins and Timothy Judge, "The Effect of Applicant Influence Tactics on Recruiter Perceptions of Fit and Hiring Recommendations: A Field Study," *Journal of Applied Psychology*, 2004, vol. 89, no. 4, pp. 622–632; Frank Schmidt and Ryan Zimmerman, "A Counterintuitive Hypothesis About Employment Interview Validity and Some Supporting Evidence," *Journal of Applied Psychology*, 2004, vol. 89, no. 3, pp. 553–561.
31. Pamela Paul, "Interviewing Is Your Business," *Association Management*, November 1992, p. 29.
32. William Tullar, Terry Mullins, and Sharon Caldwell, "Effects of Interview Length and Applicant Quality on Interview Decision Time," *Journal of Applied Psychology*, December 1979, pp. 669–674. See also Jennifer Burnett et al., "Interview Notes and Validity," *Personnel Psychology*, Summer 1998, pp. 375–396.

33. Gary Dessler, *Human Resource Management*, 10th ed. (Upper Saddle River, N.J.: Prentice-Hall, 2005), pp. 264–265.
34. Coleman Peterson, "Employee Retention: The Secrets Behind Wal-Mart's Successful Hiring Policies," *Human Resource Management*, Spring 2005, vol. 44, no. 1, pp. 85–88.
35. Edward Robinson, "Beware—Job Seekers Have No Secrets," *Fortune*, December 29, 1997, p. 6.
36. Mary Mayer, "Background Checks in Focus," *HR Magazine*, January 2002, pp. 59–62.
37. John Jones and William Terris, "Post-Polygraph Selection Techniques," *Recruitment Today*, May–June 1989, pp. 25–31. See also Richard White Jr., "Ask Me No Questions, Tell Me No Lies," *Public Personnel Management*, Winter 2001, vol. 30, no. 4, pp. 483–493.
38. These are based on Commerce Clearing House, *Ideas and Trends*, December 29, 1998, pp. 222–223.
39. Dessler, *Human Resource Management*, 9th ed., pp. 150–151.
40. Scott MacDonald et al., "The Limitations of Drug Screening in the Workplace," *International Labor Review*, 1993, vol. 132, no. 1, p. 98.
41. Sheila Hicks et al., "Orientation Redesign," *Training and Development*, July 2006, pp. 43–46.
42. "Industry Report 1999," *Training*, October 1999, pp. 37–60.
43. Jennifer Reese, "Starbucks," *Fortune*, December 9, 1996, pp. 190–200.
44. Kenneth Wexley and Gary Latham, *Developing and Training Human Resources in Organizations* (Glenview, Ill.: Scott, Foresman, 1981), p. 107.
45. Cindy Waxer, "Steelmaker Revives Apprentice Program to Address Graying Workforce, Forge Next Leaders," *Workforce Management*, January 30, 2006, p. 40.
46. William Berliner and William McLarney, *Management Practice and Training* (Burr Ridge, Ill.: McGraw-Hill, 1974), pp. 442–443. See also Stephen Wehrenberg, "Supervisors as Trainees: The Long-Term Gains of OJT," *Personnel Journal*, April 1987, vol. 66, no. 4, pp. 48–51.
47. Unless otherwise noted, this section is based on Darin Hartley, "Technology Kicks Up Leadership Development," *Training and Development*, March 2004, pp. 22–24. "The U.S. Postal Service Turns to Thinq's LMS to Streamline Operations," *Training and Development*, December 2003, pp. 72–73.
48. Helen Beckett, "Blended Skills for a Better Class of E-Learning," *Computer Weekly*, January 20, 2004, p. 20.
49. Del Jones, "More Firms Cut Workers Ranked at Bottom to Make Way for Talent," *USA Today*, May 30, 2001, p. BU01.
50. Steven Cullen et al., "Forced Distribution Rating Systems and the Improvement of Workforce Potential: A Baseline Simulation," *Personnel Psychology*, 2005, vol. 58, p. 1.
51. Kenneth Nowack, "360-Degree Feedback: The Whole Story," *Training and Development*, January 1993, p. 69. For a description of some of the problems involved in implementing 360-degree feedback, see Matthew Budman, "The Rating Game," *Across the Board*, February 1994, pp. 35–38.
52. "360-Degree Feedback on the Rise, Survey Finds," *BNA Bulletin to Management*, January 23, 1997, p. 31. See also Kenneth Nowack et al., "How to Evaluate Your 360-Degree Feedback Efforts," *Training and Development Journal*, April 1999, pp. 48–53; and "Building a Better Workforce," *HR Magazine*, October 2004, pp. 87–94.
53. Katherine Romano, "Fear of Feedback," *Management Review*, December 1993, p. 39.
54. See, for instance, Gerry Rich, "Group Reviews—Are You up to It?" *CMA Magazine*, March 1993, p. 5.
55. Romano, op. cit., p. 39.
56. Mark Poerio and Eric Keller, "Executive Compensation 2005: Many Forces, One Direction," *Compensation & Benefits Review*, May/June 2005, pp. 34–40.
57. "Employers Turn to Corporate Ombuds to Defuse Internal Ticking Time Bombs," *BNA Bulletin to Management*, August 9, 2005, p. 249.
58. "Benefits Cost Control Solutions to Consider Now," *HR Focus*, November 2003, vol. 80, no. 11, p. 1; and Johanna Rodgers, "Web-Based Apps Simplify Employee Benefits," *Insurance and Technology*, November 2003, vol. 28, no. 11, p. 21.
59. Johanna Rodgers, op. cit.
60. Douglas Shuit, "A Few Years Behind Schedule, Employee Portals Gain Ground," *Workforce Management*, 2005, p. 58.
61. Chris Pickering, "A Look Through the Portal," *Software Magazine*, February 2001, vol. 21, no. 1, pp. 18–19; and Jill Elswick, "How NCR Corp. Undertook an Internet Makeover to Improve Access to HR Information," *Employee Benefit News*, January 1, 2001, item 01008001. Ibid., p. 58.
62. "Hiring Based on Strength Test Discriminates Against Women," *BNA Bulletin to Management*, February 22, 2005, p. 62.
63. This section is based on Dessler, *Human Resource Management*, 8th ed., pp. 43–44; see also Commerce Clearing House, *Sexual Harassment Manual*, p. 8.
64. James Nash, "Beware the Hidden Hazards," *Occupational Hazards*, February 2005, pp. 48–51.
65. Michael Blotzer, "PDA Software Offers Auditing Advances," *Occupational Hazards*, December 2001, vol. 63, no. 12, pp. 11–13.
66. Jim Meade, "Web Based HRIS Meets Multiple Needs," *HR Magazine*, August 2000, pp. 129–133.
67. "Oracle Human Capital Management," www.oracle.com (accessed January 15, 2006).

CHAPTER 13

1. See http://www.whirlpoolcorp.com/about/innovation/default.asp; Michael Arndt, "How Whirlpool Defines Innovation," *BusinessWeek Online*, March 6, 2006, available online at: http://www.businessweek.com/innovate/content/mar2006/id20060306_287425.htm (accessed November 1, 2006); and Kathleen Melymuka, "Innovation Democracy," *Computerworld*, February 18, 2004, vol. 38, no. 7, pp. 31–32.
2. Warren Bennis and Burt Nanus, *Leaders: The Strategies for Taking Charge* (New York: Harper & Row, 1985), p. 21.
3. W. D. Spangler, R. J. House, and R. Palrecha, "Personality and Leadership," in B. Schneider and D. B. Smith, eds., *Personality and Organizations* (Mahway, N.J.: Lawrence Erlbaum, 2004), pp. 251–290.
4. Marc Effron, Shelli Greenslade, and Michelle Salbo, "Growing Great Leaders: Does It Really Matter?" *Journal of The Human Resource Planning Society*, 2005, vol. 28, no. 3, pp. 18–23.
5. See David Waldman, Gabriel Ramirez, Robert J. House, and Phanish Puranam, "Does Leadership Matter? CEO Leadership Attributes and Profitability Under Conditions of Perceived Incremental Uncertainty," *Academy of Management Journal*, 2001, vol. 44, no. 1, pp. 134–143.
6. See Gary Yukl, *Leadership in Organizations*, 5th ed. (Upper Saddle River, N.J.: Prentice Hall, 2002); Peter G. Northouse, *Leadership: Theory and Practice*, 2nd ed. (London: Sage, 2000); and Jean M. Phillips, "Leadership Since 1975: Advancement or Inertia?" *Journal of Leadership Studies*, 1995, vol. 2, pp. 58–79.
7. This section is based in part on Darin E. Hartley, "Technology Kicks Up Leadership Development: Bam! Some Basic Technologies Can Help Leverage Leadership Development in Your Organization," *T+D*, March 2004, pp. 22–24.
8. Loren Gary, "Pulling Yourself Up Through the Ranks," *Harvard Management Update*, October 2003, vol. 8, no. 10.
9. "Xerox Corporation: Blended Learning Prepares Leaders Around the World," Center for Creative Leadership, http://www.ccl.org/leadership/pdf/solutions/Xerox_Corporation.pdf, 2005.
10. Harold H. Kelley and John W. Thibaut, *Interpersonal Relationships* (New York: John Wiley & Sons, 1978).

11. John R. P. French Jr., and Bertram H. Raven, "The Bases of Social Power," in D. Cartwright, ed., *Studies of Social Power* (Ann Arbor, Mich.: Institute for Social Research, 1968).
12. Michelle Inness, Julian Barling, and Nick Turner, "Understanding Supervisor-Targeted Aggression: A Within-Person, Between-Jobs Design," *Journal of Applied Psychology*, 2005, vol. 90, no. 4, pp. 731–739; Kelly L. Zellars, Bennett J. Tepper, and Michelle K. Duffy, "Abusive Supervision and Subordinates' Organizational Citizenship Behavior," *Journal of Applied Psychology*, 2002, vol. 87, no. 6, pp. 1068–1076; and Steve Williams, "A Meta-Analysis of the Relationship Between Organizational Punishment and Employee Performance/Satisfaction," *Research and Practice in Human Resource Management*, 1998, vol. 6, no. 1, pp. 51–64.
13. Bill Breen, "Trickle-up Leadership," *Fast Company*, November 2001, pp. 52, 70.
14. Brian Tracy, "Grow Your Business: Seven Keys to Growing Your Business," Entrepreneur.com, November 21, 2005, available online at: http://www.entrepreneur.com/article/0,4621,324545,00.html (accessed May 13, 2006).
15. Gary Yukl, *Leadership in Organizations*, 4th ed. (Englewood Cliffs, N.J.: Prentice Hall, 1998).
16. Gary Jackson, "Moments of Truth: Global Executives Talk About the Challenges That Shaped Them as Leaders," *Harvard Business Review*, 2007, vol. 85, no. 1, pp. 15–25.
17. Jay A. Conger, "Leadership: The Art of Empowering Others," *Academy of Management Executive*, 1989, vol. 3, pp. 17–24; Jay A. Conger and Rabindra N. Kanungo, "The Empowerment Process: Integrating Theory and Practice," *Academy of Management Review*, 1988, vol. 13, pp. 471–482.
18. Based on "An Analytical Approach to Workforce Management," CRM Today, available online at: http://www.crm2day.com/library/EplVpulFAusyoHEmpq.php (accessed May 13, 2006).
19. Bernard M. Bass, *Leadership, Psychology and Organizational Behavior* (New York: Harper, 1960); Ralph Stogdill, "Personal Factors Associated with Leadership. A Survey of the Literature," *Journal of Psychology*, 1948, vol. 25, pp. 35–71; and Ralph Stogdill, *Handbook of Leadership: A Survey of the Literature* (New York: Free Press, 1974).
20. Yukl, *Leadership in Organizations*, 5th ed., op. cit.
21. Peter G. Northouse, *Leadership: Theory and Practice*, 2nd ed. (London: Sage, 2000).
22. Joshua Kendall, "Can't We All Just Get Along?" *BusinessWeek*, October 9, 2000, p. 18.
23. Daniel Goleman, Richard Boyatzis, and Annie McKee, "Primal Leadership: The Hidden Driver of Great Performance," *Harvard Business Review*, December 2001, pp. 42–51.
24. Cary Cherniss and Robert D. Caplan, "A Case Study of Implementing Emotional Intelligence Programs in Organizations," *Journal of Organizational Excellence*, Winter 2001, pp. 763–786; and Vanessa Urch Druskat and Steven B. Wolff, "Building the Emotional Intelligence of Groups," *Harvard Business Review*, March 2001, pp. 81–91.
25. Daniel Goleman, "What Makes a Leader?" *Harvard Business Review*, 1998, vol. 7, pp. 92–103.
26. Daniel Goleman, *Emotional Intelligence* (New York: Bantam Books, 1995).
27. Franz Humer, "Moments of Truth: Global Executives Talk About the Challenges that Shaped Them as Leaders," op. cit.
28. Catalyst, "Women and Men in U.S. Corporate Leadership: Same Workplace, Different Realities?" (New York: Catalyst, 2004).
29. Julie Indvik, "Women and Leadership," in Peter G. Northouse, *Leadership: Theory and Practice*, 2nd ed. (London: Sage, 2000), pp. 265–300.
30. Catalyst, "Women and Men in U.S. Corporate Leadership: Same Workplace, Different Realities?" op. cit.
31. Janet Shibley Hyde, "The Gender Similarities Hypothesis," *American Psychologist*, 2005, vol. 60, no. 6, pp. 581–592.
32. Alice H. Eagly and Mary C. Johannessen-Schmidt, "The Leadership Styles of Women and Men," *Journal of Social Issues*, 2001, vol. 57, pp. 781–797; Alice H. Eagly and Linda L. Carli, "The Female Leadership Advantage: An Evaluation of the Evidence," *Leadership Quarterly*, December 2003, vol. 14, no. 6, pp. 807–834; Alice H. Eagly and Linda L. Carli, "Finding Gender Advantage and Disadvantage: Systematic Research Integration Is the Solution," *Leadership Quarterly*, December 2003, vol. 14, no. 6, pp. 851–859; and Shibley Hyde, "The Gender Similarities Hypothesis," op. cit.
33. Bernard M. Bass, *Leadership & Performance Beyond Expectations* (New York: Free Press, 1985).
34. See, for example, James Bowditch and Anthony Buono, *A Primer on Organizational Behavior* (New York: John Wiley, 1994), p. 238.
35. Indvik, "Women and Leadership," op. cit.
36. Rochelle Sharpe, "As Leaders, Women Rule," *BusinessWeek*, November 20, 2000, pp. 74–84.
37. Nancy Flynn, *The E-Policy Handbook: Designing and Implementing Effective E-Mail, Internet, and Software Policies*, 2001, American Management Association and the ePolicy Institute; www.ePolicyInstitute.com. Available online at: http://www.epolicyinstitute.com/e_policies/netiquette.html.
38. Ralph Stogdill and A. E. Koontz, *Leader Behavior: Its Description and Measurement* (Columbus: Bureau of Business Research, Ohio State University, 1957). See also Bernard M. Bass, *Bass & Stogdill's Handbook of Leadership: Theory, Research, & Managerial Applications*, 3rd ed. (New York: Free Press, 1990).
39. Brent Schlender, "Ballmer Unbound: How Do You Impose Order on a Giant, Runaway Mensa Meeting? Just Watch Microsoft's CEO," *Fortune*, January 26, 2004, pp. 117–124.
40. Enzo Valenzi and Gary Dessler, "Relationships of Leader Behavior, Subordinate Role Ambiguity, and Subordinate Job Satisfaction," *Academy of Management Journal*, 1978, vol. 21, pp. 671–678.
41. Gary Yukl, "Towards a Behavioral Theory of Leadership," *Organizational Behavior and Human Performance*, July 1971, pp. 414–440. See also Gary Yukl, *Leadership in Organizations*, 2nd ed. (Englewood Cliffs, N.J.: Prentice-Hall, 1989).
42. Robert Blake and Jane Mouton, *The Managerial Grid* (Houston, Tex.: Gulf Publishing, 1964).
43. R. Likert, *New Patterns of Management* (New York: McGraw-Hill, 1961); R. Likert, *The Human Organization: Its Management and Value* (New York: McGraw-Hill, 1967).
44. Rensis Likert, *New Patterns of Management* (New York: McGraw-Hill, 1967).
45. Blake and Mouton, *The Managerial Grid*, op. cit.
46. Lars L. Larson, James G. Hunt, and R. N. Osburn, "The Great Hi-Hi Leader Behavior Myth: A Lesson from Occam's Razor," *Academy of Management Journal*, December 1976, vol. 19, pp. 628–641; Paul C. Nystrom, "Managers and the Hi-Hi Leader Myth," *Academy of Management Journal*, 1978, vol. 21, no. 2, pp. 325–331.
47. Kurt Lewin and Ronald Lippitt, "An Experimental Approach to the Study of Autocracy and Democracy: A Preliminary Note," *Sociometry*, 1938, vol. 1, pp. 292–300; Kurt Lewin, "Field Theory and Experiment in Social Psychology: Concepts and Methods," *American Journal of Sociology*, 1939, vol. 44, pp. 868–896; Kurt Lewin, Ronald Lippitt, and R. White, "Patterns of Aggressive Behaviour in Experimentally Created 'Social Climates,'" *Journal of Social Psychology*, 1939, vol. 10, pp. 271–299.
48. Bernard M. Bass, *Stogdill's Handbook of Leadership* (New York: Free Press, 1981).
49. Robert Tannenbaum and Warren H. Schmidt, "How to Choose a Leadership Pattern," *Harvard Business Review*, March–April 1958, vol. 36, pp. 95–101 (reprinted in May–June 1973 issue).

50. Philip Sadler, *Leadership: Styles, Role Models, Qualities, Behaviors* (London: Coopers & Lybrand, 1997).
51. Bernard M. Bass, *Transformational Leadership: Industrial, Military, and Educational Impact* (Mahwah, N.J.: Lawrence Erlbaum Associates, 1998); and J. M. Burns, *Leadership* (New York: Harper & Row, 1978).
52. Bass, *Transformational Leadership: Industrial, Military, and Educational Impact*, op. cit.
53. Shelley A. Kirkpatrick and Edwin A. Locke, "Direct and Indirect Effects of Three Core Charismatic Leadership Components on Performance and Attitudes," *Journal of Applied Psychology*, 1996, vol. 81, pp. 36–51.
54. Based on Bass, *Leadership and Performance Beyond Expectations*, op. cit.; Ronald Deluga, "Relationship of Transformational and Transactional Leadership with Employee Influencing Strategies," *Group and Organizational Studies*, December 1988, pp. 457–458; and Philip M. Podsakoff, Scott B. MacKenzie, and William H. Bommer, "Transformational Leader Behaviors as Determinants of Employee Satisfaction, Commitment, Trust, and Organizational Citizenship Behaviors," *Journal of Management*, 1996, vol. 22, no. 2, pp. 259–298.
55. Ronald Deluga, "Relationship of Transformational and Transactional Leadership with Employee Influencing Strategies," *Group and Organizational Studies*, December 1988, p. 457.
56. Frances Yamarino and Bernard Bass, "Transformational Leadership and Multiple Levels of Analysis," *Human Relations*, 1990, vol. 43, no. 10, pp. 975–995.
57. For a further understanding of charisma, see Jay A. Conger and Rabindra N. Kanungo, *Charismatic Leadership in Organizations* (Thousand Oaks, Calif.: Sage, 1998).
58. Scott W. Lester, Bruce M. Meglino, and Audrey M. Korsgaard, "The Antecedents and Consequences of Group Potency: A Longitudinal Investigation of Newly Formed Work Groups," *Academy of Management Journal*, April 2002, vol. 45, no. 2, pp. 352–368.
59. David A. Waldman and Francis J. Yammarino, "CEO Charismatic Leadership: Levels of Management and Levels of Analysis Effects," *Academy of Management Review*, 1999, vol. 24, no. 2, pp. 266–268.
60. Robert J. House and Ram N. Aditya, "The Social Scientific Study of Leadership: Quo Vadis?" *Journal of Management*, 1997, vol. 23, no. 3, pp. 409–473.
61. Bass, *Leadership and Performance Beyond Expectations*, op. cit.
62. Bass, *Leadership and Performance Beyond Expectations*, op. cit.; and D. A. Waldman, B. M. Bass, and F. J. Yammarino, "Adding to Contingent-Reward Behavior: The Augmenting Effect of Charismatic Leadership," *Group & Organizational Studies*, 1990, vol. 15, pp. 381–394.
63. Waldman, Bass, and Yammarino, "Adding to Contingent-Reward Behavior: The Augmenting Effect of Charismatic Leadership," op. cit.
64. Jim Collins, "Level 5 Leadership," *Harvard Business Review*, January 2001, p. 73.
65. Albert B. Crenshaw, "$5.5 Million Declined by Ex-Official," *Washington Post*, January 22, 1992, p. Fl.
66. Paul Hersey and Kenneth H. Blanchard, "Leadership Effectiveness and Adaptability Description (LEAD)," in J. William Pfeiffer and John E. Jones, eds., *The 1976 Annual Handbook for Group Facilitators* (La Jolla, Calif.: University Associates, 1976); and Paul Kersey, Kenneth H. Blanchard, and Dewey E. Johnson, *The Management of Organizational Behavior* (Upper Saddle River, N.J.: Prentice-Hall, 2001).
67. Frederick E. Fiedler, *A Theory of Leadership Effectiveness* (New York: McGraw-Hill, 1967).
68. Ibid., p. 143.
69. See, for example, Robert J. House and J. V. Singh, "Organizational Behavior: Some New Directions for I/O Psychology," *Annual Review of Psychology*, 1987, vol. 38, pp. 669–718; L. H. Peters, D. D. Hartke, and J. T. Pohlmann, "Fiedler's Contingency Theory of Leadership: An Application of the Meta-Analytic Procedures of Schmidt and Hunter," *Psychological Bulletin*, 1985, vol. 97, pp. 274–285; Robert T. Vecchio, "Theoretical and Empirical Examination of Cognitive Resource Theory," *Journal of Applied Psychology*, April 1990, pp. 141–147; and Robert Vecchio, "Cognitive Resource Theory: Issues for Specifying a Test of the Theory," *Journal of Applied Psychology*, 1992, vol. 7, pp. 375–376.
70. Tannenbaum and Schmidt, "How to Choose a Leadership Pattern," op. cit.
71. Ibid.
72. Ibid.
73. Robert J. House, "Leadership in the Twenty-First Century," in A. Howard, ed., *The Changing Nature of Work* (San Francisco: Jossey-Bass, 1995); and M. G. Evans, "R. J. House's 'A Path-Goal Theory of Leader Effectiveness,'" *Leadership Quarterly*, 1996, vol. 7, no. 3, pp. 305–309.
74. Gary Dessler, "An Investigation of a Path-Goal Theory of Leadership," Ph.D. dissertation, City University of New York, 1972.
75. Robert J. House, "A Path Goal Theory of Leader Effectiveness," *Administrative Science Quarterly*, September 1971, pp. 321–338; Robert J. House and Terence Mitchell, "Path-Goal Theory of Leadership," *Journal of Contemporary Business*, Autumn 1974, vol. 3, pp. 81–97; reprinted in Donald White, *Contemporary Perspectives in Organizational Behavior* (Boston, Mass.: Allyn & Bacon, 1982), pp. 228–235.
76. House and Mitchell, "Path-Goal Theory of Leadership," op. cit.; reprinted in White, *Contemporary Perspectives in Organizational Behavior*, op. cit.
77. Robert J. House and Gary Dessler, "The Path-Goal Theory of Leadership: Some Posthoc and A Priori Tests," in James G. Hunt and Lars L. Larson (eds.), *Contingency Approaches to Leadership* (Carbondale: Southern Illinois University Press, 1974), pp. 29–55.
78. Michael Arndt, "Creativity Overflowing," *BusinessWeek*, May 8, 2006, pp. 50–53; and Melymuka, "Innovation Democracy," op. cit.
79. Yukl, *Leadership in Organizations*, 5th ed., op. cit.
80. Fred Dansereau Jr., George Graen, and William J. Haga, "A Vertical Dyad Linkage Approach to Leadership Within Formal Organizations: A Longitudinal Investigation of the Role-Making Process," *Organizational Behavior and Human Performance*, 1975, vol. 13, pp. 46–78; and George Graen and James F. Cashman, "A Role-Making Model of Leadership in Formal Organizations: A Developmental Approach," in James G. Hunt and Lars L. Larson (eds.), *Leadership Frontiers* (Kent, Ohio: Kent State Univesity Press, 1975), pp. 143–165.
81. George B. Graen, Michael A. Novak, and Patricia Sommerkamp, "The Effects of Leader-Member Exchange and Job Design on Productivity and Satisfaction: Testing a Dual Attachment Model," *Organizational Behavior and Human Performance*, 1982, vol. 30, no. 1, pp. 109–131; and Robert V. Vecchio and Bruce C. Gobdel, "The Vertical Dyad Linkage Model of Leadership: Problems and Prospects," *Organizational Behavior and Human Performance*, 1984, vol. 34, no. 1, pp. 5–20.
82. William E. McClane, "Implications of Member Role Differentiation: Analysis of a Key Concept in the LMX Model of Leadership, *Group and Organization Studies*, 1991, vol. 16, no. 1, pp. 102–113; Jean M. Phillips, "The Role of Decision Influence and Team Performance in Member Self-Efficacy,

Withdrawal, Satisfaction with the Leader, and Willingness to Return," *Organizational Behavior and Human Decision Processes*, January 2001, vol. 84, no. 1, pp. 122–147 ; and Yukl, *Leadership in Organizations*, 2nd ed., op. cit.

83. Carolina Gomez, "The Leader-Member Exchange as a Link Between Managerial Trust and Employee Empowerment," *Group & Organization Management*, March 2001, vol. 26, no. 1, pp. 53–69; Carolina Gomez and Benson Rosen, "The Leader-Member Exchange as a Link Between Managerial Trust and Employee Empowerment," *Group and Organization Management*, March 2001, vol. 26, no. 1, pp. 53–69.
84. Gary Yukl and David D. Van Fleet, "Theory and Research on Leadership in Organizations," in Marvin D. Dunnete and Leaetta M. Hough (eds.), *Handbook of Research in Industrial and Organizational Psychology*, vol. 3 (Palo Alto, Calif.: Consulting Psychologists Press, 1992), p. 163.
85. Jon P. Howell, David E. Bowen, Peter W. Dorfman, Steve Kerr, and Philip M. Podsakoff, "Substitutes for Leadership: Effective Alternatives to Ineffective Leadership," *Organizational Dynamics*, 1990, vol. 19, pp. 21–38; and Steve Kerr and John M. Jermier, "Substitutes for Leadership: Their Meaning and Measurement," *Organizational Behavior and Human Performance*, 1978, vol. 22, pp. 375–403.
86. Steve Kerr and John M. Jermier, "Substitutes for Leadership: Their Meaning and Measurement," op. cit.
87. Michael Arnone, "Katrina Smashes Coast Guard IT," *Federal Computer Week*, September 1, 2005, available online at http://www.fcw.com/article90545-09-01-05-Web; and Stephen Barr, "Coast Guard's Response to Katrina a Silver Lining in the Storm," *Washington Post*, September 6, 2005, p. B02.
88. Phillip R. Harris, Robert T. Moran, and Sarah V. Moran, *Managing Cultural Differences: Leadership Strategies for a New World of Business*, 6th ed. (Boston, Mass.: Elsevier, 2004).
89. Huiching Chang and Richard G. Holt, "More Than Relationship: Chinese Interaction and the Principle of Kuan-His," *Community Quarterly*, 1991, vol. 39, pp. 251–271; and Harry C. Hui and George Graen, "Guanxi and Professional Leadership in Contemporary Sino-American Joint Ventures in Mainland China," *Leadership Quarterly*, 1997, vol. 8, pp. 451–465.
90. John Child, *Management in China During the Age of Reform* (Cambridge, U.K.: Cambridge University Press, 1994).
91. Kathleen Krone, Mary Carrett, and Ling Chen, "Managerial Communication Practices in Chinese Factories: A Preliminary Investigation," *Journal of Business Communication*, 1992, vol. 29, pp. 229–243.
92. Michael. H. Bond, *Beyond the Chinese Face: Insights from Psychology* (Hong Kong: Oxford University Press, 1991).
93. Based on Robert J. House, Paul J. Hanges, Mansour Javidan, Peter W. Dorfman, and Vipin Gupta, *Culture, Leadership, and Organizations: The GLOBE Study of 62 Societies* (London: Sage Publications, 2004).
94. Bruce J. Avolio and Surinder S. Kahai, "Adding the 'E' to E-leadership: How It May Impact Your Leadership," *Organizational Dynamics*, 2003, vol. 31, no. 4, pp. 325–338.
95. Andre Martin, *The Changing Nature of Leadership: A CCL Research Report* (Centers for Creative Leadership, 2005); and Gina Hernez-Broome and Richard L. Hughes, "Leadership Development: Past, Present, and Future," *Human Resource Planning*, 2004, vol. 27, no. 1, pp. 24–32.
96. Mary Lynn Pulley, Valerie I. Sessa, John Fleenor, and Tom Pohlmann, "E-leadership: Separating the Reality from the Hype," *Leadership in Action*, 2001, vol. 21, no. 4, pp. 3–6.
97. Linda Tischler, "Sudden Impact," *Fast Company*, September 2002, vol. 62, p. 106.

CHAPTER 14

1. See http://www.mercury.com/us/company/; Dave Dermer, "Selling Senior Execs on the Benefits of Online Incentives: Show Senior Managers How a Web-Based, Noncash Incentive Program Triggers Elevated Profits and Productivity in Their Area of Responsibility," *HR Magazine*, September 2004, available online at: http://findarticles.com/p/articles/mi_m3495/is_9_49/ai_n6206616 (accessed November 1, 2006).
2. Andrea C. Poe, "Online Recognition," *HR Magazine*, June 2002, p. 47, available online at: http://www.shrm.org/hrmagazine/articles/0602/0602agn-awards.asp (accessed November 1, 2006).
3. Richard Cyert and James G. March, *A Behavioral Theory of the Firm* (Englewood Cliffs, N.J.: Prentice-Hall, 1963).
4. See, for example, Edward W. Miles, John D. Hatfield, and Richard C. Huseman, "Equity Sensitivity and Outcome Importance," *Journal of Organizational Behavior*, December 1994, vol. 15, no. 7, pp. 585–596; Edward W. Miles, John D. Hatfield, and Richard C. Huseman, "The Equity Sensitivity Construct: Potential Implications for Worker Performance," *Journal of Management*, December 1989, vol. 15, no. 4, pp. 581–588; and Monteze M. Snyder and Joyce Osland, "Public and Private Organizations in Latin America: A Comparison of Reward Preferences," *International Journal of Public Sector Management*, 1996, vol. 9, no. 2, pp. 15–27.
5. Edwin A. Locke and Gary P. Latham, "Building a Practically Useful Theory of Goal Setting and Task Motivation," *American Psychologist*, September 2002, pp. 705–717.
6. Tommy Y. Lo, "Quality Culture: A Product of Motivation Within Organizations," *Managerial Auditing Journal*, 2002, vol. 17, no. 5, pp. 272–276.
7. Peter J. Makin and Valerie J. Sutherland, "Reducing Accidents Using a Behavioural Approach," *Leadership and Organization Development Journal*, 1994, vol. 15, no. 5, pp. 5–10; and E. Scott Geller, *Understanding Behavior-Based Safety: Step-by-Step Methods to Improve Your Workplace* (Neenah, Wis.: J. J. Keller & Associates Inc., 1997).
8. Sylvie F. Richer, Celine Blanchard, and Robert J. Vallerand, "A Motivational Model of Work Turnover," *Journal of Applied Social Psychology*, 2002, vol. 32, pp. 2089–2113.
9. Douglas McGregor, *The Human Side of Enterprise* (New York: McGraw-Hill, 1960).
10. Bo Burlingham, "The Coolest Small Company in America," *Inc. Magazine*, January 2003, available online at: http://www.inc.com/magazine/20030101/25036.html (accessed November 1, 2006).
11. Abraham Maslow, *Motivation and Personality* (New York: Harper & Row, 1954).
12. Edward E. Lawler III and J. Lloyd Suttle, "A Causal Correlational Test of the Need Hierarchy Concept," *Organizational Behavior and Human Decision Processes*, April 1972, pp. 265–287; and Mahmoud A. Wahba and Lawrence G. Birdwell, "Maslow Reconsidered: A Review of Research on the Need Hierarchy Theory," *Organizational Behavior and Human Decision Processes*, 1976, vol. 15, pp. 212–240.
13. Clay P. Alderfer, *Existence, Relatedness and Growth* (New York: Free Press, 1972).
14. Geert Hofstede, "Culture and Organizations," *International Studies of Management and Organization*, 1980, vol. 70, no. 4, pp. 15–41.
15. Ron Maiorana, "National Survey Names HIP Among Nation's Top 500 Innovative Users of Technology," HIP Health Plan, December 5, 2005, available online at: http://www.hipusa.com/about_hip/press_releases/info_week.html (accessed November 3, 2006).

16. Frederick Herzberg, *Work and the Nature of Man* (Cleveland, Ohio: World Publishing Company, 1966); see also Frederick Herzberg, Bernard Mausner, and Barbara Bloch Snydermann, *The Motivation to Work* (New York: Wiley, 1959).
17. Herzberg, Mausner, and Snydermann, *The Motivation to Work,* op. cit.
18. Herzberg, *Work and the Nature of Man*, op. cit.
19. N. King, "Clarification and Evaluation of the Two-Factor Theory of Job Satisfaction," *Psychological Bulletin*, 1970, vol. 74, pp. 18–31.
20. Richard M. Steers, Lyman W. Porter, and Gregory A. Bigley, *Motivation and Leadership at Work* (New York: McGraw-Hill, 1996).
21. David C. McClelland, *The Achieving Society* (Princeton, N.J.: Van Nostrand, 1961); David C. McClelland, *Human Motivation* (Glenview, Ill.: Scott, Foresman, 1985); and David C. McClelland, *Power: The Inner Experience* (New York: Irvington, 1975).
22. David C. McClelland and Richard E. Boyatzis, "Leadership Motive Pattern and Long-Term Success in Management," *Journal of Applied Psychology*, 1982, vol. 6, pp. 737–743; Christopher J. Collins, Paul J. Hanges, and Edwin A. Locke, "The Relationship of Achievement Motivation to Entrepreneurial Behavior: A Meta-Analysis," *Human Performance*, 2004, vol. 17, no. 1, pp. 95–117; and David C. McClelland and David H. Burnham, "Power Is the Great Motivator," *Harvard Business Review*, 1976, vol. 54, no. 2, pp. 100–110.
23. Scott E. Seibert, Seth R. Silver, and W. Alan Randolph, "Taking Empowerment to the Next Level: A Multiple-Level Model of Empowerment, Performance, and Satisfaction," *Academy of Management Journal*, 2004, vol. 47, pp. 332–349.
24. David A. Whetton and Kim S. Cameron, *Developing Management Skills* (Upper Saddle River, N.J.: Prentice Hall, 2002), pp. 426–427.
25. Thomas Malone, *The Future of Work: How the New Order of Business Will Shape Your Organization, Your Management Style, and Your Life* (Boston, Mass.: Harvard Business School Press, 2004).
26. Erik Brynjolfsson, "VII Pillars of Productivity," *Optimize*, May 2005, vol. 4, no. 5, pp. 27–35.
27. See J. Richard Hackman and Edward E. Lawler, "Employee Reactions to Job Characteristics," *Journal of Applied Psychology Monograph*, 1971, vol. 55, pp. 259–286; J. Richard Hackman and Greg R. Oldham, "Development of the Job Diagnostic Survey," *Journal of Applied Psychology*, 1975, vol. 60, pp. 159–170; J. Richard Hackman and Greg R. Oldham, "Motivation Through the Design of Work: A Test of a Theory," *Organizational Behavior and Human Performance*, 1976, vol. 16, pp. 250–279; and J. Richard Hackman and Greg R. Oldham, *Work Redesign* (Reading, Mass.: Addison-Wesley, 1980).
28. Hackman and Oldham, "Development of the Job Diagnostic Survey," op. cit.
29. Hackman and Oldham, *Work Redesign*, op. cit.
30. Brian T. Loher, Raymond A. Noe, Nancy L. Moeller, and Michael P. Fitzgerald, "A Meta-Analysis of the Relation of Job Characteristics to Job Satisfaction," *Journal of Applied Psychology*, 1985, vol. 70, pp. 280–289.
31. Ibid.; Robert W. Renn and Robert J. Vandenberg, "The Critical Psychological States: An Underrepresented Component in Job Characteristics Model Research," *Journal of Management*, 1995, vol. 21, pp. 279–303; Karlene H. Roberts and William Glick, "The Job Characteristics Approach to Task Design: A Critical Review," *Journal of Applied Psychology*, 1981, vol. 66, pp. 193–217; and Jon L. Pierce and Randall B. Dunham, "The Measurement of Perceived Job Characteristics: The Diagnostic Survey vs. the Job Characteristics Inventory," *Academy of Management Journal*, March 1978, vol. 21, no. 1, pp. 123–128.
32. Ruth Kanfer, "Motivation Theory and Industrial and Organizational Psychology," in Marvin D. Dunnette and Leaetta M. Hough, eds., *Handbook of Industrial and Organizational Psychology*, 2nd ed., vol. 1 (Palo Alto, Calif.: Consulting Psychologists Press, 1991), pp. 75–170; and Renn and Vandenberg, "The Critical Psychological States: An Underrepresented Component in Job Characteristics Model Research," op. cit.
33. Frederick P. Morgeson, Michael D. Johnson, Michael A. Campion, Gina J. Medsker, and Troy V. Mumford, "Understanding Reactions to Job Redesign: A Quasi-Experimental Investigation of the Moderating Effects of Organizational Context on Perceptions of Performance Behavior," *Personnel Psychology*, 2006, vol. 59, pp. 333–363.
34. Samuel Melamed, Irit Ben-Avi, Jair Luz, and Manfred S. Green, "Objective and Subjective Work Monotony: Effects on Job Satisfaction, Psychological Distress, and Absenteeism in Blue-Collar Workers," *Journal of Applied Psychology*, 1995, vol. 80, pp. 29–42.
35. Peter Capelli, "A Market-Driven Approach to Retaining Talent," *Harvard Business Review*, 2000, vol. 78, no. 1, pp. 103–111.
36. Clark Molstad, "Choosing and Coping with Boring Work," *Urban Life*, 1986, vol. 15, pp. 215–236; J. Benjamin Forbes and Gerald V. Barrett, "Individual Abilities and Task Demands in Relation to Performance and Satisfaction on Two Repetitive Monitoring Tasks," *Journal of Applied Psychology*, 1978, vol. 63, pp. 188–196; and Carl R. Phillips, Arthur G. Bedeian, and Clark Molstad, "Repetitive Work: Contrast and Conflict," *The Journal of Socio-Economics*, 1991, vol. 20, pp. 73–82.
37. Quoted in Theodore T. Herbert, *Organizational Behavior: Readings and Cases* (New York: Macmillan, 1976), pp. 344–345.
38. Edwin A. Locke, "Toward a Theory of Task Motivation and Incentives," *Organizational Behavior and Human Performance*, 1968, vol. 3, pp. 157–189; and Edwin A. Locke and Gary P. Latham, *A Theory of Goal Setting and Task Performance* (Englewood Cliffs, N.J.: Prentice Hall, 1990).
39. Christina E. Shalley and Edwin A. Locke, "Setting Goals to Get Innovation," *R&D Innovator*, October 1996, vol. 5, no. 10, pp. 1–6.
40. Brian Grow, "Renovating Home Depot," *BusinessWeek*, March 6, 2006, pp. 50–58.
41. Maurice Schweitzer, Lisa Ordonez, and Bambi Douma, "Goal Setting as a Motivator of Unethical Behavior," *Academy of Management Journal*, 2004, vol. 47, no. 3, pp. 422–432.
42. Lynn Sharp Paine and Michael A. Santoro, "Sears Auto Centers," Harvard Business School case 9-394-010 (Boston, Mass.: Harvard Business School Publishing, 1993).
43. Ilan Mochari, "In a Former Life: S. Kenneth Kannappan," *Inc. Magazine*, June 2001, available online at: http://www.inc.com/magazine/20010601/22711.html (accessed November 5, 2006).
44. Chuck Salter, "Chick-fil-A's Recipe for Customer Service," *Fast Company*, available online at: http://www.fastcompany.com/resources/customer/chickfila.html (accessed November 5, 2006).
45. Erik Brynjolfsson, "VII Pillars Of Productivity," *Optimize*, May 2005, vol. 4, no. 5, pp. 27–35.
46. "Johnson & Johnson," Wingspan.com, 2006, available online at: http://www.wingspan.com/default.asp?id=clients_case_jnj_edd (accessed November 1, 2006).
47. Spencer E. Ante and Jena McGregor, "Giving the Boss the Big Picture," *BusinessWeek Online*, February 13, 2006, available online at: http://www.businessweek.com/magazine/content/06_07/b3971083.htm (accessed November 5, 2006).

48. Curt Hall, "Dashboards & Scorecards Chart Business Performance," *Business Intelligence*, December 2004, available online at: http://www.softwaremag.com/L.cfm?Doc=2004-12/2004-12bizintel (accessed November 1, 2006).
49. Spencer E. Ante and Jena McGregor, "Giving the Boss the Big Picture," *BusinessWeek Online*, February 13, 2006, available online at: http://www.businessweek.com/magazine/content/06_07/b3971083.htm (accessed November 5, 2006).
50. Albert Bandura, *Self-Efficacy: The Exercise of Control* (New York: W. H. Freeman and Company, 1997), p. 3.
51. Victor H. Vroom, *Work and Motivation* (New York: John Wiley & Sons, 1964).
52. Lawrence R. Walker and Kenneth W. Thomas, "Beyond Expectancy Theory: An Integrative Model from Health Care," *Academy of Management Review*, 1982, vol. 7, no. 2, pp. 187–194; Donald Campbell and Robert Pritchard, "Motivation Theory in Industrial and Organizational Psychology," in Marvin D. Dunnette, ed., *Handbook of Industrial and Organizational Psychology* (Chicago, Ill.: Rand McNally, 1976), pp. 63–130; and Wendelien Van Eerde and Hank Thierry, "Vroom's Expectancy Model and Work-Related Criteria: A Meta-Analysis," *Journal of Applied Psychology*, October 1996, pp. 575–586.
53. Mahmoud A. Wahba and Robert J. House, "Expectancy Theory in Work and Motivation: Some Logical and Methodological Issues," *Human Relations*, 1974, vol. 27, pp. 121–147.
54. Terence Mitchell, "Expectancy-Value Models in Organizational Psychology," in Norman T. Feather, ed., *Expectations and Actions: Expectancy-Value Models in Psychology* (Hillsdale, N.J.: Erlbaum, 1982), pp. 293–312.
55. See Jerald Greenberg and Russell Cropanzano, eds., *Advances in Organizational Justice* (Stanford, Calif.: Stanford University Press, 2001).
56. See John Thibaut and Laurens Walker, *Procedural Justice: A Psychological Analysis* (Hillsdale, N.J.: Erlbaum, 1975); Jerald Greenberg and Russell Cropanzano, *Advances in Organizational Justice* (Stanford, Calif.: Stanford University Press, 2001); Jerald Greenberg and Jason A. Colquitt, eds., *Handbook of Organizational Justice* (Mahway, N.J.: Lawrence Erlbaum Associates, 2005); Jason A. Colquitt, Donald E. Conlon, Michael J. Wesson, Christopher O. L. H. Porter, and K. Yee Ng, "Justice at the Millennium: A Meta-Analytic Review of 25 Years of Organizational Justice Research," *Journal of Applied Psychology*, 2001, vol. 86, pp. 425–445; Tina L. Robbins, Timothy P. Summers, and Janis L. Miller, "Intra- and Inter-Justice Relationships: Assessing the Direction," *Human Relations*, October 2000, vol. 53, no. 10, pp. 1329–1355; and Tina L. Robbins, Timothy P. Summers, Janis L. Miller, and William H. Hendrix, "Using the Group-Value Model to Explain the Role of Noninstrumental Justice in Distinguishing the Effects of Distributive and Procedural Justice," *Journal of Occupational and Organizational Psychology*, December 2000, vol. 73, no. 4, pp. 511–518.
57. Jerald Greenberg, "Losing Sleep over Organizational Injustice: Attenuating Insomniac Reactions to Underpayment Inequity with Supervisory Training in Interactional Justice," *Journal of Applied Psychology*, January 2006, vol. 91, no. 1, pp. 58–69.
58. Jerald Greenberg, "Employee Theft as a Reaction to Underpayment Inequity: The Hidden Cost of Pay Cuts," *Journal of Applied Psychology*, 1990, vol. 75, no. 5, pp. 561–568.
59. J. Stacey Adams, "Inequity in Social Exchanges," in L. Berkowitz, ed., *Advances in Experimental Social Psychology*, vol. 2 (New York: Academic Press, 1965), pp. 267–300.
60. Paul D. Sweeney, "Distributive Justice and Pay Satisfaction: A Field Test of an Equity Theory Prediction," *Journal of Business and Psychology*," 1990, vol. 4, no. 3, pp. 329–341.
61. Kenneth J. Gergen, Stanley J. Morse, and Katherin A. Bode, "Overpaid or Overworked? Cognitive and Behavioral Reactions to Inequitable Rewards," *Journal of Applied Social Psychology*, July–September 1974, vol. 4, no. 3, pp. 259–274.
62. James L. Bowditch and Anthony F. Buono, *A Primer on Organizational Behavior*, 4th ed. (New York: John Wiley & Sons, 1997).
63. Jeanne E. Ormrod, *Human Learning*, 4th ed. (Upper Saddle River, N.J.: Prentice-Hall, 2003).
64. E. L. Thorndike, *Animal Intelligence* (New York: Macmillan, 1911).
65. B. F. Skinner, "Are Theories of Learning Necessary?" *Psychological Review,* 1950, vol. 57, no. 4, pp. 193–216; B. F. Skinner, *Science and Human Behavior* (New York: Macmillan, 1953); and B. F. Skinner, "The Science of Learning and the Art of Teaching," *Harvard Educational Review*, 1954, vol. 24, no. 2, pp. 86–97.
66. Beth Lachman, Frank Camm, and Susan A. Resetar, *Integrated Facility Environmental Management Approaches: Lessons from Industry for Department of Defense Facilities* (Santa Monica, Calif.: RAND Corporation, 2001), available online at: http://www.rand.org/pubs/monograph_reports/MR1343/ (accessed November 5, 2006).
67. Kenneth D. Butterfield, Linda K. Trevino, and Gail A. Ball, "Punishment from the Manager's Perspective: A Grounded Investigation and Inductive Model," *Academy of Management Review*, 1996, vol. 39, no. 6, pp. 1479–1512.
68. The following is based on Thomas Connellan, *How to Improve Human Performance: Behaviorism in Business* (New York: Harper & Row, 1978); and Lawrence Miller, *Behavior Management: The New Science of Managing People at Work* (New York: Wiley, 1978), p. 253.
69. See Dave Dermer, "Selling Senior Execs on the Benefits of Online Incentives: Show Senior Managers How a Web-Based, Noncash Incentive Program Triggers Elevated Profits and Productivity in Their Area of Responsibility," *HR Magazine*, September 2004, available online at: http://www.findarticles.com/p/articles/mi_m3495/is_9_49/ai_n6206616 (accessed November 5, 2006).
70. Kenneth Hein, "Anatomy of an Online Sales Incentive Program," *Incentive Magazine*, February 1, 2006, available online at: http://www.incentivemag.com/incentive/magazine/article_display.jsp?vnu_content_id=1001918194 (accessed November 1, 2006).
71. Bob Nelson, *1001 Ways to Reward Employees* (New York: Workman Publishing, 1994), p. 19.
72. Cora Daniels, "Thank You Is Nice, but This Is Better," *Fortune*, November 22, 1999, p. 370.
73. Shari Caudron, "Master the Compensation Maze," *Personnel Journal*, June 1993, vol. 2, no. 6, p. 64.
74. Nanette Byrnes, "The Art of Motivation," *BusinessWeek*, May 1, 2006, pp. 56–62.
75. Gerald Ledford Jr., "Three Case Studies on Skill-Based Pay: An Overview," *Compensation & Benefits Review*, March–April 1991, pp. 11–23.
76. Gerald Ledford Jr., and Gary Bergel, "Skill-Based Pay Case No. 1: General Mills," *Compensation & Benefits Review*, March–April 1991, pp. 24–38.
77. Caudron, "Master the Compensation Maze," op. cit.
78. W. Flanagan, "The Best Incentive Programs of 2005," *Incentive Magazine*, December 1, 2005, available online at: http://www.incentivemag.com/msg/search/article_display.jsp?vnu_content_id=1001613640 (accessed November 5, 2006).
79. Andrea C. Poe, "Online Recognition," *HR Magazine*, June 2002, p. 47, available online at: http://www.shrm.org/hrmagazine/articles/0602/0602agn-awards.asp (accessed November 1, 2006).

80. Dave Dermer, "Selling Senior Execs on the Benefits of Online Incentives: Show Senior Managers How a Web-Based, Noncash Incentive Program Triggers Elevated Profits and Productivity in Their Area of Responsibility," op. cit.
81. Andrea C. Poe, "Online Recognition," op. cit.
82. Rebecca Aronauer, "Motivation Inspiration," Salesandmarketing.com, September 11, 2006, available online at: http://salesandmarketing.com/msg/content_display/sales/e3iNwIbqvVWLdftc0pdu3MmxA%3D%3D?imw=Y (accessed November 1, 2006).
83. "Creating Simply the Best Customer Service at T-Mobile USA: The Role of Rewards and Recognition," Marketing Innovators Case Study, 2005, available online at: http://www.marketinginnovators.com/Downloads/TMobile_CaseStudy.pdf (accessed November 1, 2006); and Flanagan, "The Best Incentive Programs of 2005," op. cit.
84. Suzanne J. Peterson and Fred Luthans, "The Impact of Financial and Nonfinancial Incentives on Business-Unit Outcomes Over Time," *Journal of Applied Psychology*, January 2006, vol. 91, no. 1, pp. 156–165.
85. Nanette Byrnes, "The Art of Motivation," *BusinessWeek*, May 1, 2006, pp. 56–62.
86. John A. Byrne, "How to Lead Now: Getting Extraordinary Performance When You Can't Pay for It," *Fast Company*, August 2003, vol. 73, p. 62.
87. "Time to Take Another Look at Telecommuting," *HR Focus*, May 2002, p. 8.
88. "The Benefits of Lifelong Learning," *Journal of European Industrial Training*, February–March 1997, p. 3.
89. Kelly Dunn, "Rutgers University Creates Culture of Lifelong Learning," *Workforce*, May 2000, vol. 79, no. 5, pp. 108–109.
90. "How to Predict if Your Best Employees Are About to Walk out the Door: SAS Human Capital Management Helps Banca Carige to Retain Employees and Save Costs," SAS Success Story, available online at: http://www.sas.com/success/carige.html (accessed November 5, 2006).
91. M. Allen, "Help Wanted: The Not-Too-High-Q Standard," *New York Times*, September 19, 1999, p WK3.
92. Wonderlic Personnel Test, Inc., *Wonderlic Personnel Test & Scholastic Level Exam User's Manual* (Libertyville, Ill.: Wonderlic, 1992).
93. Byrne, "How to Lead Now: Getting Extraordinary Performance When You Can't Pay for It," op. cit.

CHAPTER 15

1. Based on an interview with Mary Lou Ambrus, Lucent's vice president of group communications, and Bill Price, Lucent's director of corporate communications, on March 1, 2006.
2. Arthur Bell and Dayle Smith, *Management Communication* (New York: John Wiley, 1991), p. 19.
3. Anne Warfield, "Do You Speak Body Language?" *Training and Development*, April 2001, p. 60.
4. Albert Mehrabian, "Communication Without Words," *Psychology Today*, 1968, vol. 2, no. 9, pp. 52–55.
5. Albert Mehrabian, *Silent Messages* (Belmont, Calif.: Wadsworth, 1971); see also Albert Mehrabian, *Silent Messages: Implicit Communication of Emotions and Attitudes,* 2nd ed. (Belmont, Calif.: Wadsworth, 1981); and Albert Mehrabian, *Nonverbal Communication* (Chicago, Ill.: Aldine-Atherton, 1972).
6. Warfield, "Do You Speak Body Language?" op. cit.
7. DeWitt C. Dearborn and Herbert A. Simon, "Selective Perception: A Note on the Departmental Identification of Executives," *Sociometry*, 1958, vol. 21, pp. 140–144; and Janice M. Beyer, Prithviraj Chattopadhyay, Elizabeth George, William H. Glick, D. T. Ogilvie, and Dulce Pugliese, "The Selective Perception of Managers Revisited," *Academy of Management Journal*, 1997, vol. 40, no. 3, pp. 716–737.
8. Based on an interview with Kenny Klepper, Medco's president and chief operating officer, and Karin Princivalle, Medco's senior vice president of human resources, March 15, 2006.
9. Peter Lawrence, "Designing Where We Work," *Fast Company*, available online at: http://www.fastcompany.com/resources/design/lawrence/050205.html (accessed March 14, 2006).
10. Tom Geddie, "Moving Communication Across Cultures," *Communication World*, April–May 1998, vol. 16, no. 5, pp. 37–41.
11. Carmine Gallo, "Lose the Jargon or Lose the Audience," *BusinessWeek Online,* December 1, 2005, available online at: http://www.businessweek.com/print/smallbiz/content/nov2005/sb20051130_272052.htm (accessed March 16, 2006).
12. Scott Kirsner, "DreamWorks Animation Couldn't Find a Videoconferencing System That Made CEO Jeffrey Katzenberg Happy—So It Built Its Own," *Fast Company*, January 2006, p. 90.
13. Tom J. Peters and Robert H. Waterman Jr., *In Search of Excellence* (New York: Harper & Row, 1982); Chip R. Bell, "Managing by Wandering Around," *Journal for Quality and Participation*, 2000, vol. 23, no. 5, pp. 42–44.
14. Alison Overholt, "New Leaders, New Agenda," *Fast Company*, May 2002, p. 52.
15. Gary Dessler, *Winning Commitment: How to Build and Keep a Competitive Workforce* (New York: McGraw-Hill, 1993).
16. Earl Plenty and William Machaner, "Stimulating Upward Communication," in Jerry Gray and Frederick Starke, eds., *Readings in Organizational Behavior* (Columbus, Ohio: Charles Merrill, 1977), pp. 229–240.
17. Michelle Conlin, "E-Mail Is So Five Minutes Ago," *BusinessWeek*, November 28, 2005, p. 111.
18. Shari Sanders, "Sailing into the Mass Market: Discount Rivals Stand at Attention—Old Navy Clothing Co. Offers Competition," *Discount Store News*, March 4, 1996, available online at: http://findarticles.com/p/articles/mi_m3092/is_n5_v35/ai_18056108 (accessed July 24, 2006).
19. Dan Patterson, "PM Portals—Show Me the Value: Improving Project Visibility Using a Web-Based Portal," *Projectmagazine.com*, July 15, 2003, vol. 4, no. 4, available online at: http://www.projectmagazine.com/v4i4/v4i4welcom1.html (accessed July 24, 2006).
20. Ibid.
21. Donald O. Wilson, "Diagonal Communication Links Within Organizations, *Journal of Business Communication*, 1992, vol. 29, no. 2, pp. 129–143.
22. Lisa C. Abrams, Rob Cross, Eric Lesser, and Daniel Z. Levin, "Nurturing Interpersonal Trust in Knowledge-Sharing Networks," *Academy of Management Executive*, November 2003, vol. 17, no. 4, pp. 64–77.
23. Grant Michelson and Suchitra Mouly, "Rumour and Gossip in Organisations: A Conceptual Study," *Management Decision*, 2000, vol. 38, no. 5, pp. 339–346.
24. Lisa Burke and Jessica Wise, "The Effective Care, Handling, and Pruning of the Office Grapevine," *Business Horizons*, 2003, vol. 46, no. 3, pp. 71–76.
25. Nicholas Difonzo, Prashant Bordia, and Ralph Rosnow, "Reigning in Rumors," *Organizational Dynamics*, 1994, vol. 23, no. 1, pp. 47–62.
26. Based on an interview with Mary Lou Ambrus, Lucent's vice president of group communications, and Bill Price, Lucent's director of corporate communications, on March 1, 2006.
27. Richard C. Huseman and Edward W. Miles, "Organizational Communication in the Information Age: Implications of Computer-Based Systems," *Journal of Management*, June 1988, vol. 14, no. 2, pp. 181–204.

28. Jennifer Stone Gonzalez, *The 21st-Century INTRANET* (Upper Saddle River, N.J.: Prentice-Hall, 1998).
29. Allison Stein Wellner, "Lost in Translation," *Inc. Magazine*, September 2005, p. 37.
30. Based on an interview with Kenny Klepper, Medco's president and chief operating officer, and Karin Princivalle, Medco's senior vice president of human resources, March 15, 2006.
31. "Pacesetters: Streamlining," *BusinessWeek*, November 21, 2005, p. 94.
32. Tracy Mayor, "Remote Control," *CIO Magazine*, 2001, at: http://www.cio.com/archive/040101/remote.html (accessed July 24, 2006).
33. Polycom, "Financial Services Firm Bear Stearns Connects Globally with Polycom Video Communications to Raise Productivity, Close Deals," available online at: http://www.polycom.com/common/pw_cmp_printScreen/0,,pw-5512,FF.html (accessed April 3, 2006).
34. Ibid.
35. Wayne F. Cascio, "Managing a Virtual Workplace," *Academy of Management Executive*, 2000, vol. 14, no. 3, pp. 81–90.
36. Nancy B. Kurland and Diane E. Bailey, "Telework: The Advantages and Challenges of Working Here, There, Anywhere, and Anytime," *Organizational Dynamics*, 1999, vol. 28, no. 2, pp. 53–67.
37. "Collaborative Software," *Wikipedia*, March 20, 2006, at: en.wikipedia.org/wiki/Collaborative_software; "Collaborative Groupware Software," available online at: www.svpal.org/~grantbow/groupware.html (accessed March 20, 2006).
38. A. B. Shani, James A. Sena, and Michael W. Stebbins, "Knowledge Work Teams and Groupware Technology: Learning from Seagate's Experience," *Journal of Knowledge Management*, 2000, vol. 4, no. 2, pp. 111–124.
39. Kenneth Laudon and Jane Laudon, *Management Information Systems: Managing the Digital Firm,* 9th ed. (Upper Saddle River, N.J.: Prentice Hall, 2006), p. 436.
40. Patterson, "PM Portals—Show Me the Value: Improving Project Visibility Using a Web-Based Portal," op. cit.
41. Ibid.
42. Ibid.
43. Niles Howard, "Information Please!" *Inc.com,* at: http://www.inc.com/partners/businessinsights/content/Intranet.html (accessed March 22, 2006).
44. Ibid. An example of a portal can be found at: http://en.wikipedia.org/wiki/Wikipedia:Community_Portal.
45. Patterson, "PM Portals—Show Me the Value: Improving Project Visibility Using a Web-based Portal," op. cit.
46. "Get Fit," *Workforce Week: Management*, March 19–25, 2006, vol. 7, no. 12, available online at: http://www.workforce.com/tools/newsletters/wfw/workforce_week_060321upload.htm (accessed July 24, 2006).
47. Pam Baker, "Interview: ExxonMobil V.P. Patricia C. Hewlett," *CIO Today*, January 17, 2006, available online at: http://www.cio-today.com/story.xhtml?story_id=033002XWE0V0&page=1 (accessed July 24, 2006).
48. Adapted from Jennifer A. Redmond, "Make Your Intranet Click," *Inc.com,* March 2002, at: http://www.inc.com/articles/2002/03/24007.html (accessed March 21, 2006).
49. "Wiki," *Wikipedia,* March 21, 2006, at: en.wikipedia.org/wiki/Wiki.
50. Ibid.
51. "Wiki," *CMS Management Systems,* March 21, 2006, at: http://www.cmswiki.com/tiki-index.php?page=Wiki (accessed July 24, 2006).
52. Ezra Goodnoe, "How to Use Wikis for Business," *InternetWeek*, August 8, 2005, available online at: http://www.informationweek.com/industries/showArticle.jhtml;jsessionid=2HDFBRPKOOPQGQSNDBCSKH0CJUMEKJVN?articleID=167600331&pgno=1&queryText= (accessed May 1, 2006).
53. "Pacesetters: Collaboration," *BusinessWeek*, November 21, 2005, p. 92.
54. "Blog," *Wikipedia,* March 21, 2006, at: en.wikipedia.org/wiki/Blog#Business.
55. Shiv Singh, "Intranet Trends to Watch for in 2006," *CIO Magazine*, December 19, 2005, available online at: http://www.cio.com/weighin/column.html?CID=15817 (accessed April 12, 2006).
56. "Pacesetters: Collaboration," *BusinessWeek,* November 21, 2005, p. 92.
57. Stanley Holmes, "Into the Wild Blog Yonder," *BusinessWeek*, May 22, 2006, pp. 84–86.
58. Allison Stein Wellner, "Lost in Translation," *Inc. Magazine*, September 2005, p. 37.
59. Scott Kirsner, "DreamWorks Animation Couldn't Find a Videoconferencing System That Made CEO Jeffrey Katzenberg Happy—So It Built Its Own," *Fast Company*, January 2006, p. 90.
60. Richard L. Daft and Robert H. Lengel, "Organizational Information Requirements, Media Richness and Structural Design," *Management Science*, 1986, vol. 32, no. 5, pp. 554–571; Richard L. Daft and Robert H. Lengel, "Information Richness: A New Approach to Managerial Behavior and Organization Design," in Barry M. Staw and Larry L. Cummings, eds., *Research in Organizational Behavior*, vol. 6 (Greenwich, Conn.: JAI Press, 1984), pp. 191–233.
61. Joseph E. McGrath and Andrea B. Hollingshead, "Putting the Group Back in Group Support Systems: Some Theoretical Issues About Dynamic Processes in Groups with Technological Enhancements," in Leonard M. Jessup and Joseph S. Valacich, eds., *Group Support Systems: New Perspectives* (New York, Macmillan, 1993), pp. 78–96; Kil Soo Suh, "Impact of Communication Medium on Task Performance and Satisfaction: An Examination of Media-Richness Theory," *Information & Management,* 1999, vol. 35, no. 5, pp. 295–312.
62. Linda K. Trevino, Robert H. Lengel, Wayne Bodensteiner, Edwin Gerloff, and Nan Muir, "The Richness Imperative and Cognitive Style: The Role of Individual Differences in Media Choice Behavior," *Management Communication Quarterly*, 1990, vol. 4, pp. 176–197.
63. Kenneth C. Petress, "Listening: A Vital Skill," *Journal of Instructional Psychology*, December 1999, vol. 26, no. 4, pp. 261–262.
64. David A. Garvin and Michael A. Roberto, "Change Through Persuasion," *Harvard Business Review*, February 2005, pp. 104–112.
65. Jay A. Conger, "The Necessary Art of Persuasion," *Harvard Business Review*, May–June 1998, pp. 85–95.
66. Jay Conger, *Winning 'Em Over: A New Model for Management in the Age of Persuasion* (New York: Simon & Schuster, 1998).
67. Conger, "The Necessary Art of Persuasion," op. cit.
68. Conger, *Winning 'Em Over: A New Model for Management in the Age of Persuasion*, op. cit.
69. Ibid.
70. Conger, "The Necessary Art of Persuasion," op. cit.
71. Larry Crump, "For the Sake of the Team: Unity and Disunity in a Multiparty Major League Baseball Negotiation," *Negotiation Journal*, 2005, vol. 21, no. 3, pp. 317–342.
72. Roger Fisher and William Ury, *Getting to Yes* (New York: Penguin Books, 1983); Roger Fisher, William Ury, and Bruce Patton, *Getting to Yes: Negotiating Agreement Without Giving In*, 2nd ed. (New York: Houghton Mifflin, 1992).

73. Carsten K. W. De Dreu, "A PACT Against Conflict Escalation in Negotiation and Dispute Resolution," *Current Directions in Psychological Science*, June 2005, vol. 14, p. 149.
74. Fisher and Ury, *Getting to Yes*, op. cit.
75. Rob Walker, "Take It or Leave It: The *Only* Guide to Negotiating You Will Ever Need," *Inc. Magazine*, August 2003, p. 75.
76. Adapted from Michael Kaplan, "How to Negotiate Anything," *Money*, May 2005, vol. 34, no. 5, pp. 116–119.
77. Roger Fisher, William L. Ury, and Bruce Patton, *Getting to Yes: Negotiating Agreement Without Giving In* (New York: Penguin, 1991).
78. Robert D. Ramsey, "Conflict Resolution Skills for Supervisors," *Supervision*, August 1996, vol. 57, no. 8, pp. 9–12.
79. Ibid.
80. Martin Delahoussaye, "Don't Get Mad, Get Promoted," *Training*, June 2002, vol. 39, no. 6, p. 20.
81. Kathryn Tyler, "Toning Up Communications: Business Writing Courses Can Help Employees and Managers Learn to Clearly Express Organizational Messages," *HR Magazine*, March 2003, pp. 87–89.
82. Adapted from Arthur H. Bell and Dayle M. Smith, *Management Communication* (New York: Wiley, 1999), p. 14.
83. Adapted from Anna Burges-Lumsden, "Body Language for Successful HR," *PersonnelToday.com*, April 5, 2005, available online at: http://www.personneltoday.com/Articles/2005/04/05/29089/Body+language+for+successful+HR.htm (accessed March 16, 2006).
84. Twainquotes.com, available online at: http://www.twainquotes.com/Word.html (accessed March 29, 2006).
85. Based on Andrea C. Poe, "Don't Touch That 'Send' Button!—E-Mail Messaging Skills," *HR Magazine*, July 2001, vol. 46, no. 7, pp. 74–80.
86. Adapted from Bell and Smith, *Management Communication*, op. cit.
87. Steven G. Rogelberg, Desmond J. Leach, Peter B. Warr, and Jennifer L. Burnfield, "Not Another Meeting! Are Meeting Time Demands Related to Employee Well-Being?" *Journal of Applied Psychology*, 2006, vol. 1, pp. 86–96.
88. Jamie Walters, "Was That a Good Meeting, or a Bad One?" *Inc. Magazine*, January 2003, available online at: http://www.inc.com/articles/2003/01/25007.html (accessed March 17, 2006).
89. "2005 Electronic Monitoring & Surveillance Survey: Many Companies Monitoring, Recording, Videotaping—and Firing—Employees," *American Management Association*, May 18, 2005, available online at: http://www.amanet.org/press/amanews/ems05.htm (accessed November 1, 2006).
90. Thomas Claburn, "Survey Suggests Employees Doubt Workplace-Monitoring Motives," *InformationWeek*, January 20, 2005, available online at: http://www.informationweek.com/story/showArticle.jhtml?articleID=57702534 (accessed March 29, 2006).
91. Ibid.
92. Ibid.
93. American Bar Association, "Some Sample Provisions and Why to Use Them," *Business Law Today*, July/August 2002, vol. 11, no. 6, available online at: http://www.abanet.org/buslaw/blt/2002-07-08/wilsonscheib.html (accessed November 1, 2006).

CHAPTER 16

1. Based on an interview with Kenny Klepper, Medco's president and chief operating officer, and Karin Princivalle, Medco's senior vice president of human resources, March 15, 2006.
2. Susan G. Cohen and Diane E. Bailey, "What Makes Teams Work: Group Effectiveness Research from the Shop Floor to the Executive Suite," *Journal of Management*, 1997, vol. 23, pp. 239–290; Daniel R. Ilgen, "Teams Embedded in Organizations: Some Implications," *American Psychologist*, 1999, vol. 54, pp. 129–139; Steve W. J. Kozlowski and Bradford S. Bell, "Work Groups and Teams in Organizations," in Walter C. Borman, Daniel R. Ilgen, and Richard J. Klimoski, eds., *Comprehensive Handbook of Psychology (Vol. 12): Industrial and Organizational Psychology* (New York: Wiley, 2003), pp. 333–375; and Bradley L. Kirkman, Paul E. Tesluk, and Benson Rosen, "Assessing the Incremental Validity of Team Consensus Ratings over Aggregation of Individual-Level Data in Predicting Team Effectiveness," *Personnel Psychology*, 2001, vol. 54, pp. 645–667.
3. Eric Sundstrom, "The Challenges of Supporting Work Team Effectiveness," in Eric D. Sundstrom, ed., *Supporting Work Team Effectiveness: Best Management Practices for Fostering High Performance* (San Francisco, Calif.: Jossey-Bass, 1999), pp. 3–23; and Thompson, *Making the Team: A Guide for Managers*, 2nd ed., op. cit.
4. Jerry Smolek, David Hoffman, and Linda Moran, "Organizing Teams for Success," in Eric Sundstrom, ed., *Supporting Work Team Effectiveness: Best Management Practices for Fostering High Performance* (San Francisco, Calif.: Jossey-Bass, 1999), pp. 24–62.
5. "Hewlett-Packard Case Study," *Microsoft TechNet*, available online at: http://www.microsoft.com/technet/prodtechnol/Visio/visio2002/case/vishpcs.mspx (accessed July 24, 2006).
6. Eric Sundstrom, Kenneth P. DeMeuse, and David Futrell, "Work Teams: Applications and Effectiveness," *American Psychologist*, 1990, vol. 45, no. 2, pp. 120–133; Leigh L. Thompson, *Making the Team: A Guide for Managers*, 2nd ed. (Upper Saddle River, N.J.: Pearson Education Inc., 2004).
7. Andrea B. Hollingshead, Joseph E. McGrath, and Kathleen M. O'Connor, "Group Task Performance and Communication Technology: A Longitudinal Study of Computer-Mediated Versus Face-to-Face Work Groups," *Small Group Research*, 1993, vol. 24, no. 3, pp. 307–333; A. B. Hollingshead and J. E. McGrath, "Computer-Assisted Groups: A Critical Review of the Empirical Research," in Richard Guzzo and Eduardo Salas, eds., *Team Effectiveness and Decision Making in Organizations* (San Francisco, Calif.: Jossey-Bass, 1995), pp. 46–78; and Thompson, *Making the Team: A Guide for Managers*, 2nd ed., op. cit.
8. Smithsonian.org, "Inventors' Stories: IDEO Innovative Product Design Team," available online at: http://invention.smithsonian.org/centerpieces/iap/inventors_ide.html (accessed April 3, 2006).
9. "Case Study: Mayo Clinic SPARC Innovation Program, Steelcase, available online at: http://www.oneworkplace.com/images/dynamic/case_studies/MayoClinic.pdf (accessed July 18, 2006).
10. Jack C. Horn, "Making Quality Circles Work Better," *Psychology Today*, August 1986, available online at: http://www.findarticles.com/p/articles/mi_m1175/is_v20/ai_4421941 (accessed July 18, 2006).
11. Colgate, "Global Procurement Mission and Goals," available online at: http://www.colgate.com/app/Colgate/US/Corp/ContactUs/GMLS/MissionAndGoals.cvsp (accessed April 20, 2006).
12. Ron Williams, "Self-Directed Work Teams: A Competitive Advantage," *Quality Digest*, November 1995, vol. 15, no. 11, pp. 50–52.
13. Charles Fishman, "Engines of Democracy," *Fast Company*, October 1999, vol. 28, p. 174.
14. Michael Macoby, "Understanding the Difference Between Management and Leadership," *Research & Technology Management*, January–February 2000, pp. 57–59, at: http://www.maccoby.com/Articles/UtDBMaL.html (accessed April 20, 2006).

15. Philip Olson, "Choices for Innovation Minded Corporations," *Journal of Business Strategy*, January–February 1990, pp. 86–90.
16. Gary Dessler, *Management: Principles and Practices for Tomorrow's Leaders* (Upper Saddle River, N.J.: Pearson/Prentice Hall, 2004).
17. Successful venture teams are sometimes spun off into their own divisions or even independent companies. Some organizations create new-venture divisions devoted exclusively to new-product development. See, for example, Christopher Bart, "New Venture Units: Use Them Wisely to Manage Innovation," *Sloan Management Review*, Summer 1988, pp. 35–43; and Robert Burgelman, "Managing the New Venture Division: Research Findings and Implications for Strategic Management," *Strategic Management Journal*, 1985, vol. 6, pp. 39–54.
18. Anthony M. Townsend, Samuel M. DeMarie, and Anthony R. Hendrickson, "Virtual Teams: Technology and the Workplace of the Future," *Academy of Management Executive*, 1998, vol. 12, no. 3, pp. 17–29.
19. Beverly Geber, "Virtual Teams," *Training*, 1995, vol. 32, no. 4, pp. 36–42.
20. Linda Rosencrance, "Meet Me in Cyberspace," *Computerworld*, January 3, 2005, available online at: http://www.computerworld.com.au/index.php/id;1948350049;relcomp;1 (accessed July 24, 2006).
21. Bruce W. Tuckman, "Developmental Sequence in Small Groups," *Psychological Bulletin*, 1965, vol. 63, pp. 384–399; and Bruce W. Tuckman and Mary Ann C. Jensen, "Stages of Small-Group Development Revisited," *Group & Organization Studies*, 1977, vol. 2, no. 4, pp. 419–427.
22. Faith Keenan and Spencer E. Ante, "The New Teamwork," *BusinessWeek*, February 18, 2002, e.Biz Supplement, pp. EB12–EB16, available online at: http://www.businessweek.net/magazine/content/02_07/b3770601.htm (accessed April 17, 2006).
23. J. Richard Hackman, "The Design of Work Teams," in J. Lorsch, ed., *Handbook of Organizational Behavior* (Englewood Cliffs, N.J.: Prentice-Hall, 1987); and J. Richard Hackman, *Leading Teams: Setting the Stage for Great Performances* (Boston, Mass.: Harvard Business School Press, 2002).
24. Hackman, *Leading Teams: Setting the Stage for Great Performances*, op. cit.
25. Ibid., p. 129.
26. Ibid., p. 130.
27. Rosencrance, "Meet Me in Cyberspace," op. cit.
27. http://www.jnj.com/careers/learn.html (accessed April 24, 2006).
28. Stanley M. Gully, Dennis J. Devine, and David J. Whitney, "A Meta-Analysis of Cohesion and Performance: Effects of Levels of Analysis and Task Interdependence," *Small Group Research*, 1995, vol. 26, no. 4, pp. 497–520.
29. Thompson, *Making the Team: A Guide for Managers*, 2nd ed., op. cit., p. 93.
30. Cheryl Dahle, "Xtreme Teams," *Fast Company*, November 1999, vol. 29, p. 310; and Thompson, *Making the Team: A Guide for Managers*, 2nd ed., op. cit.
31. Debra R. Comer, "A Model of Social Loafing in Real Work Groups," *Human Relations*, June 1995, vol. 48, no. 6, pp. 647–667; Jennifer M. George, "Extrinsic and Intrinsic Origins of Perceived Social Loafing in Organizations," *Academy of Management Journal*, 1992, vol. 35, pp. 191–202; James A. Shepperd, "Productivity Loss in Performance Groups: A Motivation Analysis," *Psychological Bulletin*, 1993, vol. 113, pp. 67–81; and Thompson, *Making the Team: A Guide for Managers*, 2nd ed., op. cit.
32. Irwin A. Horowitz and Kenneth S. Bordens, *Social Psychology* (Mountain View, Calif.: Mayfield, 1995).
33. Steven J. Karau and Kipling D. Williams, "Social Loafing: A Meta-Analytic Review and Theoretical Integration," *Journal of Personality and Social Psychology*, 1993, vol. 65, pp. 681–706.
34. Norbert L. Kerr, "Illusions of Efficacy: The Effects of Group Size on Perceived Efficacy in Social Dilemmas," *Journal of Experimental Social Psychology*, 1989, vol. 25, pp. 287–313.
35. Kipling Williams, Stephen Harkins, and Bibb Latane, "Identifiability as a Deterrent to Social Loafing: Two Cheering Experiments," *Journal of Personality and Social Psychology*, 1981, vol. 40, pp. 303–311; and Bibb Latane, "Responsibility and Effort in Organizations," in Paul S. Goodman, ed., *Designing Effective Work Groups* (San Francisco, Calif.: Jossey-Bass, 1986).
36. Robert F. Bales, *Interaction Process Analysis: A Method for the Study of Small Groups* (Reading, Mass.: Addison-Wesley, 1950).
37. Irving Janis, *Victims of Groupthink* (Boston, Mass.: Houghton Mifflin, 1972).
38. Ibid.; and Irving Janis, *Victims of Groupthink*, 2nd ed. (Boston, Mass.: Houghton Mifflin, 1982).
39. John Schwartz and Matthew L. Wald, "'Groupthink' Is 30 Years Old, and Still Going Strong," *New York Times*, March 9, 2003, p. 5; and Claire Ferraris and Rodney Carveth, "NASA and the Columbia Disaster: Decision-Making by Groupthink?" *Proceedings of the 2003 Association for Business Communication Annual Convention*, 2003, Association for Business Communication.
40. Janis, *Victims of Groupthink*, 2nd ed., op. cit.
41. Ibid.
42. Jerry B. Harvey, *The Abilene Paradox and Other Meditations on Management* (San Francisco, Calif.: Jossey-Bass, 1988). The original publication of the Abilene paradox appeared as "The Abilene Paradox: The Management of Agreement," in *Organizational Dynamics*, Summer 1974, vol. 3, no. 1.
43. J. Richard Hackman, "Group Influences on Individuals in Organizations," in Marvin D. Dunnette and Loretta M. Hough, eds., *Handbook of Industrial and Organizational Psychology*, 2nd ed., vol. 3 (Palo Alto, Calif.: Consulting Psychologists Press, 1992).
44. Douglas MacGregor, *The Human Side of Enterprise* (New York: McGraw-Hill, 1960).
45. Jon R. Katzenbach and Douglas K. Smith, *The Wisdom of Teams: Creating the High-Performance Organization* (New York: HarperBusiness, 1994).
46. Glenn Parker, Jerry McAdams, and David Zielinski, *Rewarding Teams: Lessons from the Trenches* (San Francisco, Calif.: Jossey-Bass, 2000).
47. Peter Sinton, "Teamwork the Name of the Game for Ideo," *San Francisco Chronicle*, February 23, 2000, available online at: http://www.sfgate.com/cgi-bin/article.cgi?file=/chronicle/archive/2000/02/23/BU39355.DTL (accessed April 26, 2006).
48. Ibid.
49. David Lidsky, "Fast Forward 2005," *Fast Company*, November 2004, p. 69.
50. John M. Levine and Richard L. Moreland, "Newcomers and Oldtimers in Small Groups," in P. Paulus, ed., *Psychology of Group Influence*, 2nd ed. (Hillsdale, N.J.: Erlbaum, 1989), pp. 143–186; and John M. Levine and Richard L. Moreland, eds., *Small Groups* (Philadelphia, Penn.: Psychology Press, 2006).
51. Daniel Goleman, *Emotional Intelligence* (New York: Bantam Books, 1994); and Joseph Ciarrochi, *Emotional Intelligence in Everyday Life* (Philadelphia, Penn.: Psychology Press, 2006).
52. Daniel Goleman, Annie McKee, and Richard Boyatzis, *Primal Leadership: Realizing the Power of Emotional Intelligence* (Boston, Mass.: Harvard Business School Press, 2002).

53. Chi-Sum Wong and Kenneth S. Law, "The Effects of Leader and Follower Emotional Intelligence on Performance and Attitude: An Exploratory Study," *The Leadership Quarterly*, 2002, vol. 13, no. 3, pp. 243–274.
54. Ibid.
55. Christina Gibson and Susan Cohen, *Virtual Teams That Work: Creating Conditions for Virtual Team Effectiveness* (San Francisco, Calif.: Jossey-Bass, 2003).
56. Ruth Wageman, "Critical Success Factors for Creating Superb Self-Managing Teams," *Organizational Dynamics*, Summer 1997, vol. 26, p 59.
57. Wayne F. Cascio, "Managing a Virtual Workplace," *Academy of Management Executive,* 2000, vol. 14, no. 3, pp. 81–90.
58. Jessica Lipnack and Jeffrey Stamps, *Virtual Teams: Reaching Across Space, Time, and Organizations with Technology* (New York: John Wiley, 1997).
59. Bradford S. Bell and Steve W. J. Kozlowski, "A Typology of Virtual Teams: Implications for Effective Leadership," *Group and Organization Management*, 2002, vol. 27, no. 1, pp. 14–49.
60. Joyce A. Thompsen, "Leading Virtual Teams," *Quality Digest*, September 2000, available online at: http://www.qualitydigest.com/sept00/html/teams.html (accessed January 9, 2006).
61. Bell and Kozlowski, "A Typology of Virtual Teams: Implications for Effective Leadership," op. cit.
62. Charles Manz and Henry P. Sims, "Leading Workers to Lead Themselves: The External Leadership of Self-Managing Work Teams," *Administrative Science Quarterly*, 1987, vol. 32, pp. 106–128.
63. J. Richard Hackman and Richard E. Walton, "Leading Groups in Organizations," in Paul S. Goodman & Associates, eds., *Designing Effective Work Groups* (San Francisco, Calif.: Jossey-Bass, 1986).
64. Steve W. J. Kozlowski, "Training and Developing Adaptive Teams: Theory, Principles, and Research," in Jan A. Cannon-Bowers and Eduardo Salas, eds., *Decision Making Under Stress: Implications for Traning and Simulation* (Washington, D.C.: APA Books, 1998), pp. 115–153; and Eleanor M. Smith, J. Kevin Ford, and Steve W. J. Kozlowski, "Building Adaptive Expertise: Implications for Training Design," in Miguel A. Quinones and Addie Ehrenstein, eds., *Training for a Rapidly Changing Workplace: Applications of Psychological Research* (Washington, D.C.: APA Books, 1997), pp. 89–118.
65. Connie J. G. Gersick and J. Richard Hackman, "Habitual Routines in Task-Performing Teams," *Organizational Behavior and Human Decision Processes*, 1990, vol. 47, pp. 65–97.
66. Jane Siegel, Vitaly Dubrovsky, Sara Kiesler, and Timothy W. McGuire, "Group Processes in Computer-Mediated Communication," *Organizational Behavior and Human Decision Processes*, 1986, vol. 37, pp. 157–187; Susan G. Strauss and Joseph E. McGrath, "Does the Medium Matter? The Interaction of Task Type and Technology on Group Performance and Member Reactions," *Journal of Applied Psychology*, 1994, vol. 79, pp. 87–97; and Thompson, *Making the Team: A Guide for Managers*, 2nd ed., op. cit.
67. Bell and Kozlowski, "A Typology of Virtual Teams: Implications for Effective Leadership," op. cit.
68. Deborah L. Duarte and Nancy Tennant Snyder, *Mastering Virtual Teams* (San Francisco, Calif.: Jossey-Bass, 1999).
69. This section is based on Arvind Malhotra and Ann Majchrzak, "Virtual Workspace Technologies," *MIT Sloan Management Review*, Winter 2005, vol. 46, no. 2, pp. 11–14.
70. Alan R. Dennis and Monica J. Garfield, "The Adoption and Use of GSS in Project Teams: Toward More Participative Processes and Outcomes," *MIS Quarterly*, June 2003, vol. 27, no. 2, pp. 289–323.
71. Faith Keenan and Spencer E. Ante, "The New Teamwork," *BusinessWeek*, February 18, 2002, e.Biz Supplement, pp. EB12–EB16, available online at: http://www.businessweek.net/magazine/content/02_07/b3770601.htm (accessed April 17, 2006).
72. Project.net, "The UN's Health Organization Is Bridging the 'Digital Divide' in Developing Countries with the Help of Project.net," available online at: http://www.project.net/business_case_case_studies.jsp?idno=2816 (accessed April 17, 2006).
73. Traci Purdum, "Teaming, Take 2," *IndustryWeek*, May 4, 2005, available online at: http://www.industryweek.com/ReadArticle.aspx?ArticleID=10179 (accessed July 24, 2006).
74. "Steelcase, Inc.," Groove.net, available online at: http://www.groove.net/index.cfm?pagename=CaseStudy_Steelcase (accessed July 24, 2006).
75. Rosencrance, "Meet Me in Cyberspace," op. cit.
76. http://www.jnj.com/careers/learn.html (accessed July 24, 2006).
77. Thompsen, "Leading Virtual Teams," op. cit.
78. Etienne C. Wenger and William M. Snyder, "Communities of Practice: The Organizational Frontier," *Harvard Business Review*, January–February 2000, pp. 139–145.
79. David Owens and Erick Thompson, "Fusing Learning and Knowledge at the St. Paul Companies," *Knowledge Management Review*, 2001, vol. 4, no. 3, pp. 24–29.
80. Based on an interview with Kenny Klepper and Karin Princivalle, op. cit.
81. Wenger and Snyder, "Communities of Practice: The Organizational Frontier," op. cit.
82. Based in part on Jenny Ambrozek and Lynne Bundesen Ambrozek, "Building Business Value Through 'Communities of Practice,'" *Workforce Online*, December 2002, available online at: http://www.workforce.com/section/10/feature/23/37/28/ (accessed April 3, 2006).
83. Thomas A. Stewart, *Intellectual Capital: The New Wealth of Organizations* (New York: Doubleday, 1997).
84. Ibid.
85. Patricia Gongla and Christine Rizzuto, "Evolving Communities of Practice: IBM Global Services Experience," *IBM Systems Journal*, 2001, vol. 40, no. 4, pp. 842–862.
86. John S. Brown and Paul Duguid, "Organizational Learning and Communities-of-Practice: Toward a Unified View of Working, Learning, and Innovation," *Organization Science*, 1991, vol. 2, no. 1, pp. 40–57.
87. Ambrozek and Ambrozek, "Building Business Value Through 'Communities of Practice,'" op. cit.
88. Ibid.
89. Wenger and Snyder, "Communities of Practice: The Organizational Frontier," op. cit., p. 142.
90. Charles O'Reilly and Jennifer Chatman, "Cultures as Social Control: Corporations, Cults, and Commitment," in Larry Cummings and Barry M. Staw, eds., *Research in Organizational Behavior*, vol. 18 (Greenwich, Conn.: JAI Press, 1996), pp. 157–200.
91. Jennifer A. Chatman and Karen A. Jehn, "Assessing the Relationship Between Industry Characteristics and Organizational Culture: How Different Can You Be?" *Academy of Management Journal*, June 1994, vol. 37, pp. 522–553.
92. Peg C. Neuhauser, Ray Bender, and Kirk L. Stromberg, *Culture.com: Building Corporate Culture in the Connected Workplace* (New York: Wiley, 2000).
93. Edgar Schein, *Organizational Culture and Leadership*, 2nd ed. (San Francisco, Calif.: Jossey-Bass, 1992).

94. Jennifer A. Chatman and Sandra E. Cha, "Leading by Leveraging Culture," *California Management Review*, 2003, vol. 45, no. 4, pp. 20–34.
95. Kathryn Robyn, "Acadian Ambulance Got It Done," *Emergency Medical Services*, December 2005, available online at: http://www.emsmagazine.com/publication/article.jsp?pubId=1&id=2613 (accessed April 3, 2006).
96. Richard E. Walton, "Establishing and Maintaining High Commitment Work Systems," in John R. Kimberly and Raymond H. Miles, and Associates, eds., *The Organizational Life Cycle: Issues in the Creation, Transformation and Decline of Organizations* (San Francisco, Calif.: Jossey-Bass, 1980), pp. 208–290.
97. Quicken Loans, "Quicken Loans Named to *Fortune*'s '100 Best Companies to Work For' List for Third Consecutive Year," available online at: http://www.quickenloans.com/about/press_room/news_releases/fortune_best_company2006.html (accessed April 3, 2006).
98. Michael L. Tushman and Charles A. O'Reilly, *Winning Through Innovation: A Practical Guide to Leading Organizational Change and Renewal* (Boston, Mass.: Harvard Business School Press, 1997).
99. John A. Byrne, with Mike France, in New York and with Wendy Zellner, "At Enron, the Environment Was Ripe for Abuse," *BusinessWeek Online*, February 28, 2002, available online at: http://www.businessweek.com/magazine/content/02_08/b3771092.htm (accessed April 11, 2006).
100. This table is based on Phillip Hunsaker, *Training in Management Skills* (Upper Saddle River, N.J.: Prentice Hall, 2001), p. 323.
101. Nanette Byrnes, "The Art of Motivation," *BusinessWeek*, May 1, 2006, pp. 56–62.
102. Arthur P. Brief, Benjamin Schneider, and Richard A. Guzzo, "Creating a Climate and Culture for Sustainable Organizational Change," *Organizational Dynamics*, 1996, vol. 24, no. 4, pp. 7–19; Edgar Schein, *Organizational Culture and Leadership* (San Francisco, Calif.: Jossey-Bass, 1985), pp. 224–237; and Terrence E. Deal and Kent D. Peterson, *Shaping School Culture: The Heart of Leadership* (San Francisco, Calif.: Jossey-Bass, 1998).
103. Byrnes, "The Art of Motivation," op. cit.
104. Charles Fishman, "The Man Who Said No to Wal-Mart," *Fast Company*, January 2006, vol. 202, p. 66.
105. David Faber, "With a Small-Town Culture, Wal-Mart Dominates," *MSN Money*, November 10, 2004, available online at: http://moneycentral.msn.com/content/CNBCTV/Articles/TVReports/P100061.asp (accessed April 11, 2006).
106. Tracy Mayor, "Remote Control," *CIO Magazine*, 2001, available online at: http://www.cio.com/archive/040101/remote.html (accessed April 10, 2006).
107. Denise M. Rousseau, "Why Workers Still Identify with Organizations," *Journal of Organizational Behavior*, 1998, vol. 19, pp. 217–233; and Michael G. Pratt and Peter O. Foreman, "Classifying Managerial Responses to Multiple Organizational Identities," *Academy of Management Review*, 2000, vol. 25, pp. 18–42.
108. Ambrozek and Ambrozek, "Building Business Value Through 'Communities of Practice,'" op. cit.
109. Peter Sinton, "Teamwork the Name of the Game for Ideo," *San Francisco Chronicle*, February 23, 2000, available online at: http://www.sfgate.com/cgi-bin/article.cgi?file=/chronicle/archive/2000/02/23/BU39355.DTL (accessed April 4, 2006).
110. http://www.novartis.com/about_novartis/en/index.shtml (accessed April 28, 2006).
111. Global Integration, "Case Study: Novartis," GlobalIntegration.com, available online at: http://www.global-integration.com/about/novartis_case_study.html (accessed April 28, 2006).
112. Ibid.
113. Ibid., at: http://www.global-integration.com/about/novartis_case_study.html (accessed April 28, 2006).

CHAPTER 17

1. "Supply-Chain Challenges: Building Relationships," *Harvard Business Review*, July 2003, p. 69.
2. Ron Lieber, "A Financial Data Vault Online," *Wall Street Journal*, June 24, 2006, p. B1.
3. Stephanie Strom, "Grants Given by Microsoft for Relief Aid," *New York Times*, February 22, 2006, p. A15.
4. "Leadership Challenges: A Lack of Collaboration, Motivation, Recruitment and Work Tension Top AMA Survey," *Incentives*, January 2004, no. 1, p. 12.
5. Helen Sullivan and Chris Skelcher, *Working Across Boundaries* (New York: Pelgrave, 2002), p. 42.
6. Ibid., p. 3.
7. Ibid.
8. James Austin, *The Collaboration Challenge* (San Francisco, Calif.: Jossey-Bass, 2000), p. viii.
9. Ibid., p. 3.
10. Mahesh Raisinghani, *Business Intelligence in the Digital Economy* (Hershey, England: Idea Group Publishing, 2004), pp. 82–83.
11. Ibid.
12. Frances Cairncross, *The Company of the Future* (Boston, Mass.: Harvard Business School Press, 2002), pp. 137–138.
13. Jeffrey Liker and Thomas Choi, "Building Deep Supplier Relationships," *Harvard Business Review*, December 2004, p. 108.
14. James Bamford et al., *Mastering Strategy* (San Francisco, Calif.: Jossey-Bass, 2003), p. 20.
15. Ibid., p. 13.
16. Ibid., pp. 12–13.
17. Ibid.
18. Quoted from Jens Genefke and Frank McDonald, *Effective Collaboration* (New York: Pelgrave, 2001), pp. 12–13.
19. See also Salvatore Parise and Amy Casher, "Alliance Portfolios and Managing Your Network of Business Partner Relationships," *Academy of Management Executive*, 2003, vol. 17, no. 4, pp. 25–52.
20. Bradley Kirkman et al., "Five Challenges to Virtual Team Success: Lessons from Sabre, Inc.," *Academy of Management Executive*, 2002, vol. 16, no. 3, p. 71.
21. Ibid., p. 70.
22. Cairncross, op. cit., p. 87.
23. Bjorn Munkvold, *Implementing Collaboration Technologies in Industry* (London: Springer, 2002), p. 3.
24. Ibid.
25. Ibid., p. 14.
26. "Lotus Notes and Collaboration: Plus Can Change," *Journal of Management Information Systems*, Winter 1996–1997, vol. 13, no. 3, pp. 65–81.
27. Munkvold, op. cit., p. 3.
28. Ibid., pp. 38–56.
29. Sullivan and Skelcher, op. cit., pp. 118–136.
30. Ibid., p. 50.
31. Ibid.
32. Ibid., p. 41.
33. Ibid., p. 52.
34. Adapted from James Austin, *The Collaboration Challenge* (San Francisco, Calif.: Jossey-Bass, 2000).
35. Don Mankin and Susan Cohen, *Business Without Boundaries* (San Francisco, Calif.: John Wiley & Sons, 2004).
36. Ibid., p. 102.
37. Unless otherwise noted, this is based on Mankin and Cohen, op. cit., pp. 106–148.

38. Ibid.
39. Ibid.
40. Ibid., p. 111.
41. "Supply Chain Challenges: Building Relationships," *Harvard Business Review*, July 2003, p. 69.
42. Jerald Greenberg and Robert Barron, *Behavior in Organizations* (Upper Saddle River, N.J.: Prentice-Hall, 2000), p. 378.
43. Austin, op. cit., p. 127.
44. "Supply Chain Challenges: Building Relationships," *Harvard Business Review*, July 2003, p. 69.
45. Steven Robbins, *Organizational Behavior* (Upper Saddle River, N.J.: Prentice-Hall, 1998).
46. Ibid.
47. Quoted from ibid., p. 294.
48. The following is adapted from Eileen Aranda et al., *Teams: Structure, Process, Culture, and Politics* (Upper Saddle River, N.J.: Prentice-Hall, 1998), pp. 116–117.
49. Chris Huxham and Siv Vangen, *Managing to Collaborate* (London: Routledge, 2005), p. 66.
50. "CRM ROI Review: Optimizing Returns on Customer-Centric Strategies," *SAP*, March 2004, vol. 3, no. 2, p. 11.
51. This case is quoted from and based on www.thecollaborationloop.com, "Collaboration Case Study: AT&T" (downloaded June 29, 2006).

NAME INDEX

N

O

P

Q

R

SUBJECT INDEX

J

K

L

T

A COMPLETE INSTRUCTOR AND STUDENT SUPPORT PACKAGE

FOR STUDENTS Online Study Center

Online Study Center

This website offers a plethora of valuable assets, including ACE Practice Tests; Outlines; Summaries; Glossaries; and "Your Guide to an A," which includes access to ACE+ Practice Quizzes, downloadable MP3 Audio Chapter Reviews and Quizzes, Interactive Flashcards, Interactive Games (including Crossword Puzzles, Hangman, and Skills Self-Assessments), and the Managing Now! LIVE Simulation.

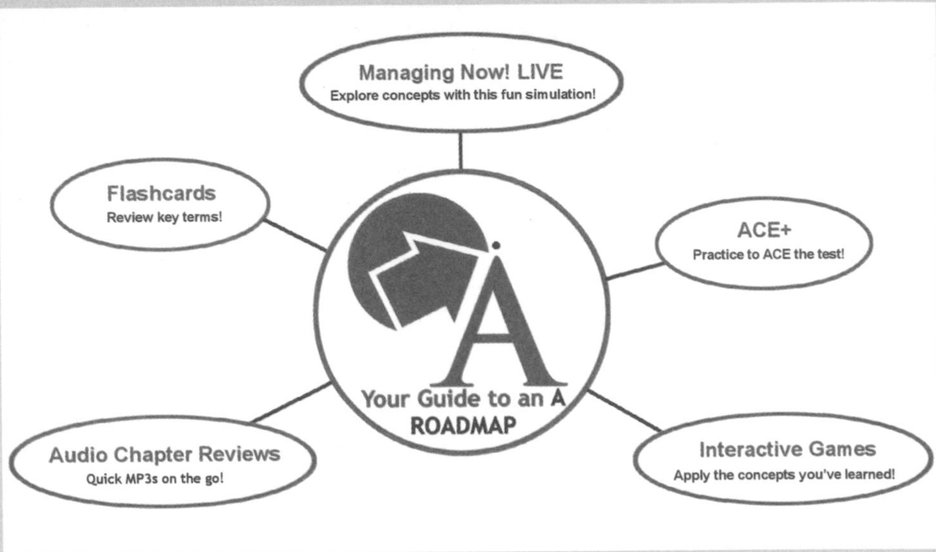

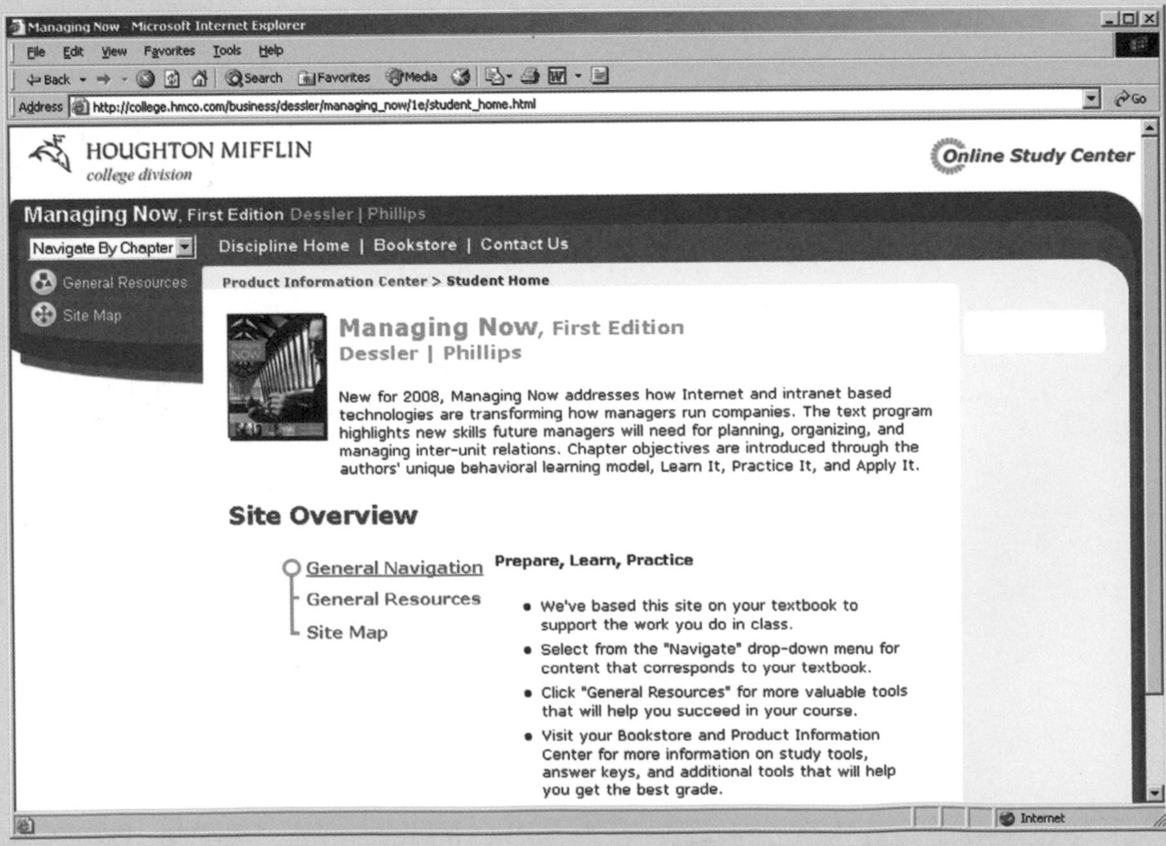